ART MAP OF EUROPE

Budapest

Constantinople

Troy

Delphi

Pergamon

Mycenae

Corinth Athens

Priene

ympia Epidauros

Sparta Tiryns

Khorsabad

Knossos

Ashur

Phaistos

Babylon

Alexandria

Jerusalem

Nippur

Gizeh Cairo

Ur of the
Chaldees

Saqqara

Beni Hasan

El-Amarna

Deir-el-Bahari Karnak

Thebes

Luxor

Edfu

ART IN THE WESTERN WORLD

ART

IN THE WESTERN

WORLD

Fourth Edition

DAVID M. ROBB

Professor of the History of Art
University of Pennsylvania

J. J. GARRISON

Late Associate Professor of Fine Arts
Michigan State University

Harper & Row ∽ *Publishers*

NEW YORK *and* EVANSTON

Contents

SCULPTURE

PAINTING

THE MINOR ARTS

Preface and Acknowledgments

Many readers of earlier editions of this book have made suggestions, directly or indirectly, that have been helpful in preparing the present edition. Special acknowledgment of such suggestions is due to my colleagues in the Art Department of the University of Pennsylvania, George Bishop Tatum and Frederick Hartt. Marvin Eisenberg of the University of Michigan has also given helpful advice.

For assistance in procuring photographs, particular thanks are extended to the following:

Mr. H. H. Arnason, The Guggenheim Museum, New York

Mr. Franklin Biebel, The Frick Collection, New York

Mr. and Mrs. Asa Bordages, Columbia, N.J.

Mrs. Adelyn Breeskin, The Baltimore Museum of Art

Mr. Kenneth John Conant, Chevy Chase, Md.

Mr. H. Lester Cooke, The National Gallery of Art, Washington, D.C.

Mr. Abbott Cummings, The Society for the Preservation of New England Antiquities, Boston

Mrs. Caroline Doskar, The University Museum, Philadelphia

M. Jean Dubuffet, Paris

M. Philippe Gangnat, Paris

Mr. Donald Goodall, The University of Texas, Austin

Mrs. Leon Jonas, Oak Lane, Philadalphia

Mr. Louis I. Kahn, Philadelphia

Mr. Patrick J. Kelleher, Princeton University Art Museum, Princeton

Miss Amelia Kelley, Trans World Airlines, Philadelphia

Mr. Paul Love, Michigan State University, East Lansing

Mr. J. P. Maher, The Philadelphia Saving Fund Society, Philadelphia

Mr. Henri Marceau, The Philadelphia Museum of Art

Miss Dorothy Miner, The Walters Gallery, Baltimore

Miss Pearl Moeller, The Museum of Modern Art, New York

Miss Elizabeth Mongan, The Alverthorpe Galley, Jenkintown, and The National Gallery of Art, Washington, D.C.

Mr. Charles Montgomery, The Henry Francis du Pont Winterthur Museum, Winterthur, Del.

The Museum Boymans-Van Beuingen, Rotterdam

Mr. Clifton Olds, San Diego State College, San Diego

Miss Therese O'Malley, Pan American World Airways, Philadelphia

Mr. Joseph L. Oppenheimer, A. A. Schechter Associates, New York

Miss I. Rice Pereira, New York

Mr. Nikolaus Pevsner, The Architectural Press, London

Miss Jessie Poesch, The University of Pennsylvania, Philadelphia

Mr. Andrew C. Ritchie, Yale University Art Gallery, New Haven

Dr. Peter Schlumbohm, The Chemex Corporation, New York

Mr. Seymour Slive, Harvard University, Cambridge

Dr. Friedrich Winkler, Deutscher Verein für Kunstwissenschaft E.V., Berlin

Mr. C. C. Wall, Mount Vernon

In general, citation of the ownership of an object is acknowledgment of permission to reproduce the photograph. Particular thanks are extended the following for allowing illustration of objects in their collections:

Mr. and Mrs. Henry Clifford, Radnor, Pa.

Dr. F. H. Hirschland, Harrison, N.Y.

Mr. Henry F. Lenning, New York and Madison, Conn.

Mr. Robert Montgomery, New York

Mrs. Carroll S. Tyson, Chestnut Hill, Pa.

Mrs. John Wintersteen, Villanova, Pa.

Miss Concetta Leone, Curator of Slides and Photographs, and Miss Margaret Lily Berg of the University of Pennsylvania Art Department have given the author the benefit of their particular skills, hereby gratefully acknowledged.

Miss Helen V. Taylor of the Art Department of the University of Pennsylvania contributed much to the preparation of the manuscript. For this, due recognition is here given.

Mrs. Jane H. Robb and Miss Sara M. Robb have been indefatigable and patient in reading the manuscript and assisting in the gathering and preparation of the illustrations. To Miss Martha E. Robb, the author is deeply obligated for the care and accuracy with which the index has been prepared.

Finally, to readers of earlier editions, the author's indebtedness to his one-time associate and collaborator, J. J. Garrison, late Associate Professor of Fine Arts at Michigan State University, will be evident. This is acknowledged in the recurrence of his name as co-author.

D.M.R.

SOURCES OF ILLUSTRATIONS

Albright Art Gallery: Fig. 546
Alinari Photo (Art Reference Bureau, Inc.): Figs. 35, 36, 49, 52, 54, 65, 70, 71, 72, 73, 77, 78, 111, 113, 114, 115, 117, 121, 123, 124, 131, 132, 151, 148, 149, 150, 152, 160, 239, 249, 251, 255, 257, 259, 267, 268, 269, 270, 272, 274, 275, 276, 277, 280, 281, 282, 284, 286 left and right, 287, 288, 290, 291, 309, 311, 312, 313, 314, 315, 316, 317, 318, 320, 321, 322, 325, 326, 329, 330, 332, 333, 334, 335, 339, 343, 362, 363, 376, 377, 381, 382, 386, 387, 388, 389, 390, 391, 392, 393, 394, 395, 396, 397, 398, 399, 400, 401, 402, 403, 405, 406, 407, 409, 410, 411, 412, 413, 414, 415, 416, 417, 420, 421, 423, 424, 425, 427, 428, 430, 431, 434, 435, 437, 438, 439, 440, 442, 450, 451, 458, 466, 467, 474, 475, 483, 486, 487, 489, 492, 564, 566, 581, 582, 591, 608.
Andrae: Fig. 21.
Photo Wayne Andrews: Figs. 194, 206, 219.
The Architectural Record: Fig. 202.
The Art Institute of Chicago: Figs. 514, 525, 536, 545.
The Art Museum, Princeton University: Figs. 283, 308, 379.
The Baltimore Museum of Art: Fig. 519.
Mr. W. Pope Barney, Architect: Fig. 224.
Cliché Paul Bijtebier: Fig. 373.
Bildarchiv Foto Marburg (Art Reference Bureau, Inc.): Figs. 254, 278, 279, 303.
The Trustees of The British Museum: Figs. 246, 247, 426.
The British Travel and Holidays Association: Figs. 146, 164.
The Buchholz Gallery, New York: Fig. 351.
C. O. Buckingham, Washington, D.C.: Fig. 190.
Caisse Nationale des Monuments Historiques: Figs. 50, 61, 76, 109, 110, 112, 156, 177, 243, 301, 305, 307, 331, 336, 485, 508.
Ediz. Vicenzo Carcavallo: Fig. 60.
Chemex Corporation: Fig. 652.
Chicago Architectural Photo Co.: Fig. 200.
Ed. L. Chiovato-Vicenza: Figs. 135, 137.
The Cleveland Museum of Art: Fig. 521.
Kenneth J. Conant: Fig. 62.
The Corcoran Gallery of Art: Fig. 340.
Country Life, Ltd.: Fig. 174.
Copyrighted Dartmouth College: Fig. 528.
The Detroit Institute of Arts: Figs. 453, 538.
Durm: Fig. 55.
Charles Eames: Fig. 649.
Photo by John Ebstel: Fig. 228.
The Essex Institute: Fig. 182.
Photo Walker Evans: Fig. 191.
Fogg Art Museum, Harvard University: Figs. 476, 491.
Copyright, Foto-Administratie, Mauritshuis, The Hague, Fig. 463.
Foto–Enit–Roma: Fig. 154.
Copyright, Fotocommissie, Rijkmuseum, Amsterdam: Figs. 460, 464.
French Government Tourist Office: Fig. 158, 170, 178.
Copyright The Frick Collection, New York: Figs. 337, 481, 494.
Isabella Stewart Gardner Museum: Figs. 432, 436.
German Tourist Information Office: Fig. 169.
Laura Gilpin: Fig. 181.
Greff, S.E.R.P., Editeur: Fig. 108.
The Solomon R. Guggenheim Museum: Fig. 223.
Dr. A. I. Hallowell: Fig. 5.
Copyright Frans Halsmuseum: Fig. 462.
Dr. Leicester B. Holland: Fig. 33.
Hölscher: Figs. 11, 12.
The Misses Rose and Ann Jarmak: Figs. 43, 153.

S. C. Johnson & Son, Inc.: Fig. 220.
Dr. Clarence Kennedy: Fig. 263.
Copyright, A. F. Kersting: Figs. 89, 90.
G. E. Kidder Smith: Figs. 217, from *Brazil Builds*; 226, from *Italy Builds.*
Dr. Fiske Kimball: Fig. 187, from *Thomas Jefferson, Architect.*
M. Knoedler & Co., Inc.: Fig. 547.
Koldewey: Fig. 23.
Richard Merrill Photo: Fig. 186.
Photograph, The Metropolitan Museum of Art: Figs. 8, 13, 14, 15 (Photograph by Harry Burton), 17.
The Metropolitan Museum of Art: Figs. 29, 40, 183, 234, 245, 250, 443, 452, 459, 470, 471, 472, 473, 490, 503, 505, 513, 533, 550, 551, 552, 554, 555, 563, 568, 569, 570, 574, 583, 586, 592, 594, 598, 605, 609, 612, 615, 616, 619, 622, 625 center and right, 628, 629, 630, 631, 632, 635, 636 right.
The Pierpont Morgan Library: Frontispiece, Figs. 465, 590.
The Mount Vernon Ladies' Association: Fig. 184.
Edit. Ugo Mugnaini: Figs. 323, 328.
Courtesy, Museum of Fine Arts, Boston: Figs. 231, 241, 248, 271, 361, 482, 531, 571.
Collection, The Museum of Modern Art, New York: Figs. 350, 352, 522, 526, 543, 647, 651.
Photograph, The Museum of Modern Art, New York: Figs. 195, 199, 203, 205, 211, 212, 213, 214, 215, 354, 524, 645, 646, 648, 649, 650.
National Buildings Record: Figs. 165, 172.
Reproduced by courtesy of the Trustees, The National Gallery, London: Figs. 375, 478.
National Gallery of Art, Washington, D.C.: Figs. 58, 338, 378, 429, 468, 477, 500, 518, 578.
National Park Service: Fig. 188.
New York Convention and Visitors Bureau: Figs. 192, 197.
Pan American World Airways: Figs. 69, 175.
Pennsylvania Historical Society: Fig. 185.
Perrot & Chipiez: Figs. 7, 9, 16.
Philadelphia Museum of Art: Figs. 173, 319, 495, 512, 520, 523, 534, 537, 600, 601, 603, 614, 617, 618, 623, 627, 634, 637, 640.
The Phillips Collection, Washington: Figs. 535, 541.
A. A. Schechter Associates: Fig. 227.
Dr. Peter Schlumbohm: Fig. 652.
Copyright Walter Scott, Bradford: Fig. 107.
Seligman: Fig. 4.
Photograph by Julius Shulman: Fig. 218.
The Smith College Museum of Art: Fig. 502.
Soprintendenza alle Gallerie di Firenze: Fig. 404.
Swindler: Fig. 562.
The Topsfield, Mass., Historical Society: Fig. 180.
Through the Courtesy of Trans World Airlines, Inc.: Figs. 10, 19, 39, 105, 153.
University Museum, Philadelphia: Figs. 20, 24, 242, 360, 556, 559, 567, 572.
Cliché Vizzavona: Fig. 510.
The Walters Art Gallery, Baltimore: Figs. 496, 498.
Dr. Clarence Ward: Figs. 86, 91, 93, 99, 100, 101.
Whitney Museum of American Art, New York: Figs. 540, 542.
Wiegand: Fig. 47.
Miss Katherine Winckler: Fig. 222.
Courtesy, Henry Francis du Pont Winterthur Museum: Figs. 633, from *American Furniture*, by Joseph Downs, published by The Macmillan Company; 638.
Yale University Art Gallery: Figs. 499, 516.
Zippelius: Fig. 46.

Chronological and Topical Concordance

The page references below are to passages of the text that refer to the general topics or styles indicated.

ART IN THE WESTERN WORLD

Introduction

What is art? What is its importance to men? If the first of these questions has been discussed at least since Plato wrote in *The Republic* about the place of the artist in society, the second has peculiarly modern implications, for only in the past few hundred years has any need been felt to justify or explain art as a significant aspect of human experience. The purpose of this Introduction is to suggest possible answers to these questions; and the authors hope it will make clear their attitude toward the material presented in the book.

As a preliminary to considering the first question—What is art?—let us note a few generally accepted definitions. One so widely encountered that it has become a platitude is the familiar expression, "I don't know anything about art, but I know what I like." To the extent that this cliché indicates the necessity of response by the observer, hearer, or reader to a work of art, whether it be a painting, a book, or a symphony, it takes account of one factor in the act of critical understanding; it is obvious that music unheard or paintings unseen can have no meaning save for the artists creating them. But in implying, as this cliché does, that individual likes and dislikes are the sole grounds for judging a work of art, there is the assumption that amusement or entertainment is its major function. Although this is undoubtedly true of some works of art, it is such a limited conception that it can hardly be felt to account for the forms which past and present have come to feel are important and significant.

Another definition of somewhat more profound implications is that art is concerned with making beauty comprehensible, capable of being perceived through the senses. This definition too contains an idea which must be involved in any statement about the nature of an art work, for it is part of the artist's purpose to reveal beauty that is often unseen by others. But it, too, raises a difficult point in assuming an absolute Beauty. This does not and cannot ever exist. A Greek of the fifth century B.C., for example, thought ideal human beauty was to be found in proportions of a mathematical character that give the figure qualities of balance and symmetry (Fig. 260), whereas a sculptor of the twentieth century A.D. finds his ideal in relationships that produce an entirely different effect (Fig. 352). The *beautiful* varies so much from person to person, from time to time, and from race to race that it becomes a term without exact meaning.

Still a third definition makes art the form resulting when ideas are expressed in such a way that they are addressed most directly to the emotions of the observer. In this definition too there is an element that must be taken into account, for the quality of stimulating emotional response is one of the most important that an art work can possess. But the character and intensity of emotional reaction are again of such illimitable variety that, taken alone, this definition omits much from consideration. Poetry, music, and the drama, for instance, usually affect the emotions of the participant far more directly than do painting, architecture, and sculpture. Few if any pictures, statues, or buildings thrill us so immediately as the performance of a play or symphony, yet it would be erroneous to conclude that an engraving by Dürer or a painting by Delacroix must be considered less effective as a work of art than a fugue by Bach or a symphony by Beethoven. We can only say that emotional appeal as such cannot constitute the ultimate and final basis for judging a work of art.

These three definitions of art have all raised points to be taken into consideration, but none are sufficiently comprehensive. In trying to formulate a more inclusive one, let us attempt to follow in a general way the procedure of an artist painting a landscape. We have all had the experience of seeing a painting of a view with which we are familiar and of realizing in its presence, possibly for the first time, that the forms of nature in that particular landscape are arranged in a way very pleasing to the eye. Upon examining the painting more carefully, we note that some details of the scene have been left out, and others have been made more prominent than we remembered them. This seems to imply that the artist has considered some details of his subject more important than others for one reason or another; he has not taken everything at its face value but has analyzed and evaluated the forms he saw, and his painting embodies the

evidence of that analysis and evaluation. This is the first step in creating a work of art, the artist's analysis of his experience of the subject. Now, returning to the painting, we next observe that the artist has sought to relate the various objects he has selected from the landscape to each other. There is space continuity, for instance, so that the observer can travel visually from foreground into middle distance and background through carefully planned passages. Or the form of a nearby tree may be repeated in another farther away, or the color of a figure in one place is employed elsewhere in such a way that the eye relates them to each other. By this process, the artist takes the forms which his analysis has shown to be significant; and by emphasizing or creating relationships between them he gives them a new identity with a reality of existence that can be grasped and understood entirely in its own terms. In analyzing his subject he has taken it apart, so to speak, and determined the importance of its various elements for his purpose; he has then put those parts together by a process of synthesis, and achieved a reality which is based upon elements of his initial experience, it is true, but which are ordered and arranged as they were not in that initial experience and therefore have become a work of art.

The experience which is the point of departure for the artist does not necessarily have to be one of sight or vision; it may be something he read or imagined. But it must be an experience in which he senses qualities that require and justify the interpretation he gives. In other words, it must be a perception of a truth, which was realized only partially or dimly before, but which his interpretation makes clear and unquestionable. For a work of art is the definition, in comprehensible form, of essential truth as the artist becomes aware of it in experience. If truth is there, no matter whether great or small, and if the interpreter is able to make its sense clear, the resultant form is a work of art. The greatness of the artist depends upon the quality and perception of his analysis of experience, the greatness of the work of art upon the completeness of the synthesis which is the tangible evidence of the artist's reaction to experience. This holds true regardless of the nature of the experience or the artist's medium. In the "Ode to a Skylark" Shelley has created a symbol of the liberating impulse that carries the spirit far above earthly things; Praxiteles' Hermes is a symbol of the ideal human form that was divinity for its creator and his time; in the Prelude to *Tristan and Isolde*, Wagner has wrought a musical symbol of the yearning passion that to him was love. Considered as intellectual analyses of experience, such forms as these have no meaning at all; if this is desired, it must be sought in scientific treatises in the fields of psychology, religion, and morals. Such forms as the above are rather persuasive and immediately recognizable concepts embodying our most intimate experiences of nature, godhood, and love.

Involved in this definition of the character of an art work is the determination of the elements which enable the observer to participate in the experience the artist has interpreted. Let us return to the painter. If he is working on a portrait, our probable first reaction is that it does or does not resemble the person he is painting. If it is a landscape, we may feel that we are seeing the actual scene, if it is one with which we are familiar, or that this tree does not look right or that house is out of place. Such reaction is determined by the extent to which the artist has succeeded in representing the appearance of the thing he is painting. Representation is an important element in art, particularly in painting and sculpture. From it we derive much of the pleasure the visual arts can give; for recognition of the thing portrayed is one means by which we identify ourselves with the experience interpreted by the artist, since by representing the objective characteristics of things, certain aspects of the truth they symbolize for him are transmitted to us. But even though representation may be a vital factor in a work of art, it is far from being the only one. Were this the case, the camera would be the greatest of artists because its lens can record the facts of appearance with the fidelity and accuracy that the most painstaking painter cannot approach. Other considerations than naturalistic appearance are involved in determining the quality of a work of art.

In speaking of the artist's treatment of the forms that make up his painting, it was suggested that one of the things he did was to create or indicate relationships between them by his manner of arrangement. Such arrangement is called design, a quality that is an absolute essential in any art form. The rules of grammar are the basis of literary design and the laws of harmony are fundamental to musical order. In the visual arts, balance, rhythm, and contrast are employed to establish the pattern of forms that is the design; they are among the formal characteristics that make clear the concept the artist wishes to express just as the design of a sentence or its grammatical structure makes clear the writer's idea. A building, a statue, or a painting must have the qualities of unity, coherence, and emphasis just as much as a poem, a story, or a sonata does. These are the qualities which a photograph almost invariably lacks; if it has them in any degree, the man who made it is to that extent an artist; when it lacks them, its detail is no more than a record of the accidents of appearance rather than a presentation of facts of inherent or relative significance.

The elements of design and representation are the foundation of every work of art. In the synthesis of ideas achieved by the artist they are present in proportions that differ in some degree in each thing he creates, depending upon the innumerable factors that go to make up his temperament; for at neither the extreme of pure design nor its opposite, naturalistic representation, is the most meaningful art to be found. If the emphasis is entirely on formal arrangement or abstract design as it appears to be in an Oriental rug, for instance, the result is a decorative arrangement of lines and colors that may be pleasing in effect; but since such an arrangement seldom provides readily grasped symbols that correspond to our own knowledge of things, it possesses little that can be related to our own experience. Everyone has attempted to find images of trees and animals in clouds and rock formations and the like. This is a natural reaction to abstract pattern which we of the western world, at least, instinctively try to vitalize by finding some relationship with things that are familiar.

"Pure" abstract design seems incapable of the universal significance that is essential in truly significant art. A statue by Brancusi (Fig. 349) or a painting by Picasso (Fig. 522) is the tangible expression of significant experience, it is true, but of a personal rather than a general nature—significant in terms of texture and surface to a sculptor or in terms of color and line to a painter. For one whose processes of comprehension are not exactly the same as those of the artist—an obvious impossibility—the painting or sculpture must stand or fall by the appeal of its purely formal elements—color, line, mass, etc.

At the other end of the scale from the Oriental rug is the photograph. As a record of the facts of appearance, it has little if any of the timeless and characteristic quality necessary if those facts are to become significant. Let us assume that two photographs of a landscape are made from the same point of view but at different times and under different light conditions. Each records what was factually true of the scene during the infinitesimal fraction of a second in which it was made, but obviously the two "true" representations will be different from each other. It is the artist's business in interpreting his experience of the landscape to correlate facts such as are objectively presented by the photographs, or better, to correlate his own observations of those facts. This correlation is the function of his design in which he emphasizes the elements he feels are basic and important and omits those that are not. The elements chosen will not be the same for two artists; they may not be the same for the same artist at different times. But just so far as the artist achieves a penetrating analysis of his experience of the subject and a complete and unified synthesis in the definition of that analysis which is the painting, just so far has he succeeded in creating a work of art. It is to achieve this end that he strives to find a consistent, ordered, and logical pattern in the facts of appearance, or imposes such a pattern upon them by the design. If he is a truly great artist, the design will seem to be inherent in the subject and inevitable in any comprehensive interpretation thereof. Consequently his painting will have a reality of its own, an even more impressive reality than the

original subject had, for it will have the balanced proportions and unity which life itself appears to have in those rare moments when we are able to coordinate and relate the fragments of experience and understand them as a coherent unity.

Two factors—objective facts of the subject which the artist attempts to bring out in his analysis, and his synthesis of the results of that analysis—must be basic in any work of art. A third factor which is frequently important in determining its expressive significance is subject matter. The objective facts in a painting like the one illustrated in Fig. 448 are two pieces of wood fastened together to form a cross upon which a dead male figure is hung, a second man standing on one side pointing his finger at the central figure, and on the other side a third man with a fainting woman; all are placed against a darkened sky; in the foreground are a kneeling woman and a lamb with its right front foot supporting a small cross. These are the objective facts of the picture; yet no Occidental Christian can see them without realizing that in such an arrangement they have a meaning that transcends objective character, for they represent the death of Christ on the cross for the salvation of mankind. This is the subject matter of the painting; in a case such as this, it possibly evokes more immediate response on the observer's part than does the pattern of form and color because it immediately calls up associations that have been rendered significant by centuries of Christian tradition. Conversely, an example of Oriental art with equally moving associations for a Buddhist might appeal to an Occidental only through its representational elements and formal design, its conscious meaning or subject matter having relatively little significance for him.

It may seem from this that art is meaningful when the subject matter is important, but this is not invariably so. An artist with little imagination may attempt to conceal that shortcoming by depending on traditional associations of subject matter to give his forms meaning they do not inherently possess. On the other hand, a twentieth-century artist may paint a vase of flowers with the same intensity of feeling that the artist of seven hundred years ago poured into his representation of the Crucifixion. In the final analysis, the greatness of a work of art must be determined by its inherent artistic character rather than by its references to external or associative values.

If we are prepared to accept the definition of art as the presentation in comprehensible form of the truth perceived by the artist in his experience of life, we can proceed to the second question posed at the beginning of this Introduction. What is its importance to men? In trying to answer this question, let us assume that we are standing before the portrait of a great man like Houdon's portait of Voltaire (Fig. 338). As we look at it, we observe the realistic way the sculptor has portrayed his appearance—the shrewd and penetrating eyes, the thin nostrils and shaggy brows, and the smile that is at once cynical and benevolent. We then observe that the factual details of hair and costume are subordinated so they do not distract attention from the face, even though they too are represented with great fidelity. Thus we have noted the representational elements in the portrait and also the design which integrates them; together, they are an embodiment of the essential idea of Voltaire as a man. Representation and design do not exist as separate things in the observer's experience but are fused in an identity which means Voltaire; for Houdon's perceptive analysis of the nature of his subject and the tangible symbol he created enables us to know for ourselves the character of the great French writer.

A different kind of reaction of necessity characterizes our experience of an art work such as a painting by Picasso (Fig. 522). Here it is clear that representational values are relatively unimportant and that psychological ones, in the sense of interpreting a specific situation, are nonexistent. Even so, certain objective characteristics are to be noted—contrasting textures of different areas of paint laid on thickly or thinly brushed, the flatness of the canvas plane

on which they are spread. And if the artist seems to have been concerned solely with problems of arrangement and design and not at all with the interpretation of psychological or physical experience, even in turning away from the picture we cannot but be conscious of a heightened awareness of brilliant reds and somber greens and the swinging rhythm of a curved line. Experience such as this may be considered very limited; it is nonetheless couched in the terms of the painter's art and cannot be excluded from critical judgment.

Such analyses as these of the infinitely complex relationship that arises between the art work and the observer are obviously open to question. These relationships are intangible and undemonstrable; they vary with each observer. One person reacts to objective facts of appearance in particular; elements of formal design are of greater importance to another. But even though the exact nature of the relationship between observer and work of art defies definition, it is no less real because of that. Representation of the objective qualities of things strikes a responding chord in our recollections and we relive the experiences of those things. The artist goes further, for his design relates representative characteristics in an ordered and logical pattern that gives the whole a greater significance than can be found in any of its parts. By availing ourselves of his analysis of experience through the synthesis that is the work of art, we are led to the observation of new truths or to reaffirmation of the validity of known truths in the light shed upon them by genius. For it is as a *human* experience, giving direction and meaning to life, that a work of art attains significance. The experience of beauty that results from complete understanding of an art work arises from the sense of enrichment, of greater breadth and depth in his own life that the participant comes to realize as its lasting and vital contribution.

ARCHITECTURE

Detail of Fig. 91.

CHAPTER ONE

Architecture: Principles of Design and Construction

Architecture is the only one of the three major visual arts that can be called practical in the generally accepted sense of the word. Sculpture and painting can be put to some practical use, it is true; much very effective advertising is made possible by them. But one of the primary purposes of architecture is to satisfy the fundamental human need for shelter, a need next only to that for food among man's instincts for preserving life. It follows from this that an example of architecture must be judged in part by the extent to which it fills the need that led to its creation.

∾ *9* ∽

This same reason provides an explanation for the many existing architectural styles; for since the needs of different periods in history and different places in the world have always differed, it follows that architectural forms designed to meet those needs and conditions must also differ.

The purpose for which a building is to be used is therefore one factor in determining its form. Another is the way it is constructed. This aspect of architecture is closely related to the science of engineering; it is possible to trace the entire history of the art through changes in form resulting from the various methods of construction employed at different times. An obvious illustration is the skyscraper; for without steel, which did not come into general use until the latter part of the nineteenth century, the lofty towers of a modern American city could never have been erected. Thus construction is an important element in determining architectural form, but it is still subordinate to function or purpose. The skyscraper would not have developed, for instance, had it not been made necessary by rising land values resulting from urban congestion; even the use of steel in its construction was more a matter of greater financial return than considerations of form, for some of the first and most distinctive tall buildings were built entirely of masonry.

In applying to architecture the general theory of art developed in the Introduction, function and construction correspond to the element of representation in painting and sculpture. The purpose a building serves is generally quite clear, and if the structural method employed is not always obvious, it can usually be determined from brief examination. These, in other words, are the facts of the idea the building is to symbolize and they correspond to the facts of appearance in the representative arts. If the theory developed in the Introduction is to hold true for architecture, it should follow that great architecture is not the result of merely good construction and utilitarian efficiency. A garage well adapted to its purpose and built solidly so it can stand for centuries if need be is not necessarily good architecture; a railroad station that provides every accommodation that is needed and is of

such a nature that its usefulness can be extended indefinitely may still fall short of architectural distinction. This is true of any building which lacks the significant element of design. Design is as important in architecture as in the representative arts and for a similar reason, since it is through design that order is imposed upon or made clear in the functional and structural facts with which the architect has to deal, relating them in a perceptible pattern of form. It is the quality of design in a building that differentiates great architecture and structures that are only tools for living.

The extent to which a building may be considered architecture thus depends upon the degree to which the three basic elements of function, construction, and design have individually and collectively contributed to its form. As was said in the Introduction; great art is formed not of design or representation alone but in an integration of the two. This is as true of architecture as of sculpture and painting. The function of a building and its mode of construction should both be clearly expressed in the design; but in addition it should possess such formal character that it will appeal to the observer in its own right. This is seen in buildings whose true architectural distinction is due to a relationship of the parts that is dictated by useful purpose but seems to be inherently and inevitably right; the result is beauty, for the forms are also expressions of the function of the building and its construction.

Architecture, like sculpture and painting, may go to the extreme of literal factualness in the treatment of form or to the opposite extreme of its sole purpose being an attractive appearance. The first produces what is called "functional" style by its adherents, and they justify their attitude by a limited interpretation of a phrase employed by Louis Sullivan, one of the greatest of American architects: "Form follows Function." As they understand this, utilitarian factors alone should be considered in designing a building, for if it is well constructed and serves its intended purpose efficiently, its form will be inherently, almost automatically, beautiful. At the other extreme are the architects who hold that the appearance of a building is the most important factor in determining its form. For them, design is unrelated to the purpose and method of building, for all that matters is to provide pleasant patterns of windows, columns, and the like. From this point of view, beauty can be put on a building like a coat instead of being inherent in the elements of purpose and structural method. Each theory fails to take some architectural fundamental into account. Functionalism in the sense here defined is overintellectual. No matter how sure the observer is that a filling station is well built and efficient for the work done there, if it is no more than that he is certain to be aware of the lack of visual coordination between its various parts—the coordination that results from good design. On the other hand, the skyscraper surmounted by a Greek temple is equally meaningless regardless of the perfection of its various formal elements, because they are not created to express the purpose and structural methods involved in building a skyscraper, but simply for the supposed beauty of the resultant forms.

Great architecture is produced only when the elements of function and construction are integrated by creative design and so acquire a significance that transcends their objective character. To the observer of a building that owes its form to such a process, understanding it comes through comprehending the synthesis of those three basic elements by the architect, a comprehension that is intellectual insofar as purpose and construction are concerned but which is transmuted by the design into the emotion connoting beauty. To undergo this experience in the presence of the Parthenon or the cathedral at Amiens and thus grasp their expressive meaning as well as the fact of their existence is to become aware of certain profoundly significant aspects of human thought and emotion.

It has been pointed out before that the materials used in building and the methods of assembling them are among the factors contributing to architectural style. Stone and wood are among the materials that have been longest in use, stone being preferred for important structures for the obvious reason that it is more durable. Brick, however, has also been in use

from very early times, either baked in the sun or fired in kilns to become almost as hard as stone. Concrete, too, was known and extensively used at least as early as the Roman period, although many of its potentialities were not realized until iron and steel came into use on a large scale in the latter part of the nineteenth century. Glass and synthetically created plastics are other contributions of modern times to the materials which can be used for building. Availability of materials is often important in determining architectural ways of thinking, as will be seen; but it should also be borne in mind that the architect's need has often led to the discovery or adaptation of materials to his purpose rather than the other way around.

Three structural principles are of paramount importance in the history of building, and in various forms and variants account for almost any imaginable type of construction. They are the post and lintel, the arch, and the cantilever. Of the three, the post and lintel is probably the earliest, although some very ancient examples of the arch have been found; the cantilever, on the other hand, came into extensive use only with the advent of steel in building, although it does occur in some mediaeval wooden roofs.

The nature of the *post* and *lintel* system is implied by its name (Fig. 1). It consists in essence

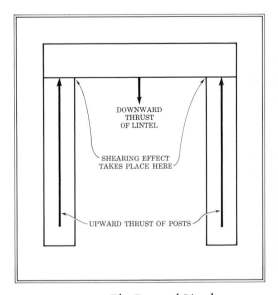

DOWNWARD
THRUST
OF LINTEL

SHEARING EFFECT
TAKES PLACE HERE

UPWARD THRUST OF POSTS

FIG. 1.   The Post and Lintel.

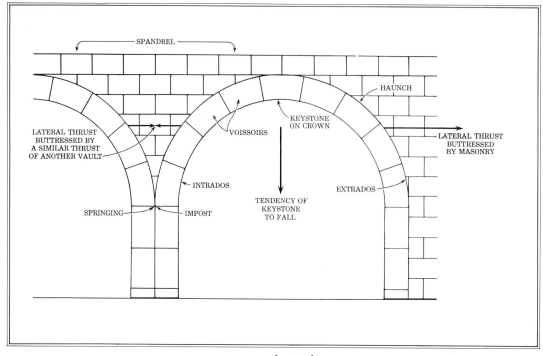

FIG. 2.   The Arch.

of two vertical members that support a horizontal one. It is the simplest of the three basic structural principles in application, for the vertical members need only be sufficiently strong to support the weight of the lintel. Even if some additional weight is placed on the lintel—as in the case of the wall over a door—the stability of the system is not threatened if its span is not too great. This suggests one of the inherent disadvantages of the post and lintel system that is particularly apparent when stone is used. A stone beam of more than a certain length in proportion to its thickness will snap of its own weight if it is supported only at the ends; this probability is heightened if there is additional pressure from above. Another disadvantage of the system is the possibility of shearing. This, too, is likely to happen if the lintel is subjected to pressure from above, in which case the end of the horizontal beam may be pinched off at the point indicated in Fig. 1. These are relatively minor disadvantages, however, and this is the most frequently employed of the three structural principles; it is

used even in modern steel-framed buildings which are composed largely of beams fastened together to form post and lintel units. In addition to being the simplest of the three principles in application, its structural effect is easily observed and it can be used to great advantage in styles that do not involve large openings or extensive unobstructed spaces.

The second structural principle is the *arch* (Fig. 2). In its simplest form, the arch consists of a semicircle of wedge-shaped blocks called voussoirs, the topmost one being the keystone. The bottom face of the lowest voussoir on each side is called an impost and the top face of the uppermost stone of whatever member supports it is called the springing. In an arch of this type, the inner and outer faces are concentric semicircles, the outer one being the extrados and the inner one the intrados or soffit. Midway between the keystone or crown of the arch and the springing is the haunch. Like the post and lintel system, the arch has some inherent shortcomings. It must, for instance, be supported on a scaffold while it is being built. Such a scaffold is called centering and is usually of the form and size of the opening to be spanned by the completed arch. The voussoirs are laid upon it and then locked in place by putting in the keystone. If the centering were then removed, the arch still would not stand; the most serious drawback of the arch as a structural principle will then become apparent. The keystone, subjected to the law of gravitation, has a constant tendency to fall; by virtue of its wedge-shaped profile it cannot fall without first pushing aside the voussoirs next to it. They are also unsupported, however, and reveal the same tendency. This ever-present thrust exerted by the central elements of an arch against those on the outer sides is a phenomenon of arcuated construction that must at all times be taken into account, for if it is not properly compensated the whole structure will collapse. This compensation is called buttressing. It may be accomplished in several ways; the basic principle of all is opposition to the lateral thrust of the arch of another force of equal strength, thus neutralizing it and establishing an equilibrium. One method of achieving this is illustrated at the right of the

FIG. 3. The Cantilever.

arch in Fig. 2, where the compensating force is the dead weight of a massive wall that smothers the thrust by sheer inertia; on the left side the thrust of the main arch is offset by that of another arch. In each case, the compensating force is applied at the haunch of the arch, the point where the accumulated lateral thrusts of the central members of the arch are strongest. At the left end, the two opposed lateral thrusts are brought together by filling the triangular space between the arches with masonry to form a spandrel. A series of such arches is called an arcade.

An Arabic proverb to the effect that an arch never sleeps is a vivid characterization of this structural form which contains a force that can destroy it; for the stability of an arch is entirely dependent upon the external buttressing force. This disadvantage is of minor importance, however, in view of its many advantages. For one thing, an arch can be built of stones too small to be used as lintels since it is a composite form in principle. Moreover, if the necessary centering is at hand, an arch can be built with relative ease over spaces that a straight lintel could span only with the greatest difficulty. And even if an arch is required to support weight other than its own, it is necessary only to provide additional buttressing for the increased horizontal thrust.

The *cantilever*, the third basic structural principle, is utilized today largely in connection with steel (Fig. 3), since its mechanical operation involves forces that subject the structural parts to many different strains—twisting, bowing, tension, compression, and the like. In the illustration, the horizontal projecting arms serve as brackets supported at one end, upon which loads may be placed or from which they may be hung, thanks to the toughness of the steel in resisting the various strains. One of the most general applications of the cantilever in modern construction is its use in skyscrapers which depend for their support upon a steel frame or skeleton (Fig. 210). From the vertical members project horizontal arms upon which the floors are laid and from whose ends the outer walls of the building are literally hung; this makes possible the continuous horizontal bands of windows in the Philadelphia Saving Fund Society Building that are at the same time striking features in its appearance and highly efficient means of illuminating the interior. Another instance of its use is the Robie House in Chicago (Fig. 203) where the porch roof is a cantilever that permits a free and unobstructed view in all directions.

The materials used in a building and the structural principle involved in assembling them are both means to an end—the disposition of the materials in such a way that they will enclose a given volume of space whose size and arrangement will be determined by the use to which the building is to be put. This disposition also involves the arrangement of the different forms that make up the building—walls and columns and doors and windows—in such a way that it can be used most effectively for that purpose. These are determined by the plan of the structure (cf. Figs. 30, 204), which indicates the arrangement of the various supporting members and openings in a horizontal sense, and by the elevation (Fig. 80), which does the same thing vertically. The construction of a building need take no more than this into account since it is concerned only with assuring stability and adequacy for the intended utilitarian purpose. But the architect must go beyond this, if the building is to have character, to be a work of art as well as merely useful. To do this, his fundamental problem is defining the volume of space in his structure by the forms that enclose it, establishing by his design a positive relationship between the solids of his building and the space involved, and going beyond the passive enclosure that is the result of construction alone. The nature of his definition of space depends on many things—the purpose of the building, the materials at his disposal, the basic ways of thinking of the time he lives in— but the character of his building will be ultimately determined by his treatment of space. The Greek's attitude toward space was negative, for the objective philosophy of the fifth century B.C. was concerned with concrete values in experience.

His architecture reflects this, for his temples (Fig. 39) are designed to be seen from the outside like sculptured forms and their interiors are almost entirely lacking in spatial definition. In the thirteenth century, on the other hand, the philosophy of the mediaeval Christian was essentially abstract and concerned with spiritual rather than material values; space was the symbol of an all-pervading God, and its presence as a positive element in the interior of a Gothic cathedral (Fig. 101) is basic to its expressive character. In contrast with both these attitudes, that of the modern world is analytical, seeking to isolate the essentials in abstract conception and concrete form alike. In architecture this results in attempts to maintain the character of both form and space as individual elements, clearly interacting yet always separate. If no great modern architectural style has appeared as yet, it is surely at least in part because the integration of these concepts, necessary if they are to acquire genuine expressive meaning, is still to be achieved.

Of all the arts, architecture is that in which social values are of most immediate importance. Bad pictures can be painted but they do not have to be seen; bad poetry can be written but no one is required to read it; bad music can be composed but it does not have to be performed or heard. Bad architecture cannot be rejected in the same way. In the absence of well-planned and comfortable houses, ill-designed and inefficient ones must be used; once an ugly office building is erected, it is there and cannot be overlooked. The obligation to society thus implied is of far greater importance than the architect's possible desire to embody an individual ideal of beauty in his building or his patron's insistence upon the satisfying of personal whims. Until this obligation is recognized and acknowledged, architecture must forswear the character and distinction that have been attained by the great styles of the past in the few periods when man's thought and expression were collectively unified and consistent.

Detail of Fig. 19.

CHAPTER TWO

Architectural Origins and Early Forms

The sheltering function of building seems first to have been provided by natural caves. But this does not mean that such caves must be considered architecture, because they lack the creatively imaginative disposition of form that is essential if the shelter is to be anything more than utilitarian. The first structures that might have been so characterized were crude huts of woven tree branches plastered with mud, or tents of skins and matting such as are found today among primitive peoples (Fig. 4). Circular because the flexible light materials the builder had were more easily woven in curves than in angular planes, the typical primitive hut was conical in profile with a pointed or rounded top. These

FIG. 4.   Primitive Reed Huts in
the Sudan.

were the crude beginnings of what might be called architectural thinking. Initially the function of these extremely simple forms was strictly utilitarian, but eventually they acquired meaning beyond their first value of mechanical usefulness. How these simple structures came to mean more than mere physical protection to those who built and owned them can only be surmised, but that they eventually had such value is clear. The concept of a life after death, for example, must have developed very early in the imaginative experience of primitive man—from dreaming of his departed ancestors who he thought could not have appeared to him unless they had more than mortal existence. Their needs as immortals he interpreted in terms of his own material requirements. One of these was protection from the harmful forces of nature; hence the necessity of similar protection for the spirit of the dead seemed only natural to him. In order for him to have such protection, he provided that his corpse should be buried in or near the house he had lived in; thus it might perform the same function of shelter for his soul. The house was then sealed up, so that its spiritual occupant might not be disturbed; the structure then took on a symbolic value as the house of the dead.

An example of the tomb as an extension of the house concept is seen in the *dolmen* which consisted of two upright slabs of stone supporting a third horizontal slab (Fig. 5). Considerable numbers have been found in various parts of Europe, particularly in Brittany in western France. The body was placed in the chamber thus formed and the whole was covered with a mound of earth, the purpose being to create a house for the dead whose shape suggested but was more lasting than the reed or skin shelters in which man lived. Because of fear that the spirit, unhappy if its shelter were destroyed, would return to trouble those still on earth, it was of the utmost importance to provide a permanent resting place for it. The dolmens are not particularly early in date—most of them are apparently later than the temples in Egypt—but they are nonetheless products of an environment and culture in a rudimentary stage of development and they illustrate one of the primary phases of architectural thinking.

Belief in the aid which could be rendered by supernatural forces in prolonging life on earth was another concept that gave early house forms more than simple utilitarian meaning. The development of a religious instinct from fetishism, in which rocks and trees and mountains are believed to have magic powers, through zoomorphism or the worship of animals, to anthropomorphism which conceives gods in the likeness of men, is a common pattern in the history of social evolution. Although initially

FIG. 5.   Carnac, Brittany.
A Dolmen (Neolithic).

FIG. 6. Stonehenge (*ca.* 1500 B.C.),
near Salisbury, England.

symbols of personal significance, the gods of an individual may in time have meaning for a group or family or even a tribe, and to these gods the fortunes of the community are ascribed. The protection and propitiation of these gods were usually the task of the chieftain, who thus also became priest. The house he shared with the god became a sanctuary. As the chieftain-priest became the incarnation of the deity he served, the place he lived in became the house of the god and thus acquired a new significance. This, in brief, is how the concept of the temple evolved; and as the house of the all-powerful it was only fitting that it should be greater and more lasting than mortals' houses but still conceived in similar terms.

The concentric circles—some partial and some complete—of upright stones connected by horizontal lintels at *Stonehenge* near Salisbury in England (Fig. 6) appear to be a primitive temple. It is called a cromlech and is so built that a stone in the innermost circle was directly in the shadow cast by another at some distance outside called the "Friar's Heel" when illuminated by the rays of the rising sun on the morning of the summer solstice when it was built. The inference that it was a place of sun worship is inescapable; the fact that its form was determined by the house designs of those who built it is equally clearly

indicated, for in nearby Wiltshire are the remains of a large circular enclosure that was evidently some form of habitation made of wooden posts thrust vertically into the ground. The actual date of Stonehenge has been determined with some accuracy at about 1500 B.C. by calculating astronomically the time when the solar phenomenon described occurred on the day indicated. As in the dolmens, however, the architectural concept involved is a primitive one, as is the fact that it was devoted to the worship of a natural force. Only in its orientation, i.e., that it is laid out with reference to the points of the compass, is there any suggestion of more than the most elementary architectural procedure.

The earliest architecture of history developed in the eastern Mediterranean area in fertile river valleys where agricultural civilizations replaced the more primitive hunting cultures of prehistory. In Egypt, for example, the stabilizing effect of a fixed and permanent society is seen architecturally in the continuity of tradition and the monumental character of the buildings erected there, to which material and social conditions contributed. The fertile fields flanking the Nile, upon which the crops were raised and the herds grazed that made life possible, are bordered by desolate and mountainous regions that were inexhaustible sources of stone for building. The annual flooding of these fields by the river renewed their fertility, and this phenomenon became a symbol of the life that comes from destruction and death, personified in the god Osiris. No less essential to the existence of the Egyptian was the warmth of the sun's rays that brought renewed life to the seemingly dead vegetation, whence it too came to be considered a force to be ingratiated and propitiated in the person of Re the sun god. These were the most powerful gods of the Egyptian hierarchy; in the manner suggested above, they were believed to be incarnate in the person of the Pharaoh, who was worshipped as a god during his life as well as after his death. So were formed the motives underlying the major architectural forms of Egypt during its long recorded history as an autonomous state. For the purposes of this discussion, that history

FIG. 7.   Egyptian Mastabas, Restored.

may be considered as divided into three major periods, the Old Kingdom from *ca.* 3200 B.C. until 2258 B.C., the Middle Kingdom from 2134 until 1570 B.C., and the New Kingdom from 1570 until 1085 B.C. Egyptian chronology was actually recorded in terms of ruling dynasties, and equivalents of modern numerical chronology in these terms are frequently encountered. The Old Kingdom was most important, for example, during the first to fifth dynasties, from *ca.* 3200 B.C. to *ca.* 2420 B.C.; the eleventh and twelfth dynasties, from 2134 until 1786 B.C. were of greatest importance in the Middle Kingdom. There were some intervening periods in which foreign influences prevailed in the country but they did little, by and large, to alter the fundamental character of Egyptian thinking.

Tombs of various types, depending upon the importance of the person buried therein, constitute the largest class of Old Kingdom architecture. Common people always were simply buried in pits or in their houses, but a nobleman's final resting place was a low massive structure of stone called a *mastaba* (Fig. 7) from the sloping or battered walls that make it resemble the Arabic benches from which the name is derived. Rectangular in shape and usually laid out with its four sides facing the cardinal points of the compass, the mastaba has two entrances as a rule, one of which is an actual door and the other a false one; these are for the most part on the north or east sides. The internal arrangement varies, but certain elements are always present

FIG. 8.   Mastaba of Perneb (*ca.* 2500 B.C.), from a Model.

FIG. 9.   Saqqara.   Mastaba of Ptahotep (*ca.* 2600 B.C.).   "False Doors."

(Fig. 8). These are a chapel or offering room in which presents were made to the spirit of the deceased; a separate chamber—the serdab—where a statue of the dead man was placed and which was often accessible only through very small apertures; and a shaft that runs vertically through the mass of the mastaba down into the ground where the actual burial chamber was located. This shaft, whose opening can be seen in the flat top of the mastaba (Fig. 7), was filled with stones after carefully contrived barriers or portcullises were lowered following the final installation of the sarcophagus, the purpose being to prevent as far as possible the grave being rifled for the riches buried with the deceased. Another false door was an invariable feature of the chapel or offering chamber (Fig. 9); through it the spirit of the dead man came to partake of the food that first was actually brought to him but later was carved and painted on the walls of the chamber along with the innumerable details of the daily activity involved in producing it.

The statue in the serdab was placed there for comparable reasons—to provide the spirit with a body if the dreaded possibility of the mummy in its sarcophagus being damaged should materialize. The whole character of the mastaba is thus seen to result from material and magical efforts to insure the personal immortality which the Egyptian passionately hoped and prepared for during his life on earth.

A mastaba such as the one described might have been built in the fourth or fifth dynasties of the Old Kingdom. Certain of its elements may have been present in earlier tomb structures, but built in brick or clay rather than stone. The way the form of the mastaba was determined by the more elemental concepts and structural practices of earlier periods is one of its significant characteristics from the point of view of the evolution of architectural thinking. The tomb was the house of the soul, so it follows in its general character the house of the man who built it. This house was very likely made of sun-dried mud brick laid in walls that were thick and heavy and sloped backward because they had to be thicker at the base to be stable; and it was in this same form that the mastaba was built, with cut stone walls encasing a rubble fill even though they would have lost no structural strength by being vertical. Similarly traditional in their elements are the "false doors" of the chapels in a mastaba (Fig. 9) which show in conventionalized forms the front of a house; here, symbolically, the actual house of the dead where are carved in stone the various elements that went to make up a façade—the screens of matting or the panels of small pieces of wood that formed the walls, the bound reeds used for mouldings on the angles, and the tips of others projecting above and bending forward to form a concave cornice. In some cases, there is a cylinder at the top of the false door itself with a rope and matting pattern. This represents a rolled-up screen of reeds that served as curtain in the house door. The plan of the mastaba also refers directly to that of the Egyptian house. The chapel or offering chamber is the principal room, the serdab the private room, and the

underground burial chamber a direct continuation of the primitive practice of interment beneath the floor of the dwelling.

Like the houses of mortals, those of the dead were grouped together in cities or necropoli (Fig. 11). In the Old Kingdom, these necropoli were usually on the west bank of the Nile—the "land of death"—two very important ones being at Saqqara and Gizeh where long rows of mastabas form regular patterns of streets. The social and religious tradition of Egypt demanded an adequate symbol of rank and importance even in death, and the tomb of the king was of necessity more important than those of men of lesser degree, a concept which undoubtedly suggested building a second mastaba on top of the lower one and continuing this process until a suitable form was created. This, thanks to the inclined walls of the mastaba form, was a pyramidal mass with stepped sides such as was built at Saqqara by the architect Imhotep for King Zoser, who reigned in the early part of the third dynasty in the Old Kingdom. The *Stepped Pyramid* (Fig. 10) is the central element in a vast complex of buildings erected with the intention of reproducing in stone as the permanent resting place of Zoser's soul the structures of wood, brick, and reeds of his fortified palace at Memphis. The ensemble as a whole is important as the earliest known instance of the forms of earlier architecture being translated from less durable materials into stone, and as an illustration of how the pyramid as an architectural type was developed from the mastaba.

The *Great Pyramids* (Fig. 11) at Gizeh were among the wonders of the ancient world, a distinction they retain today. Built in the fourth dynasty of the Old Kingdom—between 2680 and 2565 B.C.—they were the tombs of the Pharaohs Khufu, Khafra, and Menkaura and were built in that order, the Great Pyramid of Khufu being the northernmost and largest of the three. That of Menkaura, the latest and smallest, is not shown in the illustration, which is a restoration of part of the necropolis at Gizeh. The huge bulk of Khufu's pyramid—756 feet at the base and 481 feet in height when its original casing was in place—makes it the largest mass of

FIG. 10. Saqqara. Imhotep, The Stepped Pyramid of Zoser (*ca.* 2750 B.C.).

FIG. 11. Gizeh. The Pyramids of Khufu and Khafra, and the "Portico"
(2700–2600 B.C.), Restored.

stone in the world assembled by human hands. This it is in a literal sense, because the Egyptian builder's elemental mechanical equipment could have been of only little effectiveness in handling the limestone blocks averaging two and a half tons in weight that make up the core. A system of corridors and passages within its mass provided carefully disguised means of access to the burial chambers of the king and queen. These were ingeniously built with triangular roofs so constructed as to divert the pressure of the enormously heavy masses of stone above away from the openings. The passages were lined with slabs of finely cut limestone of very precise dimensions which have been romantically interpreted as prophesying future history but are of more significance in revealing the extraordinary technical skill of the Old Kingdom stone masons. The present rough exterior of the Great Pyramid once had a casing of highly polished slabs of stone similar to that of which a part can still be

seen on the adjoining Pyramid of Khafra. The glittering effect of this casing under the sun's rays was undoubtedly planned to make it a symbol of Re, the sun god, who was worshipped in Lower Egypt during the Old Kingdom period in the form of a gleaming obelisk with a tip of the same pyramidal form as Khufu's tomb.

The Old Kingdom pyramid provided only for interment in the burial practices of ancient Egypt. The functions of the serdab with its statue and the offering chamber of the mastaba had to be discharged in other ways. Close to the east side of the second pyramid, that of Khafra, is a structure that served as its chapel. It is of considerable size and contains various rooms with serdabs and false doors, presumably similar in purpose to the comparable forms in a mastaba but on a larger and more elaborate scale. It is now in such a ruinous state that little but its plan can be made out, but it is connected by a covered causeway with a somewhat smaller and

FIG. 12. Gizeh. The "Portico"
(*ca.* 2600 B.C.), Interior, Restored.

better-preserved structure about a quarter of a mile distant which apparently resembled it somewhat in plan and appearance. This structure lies near the famous statute of the Sphinx (Fig. 11) and is sometimes called its temple; it was probably intended as a *portico* (Fig. 12) or monumental approach to the ruined shrine-temple nearer the pyramid itself. Inside are two halls whose plan forms a T, in which square monolithic piers of granite support the roof; these are impressive alike in their massive proportions and the simplicity of their forms which are unobscured by any carved or painted ornament. As the earliest known examples of isolated stone supports, these piers are historically important; the fact that small pegs or dowels are carved at their tops and that cramps were used to bind the architrave blocks together shows that the conception underlying their form is still based on wood-joining practice. The exterior, which was nearly forty feet in height, must have resembled a large mastaba in appearance; its battered walls with rounded corners and the flat roof are in the the tradition of mud-and-brick rather than stone construction.

There is reason to believe that temples were built during the eleventh and twelfth dynasties of the Middle Kingdom (2134-1786 B.C.), but as they were of brick for the most part, they have not survived in a state that permits more than archaeological discussion. In the *Rock-Cut Tombs* (Fig. 13) at Beni-Hasan about 125 miles up the river from Gizeh, however, there are examples of a Middle Kingdom architectural type of great distinction and impressiveness. Hewn literally from the live rock of the eastern bank of the river, these were the final resting places of the chieftains of the Oryx nome, one of the most powerful tribes in the feudal society that in the Middle Kingdom replaced the monarchic system of the Old Kingdom. Originally with external courtyards, partly built and partly cut from the rock, these tombs preserve in their general plan the traditional elements of the Egyptian sacred structure that originated in the house-court, vestibule or portico, hall with pillars, and a private or sacred chamber. In the rock-cut tombs, the latter is the main interior room and the smaller one at the rear which originally contained the statue of the deceased (Fig. 14), the mummies being placed in a pit in the floor of the main hall. Many details in these

FIG. 13. Beni-Hasen. The Rock-Cut
Tombs (*ca.* 1800 B.C.).

tombs reflect forms originally created in materials other than the stone in which they appear. Both external and internal columns are polygonal in section, with eight or sixteen sides—a form which might appear to have originated from cutting the corners from a square beam but which seems rather to have been originally a composite resulting from binding a number of reeds together and filling the interstices between them with mud for plaster which was then smoothed off to a plane surface. The little blocks below the horizontal member at the top of the façade likewise appear to have originated in wooden construction, in the projecting ends of small roof beams. Within, the flattened arches of the ceilings in the main hall are painted in diaper and checkered patterns that reproduced those of woven matting roofs such as actually covered the houses of the Oryx chieftains. Other than this, the painted interiors of these rock-cut tombs continue the older tradition of detailed and lively portrayal of the life at the time for the sake of the spirits of those buried in them (cf. Fig. 356).

The mastabas and pyramids of the Old Kingdom and the rock-cut tombs of the Middle Kingdom were imposing and impressive monuments to the greatness of their builders, but massiveness and inaccessibility proved insufficient to ensure the preservation and permanent repose so deeply desired. Thus in spite of centuries-old traditions which tended to enforce the practices and crystallize the forms that had been hallowed by unquestioning usage over a long period of time, a change in the character of the Egyptian tomb occurred in the New Kingdom that provided more adequately for protecting the mummy but removed the tomb as a type from the category of architecture. It was then that the rulers of Egypt began to make their tombs in the form of long underground corridors, frequently complex in plan. Many of these are found in the cliffs of the Valley of the Kings in the Libyan desert west of Deir el-bahari not far from Thebes, then the political capital of the country. That concealment was the chief motive for the form of these underground tombs is indicated by an inscription in the tomb of an architect of one of the earliest of them: "I attended the excavation of the cliff-tomb of His Majesty alone, no one seeing, no one hearing." The occasional success of the designers is proved by the discovery in 1923 of the shaft tomb of Tutankhamen, a minor ruler of the eighteenth dynasty, which, only slightly disturbed, provided one of the richest treasures in the history of Egyptology (cf. Fig. 553). However, the ingenuity of the designers in concealment has been equaled by that of many would-be looters in discovery for the majority of the graves now known have long since been despoiled.

With the place of actual burial purposely deprived of its character as a monument in the

FIG. 14. Beni-Hasan. The Rock-Cut Tomb of Amenemhat I (*ca.* 1975 B.C.), Interior.

interests of more effective concealment, the temple or shrine in which the name and divinity of the deceased ruler could be properly venerated became more important. As early as the eighteenth dynasty, the Theban rulers erected their mortuary temples at Deir el-bahari on the plains between the west bank of the Nile and the cliffs at the edge of the Valley of the Kings, actually at some distance from the tombs themselves. Particularly notable, and one of the outstanding monuments of Egyptian architecture (Fig. 15), was the *Temple of Queen Hatshepsut* (d. 1479 B.C.) It was designed by the architect Senmut as a series of terraces with columnar porticoes com-

bined with rock-cut chambers in the cliff against which the temple is set; these are chapels to the gods Hathor, Anubis, and Amon, as well as to Hatshepsut herself. Of monumental proportions—the upper terrace is more than 300 feet in width—the structure as a whole is nonetheless a repetition of the basic architectural elements previously noted, the portico, columnar hall, and private chamber. Important details are the columns of the terrace porticoes—square or sixteen-sided—the use of statues as supports, and the carved and painted accounts on the wall of the upper terrace of the birth of Hatshepsut and the expedition to the land of Punt which, like

FIG. 15. Deir el-bahari. Senmut, The Temple of Hatshepsut (*ca.* 1500 B.C.), from the East.

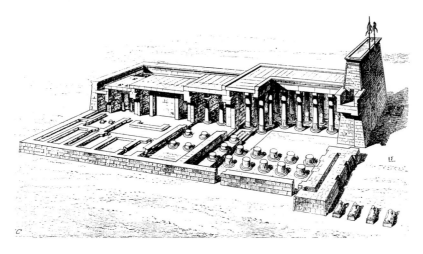

FIG. 16.   Karnak.   The Temple of Khons (*ca.* 1100 B.C.),
Restored Perspective View.

the temple itself, was supervised by her architect Senmut.

Other than the mortuary temples which it was the duty as well as the privilege of Egyptian rulers to erect in their capacity as incarnations of divinity, there were buildings consecrated to the gods themselves; these were both great in number and impressive in form in the New Kingdom. Chief among Egyptian deities was the sun god, Amon-Re; his temples, administered by a powerful priesthood ever-increasingly jealous of prerogative and confirmed in privilege, were the largest and most important in the country. This was natural, in accordance with the belief that the temple was the house of the god and that its glory should be proportionate to his greatness, a fact which also confirms the conceptual identity of mortal and divine houses. One of the Egyptian temples, smaller but illustrating the basic elements with more than usual clarity, is that erected to *Khons* (Fig. 16) at Karnak near Thebes by Rameses III in the twentieth dynasty, *ca.* 1100 B.C.

The temple is approached by an avenue of sphinxes leading up to a massive gate-wall called a pylon; this is a structure with sloping or battered walls heavier at the base and topped by a concave cornice. A portal opens into a court with colonnaded covered galleries on the sides. Steps

in the gallery opposite the portal lead to a chamber, the hypostyle hall; it is as wide as the temple and its roof is supported by numerous columns. A door at the rear of this hall leads to the sanctuary proper. This was generally a rather small room surrounded by many others in which the treasures of the temple were kept. Deviations from this basic type are common; in fact, there is no other temple so typical in character as that of Khons. Modifications, however, almost invariably involve duplications of one or more of the essential elements—two courts instead of one, or a hypostyle hall so large as to overshadow the rest of the structure; but the fundamental plan is hardly ever changed except in buildings that have other purposes. The longitudinal axis of the plan for example, is characteristic of the Egyptian temple, and any variation can be explained by particular physical circumstances that could not be modified.

The construction of an Egyptian temple involved the post and lintel principle exclusively. There is evidence that the arch was known to Egyptian builders, but its use was limited to certain types of tomb and to utilitarian structures; its monumental potentialities were realized hardly at all. In contrast, the possibilities of the column for impressive effect were extensively developed by the New Kingdom builders, as can be seen in the colonnade and forecourt of *The Temple of Amon-Re* (Fig. 17) at Luxor. This temple, one of the largest in Egypt, was begun by Amenhotep III, of the eighteenth dynasty. The colonnade leading to the original entrance pylon, now in ruins, was added later by the same monarch; its columns are surmounted by bell-shaped capitals resembling the open flower of the papyrus plant, and those of the forecourt beyond are in the form of buds of this plant. These were not the only foliate forms the

Egyptian used to decorate his columns; he also used lotus blossoms and palm leaves.

Visually the capital provides a transition from the vertical of the column shaft to the horizontal of the lintel resting on it; the same visual function is performed in the simpler columns of the rock-cut tomb at Beni-Hasan (Figs. 13 and 14) by the rectangular blocks interposed between lintels and columns. It is doubtful, however, if the Egyptian builder was conscious of these considerations, for the column and

FIG. 17. Luxor. The Temple of Amon-Re (*ca.* 1400 B.C.), from the North.

capital as he used them were simply traditional structural elements whose forms had been determined by primitive practice using other materials than stone. What these forms were is suggested by certain details of the columns themselves. At the top of the shafts immediately beneath the swelling of expanded and bud capitals alike is a series of horizontal bands; the shafts of the bud columns are not simple cylinders but are carved in vertical stemlike members which cut in perceptibly at the base. If a cluster of long-stemmed papyrus buds growing from a single root be imagined as bound around just below the buds themselves, the source of the form executed in stone by the eighteenth-dynasty builder will at once be suggested.

The architectural piety of the Egyptian is further indicated by another major element in the temple form, the *pylon* (Fig. 18). This example is from a temple erected at Edfu in honor of the god Horus; and although it is much later than the New Kingdom temples already discussed—it was begun in 237 B.C. and finished by 212 B.C.—it repeats the basic pattern of the earlier structures. The vertical slots at the base of the pylon were sockets to hold the staves of banners on festal days. Both inner and outer faces are liberally decorated with figures in the characteristic sunken relief used by the Egyptian for wall ornament. These deal with the achievements of the ruler who built the temple; they are here ascribed to the power given him by Horus, represented as a human figure with a hawk's head. The pylon itself consists of two towers with a doorway between them, a form with a traditionally symbolic value as the "Horizon of Heaven" which it is sometimes called in inscriptions; its sloping walls are likewise traditional, repeating the characteristics of construction in woven matting with a strengthening core of mud that might well have been used earlier. Around the edges of the pylon runs a cylindrical moulding which close view shows to have a recurrent pattern of horizontal bands connected in groups by others that slant across the principal moulding. This, too, is a stone translation of a form made originally of less permanent materials —a bundle of reeds placed on the edges of the

FIG. 18. Edfu. The Temple of Horus (237–212 B.C.), Main Pylon.

original matting and mud wall to protect them from damage. The Egyptian pylon was usually crowned with a projecting concave cornice (cf. Fig. 16), although it has been broken off at Edfu; the preferred decoration for this cavetto cornice, as it is called, was a pattern of leaves, a characteristic that points to its ultimate derivation from the reed parapets on primitive houses.

By perpetuating in durable stone the forms his ancestors had created and made in less permanent materials, the Egyptian architect provides an illuminating example of the unquestioning acceptance of conventions rendered significant by tradition which constitutes the primary characteristic of all Egyptian art. This is no less true of the temple plan as a whole; this plan was thought of as that of the god's house which in principle is simply a larger and more permanent dwelling composed as was the house the Egyptian himself lived in. The forecourt, the porticoed vestibule opening into the great hall, and the private chamber of the god all had their counterparts in the smaller and less distinguished house of the mortal. As has been said, these are the fundamental elements in the plan of every Egyptian temple, regardless of apparent variations or added complexities that are the consequence of repeating one or more of the basic

FIG. 19. Abu Simbel. The Temple of Rameses II (1257 B.C.), Façade.

forms without altering either function or traditional symbolic value.

The addition of ornament to utilitarian forms apparently was practiced from earliest times, and the decoration which is an element of Egyptian architectural style is one of its outstanding characteristics. It is seen in the figures carved in raised or sunken relief on façades (Fig. 18) and columns where their effect is often accentuated by color, and in the mouldings on the angles of pylons and the cavetto cornices surmounting them, as well as the foliate forms used for column capitals. The symbolic origin of Egyptian decoration cannot be doubted. The lotus and papyrus blossoms that adorn the columns are conventionalized references to the fetishes of fertility that were later symbolized by bundles of flowers hanging from the supporting posts of the priest's house in the annual celebration of the resurgence of life brought by sun and river to the apparently lifeless vegetation of the Nile valley. The reliefs carved on walls and columns originated in the practice of scratching in the mud of the house wall or plastered reed column pictographic symbols that recorded the owner's attainments and good deeds; those on tomb or temple are simply more permanent records in stone, but their purpose is the same. This is the motivation of the great seated figures in front of the *temple* (Fig. 19) that *Rameses II* had carved from the solid rock of the west bank of the Nile at Abu Simbel in 1257 B.C. The façade was cut in the stone, as well as the inner chambers of the temple, and is conceived as a pylon complete with bound-reed and cavetto mouldings surmounted by a row of dog-headed apes. These animals were sacred to the rising sun in whose honor the structure was ostensibly created and whose statue stands in a niche in the center of the façade. It is far overshadowed, however, by the four colossal statues of Rameses himself—sixty-five feet in height—representing the monarch in the royal enthroned pose; smaller figures representing his family appear around the legs of the colossi. Other figures in relief on the façade and bands of hieroglyphic inscriptions denote the Pharoah's nominal homage to the god, but the walls of the inner rock-cut chambers are crowded with pictorial and inscribed praises of the ruler himself.

In the magnitude of its dimensions—the façade is 119 feet wide and 100 feet high—whose laborious execution by cutting away the stone of the cliff was made possible only by almost unlimited slave labor, the temple at Abu Simbel is a characteristic instance of the preoccupation with size and bulk that existed from the very beginning in Egyptian art in expressing a primitive desire for certainty and permanence in a world of transient values. If this size is not at first apparent either in illustrations of the monuments or in their actual presence, it is due to the lack of scale in both individual forms and ensembles. Scale is the quality in the design of a building that allows its size to be sensed and creates the visual impression of bigness or smallness. A building may be enormous in bulk yet seem very small, or—as is usually the case with Egyptian forms—be devoid of any inherent proportion so that it may seem either large or small. Giving scale to architectural design is one of the most important functions of ornament, but the Egyptian architect was oblivious to it, for the function of his ornament, like that of the building of which it was a part, was symbolic and not aesthetic.

Finally to be noted is the way in which the architectural forms of ancient Egypt reflect the communal beliefs of those who built them. From the exterior, the temple was an extended, low-lying mass of masonry inside high walls through which the ordinary man might never pass. Unrelieved by openings save for that in the pylon, its massive proportions and forbidding aspect must have impressed the beholder with the extraordinary power of its inhabitant, an impression enhanced, were he privileged to enter the courtyard, by the mysterious gloom of the hypostyle hall with gigantic carved forms dimly outlined on wall and column where the all-powerful dweller in this divine palace could reveal himself on occasion to his court, and which led in turn to the even more profound darkness of the sacred shrine where the god actually lived. But surrounded as the Egyptian was by symbols made significant by centuries-old tradition, symbols he unconsciously employed in his own humble dwelling but here of a size that he could not hope to emulate, and created in a medium far more permanent than the mud bricks and reeds to which he was limited, he must have felt that here was the house of one who would exist long after he had vanished from the earth and to whom he therefore willingly acknowledged the allegiance that made possible the rigidly conventional way of thinking that was at once the strength and weakness of Egyptian culture.

The second of the great preclassical cultures whose architectural style reveals the change from temporary and primarily utilitarian buildings to monumental and more lasting ones with the shift from a nomadic life to an agricultural one developed in Mesopotamia. Here as in Egypt the fertile valleys of rivers—the Tigris and Euphrates—provided both sustenance for mortals and pliable materials in the form of reeds which, used in bundles or woven into matting and plastered with mud, were the building substance in earliest times. Sun-dried brick was developed relatively early and became the most prevalent medium, but the influence of the early forms persisted. Another element of the early house form that continued as a salient characteristic of monumental Mesopotamian building was the courtyard; originally formed by walls built around the house for protective purposes, it became in time a controlling factor in the large city-palaces and temples. Fetishism with its deification of natural objects must also be taken into account in the origins of Mesopotamian architectural forms; for the staged towers called *ziggurats*, of which an early example dating from the third millennium B.C. has been

FIG. 20.   Ur in Chaldaea.   The
Ziggurat (*ca.* 2100 B.C.), Restored.

sufficiently excavated at Ur in Chaldaea (Fig. 20) to
permit reconstruction of its original form, appear
to be the work of people investing mountains
with religious meaning. This concept eventually
is modified to make the ziggurat the house of the
god, in which capacity it is associated with that
of the king-priest.

The "Land of the Two Rivers" was much
fought over in ancient times and the culture that
flourished there was a composite one in which the
influences of different races and tribes prevailed
at one time or another. Certain traditional forms
persisted in the architecture, however, as in the
great *palace* at Khorsabad (Fig. 21). Dedicated
by *Sargon II* in 706 B.C., it embodied many
features of the older styles of the region which is
Assyria, the northern part of Mesopotamia. The
palace, part of a fortified city, was built on an
artificial mound some fifty feet high that
straddled the walls of the city. Generally rectangular in plan, it is oriented by angles since the
corners are directed toward the cardinal points
of the compass. Otherwise the plan is notable
for its asymmetry. Its 209 rooms are grouped or
agglomerated around open courtyards instead of
being laid out with reference to a central axis;
in general, the arrangement is determined by the
use to which the different groups were put. At
the left of the illustration, in the south angle, are
the women's quarters or harem, somewhat apart
from the main part of the palace. Directly
across the principal court from the harem and

in the east angle of the palace are storerooms and
offices, the administrative section; the men's
quarters are on the northwest side of the same
court. In this same direction are the monarch's
private apartments, near the chambers of state
where the reception rooms used on great ceremonial occasions were located. These latter are
grouped around the rather long and narrow
court which is reached through a portal flanked
by towers opening from the upper level of the
mound. This general layout maintains the traditional relationship of enclosed room to surrounding courtyard. Also included in the palace
form, however, is the ziggurat, located at
Khorsabad in the angle between the harem and
the men's quarters on the southwest side of
the palace; its form here—a rectangular tower
ascended by ramps that spiral up its sloping sides
—is no more than a conventionalized erected
mound such as had been built centuries before at
Ur (Fig. 20) in a somewhat less rigidly organized
form. It was used specifically as a platform from
which the astrologer-priests could make the
observations of stars that guided the policies of
the ruler.

The rooms of the palace were not very large
for the most part; they were usually long and
narrow, with heavy walls from twelve to twenty-
eight feet thick built of mud brick and faced
with stone. As a rule they were covered with flat
roofs made of mud and supported by beams of
such wood as was locally available or could be

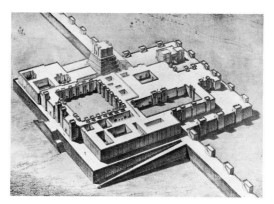

FIG. 21.   Khorsabad.   The Palace of
Sargon II (706 B.C.), Restored.

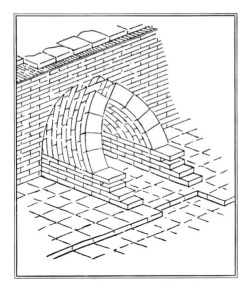

FIG. 22.   The Laminated Vault.

imported. Certain rooms were probably vaulted, notably the royal chamber. The curving profile of its vaulted ceiling appears to have resulted from attempts to reproduce the rounded matting coverings of the mud and reed huts of earlier times. The true vault with voussoirs and key-stone (cf. Fig. 2) was used in some instances and the corbeled type in others where the courses are laid so that each one projects slightly beyond the one beneath, diminishing the span until it is closed in at the top. Still another type of vault, the *laminated vault* (Fig. 22), was apparently extensively developed for utilitarian purposes in Mesopotamia—for covering underground chambers, drains, and the like. Built of mud bricks laid at an angle so that the courses lean on each other and are supported at the end by a wall, this type of vault had the great advantage of requiring no centering or wooden scaffold for support while being built. The bricks, which were sun-dried, were moistened slightly to make the faces sticky and cement them to those on which they rested until the next course anchored them in place by its weight.

Clay in the form of glazed and enameled brick supplied the decoration as well as the substance for the walls of Mesopotamian buildings. The *Ishtar Gate* (Fig. 23) in the northwest wall

of the city of Babylon was built in the time of Nebuchadnezzar, about 570 B.C. The walls are of crude brick, faced with others modeled in relief with lions and bulls and painted with an enamel that became hard and glassy when fired in an oven. This process involved taking the brick facing down after it was modeled, firing it, and putting it back in place, but the striking color effects obtained were apparently much desired. The background is blue, the animals are brown and yellow, and accents of red and white appear in the margins. These enameled and colored bricks were used in facing the ziggurat walls as well—a different color for each level identifying it with a certain god in the Mesopotamian hierarchy. Besides the decoration thus provided, carved reliefs of stone were often used to ornament Mesopotamian buildings. Largely concerned with glorifying the ruler by citing his great accomplishments, the details of these reliefs indicate the character of the Mesopotamian monarchs—savage and warlike on the

FIG. 23.   Babylon.   The Ishtar Gate (*ca.* 570 B.C.), as Restored in Berlin.

one hand and passionately fond of the battle and hunt (Fig. 246), yet at the same time given over to a degree of Oriental luxury that led to creating in this same city of Babylon the fabulous Hanging Gardens that were one of the wonders of the ancient world.

The absence of the tomb as a monumental type in Mesopotamian architecture is in direct contrast with Egyptian practice. The extraordinarily developed cult of the dead which explains so much of the Egyptian way of thinking had no counterpart in Mesopotamia, where house burial was practiced with few exceptions. At the same time, however, the ruler's association with the god was very close; his dual role as chief priest of deity and monarch invested his dwelling with significance and religious meaning, as the incorporation of the ziggurat—the sort of thing that the Biblical writer doubtless had in mind in describing the Tower of Babel—in the king's palace makes quite clear (Fig. 21). The controlling concept was therefore the house, enlarged and made more permanent for ruler and god and taking its larger meaning from the religious values with which it then became invested. Thus it is clear that the attitudes of the Egyptian and the Mesopotamian were similar in principle however the forms in which they were embodied may have differed.

The third great cultural area of the pre-classical Mediterranean world is the Aegean, the chief centers being the island of Crete, the southern mainland peninsula of Greece, and the western shores of Asia Minor, as well as many islands in the Aegean Sea. Certain features are common in the culture of the area as a whole. Its religion, for instance, involved the worship of primeval forces such as the Earth or Snake Goddess (Fig. 248), symbolized by snakes and by a curious object resembling a double-headed axe, and also the bull, apparently the symbol of a fertility cult. Similar too are certain architectural forms that appear over the entire area, whereas others seem to be more regional. In general, however, the inhabitants of Crete were less given to warlike pursuits than people on the mainland; the latter were in constant danger of attack from which the islanders were protected

by the sea, a fact which explains some of the differences between the buildings of the island and those on the mainland.

At Knossos on the north coast of Crete the legendary palace of King Minos was a vast conglomerate of building known in antiquity as "The Labyrinth," meaning the House of the Double-Axe. It was the fabled lair of the Minotaur whose slaying brought fame to Theseus, one of the great legendary heroes of Athens; in his time the Minoan palace was already old. The structure revealed by exhaustive excavations in the early twentieth century shows evidence of many rebuildings; it reached the stage indicated in the plan between about 1950 and 1400 B.C. The catastrophe that reduced it to ruins—an earthquake, possibly, of which the building had experienced many, or an invasion—apparently occurred about 1400 B.C. The *plan* (Fig. 24) is agglomerative, with groups of rooms around a roughly rectangular central area or plaza with a north-south long axis. This plaza is actually the top of a mound formed by many rebuildings on the site which have raised its level perceptibly. The variation in levels of the site as a whole makes possible the different heights of the stories on the east and west sides of the central space. On the east the slope was increased by considerable excavation and there are three levels through which a monumental staircase provided access to the plaza. On the west there were only two stories.

The domestic quarter of the palace is immediately east of the central plaza. It had quite elaborate facilities, including lavatories, running water, and a very efficient drainage system; porticoes and terraces formed by the flat roofs supplied pleasant open areas throughout. Here as elsewhere in the palace, rooms on the lower levels were lighted and ventilated by shafts or wells that rose through the entire structure. North of this area but still on the east were service quarters. One of the main approaches to the palace was from the sea on the north side of the plaza; on the west were the ceremonial rooms. The lower story on the west in the plan is divided by a north-south corridor, with a series of long narrow storage chambers to the west, and

FIG. 24.   Knossos.   The Palace of Minos (*ca.* 1950–*ca.* 1400 B.C.), Plan.

various cult rooms to the east including the *Room of the Throne* (Fig. 25) which has been partially restored. The upper level of this part of the palace has also been partly restored on the basis of details carefully observed during excavation, when the accumulated layers of material deposited by the gradual collapse of the structure were identified and their original use determined. Here are many of the most ancient portions of the structure, and the decoration of the various rooms leads to the conclusion that this whole wing was the ceremonial house of the Priest-King Minos, the hereditary name of the ruler of Crete. The clearly defined functions of the various parts of the palace and the archaeological evidence of their construction in different periods are grounds for concluding that the ensemble was once a series of separate and unrelated groups of buildings which were later made into a single structure of rather casual unity.

The Cretan builders utilized columns extensively, making them of both stone and wood. Walls were of mixed materials—sun-dried brick and rubble or conglomerate for the most part, with wooden beams to stiffen them. Stucco, brick, and stone were used to face the walls as a rule and in many cases they were painted as well, as appears in the Room of the Throne (Fig. 25), where one wall has been left undecorated to expose the structural materials. Wood was used for door frames and columns; and stone for parts subjected to wear, like door jambs and sills, and also for column bases. The restored columns in the Room of the Throne stand near a low balustrade that separates the room proper from a small enclosed basin probably used for ritual purposes; the columns are of wood and taper from top to bottom, unlike most later column types (cf. also Fig. 26). The form used here is based on evidence from charred remains of the original shafts and from columns in some of the decorative wall paintings. They are surmounted by heavy circular capitals of rather awkward profile and by rectangular abacus blocks. Not all Minoan columns were like these, and the origin of this particular type is not certain; it may have originated in the feeling that the butt ends of tree trunks,

the first such supports, were stronger for supporting horizontal loads than the smaller top ends.

Much of the effect of Minoan building is due to its decoration. This was predominantly painting for which the stuccoed or plastered walls offered ample areas; for example, the royal seat in the Room of the Throne was originally flanked by two griffons in a landscape of plant forms against a background of brightly colored undulating bands. These were probably of symbolic importance as are other paintings in the palace—stately processions of figures participating in some ceremonial rite or in bull-baiting (Fig. 359), which seems to have been part of Minoan religious practices. Elsewhere flowers and marine and animal forms are wrought into effectively stylized patterns (Figs. 557, 558). The color scheme of these paintings is simple as a rule, but the hues are brilliant, giving a note of gayety to rooms which were usually lighted only indirectly through the light-wells.

The various elements of the palace at Knossos that have been mentioned indicate certain characteristics of the culture that produced it—materialistic in the concern for physical comfort and well-being evident in the plan and details of the domestic area, gay and pleasure-loving

FIG. 25.   Knossos.   The Palace of Minos, Room of the Throne
(ca. 1400 B.C.), Partially Restored.

from the engaging paintings on the walls, yet conforming to the same principles of worship and religious belief that characterized its Egyptian and Mesopotamian contemporaries. Fetishism is apparent in the stone pillars inscribed with the sacred double axe in certain small dark rooms that were probably shrines; the cult of the Earth Goddess with her snakes is a manifestly elemental form of belief. The character of the west wing of the palace is an architectural suggestion of the same idea, for its complex plan and the apparently ritualistic function of many of its rooms testify to a pious traditionalism that preserved unchanged the sites used by countless generations, incorporating them only very nominally in the final ensemble when judged by purely aesthetic standards, but justified by the symbolic significance of the regions involved. This was made possible in considerable degree by the consistency of Minoan culture from earliest to latest times, itself the consequence of the geographical isolation of the islanders and their relative freedom from attack.

The Aegean culture of the mainland is known as Mycenaean because many of its monuments were found at Mycenae in Greece. It is roughly contemporary with that of Crete but reached its climax somewhat later—between 1350 and 1200 B.C., after the catastrophe that reduced the island palaces to ruins. It was not as consistent in character as the civilization of the Minoans because the region in which it developed suffered many invasions by neighboring tribes. These seem to have occurred relatively frequently from the time it was first known to be inhabited after the palaeolithic period. They brought to the peninsula of Greece the changing forms and practices of peoples from the regions to the north and northeast as well as from the Mediterranean, and the Mycenaean culture that existed from the end of the fourth millennium B.C. until the end of the second reveals not only many traits also seen in Crete but others that have no counterparts there. Thus although many decorative motives are common to both mainland and island styles of painting, and the downward tapering column is found in Mycenae and Tiryns as well as at Knossos, there are notable differences as well.

FIG. 26. Mycenae. The Lion Gate
(*ca.* 1350 B.C.)

Necessity for protection from military attack was responsible for some features of mainland Aegean architecture that have no counterpart in Crete. Thus the city of Mycenae, the home of Agamemnon, the famous Greek hero of the Trojan War, was a fortified citadel surrounded by enormous walls of massive, boulderlike stones shaped roughly in what is called cyclopean masonry from the classic Greek legend that such walls were built by the race of giants called the Cyclops. The *Lion Gate* (Fig. 26) was the main entrance—an impressive portal over ten feet high made of three enormous blocks of stone that serve as posts and lintel. Above, the side walls are corbeled over the lintel to frame a triangular slab of stone carved with two rampant lions on either side of a column. This gate is at the end of a deep approaching passage between walls from which attackers could be fired on from both sides, an indication of the constant need for protection that was a major consideration in planning the fortress palaces that are the mainland counterparts of the relatively undefended structures in Crete.

Near Mycenae are several tombs of a type that was not unknown in Crete and is not the only kind found on the mainland. They are nonetheless of great intrinsic importance and are

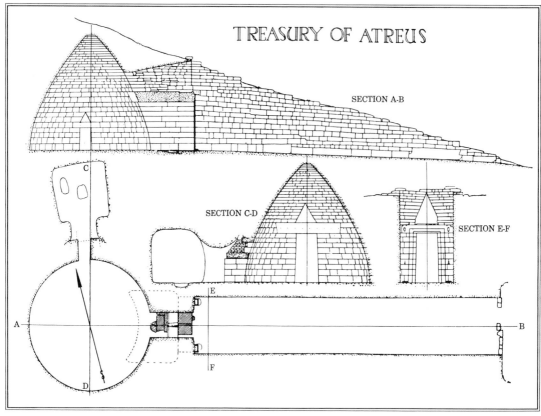

TREASURY OF ATREUS

SECTION A-B

SECTION C-D

SECTION E-F

FIG. 27.   Mycenae.   The Treasury of Atreus (*ca.* 1325 B.C.), Plan and Sections.

among the most spectacular examples of pre-classical architecture in Greece. These are the so-called "beehive tombs," of which the one called the *Treasury of Atreus* (Fig. 27) by its discoverer, the archaeologist Schliemann, is characteristic. The principal chamber is circular and has corbeled walls of finely cut stone blocks laid in circular courses successively smaller in diameter. The resulting elliptical section in elevation explains the popular name for the type. Within, these walls were dressed to a smooth surface which was presumably ornamented with bronze medallions fastened with pins in holes that can still be seen. At one side, a small door led to an irregularly shaped room that may have been the place of burial. On the outside, this chamber was partially covered by a mound of earth; a long passage in it led to the entrance portal, enough of whose decoration has been recovered in excava-

ting to permit some knowledge of its original appearance. The lintel—a huge block of stone some twenty-six feet long, sixteen feet wide, and four feet high and weighing about a hundred tons—was relieved of weight from above by a triangular corbeled opening filled by a slab of red porphyry carved in an all-over spiral pattern. The opening was flanked by applied half-columns of gray alabaster with spirals and chevrons on the downward tapering shafts, and cushionlike capitals semicircular in profile.

Not the least interesting detail of the Treasury of Atreus is the slight decrease in the width of the portal at the top, a feature also seen in the opening of the Lion Gate (Fig. 26). The former is about six inches narrower at the lintel than at the base, the latter about a foot. Such deviations from the vertical in the jambs of portals are rare in preclassical architecture except in Egypt, and it is probable that the appearance of such a form in Greece at this time (*ca.* 1300 B.C.) is due to Egyptian influence, a probability supported by other considerations noted elsewhere (cf. Fig. 559). Egyptian example may also have inspired the fine masonry of the "beehive tombs" and the relieving triangle above the portal lintels. There is scant precedent, in any event, for structural procedures like these in the rather indifferent stonework of Mycenaean building before the fifteenth century B.C.

Another mainland architectural type of the Aegean period that not only has no immediate Cretan parallel but is of great significance in the background of the later classic Greek temple is the *Megaron* (Fig. 28) or chief hall of the fortified palace at Tiryns, shown here restored. A more or less isolated structure, rectangular in plan, it was entered through a portico of two columns between projecting side walls that opened between rectangular piers into a vestibule; from here a single door led to the megaron proper. The principal room was over thirty feet long; a fixed hearth in the center was surrounded by four columns that supported the roof rafters. The walls were of sun-dried brick reinforced with wooden beams. Wood was also used for

the columns and as facing for the door jambs, but walls and columns alike rested on bases of stone that are still in place. The structure was probably covered by a gabled roof—a fact that distinguished it from the Cretan houses which were invariably flat-roofed, and also from the purely domestic structures at Tiryns itself, for the megaron was the ceremonial house, the symbol of the authority of the chief. As such, its form was traditionally determined, and its contrast with other buildings of the palace from which it was isolated in plan made clear its particular significance. The probability that the "beehive tombs" and the gabled-roof megaron both evolved from earlier conical house types is considerable. Their distinction from the flat-roofed houses of mud brick and rubble with wood bonding that appear to have been the prevalent type in Crete, as well as for utilitarian or nonceremonial structures on the mainland, is clear indication of the mixture of traditions in the Mycenaean branch of Aegean culture.

The different names applied by the Homeric poet to the Greeks who fought the Trojans—Achaeans, Dorians, Danaans, and Argives—in the second book of the *Iliad* are likewise evidence of the varied origins of the peoples inhabiting the

FIG. 28.   Tiryns.   The Megaron (*ca.* 1225 B.C.), Restored.

peninsula of Greece during the closing years of the Aegean period, for the generally accepted date of the Trojan War—the second decade of twelfth century B.C.—would make it contemporary with the greater part of the structures discussed in the foregoing paragraphs. Moreover, more than a few passages in the *Iliad* and the *Odyssey*, particularly the latter, refer to buildings that have the characteristics of those found at Mycenae and Tiryns and other mainland citadels of this period. The picture there painted of a country divided among a number of feudal lords is significant too, for although the circumstances of the fall of the Mycenaean fortified palaces are far from clearly defined, the fact that

they fell to foreign invaders is certain. This occurred in all likelihood about 1100 B.C., after which follows a period in Aegean history of which only the scantiest knowledge is available. Such building as there was could hardly have been other than most impermanent in character, the work of hunters and fighters who only slowly adopted agricultural ways. But the earlier buildings still existed; and when the assimilation of the invaders to the soil had finally been consummated, they were not without influence in determining the character of later forms. Not the least significant thing about the Mycenaean age is the fact that upon its foundations the culture of Hellenic Greece was to rise.

Detail of Fig. 39.

CHAPTER THREE

Greek Architecture

The architectural style developed in Greece after the dark ages
that followed the destruction of Aegean culture has at least one
characteristic in common with the way of building that preceded
it there and with the majority of preclassical styles—the use of
the post and lintel system of construction. Also as in most of the
earlier architecture, the chief concern is for the exterior of the
building; the interior is relatively unimportant. This may have
been in part the result of the outdoor life that a temperate
climate encouraged the Greek to lead. In any event, the lack of
distinction in interior treatment in comparison with the distinction in the treatment of exteriors is an outstanding trait of Greek

architecture. In this and in other characteristics mentioned elsewhere, this architecture is the product of an attitude that is still primitive in many ways; but in the refinement of structural forms and decoration and in the clarity and logic of their presentation is embodied the outstanding contribution of Greek thought to western culture, and the primary reason for considering it the culmination of the primitive point of view becomes clear.

Clarity of effect, logical construction, and refinement of detail are qualities which characterize the Greek way of thinking in all its expressive forms, but many other values were sacrificed to attain them. One of these was variety. Greek architecture expended its energy in creating very few types of buildings, notably the temple and the theatre; not more than a dozen subjects were considered worthy of treatment in Greek tragedy; and Greek sculpture was limited almost entirely to representation of the human body. These limitations, however, were conscious, self-imposed by the Greek temperament which sought to master the world by knowing it but could know it only through rational simplification. A similar limitation is apparent in the anthropocentric philosophy of the Greek, which held that man is the measure of all things. This concept is combined with the emphasis on

intellectual procedure and reasoned understanding that is implied in the idea that knowing is the final phase of evaluating experience, whereby is established the attitude expressed architecturally in shapes that are precise, logically organized, and designed with an infallible sense of formal proportion.

Although the Greek temple (Fig. 29) little resembles its Egyptian counterpart (Fig. 16), the conceptual process which established its basic form was much the same. Evidence for the early stages of the evolution that resulted in a building like *The Parthenon* (Fig. 29) is found in archaeology rather than in the history of art, but it is certain that the earliest Greek temples were like the Egyptian in resembling the houses of the time but were larger and their construction was more permanent. Some of these may have been built as early as the tenth century B.C.; their scant remains indicate that they were apparently little more than round or elliptical huts. A subsequent stage has elongated walls on the sides but retains a curved or apsidal end which eventually is squared, producing a rectangular plan. At this stage, the Greek house-temple must have been very similar in appearance to the Mycenaean megaron (Fig. 28), existing examples of which may indeed have influenced the early Greek builders. The Greek temple had walls

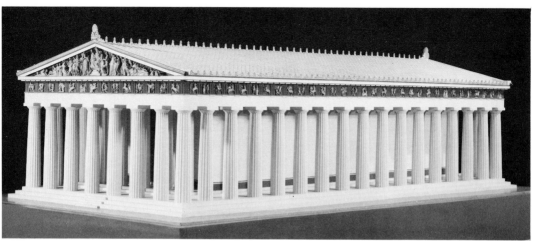

The Metropolitan Museum of Art, Purchase, 1890, Levi Hale Willard Bequest.

FIG. 29.   Athens.   The Parthenon (447–432 B.C.), Restored Model.

enclosing the room that contained the image of the god; this was entered through a portico of columns enclosed between the projecting ends of the side walls, and was covered in all likelihood by a roof that curved up or may even have been gabled. The next step in the development of the monumental temple form in Greece was apparently the surrounding of the building with a row of columns. This stage was reached in all probability about 750 B.C., for it is found in the temple of Hera at Samos, dating from that time and one of the oldest Greek temples of which there are more than the most fragmentary remains. This marks the final stage in the assembling of the various elements that made up the Greek temple scheme. Henceforth the efforts of Greek builders were directed toward refining these elements to achieve the most ideal and perfect effect.

The heart of the Greek temple plan was the sanctuary in which stood the statute of the deity to whom it was dedicated. Known as the *cella* in a Greek building, it may be the entire walled-in part of a small temple, but it is somewhat more developed in such a structure as the Parthenon (Fig. 30), being in two sections. The principal room is entered from the eastern end and is the shrine in which the statue of Athena was placed; the smaller chamber at the western end is the treasure room. In a temple as large as the Parthenon, the cella and the treasure room are surrounded on the outside by a peristyle, the free-standing columns that provide a covered passage around the walled-in portion of the temple; smaller temples usually have columnar porticoes only at one or both ends such as form the inner porches of the Parthenon. No fixed rule determined the number of these columns; there are eight on each end of the Parthenon, but six is more usual, and larger structures have as many as ten or twelve.

The most distinctive external feature of the Greek temple, both structurally and decoratively, was the column, whether Doric (Fig. 31) or Ionic (Fig. 32) in style. These names are taken from the geographical areas where the two forms are most frequently found. The Doric was used chiefly in the western part of the Greek world

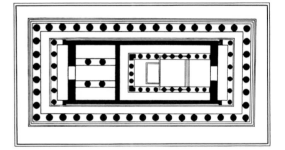

FIG. 30.   Athens.   The Parthenon, Plan.

that was settled by the Dorians; the Ionic predominated in the eastern or Ionian region. It was from the mingling of these races that the Greek of the fifth century was descended, and his architecture indicates this in using Doric and Ionic forms side by side and even combined in the buildings on the Acropolis in Athens (Fig. 36). Both types apparently developed along somewhat similar lines but without much interaction until the two regions were given temporary political unity by the founding of the Athenian Naval Confederacy after the defeat of the Persians in the battle of Salamis in 480 B.C.

Before examining the two basic Greek columnar types more closely, we should note that both forms are planned in accordance with rules which regulate not only the details of the column but also its relationship to other parts of the building. This relationship is known as the order, a term that implies the entire organization of the building and is not limited to the column alone. A third order in Greek architecture that first appeared late in the fifth century B.C. was the Corinthian; in Greek architecture it was a variation of the Ionic, differing from it only in the form of the capital.

The *Doric order* is the simpler of the two principal Greek types and the more straightforward in expressing the function of its various elements (Fig. 31). The base is a series of steps—usually three—from which the superstructure of the temple rises. The shafts of the peristyle columns rest directly on the topmost step which is usually called the stylobate, although this term

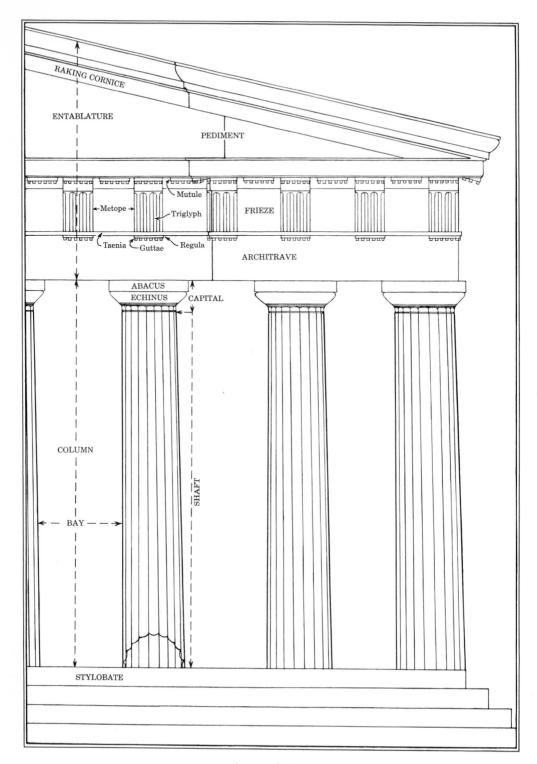

FIG. 31. The Greek Doric Order.

CORNICE

FRIEZE

ARCHITRAVE

CAPITAL

ABACUS

CUSHION

VOLUTE

NECKING

BASE

STYLOBATE

FIG. 32.   The Greek Ionic Order.

is specifically applicable only to the portion immediately under the columns. These shafts are circular in section and taper slightly toward the top; there is a very slight bulge or outward curve, called entasis, which reaches its greatest deviation from a straight line about one-third of its height above the stylobate. The surface is also grooved vertically with a series of hollows —usually twenty in number and elliptical in section—called flutes; the sharp edges where they meet are called arrises. Near the top of the shaft, the arrises are cut by a horizontal groove above which the shaft flares slightly in the necking where the flutes die away. A series of horizontal grooves above the necking separates it from the even more pronounced flare of the echinus whose elliptical profile leads to a heavy square slab called the abacus. Necking, echinus, and abacus make up the capital, which combines with the shaft to form the column. The space or intercolumniation between two columns is called a bay.

Above the columns and resting directly on the abacus blocks in a Doric building is a plain horizontal beam called the architrave. It is surmounted by the taenia, a continuous rectangular moulding, from whose lower face a small block with six pegs depends over each column and each bay; the blocks are regulae and the pegs guttae. Above the architrave is the frieze of alternate triglyphs—the panels with flutes—and metopes; these latter may be plain or carved in relief (cf. Figs. 259, 264). The cornice projects immediately above the frieze, its soffit or lower face slanting to continue the line of the roof; it has pegged slabs or mutules on the soffit, one for each triglyph and each metope. Above the cornice is a moulding along the sides of the building that has decorated openings for water spouts (Fig. 29); it slants up on the ends to form the top of the gable. This slanting moulding is called the raking cornice; the flat triangle it forms with the horizontal cornice is the pediment, in which sculptured figures were often placed (cf. Fig. 256). All the parts of the order above the columns together form the entablature.

Many details of the Doric order, like those in Egyptian building, suggest construction in material other than the stone in which they are best known, and there is ample justification for the conclusion that they evolved when traditional structural elements once made of wood or brick were reproduced in more durable materials. The capital, for instance, must originally have been a slab of wood placed between a supporting tree trunk and a lintel to keep it from splitting; a similar form is part of the Minoan column (Fig. 25), whose capital may well have suggested the form of the Doric echinus. The peglike

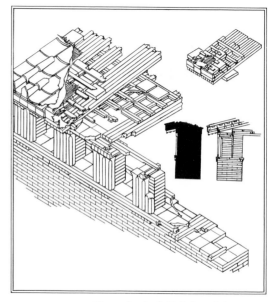

FIG. 33. Hypothetical Origin of the Doric Entablature.

guttae on taeniae and mutules are also reminiscent of wood-joining practice in fastening one plank to another. Other details, notably the triglyph and metope frieze, seem to have developed from forms in which both brick and small pieces of wood were used. L. B. Holland's ingenious and plausible suggestion regarding the hypothetical origin of this feature of the Doric order (Fig. 33) is based on such an assumption made after examining and correlating many measurements in existing examples of the order. Elements like the regula, taenia, triglyph cap, and mutule, for example, are all nearly equal in size. This suggests a basic unit of measurement or module such as could have been supplied originally by some small linear value—the thickness of a brick, for example—which is the mathematical root of all the larger dimensions of the building. In a brick wall surmounted by a roof, the openings near the top which may have been made to let smoke out of the interior would have been ten bricks in height and separated by small piers upon which the roof rafters were supported and which were faced with blocks of wood with chamfered corners as protection from wind and rain. This supplies the triglyph of the frieze, the metope being an opening, which, indeed, is the meaning of the word metope in Greek. Other than the suggestions inherent in the order itself, there is also literary evidence of forms originally in brick and wood in Doric buildings. In a guidebook of the ancient world, Pausanias, a Greek traveler of the second century A.D., mentions seeing a wooden column at the entrance to the treasure room of the temple of Hera built at Olympia about 580 B.C.; the cella walls of this temple are known to have been of sun-dried brick on a base course of stone. As was the case with the similar translation of forms in Egypt, the motive was desire for greater impressiveness and permanence in the house of the god than human habitations provided.

The proportions of the *Ionic order* (Fig. 32) are not as heavy as the Doric. The shaft is from eight to ten times the greatest diameter which is at the bottom, whereas the Doric shaft is about five or six times its greatest diameter as a rule. Another point of difference is the invariable use of a base between the Ionic shaft and the stylobate. This base is variously constituted, but the arrangement in the diagram, in which two convex mouldings are separated by a concave moulding, is more usual in Greece proper. Twenty-four flutes of semicircular section separated by flat fillets instead of the sharp Doric arrises are found on the shafts which taper, may have slight entasis, and are terminated at the top by a moulded necking. The capital of the Ionic order is its most individual feature. A band or echinus rests on the necking of the shaft and is

usually carved with a pattern of alternately oval and pointed forms making an egg-and-tongue moulding. The cushionlike form resting on the echinus droops over its sides in two hanging spiral scrolls or volutes; upon it rests a square thin abacus whose edge is moulded.

Like the Doric order, the Ionic entablature consists of architrave, frieze, and cornice, but the detail of each is different. The architrave has three horizontal bands, the upper two of which are stepped slightly forward; and its upper edge is moulded, with the leaf and tongue in this case. The frieze above it may be either a continuous band of relief sculpture or a series of small blocks called dentils; the example shown in Fig. 32 originally had such a band, although the figures are not represented in the diagram; late examples, after the fourth century B.C., sometimes have both figured frieze and dentils in the same order. The cornice and raking cornice have the same general form as the comparable elements in the Doric but differ in their mouldings. An origin in forms initially composed of brick and small pieces of wood may be assumed for the Ionic types as well as for the Doric, the voluted capital being originally a saddle block on top of a wooden shaft, and the dentils of the frieze the projecting ends of roof beams.

The Corinthian order which the Greek used as a variation of the Ionic in the latter part of the fifth century and during the fourth involves all Ionic elements but the capital. For this was substituted a form composed of a core shaped like an inverted bell with rows of leaves around the bottom and volutes springing from the center of each side as well as at the angles where they support a rather heavy abacus block with concave sides (Fig. 34). The leaves are adapted from the acanthus plant, a perennial that still abounds in Greece and which also suggested the motives in some Greek mouldings. Unlike the Doric and Ionic capitals, the Corinthian was not developed from an originally structural form but apparently served from the outset as a decorative element. Its invention was attributed by classic tradition to a bronzeworker named Callimachus; the character of its details—both leaves and scrolls— suggests metal models. First used in interiors, its

Epidauros Museum.

FIG. 34.   Corinthian Capital from
the Tholos (*ca.* 360 B.C.).

popularity in the Hellenistic period of the third
century B.C. and afterwards, when it almost
completely replaced the Doric and Ionic, was
partly due to its easy adaptation to certain problems in designing the angles of peristylar buildings in both Doric and Ionic styles. In the Doric,
the problem is to achieve a satisfactory compromise between structural tradition and decorative
perfection in the relationship between the angle

column of the peristyle and the end triglyph in
the frieze. In the Ionic, the basically two-sided
volute pattern of the scrolls is not as effective in
giving a sense of support to the top of the shaft
when seen from the side as from the front. As
long as the Greek was willing to strive for the
visual perfection that characterizes the design of
fifth-century buildings, these problems were
faced and disposed of, if not solved to perfection;
with the waning of this idealism in later periods,
the easier way of avoiding them altogether,
made possible by the Corinthian capital, was
preferred.

The history of Greek architecture which
reaches it climax in the fifth century B.C., reveals
an even and logical progression that is one of
the factors differentiating it most vividly from
the static and unvarying forms of Egyptian
building. An early temple like *The Basilica* (Fig.
35) at Paestum, built about 550 B.C. in a Greek
city a little south of Naples on the west coast of
Italy, is a good example of the archaic phase of
the Doric style. One detail thus characterizing it
is the odd number of columns in the façade
colonnade. This results from the elemental
practice of having a row of columns running the

FIG. 35.   Paestum.   The Basilica (*ca.* 550 B.C.).

length of the cella to aid in supporting the roof. Carried out to the peristyle at each end, this results in a column in the center. The visual effect of placing a solid on the axis of the symmetrical façade is seemingly to divide it in half and so impair its unity. The shape of these columns is another archaic characteristic; the taper and entasis are so pronounced that the shafts seem almost too weak to support the entablature in spite of their heavy proportions in which the height is but 4.4 times the greatest diameter. The broad flare of the echinus and the thickness of the abacus block are other details whose exaggeration indicates a style in its formative stages, reproducing as they do the descriptive characteristics of wooden forms but with the ponderous proportions which the structural limitations of stone imposed. This is the point in the evolution of Greek architectural style that corresponds to the way of thinking revealed in the massive forms of Egyptian building, but beyond which the Egyptian never went.

The most complete and perfect statement of the ideals of Greek architecture corresponds in time with the highest achievements in all Greek thought, in the Golden Age of the fifth century

B.C. The country's political independence had been made possible by Persia's defeat at Marathon and Salamis in 490 and 480 B.C.; and the sense of national individuality that began to develop in consequence found expression in the formation by the previously disunited city-states of a naval federation in which Athens played the dominant role from 461 to 430 B.C. Under the leadership of Pericles, funds raised by the federation to build a huge fleet were diverted to other ends, including the monumental embellishment of the *Acropolis* (Figs. 36, 37) in Athens, the great hill of rock that is the heart of the city. A rugged, irregular mass of stone, approximately 1000 feet in its longest dimension from west to east, it provided an unsurpassable site for the monuments erected upon it.

The main approach to the Acropolis from the city below was at the west through a monumental gate or entrance portico called *The Propylaea* (Fig. 38). Begun in 437 by the architect Mnesicles, the work had to be abandoned in 432. Although the unfinished building has suffered much damage, the principle forms can be observed as a result of restorations that have given the façade facing the Acropolis something of its

FIG. 36.   Athens.   The Acropolis, from the Southwest.

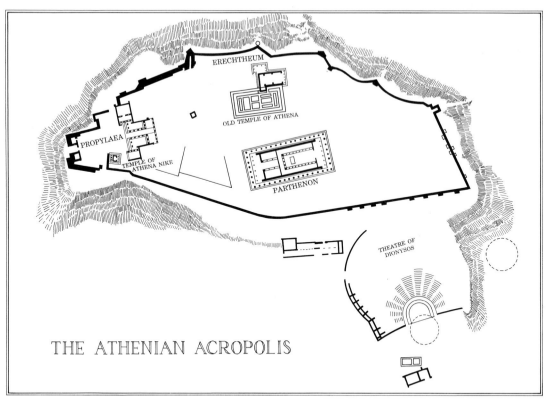

FIG. 37. Athens. The Acropolis, Plan.

FIG. 38. Athens. Mnesicles, The Propylaea (437-432 B.C.),
from the East.

original character. It was conceived as a gabled structure with Doric columns forming porches on west and east fronts, flanked by smaller buildings of which only one on the outer side was completed; the others were obstructed by previously existing structures on the site required for the entire project and had to be left incomplete. The central bay of each façade was one triglyph and metope wider than the others to permit the passing of chariots in ceremonial procession; pedestrians used the openings on the side. This central passage was flanked by columns that supported the roof; these were Ionic rather than Doric because the more slender proportions of that order made possible greater height for a given base diameter. The Propylaea is one of the first known buildings in which both orders are used. The general arrangement was traditional for entrance porticoes, but its perfection of structural and decorative detail was such that the Athenians took even greater pride in it than they did in the Parthenon.

Passing through the Propylaea, the observer beholds *The Parthenon* (Fig. 39) to his right on the south edge of the rocky plateau which is the summit of the Acropolis. The most complete example of the Doric style in temple architecture ever built, it was begun by Iktinos and Kallikrates in 447 B.C. and completed fifteen years later. Approximately 100 feet wide on the stylobate and nearly 230 feet long, it had eight columns on the front and seventeen on the sides, counting the angle columns in each figure. Inside the peristyle, a second row of columns at each end formed inner porticoes (cf. Fig. 30) from which wooden framed doors led into the cella at the eastern end and the treasure room at the west. Above these inner portico columns, the usual Doric frieze of triglyphs and metopes was replaced by a continuous figured frieze in the Ionic manner (Fig. 265), which also encircled the entire cella; it represented the Panathenaic procession, a quadrennial celebration in honor of Athena to whom the temple was dedicated. Nothing remains today of the interior walls and columns of the cella, but descriptions make approximate restoration possible (Fig. 40), although some details such as the source of illumination

FIG. 39.   Athens.   Iktinos and Kallikrates, The Parthenon (447–432 B.C.),
from the Northeast.

FIG. 40. Athens. The Parthenon,
Interior, from a Restored Model.

amount and quality to that of any other temple in the Greek world. The mouldings that are used in great profusion throughout the building are of similar perfection. Color was used as an accessory to carving in all parts of the building as some remaining patches indicate; the effect (cf. Fig. 29) must have been very different from the monotonous whiteness that is the current notion of Greek architecture.

The construction of the Parthenon reveals an astounding degree of technical skill. Earlier temples like the Basilica at Paestum were usually built of some material like coarse limestone covered with a thin layer of marble stucco; but the Parthenon was of marble throughout, except for the wooden door frames, doors, and roof timbers. No mortar was used anywhere; the columns were built up in horizontal sections or drums fitted together with joints so tight they can hardly be seen. The blocks of marble forming the walls were laid with similar care, with adjacent faces highly polished and held together by iron cramps let into slots and fixed in place with melted lead. The marble used in its construction —and for all the fifth-century buildings on the Acropolis—was quarried from nearby Mount Pentelicus; it contains a considerable amount of iron and has weathered to a rich golden brown. Its very fine grain made possible certain minute and delicate refinements of form that contribute greatly to the building's distinction.

Some of these refinements have been mentioned previously—the entasis of the columns, the subtle, almost imperceptible swelling of the shafts which makes them seem to yield slightly under the weight upon them with the result that they appear to be alive and elastic instead of stiff and inert as would be the case if the profiles were mathematically straight. The same effect is achieved in the building as a whole by making the surfaces of stylobate and entablature curve slightly upward in the center of façades and sides. The curvature is very slight—about two and three-quarter inches on the fronts and about four on the sides—but its part in the effect is perceptible nonetheless, for it and other similar refinements are responsible for the impression of life and vitality in the structure. Other minute

are controversial. The heroic ivory and gold statue of Athena made by Pheidias stood near one end of the cella, which was surrounded on three sides by a double range of Doric columns that probably supported a flat timber ceiling under the gabled roof; four Ionic columns apparently performed the same function in the smaller treasure room at the western end.

Sculptured figures and carved mouldings were an integral part of the Parthenon design. The frieze around the wall inside the peristyle has been mentioned. In addition each metope (Fig. 264) of the building was carved—ninety-two in all—and there were groups of figures in the round in both east and west pediments (Figs. 261, 262), a body of sculpture superior in

variations from mathematical regularity occur in the columns, whose axes are not strictly vertical but tilt slightly inward, and the diminution in width of the space between the angle columns and those adjacent on each side. None of these variations are so great as to be obtrusive; a casual glance would lead an uninformed observer to conclude that everything in the design of the building was mathematically exact and regular—an impression the architects wished to create. But they also wanted the structure to have a sense of life and organic unity which it would have lacked had it been no more than mathematically correct; the way they achieved this was by these minute variations from mathematical exactitude. Nothing illustrates better the pains the fifth-century Greek took to create plastic forms characterized alike by the semblance of mathematical perfection and of organic life than these meticulously calculated and executed effects.

Comparison of the Parthenon with the earlier Basilica at Paestum (Fig. 35) will make clear both the objective differences in detail of the two buildings and the ultimate formal purpose of the Doric architect. The exaggerations of mass and contour in the columns of the Basilica have disappeared, the Parthenon shafts being more slender, the tapering and entasis less pronounced, and the bays of the peristyle somewhat wider. These qualities all contribute to an effect of organically articulated form rather than mere massiveness, of subtle refinement rather than bulk. That this was the ideal toward which the Doric style was directed and that it was attained in the Parthenon is indicated by the fact that no changes of any importance in the order as seen here were made in later examples. Whatever could be said with the Doric vocabulary has been said once and for all in the Parthenon. Any attempt to enlarge or change it assumes a different ideal and another expressive idiom.

On the north side of the Athenian Acropolis almost directly across from the Parthenon stands the building which is the ultimate of the Ionic way of thinking in architecture. *The Erechtheum* (Fig. 41) was begun about 421 B.C.; but like the Propylaea and unlike the Parthenon, it was

FIG. 41. Athens. The Erechtheum (421–406 B.C.), from the Southeast.

never finished except for the part now standing, which was completed about 406 B.C. The building occupies an extremely uneven site which slopes sharply to the northwest; as a result, the floor of the north porch—the one seen through the columns in the illustration—is about ten feet below that of the east porch. This circumstance the architect had to accept, however, for the temple was erected to commemorate an extremely significant event in the legendary history of Athens which occurred on that spot—the contest between Athena and Poseidon to determine which of them should be the patron deity of the city. Poseidon struck the rock with his trident, causing his gift to mankind, a horse, to spring out; on this he staked his claim. When Athena responded by making an olive tree grow nearby, she was awarded the decision. The mementos of this contest—a spring of salt water on the spot where the horse emerged, and an olive tree—had to be taken into account in laying out the building.

The cella of the Erechtheum was a rectangle about sixty feet long and something over thirty feet wide; it was entered from the east. Like the Parthenon, its inner walls no longer stand and no indications of their arrangement remain. However, the cella must have been subdivided, since at least three deities were worshipped there —Athena, Poseidon, and Erechtheus in whose honor it was named, a legendary semidivine being who was reared by Athena and established her worship in Athens. There are three porches, on the east, north, and south sides; those to the east and north have Ionic columns, but these are replaced by statues of maidens called caryatides in the porch to the south. The original plan may have called for another chamber to the west, equal in size to the one built. Had it been constructed, the ensemble would have been symmetrical on the short north-south axis, and the north porch and that of the caryatides would have been in the center of the long sides. However, the area to the west of the finished portion of the building was consecrated to another deity whose priests would not yield their rights and the Erechtheum perforce remained uncompleted.

The site of the Erechtheum created such

difficult problems in planning that its architect apparently gave up all hope of achieving a harmonious and unified structure like the Parthenon and instead lavished his best efforts upon decorative details. For all its simplicity of character, the south wall of the cella is beautifully proportioned, and its fine-grained Pentelic marble lends itself admirably to the minute detail of the base and cornice mouldings. A notable feature of the building is the door into the cella from the north porch (Fig. 42), historically important as the first portal in Athens to be framed in stone instead of wood, and luxuriously decorated with mouldings and rosettes. The Ionic capitals of the six columns that support this porch are among the most elaborate and beautifully executed in Greek building (Fig. 32), with the triple spiral of the volutes and the delicate lotus and palmette moulding on the necking of the shafts. Other

FIG. 42. Athens. The Erechtheum. Door of the North Porch.

FIG. 43. Athens. The Erechtheum,
The Porch of the Maidens.

decorative details of the building include a palmette frieze along the top of the walls and, originally, a continuous band of white marble figures against a background of black Eleusinian limestone in the entablature.

The small porch on the south side of the Erechtheum (Fig. 43) differs from those on the north and east fronts in that figures of maidens instead of columns support the architrave. This practice of substituting human for architectonic forms is not without precedent in earlier Ionic Greek buildings, but it was not general, possibly because of a temperamental reticence in imposing mechanical functions upon an organic form. The Maidens of the Erechtheum are in no wise crushed beneath their burden, however, for the relationship of the straight drapery folds over the legs supporting the weight—the outer one in each case—and the balancing curves over the other legs creates an abstract rhythm of upward movement that successfully gives the impression of adequate support for the entablature. Furthermore, the bulk of the entablature is reduced in actuality, as well as in its visual weight, by omission of the figured frieze that appears elsewhere in the building; a row of dentils is used instead.

Like the Parthenon that is its Doric counterpart in perfection, the Erechtheum marked the end of a certain way of thinking, one that preferred an opulence of effect inconsistent with Doric austerity. Later taste found even the Ionic

somewhat overrestrained. These are the general circumstances that account for the later popularity of the Corinthian order which was first used in the late fifth century B.C.; one of the finest examples of it in Greek times—that in the Tholos at Epidauros (Fig. 34)—was executed about 350 B.C. The order was first used exclusively in interiors. The earliest instance of its use on exteriors is *The Choragic Monument of Lysikrates* (Fig. 44) erected in Athens in 334 B.C. as the monumental support of a bronze tripod awarded the winner of a choral contest. Upon a square base or podium is a circular cella surrounded by six columns recessed in the wall, though free from it. The bases and shafts are identical with those of the north porch of the Erechtheum, but the capitals consist of acanthus leaves and spiral volutes in an even more complex pattern than those in the example from Epidauros (Fig. 34). They support an entablature that is also made up of Ionic elements but which combines dentil and figured friezes in a way that has no precedent in fifth-century design. A single slab of marble carved in imitation of tiles covers the monument and is

FIG. 44. Athens. The Choragic
Monument of Lysikrates (334 B.C.).

FIG. 45. Epidauros. Polykleitos the Younger, The Theatre (*ca.* 350 B.C.).

surmounted by an elaborate finial of acanthus leaves that supported the bronze tripod for which the structure as a whole was the base. Although the monument is Greek and the details follow fifth-century models, the general effect, more ostentatious than earlier designs, indicates a tendency that is even more pronounced in the architecture of the later Hellenistic and Roman periods.

Among western civilization's most precious inheritances from Greece are the tragedies and comedies by its great playwrights such as Aeschylus, Sophocles, and Aristophanes. The origins of Greek drama are obscure and controversial, and no less so are those of the structures in which it was performed, except that both were related to the worship of Dionysos. A theatre with permanent seats that was built on the south slope of the Acropolis in the fifth century B.C. is apparently the first example of what became a characteristic Greek architectural form. Its present state is largely the result of modifications and rebuildings, but part at least of the *Theatre* (Fig. 45) at Epidauros is as originally designed. It was built about 350 B.C. after the designs of Polykleitos the Younger, who was also the architect of the Tholos in the same place whence, as was just said, came one of the finest of fourth-century Corinthian capitals (Fig. 34). Its plan is typical of all Greek theatres in being built around a circular orchestra with an altar in the center dedicated to Dionysos; the action of the play took place around this altar. The seats rise in

concentric curves from this orchestra and are supported on a hill which naturally or as a result of excavation slopes inward to form concentric banks that are a little more than semi-circles. On the other side of the orchestra from this auditorium was a rectangular building whose foundations are still visible. This was not a stage as in the modern theatre, but served as the background of the action in the orchestra, taking the place of the temple façade that had a similar function in the earliest dramatic performances; it probably also acted as a sounding board to enhance the acoustic properties which were always given very careful consideration. Character was imparted to this background building by the use of orders, usually Doric but sometimes Ionic; otherwise the architect's chief concern was to arrange the auditorium seats so the dramatic production could be seen and heard easily. The Greek theatre like the temple served a lofty function; hence it would be a mistake to consider it simply a place of entertainment and amusement as it is today.

In selecting a site naturally adapted to the particular requirements of his structure, the Greek theatre designer followed the usual procedure of his time. It would be difficult, for example, to imagine the buildings on the Athenian Acropolis (Fig. 36) on any sites that would reveal them to better advantage; the identity of each one is clearly established in its own individual terms like so many sculptured forms distinct against the sky. This formal self-sufficiency is, indeed, one of the outstanding characteristics of Greek buildings of the Golden Age and of other Greek art forms of that time too, as will be shown elsewhere; it is a direct expression of the Greek's enjoyment of organically conceived plastic form controlled and directed by the same unerring sense of proportion that made solving a problem in geometry a genuine pleasure to him. There is another aspect of this self-sufficient perfection of the Greek building, however, one that reveals its limitations as an attitude and also those of the period which accepted it as an ideal. A glance at the plan of the Acropolis (Fig. 37) will establish the fact that in laying out their buildings the architects showed no concern whatsoever for their communal effect. The Propylaea, Parthenon, and Erechtheum each have a different axis of their own. They are forms that can be understood only as isolated entities, and not in any other way; for if a relationship to some other object is needed to establish the significance of the object in question, obviously that significance is not inherent and complete.

The conception of a building as isolated from its surroundings and uninfluenced by them is elemental; and to the extent that Greek architecture exemplifies this, it is a primitive architectural style. But at the same time, it is also the most highly developed phase of primitive architectural style, for it represents an ideal of form that is organically integrated and organized—a whole that is the sum of its parts instead of being only a statement about them like the Egyptian temple (Fig. 16), which is as objective as the Greek in its detail but in which there is no controlling formal relationship between various parts except for the simple order of the axis. If the Greek did not wish to perceive the possibility of an organic relationship between his building and its surroundings comparable to that realized with such perfection within the building itself, this is only characteristic of an attitude which accepted the facts of nature as fixed and permanent values that had to be recognized and understood, and that could be controlled and directed but not modified. A later generation than that of the fifth-century Athens of Pericles and Iktinos was to question this concept.

When the Hellenistic city of *Priene* (Fig. 46) in Asia Minor was laid out late in the fourth century B.C. no effort was made to develop a pattern from nature as earlier Greek planners would have done; instead, a pattern was imposed on the natural site. The fortification walls are irregular because they follow the conformations of the terrain; but the city within is laid out in regular blocks divided by streets which run due east and west the length of the city and north

FIG. 46. Priene.   The City (late 4th cent. B.C.), Restored.

❧ 55 ❧

and south across it. The latter slant so steeply up the hill that most are negotiable only by steps, yet there is no trace of the difference in level in the relationship of the buildings to the plot plan as a whole or to each other. Moreover, the most important single element in the plan is not a building but the open market square or agora; the temple and precinct of Athena are given places of importance but without in any way modifying the basic compositional scheme of rectangular blocks separated by streets. The plan of Priene is important as one of the first attempts to lay out an entire city in accordance with a preconconceived scheme instead of following the natural conformation; the grid-iron that resulted has been developed in many more modern cities.

Two characteristics stand out in reviewing the architectural style of the Greeks. The first is its objectiveness. Nothing has to be added to the statement of function visibly implicit in the various forms in order to understand the part they play as details or as a whole. It is this objectivity that underlies the almost exclusive preoccupation of the Greek builder with post and lintel construction instead of the arch whose manner of operation cannot be so clearly grasped visually because comprehension of the objectively intangible lateral thrusts is essential to understanding its form. This makes for simplicity of form as well, but within that simplicity of the Greek design as a whole is great complexity of detail. This is the second outstanding quality of the Greek way of thinking in architecture, that from complex and involved detail it distills fundamental simplicity and unity of effect. It thus becomes a manifestation of a high order of the purpose of all Greek creative activity—to attain infinite variety and refinement within a consciously restricted expressive scope. The self-imposed limitations in attaining this goal make the Greek way of thinking seem far removed from application to modern problems, for contemporary life is so complex that the conscious simplification which to the Greek seemed justified by the harmonious character of the results cannot be reattained. But the beauty of clear and logical thought continues as a constant element in the forms of Greek architecture and an imperishable reminder of the enrichment of experience that, now as then, is a possible consequence thereof.

Detail of Fig. 52.

CHAPTER FOUR

Roman Architecture

The Greek of the fifth century B.C. lived in a world of thought infinitely refined and purposely limited. He hoped to master and control that world by restricting his experience of it to what was concrete and by investigating its objective characteristics as penetratingly as he could. As has been seen, this world was of but short duration; its perfectionism was compromised almost at the moment of its achievement. The diffusion of Greek thought following the conquests of Alexander the Great (356-323 B.C.) is the outstanding cultural phenomenon of the Hellenistic period—the third and second centuries B.C.—when the ways of thinking in architecture might be characterized as basically Greek but colored by regional distinctions; the result was forms that were very different in expressive content from those in which the original types were created. Destined to become the foremost of these regional architectural styles was that of Rome. After a period of internal consolidation and external expansion the high points of which were the destruction of Carthage and the conquest of Greece in 146 B.C., Rome became the dominant political and cultural force in the Mediterranean world and remained so for the better part of six centuries. Architecturally this dominance is symbolized by a remarkable consistency of style over almost the entire western part of Europe in the north and in the lands bordering the Mediterranean, from Spain in the west to Syria in the east as well as a considerable portion of northern Africa. The contrast between the vast area of Roman architectural style and the geographically limited Greek manner is only one of the significant differences between them.

Having somewhat the same relationship to the culture of Rome as that between the Aegean period and Hellenic Greece was the civilization of the Etruscans, the most powerful of the various peoples in the Italian peninsula before the Romans. There are only few remains of their architecture, but the Etruscans are known to have used the stone arch effectively, particularly in walls, and also to have employed post and lintel forms. Among the most impressive examples of their buildings that have been preserved are tombs, some rock-cut and others built of stone. Their painted decoration has some points of similarity with the archaic phases of Greek art, but their architectural character is directly the result of translating wood idioms into stone, the basic type being the house. The *Etruscan Temple* (Fig. 47), however, was apparently never carried to that point; it was almost always of wood, with some portions, notably the entablature, protected by a casing of terra cotta. The preservation of such buildings being manifestly impossible, the appearance of the temple can only be conjectured; but there is reasonably dependable evidence from two sources —small votive models made of terra cotta and the description of an Etruscan temple by Vitruvius,

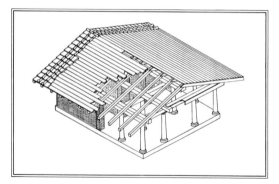

FIG. 47.   Etruscan Temple, After Vitruvius.

who wrote a book on Greek and Roman architectural theory in the first century A.D. The building is almost square, with a porch of free-standing columns at one end and sanctuaries at the other; the whole was raised above the ground on a rather high platform ascended by steps. The roof was made of wooden beams and rafters covered with tiles. Since such a superstructure was relatively light, wooden columns were generally used, especially in the earlier period. Even when stone supports came into use the retention of the wood entablature permitted the wide spacing of the columns that is a salient characteristic of the style. The usual Etruscan order was a variant of the Doric from which it may have been derived; the chief differences in Vitruvius' "Tuscan" column are the shaft, which is plain and without entasis, and the compound moulded base, whose height is equal to half the diameter of the shaft. As will shortly be apparent, certain characteristics of the Etruscan temple reappear in Roman forms, supplying a number of features that distinguish them from Greek examples.

The orders were used extensively in Roman building and the same types occur that are found in Greece, but with characteristic changes (Fig. 48). The Doric and Ionic were used only rarely and then in forms somewhat lighter in proportion than in Greek examples. The Roman Doric shaft has a base, the echinus is a simple quarter-round moulding, and the entablature is relatively thin. Figured and dentil friezes were regularly used together in the Roman Ionic; and the flutes of the shaft, when they occur, are grooves of semicircular rather than elliptical section. They were commonly omitted in Roman columns, possibly because of the preference for colored and veined marbles over the more uniformly toned varieties in most Greek buildings; in the latter the flutes have an important function in visually defining the column. Most popular of the Roman orders was the Corinthian, a fact which is not surprising in view of its growing popularity in later Greek and Hellenistic design. Its inherently rich appearance was often augmented by various additions to the basic acanthus leaves and volutes; one quite extensively employed was the so-called "Composite" capital in which Ionic scrolls are placed over the rows of leaves. This order first appeared on the *Arch of Titus* (Fig. 49), built in Rome about 82 A.D. to celebrate the conquest of Jerusalem in 70. Another Roman addition to the orders was the console or modillion—a scrolled bracket under the horizon-

tal and raking cornices (Fig. 48, F)—which also heightened the decorative effect of the order as a whole.

No less important than the changes the Romans made in the details of the orders is the different way they used them. In any Greek building of the fifth century (Figs. 38, 39, 41) the column is a structural fact. It is used as a supporting member and its physical function is defined by its form; for, standing free as it does, it is at once apparent that what rests upon it is sustained by the column and by the column alone. This is true even of the Monument of Lysikrates (Fig. 44) in which the columns are recessed in the wall of the circular cella but are nonetheless clearly distinguished from it. In contrast, the composite columns of the Arch of Titus (Fig. 49) are an integral part of the rectangular piers. They are not in the round but attached to the wall, and are clearly far from supporting the superstructure; that function is performed by the piers and the barrel vault

FIG. 48. The Greek and Roman Orders Compared.

FIG. 49. Rome. The Arch of Titus
(*ca.* 82 A.D.).

spanning the opening. Thus the function of these columns is primarily descriptive—the column being a decorative symbol which, when applied to the pier, expresses its supporting function in a way the basic form of the pier itself could not.

The *Maison Carrée* (Fig. 50) at Nîmes in southern France was completed in 16 B.C. It is the best-preserved Roman temple extant, and typically characteristic. It stands on a podium or base ascended at one end by a flight of steps, like the Etruscan temple (Fig. 47) which it also resembles in having a porch of free-standing columns. The order is continued on the outside of the cella which is the entire width of the structure for two-thirds its length of about eighty-six feet; in the form of applied Corinthian half-columns, the order has the same descriptive purpose here as it does in the Arch of Titus. Possibly it is even more appropriate in stating

the function of the temple wall in supporting the entablature in addition to performing the more basic duty of enclosing the internal space of the sanctuary. The proportions of the entablature are more Greek than is usually the case in Roman structures, but the rich *rinceau* or band of foliage used for the frieze differs from the Greek figured type and the cornices are provided with modillions. The column shafts are monolithic instead of being built up in drums, another feature distinguishing the usual Roman practice from the Greek. The Maison Carrée is one of the few Roman buildings in which linear refinements like those of the Parthenon are present; there are convex curves in plan on the long sides, and variations in the intercolumniations on all four fronts. The fact that the temple was built under Augustus Caesar, who is known to have had great enthusiasm for Greek ideas, may explain the presence of refinements in this case at least.

The Roman temple differs from its Greek counterpart not only in details of design but also because it was usually an element of a large-scale plan involving other buildings. The Greek ideas of this sort have been noted elsewhere, as well as the rather casual relationships that resulted, as in the arrangement of buildings on the Athenian Acropolis (Fig. 37). When its plan is compared with that of a typical Roman forum (Fig. 51), a difference is immediately apparent.

The forum in a Roman city was the principal place of public gathering. There is reason to believe that it developed from the open space or parade ground in the center of Roman military camps which were laid out in rectangular walled areas with two principal streets intersecting at right angles; this basic scheme seems to have been the point of departure for many Roman city plans as well. In the military camp, this space was dominated by the headquarters; in the city forum, the temple was the central element in a scheme that was as symmetrical with respect to it as the site permitted. In *Trajan's Forum* (Fig. 51), which was designed and laid out by Apollodorus of Damascus in the early second century A.D., nothing was permitted to interfere with carrying out this balanced scheme;

FIG. 50.   Nîmes.   The Maison Carrée (16 B.C.).

the result was one of the most grandiose large-scale architectural compositions in Roman times. A monumental gate led into an open court with columnar porticoes on three sides behind which to right and left buildings were laid out in semicircular plan; this court was the forum in the specific sense. Beyond it lay the Basilica Ulpia, a structure whose main axis was at right angles to that of the forum, roofed over and surrounded within by colonnaded aisles; at each end were large apses where legal court was held. Continuing on the principal axis, beyond the Basilica Ulpia was a smaller open court with the memorial column Trajan erected to celebrate his victory over the Dacians; two buildings that were entered through porches at the sides were libraries. At the rear of this court, Hadrian, Trajan's successor, erected a temple to his memory; like all the other principal buildings in the ensemble it is placed symmetrically on the principal axis; it is similar to the Maison Carrée in being on a high podium with steps at one end and a porch of free-standing columns.

The scheme of Trajan's Forum reveals an attitude different in principle from anything comparable with it in either Greek or Hellenistic architecture. The Greek in planning his building sought only a site that would enable it to appear to best advantage as an isolated form; he tried to develop a pattern from nature, and the axis of his structure was a controlling element only in its individual design (Fig. 37). The Hellenistic designer attempted to impose a pattern upon nature (Fig. 46) by laying out his buildings in a preconceived scheme but giving no pronounced accent to any one. The Roman builder makes everything subordinate to the axis in planning; he takes even less account of natural conformation than his Hellenistic predecessor, and strives for the complex and abstract symmetrical perfection that was his ideal with no concern for anything but achieving an overwhelming effect. It is the part the temple plays in such centralized ensembles that in large measure determines its form. The subordination of all design elements to the façade that results when it is accessible only from the front is characteristic of the Etruscan temple too (Fig. 47), but it remained

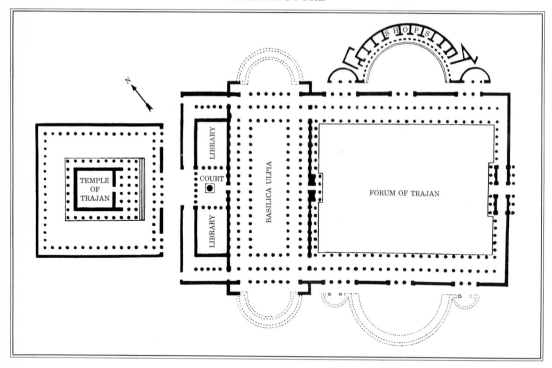

FIG. 51. Rome. Apollodorus of Damascus, The Forum of Trajan (112 A.D.).

for the Roman to carry to their logical conclusion the implications of the form with respect to large-scale planning.

In the forum with its varied architectural forms and its grandiose effects, the Roman reveals a quite different concept from the limited perfectionism of the Greek, and the variety of Roman building types makes this contrast even more apparent. One of these is the amphitheatre, a huge bowl-like structure in which great public spectacles like gladiatorial combats took place. Of those which have been preserved in whole or in part, the largest is the *Colosseum* (Fig. 52) in Rome, built between 75 and 82 A.D. From the outside, it consisted originally of an elliptical three-storied range of arches and piers surmounted by a wall without openings. All are decorated with orders—Doric on the ground level, Ionic for the second story, and Corinthian for the third and fourth. The three lower orders are of columns whose shafts are three-quarters free of the pier; the fourth is of flat pilasters rectangular in section. Like the applied columns of the Maison Carrée (Fig. 50), those of the Colosseum are

descriptive rather than structural. Their relationship to the piers behind them indicates the supporting function of those piers, for the fact that the arches still stand even in places where the applied columns have been removed makes it clear that the piers are the essential structural elements.

The arches in the outer wall of the Colosseum are not the only features that are visible in its construction. Behind them are vaults—long, uninterrupted semicircular ceilings of masonry which cover the corridors and passageways inside the structure; some have been exposed by the removal of the outer shell of piers and orders. The vaults of the outer corridors are of two types—barrel and groined (Fig. 53, A,B). The barrel vault is the simpler of the two, resembling nothing so much as a series of arches set face to face; the groined vault is formed by the intersection, at right angles, of two barrel vaults of equal span and height, the resulting diagonal lines being the groins. The groined vault is sometimes called a cross vault. In both cases, since the arch is the basic structural principle, buttressing

FIG. 52. Rome. The Colosseum (75–82 A.D.).

is essential to the stability of the vault. That of the barrel type must be continuous because its thrusts are exerted throughout its entire length; in the groined or cross vault, buttressing is needed only at the angles since the thrusts of the two barrel elements that make it are mutually deflected along the groin. In the ground story of the Colosseum there are two elliptical corridors which are both barrel vaulted; the lateral thrusts of the outer one are absorbed by the heavy wall over the arcade on the outside and by those of the inner vault on the inside. This is buttressed

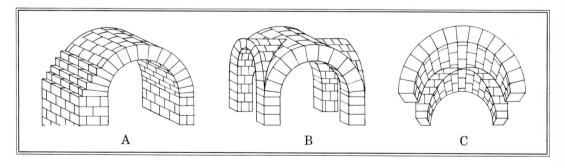

FIG. 53. Barrel and Groined Vaults

in turn on the inside by the ends of other vaults perpendicular to it which covered the passages leading into the interior of the amphitheatre and also supported the marble seats in the two lower sections.

The vault in a structure like the Colosseum was of considerable value. It made possible, for example, relatively unobstructed passageways that would have been impossible if the heavy mass of the upper stories had been supported by lintels on posts. Another practical advantage was the fact that it could be built of concrete instead of stone, with consequent great saving in cost. Roman concrete was a mixture of small stones or broken bricks combined with a cement made of volcanic dust mixed with water; this was poured in moulds—first a layer of brick and stone and then the dust and water mixture until the form was complete—where it hardened into a homogeneous mass of surprising strength and durability. Reinforcements of brick or cut stone were often put into the moulds before pouring. As an inexpensive medium lending itself to vast structural projects, concrete was admirably suited to the Roman architectural temperament which found satisfaction in the large and grandiose. The great public buildings of the Empire, which could not possibly have been built in any other medium known at the time, have no equal for sheer massiveness until the structures of the late nineteenth and twentieth centuries constructed with the aid of steel. They were cheap to build, moreover, since otherwise useless material could be employed in the concrete mixture; many buildings in Rome erected after Nero's famous fire in 64 A.D. are of concrete; the stones in them show signs of having been burned and hence were useless as structural material in their own right. In buildings monumental in character, the concrete walls and vaults

FIG. 54. Rome. The Basilica of Maxentius (310–*ca.* 320 A.D.).

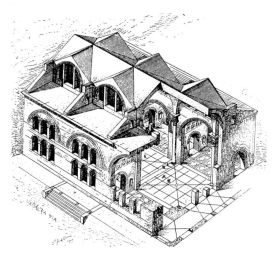

FIG. 55. Rome. The Basilica of Maxentius, Restored Perspective.

were faced with cut stone or brick laid in a pattern—a type of ornament that parallels the applied order in principle.

Characteristically Roman in function, size, structural character, and material is the *Basilica of Maxentius* (Figs. 54, 55), begun in 310 A.D. by the emperor for whom it is named, although it is also associated with his successor, Constantine, who finished it about 320. It stands between the Roman Forum and the Colosseum; and even in ruins, the structure is impressive. The Roman basilica was designed to accommodate large gatherings for various purposes—as places of business, law courts like the Basilica Ulpia in Trajan's Forum (Fig. 51), and so forth. The problem of providing unobstructed shelter on the scale involved required vaulting, although some earlier examples—again like the Ulpia— were roofed with timber ceilings supported on columns. The size of the building was also a factor in concrete being used in constructing it, for it is 265 feet long and 195 feet wide, and the height to the top of the groined vault over the central aisle is 120 feet. The choice of a groined vault to cover the central aisle was dictated by the necessity of lighting the interior. A barrel vault must be buttressed its entire length, and openings in the sides above the level of the vault

spring would weaken it; but with a groined vault the openings in the sides can be as large as the entire arch if desired, because the thrusts are concentrated at the angles. In the Basilica of Maxentius, the large semicircular windows in the upper level are in the sides of the groined vaulted bays of the central aisle which were covered on the outside with gabled roofs of tile to protect the masonry of the vaults. The thrusts of the vaults are buttressed by the sloping walls above the side-aisle roofs between the large windows, those being the points where they are concentrated. The side aisles were covered with barrel vaults perpendicular to the principal one of the building; those over the north aisle are still intact after centuries of neglect (Fig. 54), an impressive tribute to the durable concrete of which they are made.

A planning and construction problem similar to that involved in the Basilica of Maxentius arose in another characteristically Roman type of building—the public baths which were the centers of Roman social life as the basilicas were their places of business—for here also large crowds of people had to be accommodated in an enclosed space. The groined vault was extensively employed in the principal rooms, as can be seen in the illustration of the concourse of the *Baths of Caracalla* (Fig. 56), built chiefly between 211 and 217 A.D. Here, as was generally the case with Roman buildings purposely impressive in character, the concrete walls and piers and vaults were faced with thin slabs of marble or covered with moulded stucco; and the huge Composite columns surmounted by partial entablatures which seem to support the vaults are likewise no more than decorative.

Concrete as the basic material and the arch principle of construction in yet another form— the dome—are the outstanding structural characteristics of another Roman building of great importance, the *Pantheon* (Figs. 57, 58). Historically it is of interest in being the oldest roofed building of monumental character in the world that is still intact, the major portion—the rotunda and its dome—having been erected by Hadrian about 120 A.D. It is built of brick and concrete with a stone facing. The exterior (Fig. 57) is

FIG. 56. Rome. The Baths of
Caracalla (211-217 A.D.), Restored.

impressive chiefly by virtue of its great bulk,
for the dome is so low that it can hardly be seen
from the narrow side streets and it is almost
entirely cut off from view in front by the porch
of sixteen columns surmounted by a broad pediment. The interior (Fig. 58) is as high as it is
wide at the greatest diameter—141 feet—the
dome being something less than a hemisphere for
the circular wall supporting it rises to a height of
about 75 feet. This wall is in two levels, separated
by a full entablature resting on Corinthian
columns and pilasters which stand in and frame
respectively a series of deep recesses in the thickness of the wall itself. Above the columns framing
the recess immediately opposite the entrance
portal, the entablature breaks out from the wall
in a characteristically Roman way. The upper
level of this wall is decorated with pilasters that
frame niches and panels and support a cornice
from which the dome rises. Its inner surface is

faced with concrete and is decorated with a
pattern of rectangular recessed panels known as
coffers, a motive also used in the vaults of the
Basilica of Maxentius (Fig. 54) and the Baths of
Caracalla (Fig. 56). The reduction in mass of
vault or dome effected by this device is its structural function; in the Pantheon, the coffers are
decorative as well in emphasizing the upward
overarching lines of the cupola and focusing
attention upon the circular opening at the top.
This opening, called an oculus, is about 29 feet in
diameter and is the only source of light in the
interior.

The construction of the Pantheon is very
ingenious. The recesses in the circular wall supporting the dome are so deep that it is actually
converted into a series of eight heavy piers.
Upon these piers is concentrated the weight
of the wall above and the dome by a system
of arches built into the thickness of the wall
itself—arches which are both radial and tangent
to the circumference of the dome and wall.
When used in this way, they are called discharging
arches because they carry the crushing weight
upon them away from the space they span to the
members by which they themselves are supported.
The Pantheon is thus not an inarticulate mass of
brick, stone, and concrete but a highly organized
system of arches clothed in a skin of facing
material. Although the concrete became a hard
and homogenous mass as soon as it dried out in
the forms, the lateral thrusts of the dome are
carefully buttressed by the stepped masses visible
at its springing on the exterior (Fig. 57), an
indication of the careful study given to the purely
structural problems of the building.

Interesting though these technical considerations are in explaining how the Pantheon was
built, they are subordinate in importance to the
effect created by the form to which they contribute. The Pantheon was one of the first
buildings to be consciously composed as an
interior—as a volume of space that is given
character by the solids enclosing it. In it, this
character is balanced geometrical unity, created
by equality of height and diameter and isolated
by the cupping and defining effect of the dome
that is emphasized by the coffered pattern of its

surface and given scale by the precisely limited indication of external space provided by the oculus at the top. So powerful is the sense of enclosure created by the interior design of the Pantheon that its space seems almost a tangible substance to be isolated and handled as objectively as any Greek architect treated column or architrave. In his endeavor to compose architecturally with elements that are specific and comprehensible through the senses, the Roman reveals himself of the same classic stock as the Greek; in his extension of that conception to include imponderable space as well as tangible and plastic forms the difference between his broadened point of view and the purposely limited one evident in Greek design is equally apparent.

The circular domed interior of the Pantheon is as impressive a formal unity today as when it was built. To the man of those days—and indeed until the end of the Renaissance when Palladio

spoke of it as bearing "the figure of the world" —it had profound symbolic meaning as well. Dio Cassius, a Roman historian of the early second century, accounts for its name, which means a house of all the gods, as follows: "It is called thus possibly because it included images of many gods in its statutes . . . but I believe that the reason is the similarity of its cupola-form to the heavens." The peculiar significance of circular buildings as commemorative or memorial structures in ancient times has been pointed out elsewhere (cf. pages 37-38). The Romans subscribed to this concept, as in the well-known Tomb of Hadrian, now the Castello Sant'Angelo in Rome; it is continued in the mausoleums and baptisteries of the Middle Ages whose plan is invariably of a central type, i.e., circular or polygonal. There is reason to believe that the rosettes in the Pantheon dome coffers were gilded originally, emphasizing the skylike, astral character of the whole. This idea too was

FIG. 57.   Rome.   The Pantheon (*ca.* 120 A.D.)

FIG. 58. Rome. The Pantheon, Interior, from the
Painting by G. P. Panini.

apparently used in the domed buildings of the
Middle Ages (cf. Fig. 74). It is hardly to be
doubted that the appropriateness the dome has
been felt to have through the ages for buildings
of monumental character and specific significance (cf. Figs. 163, 190) is only a reflection of the
meaning attributed to it since earliest times.

The impression of a materialistic people
created by the Roman public buildings is reinforced by observation of the houses they lived
in. The Greek of Pericles' time in Athens was
privileged to gaze every day at temples of surpassing beauty, but he lived in a house that was
little more than a place to eat and sleep in and
so lacking in monumentality and permanance
that only the scantiest remains exist today. By

contrast, Roman houses, though based on Greek prototypes, were relatively pretentious. The type of house found in excavating the city of Pompeii from the lava and ashes that buried it when Mount Vesuvius erupted in 79 A.D. is not the only kind the Romans built, but these remains permit a quite accurate restoration of the original forms (Fig. 59). The outside was unimpressive because the narrow streets in the residential district of the city permitted little but the necessary enclosing walls and entrances. Within, the average house was divided into two main parts. The first, built about an open court that was entered from the street through a passageway and surrounded by columnar porticoes, is called the atrium. It usually had a fountain in the center, and was the semipublic portion of the building where the owner often carried on his business. At the back of the atrium was another passage, usually with a recessed niche or small room at one side in which the household gods were enshrined. This led to the second main part of the house which was also a porticoed court but it was called the peri-style (Fig. 60); it was often treated as a garden with shrubs and plants and decorated with sculpture. This was the domestic center of the building. Dining, reception, and retiring rooms were on the first floor, the bedrooms and the like on the second. At the rear of the peristyle court was located a large hall or salon which frequently overlooked another garden back of the house. The walls of this court and of the rooms opening from it were often elaborately painted (Fig. 364) with episodes from myth and legend or with landscapes. The whole was well designed for ease in living with considerable regard for privacy and comfort.

Some of the most impressive examples of Roman building were entirely utilitarian and made no pretense to architectural distinction. Such are the aqueducts by which water was brought, frequently from distant points, to the cities of the Roman Empire. They were water channels, open or enclosed and lined with concrete or finely jointed stone, which were carried on arches where they appeared above ground or through tunnels in the mountainous regions

FIG. 59. Typical Pompeiian House, Restored.

FIG. 60.   Pompeii.   The House of the Vetii (1st cent. A.D.),
The Peristyle.

where the water usually originated. Its flow was insured by sloping the level of the channel from its source to its end. The *Pont du Gard* (Fig. 61) near Nîmes, an important Roman provincial city in southern France, is part of one of these aqueducts. Built in the first century A.D., the entire system was more than twenty-five miles long; it ran underground for the most part but crossed the river Gard on a series of superimposed arches some 900 feet long and about 180 feet high. These arches were built of stone, laid in vertical slices on wooden centering; this centering was used only in the head where it was supported by still visible projecting courses, a procedure that in its economy is characteristic of Roman structural practice. No attempt was made to give the Pont du Gard formal architectural character in the usual Roman manner by applied ornament; but its fine proportions, the skillfully varied dimensions of the two lower ranges of arches, and the strong rhythm set up in the heavy piers topped off by the smaller arches above give it great distinction nonetheless. Comparison with a modern bridge (Fig. 197) reveals the parallel in

method and effect of similar structures built with other materials and utilizing different principles but motivated in much the same way.

Of all the historical styles, Roman architecture is nearest to the modern taste. In its utilitarianism, its striving for grandiose effects, and its frank divorcing of structural and ornamental facts, there are many parallels to average contemporary building. But it also produced many different types, some of which have proved capable of being adapted to the needs of other and later civilizations. The football stadium of today is only a variation of the Roman amphitheatre (Fig. 52), and the vaulted halls of the public baths have served as models for the concourses of innumerable railroad stations; a notable instance is the Pennsylvania Station in New York whose design was originally based directly on that of the Baths of Caracalla in Rome (Fig. 56). Such parallels as these suffice to show the eminently practical point of view of the Roman architect. For him the form of a building was established primarily by practical considerations of usefulness and stability, and

FIG. 61.   Nîmes.   The Pont du Gard
(1st cent. A.D.).

determined by its plan and the materials used in its construction. His conscious conception of architectural character in a formal sense is seen in the striving for size and ostentation in his monumental structures, effects achieved by sheer bulk and lavish use of applied decoration. Both these qualities are overshadowed in ultimate significance, however, by the space concepts that are, in the final analysis, the Roman's most important contribution to the art of building. Whether the problem involved relating the exterior design of a structure to its environment or giving character to its internal volume, the Roman architect was the first to sense the value of space as an architectural element and it has been a factor in the art ever since.

Detail of Fig. 70.

CHAPTER FIVE

Architecture of the Early Middle Ages

The grandeur of Roman architecture was a reflection of Roman military strength and economic power, and as long as those were maintained, the character of Roman building was consistent. Even at the moment when such a characteristic example of this style and attitude as the Basilica of Maxentius (Fig. 54) was in process of construction, however, there were positive indications of change in the life and thought of the Roman Empire. In 313 A.D. a royal edict issued at Milan in northern Italy gave official status to a religious cult that had existed in Rome for many years but had never attained such recognition before—Christianity. Ten years later, in 323 A.D., the emperor

Constantine himself professed Christianity, and it thenceforth became the state religion, a position of eminence it maintained for many centuries. If recognition of Christianity was not in itself an indication of the declining power of the Roman state—as might be inferred from the legend of Constantine's conversion on the battlefield when he renounced the pagan gods of Rome to avail himself of the help of God— the fact that seven years later Constantinople was established as capital of the Empire, located in the Near East at the juncture of the Bosporus and the Sea of Marmora, clearly reveals that the rigid political and social discipline that was the core of Roman civilization no longer existed. The subsequent history of the Western or Latin Empire bears this out. Rome fell to Alaric, a German chieftain, in 410, and the once vast empire north of Italy was almost completely dismembered by Vandals, Goths, and Franks during the fifth century. In 476, another German leader, Odoacer, ascended the throne of the Western Empire. Although the relations he established with the Eastern Empire were maintained by Theodoric the Goth and were even strengthened briefly during the sixth century when Justinian reigned in Constantinople (527- 565), there was no effective opposition to the incursions of yet another barbarian tribe— the Lombards—in 568. This date marks the end of even the smallest pretense at maintaining the political autonomy of the Western Empire.

In contrast to this history of progressive secular decadence, the fortunes of the Church mounted almost from the time it was recognized. Its doctrines appealed strongly to those revolted by the spiritual and moral laxity of the times and the integrity of its leaders won many converts. Often it was the churchman who stayed to meet the invaders when officers of the Empire fled their posts—it was Pope Leo I who faced Genseric the Hun at the gates of Rome in 455. The relationship thus suggested epitomizes the culture of the Middle Ages. The spiritual power of the Church was substituted for the secular power of the Roman Empire, and for the better part of a thousand years such continuity and consistency of thought as there was in western Europe existed within the walls of churches and monasteries.

In the Western or Latin Empire, the architecture of Christianity understandably derived at first from that of Rome as far as comparable elements or types of building are concerned. The Christian architect's problem was not without certain parallels in Roman building, for the first requirement of a church was to provide an enclosed space wherein the faithful might partake of the sacraments and hear the Word of God. The type of building developed to meet these requirements is called a basilica (Figs. 62-64); its form apparently was based on elements from several sources, notably the Roman house and basilica. It may seem strange at first that the Church fathers did not hesitate to avail themselves of pagan ideas in creating the earthly shrines of their faith; but this is directly paralleled in the forms of the faith itself, for many Christian practices were taken over almost directly from the pagan cults that flourished in Rome during the first centuries of the Christian era. Furthermore, when the first Christian edifices were being built in the West, practical considerations weighed more heavily than spiritual scruples. The Church urgently needed buildings of its own so that the cult might be properly housed; and it drew upon all available sources for ideas for design and also for building materials, a fact apparent not only in the form and general character of the buildings but also in much of their undeniably poor construction.

The *Old Basilica of St. Peter* (Figs. 62-64) at Rome was built over the saint's tomb in a cemetery not far from the Gardens of Nero, the emperor who ordered his execution. Erected at the order of Constantine, it was built between 324 and 354; the work actually began, it seems, about 330. This basilica was demolished in the early sixteenth century to make way for the Renaissance structure of the same name (Fig. 130), but its form is well known from drawings and descriptions, and the various restored plans and other views give a possibly more informative impression of the appearance of a typical Early Christian or Latin basilica than any single existing structure does. It consisted in general of two parts which are shown clearly in the perspective view and the plan—the atrium and the church proper.

The atrium is the open court in front of the church surrounded by columnar porticoes; there is a fountain in the center. In these respects it resembles the similarly named part of the Roman house (Fig. 59) from which it was probably derived, since the form provides for certain features of the rites celebrated in the church which had doubtless been developed when such celebrations were held in the houses of the faithful. In the Christian basilica, the atrium was a place where persons could assemble who were not qualified to participate in the ritual inside the church, such as the penitent or the unbaptized. Architecturally, it secluded the building from the turmoil of the street. The portico of the atrium which gave access to the church proper is known as the narthex; it sometimes appears alone as an entrance porch in churches that do not have complete atriums.

The church of St. Peter's was divided internally into five aisles (Fig. 64) extending almost its entire length and separated from each other by rows of columns. The central and largest of these is called the nave; the others are the side aisles. The number is not fixed, for only the largest churches had five; as a rule the nave was flanked by one aisle on each side but in some very small churches there was only a nave. At the end of the nave and side aisles opposite the entrance is another aisle or space whose long axis is at right angles to that of the main body of the church; it is shown in the exterior view, covered by the gabled roof perpendicular to that of the main arm of the building. It is called the transept and is found as a rule only in the largest of the Latin basilicas; it usually projects beyond the side-aisle walls, giving the plan the shape of a capital letter T. Opposite the nave and across the transept is a semicircular space called the apse. In it or directly in front of it stood the altar; the bishop's throne was placed against the

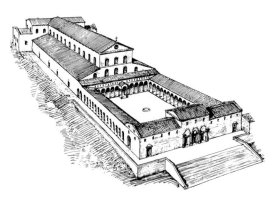

FIG. 62.   Rome.   Old St. Peter's
(ca. 330-354),
Restored Perspective View.

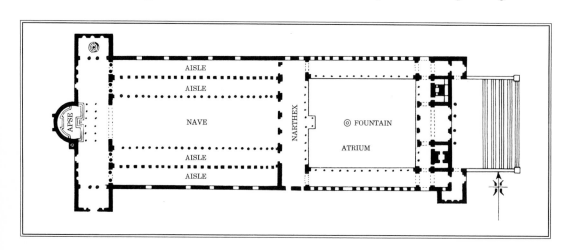

FIG. 63.   Rome.   Old St. Peter's, Plan.

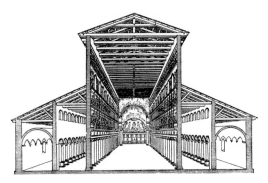

FIG. 64. Rome. Old St. Peter's,
Interior Elevation, Restored.

semicircular wall and flanked by the seats of the lesser clergy.

The interior elevation or vertical design of an Early Christian basilica like the Old Church of St. Peter (Fig. 64) consists of rows of columns between the nave and the aisles; those flanking the nave are the nave arcade and support a wall pierced by a row of windows. This row of windows is called the clearstory; it supplies direct illumination for the nave. Light for the side aisles comes from windows in the lower outer walls which also support the slanting roofs over them. These as well as the gabled roofs over nave and transepts are supported by triangular trusses of wooden beams which rest directly upon the walls.

Simple as the basilican church may seem, it is of great importance as a type, for it is the fundamental scheme of nearly all Christian churches. The building is invariably oriented unless unavoidable conditions make it impossible. The usual Christian practice is to place the entrance at the west and the altar and apse at the eastern end —a procedure which was established during the fourth century, although some of the first Christian basilicas like Old St. Peter's are oriented in the opposite direction. In either case, axial orientation is one of the points that distinguish the Christian basilica from the pagan building type of the same name (Fig. 51, 54, 55) and from which certain of its features were apparently taken. As was pointed out earlier, the Roman law and business basilicas were places for the accommodation of large crowds and as such

they were the logical model for the Christian meeting house. Although some of the Roman basilicas were vaulted (Fig. 55), most of them, like the Basilica Ulpia (Fig. 51), apparently had wooden roofs resting on clearstoried walls supported by columns; the interior division into spaces corresponding to nave and side aisles with apses at the ends is also quite clear.

The changes made by the Christian builders are of great importance, as indications of the differing significance of the various forms. The entrance to the pagan basilica was usually in the center of one of the long sides. From that point the interior gave an effect of static symmetry, the columnar arcades carried around the ends and the apses behind them completing the effect of balance and equilibrium; this is evident in the plan of the Basilica Ulpia in Trajan's Forum (Fig. 51). The entrance to the Christian basilica, however, is in one of the ends; a single apse opposite is made visible by omitting the returned colonnades. The apse thus becomes the focus of the interior design—the goal toward which the movement created by the rhythmic succession of the columns inevitably tends. To state it in strictly formal terms, the distinction between the Roman basilica interior and the Christian type is that between a design unified by symmetrical balance of plastic forms and one unified by an axis of movement; expressively, the distinction is between emphasis on visible and objective elements on the one hand and abstract and intangible sensation on the other. The significance of these distinctions is their intimation of a new orientation of thought in the western world, an orientation that reaches its clearest exposition in the Gothic cathedral of the thirteenth century.

From a structural point of view, the Early Christian basilica was very simple. In the first to be built, the nave arcade columns supported straight lintels (Fig. 64) which were often taken from pagan buildings and used with little concern for the consistency, or lack of it, in the carved patterns. Later, semicircular arches were substituted for the architraves as in the church of *Santa Sabina* (Fig. 65) which was begun in 425. Apses were covered with half-domes of masonry,

FIG. 65. Rome. Santa Sabina (425), Nave, Looking East.

but there was invariably a wooden roof over nave and side aisles. This roof was structurally the least satisfactory part of the building; its liability to destruction by fire was both very great and ever present, if the numerous contemporary records of churches being struck by lightning and completely destroyed can be trusted. It may seem strange that the fireproof masonry vaults used so skillfully by Roman architects were not used by Christian architects, for there is evidence of such structural methods even after the first churches were built. The explanation is not far to seek. As was pointed out earlier, the Roman buildings from which the Christian basilica derived were usually roofed with timber, and coverings of this material were generally associated with this type of building. Furthermore, wood was relatively plentiful and a trussed roof could be constructed more easily, rapidly,

and cheaply than even the simplest vault—considerations that weighed more heavily than both the relative impermanence of the wooden roof and its incoherent relationship to the rest of the interior, as is obvious in the view of Santa Sabina. The walls, usually of rubble faced with coarse stone or brick in the Roman manner, were not very heavy as a rule.

The exterior of the Latin basilica is rarely impressive. The principal façade was sometimes decorated with mosaic, but there was seldom anything more on the sides than wall arcades framing the clearstory and side-aisle windows (Fig. 71). The interior, on the other hand, was the object of extensive decoration designed to amplify and accentuate the focusing effect of the columnar arcades, thus expressing the significance of the altar as the heart of the design. This preferably took the form of mosaics on the walls below and around the clearstory windows; although those originally in Santa Sabina (Fig. 65) no longer exist, other examples still in existence illustrate their effect. The mosaics consisted of scenes and figures executed in small cubes of colored glass held fast in the plaster of the wall (Fig. 365). They are found in the apse as well (Fig. 72). The glow of shimmering and luminous color they impart to the interior contributed greatly to the abstract and immaterial atmosphere appropriate to Christian thought. This may possibly not have been a conscious factor in determining the character of the basilica, for mosaic decoration was common in Roman buildings as well; it is known, furthermore, that the ostensible purpose of such decoration was to inform those of the faithful who could not read. But the introduction of color and light in the basilican interior provided intangible expressive elements in the design that complement the axis of movement in the nave arcade. For the better part of a millennium the history of European architecture was concerned with attempts to create an adequate synthesis of these elements in the interests of a more comprehensive interpretation of the Christian ideal of emotional belief.

While the western or Latin portion of the Roman Empire experienced the parallel phenomena of political decline and the growth of the Christian Church, the Eastern Empire—its capital at Byzantium was renamed Constantinople—pursued a course that avoided the physical disruption inherent in the recurring attacks of invaders that so effectively undermined the power of Rome. This it owed to the relative protection from the wandering Teutonic and Slavic tribes afforded by its geographical location. There were still social and economic factors to contend with, however, and the rulers following Constantine (272-337) were weak for the most part. Not until the reign of Justinian I (483-565) which began in 527 is there a consistent architectural expression of the mingled classic, Oriental, and Christian elements that constituted Byzantine culture.

Christian architecture of the eastern or Byzantine style was developed to meet require-ments like those of the Latin west, as far as function was concerned. As has been noted, the basilican plan with its longitudinal axis provided best for these requirements. There are a few structures of this type in the Byzantine area such as the church of St. Demetrius at Salonica in Greece and St. John of the Studion in Constantinople; both date from the fifth century and are similar to the west Christian buildings of the fourth and fifth centuries in Rome in having naves and side aisles with columnar arcades and wooden roofs.

Obviously, however, there are considerable differences in plan (cf. Figs. 63, 67) and interior (cf. Figs. 65, 68) between Latin and Byzantine Christian basilicas. The most significant of these is the incorporation of a dome in the Byzantine scheme. Recent studies on the symbolism of architectural forms, notably those of E. Baldwin Smith, point out the traditional importance of the dome as a significant form in the architecture of the Orient and the Near East where from earliest times it was associated with ideas of divinity and royalty. There is conclusive evidence that wooden domes were used for pre-Christian palaces and temples in these regions, and it was only natural that the form should be thought essential in Christian churches. But the problem of translating the form from wood into masonry was difficult, particularly when its circular shape had to be adjusted to the rectangular areas of the basilican plan.

As the Romans used the dome in the Pantheon, the problem of its relationship to the supporting walls was simple because the plan of the structure as a whole was circular (Fig. 57). As the Byzantine builders employed it in the basilica, the problem was very difficult because the most that could be done in laying out the plan was to create a square area over which to place the dome as effectively as possible. The nature of the problem is evident in the first diagram in Fig. 66, where such a square is lettered $ABCD$. The sides are four arches, as indicated in the fourth diagram; the circle E in this square is the base of a dome whose diameter is equal to the sides of the area; the dome outside this square—FGH—has a diameter equal to its

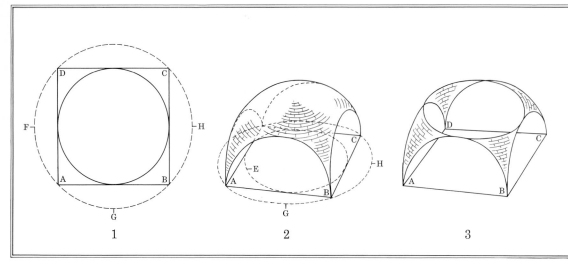

FIG. 66.   The Spherical Pendentive.

diagonal. It is obvious that a dome of either diameter cannot be fitted directly to the supporting arches. One method of solving the difficulty was building a squinch at each angle of the area; this is done by laying a lintel across the corners, reducing the square to an octagon, and repeating this process. This builds up the supporting base above the level of the arch tops and at the same time increases the number of angles in the base polygon until it approximates a circle. This method of transforming a square base into a circular one is good as a utilitarian measure but is not particularly effective in appearance; it was a makeshift at best and is found as a rule only in buildings rather elemental in character.

The most satisfactory method of fitting a circular dome to a square base is by spherical pendentives. In geometrical terms, a spherical pendentive is a triangular section of a hollow hemisphere whose diameter is equal to the diagonal of a square inscribed in it. How a series of pendentives looks when arranged to form the support of a dome is shown in the third diagram in Fig. 66; their theoretical formation is indicated in the second where a dome whose diameter is equal to the diagonal of the square to be covered is shown with four segments cut from it on lines corresponding to the sides of the square base, i.e., *AB*, *BC*, *CD* and *DA*. The form in the

second diagram is mechanically sufficient because it is a domical covering fitted to a square area. In some *pendentive domes* the curve from one angle to the one diagonally opposite is a complete semicircle. The more usual and more impressive treatment, since it permits any desired height, is indicated by the third and fourth diagrams. In the third, the top of the pendentive dome in the second diagram has been removed, leaving a circular base supported by the triangular sections that are the pendentives at the four angles; upon this base a cylinder called a drum can be built to any height and finished off with a hemispherical dome, as shown in the fourth diagram. Like all arches, those that frame the area to be covered must be adequately buttressed, as must also the dome since it functions mechanically like a number of arches intersecting at a common center.

The most impressive example of a dome on pendentives is the one in the church of *Hagia Sophia* (Figs. 67-69) or Divine Wisdom in Constantinople. Begun by order of Justinian I in 532 to replace an earlier structure on the same site that had been destroyed by fire, it was dedicated with impressive ceremonies five years later on December 27, 537. The architects were Anthemius of Tralles and Isidorus of Miletus, both from regions with a long tradition of

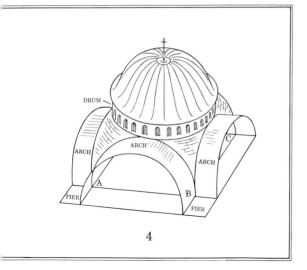

4

rather than semicircular shape and hence more difficult to buttress. The dome was rebuilt by Isidorus the Younger, a nephew of one of the original architects. He gave it a somewhat steeper pitch and also increased the size of the buttressing piers on the minor axes of the structure; as a result of these precautions, his dome is still standing in spite of some further small displacements.

The exterior of Hagia Sophia falls short of the interior in distinction (Fig. 69). The four slender spires are minarets built when the church was turned into a mosque after the fall of Constantinople to the Turks in 1453 and must be left out of account. From the outside, the dome gives little impression of its actual height—180 feet above the floor level. This is in part due to its shape, which is less than a complete hemisphere

vaulted and domed buildings. The church lies on a northwest-southeast axis with the apse pointing in the latter direction; its plan, almost square, measures about 240 by 250 feet exclusive of the narthex and apse. This area is reduced by a series of groined vaulted aisles on the sides to the main spatial volume of the interior or nave, which is about 240 feet long and 107 feet wide. Except for the spaces immediately inside the portal and in front of the apse, this is covered by a dome on pendentives equal in diameter to the width of the nave, and by two half-domes flanking it on the principal axis of the structure (Fig. 67). These half-domes are also buttresses, for they oppose their masses against the thrusts exerted by the principal dome along the building's main axis. In this they are aided by smaller half-domes; those at the east end may be seen in Fig. 68. The side thrusts of the central dome are not so effectively handled, for they are opposed only by the heavy arches connecting the piers at the angles of the space covered by the dome and the massive piers at these same points on the exterior (Fig. 69). Possibly this inadequate buttressing of the dome's side thrusts was responsible for the collapse of the original dome in 558, although it is probable that the dome itself was somewhat shallower than the one now over the building and that the supporting arches were in catenary

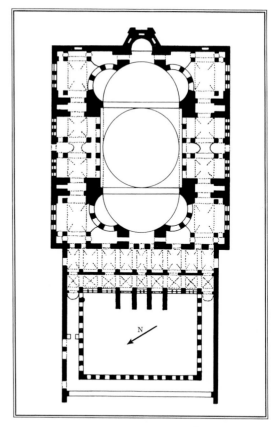

FIG. 67. Constantinople. Hagia Sophia (532-537), Plan.

FIG. 68.   Constantinople.   Anthemius of Tralles and
Isidorus of Miletus, Hagia Sophia, Interior.

and is dwarfed by the huge pier buttresses on the cross axes of the building. These latter are impressive as sheer bulk but are inconsistent in their relationship to the dome which should be the crowning feature of the structure. This it would have been on the outside as it is within if it were higher—either by resting on a taller drum or by having a steeper pitch—but the magnitude of the dimensions apparently precluded either treatment.

The interior of Hagia Sophia in Fig. 68 shows it as a mosque before it was secularized in 1934 Color is an important element in the effect— from the marble and porphyry columns of dark green and red, from the veneer on walls and piers of similar materials sliced in thin slabs and applied so the veining forms regular patterns, and from the mosaics on the pendentives and domes. In the illustration only two of the great archangels in the pendentives can be seen, for most of the figured ornament was covered with plaster or otherwise obscured when the structure was converted to a Mohammedan mosque, a

process that has been reversed with its transformation, beginning in 1934, from a place of worship to a museum of Byzantine art.

The initial impression given by the interior is a single vast domed space—an impression which yields to one of complexity as the relationship of the minor domes and the colonnaded aisles and galleries to the central cupola is perceived, but without sacrificing the effect of great size. This is created by the fine scale resulting from the interacting rhythms of forms and volumes of space in the columns and piers and in the domes and windows. In the effect of space enclosed by form that is the basic concept of the interior of Hagia Sophia, there is a parallel to the Roman Pantheon (Fig. 58) created some 400 years earlier. But the pattern of space volumes in the Byzantine church is more complex and subtle than that in the Roman temple, and the definition of the enclosing forms is blurred and softened by the gleam and color of the patterned marble and mosaic surfaces, as if the architects' intention had been to emphasize the emptiness of the space as the significant element of the interior. To this effect the row of windows in the base of the dome contributes powerfully, seeming by its diffusion of light almost to separate the cupola from its supports and suggesting to Procopius, a writer who described the building shortly after its completion, that the dome appeared "as if suspended by a chain from heaven." But the forms that enclose and articulate the space volumes remain definite and comprehensible in spite of the ambiguousness of line and surface induced by the color and gleam of mosaic and veneer; with his classic heritage of rationalism the Byzantine could never completely forswear the significance of the tangible and concrete. Classic too is the static balance of volumes created by raising the Oriental dome on pendentives over the Latin basilica, for the vitalizing horizontal movement which the western Christian architect introduced in the classic basilican plan is overwhelmed in the domed structure by the centralized and vertical axis. If the marvelous unity of the Byzantine structure seems more impressive than the inchoate form of the western church, it is nonetheless the ultimate statement of an attitude that long persisted but never surpassed its first comprehensive expression, whereas the humble Latin basilica was the first step toward the realization of the most expressive religious architectural form the Occidental world has seen—the Gothic cathedral.

Justinian reigned over the Roman Empire from his eastern capital, but exercised a measure of control over some parts of the western kingdom that had been recaptured from the Goths. At this time the western capital was Ravenna, a city north of Rome that lay on the east coast of Italy on the Adriatic Sea. A number of buildings erected there in the first half of the sixth century reveal the mingling of Latin and Byzantine elements. One of these was the church of *San Vitale* (Fig. 70), an octagonal structure covered by a dome adjusted by squinches to the eight-sided base. It was begun in 526 and consecrated by Justinian himself in 547. Being octagonal, it follows that it has a vertical rather than a horizontal axis and is thus of the central rather than the basilican type—a kind of building

that was used in the west for some rather specialized purposes such as baptisteries but seldom for a church in the general sense. There is some reason to believe that this type was used at San Vitale because the church was part of the royal palace ensemble at Ravenna, particularly since the domed octagon was once flanked by towers, another architectural form traditionally associated with royalty. Much of the interior has been redecorated in a debased Renaissance style but the original mosaics of the sanctuary are still to be seen (Fig. 365), including representations of Justinian and his queen Theodora, accompanied by members of the Byzantine court, performing the consecration rites. Other Byzantine characteristics include the capitals of the columns between the central domed space and the aisle that surrounds it. These are shaped like inverted truncated pyramids with rectangular faces rounded to a circular base fitting the shaft; they are decorated with various patterns cut into the surface of the basket-shaped block and emphasized by the black backgrounds. Above these capitals are other inverted truncated pyramids upon which the arches rest. Known as stilt-blocks or pulvins, they concentrate the weight of the superstructure upon the column shafts,

Photo by Pan American.

FIG. 69.   Constantinople.
Hagia Sophia, Exterior.

FIG. 70.   Ravenna.   San Vitale (526–547),
Interior.

thus sparing the capitals the varied thrusts to which they would be subjected if the arches sprang directly from them. There is some precedent for the stilt-block in the partial entablatures used by the Romans over columns from which arches were sprung, but its form at San Vitale is characteristically Byzantine.

The church of *Sant' Apollinare in Classe* (Figs. 71, 72) near Ravenna illustrates even more clearly than San Vitale the mingling of Latin and Byzantine elements in the architecture of Justinian's western capital. Built between 534 and 539 and consecrated in 549, it is basilican in plan and has wooden roofs like those of the Roman churches of the fourth and fifth centuries. It lacks transepts, however, and has three apses instead of one (Fig. 71); this is an eastern characteristic as is also the fact that they are polygonal on the exterior and semicircular within. The bell tower or campanile a short distance from the north side of the building is a later addition. Inside (Fig. 72), the Corinthianesque capitals of the nave arcades are surmounted by Byzantine stilt-blocks; the soffits or lower surfaces of the arches have a coffer pattern of Roman origin. Above the arcades, in a band on the lower clearstory wall, are mosaic portraits of the bishops of Ravenna; on the half-dome of the apse and the arch in front are representations, also in mosaic, of Christ and the apostles—the latter symbolized by lambs—and the patron saint of the church. The interior is much like that of the early fifth-century Roman church of Santa Sabina (Fig. 65) in every respect.

Sant' Apollinare in Classe is an architectural symbol of the Latin-Byzantine cultural fusion Justinian was able to effect in his western capital. It is also the ultimate statement of the basically Hellenic-Christian concepts underlying those cultures. In 568, less than twenty-five years after its consecration, an invading horde of Lombards from the north overran the Italian peninsula as far as Tuscany, leaving only isolated regions under Empire control. These included Rome and Ravenna and Venice. In Venice, a late reflowering of Byzantine architectural ideas in the west produced one of the best-known examples of the style, the church of San Marco.

FIG. 71. Ravenna. Sant' Apollinare in Classe (534-539), from the Northeast.

Begun in 1063, it was modeled on the Church of the Holy Apostles in Constantinople; but in spite of its structural and decorative impressiveness, its influence on later mediaeval architecture in western Europe was not extensive. For the rest, in the sixth century Italy entered a period that was truly a dark age; the only ray of light came from the Church in the organized monasticism that was one of the distinctive phenomena of the early Middle Ages. Monasticism, a direct outgrowth of the impact of Christianity upon the declining world of classic antiquity, originated in the fourth century in the eastern Mediterranean area and spread rapidly through the west in the fifth and sixth centuries. The codification of monastic practice established in 526 by St. Benedict at Monte Cassino in southern Italy was the first attempt at regulating the procedure to be followed by those who wished to withdraw from a confused and chaotic world to seek spiritual regeneration. Its aptness to the times is indicated by the great number of monasteries that followed the Benedictine rule that were founded in northern Europe as well as Italy in the latter part of the first Christian millennium. If it is exaggeration to suggest that only in them

FIG. 72.   Ravenna.   Sant' Apollinare in Classe, Nave.

was to be found any perception of the significance of spiritual experience during this period, it
cannot be denied that they had an important
part in preserving the small amount of ancient
culture that was kept alive.

In the circumstances prevailing in the so-
called Dark Ages, it is not surprising that architecture came almost to a standstill. In the few
buildings erected, however, there are certain
features of some importance. This is true of the
church of *Santa Maria in Cosmedin* (Fig. 73) in
Rome, begun in 772 and finished in 795. Basilican in plan and having the tri-apsidal eastern end
as in Sant' Apollinare in Classe (Fig. 71), the
interior is notable for two details. The first is the

space enclosed by a parapet of marble slabs at the
end of the nave immediately in front of the altar;
this is the choir, where participants in the service
had their place. The second is the substitution of
rectangular masonry piers for some of the
columns in the nave arcade. This may have been
due to failure to find enough Roman columns
to complete the arcades—they are made up for
the most part of pilfered material—and to inability to make satisfactory copies, or the piers
may have been introduced for additional strength
needed to support the clearstory walls. In any
event, the pier made a fortunate contribution to
the expressive character of the nave, for it significantly altered the rhythmic progression

toward the altar and apse which has been noted as the characteristic feature of the Christian basilican interior. This it did by introducing pauses—points upon which the eye rests momentarily—in the rapid, unaccented movement of the earlier interiors (Figs. 65, 72); and in slowing up the progression it created a more profound sense of awe and reverence in the ultimate apprehension of its goal. This effect is not completely attained, it is true, in the rather unprepossessing interior of Santa Maria in Cosmedin, but the incipient vertical motive there introduced in what was previously an unequivocally horizontal architectural composition is an important innovation. On the outside, the Latin basilica underwent changes of comparable character. During this same period of the eighth and ninth centuries, the practice of erecting bell towers or campaniles was initiated; that of Sant' Apollinare in Classe

at Ravenna (Fig. 71) is an example. Although that campanile is not an integral element in the exterior design of the building, the significant fact is that a vigorous vertical accent was felt to be necessary in what was otherwise a predominantly horizontal composition.

The modifications of the basic basilican scheme in the campanile of Sant' Apollinare in Classe and the piers in the nave of Santa Maria in Cosmedin are important as indications that these builders realized the unsatisfactory character of the basic type as an expressive form. It was not, however, in the section of Italy that remained part of the Roman Empire that the full possibilities of the modified and developed basilica were realized, but in the region north of the Alps and in the parts of Italy culturally allied to it. Structures in Spain, France, and England dating from the seventh and eighth centuries reveal attempts

FIG. 73.   Rome.   Santa Maria in Cosmedin (772-795), Nave.

to adapt regional building methods to basilican forms. They are very interesting as archaeological monuments but have little distinction as works of art, for they are simple edifices of brick, rubble, and timber for the most part, with little ornament except for rudely carved slabs and capitals and some polychrome materials for the walls.

FIG. 74. Aachen. Odo of Metz, Charlemagne's Chapel (792-805), Interior.

Not until the time of Charlemagne (724-814) are there any buildings comparable in character to the Christian structures thus far considered. The *Chapel* (Fig. 74) built at his command in Aachen, his capital city in the Rhineland, was his palace church and his mausoleum as well. Erected between 792 and 805 after the design of Odo of Metz, it is of the central type, a sixteen-sided polygon in plan on the ground level with two-storied annular aisles, the lower being covered with alternate rect-

angular and triangular groined vaults. An octagonal dome above raises the total height to four stories. Although the building has been much altered since it was erected, enough of the central portion remains to indicate some points of resemblance to San Vitale in Ravenna (Fig. 70). Most notable of these is the flanking of the dome by a twin-towered façade, the same royal symbolism found in the Ravenna church. The variants are no less important than the resemblances. Structurally the Carolingian building is much simpler than the church in Ravenna and its general proportions are somewhat heavier, although the Byzantine building must have been known to the Germans because some of their materials came from Ravenna. That they chose a central type of building with a vertical axis as their model may have been dictated by the somewhat specialized purpose of the chapel, but the increased height—from three stories in San Vitale to four at Aachen—was hardly a matter of chance, for it was in accordance with the already mentioned definite tendency toward stressing vertical elements in the basilican buildings of the time.

Charlemagne's Chapel was the finest building of its period in northern Europe. Evidently it greatly impressed the men of its own and subsequent times, for many simplified copies were built in later years. As an architectural illustration of Charlemagne's attempt to re-create the political structure of the Roman Empire, its lack of distinction exemplifies the unintegrated thought of a time which sought its expression in forms that were incapable of embodying it, either political or artistic. For although the Latin and Byzantine elements in the amalgam of mediaeval thought supplied at least a classic common denominator to the Christian of Rome or Ravenna or Constantinople, they offered only little to the Teuton whose whole manner of thinking was couched in different terms. The time had not yet come when these various dialects of antique, Christian, and northern origin could fuse into a new language. Charlemagne's "renaissance" produced many works of art; but insofar as the motivating impulses were limited in expression to the modified classic forms and idioms then current, they failed in finding adequate vehicles through which they might become comprehensible.

In the architecture of the early Middle Ages, the shift in emphasis—from static and sculptural mass composed for its external effect that was exemplified most convincingly in the Greek temple, to a conception of interior space given character by scale and proportion that was the Roman contribution to the art of monumental architectural design—is carried still further. But in becoming the instrument of a mode of thought that was intuitive and emotional rather than logical and intellectual, the static perfection of classic architecture perforce underwent certain modifications, of which the establishment of an axis of movement in the basilican interior was the most significant. If the resultant forms are inchoate in design and confused in effect, there is in them nonetheless the germ of an architecture which eventually became the only rival, in its expressive unity and comprehensiveness, of the mode evolved by the Greeks of the fifth century B.C.—the Gothic.

Detail of Fig. 90.

CHAPTER SIX

Romanesque Architecture

The architectural styles of Christian Rome and Byzantium were created in the first attempts to adapt the building idioms of antiquity to the needs of the Christian Church. They are manifestations of the same point of view that framed the theology of the early Church by striving to clothe the spiritual ideals of the new faith in the garb of classic thought; in theology and architecture alike, the disharmony between the antique forms and the Christian beliefs they were expected to express was fundamental. So long as Christian architecture had to be cast in a classic mould, so long was it inevitable that the integration of design and function essential to significant expression would fail of attainment, an exact parallel to the failure of ancient philosophical dialectic to supply an adequate vehicle for the expression of Christian faith.

These are the underlying reasons for the lack of integration in nearly all fields of European thought from the fall of Rome until about 1000. This was the blackest night in the history of European culture; the only ray of light, feeble as it was, was cast by Charlemagne's short-lived "renaissance" of the early ninth century. The artificiality of the culture he attempted to create has already been noted in pointing out the comparative isolation, save for a few attempts at imitation, of his chapel-mausoleum at Aachen (Fig. 74); it is further indicated by the fate of his kingdom when his death removed the coalescing force of his personality. In the century after his death, political Europe was in near anarchy, without central or recognized authority.

By contrast, the power of the Church was stable and widespread. Nothing illustrates more vividly the shifting of the foundations of European thought from the objective and material values of classic antiquity to an intangible and spiritual ideal than the humbling of Henry IV of Germany before Pope Gregory VII at Canossa in 1077 in the final resolution of a bitter conflict over the investiture of churchmen by temporal authorities. In such circumstances, when even the world's mightiest rulers could not but abase themselves before the power of the Church, it is easy to perceive its domination of all human activity and to understand how within its walls surcease could be found from the trials of life in a society seemingly incapable of any temporal certainty or stability. It was in the monasteries that the soul that longed for spiritual peace could find refuge. In them was cherished all that remained of the once vigorous and creative intellectual life of the ancient world. And from the seed carefully nurtured there the new life of the Middle Ages grew, shaped by the synthesis of various contributing cultural elements that was first apparent about 1000.

Architecturally, the consequence of this synthesis is implied in a striking passage in a chronicle of the times written by an eleventh-century monk, Raoul Glaber, who likened the effect of the great number of new churches built after 1000 to a white garment spread over all Europe. A superficial explanation of this phenomenon holds that it followed the uneventful passing of the year 1000 during which, according to earlier popular superstition, Christ would return to earth for the Day of Last Judgment. Rather more significant is its indication that the integration of thought necessary for the creation of an expressive architectural style was beginning. Charlemagne had attempted to bring about such an integration by political fiat but had failed. Now it was evolving in its own way, and with it came the need for expression always felt when there is consciousness of deep and profound significance in human experience.

Romanesque is the term applied to the period in which the forms created by this need began to assume definite and individual character. In general, the Romanesque period may be considered as lasting from about 1000 until around 1200, even though in some parts of western Europe forms anticipating the succeeding Gothic appear as early as 1150 and in others the Romanesque continues until far into the thirteenth century. The name Romanesque is used because many of the forms created in this period are clearly derived from or influenced by Roman examples. This was natural in view of the fact that western Europe at this time was largely peopled by races of mingled Roman and barbarian stock. Latin, for example, was the common language, even though it was varied in different regions by local idioms. This provides an immediate analogy in the various Romance languages to the numerous local schools or regional types of Romanesque art. All based on Latin, the languages are distinguished from one another by the local differences that make them the modern Latin dialects of French, Italian, or Spanish, corresponding to modern political entities that are themselves often based on Romanesque feudal divisions of the eleventh and twelfth centuries. In the same way, Romanesque architecture, although based on and related to that of Rome, has many different aspects resulting from modifications of the Roman style by local traditions. Thus there is actually not one

FIG. 75. Clermont-Ferrand.
Notre-Dame du Port (*ca.* 1100), Plan.

Romanesque style but many; in nothing is Romanesque differentiated so distinctively from its classic source as in its abundant variety. In Roman times, an arch of triumph in France might be exactly like one in Africa; public baths built by the Romans in England differ in no essential from their counterparts in Italy. By contrast, in the eleventh and twelfth centuries there were no less than eight clearly defined regional architectural styles in France alone; Italy had at least three; and there are other distinctly individual traditions in the buildings of Spain, Germany, and England, to mention only the most important.

For all the regional distinctions in Romanesque architecture of the eleventh and twelfth centuries, certain characteristics are more or less common. A typical Romanesque church plan (Fig. 75) is basilican; i.e., it is composed horizontally rather than vertically, and contains features found in similar structures of the fourth and

fifth centuries (cf. Fig. 64). A nave with side aisles is the principal part of the building, and many have transepts, though this is not invariable (Fig. 85). A point of contrast with the Early Christian basilica is the part beyond the transept, where the choir appears to be an extension of the nave. Around the choir, too, is an aisle—the ambulatory—seemingly an extension of the side aisles across the transept. Both these additions to the Early Christian basilican plan apparently evolved to meet the expanding liturgical requirements of the monastic churches of the time. Earlier structures have special enclosures for those participating in the service; there is one in the late eighth-century interior of Santa Maria in Cosmedin at Rome (Fig. 73), but its form is somewhat tentative. The ambulatory and the small apses opening from it (also called radiating chapels) seem to have developed in connection with the cult of relics that supposedly invested some part of a holy man's body or some object identified with him with power to perform miracles or confer grace upon those who visited it in an appropriate frame of mind. Investigations begun in 1939 have provided sound reasons for believing that Pope Gregory I constructed such an ambulatory around the shrine where Saint Peter was venerated in the basilica in Rome that bears his name (Figs. 62-64) when the Pope enlarged Constantine's more modest monument between 594 and 604. So also, the ambulatories that are an almost invariable feature of the monastic churches of the later Middle Ages permit the faithful to circulate freely about the altars where relics are kept without disturbing a service that may be going on. The probability that the chevet—the term applied to the ensemble of choir, ambulatory, and radiating chapels—was a result of the cult of relics is strengthened by the presence of chevets in a considerable number of churches on one of the most famous pilgrimage roads in the Middle Ages, that leading to the putative tomb of Saint James the Greater at Compostela in northwestern Spain.

In the Romanesque elevation, the most evident point of contrast with an Early Christian building is a third story consisting of a second row of arches on columns or piers between the nave arcade and the clearstory (Figs. 76, 91). This is called a triforium gallery. Such galleries are not unknown in the Christian basilicas in Rome but they occur chiefly in churches where the Oriental practice of segregating women made it necessary to provide separate places for them. As a rule the wall was unbroken between the nave arcade and the clearstory windows (Figs. 64, 65, 72, 73) and was covered with mosaics or paintings in fresco. In Romanesque building, the open triforium may have been introduced to lighten the weight supported by the nave piers as at Vignory (Fig. 76), where there is no practical gallery but the walls are of considerable thickness. It is not an invariable feature of all Romanesque churches, for some buildings have no triforium, whereas in others it takes the place of the clearstory (Figs. 79, 80); nevertheless, its contribution to the expressive character of the interior was considerable, as will be brought out elsewhere.

The *Church at Vignory* in France (Fig. 76), built about 1050, reveals the Romanesque characteristics of plan and elevation that have been noted—the three-part elevation of the nave, the choir and the ambulatory separated from it by the columns supporting the semi-dome of the apse; the radiating chapels beyond it are not visible in the illustration. The nave has a trussed wooden roof and the side aisles are similarly treated. The nave system is distinguished from that of older basilicas in consisting of piers, a form seen in the nave of Santa Maria in Cosmedin (Fig. 73) but used here alone instead of with columns. This is another characteristic of Romanesque architectural style that distinguishes it most clearly from preceding modes, for the pier is the preferred isolated support in the majority of the northern schools of building in the later eleventh and twelfth centuries. A direct visual consequence of using piers in the nave system and repeating them in the triforium is the vertical element thus introduced in the interior elevation. This too was suggested in tentative fashion in Santa Maria in Cosmedin, but it is much more apparent here, as will be evident if it is compared with any Early Christian basilican nave (Figs. 65, 72) where the whole effect is horizontal move-

ment. At Vignory, the vertical relationship of the openings in the nave elevation is rhythmic, ascending from the wide arches in the nave arcade through the smaller ones of the triforium to the clearstory. Each such vertical group makes up a bay, and the composition is conceived as a series of these bays instead of a single continuous plane as it is in the earlier basilicas in consequence of the more rapid rhythm created by the quickly repeated accents of the slender columns.

The *Cathedral at Pisa* (Figs. 77, 78) is an example of Tuscan Romanesque, one of the three regional styles of Italy. Begun by Buschetus in 1063 and consecrated, although unfinished, in

FIG. 76. Vignory. Church (*ca.* 1050), Nave.

FIG. 77. Pisa. Cathedral (1063-1272),
Nave.

characteristic of the Tuscan school. The campanile, another characteristic Italian features, is the famous Leaning Tower. Like the Cathedral, its external decoration consists of colonnette arcades; the ensemble is one of the most striking in mediaeval architecture.

In both the church at Vignory and the Cathedral of Pisa, the tendency toward greater height, both actual and apparent, that appeared in tentative form in certain churches in the later Dark Ages is carried further by increasing the number of levels in the nave elevation and stressing the vertical elements in its design. There still remained the problem the Christian basilican type of building always raised, namely, working out a roofing method that would contribute in some degree to the expressive effect of the church interior. This the timber roofs at Vignory and Pisa do not do any more than those of Santa Sabina and Santa Maria in Cosmedin in Rome Sant' Apollinare in Classe in Ravenna (Figs. 65, 72, 73). Wooden roofs of this type also presented a practical problem that was probably of more immediate and conscious concern to Romanesque builders than their lack of expressive character—their relative impermanence and liability to destruction by fire. The task confronting the architects of the eleventh and twelfth centuries was to find a roofing method that would solve these difficulties; the ultimate solution was masonry vaults. The character of mature Romanesque architectural style is determined in the final analysis by combination of the basilican plan and the stone vault in one form or another.

Vaulting had been extensively developed by Roman architects, and in the parts of northern Europe colonized by the Romans their traditions of building had never been entirely forgotten. In southern France and eastern Spain, for example, there are many small churches of the late tenth and early eleventh centuries with crude masonry vaults that are simplified and provincial versions of monumental Roman prototypes. They were not sturdy enough, however, to be used over larger and higher naves such as the one at Vignory. Romanesque vaulting has many characteristics of its own that distinguish it sharply from Roman practice and that were

1118 though somewhat modified in the thirteenth and fourteenth centuries, the nave elevation is in three levels with a triforium arcade of columns and piers like that at Vignory; however, the lower supports are columns. In this respect, the Cathedral of Pisa resembles the Christian basilicas of the fourth and fifth centuries (Figs. 65, 72) and it is like them too in having a wooden roof over the nave. The effect is one of greater height. The interior decoration consists largely of alternate bands of light and dark marble, a material abundant in central Italy where Pisa is located and extensively used for architectural purposes at all times. Similar marble facing gives the exterior of the building its character (Fig. 78), whether as polychrome inlay or in the decorative colonnades developed independently by builders in the late eleventh and twelfth centuries. The church of *Notre-Dame du Port* (Figs. 75, 79, 80) at Clermont-Ferrand, begun about 1100, shows the simplest vault that can be used. The plan is the developed basilican form and the nave vault is the semi-cylindrical type called a barrel vault (cf. Fig. 53, A); there are similar vaults over the straight portion of the choir and the transepts. The elevation, however, is in only two levels, a fact explained by the mechanical necessity for buttressing the thrusts of the nave vault. This must be continuous for its entire length and it must be applied at or near the haunch, the point where the lateral thrusts are strongest. At Notre-Dame du Port, the half-barrel vaults over the galleries above the side aisles perform this buttressing as well as covering the triforium galleries (Fig. 80) which are here the upper story of the interior elevation. The way this buttressing is achieved will be clear if the triforium vaults are thought of

as leaning against that over the nave and also as transmitting its thrust to the thick outer wall which is sufficiently heavy to absorb it and make the system stable.

A barrel vault such as that over the nave of Notre-Dame du Port was a satisfactory mechanical means of avoiding the fire hazard of a wooden roof, but its construction was costly. The side walls supporting it had to be very thick to absorb the lateral thrusts. Furthermore, until a barrel vault is completed it must be held up by centering, a wood scaffold on which the fabric or web of the vault is laid. In a building of any size, the centering for a barrel vault requires almost as much timber as a roof would—sometimes even more—and this was a considerable expense where wood was scarce. In such regions means were sought for erecting vaults with a minimum of centering as well as evolving vault types which would not require the excessively heavy side walls of Notre-Dame du Port.

FIG. 78.   Pisa.   Buschetus, Cathedral and Leaning Tower.

FIG. 79. Clermont-Ferrand. Notre-Dame du Port, Nave.

Saint-Sernin (Fig. 81) at Toulouse is vaulted so as to avoid the drawbacks of the simple barrel vault that have been mentioned. Begun about 1080 and finished in the twelfth century, its nave is spanned by a series of arches connecting opposite piers that provide permanent support for the web of the barrel vault which rests directly upon them. These transverse arches or ribs made it possible to reduce somewhat the thickness of the side walls and to lighten the vault itself. Furthermore, since the transverse arches divide the nave vault into sections corresponding to the bays, each bay could be built individually, one set of centering being used for each in turn. As in Notre-Dame du Port, the lateral thrusts of the vault are buttressed directly by half-barrel vaults over the triforium gallery. Since these thrusts are slightly greater at the points where the transverse arches occur, the outer walls are strengthened there by strips of masonry called salient buttresses which rise the entire height of the wall on the outside.

The use of transverse arches provided a means of reducing the weight and costliness of barrel vaulting, but another great disadvantage remained—the difficulty of providing adequate illumination in a building thus covered. In both Notre-Dame du Port and Saint-Sernin, the naves are very dark. There can be no windows in the vault itself for its stability would be seriously impaired by any openings; the only light in the nave comes from the door at the end or indirectly through the side-aisle and triforium windows. Nor can these latter be very large because the walls must be heavy to sustain the thrusts of the nave and triforium vaults above; their opening can be somewhat enlarged by splaying or cutting the sides and bottoms away at an angle (cf. Fig. 80), but even this does not admit much light. A row of windows opening directly into the top of the nave—a clearstory—would have met this lighting difficulty, but this was impossible in either Notre-Dame du Port or Saint-Sernin because the nave vaults would have had to be raised considerably above the level of the triforium and the buttressing function of the vaults over the galleries would therefore have been lost.

FIG. 81. Toulouse. Saint-Sernin (*ca.* 1080-12th cent.), Nave.

FIG. 80. Clermont-Ferrand. Notre-Dame du Port, Section.

Thus it is clear that although the barrel vault either in its simple form or with transverse arches adequately solves the mechanical problems of roofing a church with masonry, the difficulties of illumination are such that the expressive character of a church thus covered is decidedly limited.

The groined or cross vault provided Romanesque builders with the solution of the problem of lighting their masonry-covered churches (Fig. 53, B, C), a form inherently applicable to the rectangular bays of the nave formed by the piers of nave and triforium galleries and transverse arches. Providing windows in the side walls of a building with a groined vault is not difficult, for the thrusts in any given bay are concentrated at the angles and all the space between

FIG. 82. Morienval. Church
(*ca*. 1080), North Side Aisle.

by the long and unsupported elliptical curve of the groin line when such a vault was built over the relatively wide span of a nave, with its understandable tendency to sag. In any event, not until another vault form—the ribbed vault—was evolved could Romanesque builders construct large buildings completely roofed with masonry and adequately illuminated.

The ribbed vault has something of the same relationship to the groined type as a barrel vault with transverse arches to a simple one. The distinguishing characteristic is a set of ribs or arches (Fig. 83), built in advance on a separate centering, upon which the vault web is laid. There are six of these arches in a ribbed vault; two parallel the nave axis and are called the longitudinal ribs, two span the nave and are called the transverse ribs, and two cross the nave diagonally and are called the diagonal ribs. If the bay is square and the arches semicircular, as is usually the case in Romanesque buildings, the diagonal ribs will rise higher than the others, assuming a common springing level, since their radius is longer. As a result, the vault will be domical in shape (Fig. 84). The four triangular cells formed of the vault web by the diagonal ribs are called severies.

Among the earliest extant buildings with a ribbed nave vault is the church of *Sant' Ambrogio* (Figs. 85-87) at Milan, a characteristic example of North Italian or Lombard Romanesque style. Its vaults were almost certainly first built in the last quarter of the eleventh century. Although the present ones are undeniably the result of later rebuilding and subsequent restorations, the foundations make it clear that vaults of this type were planned from the outset. The plan (Fig. 85) is a modified basilican type without transepts. Two side aisles flank the nave of three large bays; a crossing with an octagonal dome on squinches leads to the short choir with a large semicircular apse, flanked by two smaller ones at the eastern ends of the side aisles. The elevation is in two parts—the nave arcade and the triforium galley (Fig. 86). The nave vaults are ribbed and domical in shape; the supporting piers are compound forms made up of a rectangular core or nucleus to which columns and

may be left open if desired (cf. Fig. 55). Furthermore, the groined vault is even more economical than the barrel vault with transverse arches since it requires buttressing only at the angles, and the massive side walls necessary in barrel-vaulted structures can be considerably lightened.

Groined vaults were used by the Romans over their great public baths and basilicas (Fig. 56) and they are found quite early in Romanesque building, but on a smaller scale than vaulting a nave would have involved. At Notre-Dame du Port, the side aisles are covered with such vaults (Fig. 80), as indicated in the plan (Fig. 75) by the diagonal lines in each bay; there is another example in the north side aisle of the parish church at *Morienval* (Fig. 82) where the transverse arches separating the bays of the side aisle are also visible. In this form, the groined vault was widely used in Romanesque building from the beginning, often over the side aisles of churches whose naves still had wooden roofs, an example in point being the Cathedral at Pisa. There is no reason in principle why groined or cross vaults could not have been used over naves as well as side aisles, but they seldom were. The probable explanation is the difficulty presented

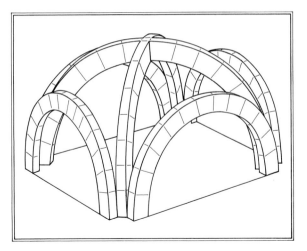

FIG. 83. Ribs of Four-Part Vault
with Semicircular Arches.

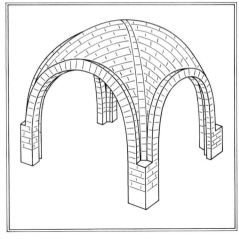

FIG. 84. Four-Part Vault with
Semicircular Arches.

pilasters are applied. These applied members are the ostensible supports of the vault ribs above, there being one for each of the arches forming the armature upon which the vault web is laid. It is because the foundations of these piers have the characteristic compound section even in their lowest courses that the probability of ribbed vaults being planned from the outset can be assumed. This organic conception, wherein the character of the structure as a whole is indicated by the elements in the plan, is the most significant characteristic of the building.

The Sant' Ambrogio nave vaults are buttressed by groined vaults over the triforium galleries, augmented by heavy walls of masonry over the transverse arches separating the triforium bays. These carry the thrusts concentrated at the nave vault angles to the outer walls where salient buttresses are placed, as shown in the plan; such walls are called diaphragm walls. The nave vaults are domical because the bays they cover are square, and consequently the semicircular diagonal ribs rise above those on the sides. A sequence of domical vaults is not particularly pleasing in effect, because the curving crown lines tend to stress each unit as a separate form rather than as part of a continuous

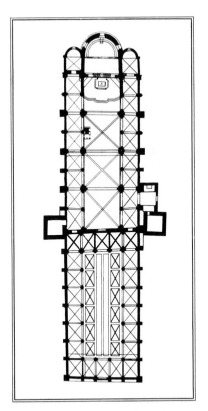

FIG. 85. Milan. Sant' Ambrogio
(begun *ca.* 1080), Plan.

FIG. 86.   Milan.   Sant' Ambrogio, Nave.

whole. This could have been avoided by depressing the diagonal arch crowns to the same height as the transverse and longitudinal ribs; the resulting profile, however, would have been elliptical, which is both harder to build and harder to buttress since flatter arches always exert more lateral thrust than steeper ones. This consideration, no doubt, led to sacrificing appearance to ease of construction and stability in these early ribbed vaults.

Another detail of the nave system at Sant' Ambrogio is the alternating of large and small piers in the arcade. The large ones obviously support the ribs of the nave vaults, but the smaller ones have no apparent relationship to them. They are necessary, however, for the vaulting of the side aisles and the triforium galleries, for without such divisions the bays would be oblong (cf. Fig. 85)—as long as each nave bay but only half as wide. It is exceedingly difficult to erect a groined vault with semicircular arches over a bay of such shape, for in this case three pairs of different-sized arches would be required and the vault web would have to be adjusted to three levels. There is such a vault in the north side aisle at Morienval (Fig. 82); although only a simple groined vault, its lower surfaces are warped and twisted in spite of efforts to make the crown level by springing the arches from different heights—indicated by the varying levels of the capitals—and by stilting the transverse arches. Instead of trying to vault an oblong bay, the builders of Sant' Ambrogio divided the awkward space into easier square units by placing small piers between the large ones that supported the nave vaults and springing transverse arches across the aisles and triforium galleries, thus dividing them into small square bays half as long on a side as those of the nave. It was comparatively easy to cover these with groined vaults. This arrangement of large and small piers is called an alternate system; its effect in Sant' Ambrogio is not entirely satisfactory because the relationship of the small piers to the large ones and to the main vaults of the structure is not at all clear when they are seen from the nave.

Lack of formal integration in the design of the nave is not the only evidence that the builders of Sant' Ambrogio were groping their way in using ribbed vaults; the darkness of the interior is the result of omitting the clearstory which in principle is entirely feasible with such construction. Once more it was a question of sacrificing effect to structural considerations, for the buttressing of the nave vaults by those over the triforium galleries and their supplementary diaphragm walls was no more than sufficient in any case. The builders doubtless were aware of this and were understandably timid about raising the heavy arches of the nave vault higher than those of the triforium galleries to provide a clearstory, particularly since the first ribbed vaults of the building had collapsed. The construction at Sant' Ambrogio, however, is historically very important in spite of its tentative and hesitating character; it should not be underestimated, for the two basically Romanesque problems are definitely faced in it—the ribbed vault and the potential illumination of the structure it covers.

Externally, Sant' Ambrogio is of interest in having an atrium (Fig. 87), one of the few Romanesque examples of what was a typical feature of the earlier basilicas (cf. Figs. 62, 67). The porticoes are covered with groined vaults with transverse arches as are the side aisles within, and buttressed by strips of masonry applied to the outer walls. The narthex and the open gallery above it make up the façade of the building. The decoration is limited to rows of small stone brackets called corbels which are connected by arches; these appear on the cornice separating the two levels of the façade, its raking cornice, and at the various stages of the north tower, which is the later of the two, the south one dating from the ninth century when an earlier building was erected on the same site. There is a certain amount of carving on the principal portal of the church and the capitals of nave and atrium, but by and large there is not as much ornament as on some Romanesque buildings.

Not all the schools of Romanesque building were equally advanced as far as the problem of a vaulted church with adequate interior illumination was concerned. Most of the church of *Notre-Dame la Grande* (Fig. 88) at Poitiers in France was built in the twelfth century, but its nave is covered with a heavy barrel vault that

FIG. 87. Milan. Sant' Ambrogio, Atrium and Façade.

springs directly from the level of the arcade in such fashion that even the triforium gallery is omitted. It is notable, however, for the lavish sculptural decoration which makes the façade one of the most richly ornamented of all Romanesque examples. In the gable is a statue of Christ as judge of the world on the day of Resurrection; the arcades in the middle levels enclose figures of the twelve apostles and of Saints Martin and Hilary; and the spandrels between the arches on the ground level are filled with reliefs pertaining to the life of the Virgin to whom the church is dedicated. Although the immediate purpose of such decoration was to instruct those who could not read, its value in the architectural effect is unmistakable. Here it emphasizes the flatness and massiveness of the façade wall, for the portal and its flanking arches are recessed in the thickness of the wall itself. If the façade seems to lack organic relationship with the rest of the building, it nonetheless contains the elements of the basic mediaeval church front as it was developed in France, with its triple arch motive on the ground level, the figured arcades above, and the two flanking towers. It is thus an example of the initial decorative phase of mediaeval architecture, as Sant' Ambrogio exemplifies the inception of its final structural character.

One reason for the importance of Sant' Ambrogio in the history of mediaeval building was mentioned earlier. Another is the fact **that**

FIG. 88   Poitiers.   Notre-Dame la Grande (*ca.* 1135-1140), from the Southwest.

FIG. 89.   Durham.   Cathedral (1093–1133), from the Southwest.

it is one of the first structures in which the solution of the basic structural problems of the Romanesque style is suggested. It is only suggested, however, for three features of the nave design are open to criticism—the domical vaults with the halting and ineffective rhythm that results from the uneven crown line, the lack of coherent relationship between the vaults and the alternate system of the nave supports, and the darkness of the interior due to omission of the clearstory. The ultimate solution of these problems was not achieved in Italy, but in buildings

FIG. 90. Durham. Cathedral, Nave, Looking East.

of the Anglo-Norman group erected in the late eleventh and twelfth centuries—the Cathedral at Durham in northern England near the Scottish border, and the churches of *Saint-Étienne* and *La Trinité* at Caen in Normandy, in northwestern France.

 Durham Cathedral (Fig. 89), one of the most impressive and important Romanesque structures in Europe, has a magnificent site on the river Wear; its massive form was aptly termed "part house of God, part fortress against the Scots." Begun in 1093 at the eastern end, the high vault over the choir was finished by 1107; that over the nave (Fig. 90), by 1133. Although the present choir vaults date from the thirteenth century, they follow the same pattern as the originals but have better masonry in the webs. Both the choir and the nave vaults are important because they are the earliest surviving ribbed vaults outside Italy. They are supported on alternately compound and cylindrical piers, with two sets of diagonal ribs to each bay; the result

FIG. 91.   Caen.   Saint-Étienne (begun *ca.* 1068;
Vaults *ca.* 1115), Nave.

is a pattern of seven cells or severies. Their principal buttressing is the thick clearstory wall, but
this is supplemented by a series of arches in the
triforium gallery—full for the choir, half for the
nave—over the ribbed vaults; these arches also
support the wooden roof over the triforium.
Thanks to the vault and buttress system, a clearstory is possible; hence the interior is admirably
illuminated. Otherwise, the characteristically
English decoration of columns and mouldings—
the zigzag chevrons and the lozenge patterns,

for example—could hardly be seen. These do
much to enliven edges and surfaces and contribute in no small degree to the sense of movement that animates the interior as a whole.

A further step in realizing the potential of
the ribbed vault was taken in the construction of
Saint-Étienne at Caen (Figs. 91, 93). Begun in the
latter part of the eleventh century by order of
William the Conqueror in expiation of a vow
he had made, it was first consecrated in 1073 as
part of a monastery from which it received the

FIG. 92. Caen. La Trinité,
Buttressing Arches in the Triforium
Gallery (*ca.* 1125).

name of *Abbaye-aux-Hommes* in addition to its dedicatory title. Although William's church had a wooden roof, it was rebuilt with the present nave vaults by about 1115 (Fig. 91). It and Durham both differ from the nave of Sant' Ambrogio (Fig. 86) in having better illumination. A clearstory above the triforium gallery opens directly through the sides of a sexpartite ribbed vault. These were formed by springing a transverse arch across the nave in the middle of what would otherwise be a four-part vault like the one at Sant' Ambrogio, the extra arch being supported by the smaller intermediate pier in each bay of the alternating system. The resulting division of the web into six severies give this type of vault its name.

Addition of the intermediate transverse arch which makes a six-part vault from the four-part ribbed type established a relationship between the small piers of the nave system and the principal vaults. It also supplied additional support for the vault web and made possible the depressed diagonal ribs in each bay at Saint-Étienne. This in turn allowed the web to be laid with a level crown, thus avoiding the domical effect which is so obtrusive at Sant' Ambrogio. It was probably confidence in the added support provided by the additional transverse rib that led the builders of the Abbaye-aux-Hommes to venture a clearstory also in their vaulted structure, a further adjunct to the expressive effect of the interior.

The sexpartite vaults did not eliminate the necessity of buttressing, however. At Saint-Étienne the nave is buttressed by half-barrel vaults over the rather tall triforium galleries, as in Notre-Dame du Port (Fig. 80). Since the counterthrusts of these half-barrel vaults are continuous for their entire length and the lateral thrusts of the ribbed vaults are not continuous but are concentrated at the angles, it follows that there is actually more buttressing in the Abbaye-aux-Hommes than is needed. This was noted by the builders of another church in Caen, *La Trinité* (Fig. 92) or the *Abbaye-aux-Dames*, which was erected by order of Matilda, wife of William the Conqueror. The nave is generally similar in plan and elevation to the brother church and has a parallel history, having first been roofed with wood and then rebuilt around 1115 with a variant of the sexpartite ribbed vault. Instead of using a continuous half-barrel vault over the triforium as at Saint-Étienne, the builders followed the example in Durham. A series of half-arches connecting the nave piers with the external salient buttresses was constructed and covered with a slanting roof; at the same time, the height of the triforium gallery was reduced since, unlike the Abbaye-aux-Hommes, it was not to be used for spectators. The economy resulting from eliminating the greater part of the half-barrel triforium vault was an immediate advantage. More important, however, was the establishment at Durham and at Caen of a new structural concept, the free buttress, which was destined to develop into the flying buttress, an essential feature of Gothic style.

The *façade of Saint-Étienne* (Fig. 93) is a Romanesque example of a motive seen in less impressive form at Sant' Ambrogio (Fig. 87) and Notre-Dame la Grande at Poitiers (Fig. 88). This is the flanking of the entrance of the building by monumental twin towers, a form that can be traced back to earliest times (cf. Fig. 23). That such a tower has a utilitarian function is indisputable; it houses the bells that call the faithful to service in a Christian church. But its symbolic function is even more significant. In early times, as has been seen (cf. page 32), the arched and towered portal stood for the arch of heaven. An inscription on St. Martin's Church at Tours (470-474 A.D.), one of the first Christian buildings in France, referred to its towered bulk as "the true temple of God and gate of heaven." To mediaeval man, the turreted building also symbolized imperial power, as in the royal churches at Ravenna (Fig. 70) and Aachen (Fig. 74); the same concept appears in the Norman context of the Bayeux Embroidery (Fig. 596) which shows King Harold of England seated between the twin cupolas of his palace. It was inevitable that a form with such traditional meaning should ultimately be associated with the house of the King of Kings. Moreover, its form contributes to the vertical effect which has been mentioned elsewhere as the characteristically northern expression of Christian spiritual aspiration.

It was in the Romanesque period that the various traditions of thought and feeling in the culture of the Middle Ages began to amalgamate into new conceptual patterns, when, as it were, a new language begins to form in the fusion of traditional dialects of Greek and Latin and Teuton and Anglo-Saxon. Architecturally, this is apparent in the changes in the basilican interior when the orientation of the structure toward the apse added movement to the static classic prototype, and in the increasing vertical effect achieved by substituting piers for columns and masonry vaults for timber roofs. The even spacing of the piers in the Romanesque interior (Fig. 91) still creates a horizontal movement toward the altar, but it is slower than in the Latin basilica (Fig. 72), because of the increased expressive importance of vertical elements in the nave design. Simple piers supporting the triforium galleries and the clearstories are no longer sufficient (cf. Fig. 76); they are compounded and the applied shafts are carried up from the ground level into the vaults, where they diverge in the diagonal ribs. Their intersection becomes the central point of a spatial volume defined by the piers, walls, and vaults, a bay from which one moves into the next bay, and so on to the culminating experience of the sanctuary. The rhythm of this movement is more complex and ordered than the simpler and unvarying drive of the Early Christian arcade (Fig. 65). For that

very reason, it is an experience charged with more profound meaning, allowing fuller comprehension of the significance of the forms. This is the greatest importance of the ribbed vault—that it made a crucial contribution toward the realization of articulated form in space, the ideal implicit in western Christian architecture from the beginning. Its usefulness as a technical innovation was incalculable, but it can hardly be doubted that the mechanical invention was inspired by the expressive conception.

Within its own terms, the Romanesque is an autonomous, individual style, capable of creating forms like the towered mass of Durham (Fig. 89) and the nave of Saint-Étienne (Fig. 91)

FIG. 93.　Caen.　Saint-Étienne, Façade

that are unrivaled in impressiveness. The fact that some inconsistencies still remain in no way detracts from this. In Saint-Étienne, for instance, the vertical movement of the piers is directly met and turned back in the overarching semicircles of the vaults. There is active opposition between the aspiring verticals of the wall shafts leading up to the vaults, and the suppressive effect of the inflexible arches they support. To return to an earlier analogy, the Frenchman at Caen still speaks with a Latin accent, even though the words he uses and their grammatical organization are mediaeval French. Aware as he was of the profound significance in the transcendental spirituality of the Christian faith, he sought an architectural symbol thereof by directing his building upward toward the infinite space that to his emotional being connoted ultimate reality. But the aspiration in this architectural symbol of his belief is thwarted by precisely the forms he retained from his Latin ancestors—the rounded arches of his vaults and openings and the large volumes of space they imposed upon him. And it was precisely these elements of the Romanesque architectural vocabulary that were transformed in the development of Gothic style.

Detail of Fig. 100.

CHAPTER SEVEN

Gothic Architecture

During the twelfth and thirteenth centuries, the Church maintained its dominance in Europe as the great unifying element in mediaeval culture. It was Pope Urban II, for example, who in 1095 launched the first of the crusades to recapture the Holy Land from the Turks, possibly the most spectacular expression of Christian faith in the history of the Church. If later crusades were not always animated by the highest motives, their ostensible purpose was nonetheless spiritual. The resulting revival of intercourse with the East, however, had significant consequences of a different character. In Italy, for example, the stream of crusaders to and from Palestine brought much industry and commerce that lifted many of its cities to heights of commercial power which were maintained until the discovery of the New World in the late fifteenth century and its exploitation thereafter. Elsewhere in Europe, the beginning of a secular and civic spirit is also evident in the gradual change from the feudal and agricultural world of the tenth and eleventh centuries to one in which the man of business and commerce was the dominant figure. Politically, too, there were changes. If the barons and dukes of France and England apparently owed no more than nominal allegiance to their kings, the fact remains that a single ruler's right to their loyalty was recognized. The formation of modern European states is at least foreshadowed in the shifting and confused history of the time. All these factors are directly involved in the development of the Gothic cathedral which is no longer the church of a monastery, as were the majority of Romanesque buildings, but is in a town or city under the patronage of secular rulers and commercial guilds rather than the abbots of religious orders.

It was in the Gothic period that mediaeval Europe came of age culturally speaking, when the merging streams of classic, Oriental, and northern thought gave rise to the second great and comprehensive philosophical system in the history of the western world. For the man of the thirteenth century was sure of the world he lived in, just as was the Athenian of the fifth century B.C. The difference between those worlds was great. For the Greek, the real was the objective, and his understanding of experience came from perceiving through the senses the qualities that gave things meaning. There is no less consciousness of things in the thirteenth century, but they are evaluated in a different way; their reality lies not in their objective qualities but the degree in which they are elements of a system that itself is a symbol of abstract and ultimate realities.

The architectural expression of this attitude resulted in the establishment of a vital relationship between the physical fabric of the church building and the space that it occupied and that filled it; for to mediaeval man space was the symbol that, more than any other, connoted the all-pervasive principle of God who exists in and gives significance to all things. In an incipient form, this ideal is the motive behind the ever-increasing emphasis on height and verticality in the changing forms of mediaeval architecture. Its most complete and monumental expression is found in the Gothic architecture of France in the early thirteenth century.

Romanesque builders were unable to attain completely the effect of height held ideal by the northern temperament because they were hampered by the semicircular arches usually found in their methods of vaulting. One consequence of this type of arch already mentioned is the lid-like effect of the vault which turns back the upward movement in the vertical elements of the compound piers and their shafts. Another was the wide spacing of the supports which was unavoidable with such arches, for the length of a bay must be equal to its width if semicircular arches of equal height support its vault. Even the sexpartite vault with its alternating system is not a completely satisfactory solution (cf. Fig. 91), and the considerable separation of the piers introduces an element of horizontal movement that cannot be avoided. In order to achieve an effect of greater height in the interior and to render it more unified, the Gothic builder made two important changes in the Romanesque structural system. He introduced the oblong bay and the pointed structural arch. Substituting individually vaulted oblong bays for square ones considerably reduced the width of each one in relation to the nave span, and restrained the horizontal movement created by the more widely separated piers of the square bay. To cover these oblong bays, he used ribbed vaults laid on pointed instead of semicircular arches (Figs. 94, 95), for semicircular arches can be used over such a bay only with the greatest difficulty (cf. Fig. 82). The greater adaptability of the pointed arch in such circumstances is the fact that within rather wide limits it can be made to rise to any height above the springing, regardless of its span, whereas the height of a semicircular arch can be no greater than its radius above the springing. Thus where the Romanesque builder had to juggle stilted semicircular arches springing from various heights to make his vault crowns level when he tried to use them over oblong bays, or else weaken the longer arches by depressing their crowns to the height of the shorter ones, the Gothic builder could vary the pointed arches in pitch to rise to any level and the three sets in a given vault (Fig. 94) are all more or less the same height. This means of building a vault that has an even crown but involves no loss of structural strength is one of the triumphs of Gothic engineering (cf. Figs. 84, 95), for not only was this vault lighter and easier to build than the heavier Romanesque forms but it could be raised to much greater heights.

(Fig. 80); even in the Abbaye-aux-Dames at Caen where the buttresses are no longer related to the roofing, they are still associated structurally with the triforium gallery. This means that the nave vault cannot rise very far above the triforium level; although it is sufficient to permit a clearstory, the nave vault crown at the Abbaye-aux-Dames is only about sixty-five feet above the floor.

It was from the buttressing half-arch concealed under the triforium gallery roof at Durham and the Abbaye-aux-Dames (Fig. 92) that the characteristic Gothic buttressing device

FIG. 94.   Ribs of Four-Part Vault
with Pointed Arches.

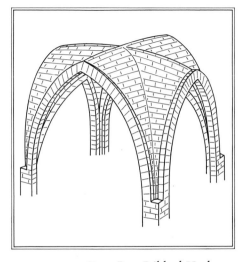

FIG. 95.   Four-Part Ribbed Vault
with Pointed Arches.

By substituting oblong for square nave bays, the Gothic builder was able to subordinate the horizontal rhythm still present in the Romanesque interior as an inheritance from the Latin basilica; and by using pointed instead of semicircular arches, he could accentuate the effect of upward movement and increase the actual height of his vaults. The possibilities along these lines would still have failed to be fully realized, if adequate buttressing for the higher vaults had not been developed. In the most organic Romanesque styles, the buttressing of the nave vaults was a function of those over the triforium gallery

evolved once it was divorced both structurally and formally from its traditional association with the triforium. The realization that the half-arch could be brought out from under the triforium gallery roof and placed at any desired height marked the creation of the flying buttress; and only the inherent structural limits of stone restricted the loftiness of buildings whose vaults it stabilized. At *Saint-Germain-des-Près* (Fig. 96) in Paris, flying buttresses were built to sustain the chevet vaults shortly after the middle of the twelfth century. They are rather heavy and awkward in appearance, but this is natural in

FIG. 96.   Paris.   Saint-Germain-des-Près, Flying Buttresses (*ca.* 1160).

using a new structural device whose potentialities were as yet not realized. It soon became apparent that the effectiveness of the flying buttress lay in the rigidness of the masonry bar rather than its weight; and when the nave buttress of *Amiens Cathedral* (Fig. 97) were built in the second quarter of the thirteenth century they were slenderer in proportion and more decorative in effect, the weight required to absorb the nave vault thrusts being concentrated in the pier buttresses that rise beyond the side-aisle wall. The struts have been doubled, one abutting the clearstory at the level of the vault springing and the other at the haunch. The flying buttress is the only major structural innovation in Gothic building, for Romanesque architects had used both pointed arches and oblong vaults, though without fully realizing their structural and expressive potentials. This realization was achieved when all three were used together, during the first half of the thirteenth century, in northern France.

From the beginning of organic vaulted construction in mediaeval building, the problem of illumination had been as important as those of engineering and the attainment of greater apparent and actual height. Perfection of the Gothic structural system solved this problem too, for the diagramed section of the cathedral (Fig. 97) shows clearly that there are almost no wall areas. The principal supports of the building are piers, whether the compound ones in the nave system or the heavy ones of the flying buttress bases. These piers have thus assumed one of the traditional functions of the wall—support. They also play a part in screening, the other function of the wall, since they sustain the thin sheets of glass that are the windows. The perfected Gothic building is a cage or skeleton of organically articulated stone piers, vault ribs, and buttresses, with planes of colored glass like an enclosing membrane between the solid supports. These planes of glass, in jewellike and brilliant patterns whenever possible (Fig. 371), contribute significantly to the expressive effect of the Gothic cathedral.

Much of the interest of Romanesque building lies in the different ways of approaching various structural and expressive problems; the beauty of the Gothic lies in the faultless logic of their final solution. Except for the flying buttress, the Gothic builder uses the same architectural elements that his Romanesque predecessor did, but he uses them with greater knowledge and keener perception of what can be done with them structurally and a clearer understanding of the values he is attempting to express. In the completeness of its statement of all these things, there is no more characteristic or monumental example of Gothic design than the Cathedral of Notre-Dame at Amiens in northwestern France which was begun in 1220.

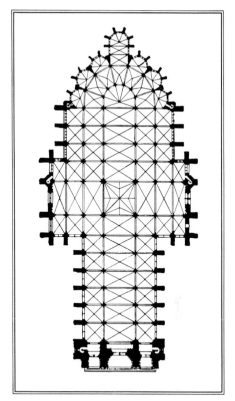

FIG. 98. Amiens. Cathedral, Plan.

FIG. 97. Amiens. Cathedral
(1220-*ca.* 1300), Section.

The *Plan of Amiens Cathedral* (Fig. 98) contains many of the elements noted in the Romanesque type (Fig. 75) but in general is more elaborate. This is most apparent in the chevet, where doubled aisles flank the choir, there is a vaulted ambulatory with radiating chapels, and the choir has a semicircular apse that is covered not by a simple half-dome but by a very complicated ribbed vault. Without the pointed arch, many of the vault forms used over the irregularly shaped bays of the Gothic chevet could not have been built; indeed, it may have been over such bays that the arch was first used with a ribbed vault. The plan of Amiens is characteristic in showing the elimination of the wall as a means of support; for between the heavy black bars representing the flying buttress piers there are only light lines indicating glass windows. The effect is almost that of sections of the wall turned at right angles to the plane which would enclose the

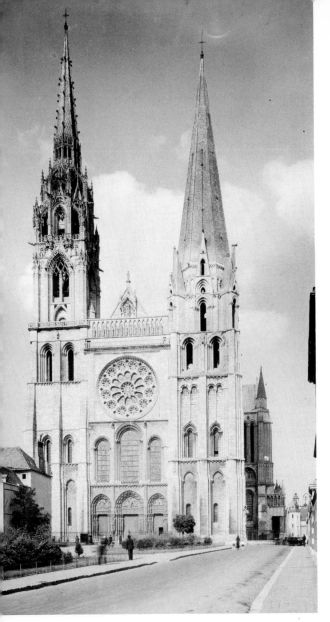

FIG. 99. Chartres. Cathedral
(begun *ca.* 1145), Façade.

inner space of the building, making them instead into the piers supporting the flying buttresses.

As an example of the High Gothic façade, that of *Amiens* (Fig. 100) is the culmination of an evolution that can be traced from the Romanesque type at Notre-Dame la Grande at Poitiers (Fig. 88) and the Abbaye-aux-Hommes at Caen (Fig. 93) through that of the *Cathedral at Chartres* (Fig. 99) which is between the Romanesque and Gothic in both time and style. At the Abbaye-aux-Hommes and Chartres, the hori-

zontal and vertical divisions into three parts correspond in plan to nave and side aisles and in elevation to arcade, triforium, and clearstory. These are the basic features at Amiens as well, but they are treated with greater refinement and integration of detail and with a more consistent vertical feeling throughout. At Saint-Étienne, whose façade was largely completed by 1077, solid wall masses are still dominant, for the windows and portals are small. The façade at Chartres is about seventy years later in date and is transitional between the Romanesque and Gothic. There is a more vertical feeling that results from emphasizing the angle towers and doubling the buttresses; and although something of Romanesque massiveness remains, the portals and windows are proportionately larger. The rose window which at Chartres replaces the three upper arched ones at Saint-Étienne is an example of a very popular and widely used Gothic decorative motive. The spires on the towers are of different periods; that to the south dates from the late twelfth century, but the northern one was not erected until early in the sixteenth century.

Amiens is the climax of the development suggested by the Romanesque and transitional façades (Fig. 100). It is not complete because the crowning spires of the towers were never erected; but even their absence cannot detract from the complete integration of structure and ornament here achieved. The three-part division of the façade is prominent. Each part has its own portal that is no longer recessed in the wall as at Caen and Chartres but projects outward in a deep porch whose sides are lined with statues representing personages of Biblical and Church history (Fig. 300). Two things stand out in the general impression created by this façade. The first is the complete disappearance of the wall as a structural member, its supporting function being taken over by the great isolated piers and its screening effect being achieved by the arcades and figures between the piers. The second is the pronounced verticality of the façade as a whole. No horizontal line is permitted to continue unbroken for more than a relatively small portion of its total width, for the carved stringcourses

FIG. 100. Amiens. Robert de Luzarches, Cathedral,
Façade.

and the decorative arcades come out and around the buttresses in such a way that from the ground they seem to be a succession of horizontal units rather than single and continuous bands. This effect is heightened by the way the peaked porch gables cut across the heavy carved moulding immediately beneath the open arcade under the row of figures about halfway up the façade. These horizontal arcades are a significant Gothic addition to the mediaeval church façade, for they have no immediate prototype in Romanesque designs. Their meaning and importance have been established by Baldwin Smith (*Architectural Symbolism in Imperial Rome and the Middle Ages*, p. 37): "The proof that the Gothic churchmen and builders were . . . aware that a crowning arcade had celestial and royal implications over the 'Royal Door' and between the towers of a triumphal 'Porta coeli' is the way in which they made its symbolism more explicit by the sculptural introduction of a 'King's Gallery'—for their crowns identify these as royal persons."

The deep porches of the Amiens portals (cf. Fig. 300) are one of the most characteristic forms in Gothic façade design and are effective in establishing a direct relationship between the exterior and interior of the building. At Saint-Étienne (Fig. 93), the portals are little more than holes cut in the massive façade wall, emphasizing its space-enclosing function. At Chartres (Fig. 99), the recession of the portals almost suggests that the wall is being pressed inward by the space outside the building, and its heaviness is still a basic factor. At Amiens, on the other hand, the porches are a transition from exterior to interior space with no sharply marked line of demarcation, a prime example of the integration of form with space that is the ideal in the whole form of Gothic building.

Other details of the façade contribute to the same effect. The pronounced verticality of the design as a whole leads the eye upward from the tangibly heavy piers at the base to the intangible space that surrounds and pervades the towers. At the same time, as these forms appear to grow lighter in their ascent, they also seem to merge with the space around them. The transitional south tower at Chartres appears heavy and solid

to the tip of the spire, whereas its Gothic counterpart seems to dissolve into the space around it, an impression resulting from the softening of its outlines by the small curling leaves, called crockets, growing out of them. At Amiens, every straight line of gable or pinnacle, stringcourse or capital, is broken by these foliate forms which are realistic to a degree in reproducing the forms of leaves and plants of the French countryside—all this to enhance the effect of the building as part of and one with the space which surrounds it.

In the *Nave* of Amiens (Fig. 101), the fusion of form with space is equally apparent. The elements of the design are inherited from the Romanesque—nave arcade, triforium gallery, and clearstory—but now even the vestigial remains of the horizontal rhythms (Fig. 91) have disappeared. Pointed arches and oblong bays narrow the spaces between the piers so the eye perceives only a succession of vertical accents in the shafts. The proportionate height of the arcade is greater and its pointed arches contribute in no small degree to the upward movement that is carried further by the applied shafts whose vertical continuity is unbroken and which lead the eye directly to the shadowed pointed vaults. All horizontal lines are subordinated to vertical lines; stringcourses separating arcade from triforium and triforium from clearstory come out around the shafts and die away completely in the crossing piers whose vertical lines rise from the ground to the spring of the vault where bands of foliage mark their functional change into the supporting arches of the crossing vault.

The final effect of form merging with space which is achieved in the Gothic façade by crockets and pervasive penetration is established in the interior by color from the stained glass windows (cf. Fig. 371). This was the form in which painting entered the decoration of the cathedral and the subject matter was chosen from Bible and Church stories to instruct the illiterate. Its importance as an adjunct to the architectural effect must have been recognized as even greater than its dogmatic value, for many of the details are at such a distance as to be unidentifiable. The greatest value of the stained-glass windows was in diffusing and softening the

FIG. 101.   Amiens.   Cathedral, Nave.

light from the clearstory openings, for otherwise the structural details of the interior would have been overobtrusive. The original glass is no longer in the windows at Amiens and the effect of the nave is impaired by its absence, for the bones of the structural skeleton stand out too clearly. But in a Gothic nave with its proper complement of colored light, such as that of Chartres Cathedral, the structural forms lose their material concreteness in the same way that the otherwise insistent lines of the spires and pinnacles of the façade are diffused by the crockets. All these things contribute to a final experience—pure color almost completely unrelated to form. The eye of the observer is drawn upward by the massive piers which seem to become lighter the higher they rise, as their vigorous outlines are diffused by the irregular patterns of radiant color pouring from the windows. The lines of the pointed arches lead the observer's eye and spirit ever upward until they are enveloped in the luminous dusk that pervades the upper reaches of the nave and in which every tangible quality and objective characteristic is lost. Thus is realized in the Gothic nave the final achievement of the aspiration toward the infinite that first faintly stirred the souls of the men who built the Latin basilicas and was the guiding ideal of their successors throughout the Dark Ages and the Romanesque period. Only in this way could man's hope for ultimate identification with God be expressed in architecture; and never has it been more completely set forth in stone and glass than in the Gothic cathedral.

In dominating the mediaeval city as it did, the cathedral was an architectural symbol of the Church's authority over all human activity in the thirteenth century. It was by virtue of this dominance that a truly communal spirit prevailed, for the spiritual values of Christian faith gave significance and meaning to all aspects of western thought. In such a community of feeling, the importance of any one individual was very slight, a fact which is given point by the anonymity of most mediaeval artists. Occasionally a name is known such as that of Robert de Luzarches, but this is an isolated fact in itself; for there is no intimation as to his personality, and

he has no existence as an individual because his achievement in designing the cathedral at Amiens was not for his personal glory but that of the Church. This subordination of the individual to the Church carries over into the arts as well; architecture is dominant and the other arts are subservient to it. There is relatively little sculpture that was not intended as part of a building (cf. Fig. 302) rather than being done for its own sake, and painting hardly existed except on the walls and in the windows (Fig. 371) of churches and on the pages of religious books (Fig. 370).

Moreover, the cathedral itself was not a self-sufficient entity. Its forms were evolved not as ends in themselves but as aids to the intuitive perception of the spiritual principle that gives them meaning; for their aspiring verticality involves a denial of certain objective architectonic values that directly parallels the denial of significance in much human experience that was demanded of mediaeval man by his faith. The wall, for example, by virtue of its various physical and aesthetic characteristics is a basic architectural element in enclosing and defining space; yet in the Gothic cathedral space is defined by formless and weightless color. The massive stone vaults seem poised in mid-air, so lightly do they rest upon the slender shafts that ostensibly support them, nor do the vaults themselves define and enclose the space over which they hover. Furthermore, it is impossible to perceive the form of the cathedral in its entirety as a rational unity. The flying buttress, for instance, has no immediately apparent structural function because the thrust of the invisible interior vault must supply in imagination the reason for its existence. In other words, the identity and unity of the cathedral are to be felt rather than understood; and if that feeling is to be complete, the reality of sensuous experience must be denied. The observer is asked to *believe* that the gables and spires of the façade dissolve in the space around them and that the heavy stones of the vaults hover over the nave without support even though this directly contradicts the sensory evidence by which he *knows* that such things cannot be.

French architecture after the thirteenth century shows a reaction away from the spiritual

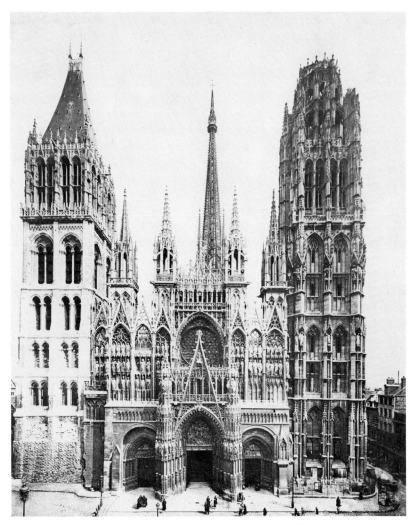

FIG. 102.   Rouen.   Cathedral, Façade
(early 16th cent.).

abstractions of High Gothic style. The façade of *Rouen Cathedral* (Fig. 102), completed in the first quarter of the sixteenth century, shows a significant change from the thirteenth-century conception of the Gothic façade with its identity of structural and ornamental forms. Here decoration and construction are divorced and the separate character of the two elements is clearly established. The ornament is now a lacy screen of stone standing clear of the wall behind, which has recovered its basic function of space enclo-

sure. No longer do the statues appear to grow from the portal embrasures as they do at Amiens (Fig. 100). They are free, complete in themselves, existing in their own right rather than as forms subordinate to an architectural scheme. In other words, by the sixteenth century the arts had been freed from the expressive limitations imposed by High Gothic philosophy; sculpture and painting could pursue their proper aims, as will be pointed out elsewhere (page 353 ff.), and architecture was no longer forced to deny the reality of its

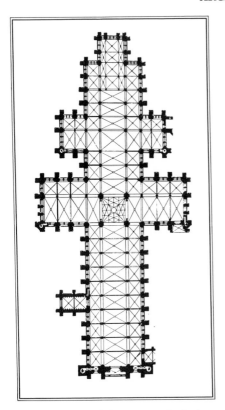

FIG. 103. Salisbury. Cathedral (begun 1220), Plan.

stems from its greater narrowness, its width through nave and side aisles being 78 feet against 104 at Amiens. The transepts are doubled in the English building too, and the chevet or eastern end is rectangular instead of rounded as in the French one. From the exterior (Fig. 104), Salisbury is low and long and picturesque in outline, instead of having the vigorous masses and pronounced verticals of Amiens. The whole is dominated by the lofty spire of the crossing tower which reaches a height of 404 feet. The façade at Salisbury lacks the comprehensive integration of ornament and structure which characterizes the French Gothic building; it is intrinsic qualities for the sake of abstract emotional sensation.

Earlier in this chapter it was said that the most comprehensive and monumental expression of the architectural attitude called Gothic is found in French buildings erected in the early thirteenth century. Decorative and structural forms of similar character were used elsewhere in Europe at the same time, but seldom with the same overwhelming effect. In England, for example, Gothic buildings always retain something of the broad low proportions of the Romanesque; they lack the aspiring and vertical character of contemporary French examples. *Salisbury Cathedral* (Figs. 103-105) was begun in 1220, the same year as Amiens; a comparison of the two provides characteristic points of contrast. The plan seems much longer than that of Amiens (cf. Figs. 98 and 103), although both are actually 450 feet long; the different impression of Salisbury

FIG. 104. Salisbury, Cathedral. Façade.

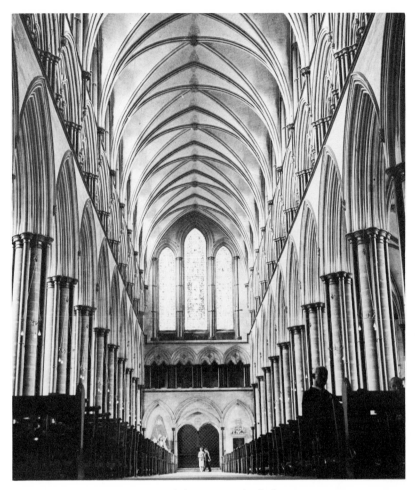

FIG. 105.   Salisbury.   Cathedral, Nave.

little but a screen wall concealing the building behind it. But its setting in a broad lawn or close permits the effect of the structure as a whole to be grasped to an extent rarely if ever possible in France, where the cathedrals are as a rule completely hemmed in by other buildings.

Structurally an English Gothic cathedral like Salisbury is not an organically integrated skeleton of piers, buttresses, and ribs but depends largely on heavy walls to sustain the vaults. In English buildings, the flying buttress has neither the structural nor the decorative effectiveness it has in French examples; it seldom is used except in buildings designed by French architects or influenced by French methods. Nor are English

buildings as tall in fact or effect as their French counterparts. In the *Salisbury Nave* (Fig. 105) the horizontals of nave arcade, triforium, and clearstory are quite pronounced, and the applied shafts of the compound piers do not rise to the vaults but relate only to the nave arcade. In direct contrast to the diffusion of line by luxuriant and naturalistic foliage so noteworthy in the French interior (Fig. 101), in the English example line is emphasized by the multiple mouldings of the arches and the precise contours of the polished black Purbeck marble shafts against the lighter color and matte surface of the limestone piers.

Another specifically English Gothic feature that evolved from certain features of the nave at Salisbury is the decorative vault rib. In the four-part vaults at Salisbury, all the ribs are structural, as they are at Amiens. But the vault is much lower—only 81 feet, whereas that at Amiens is 140—and the plain surfaces of the panels between the ribs are rather obtrusive. Later English builders break up these plain surfaces in a characteristic way—with linear patterns created by adding more ribs to the vault. At first these are sprung from the bay angles, as in the early fourteenth-century nave vaults of *Exeter Cathedral* (Fig. 106), where as many as

FIG. 106. Exeter. Cathedral (*ca.* 1350), Nave.

eleven ribs develop from a common point. The resultant richly textured surface in which color also plays an important part has a distinction that is only slightly suggested in even the best illustrations.

More complicated still are the nave vaults of *Canterbury Cathedral* (Fig. 107). Begun in 1379 when the remaining portion of the late eleventh-century church was replaced by the present structure, they were built in the time of Chaucer, whose *Canterbury Tales* interpret the spirit of the pilgrimage to Thomas à Becket's tomb that made

this one of the most famous shrines in the later Middle Ages. Here the ribs are multiplied to a point where the original four-part vault can hardly be discerned in the lively play of lines on its surface. The stonecutting skill necessary to build a vault of this type has never been surpassed, for each block had to be shaped to its particular purpose before being set in place. The result may not have the organic character of a French High Gothic interior; but the delicacy of the forms and the spare precision of outlines in the bewilderingly complex shapes combine with the clear definition of space in the whole to achieve an effect of great elegance.

In discussing late Gothic architecture in France in connection with the façade of Rouen Cathedral (Fig. 102) the difference was pointed out between the self-sufficiency of its structural and decorative elements and the abstractly architectonic unity imposed on comparable elements of thirteenth-century structures. This change was symbolic of the gradual shift from the predominantly spiritual and abstract values in High Gothic thought, as summed up in the scholastic philosophy of Thomas Aquinas, to more material and secular ways. Another aspect of this is the decreasing emphasis on religious architecture in the fourteenth and fifteenth centuries in France and a correspondingly greater interest in secular building. Such structures had been built much earlier, it is true. The fortified city of *Carcassonne* (Fig. 108) occupies a site used for defensive purposes from Roman times, but its present form is largely the result of construction in the late thirteenth and fourteenth centuries; although greatly restored in the nineteenth century, the ensemble remains an impressive secular monument of the Gothic period. The heavy outer walls with their picturesque towers and bastions are irregular in plan to take the maximum military advantage of the site. In this respect, the mediaeval fortified city is like the Hellenistic (Fig. 46); but within the walls of Carcassonne there is no such artificial order as there is in Priene, for the controlling factor is conformity of the individual buildings to the peculiarities of level and orientation in the site as a whole. Designed primarily for protection, the inner and outer fortifications

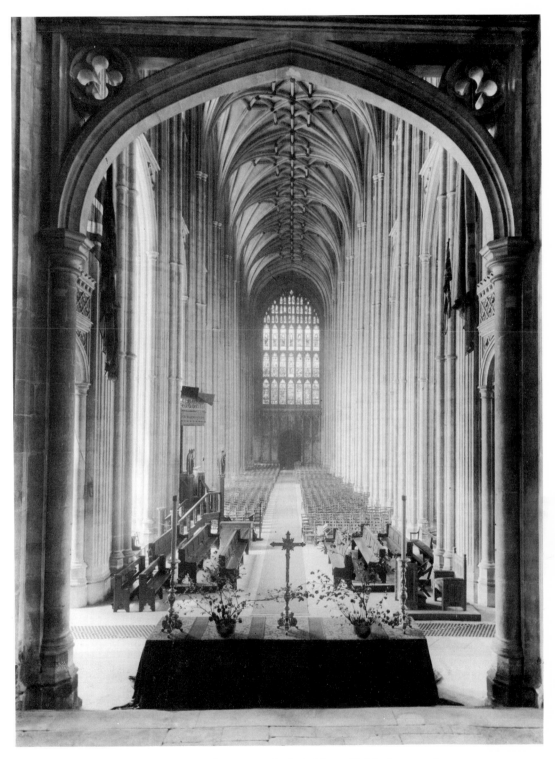

FIG. 107.   Canterbury.   Cathedral, Nave (finished *ca.* 1410).

FIG. 108.   Carcassonne.   The City
(late 13th-14th cents.).

FIG. 109.   Cahors.   Pont Valentré
(begun 1308).

are clearly the principal elements in the ensemble, but it is characteristic that the church also should be a building of some importance. Individual forms in mediaeval military architecture often reveal a similiar harmony with their settings. The *Pont Valentré* (Fig. 109) at Cahors in southwestern France was built in the fourteenth century across the river Lot; its six pointed arches are of unequal span determined by the conformation of the river bed, and a comparable asymmetry is also present in the two heavy towers which straddle the roadbed. Of utmost simplicity in design and with no ornament whatsoever, the structure as a whole nonetheless produces an impressive effect that results from the related planes of piers and arches, the strong rhythm of the openings, and the massive proportions. The fundamentally organic character of Gothic architectural forms is indicated by the distinction with which a strictly utilitarian structure like the bridge can be designed in accordance with the same basic principles as the cathedral with its immaterial and abstract expressive values.

It was only natural for the growing secular interests of the fourteenth and fifteenth centuries in Europe to be reflected architecturally in a more impressive type of domestic architecture. One of the best examples in this category of French building is the *House of Jacques Cœur* (Fig. 110) in Bourges, which was built in 1443. Jacques Cœur, a prosperous banker and leading citizen of Bourges, became master of the mint and ambassador of Charles VII of France (cf. Fig. 381). His dwelling is a striking indication of the importance a layman could attain in the fifteenth century. The house is an irregular pentagon built around an open court that is reached through the large arched opening in the façade which itself is bent to conform to the angle in the street. Other notable characteristics of the exterior are the steeply pitched irregular roofs asymmetrically grouped over the different rooms, and the elaborate decorative detail of window tracery, crockets and pinnacles, and sculptured figures. Within, a notable feature is the arrangement of rooms for maximum ease and convenience of use and circulation. Spiral staircases covered by complicated ramping vaults are located in small

FIG. 110.   Bourges.   House of Jacques Cœur (1443).

towers like the octagonal one on the street front that ascends to the chapel behind the pointed window with flamboyant tracery in the main pavilion of the façade; other rooms with clearly defined purpose account for the remaining details of the building's exterior. Lavishly ornamented within, with richly carved doors and painted ceilings above paneled walls hung with elaborate tapestries (cf. Fig. 600), Jacques Cœur's house provided a sumptuous setting for a scale of living befitting the prominent position of its bourgeois owner, a scale to which only feudal lords or princes of the Church could have aspired in earlier times.

A further manifestation of the increasingly secular character of mediaeval culture in the Gothic period is the number of civic buildings erected. The *Palazzo Vecchio* (Fig. 111) in Florence was begun in 1298 after the designs of Arnolfo di Cambio as the city's town hall, a function it still performs. The impulse the crusades gave to commerce and industry in Italy was mentioned at the beginning of this chapter; a monumental structure like the Palazzo Vecchio built relatively early for strictly secular purpose is one indication of this. In form it is an enlargement of the Florentine residential building type and it retains much of the fortresslike character

FIG. III. Florence. Arnolfo di Cambio, Palazzo
Vecchio (begun 1298).

appropriate in a city periodically convulsed by internal strife; the bloody struggles of the Guelphs and Ghibellines who replaced each other in sanguinary alternation as the ruling factions in Florence during Dante's time are symbolized by the contrasting square and notched crenellations surmounting the main mass and the tower respectively. Otherwise, the chief external characteristics are the rusticated walls of large roughcut blocks of stone, the windows with their double openings, the graceful slender tower in which hung the bell that called the Florentines to the defense of their city, the heavy mass of the building itself, and the characteristically Gothic asymmetry of the design as a whole.

The Norman city of Rouen in France is associated historically with Joan of Arc, who met her death there in 1431 while it was held by English troops. Later, its importance increased rapidly and some of the buildings erected or completed in the latter part of the fifteenth century are among the most impressive examples of late French Gothic or flamboyant style. The façade of the cathedral (Fig. 102) is one of these. Another is the *Palais de Justice* (Fig. 112), begun in 1493 as the seat of the *Parlement* of Normandy; the central and left wings were finished by 1508, the architects being Jacques and Robert Leroux. Like the Palazzo Vecchio in Florence, the building is an enlargement of the current domestic type (cf. Fig. 110), for it is built around a large court rather irregular in plan. The main block of the structure is at the back, with two projecting wings connected by a screen wall with a portal that closes in the court. Characteristic details of this late or flamboyant phase of Gothic style in France are the reversed curves of the pinnacle gables and the flattened arches of the windows on the ground level and in the principal story. Like the ornament on the façade of Rouen Cathedral, that of the Palais de Justice is a screen of lacelike stonework relatively independent of the wall. Even though many of the forms apparently are used primarily for decorative effect—such as the flying buttresses of the dormer gables in the roof—the richness of the resulting impression is undeniable. As a whole, the relatively simple design of the side-wing façade is an effective foil to the more elaborate one of the main part of the structure.

Infinite variety is the keynote of Gothic style whether in the details of a single structure or the different types of building. This is a clue to the fundamental purpose of all creative thinking of that time—to construct a system in which the multiplicity of nature should be resolved into

FIG. 112.   Rouen.   Jacques and Robert Leroux,
Palais de Justice (begun 1493).

order as a symbol of the pervading unity that was God. It is because of the Gothic architect's success in creating such a symbol that the cathedral of the thirteenth century makes it possible to realize the validity of religious experience to an extent not approached before or since. Whether Christian or unbeliever, the observer cannot but feel a powerful emotion created by the soaring lines and luminous color and the resultant sense of being enclosed in illimitable space. The nature of this emotion, which can be called only religious in character, has never been more clearly stated than in the words of Suger, abbot of the monastery of Saint-Denis near Paris and one of the great personalities of the Middle Ages: "When the house of God, many colored as the radiance of precious jewels, called me from the cares of this world, then holy meditation led my mind to thoughts of piety, exalting my soul from the material to the immaterial, and I seemed to find myself, as it were, in some strange part of the universe which was neither wholly of the baseness of the earth, nor wholly of the serenity of heaven, but by the grace of God I seemed lifted in a mystic manner from this lower towards that upper sphere."

Detail of Fig. 119.

CHAPTER EIGHT

Architecture of the Renaissance in Italy

During the Middle Ages, whatever consistency there was in European culture can be ascribed almost entirely to the influence of the Church. As already noted, it was the sole institution, after Rome's decline as an autonomous political and economic entity, with such comprehensive authority in Europe, that it could give direction to the thought and feeling of the period; and in so doing, it was instrumental in creating the most abstract and spiritual philosophy in the western world. At the same time, the secular elements in mediaeval culture must be recognized; although always subordinate to the spiritual, their importance increased considerably in the fourteenth and fifteenth centuries.

as was noted in the increasing number and distinction of nonreligious structures that were built. The inevitable outcome of this trend was the eventual reversal of the relative importance of religious and secular elements in European culture. This was first apparent in Italy, and it began to be clear in the early fifteenth century, in the period known as the Renaissance.

A partial explanation for the initial appearance of the Renaissance way of thinking in Italy is found in that country's economic history. Throughout the entire mediaeval period, the most traveled trade routes with the East went through Italy, and it was as trading posts on these routes that many north and central Italian cities became organized communities with unified civic governments. Venice and Milan, Florence and Pisa were among the leaders; all owed their importance to the flourishing trade in goods from the Orient, the manufacture of wool and leather, and the establishment of banking facilities and other institutions basic to commerce that ultimately gave them control of much of the business of the Occidental world.

Paralleling these background economic factors was the early establishment in Italy of political institutions somewhat different from those elsewhere in Europe. The feudal aristocracy that developed in France and Germany and England in the wake of Charlemagne's dissolving empire was never as widespread or as powerful in Italy. Civil bodies called communes which are similar in some respects to the city-states of classic Greece were founded in Italy appreciably earlier than any comparable development occurred in northern Europe. Many of these communes were eventually dominated by individuals or families—the Sforzas of Milan, the Gonzagas of Mantua, the Malatestas of Rimini, and the Medici of Florence; but even they owed their authority nominally to the free choice of the communes. In Florence, at least the simulation of democratic procedure in government was a basic factor in the Medici's firm grasp upon the affairs of the city during the fifteenth century.

Important though economic and political factors are in contributing to the Renaissance, they are not sufficient in themselves to explain it or its development. The literal meaning of the word Renaissance is "rebirth"; and in its use to characterize the period as a whole there is a direct reference to the reappearance of interest in the classic past. This has been accounted for as resulting from the sudden discovery of many examples of antique art, long-buried statues, or treasures of Greek and Roman literature that had lain unread for centuries in monastery libraries. According to this theory, the Renaissance was the result of attempts to emulate this beauty of past ages, revealed anew to the eyes of mediaeval man, and to revitalize the forms originally created in expressing the ideals of the classic world. This conception of the Renaissance derives some support from the undeniably classic character of many elements in it, but it is superficial and inadequate as a complete explanation.

The character of Renaissance culture indicates the redirection of European thought away from the abstract spiritual values of mediaeval culture toward more material ways of thinking. In the Middle Ages, man was of no importance except as a part of the Church; the physical earth was only a proving ground for the soul, for there it was prepared for the ultimate realities of the next world. In the Renaissance, man's inherent dignity was once again perceived in a way comparable in some respects to the way classic antiquity had perceived it. Moreover, the world he lived in was no longer thought to be only a symbol but was considered to have fundamental and intrinsic significance. The interest in nature that is apparent in Renaissance thinking may at first seem to be the logical outcome of the realistic view of material forms in the Middle Ages. But mediaeval realism reflects the then prevalent conception of nature as a manifestation of divine purpose, whereas Renaissance realism is scientific in the modern sense in being born of a searching inquisitiveness about things believed to have meaning in and of themselves rather than as symbols in a previously determined abstract order. It was in the Renaissance that an objectively analytical point of view toward nature appears for the first time; and as the most important institution therein, man once more becomes the focal point of human interest instead of a cog in a theological machine. This basic humanism distinguishes Renaissance thought from that of the Middle Ages far more significantly than its classicism.

At the same time, it is the humanism of the Renaissance that gives its art forms their undeniable affinity with those of classic antiquity. The essentially symbolic character of mediaeval art made it a poor vehicle at best for expressing ideas involving an objective interest in man and nature, whereas classic art is conditioned in large measure by precisely such interests. Therefore, instead of saying that the discovery of classic art was instrumental in creating the Renaissance point of view, it is more nearly correct to say that it was the emergence of that point of view that made possible the rediscovery of the principles of classic art. This is borne out by the fact that during the Middle Ages the knowledge of antique art in Europe was fairly extensive and there were even some attempts to reproduce its forms (cf. page 361), but this did not stimulate a renaissance like that of the fifteenth and sixteenth centuries in Italy. Mere knowledge of the forms was not enough; the first requisite was an attitude sympathetic to and capable of understanding them. This consideration provides another explanation for the initial appearance of this appreciation and understanding in Italy instead of elsewhere in Europe where economic and political conditions may have been quite as favorable. The classic habit of thought was always strong in Italy, even in the Middle Ages. Romanesque and Gothic buildings in Italy often seem more like classic skeletons clothed in mediaeval details than anything else (cf. Fig. 77) and this is even more apparent in some Italian mediaeval sculptures (cf. Fig. 309). For Italy, the Renaissance was simply a reversion to the classic point of view that was Italy's rightful heritage.

It should not be assumed from this that Renaissance architectural style was created by copying Roman buildings. Rather it was primarily a matter of using classic decorative vocabularies—and structural elements to a lesser degree—in ways that, as will be seen, are basically different from those of Rome and Greece. For the Renaissance architect, limited by his heritage of mediaeval structural technique, could not reproduce the forms of antique architecture as, having greater resources of verbal expression, the literary humanists of the time could copy those of ancient literature. Moreover, the classic models available to the Renaissance designer were largely Roman, because, culturally speaking, Greece was part of the Orient at that time; not until three and a half centuries later did Greek art become well enough known in western Europe to have any appreciable influence upon creative efforts there.

In the increasingly material culture of Europe in the fifteenth and sixteenth centuries, the dominance of the Church was progressively lessened in a theological sense, and religious thought was quite different from what it had been during the Middle Ages. The Reformation, the great revolt against the Church's spiritual authority, was in fact directed against its prevailingly profane principles at a time when it competed with temporal rulers for worldly power—a far cry from conditions in 1077 when Henry IV of Germany had acknowledged his subordinacy to Pope Gregory VII in the snows at Canossa and thus provided a symbol of the Church's supreme control of human destiny. But the atmosphere was too rarefied in the world of the spirit in the Middle Ages, when the value of the individual was determined by the part he was willing to play as an insignificant and anonymous unit in an intellectually perfect but abstract order maintained by inexorable principles. A reaction against the impersonal systematizing of mediaeval thought is apparent even before the end of the Gothic period; its effect on architectural style, already noted, will be seen again (cf. pages 353 ff.) in the sculpture and painting of France in the fourteenth and fifteenth centuries. A similar quality is the animating spirit of François Villon's poetry; in a more genial form it infuses the doctrines of Saint Francis of Assisi with a kindly spirit far different from the austere principles voiced by Bernard of Clairvaux. It is such changes in sentiment as these that distinguish the place of religious thought in Renaissance Europe from the place it held in the Middle Ages; it is now a part of human experience but not all of it; spiritual values still have significance, but material ones must also be taken into account.

Renaissance humanism also explains the final distinction between the arts embodying its principles and those of the Middle Ages, a distinction that is immediately apparent in considering the monuments themselves, namely, the importance of the creators of those forms as individuals. In the mediaeval period, as has been said, the individual was submerged in the community; in the Renaissance, he emerges from that impersonal social order and claims the right to express his ideas in his own way thus creating in the arts the concept of the modern, self-conscious artist. Previously the arts had been the expression of communal rather than individual experience; this is true of the classic as well as mediaeval styles. This does not minimize the importance of men like Iktinos and Kallikrates who built the Parthenon, or of Isidorus of Miletus and Anthemius of Tralles, the designers of Hagia Sophia, or of Robert de Luzarches who was the architect of the cathedral at Amiens; rather it emphasizes the fact that their names are gleams in the anonymous gloom that obscures those of most of their contemporaries. All this is changed in the Renaissance. The architect no longer builds solely for the greater glory of the country or city he lives in, or for the greater glory of God; he builds to win honor for himself in this world and in order that his name may live on in history after his death.

THE EARLY RENAISSANCE

It is perhaps symbolic that the year 1401— the first in the fifteenth century—should have witnessed what can well be taken as the beginning of Renaissance art, a competition directed by the governing body of Florence to determine the artist who should execute a pair of bronze doors for the Baptistery there (cf. pages 362-364). Two projects were chosen for the final stage in the contest, one by Lorenzo Ghiberti and the other by Filippo Brunellesco di Brunelleschi (1377-1446), both men of good standing in the city's goldsmiths' guild to which all sculptors belonged. The final award went to Ghiberti. Such was Brunellesco's chagrin that he determined to seek success in a field where his supremacy would be unchallenged. Accordingly he went to Rome in 1403, taking with him a youth named Donatello (cf. pages 367 ff.) who was destined for great distinction as a sculptor; here for a number of years he studied and measured the great examples of Roman architecture.

Brunellesco's researches in the methods and forms of Roman architecture came to fruition in 1420 when, after three years of argument, he was commissioned to build a dome over the crossing of the *Cathedral of Florence* (Fig. 113). This huge building, approximately 500 feet long, had been begun in 1296 in the Tuscan Gothic style whose chief characteristic was a lavish use of colored marble for decoration similar to that in Roman architecture; the designer was Arnolfo di Cambio, who also designed the Palazzo Vecchio in Florence (Fig. 111). Arnolfo died shortly after work started on the building and his place was taken in 1336 by Giotto the painter (cf. pages 454 ff.) who designed the beautiful campanile at the western end of the structure. Work continued under various supervisors during the fourteenth century. The structure was complete up to the level of the dome springing when Brunellesco returned to Florence from Rome in 1417, but the cupola itself was lacking. Its construction presented considerable difficulties; its base was 180 feet above the floor of the building and nearly 140 feet in diameter; the area to be covered was octagonal and the dome had to be built without centering to keep expense at a minimum. With his knowledge of Roman methods of construction, Brunellesco professed ability to erect the dome; but an obstacle to his being awarded the commission appeared in the refusal of the *Opera del Duomo*—a committee that had final and absolute decision regarding everything pertaining to the physical fabric of the building, as was commonly the case in mediaeval

FIG. 113.   Florence.   Cathedral (1296-1461), from the Northwest.

times—to permit him to proceed until his plans had been submitted to and approved by its members. This Brunellesco refused to do; if he did this, he said, credit for the project that he felt should rightfully be his would go to the *Opera*. The resulting three-year struggle between architect and committee was symptomatic of the conflict between the old and the new orders, mediaeval impersonalism against Renaissance individualism. Symbolic too was the outcome, for Brunellesco won, and his name has ever since been associated with the dome of Florence Cathedral.

In its final form, the cupola is the result of combining classic and mediaeval structural methods, with the latter predominant. It is a skeleton of ribs—eight massive ones rising from the angles of the octagonal base and two in each space between, making a total of twenty-four —that support blocks of stone. The whole is pointed in profile to lighten the lateral thrusts which are contained by belts of stone and wooden beams bolted together that circle the dome near its base; these belts are buried in the masonry, but even though invisible they are nonetheless essential to the stability of the structure. The dome is thus not a dome at all in the sense that comparable forms in Roman or Byzantine building are (Figs. 57, 69); rather it is an eight-sided vault whose thrusts are compensated in the manner usual in Italian Gothic construction, by tying the ends of the arches together. The high pitch of the sides of the dome also aided in building it without centering, for the ribs and the filling could be raised without external support to a considerable height; the small amount of scaffolding necessary to close in the opening at the top was then hung from the ribs themselves. It was completed by 1436 except for the lantern tower at the apex; this was finished in 1461, fifteen years after Brunellesco's death.

In view of Brunellesco's long studies of Roman architecture, it might be thought that the Florentine dome would have been very much like that of the Pantheon in Rome (Figs. 57, 58) and some features are similar. But there is considerable difference in the effects created, especially externally. The dome of the Pantheon is chiefly impressive when viewed from within, whereas that at Florence is the dominant feature of the exterior, its curvilinear form being admirably set off by Giotto's slender square campanile at the western end. In order to dominate the considerable bulk of the building supporting it, the dome had to be rather high; it rises more than 100 feet above its 180-foot-high base. In the interior, the actual height is so great that its effect would be somewhat impaired were there not an inner dome a little lower than the one visible on the outside but supported by the same ribs that sustain the outer one. Since the fifteenth century, nearly all monumental domes have been built in accordance with these principles.

The impression of external size and loftiness in the Florentine dome is an outstanding difference between it and earlier examples of the same architectural form such as the Pantheon at Rome and Hagia Sophia at Constantinople (Fig. 69). In them, exterior effectiveness was sacrificed to structural necessity, for the crowning domes are hemmed in by the buttressing masses essential for stability. This mechanical function is performed for Brunellesco's dome by the girdles of stone and timber buried in the masonry; its beauty of form is thus obtained at the expense of a complete statement of structural

fact. This is one of the most significant differences between architectural thinking of the Renaissance and that which was responsible for the Greek and Gothic styles. In both the latter, beauty of form is a concomitant of construction; the essential character of a building erected in accordance with the principles that govern either of these can be grasped only if the structural factors involved are understood. In Renaissance architecture, problems of construction play a lesser part in determining the form of buildings. The dome of the Cathedral of Florence is really a vault, but the buttressing essential for stability contributes nothing to the visual effect, concealed as it is in the masonry. In thus subordinating structural facts to formal effects, Brunellesco's attitude is typical of that of Renaissance architects in general who strove to realize preconceived ideals of beauty instead of thinking primarily in terms of construction that had to be integrated and unified in the final effect.

A chapel built by Brunellesco for the Pazzi family of Florence (Figs. 114, 115) illustrates the Renaissance architect's preoccupation with problems of formal design rather than construction even more clearly than the dome of the Florentine Cathedral. Although built in the Gothic cloister of Santa Croce (the façade and tower of which can be seen above the roof of the Cathedral in Fig. 113), it is completely in the Renaissance manner; it was probably the first ecclesiastic example, for it was begun sometime between 1420 and 1429. Rectangular in plan, it is covered by a dome on pendentives, flanked by barrel vaults on the cross axis. There is a smaller dome in the center of the entrance portico or loggia; it too is flanked by barrel vaults which extend to the outer ends of the porch and are masked by the pilastered and paneled wall above that rests on the Corinthian columns of the portico. Here more than in the Cathedral dome the results of Brunellesco's Roman studies are apparent; the dome on pendentives is Byzantine, but the coffered ornament that covers it is in the best Roman tradition (cf. Figs. 56, 58), as is also the Corinthian order, in both general proportions and the detail of the capitals. Further direct

FIG. 114. Florence. Brunellesco, Pazzi Chapel (*ca.* 1420-1429).

references to Roman usage are the band of strigils or wavy flutings at the top of the masking wall and the triangular pediment of the portal.

Other than the dome over the interior, of which only an angle pendentive is shown in Fig. 115, the most striking feature of the internal design is the decoration. Applied pilasters on the walls support an entablature from which moulding and framing arches rise on each of the principal walls and in the niche where the altar stands. Between the pilasters are panels with arched heads and sculptured medallions; and the shallow barrel vaults that flank the central dome on the cross axis of the interior are ornamented with panels enclosing rosettes. The architectural elements in the decoration are in the classic tradition—Corinthian pilasters, the entablature above, and the panels with rosettes. As

ornament, their effectiveness is heightened by the contrast between the gray-green color of the stone they are carved from, and the cream of the stucco walls. It is easy to see that the character of these principal features of the interior is determined not by structural necessity but solely by a desire to create a pattern of form and color that will be effective by virtue of pleasing tones and proportions. The latter are realized by using simple geometrical shapes as the basis of the design and repeating them throughout; the half-circle of the panel heads, for instance, echoes the larger motive of the barrel vaults and arches supporting the dome, and the rectangles framed by the pilasters are of the same dimensions and proportions as those formed by the exterior portico columns. In the façade there is similar concern for mathematically coordinated forms;

FIG. 115.   Florence.   Pazzi Chapel, Interior.

the height of the applied pilasters on the upper masking wall with its architrave is one-half that of the columns beneath with their architrave, and the wall itself is divided into almost exact squares by the pilasters. Here, too, semicircular arches provide a curvilinear foil for the predominant rectangularity of the balanced and symmetrical whole.

Inasmuch as Brunellesco's intention was to produce a visually pleasing design by these various relationships, the result may be legitimately criticized if this end is not attained. For example, the mathematical relationship between the pilastered wall above the colonnade and the colonnade itself is overstudied and obvious, and contributes in some degree to the impression that the wall is too heavy for its supports. This it is in fact as well as appearance, for some of the columns have split under the weight that rests on them. Their equal spacing on either side of the

central arch is also debatable, because it prevents any suggestion of framing the composition as a whole; this can be achieved in such a pattern only by stressing the outer accents in one way or another. As was the case in classic peristylar compositions (cf. Fig. 39), the problem of the angle support, whether in loggias such as this or in courtyards surrounded by arcades, challenged many Renaissance architects. Finally, the façade is open to criticism for its lack of scale; there is little intimation of its actual size, which is not inconsiderable, for the columns of the portico are nearly twenty-five feet high, whereas its apparent size is if anything quite small.

Brunellesco is said to have been animated by a desire "to restore to light the good manner of architecture," meaning the classic; hence it is important to realize the differences in principle between his way of thinking and that of the Middle Ages with which, in the Pazzi Chapel, he was consciously breaking. Most obvious of these is his use of classic decorative motives which have little or nothing to do with the construction of the building. Also different is the balanced symmetry of the design as compared with the picturesque asymmetry of comparable mediaeval forms. But we should not assume that Brunellesco is thinking as a Greek or Roman would, in spite of his accuracy in reproducing certain elements of their architectural styles. This building lacks the organic integration of construction and decoration that would be found in a Greek temple, for instance; and even a detail like the applied order which seems to parallel Roman usage he uses not as a form descriptive of structural function but for decorative reasons. His use of classic forms was motivated by an almost naïve delight in revealing his knowledge of them; but his way of using them is quite mediaeval because the effect is not an inherent and organic unity but a piling up and multiplication of decorative detail. The undeniable charm of the building lies in the freshness and novelty of his treatment of this detail which is eloquent of the new and vivacious interest of the Renaissance in both its classic past and its —for that time—modern present.

It was characteristic of the Renaissance that secular architectural forms should have attracted attention early as worthy of monumental treatment. A number of palaces were built in the first half of the fifteenth century in Florence for the wealthy burghers then becoming the most influential class in the city. One was the *Medici-Riccardi Palace* (Figs. 116, 117), begun in 1444 by Michelozzo Michelozzi (*ca.* 1396-1472) for his patron Cosimo de' Medici, then the foremost citizen of Florence. It was finished by 1459. The building was acquired by the Riccardi family in the sixteenth century (hence the hyphenated name) and underwent modifications in design in 1517, when some of the original arched openings of the ground story were transformed into pedimented windows. In 1715, the original length of ten bays was increased to the present seventeen. In plan a hollow rectangle, it is built around a court like the earlier Palazzo Vecchio (Fig. 111) and the later Farnese Palace in Rome

(Fig. 124); the façade rises directly from the street.

Externally, the chief features of the Medici-Riccardi Palace are the rustication of the wall surface, the treatment of the window openings in the second and third stories, the use of mouldings to distinguish the different levels in elevation, and the crowning cornice (Fig. 116). Of these, the first two are more or less traditionally Florentine. The windows are divided by mullions into two lights; and if the mullions themselves are in the form of Corinthian colonnettes, the divided window opening is found in earlier buildings like the Palazzo Vecchio (Fig. 111). The rough stone of the lowest story is also present in the older

FIG. 116. Florence. Michelozzo, Medici-Riccardi Palace (1444-1459).

FIG. 117.   Florence.   Medici-Riccardi Palace, The Court.

structure. There, however, it is uniform on all levels, whereas Michelozzo differentiated the the three stages of his elevation by varying the surfaces. They are massively irregular on the ground story; there are smooth faces on the second, but the joints between the stones are emphasized by beveling the angles; the third is smooth-faced throughout. In his treatment of the exterior, Michelozzo created a sense of scale, for the different parts are at the same time related to and differentiated from each other. The horizontal accents in the mouldings or stringcourses between the stories also aid in giving scale to the structure whose external bulk is dominated by the bold and massive cornice. These two features—the stringcourses and the cornice—have no precedent in mediaeval Florentine building. Their detail is classic—the dentils of the mouldings and the modillions of the cornice, for example;

and their general function in the design parallels that seen in Roman practice, for their use enabled Michelozzo to invest his building with a formal unity quite different from that of the mediaeval palace from which he took some features. In its self-contained symmetry, the exterior of the Medici-Riccardi Palace represents a compositional ideal inherently classical in feeling just as does Brunellesco's Pazzi Chapel (Fig. 114), but with more character from its effective scale that is due in part at least to the retention of some traditional elements.

Many classic details are also to be noted in the *Court* (Fig. 117) of the Medici-Riccardi Palace. Vaulted porticoes surround it, the colonnade arches springing from columns with modified Composite capitals as in certain late Roman examples. The arches are moulded on their external faces and the same profile is repeated horizontally in the entablature resting upon them. As in the Pazzi Chapel façade, structural considerations play no part in determining the form, for the groined vaults of the porticoes are built with tie rods instead of buttresses to offset their thrusts. Also, as in the design by Brunellesco, the arcade lacks an impression of adequate support at the angles in consequence of the uniform spacing of the columns and in seeming too light for the walls above. These are evidence of unfamiliarity with the basic principles of a structural vocabulary that is still appreciated more than it is understood; later architects improved upon these effects because of greater understanding. But here as in the sculpture and painting of the early fifteenth century in Florence (cf. pp. 362-371, 467-469) there is the charm of freshness and the appeal of a naïve vision that offset much that may rightfully be said by way of academic criticism.

The Medici-Riccardi Palace is important in the history of architecture for it represents the first stage in the transition from the mediaeval fortress concept of domestic architecture to the city house. As one of the first buildings in Renaissance style to incorporate such ideas, it was influential in creating a type which was continued in Florence until far into the sixteenth century and was a potent factor in determining the style of many important buildings in other parts of Italy as well. Significant too is its role as the home of the Medici family, which probably contributed as much as any comparable group to the formation of Renaissance culture of the fifteenth century; within its walls occurred incidents that vitally affected not only Florentine history but that of the entire western world. The art treasures it once housed are the nucleus of one of the greatest extant collections of Renaissance sculpture and painting; and the picturesque Procession of the Magi painted on its chapel walls by Benozzo Gozzoli (Fig. 405), in which members of the Medici family are represented as some of the Wise Men from the East, is a priceless source of knowledge regarding the costumes and customs of that time.

Brunellesco and Michelozzo were of the first generation of Renaissance architects in that the classic style was a source of pleasure and inspiration to them. It was likewise an inspiration to Leon Battista Alberti (1404-1472), but that he made somewhat different use of it is seen in the façade of the *Rucellai Palace* (Fig. 118) in Florence. Begun in 1446 and completed in 1455, it follows the Medici-Riccardi Palace in its three-storied elevation and in details like the window openings whose frames are flush with the wall and divided by colonnette mullions. The effect is less massive and more ornate than in Michelozzo's palace, however, and the primary decorative scheme is not rustication but a system of superimposed pilasters of modified Doric and Corinthian types. These are used in the Roman manner (cf. Fig. 52), with one order, including a complete entablature, for each story. In this use of the orders, Alberti developed a motive that became extremely popular in the later fifteenth century and was further elaborated in the sixteenth. One difficulty was the treatment of the main cornice. Although it is the entablature of the topmost order, it had to be much more massive in proportion than the corresponding features of the lower levels in order to cap the building as a whole with any degree of success but it could not be entirely out of scale with the order of which it is theoretically a part. In trying to effect a compromise between these formal requirements, Alberti had to forego the bold and vigorous profile of Michelozzo's cornice on the Medici-Riccardi Palace and his structure is somewhat less forceful in character as a result.

Other than the innovation of the superimposed pilasters applied to the wall, the decoration of the Rucellai Palace façade consists of rusticated surfaces, framed by the orders, which are similar to that of the second story of the Medici-Riccardi Palace (Fig. 116), and continuous friezes of delicate arabesques in low relief in the entablatures that correspond to the stringcourses in Michelozzo's design. The rustication is only simulated in some places, notably the arched window heads, the pattern of the supposed joints being determined not by the size of the stone blocks but by the desire to produce an even and uniform effect; this reveals the Renaissance tendency to divorce structure and

FIG. 118. Florence. Alberti, Rucellai Palace
(1446-1455).

ornament that has been noted elsewhere. As a study in formal relationships other than those mentioned, Alberti's design is notable for its fine balance of solids and voids and for the effective rhythm resulting from slight variations in the widths of the bays framed by the applied pilasters, those enclosing the doors being a little wider than the others. It is by this device that Alberti obtains variety and suggests scale in his façade which is as notable for its lyric delicacy as is Michelozzo's for its rugged boldness. Although in both the Medici-Riccardi and Rucellai Palaces, the original interiors have been modified, rooms of the period in other palaces (cf. Fig. 613) make it possible to complete in imagina-

tion the settings of fifteenth-century Florentine life.

The greatest difference in principle between Alberti's use of classic architectural forms and that of Brunellesco and Michelozzo is his employment of them in accordance with Roman theory. Brunellesco and Michelozzo were craftsmen first of all, trained in the use of their hands and capable of demonstrating by example just how a stone should be cut and laid. Alberti was a scholar and humanist, versed in Latin, and an accomplished author, mathematician, painter, sculptor, and poet as well as architect. In this last capacity, he was a designer and director in the modern sense, rather than the master mason of mediaeval times to which Brunellesco and Michelozzo are more comparable. His scholarly interests led him to a profound study of the writings of Vitruvius, the Roman architectural theorist of the first century A.D., a manuscript copy of which had been found and identified in the Swiss monastery of Saint Gall in 1414. Alberti's own theories of architectural design as set forth in the book he wrote, characteristically in Latin and called *De Re Aedificatoria* or *Concerning Building*, are deeply colored by the principles of the Roman writer. Alberti's book, composed about 1450 and published in 1486, was instrumental in establishing his own somewhat academic theories as a fundamental factor in subsequent Renaissance architectural practice. In making classic usage as well as classic forms the basis of his creative thinking, Alberti re-

sembled many artists in other fields during the later fifteenth century in Italy; the implicit principle of creation in accordance with a preconceived and consciously maintained ideal of beauty is in direct contrast to the intuitively felt and emotionally realized concepts of the Middle Ages.

The character of Renaissance conceptions of architectural beauty is clearly revealed in Alberti's remodeling between 1450 and 1468 of the thirteenth-century church of *San Francesco* (Fig. 119) in Rimini. The project, undertaken for Sigismondo Malatesta, the Tyrant of Rimini, was calculated to appeal to Alberti's classical and humanist tastes; for the remodeled structure was to be a hall of fame in which Sigismondo, his mistress Isotta, and the members of his "academy," founded to study the masterpieces of

FIG. 119. Rimini. Alberti, San Francesco (1450–1468).

classic literature, were to be buried. Over the brick core of the earlier building Alberti spread a marble veneer that would have transformed the façade into a veritable Roman arch of triumph had the projected upper story been completed; the design was a direct adaptation of a Roman gate in the walls of Rimini that still stands. It is probably the first Renaissance building in which an effort was made to reproduce the general form as well as the details of a classic architectural type. The full entablature breaking out over the semi-detached columns of the façade creates an effect compararable in ostentation to that in many late Roman buildings, an impression intensified in the carving of the richly moulded and pedimented doorway. A great deal of its sculptured ornament was done by Agostino di Duccio, and its lightness and delicacy do much to relieve what would otherwise be a rather dry design. The niches along the side were to receive the ashes of Sigismondo's associates in sarcophagi copied after those of classic Roman times.

Florentine artists were the first in Italy to develop consistent Renaissance styles, and in Florence is the character of the Early Renaissance phase of the arts most clearly and comprehensively defined. Its commercial importance and economic power as one of the great centers of banking and wool manufacture in the fifteenth century may have been partly responsible for this; but it can hardly be doubted that the city's free and democratic atmosphere which encouraged originality of thought and intellectual curiosity did much to further imaginative creativeness and a receptive attitude toward its results. Such an atmosphere did not exist everywhere in Italy at this time. In Venice, for instance, although the economic picture was highly favorable in consequence of the city's flourishing trade with the Near East, originality of thought was not encouraged by a government theoretically republican but actually an oligarchy exercising despotic control and having final judgment over all aspects of life in the city and its possessions. The restraining effect of such circumstances upon Venetian architecture is evident in the continuation of many mediaeval forms long after the innovations of Brunellesco and Michelozzo had given way to other and later styles in Florence. Furthermore, there were no classic remains in Venice; it had not been a Roman city but was founded in 568 by inhabitants of northern Italy fleeing from invading Lombards. They thus lacked the direct classical heritage the Florentines were so proud of. Renaissance motives are an importation there in a certain sense as compared with the way they were regarded in Florence and even elsewhere in northern Italy as for instance in Milan, where a rather important school of architecture had its center.

An example of the tardy appearance of Renaissance architectural style in Venice is the *Vendramini Palace* (Fig. 120) on the Grand Canal, designed by Pietro Lombardo (1435-1515). It was begun in 1481, by which time the classical habit had been firmly established in Florence by Brunellesco, Alberti and others; but the Venetian palace still retains so characteristic a mediaeval motive as the traceried window with a dividing mullion, though framed by superimposed orders of engaged columns on pedestals and with entablatures for the dividing courses between stories. A characteristically Venetian effect created by these orders is the triple division of the façade resulting from doubling the columns framing the outermost bays; this tripartite pattern, which appears in the earliest preserved examples of Venetian palace architecture, persisted until the eighteenth century. Otherwise the most characteristic feature of the Venetian palace as compared with the Florentine (Figs. 116, 118) is the pronounced openness of the façade, with its large and ample windows. These look out as a rule from spacious salons on the second and third floors, over the Grand Canal which was the principal "street" of the city. The fact that they are a more or less invariable characteristic of Venetian domestic structures is a reflection architecturally of the civic peace imposed by the arbitrary power of the city's Council of Ten, as compared with the turbulence in Florence where a less open street façade was a wise precaution against flying stones and other missiles even in the fifteenth century.

The naïve pleasure with which Brunellesco and Michelozzo regarded the art of classic antiquity gave way to Alberti's scholarly enthusiasm in the mid-fifteenth century. The closing years of this period brought further developments along this line in the work of Donato Bramante (1444-1514). Born in Umbria in central Italy, Bramante was a painter in his youth; he possibly studied this art under Piero della Francesca (cf. Fig. 402) and certainly he was influenced by Mantegna (cf. Fig. 406), two of the most creative and classically-minded masters of painting in the fifteenth century. It was in Milan in northern Italy, however, that Bramante began his architectural career; here he designed the church of *San Satiro* (Figs. 121, 122) built between 1482 and 1487. Part of the ensemble is the Cappella della Pietà; its plan is of the central type; with a circular lower level resolved into a Greek cross in the four gabled arms of equal length in the second stage, the whole terminating in an octagonal drum which is surmounted by a slender cylindrical tower and pinnacle. The central plan had great attraction for later Renaissance architects, for it gave them an opportunity to develop monumental compositions of form and space in a way impossible with the basilican type. This is apparent in the exterior of the Chapel (Fig. 121), which is quite imposing although of rather modest dimensions, a consequence of the relationships between the various parts of the structure which were determined by giving its silhouette as a whole the form of an equilateral triangle. Within this basic geometrical form the applied pilasters—their shafts decorated with arabesques of vases and foliage on the lower level where they frame alternate wide panels and narrow niches, and bent around the angles of the octagonal drum above—define and accent the plastic patterns formed by the different parts of the building. In the *Baptistery* (Fig. 122) of San Satiro, on the other hand, the problem was to define interior space and give it adequate scale. An octagon in plan, this quality of the space volume is established by bending the angle pilasters; the desired effect of scale is secured by judicious adjustment of the proportions of the upper order to those below. Again arabesques

decorate the pilasters—delicate patterns of lightly carved but crisply defined leaves. The medallions flanked by groups of *putti* or nude infants in the panels between lower and upper stories are classic in type and strongly individualized in detail, suggesting that Bramante may have known and admired the sculpture of Donatello (cf. Fig. 317) with its antique overtones, as well as the paintings of Mantegna and Piero della Francesca.

FIG. 120.   Venice.   Pietro Lombardo, Vendramini Palace (begun 1481).

About 1500, Bramante was called from Milan to Rome to undertake certain architectural works for the pope, a circumstance that made him a transitional figure from the Early Renaissance style still apparent in his Milanese designs to the High Renaissance manner of which his Roman buildings are in many ways the initial statement. The differences between the two phases will be discussed elsewhere. Here it suffices to note that the fifteenth-century architects of the Early Renaissance worked chiefly in Florence and northern Italy; only toward the

FIG. 121. Milan. Bramante, San Satiro,
Cappella della Pietà (1482-1487).

close of that period do they reveal more than enthusiastic observation of the immediate and obvious characteristics of classic architectural form. Brunellesco's Pazzi Chapel and Michelozzo's palace for the Medici family have many classic details of ornament, but the basic compositional schemes and the use of ornament are dictated by the designer's feeling rather than by comprehension of the larger plastic relationships that are as much a part of antique architectural procedure as its decorative detail. Alberti and Bramante reveal some perception of these more fundamental qualities of architectural expression. Although the ornament on their buildings has much of the lightness and exuberance typical of Early Renaissance design in general, it is used as an accessory to well-designed and planned structures that are given character more by effective relationships of mass and space than by surface decoration. It is from their practice and theories that the Italian High Renaissance style developed.

FIG. 122.   Milan.   Bramante, San Satiro, Baptistery.

THE HIGH RENAISSANCE

With the turn of the sixteenth century, Rome became the chief artistic center in Italy, and the High Renaissance style whose chronological span falls within the first half of the century is first and foremost a Roman phenomenon. During the Middle Ages, Rome only indifferently reflected its spiritual importance as the seat of the Church. Possibly its physical fortunes reached their lowest point during the so-called "Babylonian Captivity" from 1305 to 1377, when the papacy was moved to Avignon in France. After its return to Rome, a number of fifteenth-century popes took steps leading to the artistic regeneration of the city. Nicholas V (1447-1455) called Fra Angelico from Florence to paint his chapel walls with frescoes depicting the lives of Saints Stephen and Laurence. Sixtus IV (1471-1484) imported a Florentine architect to build the Sistine Chapel in the Vatican Palace between 1475 and 1481, and painters from Tuscany and Umbria to decorate it. Other popes such as Pius II (1464-1471) and Alexander

FIG. 123. Rome. Bramante, San Pietro in Montorio,
Tempietto (1502).

VI (1492-1503) encouraged humanistic and secular interests in the papal court that frequently involved practices not at all consistent with its spiritual character but which created an atmosphere favorable to the attitude reflected in High Renaissance style. The names of three popes are directly associated with this by virtue of their patronage of the arts—Julius II (1503-1513), Leo X (1513-1521), and Clement VII (1523-1534). The rise of Rome as the chief artistic center of Italy in the sixteenth century and of the popes as the chief patrons of the arts is paralleled by the decline of Florence and the Medici family from the artistic eminence they had attained in the fifteenth century. The death of Lorenzo the Magnificent in 1492 and the ensuing unrest in the city, well symbolized by Savonarola's abortive attempts at reform and the banishment of Piero de' Medici, indicate in some measure the circumstances of the decline of Florence in worldly and creative fortune. Although a number of outstanding artists of the early sixteenth century are Florentine in background and training, and there are High Renaissance monuments there of great importance, the leadership is found elsewhere, largely in Rome.

Bramante is the first name in the history of High Renaissance architectural style in Rome; and his first building there—the *Tempietto* of *San Pietro in Montorio* (Fig. 123) which was finished in 1502—is an outstanding example of High Renaissance design. Like the earlier buildings of San Satiro in Milan (Fig. 121), it is centrally planned and of rather small dimensions, the outside diameter of the peristyle being only twenty-nine feet; but here the resemblances stop. Where the earlier one is made up of varied plastic forms—circular, rectangular, and octagonal— the Roman church is composed entirely of curvilinear patterns in the circular sanctuary and its surrounding peristyle surmounted by a dome resting on a tall drum. The order, too, is less ornate than in the Milanese structure where it consisted of arabesque paneled pilasters; here the sixteen columns of the peristyle are purest Roman Doric, complete with entablature and frieze whose detail is of the greatest accuracy.

The balustrade crowning the lower level of the exterior provides a visual transition to the drum with its recessed niches and the dome. As an example of architectural design intended primarily for monumental effect (it was erected on the spot where it was once believed Saint Peter was executed), the Tempietto lacks inherent scale, for when viewed as an isolated building there is nothing to indicate its size. However, it was planned to be part of an ensemble in a colonnaded court where its simple dignity would have been more adequately accommodated than in its present surroundings.

Monumental formality has replaced picturesqueness as the chief characteristic of architectural design, and logic and reason, rather than charm and gayety, are the basic expressive aim. These are the fundamental differences between the Cappella della Pietà of San Satiro (Fig. 121) and San Pietro in Montorio (Fig. 123). In adopting this new attitude, Bramante exemplifies a phenomenon that recurs again and again in the Renaissance, among painters and sculptors as well as architects—the development of a more monumental, serious, and significant style upon coming to Rome. The reason for this can hardly be specified; it may have been the artists' intuitive perception of the traditional significance of the Eternal City and a feeling that their contributions thereto should acknowledge its venerable spiritual supremacy. However this may be, the more monumental quality of High Renaissance architecture is its most distinguishing characteristic, and with it there is a growing appreciation of the need for designs that are well unified and consistent in formal qualities rather than merely superficially attractive. This involved among other things an extensive development of architectural theory as well as structural practice; and the influence of writings like those of Alberti becomes increasingly more important as the sixteenth century moves on.

In the field of domestic architecture, the *Farnese Palace* (Figs. 124-126) in Rome illustrates certain features of the High Renaissance style. Built for Alessandro Farnese, then a cardinal and later Pope Paul III, it was begun in 1517 after the designs of Antonio da San Gallo the Younger

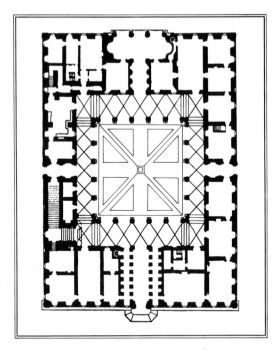

FIG. 124. Rome. Antonio da San
Gallo the Younger,
Farnese Palace (1517), Plan.

(1485-1546). He was a Florentine, nephew of two fifteenth-century architects of the same surname from whom he had received his early training; he completed it by work with Bramante. His plans were followed only for the first and second stories; the third with its cornice was designed by Michelangelo Buonarroti (1475-1564). The plan is a hollow rectangle (Fig. 124), symmetrically disposed on both major and minor axes. In this it is more or less traditional, for, as has been noted, the fifteenth-century Florentine palaces have the same general arrangement (Fig. 117). Also reminiscent of Florentine practice is the absence of superimposed orders in the façade design, although elsewhere in Italy and even in some earlier sixteenth-century Roman palaces, the order was used in the manner of Alberti and Bramante. Florentine too is the heavy cornice, massive in proportions and bold in projection, following the general pattern of Michelozzo's Medici-Riccardi Palace (Fig. 116) which Michelangelo must have known well, because, as

noted elsewhere, it was he who was engaged to modify the ground story of the Florentine structure in 1517.

The rustication and applied orders on the façades of Early Renaissance palaces (cf. Figs. 116, 118) make them largely studies in contrasting tone and texture. These are not found on the Farnese Palace façade; it is rather a study in proportion and mass, framed by the cornice and the alternately long and short projecting stones or quoins at the angles, unified horizontally by the carved and moulded stringcourses between the stories, and given interest by the plastic patterns of the window frames. These are treated in differing ways—with flat architraves and sills on consoles in the first story, with applied colonnettes on projecting bases and alternately triangular and curved pediments in the second, and with round arched openings under broken triangular pediments in the third. Whatever the design, the window is a positive plastic motive by virtue of such treatment, as compared with the neutral effect of the openings in an Early Renaissance façade which are flush with the wall surface. In making a formal problem of fenestration or the handling of windows, instead of letting openings be determined by their practical function as transmitters of light and air to the interior, the concern of High Renaissance architects with perfection of appearance as a primary aim is obvious. Somewhat weak in the façade ensemble is the entrance motive, for it is lacking in adequate scale, a limitation imposed by the need to respect the rhythmic pattern of the windows in the lower and second stories.

The court of the Farnese Palace (Fig. 126) is reached through an elaborate columnar vestibule whose Doric order and coffered vault appear to have been inspired by details of the ancient Roman Theatre of Marcellus from which much of the stone in the Renaissance palace was taken. The Colosseum (Fig. 52) was also looted for this purpose and the design of the court clearly indicates considerable study of the older structure. It is in three stories with vaulted arcades on the ground level and walls with windows above. Applied orders appear throughout—Doric and Ionic columns for the first and second floors and Corinthian pilasters for the third—in the same relationship as that on the exterior of the Colosseum, to which the treatment of the base courses and entablatures is also to be referred. Pediments are used over the windows as on the façade, but the framing colonnettes are omitted in the interests of scale which would have been impaired by too close juxtaposition of the small orders appropriate to the windows and the larger ones on the walls. The angle support which so taxed fifteenth-century architects in designing arcaded courts (cf. Fig. 117) is solved here by using piers instead of columns, those at the corners being larger and angular in section so they enable the arcade to turn at right angles. The more massive and dignified effect of the Farnese court in comparison with that of the Medici-Riccardi Palace and its more consistent classicism in detail are further illustrations of the differing architectural ideals of the Early and High Renaissance.

Symmetry of effect was a primary quality in the rational High Renaissance ideal of architectural distinction. This was not difficult to achieve in the Farnese Palace, for the plan is symmetrical. In the double *Massimi Palace* (Figs. 127, 128), in Rome the problem confronting the architect

FIG. 125. Rome. Antonio da San Gallo the Younger and Michelangelo, Farnese Palace (1517-1546).

FIG. 126.   Rome.   Farnese Palace, The Court.

Baldassare Peruzzi (1481-1536) was much more difficult. The site had traditionally been occupied by the palace of this family, one of the oldest in Rome, and Peruzzi was called to build two houses on it (for the households of Pietro and Angelo Massimi) in place of an older structure destroyed in the sack of Rome in 1527. The street upon which the palaces fronted was narrow and curved, a fact responsible for the striking bowed façade of Pietro's portion of the establishment (Fig. 128), the one to the right in the plan. This façade extends beyond the much narrower structure of which it is actually the front, but in the interests of symmetry such a solution was unavoidable. It is also clear that the façade as a whole can hardly be said to have been composed above the first row of windows, for those in the third and fourth stories are little more than openings in the wall. The narrowness of the street explains this, for a tall façade of monumental proportions could not have been as effective as the

Farnese Palace was on its large piazza. For the same reason and because of Peruzzi's realization that the façade would have to be effective at close range, the details of orders and mouldings are executed throughout with a delicacy and refinement that agree beautifully with the modest scale of the structure. At the same time, the entrance portico with its coupled freestanding Doric columns—possibly a reference to the family's full name which was Massimi *alle Colonne*—is one of the most dignified and impressive in the domestic buildings of the High Renaissance in Rome. It continues the rhythm of alternate wide and narrow bays of the side-wall pilasters in a motive similar to that used by Alberti in the façade of the Rucellai Palace (Fig. 118) and also by Bramante in several of his Roman buildings.

The High Renaissance palaces of Rome are effective symbols of the culture that produced them in their dignity and measured proportions

—creations of the attitude set forth as ideal in Baldassare Castiglione's *Cortegiano* or "The Courtier." But there is another side to the High Renaissance temperament—that expressed in the unscrupulous opportunism of Machiavelli's *The Prince* and the crafty blackguardism of Aretino's polemics. This too was not without architectural expression, for the vaulting ambition and unfettered personal pride of Julius II was responsible for one of the most characteristic examples of High Renaissance style, the present basilica of *St. Peter's* (Figs. 129-132) in Rome which is on the site once occupied by the structure of the same name erected by Constantine (Figs. 62-64) nearly 1200 years before. This venerable building, one of the most important monuments of the early Church through its commemoration of the first bishop of Rome, had suffered much

FIG. 128. Rome. Massimi Palace (begun 1535).

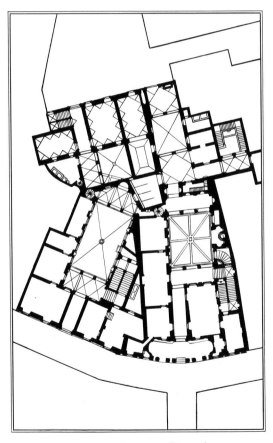

FIG. 127. Rome. Peruzzi, Massimi Palace, Plan.

during the later Middle Ages; a project to reconstruct it had actually been initiated, possibly by Alberti, at the command of Pope Nicholas V in 1454. This was never carried beyond the preliminary stages, however, and the old basilica was in considerable disrepair by the end of the fifteenth century.

In 1505, Julius II commissioned Michelangelo to create a monumental tomb for him in the Constantinian church (cf. pages 378-379). So huge was the projected mausoleum that the building in its existing form could not have contained it; the ambitious pontiff characteristically ordered it demolished and replaced by a larger one. A competition to determine the architect was won by Bramante and the first stone was laid in 1506. It was to be a structure of the central type for which Bramante had a particular fondness, as noted in discussing his designs for San Satiro in Milan and San Pietro in Montorio in Rome—a Greek cross with four equal arms and a dome over the crossing where the tomb was to stand. Three other men were associated with him on the project, Giuliano da San Gallo, Fra Giocondo of Verona, and Raphael, Bramante's nephew, who is better known as a

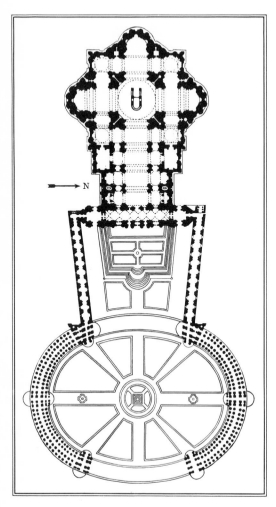

FIG. 129. Rome. St. Peter's
(1506-1667), Plan.

Michelangelo was appointed directo˜ of the construction in 1546, and the general character of the western end of the building (which faces east instead of west, as did the Constantinian basilica) is the result of his ideas. He reverted to a Greek cross plan, with an entrance portico of free-standing columns at the end of the eastern arm, so arranged that the tremendous dome he planned over the crossing would dominate the structure from every point of view. At his death in 1564, the outer walls and the internal ordinance were completed. The small flanking domes around the principal one were built from his plans by Vignola between 1564 and 1585, and the large one by Giacomo della Porta between 1585 and 1590, with slight modifications of Michelangelo's original design, which is still preserved in the form of a large-scale wooden model. In 1605 it was thought necessary to lengthen the eastern arm of the structure to provide more space for the great ceremonies celebrated in it. This was done by Carlo Maderno, who added three bays to Michelangelo's plan, with a vestibule that carried the façade, also designed by him, much farther from the dome than Michelangelo's portico would have been (Fig. 130). Finally, in 1667, the Doric colonnades enclosing the vast piazza in front of the building were added by Gian Lorenzo Bernini (1589-1680). It is perhaps an appropriate comment on the futility of human ambition that the motive that impelled Julius II to destroy the Constantinian basilica and decree the erection of the present structure—an adequate setting for his stupendous mausoleum—was not consummated; the pontiff's remains lie under an obscure and insignificant slab in the church. The magnificent tomb planned by Michelangelo was never completed; only an unhappy reduction of it is now to be seen in San Pietro in Vincoli.

Comparison of the façade and apse of Saint Peter's (Figs. 130, 131) shows the extent to which Maderno's façade impairs the effect planned by Michelangelo in which the dome would have dominated the structure. From the Piazza di San Pietro, only a portion of the drum is visible and the dome appears to have no base; thus a

painter (cf. Figs. 427-430) but also was active as an architect. The four piers to support the dome were completed according to Bramanate's plans and the general proportions of the nave were established by 1514 when he died. The work was carried on by his associates but they all died by 1520 and construction was halted for some time. Between 1520 and 1546, Baldassare Peruzzi and Antonio de San Gallo the Younger were successively in charge of the building and introduced considerable modifications of Bramante's plan, but actual work went little further than some reinforcement of the crossing piers and arches.

proper transition from the horizontal lines of the façade cornice to the mounting arches of the cupola is not achieved. From the west, however, the monumental grandeur of Michelangelo's design is immediately apparent (Fig. 131). The walls of apse and transepts are decorated with applied Corinthian pilasters 90 feet high which rise from a basement course and are surmounted by an entablature with an attic story above, the total height from the ground to the top of the attic story being nearly 170 feet. Over these towering cliffs of masonry rise the small domes above the angle chapels which prepare the eye for the bold curves of the principal cupola that with its lantern tower rises to a height of 450 feet. Like Brunellesco's dome for the cathedral of Florence (Fig. 113), that of Saint Peter's is in two shells —the outer one of somewhat steeper pitch than the inner one, assuring its supremacy as the domin-

ant element in the external effect. It is supported on sixteen ribs which are visible both within and without; the lateral thrusts are buttressed by the coupled columns of the drum and by girdling iron chains embedded in the masonry. No dome of such stupendous proportions had been attempted before; and the impressiveness of Michelangelo's solution of its structural and formal problems makes the cupola of Saint Peter's at once the historical climax of the evolution of the dome as an architectural element—led up to by those of the Roman Pantheon (Fig. 57), Hagia Sophia (Fig. 69) and the cathedral of Florence (Fig. 113)—and the archetype of the form in succeeding periods (cf. Figs. 163, 190).

No less grandiose than the dimensions of the exterior are those of the interior (Fig. 132). The Corinthian pilasters of the nave piers are nearly 85 feet high and the entablature adds

FIG. 130. Rome. St. Peter's. Maderno, Façade
(1605-1613): Bernini, Piazza (begun 1656).

FIG. 131. Rome. St. Peter's. Michelangelo and
Giacomo della Porta, The Dome (1558-1590).

another 20 feet. The crown of the coffered barrel vault rises 150 feet above the floor level—higher than the vaults of Amiens Cathedral which were among the loftiest completed in the Middle Ages (Fig. 101). This huge size in the supporting members of the structure was necessary in view of the great physical forces involved in its construction, but it is actual rather than apparent size. The formal problem is once again scale and this the interior lacks to a marked degree, for the real size of the various elements cannot be grasped directly. It is only after the original impression of the interior has been many times renewed that its immensity can be comprehended—that ten-foot-long decorative cherubs are realized to be that large and that orders of such height can be felt to be really so lofty. The interior dimensions as they stand were established by Bramante, whose plans were followed in building the crossing piers where the gigantic order was first used. Had Michelangelo's equal-armed Greek cross plan been left unmodified, the internal effect of the dome would have done much to create an adequate impression of the huge spatial volume of the interior, but the increased length of the nave resulting from Maderno's added bays deprives it of nearly all its effect from any but nearby points.

In striving for largeness of scale, the architects of the High Renaissance made frequent use of the orders, as has been seen; and when the building was on a basically human scale, the treatment of the orders could follow that of the classic builders as in, for example, the court of the Farnese Palace (Fig. 126). Orders of such dimensions as those could have been used on the craglike walls of the apse at Saint Peter's (Fig. 131) only by repetition and superposition, breaking up the wall surfaces into many small units whose total effect would have been inherent smallness of scale. It was no doubt to emphasize the massive simplicity of the walls and the space volumes they enclose that Michelangelo used a single order instead, making it rise through both stories of the elevation below the attic. When columns or pilasters are used in this way to include more than one story, they are called giant orders; this is one of the most individual architectural conceptions of the High Renaissance. In Saint Peter's, the giant order of the exterior was doubtless dictated by the colossal pilasters planned for the interior by Bramante, although these are limited to one story in elevation. In the group of buildings called the *Campidoglio* (Fig. 133) on the Capitoline Hill in Rome which was begun by Michelangelo in 1546, the device was used with great success as the basic unifying motive relating the three façades in a monumental and well-composed group. At the back of the piazza whose sides diverge from the steps by which the hill is ascended (Fig. 134) is the Palace of the Senate; its façade dominates the group from a high podium above which the giant order of Corinthian pilasters rises through two stories to support an entablature crowned

with a balustrade. The end bays of this building project slightly beyond the wall plane to frame the façade as a whole, and the central axis is emphasized by the doorway approached by stairs from both sides. The proportions of the different parts of the façade are determined by a simple but effective system of compositional lines based on 90-degree-angle relationships, another factor that contributes to the monumental homogeneity of the whole. To the right is the Palace of the Conservatory and to the left the Capitoline Museum; giant orders and crowning balustrades are prominent features in their designs too, as well as the pedimented windows. The group composition is aided by these reiterated devices; and the whole is a characteristic example of High Renaissance ensemble planning of great unity and impressiveness.

Michelangelo's activity as an architect came toward the end of his career, largely in the second third of the sixteenth century. His free and individual treatment of classic elements represents one of the principal trends in the architecture of the period and is in contrast to the stricter observance of antique procedure that characterizes the work of a number of contemporary designers, notably Andrea Palladio (1518-1580). Born in northern Italy and chiefly active in his native city of Vicenza, Palladio was a devoted student of Vitruvius, the Roman theorist, and of Alberti whose *De Re Aedificatoria*, published in 1485, had become one of the recognized authorities on architectural design in the sixteenth century. His own writings—notably the *Quattro Libri dell' Architettura* or "Four Books on Architecture," published in 1570, in which he undertook a detailed and meticulous collation of Vitruvius' theories with existing monuments—were destined to become even more influential than earlier works, and are one of the foundations of academic architectural procedure throughout Europe in the seventeenth and eighteenth centuries.

Palladio's practice reveals his veneration for classic precedent as clearly as his writings. His first important commission was to remodel the city hall of Vicenza, built in Gothic style in 1444. Palladio's reconstruction, begun in 1549,

FIG. 132. Rome. St. Peter's. Bramante,
Michelangelo, and Maderno, Nave.

resulted in the structure known today as the *Basilica* (Fig. 135) since it was his purpose to reproduce in some degree the Roman architectural type of that name. Little was done to the interior, but the exterior was transformed into a series of arcades with orders applied to the older façade, consisting of Doric engaged columns on the first story and Ionic above, both supporting entablatures to frame the arched openings between. The orders are adapted to the

height and span of the existing Gothic framework by arches springing from smaller intermediate columns within the arcade openings, these columns being connected with those of the main order by small entablatures. The resulting form of an arched opening flanked by two smaller rectangular ones is called the "Palladian motive." Like the giant order, it is a characteristic High Renaissance adaptation of classic elements. It became very popular through the wide

to give them a heavier accent, and prevented from monotonous overhorizontality by carrying the vertical lines of the applied orders through the entablatures up into the sculptured figures on the crowning balustrade.

Profound and sincere as was Palladio's admiration for antique architectural procedure, it was inevitable that his style should reveal the formal ideals of his own period. The *Palazzo Valmarana* (Fig. 136) in Vicenza, built between 1556 and 1566, is one of his many town houses. The order of pilasters rises above a basement and through two stories, and is surmounted by a broken entablature and an attic. A smaller order frames each bay of the first story within the shafts of the giant one, enhancing its scale and contributing to a richness of texture in which the relief sculptures over the windows in the four central bays and the carving in the portal spandrels also play a part. At the angles only the first-story order appears, surmounted by sculptured figures, instead of continuing the giant order to the ends of the façade. This modification of the basic design is explained by the fact that the building is not an isolated structure like some of the Florentine and Roman palaces discussed previously (cf. Figs. 116, 125) but is connected with others on both sides; what might be considered a weakening of the plastic elements in the façade pattern at the angles is the result of conscious planning to relate it to its setting. Such an attitude as this foreshadows the seventeenth-century concern with composition in space as well as form and is a parallel manifestation of Michelangelo's plan of the Campidoglio (Fig. 134).

A similar preoccupation with establishing a relationship between structure and surroundings is apparent in many of Palladio's country houses. One of the best known is the *Villa Rotonda* (Fig. 137) near Vicenza, built for the Capra family between 1552 and 1591. On the order of a summer house, the planning is simple, the various rooms being laid out in a symmetrical centralized scheme around the space covered by the dome. On the exterior, the dome, based on that of the Roman Pantheon (Fig. 57), rests on a square base with porticoes of free-standing

dissemination of Palladio's theories and the effectiveness of his designs and also because it provides a means of combining arch and column in a single motive of considerable expressive value from a structural point of view. As used by Palladio in the Basilica, it gives scale to the main order and richness of effect to the façade as a whole. The façade is well unified by the use of the motive in each bay, successfully composed in length by reducing the width of the end bays

FIG. 133.   Rome, Capitoline Hill.   Michelangelo,
The Campidoglio (begun 1546).

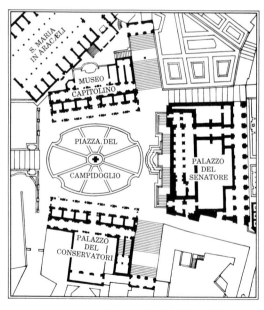

FIG. 134.   Rome, Capitoline Hill.
The Campidoglio, Plan.

Ionic columns and pedimented fronts—one of
the early examples of this most classic of Renaissance architectural motives. In ornament and
proportions these porticoes are faithful reflections
of antique conceptions; but in their relationship

FIG. 135.   Vicenza.   Palladio,
The Basilica (begun 1549).

to the mass of the structures they are similar to the device in the angle orders of the Palazzo Valmarana (Fig. 136), since their projection establishes the building as part of its surroundings. As one of Palladio's most classically perfect buildings, the Villa Rotonda was much admired by academically-minded architects of later generations and it was the prototype for many English and American buildings in the eighteenth century; in 1792 Thomas Jefferson used it almost verbatim—plan, porticoes, and dome—for a projected house for the President of the United States.

The buildings of Michelangelo and Palladio are outside the chronological limit of the mid-sixteenth century set for High Renaissance style. The tendency toward individualistically free use of classic elements in the one and the academically pure handling of the same elements in the other is in its way a symbol of the changing values in European thinking in the late sixteenth

FIG. 136.   Vicenza.   Palladio, Valmarana Palace (1556-1566).

FIG. 137.   Vicenza.   Palladio, Villa Rotonda (1552-1591).

century. The economic and political fortunes of Europe were confused and disordered under the impact of new geographical and scientific discoveries; under vacillating leadership and driven by the Reformation sentiment developing in northern Europe, the Church had renounced the major part of its claim to temporal power but had not as yet perfected a spiritual canon for its policies. This is the background against which the baroque phase of Italian architecture that evolved in the seventeenth century must be placed if it is to be seen in proper perspective. This phase is considered in a later chapter after considering developments in European architecture outside Italy during the sixteenth century, primarily in France and England.

Detail of Fig. 139.

CHAPTER NINE

Architecture of the Sixteenth Century in France and England

In the fourteenth and fifteenth centuries in France, the cultural synthesis achieved in the thirteenth century and symbolized by the Gothic cathedral was breaking down. The progressive modifications of mediaeval style in French art of the fifteenth century reveal a point of view somewhat like that of the Early Renaissance in Italy, though not expressed in the classical idioms current in the southern peninsula. Thus comparison of Rouen Cathedral (Fig. 102) and San Francesco at Rimini (Fig. 119) hardly suggests that the Italian church was fifty years earlier than the French if both are judged by their classic elements; and Jacques Cœur's house in Bourges (Fig. 110) has little in common, formally speaking, with the contemporary Medici-Riccardi Palace in Florence (Fig. 116). French and Italian buildings are alike, however, in being expressions of a spirit of individualism different from the communal principles of the thirteenth century, and they are alike too in being modifications of the earlier styles of their respective countries along lines indigenous to the regions.

In Italy, as already pointed out, Renaissance classicism was in many respects a reversion to its rightful formal heritage that was only natural when the dominance of Gothic style was broken in the late fourteenth and early fifteenth centuries. The only reason that Rouen Cathedral and Jacques Cœur's house show no such definite break with the immediate past in French style is that there the inborn formal tradition was mediaeval just as it was classic in Italy.

RENAISSANCE ARCHITECTURE IN FRANCE

If sixteenth-century French architecture had continued the trends apparent in the preceding century without coming under the influence of Italian ideas, a northern style as individual as the Italian but with its own formal idioms might conceivably have resulted. The reasons why this did not occur are found in the history of the times. The spirit of nationalism which began to develop after the English were driven out in 1453 by French troops inspired by the heroic patriotism of Joan of Arc soon found expression in ambitious projects for new conquests and territorial expansion. Various French rulers beginning with Charles VIII in 1495 attempted to establish claims by feudal rights to different regions in Italy. Under his successors, Louis XII, Francis I, and Henry II, a series of military campaigns took thousands of Frenchmen across the Alps into the southern peninsula. It was inevitable that they should have been much impressed by the vivid beauty of Italian art forms whose like had never been seen in France. The Renaissance ideal had by then been firmly established in all parts of Italy; and it was only natural that its forms should appeal strongly to a national temperament that also had a classic background and could react to the revitalized ideals of classic antiquity with an enthusiasm almost comparable to that of Italians in achieving the rebirth of these ideals.

It was through the interest of Frenchmen thus inspired that Italian styles were brought to France early in the sixteenth century, and their novelty and grace soon won such a following that the native modified Gothic tradition of Rouen and Jacques Cœur's house (Figs. 110, 112) was abandoned. This was not equally true in all parts of France, to be sure, nor of all types of buildings. In the provinces the old tradition continued after it had died out in the cities, and the Gothic style was used for churches long after secular design had embraced the new mode. But enthusiasm for the Italian forms was widespread among both aristocracy and royalty. The great châteaux built in the Loire valley for Francis I and his nobles during the first part of the sixteenth century for the hunting expeditions of which he was so fond show without exception the taste for Renaissance style that appeared first in court circles but soon became much more widespread and popular.

The first examples of French Renaissance architecture represent chiefly a combination of mediaeval structural principles and Italianate decorative forms. As was said earlier, French design of the later Middle Ages tended to separate construction and ornament, so when classic idioms were substituted for mediaeval there was no very violent break with prevailing concepts of architectural composition. Thus in the façade of the château at *Azay-le-Rideau* (Fig. 138), which was built between 1518 and 1524 as a shooting lodge in the Loire valley, acanthus leaves are used instead of the native flora of Gothic style, openings are framed by pilasters instead of the shafts that have a similar function on the façade of Jacques Cœur's house (Fig. 110), and there are classicizing pediments instead of gables with crockets and finials over the dormer windows. The character of this ornament suggests that the sources of the motives used by the French craftsmen were north Italian Renaissance buildings (cf. Fig. 122); light and delicate arabesques of foliage are used extensively, often framing the salamander which was Francis I's heraldic device. On the other hand, the heavy round towers at the angles are like the donjons of a fortified feudal castle, and the irregular silhouette of the steeply pitched roof with its conical towers of picturesque outline and the suggestion of battlements in the bracketed cornice recall earlier French practice. Nor does the L-shaped plan have the symmetry of Italian models (cf. Fig. 124); rather it is an adaptation of the traditional French court arrangement with its screen entrance wall (cf. Fig. 112).

Azay-le-Rideau is an example of the Early Renaissance style in French architecture which is found in buildings erected for the most part between 1495, when the troops of Charles VIII returned from Italy and brought with them the first inklings of Renaissance ideals, and about 1545. The succeeding High Renaissance lasted until approximately 1590; it began in the reign of Francis I, who died in 1547, reached a climax under Henry II from 1547 until 1559, and declined under Charles IX and Henry III between 1560 and 1589. As in the preceding Early Renaissance, the influence of Italian ideas is strong, but it differed in deriving from the Roman style of Bramante and his followers rather than from the north Italian models which had previously attracted the French. It follows that French Renaissance design during the second half of the sixteenth century is distinguished by greater formality and more complete understanding of classic architectural idioms. Two factors were immediately responsible for these developments. The first was the importation of Italian architects to France in the service of Henry II's queen, Catherine de' Medici of the famous Florentine family. Foremost among them were Primaticcio and Serlio. Although neither of them could be considered the equal of Michelangelo or Palladio, both were competent designers and well versed in the academic Italian High Renaissance

tradition; Serlio's influence was extended as much through his theoretical treatises as the buildings constructed from his plans. The second factor in the change from naïve picturesqueness to academic formality in French architecture was the increasing travel and study which made Frenchmen better acquainted with Italian examples; Pierre Lescot, Jean Bullant, Philibert de l'Orme, and Jacques Androuet du Cerceau all spent considerable time in Italy, where they observed and assimilated current principles of design. The last three also wrote handbooks that were as important in disseminating those principles as the similar works of their

FIG. 138.   Azay-le-Rideau.   Château
(1518-1524).

Italian contemporaries. In either case, it is significant that it was the restrained and academic Italian practice of Palladio rather than the free and quasi-baroque manner of Michelangelo that contributed to the theories developed and accepted in France at this time.

One of the most distinguished examples of French High Renaissance style is the *Court of the Louvre* (Fig. 139) in Paris, designed by Pierre Lescot (*ca.* 1510-1578) in rebuilding the Gothic castle which was the royal palace in Paris. The nine bays of the south part of the western façade of this court were built between 1541 and 1548. This was planned as the principal wing of a

FIG. 139.   Paris.   The Louvre.   Lescot, Court, Southwest Front (1541-1548).

structure facing a court, with two subordinate side wings and a front screen wall, the traditional French domestic plan. Later enlargements brought the court up to its present size, four times that planned by Lescot; however, his designs were repeated in the later additions and the effect of the whole is consistent although less impressive in scale than it would have been if the original dimensions had been retained. In the nine bays Lescot designed, the applied orders with entablatures and carved friezes on the two lower stories are surmounted by a low attic and crowned by a balustrade. The end and center bays are accented by being framed with coupled columns instead of single pilasters; they thus become slightly projecting pavilions that function formally like the angle towers at Azay-le-Rideau. The orders also differ from those of the

older building, and the pedimented windows they enclose are similar to those used by sixteenth-century Italian architects (cf. Fig. 125). By emphasizing the end and central bays, however, Lescot introduced a vertical element in the design, and in this he is French rather than Italian. French too are the relatively large windows and the extensive use of sculpture. This is the work of Jean Goujon (ca. 1510-ca. 1568). Lescot's collaborator in the project and an architect of some distinction in his own right as well as a leading French sculptor of the time (cf. Fig. 331). In the finely executed details and their relationship to the ensemble, in the well-calculated proportions and the decorative variety of a restrained and dignified scheme, Lescot's wing of the Louvre ranks with the Italian masterpieces of the High Renaissance. As pure and scholarly in classical detail as Palladio's work, the design is still essentially French in spirit, not a mere aping of the mannerisms of other styles. This is particularly true of the way engaged columns distinguish the end pavilions from the pilastered bays between; this imparts a characteristically French emphasis to the angles of the façade, but does so by using well-understood classic forms.

Another example of French High Renaissance style that illustrates the ready apprehension of new developments in Italy is the entrance portico in the court of the *Château* at *Ecouen* (Fig. 140), near Paris. Designed by Jean Bullant (*ca.* 1512-1578), it was built for Anne de Montmorency, High Constable of France and one of the most impassioned admirers of Italian art in his day. He was well pleased, no doubt, by the giant orders with which Bullant flanked the principal court entrance of his château. The first example of the motive in French building, this portico dates probably between 1552 and 1564. The inspiration for the order obviously was Michelangelo's Campidoglio buildings in Rome (Fig. 133) which were begun in 1546, although Bullant used applied columns instead of pilasters. This detail reveals a more academic conception of classic form than the Italian example; it was obviously dictated by enthusiasm for the motive rather than by desire to develop a formally integrated ensemble, for there is no very effective relationship between the portico and the wall behind it. However, this does not reduce its significance in indicating the increasingly Italianate taste of French patrons and architects alike. This is also evident in the original emplacement in the arched niches between the columns of the two famous figures by Michelangelo called the Bound Slaves (Fig. 325) which the High Constable bought after being discarded by the sculptor when he was forced to reduce the great mausoleum of Julius II for which they had been intended.

Conditions in France during the reigns of Charles IX (1560-1574) and Henry III (1574-1589) were not favorable for building on a large scale, for the religious wars of the time drained financial resources and creative imagination alike. Possibly the most significant architectural activity of this period was not the construction of buildings but the writing of books on architectural theory and principles. The straitened economic circumstances in France when Henry IV ascended the throne in 1589 was a restriction which even that enlightened monarch could not overcome to any considerable extent. However, before his death in 1610, plans had been begun that were to change the city of Paris from a mediaeval town with dark and narrow streets to the city of broad vistas and great *places* it is today. A typical example of what Henry IV did to modernize the city was the construction of the Pont Neuf, connecting

FIG. 140. Ecouen. Château. Bullant, Portico in the Court (1552-1564).

the west end of the Ile de la Cité with both banks of the Seine. The tip of the island was replanned in 1607 in conjunction with the project and became the Place Dauphine. The building façades of brick with stone trim above simple but well-proportioned arcades may have been inspired by contemporary structures in the Low Countries; they are similar in effect, in any event, and initiated the practice of designing open spaces with controlled designs for the surrounding buildings that continued through the seventeenth and eighteenth centuries.

RENAISSANCE ARCHITECTURE IN ENGLAND

The development of Renaissance architecture in England offers many parallels with that of France although it began somewhat later and the two styles are distinct in character. A partial explanation for the tardy appearance of Renaissance style in more than isolated examples in England is that building during the later Middle Ages was not interrupted there by wars as it was on the Continent. The sixteenth century began with no apparent wane in the vigor and originality of the Gothic style in England. Some of its most distinguished examples—the Chapel of Henry VII at Westminster in London, for example—were begun after the High Renaissance was in full swing in Italy. The long-continued vitality of mediaeval style, along with England's geographical isolation and natural conservatism, delayed the appearance of Renaissance ideas there until long after they were firmly established in nearly every other country in Europe.

During the fifteenth century, a characteristic type of country house had evolved in England, and the Renaissance concept of worldly-being was an architectural factor there long before its artistic expression appeared. An example is *Compton Winyates* (Fig. 141), which dates from around 1520. As usual with domestic buildings of the time, it is built around a court; the general arrangement is irregular and picturesque to a degree, with the steeply pitched roofs and clustered chimneys, battlemented towers and ample windows which were a necessity in a northern latitude. A structural feature to be noted is the mixture of materials—stone, brick, wood, and plaster—in attractive patterns of contrasting color and texture. This is not done because of any self-conscious desire for romantic charm, but is the result of using the material at hand in the most effective way. The same principle prevails in the plan that is centered about a lofty, timber-roofed hall with a platform at one end of the family table; other members of household are provided for in the longer portion of the room. The other rooms—kitchen and service quarters, chapel, drawing-room and bedrooms—are functionally related to the hall. The whole has a quality of organic growth from practical necessities and does not show as much Italian Renaissance influence as might be found in a contemporary French building like Azay-le-Rideau (Fig. 138).

Lord Leycester's Hospital (Fig. 142) at Warwick is another case in point. Here the absence of Italian forms is even more significant because it was rebuilt in 1571. Like Compton Winyates, the main façade is irregular and picturesque, with steep roofs and clustered chimneys—the result of additions to the original structure required by the changing circumstances of its use. The method of building is known as half-timbered work.

FIG. 141. Compton Winyates (begun *ca.* 1520).

FIG. 142. Warwick. Lord Leycester's Hospital (1571).

The structure consists of a frame of heavy wooden posts, joined by horizontal and diagonal beams; the spaces between are filled with brick or other material that was sometimes, as here, covered with stucco on the exterior. This was the favored method of erecting small buildings and domestic structures in mediaeval England; it was sometimes used in connection with masonry in larger ones as well, as at Compton Winyates where it is seen in the gables (Fig. 141). It continued to be used for buildings of this type throughout the Elizabethan and subsequent periods in English history and is sometimes referred to as the Tudor style.

As in France, the influence of the Italian Renaissance first appears in decorative details; and also as in France, it appears in buildings for royalty and aristocracy. The tomb of Henry VII dates from 1516 and lies under the flamboyant Gothic vaults of the chapel he added to to Westminster Abbey in London, but its detail is Italian Renaissance and is probably the first example of it in England; it was the work of Pietro Torrigiano, a Florentine sculptor who was forced to leave his native city after a brawl with Michelangelo. Other Italians were imported to meet the demands created by the fashion; they often worked side by side with native artisans on such buildings as Hampton Court Palace, which was built by Cardinal Wolsey and Henry VIII between 1515 and 1536. The character of English Renaissance architecture in this phase is similar to that of contemporary France, for it is a matter of Gothic construction overlaid with Italian detail. Probably the finest example of it is the rood screen in King's College Chapel at Cambridge. The building in which it stands is in the late Gothic style throughout; but the screen, which probably dates between 1532 and 1536, has hardly any mediaeval detail.

Political conditions in England under Henry VIII and his immediate successors were not conducive to further development of these beginnings of Renaissance style such as that which occurred in France under the patronage of Catherine de' Medici. Religious reasons made the Italian workmen responsible for the first Renaissance examples unwilling to remain in the country; even if they had remained, financial conditions would have prevented any extensive building activity. Not until the reign of Elizabeth I (1558–1603), when there was greater economic and cultural stability, did further developments take place—in the period of England's beginning greatness as a world power, the time of Shakespeare and Marlowe.

There are two particularly noteworthy features in the architectural picture of Elizabethan England: very little ecclesiastic building, with country houses predominant in domestic design, and a generally more extensive knowledge of continental Renaissance styles. In some buildings

like *Longleat* (Fig. 143), which was built between 1568 and 1579, Italian precedent was followed very closely. The plan is symmetrical; the chief exterior ornament consists of superposed classic pilasters that are academic in proportion and detail, the whole being crowned by a balustrade in the best Italian High Renaissance manner (cf. Figs. 133, 135). Originally this latter may not have been present, for apparently the house first had gables extending from front to back; these were subsequently replaced by the present flat roof, even though the gabled type was better adapted to prevailing climatic conditions. Certain indigenous features are still present; the projecting bays introduce a vertical note, and the clustered chimneys are a reminder that in England heating was a necessity for which provision had to be made even at the cost of academic formalism. But the main entrance is through a portico with columns and a broken pediment and is approached by a broad flight of steps quite in the manner of the Italian sixteenth century.

The Italianism of Longleat is the exception

FIG. 143.   Robert Smythson, Longleat (1568-1597).

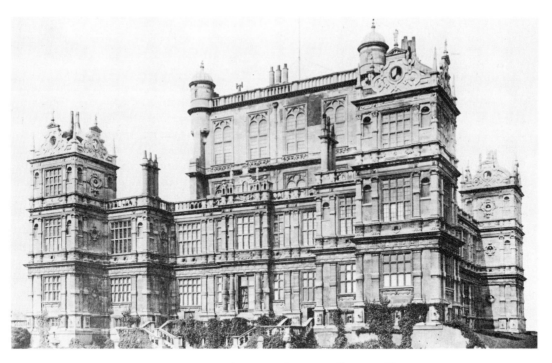

FIG. 144. Robert Smythson, Wollaton Hall
(1580-1588).

rather than the rule, however, in late sixteenth-century English building. For the most part, the predominant Renaissance influence in this period comes from the Low Countries—from Flanders and Holland—a fact explained in part, at least, by the political circumstances of the times. Henry VIII's conflict with the Church was continued by Elizabeth, and the rise of Protestantism in England was marked by increasing sympathy with similar movements in the Low Countries then fighting for their independence from Spain. Many refugees from those countries found their way to England, among them artisans who brought their own regional versions of Renaissance style as well as handbooks like J. Vredeman de Vries' *Architecture* and *Compartimenta* published in Antwerp in 1563 and 1566. *Wollaton Hall* (Figs. 144, 145) in Nottinghamshire, built between 1580 and 1588, exemplifies this Netherlandish influence. Designed by a certain Robert Smythson, the plan (Fig. 145) is symmetrical on both axes but is unusual even

for houses of this period in that the great hall is the nucleus around which the other rooms are grouped on lower levels and with symmetrically

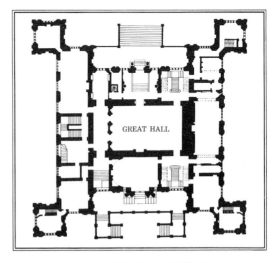

GREAT HALL

FIG. 145. Wollaton Hall, Plan.

FIG. 146.   Hatfield House (1607-1611),
The Long Gallery.

are also Flemish in origin. The expansive windows with their mullions are English, however; and the general picturesqueness of the sky line with its chimneys, towers, and pinnacles is likewise at variance with the Renaissance character of much of the detail.

One of the most individual features of country houses built in Elizabethan and Jacobean England is the *Long Gallery* (Fig. 146), a room that as its name implies was very long and was almost always on the top floor. The long gallery of Hatfield House which was built between 1607 and 1611 is typical of these rooms in being paneled, or hung with tapestries, and in having the ceiling decorated with moulded plaster in elaborate designs. Very prominent, too, is the fireplace with its elaborately decorated overmantel. The origin of the long gallery is not clear. Possibly it was intended as a place to display paintings, as many of them now do, or to stage pageants and masques for visiting royalty, or even to provide space for exercise because the long gallery usually is in a part of the house where space is not at a premium. In any event, it is one of the chief elements of English houses of the late sixteenth and early seventeenth centuries in which there is still concern for convenience and facility in planning, and where Renaissance ideas appear chiefly in decorative details or, at the most, in the generally symmetrical disposition of the mass of the building as a whole.

In the sixteenth and early seventeenth centuries, whatever there is of Renaissance character in English architecture is at the most an indirect reflection of Italian usage, for the most part through the intermediary of the Low Countries on the Continent. To be sure, some Italian craftsmen came to England, and a few Englishmen like John Shute and John Thorpe went to Italy and made some studies of current practice there. But the influence of these men counted little in the generally conservative trends of Elizabethan and Jacobean design. Not until the first quarter of the seventeenth century was almost over were Italian Renaissance ideas understood for what they really were in English architecture.

placed towers at the angles (Fig. 144). The gables of these towers are good examples of the Flemish influence on English design, consisting as they do of pediments supported by scrolls, flanked by small obelisks, their flat surfaces decorated by ribbon-like patterns known as strap-work. Orders are used in profusion for the external decoration— a separate one for each story in elevation with entablatures that serve as stringcourses between the stories; the flat bands across the shafts

Detail of Fig. 149.

CHAPTER TEN

Architecture of the Seventeenth Century

The political and economic background of European seventeenth-century architecture is as complex and involved as the artistic styles developed during that period. It was then that England laid the foundations upon which was to rise the empire that reached its greatest heights as an international power in the nineteenth century. Torn by the religious wars in the late sixteenth century, France achieved in the seventeenth the most complete and absolute cultural autonomy to be seen until the dictatorships in the twentieth century. On the other hand, Germany continued as before to be little but an inchoate assemblage of minor political divisions; and Spain, perhaps the most powerful of all European countries in the sixteenth century, gradually lost all but the shadow of its one-time glory. The political picture in Italy in the seventeenth century is even more one of principalities continuing age-old antagonisms than was true in preceding centuries, if that is possible. But with all its worldly and temporal dissensions, Italy remained, along with Spain, the most Catholic of countries; and the continuing dominance of the Roman Church finds expression in the powerfully expressive architectural style which developed there during the seventeenth century. This is known as the baroque.

BAROQUE ARCHITECTURE IN ITALY

The term "baroque" which is applied to the architectural style that prevailed in Italy between approximately 1580 and 1730 was once used in a derogatory sense as being contrary to good taste. It has come to mean the quality of a work in which the artist seeks to transcend the limitations inherent in his medium in the direction of a more fluent medium and so achieve more dramatic and spectacular effects. Thus baroque can be applied to sculpture that strives for the qualities of painting, or to painting that seeks to explore the dynamic spatial patterns of the stage. In architecture it refers to the increasingly free use of classic elements to create patterns of plastic form and spatial depth suggestive of sculpture and painting; however, not all buildings of this period have the exaggerated characteristics usually associated with the term baroque. When least distinctive, the baroque style is bombastic and not undeserving of the criticism that it is a degenerate phase of the High Renaissance manner. But at its best, it is at the same time varied and unified in its plastic and spatial elements and exciting in a way unsurpassed in any previous or subsequent style. At no other time in the history of architecture were designs created with so much regard for their effect as dramatic spectacle; it was with this in mind that the baroque masters strove for and frequently attained a new synthesis of the arts by using painting and sculpture as integral features of their architectural designs. More than this, even purely architectonic forms were employed to attain effects closely akin to those of the representative arts. A column may be twisted or a pediment broken, denying inherent architectural functions to realize an effect comparable in plasticity to that of a sculptured figure. A façade is designed in many planes that create a play of light and shade, thus suggesting three-dimensional depth as in a painting.

To understand the change from the static and dignified reticence of the High Renaissance to the dynamic and spectacular effects of the baroque, we must look at the history of the late sixteenth and seventeenth centuries. This was the time of the Counter-Reformation when the Church was marshaling all its resources against the ascetic and intellectual Protestantism that was undermining its power in northern Europe. In the extended actions of the Council of Trent between 1545 and 1563, the naïve and childlike symbolism of the Middle Ages was formally banned. The simple faith of Franciscan and Dominican doctrines was subordinated in the spiritual order of the Church to the devices by which Ignatius Loyola (1493-1556) in his "Spiritual Exercises" sought to bring Christian belief to physical realization and make it an aesthetic pleasure. It was only natural that the tremendous emotional resources of the arts should have made them a powerful instrument in achieving these ends. This was not new, for the Church had always utilized the arts as a means of addressing the faithful, to instruct the worshiper or create a proper attitude in him. In the Middle Ages, the melody of Gregorian plain song and the color of stained glass aided in elevating the spirit of the devout to that part of the universe, not wholly of earth or of heaven, of which Suger speaks. In the seventeenth century the motet by Palestrina and the complex patterns of architecture with sculpture and painting that were the baroque church led to the same result. In both periods, the architectonic ideal was a synthesis of the major visual arts; and it was in effective

FIG. 147. Florence. San Lorenzo. Michelangelo,
The Medici Chapel (1519-1534).

relationships between architectural, sculptural, and pictorial elements that the most comprehensively expressive results were attained. But if the formal principles of the two periods seem to have something in common, their motivation reveals a profound and significant contrast. The spiritual truth apprehended intuitively in the forms of the mediaeval building was itself the product of the intellectually created system of scholastic philosophy, whereas the baroque structure is conditioned from the outset by an intent to stimulate the emotions and to overwhelm by the suddenness and violence of its impact on the physical senses.

Intimations of the baroque appear in certain phases of High Renaissance architectural style, more particularly in buildings designed by Michelangelo which in some ways directly anticipate seventeenth-century methods. In the *Medici Chapel* (Fig. 147) he designed as a mausoleum for the famous Florentine family in the New Sacristy of San Lorenzo and built between 1519 and 1534, nearly all the elements are classic in character but are used in a far from classic way. Thus the coupled pilasters flanking the central seated figure on the right wall support nothing and their own supports are uncertain because their bases are obscured by the heads of the nude figures reclining on the sarcophagus. As an architectonic system this arrangement of forms seems unstable; and this, combined with the physical magnitude of all the shapes that are crowded into the relatively small room, creates an effect of strain and discord that is increased by the angular lines and violent distortions of the gigantic sculptured forms on the sarcophagus. In a sense this is sculptural rather than architectonic design, for the whole is conceived in sculptural terms as a setting for the carved figures. But in creating a design that would be emotionally expressive because of its arbitrary and nonstructural use of the elements involved,

Michelangelo indicated possible expressive values in architecture that were realized even more completely by the baroque masters of the seventeenth century. If the paintings originally planned for the niches flanking the central figure had been executed, the baroque synthesis here seen in embryo would have been suggested even more directly.

If baroque effects of form are forecast by Michelangelo in the Medici Chapel, his design for the Roman Campidoglio (Figs. 133, 134) shows in incipient form the baroque treatment of space. The façades of the Capitoline Museum and the Palazzo dei Conservatori on the sides are neither parallel with each other nor perpendicular to the Palazzo del Senatore at the rear but diverge from the point of view of a spectator at the summit of the steps which lead to the top of the hill. This divergence creates an impression of outward expansion—as if the space defined by the forms were not passive and static but had an organic life of its own that complements the dynamic architectural forms. Also contributing to the effect of space as a plastic and dynamic element in the Campidoglio group is the oval pavement design which centers about and radiates from a Roman equestrian statute of Marcus Aurelius.

The seventeenth century in Italy witnessed a more pronounced treatment of form and space by baroque masters along the lines suggested by these works of Michelangelo. The arrangement of the great colonnades enclosing the piazza of St. Peter's in Rome (Figs. 129, 130), for instance, was dictated by the desire of its designer, Gian Lorenzo Bernini (1589-1680), to achieve an effect of space as a living and pulsating force which he apparently conceived in terms of almost mystic symbolism, enclosed within the colonnades as the world is embraced by the arms of Christ. Built between 1656 and 1667, the columns are Doric and classic in detail, but the plan as a whole (Fig. 129) is baroque in its combination of an ellipse with the obelisk in the center and fountains at the foci and the straight but diverging planes of the colonnades connecting it with the façade of the building. This choice of elements that are complex rather than simple

geometrical forms—the ellipse instead of the circle and the trapezoid instead of the rectangle —is characteristically baroque and again is motivated by a desire for dynamic space effects. A pattern of radiating lines in the pavement, similar to that of the Campidoglio, was introduced for similar reasons. The central obelisk, placed on the axis of building and piazza, is the anchor for the whole composition and the point of departure into the space patterns defined by the colonnades whose dramatic expansive effect does much to mitigate the ineptitude of Maderno's façade by giving scale to its formally inert bulk.

Bernini was one of the foremost sculptors of his time (cf. Figs. 333, 334) and much of his architectural work has the quality of sculpture. This is true of the canopy or *Baldacchino* over the high altar of St. Peter's in Rome (Fig. 132); it dates between 1624 and 1633. Measuring 100 feet in height—more than the façade of the Farnese Palace (Fig. 125)—it would nonetheless be dwarfed by the gigantic structure in which it stands were it not designed in a typically baroque manner to create an impression of size commensurate with its surroundings. This was done by introducing apparent movement into the design in the spiral columns which support an open crown and establish a silhouette that draws the eye up and through and past the curving scrolls at the top into the vast dome. The scale that is sensed in the crossing of the structure is a consequence of Bernini's designing the baldacchino as an accessory to it, for giving scale by movement is one of the most baroque devices of his formal imagination.

Light as well as movement played an important part in the dramatic and spectacular effects with which the baroque architect sought to induce the faithful to participate in the thrilling experience of Christian belief. This is evident in the nave of the first church built in Rome for the Jesuit Order—the *Gesù* (Fig. 148). Begun by Giacomo Barozzi da Vignola (1507-1573) in 1568, it was completed after his death by his pupil, Giacomo della Porta, and the structure was consecrated in 1584, although the present decoration was not finished until 1683. The building was the parent church of the Jesuit Order and

FIG. 148.   Rome.   Vignola and Giacomo della Porta, The Gesù (1568-1584).

as such was very influential. The type was employed with local modifications wherever the numerous missionaries of the Order went, a fact responsible for the presence of structures of this type during the seventeenth and eighteenth centuries in such widely separated places as Mexico City in North America and Macao in southeastern Asia. The nave is broad with slightly projecting transepts—reflection of the importance of the sermon in the Jesuit service—and is covered by a barrel vault with smaller penetrating ones from the clearstory windows. This vault was originally plain—the present painted and stucco figures are a later addition—and was

a strongly directive force guiding the observer's attention toward the central dome and the apse. The bold cornice from which the vault springs also contributes to this effect of movement in depth; the applied pilasters of the piers and the openings into the small side chapels are subordinated to it in the design so that the dominance of the nave space would not be weakened. This spatial volume is enlarged into the domed crossing, reduced to narrower proportions by the arch of the choir, and finally closed in by the semi-dome and surrounding wall of the apse. The effect of movement created by the solid forms of the interior is given further emphasis by

FIG. 149.   Rome.   Santa Maria della Pace,
Pietro da Cortona, Façade (1656).

the light—ample but diffuse in the nave, concentrated and intense in the crossing from which the eye escapes with relief into the semi-gloom of the apse. The nave is thus seen to be designed primarily in terms of space, articulated and unified by the plastic elements of vaults and mouldings and by the lighting, the ultimate purpose being to focus attention upon the altar which in this way becomes the heart of the building in fact as well as symbolically in sheltering the blood and body of the Savior.

The dualism of High Renaissance architectural style, in its free adaptation of classic forms as in Michelangelo's work on the one hand, and their more restrained use as in Palladio's buildings on the other, is continued in the baroque of the seventeenth century. The reticence and severity of detail in Bernini's colonnades for the piazza of St. Peter's (Fig. 130) are typical of the latter, as is also the façade of *Santa Maria della Pace* (Fig. 149) in Rome, designed by Pietro da Cortona (1596-1669) and built in 1656. The semi-circular portico has coupled Doric columns and an unbroken entablature of classic simplicity, but the upper level is composed somewhat more freely. Between the framing pilasters the wall seems to swell out, applied columns are directly juxtaposed with pilasters, and the triangular gable that crowns the façade as a whole encloses a curvilinear one whose horizontal moulding is broken to permit the insertion of an irregular cartouche. Both these forms—the broken pediment and the cartouche—were favorite baroque compositional devices. Two concave wings project from the sides of this central unit and serve as foils to its convexity. The whole is typically baroque in its effect of dynamic space which seems to force the façade out, the opposing curves of the side wings creating a complementary effect of yielding to pressure from the space in front of the building. This formal and spatial complexity that calls for several points of view from which the structure must be seen to be fully comprehended is also typically baroque. When compared with a High Renaissance façade like that of the Farnese Palace (Fig. 125) or Peruzzi's Massimi Palace (Fig. 128), the contrasting formal qualities of the two styles are evident. Like the baroque façade, Peruzzi's plan curves, but the curve is simple and gives the effect of an unbroken plane which controls and determines the character of the openings. Moreover, nothing in either of the sixteenth-century façades indicates the plastic bulk of the structure behind them, for they are inherently two-dimensional and as such are complete and self-sufficient. At Santa Maria della Pace, oblique angles of view cannot be avoided and each carries with it implications of others; the observer must see the structure in its three-dimensional entirety before he has any sense of completeness. At the same time Pietro da Cortona's style retains a strong feeling for forms which are clearly defined and plastically solid.

In his own time, Francesco Borromini (1599-1667) was considered the equal of Bernini and Pietro da Cortona, and his designs for the church of *San Carlo alle Quattro Fontane* (Fig. 150) in Rome are among the most striking in the free category of baroque architecture. The

FIG. 150. Rome. San Carlo alle Quattro Fontane. Borromini, Façade (1662-1667).

façade, dating between 1662 and 1667, was the last part to be built, although the building was begun in 1638. The poverty of the mendicant order for which the church and its monastic adjuncts were built was responsible for the delay in completing them and was also a factor in determining the site—on a narrow street intersection with fountains on each angle which gave the church its name, *alle Quattro Fontane;* one of the fountains is incorporated in the church building itself. The façade is hardly as wide as a single

FIG. 151. Venice. Longhena, Santa Maria della Salute
(begun 1631).

pier in St. Peter's nave. Such physical restrictions would make it appear impossible to achieve an effect of such intensity as Borromini's design has; nor could it have been done with the idioms of the High Renaissance or even of Bernini and Pietro da Cortona, whose ideas are best realized in large forms and ample spaces. Borromini's façade is organized around the eight columns— four in each story—between which the wall and entablatures and cornices protrude and recede in wavy planes. The movement thus created is brought to a focus by the sculptured figures in the lower and upper levels, producing an effect of mounting tension that comes to a climax in the oval medallion framed by an upward projection of the top balustrade. Borromini gave character to the façade of his building in the same way that Bernini gave scale to the baldacchino in St. Peter's (Fig. 132), i.e., by movement. It is attained at the cost of such traditionally architectonic qualities as solidness and weight, for the walls seems more like a tenuous membrane rippling under the impulses of pulsating space than something made of stone, but it is undeniably very striking. The contrasting planes of the façade also create varied and shifting effects of light and shade in the manner of a sculptural composition; this along with the combination of sculpture and painting makes the façade of San Carlo alle Quattro Fontane one of the most distinctive examples of the baroque principle in architectural thinking.

Although Italian baroque style was born in Rome, where it can be studied most comprehensively, there are significant examples in other Italian cities too, notably Venice. There, in 1631, work began on the church of *Santa Maria della Salute* (Fig. 151), designed by Baldassare Longhena (1598-1682). The site, at the entrance to the Grand Canal, is important and the architect made the most of it. The plan is unusual for its time—a central octagon with surrounding ambulatory for the main part of the building that leads to the sanctuary behind. Both these parts of the building are domed; the smaller one over the sanctuary is partly concealed by the main one in the illustration. Longhena apparently based the design of the principal dome on that of St. Peter's in Rome (Fig. 131), but used the great scroll buttresses to relate it to the octagon beneath. For the triumphal arch of the chief entrance, and for the two chapels that flank it, Longhena found inspiration in Andrea Palladio's designs for two churches in Venice not far from the Salute. But Longhena adapted these motives to his own use and contrived one of the most coherent relationships of external and internal design in any building of the period.

The central motive of the entrance portal, the arch with its flanking order, is repeated in the arcaded octagon of the interior of Santa Maria della Salute (Fig. 152), and is echoed in the spaces that recede toward the sanctuary. Rudolf Wittkower has pointed out Longhena's utilization of devices from stage scenography in this interior, carefully relating plane to plane and form to form to lead the eye into depth. The importance of this for later Italian baroque design is great, for by the end of the seventeenth century Longhena's scenographic concepts dominated architectural thinking even in Rome.

It was only natural that the feeling for space

FIG. 152.   Venice.   Santa Maria della Salute, Interior.

FIG. 153. Rome. De Sanctis, The Spanish Stairs
(*ca.* 1700; 1723-1725).

as a vital element in architectural design and the sense of the dramatic and grandiose that is part of seventeenth-century thinking should have stimulated interest in large-scale planning—the gardens and surroundings of individual buildings, and even entire cities. In the latter category are the various modifications of Rome, from the unplanned and formless conglomeration of ancient and contemporary buildings that it was at the close of the sixteenth century to its present form in which avenues command long vistas that are dominated by great buildings and accented by spacious piazzas. The importance of Michelangelo's Campidoglio design (Figs. 133, 134) as an example of group planning has already been noted; Bernini's colonnaded piazza of St. Peter's (Fig. 130) is another baroque concept of large-scale architectural relationships. In both these cases, the planning was intended to empha-

size the dominance of given buildings. In other cases the city as a whole was the controlling form, its avenues being designed not only to facilitate circulation but also to create the expansive and exciting vistas so congenial to the baroque temperament. Thus from the Porta and Piazza del Popolo, the principal entrance to Rome from the north in the seventeenth century, three radiating streets led past two impressive baroque churches that were particularly designed to provide a monumental approach to the city. This was only one feature of a comprehensive plan of avenues and piazzas that was drawn up about the middle of the century. Around 1700, the widely swinging *Spanish Stairs* (Fig. 153) that rise from the Piazza di Spagna to the Pincian Hill were begun by Alessandro Specchi to connect that part of the city with an area then being built up; they were completed by Francesco de

Sanctis in 1723-1725. They provide one of the most familiar views of modern Rome and one of the most striking, with an axis of movement in depth relating the obelisk on the upper level to the fountain in the piazza below. This fountain was designed by Bernini, who was as noted for fountains as for his buildings (cf. Fig. 335). The use of fountains and obelisks as accents in baroque ensembles of avenues and squares is a major feature of seventeenth-century large-scale planning. Undulations of surface and contour in steps and balustrades have the same formal function as in buildings (cf. Fig. 150); that is, they contribute movement and a sense of organically vital space.

Landscape architecture also reflects the preoccupation of baroque architects with movement and space and light, as is evident from the gardens of many country houses or villas of the time. Those of the *Villa Torlonia* (Fig. 154) at Frascati near Rome were designed by Carlo Rainaldi (1611-1691) in a series of ramps and terrances laid out along axes usually marked by cascading streams of water. The never-ending movement of flickering light and the water flowing over rocky surfaces or shooting up in plumes of spray were understandably congenial to baroque taste; as in the urban squares just discussed, the gardens of the period were extensively accented with fountains. Such effects in architecture and garden design reveal the same expansive interests that led to equally notable developments in landscape painting in the seventeenth century (cf. pages 549 ff.).

The closing years of the seventeenth century and the beginning of the eighteenth saw Italy yield to others the pioneering role it had played in architecture since the Renaissance began in the fifteenth century. With the country divided politically, and its one-time economic supremacy lost to the nations that controlled the New World its artistic vitality slowly ebbed and its

FIG. 154. Frascati. Villa Torlonia. Rainaldi, The Gardens.

artists could do little more than accept ideas from France where the Academy ruled supreme. Under this influence, Italian architecture subsided into sterile and ineffective classicism in the later eighteenth and nineteenth centuries; only an occasional building showed a trace of the one-time creative spirit.

FRENCH ARCHITECTURE OF THE SEVENTEENTH CENTURY

The assassination of Henry IV in 1610 brought his nine-year-old son Louis XIII to the French throne, but for some years the country was governed by a regency under Henry's second wife, Marie de' Medici. It was for her that the *Luxembourg Palace* (Fig. 155) in Paris, one of the most important buildings to be erected in France during the first quarter of the seventeenth century, was designed by Salomon de Brosse (1571-1626). Begun in 1615 and completed by 1624, it follows the usual plan for a French town house of the period—a forecourt with a monumental entrance pavilion closed in on the sides by wings somewhat lower than the main part at the rear of the court. A distinctive feature is the heavy rustication of walls and piers, possibly introduced to resemble the Pitti Palace in Florence whence Marie had come. However this may have been, the structure's uniform roof line, achieved by suppressing the pavilion and

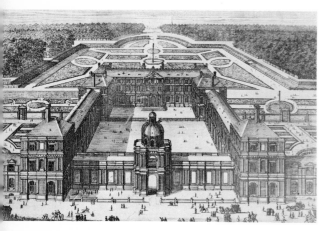

FIG. 155.   Paris, Salomon de Brosse, Luxembourg Palace (1615-1624).

end bay pattern found in earlier designs like Lescot's Louvre (Fig. 139), testifies to de Brosse's appreciation of the monumental potentialities of simplified mass relationships that he undoubtedly derived from his study of the Italian High Renaissance masters. In addition to having architectural distinction, the Luxembourg Palace is a notable example of the baroque synthesis of the visual arts, for the long gallery in one of the side wings was originally decorated with brilliantly conceived paintings by Peter Paul Rubens (cf. pages 532 ff.) celebrating the married life of Marie and Henry IV. These are now in the Louvre Museum.

If the parallel between the evolution of architectural style in France and in Italy during the early seventeenth century had continued, an even more extensive development along baroque lines than the Luxembourg Palace represents might have occurred in the reign of Louis XIII (1610-1643). There was instead a pronounced reaction toward formalism and academicism to which several factors contributed. One was the tradition of systematic and logical French thought, expressed earlier in the rational synthesis of Gothic style—the product of a temperament to which the unrestrained emotionalism of the more extreme forms of Italian baroque would have been distasteful. This same sense of rule and order found expression in the political structure developed in France in the seventeenth century; it brought more and more power into the hands of fewer and fewer persons until Louis XIV could say in all truth, *"L'État, c'est moi,"* for in him as an individual was vested absolute power over all human activity in the land. This was exercised through highly organized institutions that had complete authority in their respective fields. The Academy of Letters was founded in 1635 "to give certain rules to our language and to render it pure"; a similar purpose in the field of the visual arts led to the establishment of the Academy of Painting and Sculpture in 1648, and of Architecture in 1671. Although they may be said to have come into existence in response to inherently French sentiments, they ultimately expressed their ideas in forms which had little to do with French ways of thinking.

It was a more or less foregone conclusion that the classic style should be sanctioned by the Academy. Over a century of close artistic relationships with Italy had confirmed the classic habit in French minds, and it was only natural that the academic phases of Italian design would be most attractive to temperaments already disposed to value "reason" and "good sense" as evidence of logic. The writings of Palladio were translated into French in 1650 and became one of the foundation stones of French architectural theory. More and more, Frenchmen went to Italy whenever possible; there they studied the buildings of classic antiquity, and also the interpretations of those forms in the work of High Renaissance masters. It was to provide controlled instruction in understanding these models that the French Academy in Rome was founded in 1677; here students who had shown themselves capable were enabled by the state to continue their studies. As a result, French architectural thinking was dominated for many years by the theory that only in classic usage and its interpretation by academic Italian and French theorists could there be an acceptable ideal of structural beauty.

The foundation of the Academies was of considerably more than merely historical significance, for they marked the final uprooting of creative activity from its traditional place in the social fabric, in the thoughts and emotions of the people. This separation began in France when the Italian style was imported in the early sixteenth century; it became final when the arts came under royal patronage through the intermediary of the Academies and artists became a class apart, owing allegiance only to the abstract ideal imposed upon them by academic regulations. This ideal was *a priori* perfection based on the art of classic antiquity as seen through the eyes of Italian and French theorists—a concept which of necessity takes account of nothing but preconceived formal and expressive values and makes little if any provision for tradition and individual inspiration. It is from such a concept too that the notion of the art critic developed. Works of art are evaluated today by many criteria other than those of the French Academy in the seventeenth century; but the mere fact that there is still current the notion that only the select few to whom the mysteries of art have been disclosed are qualified to judge it is evidence of the persisting academic concept of art as something resulting from the application of rules of formal design. The reduction of the process of artistic creation to compliance with reasoned and theoretical principles and rules instead of its being developed by the inductive training of hand and eye was one of the most pernicious consequences of academic supervision of the arts. The consistent unity that has characterized French official art from the closing years of the seventeenth century to the present is another —a unity achieved by raising the quality of much work that undoubtedly would otherwise have been very poor but at the cost of circumscribing genius to the point of smothering it.

The ideals of the French Academy of Architecture are evident in the wing added by François Mansart (1598-1666) to the *Château* (Fig. 156) at Blois between 1635 and 1638 for Gaston d'Orléans, Louis XIII's brother. Earlier parts of the structure, like the spiral staircase at the right in the illustration, are in the older manner of Francis I. Mansart's wing, in the purity and sobriety of its design, was planned without thought of being consistent with these portions. The order is used in a restrained form, with coupled pilasters and unbroken entablatures on each level in the canonical relationship of Doric, Ionic, and Corinthian on first, second, and third stories respectively. The roof is rather steeply pitched, but there are no dormer windows as there would have been in the sixteenth and earlier seventeenth centuries. The quietness and simplicity of the effect contribute to the sense of repose created by the prevailing horizontality of the design, and the form as a whole is given monumentality by the well-studied proportions. Only in the sculptured figures on the pediment in the second story of the entrance bay and the curvilinear gable of its third story is there any suggestion of baroque exuberance in this well-nigh perfect architectural embodiment of Gallic ideals of reason and logic.

The Gaston d'Orléans wing was built late in the reign of Louis XIII before power had been completely centralized in the person of the king as it was later. That such an imposing structure could be erected for anyone but the king is one indication of this, for under Louis XIV, who reigned from 1643 to 1715, nearly all the great architectural creations in France were motivated more less directly by his imperialistic ambition or that of his immediate advisers. Among these were the enlargement of the royal palace of the Louvre in Paris and of the château at Versailles, which became one of the largest buildings in seventeenth-century Europe by virtue of Louis'

FIG. 156. Blois. Château. François Mansart,
Orléans Wing (1635-1638).

interest in it. He was not so much concerned with the building in Paris, but his minister Colbert felt it essential to royal dignity that there should be a monumental residence for the king in his capital city. Lescot's mid-sixteenth-century building (Fig. 139) had already undergone a series of alterations and enlargements that quadrupled the area of the court of honor he designed and connected it with the palace of the Tuileries nearly a third of a mile away, but its eastern front still lacked an appropriately imposing external façade. Various plans for its completion were submitted

FIG. 157. Paris. The Louvre. Perrault,
The Colonnade (1667-1670).

in a competition entered by nearly every important architect in France, but none of the plans were felt to have the necessary grandeur; hence in 1665, Gian Lorenzo Bernini was asked to come from Rome to Paris to undertake the project. Although he was received with the acclaim due an architect recognized as the greatest of his time, his suggestion for the façade was not acceptable because it could not be built without destroying practically all the existent structure. Its cornerstone was laid, but the design was discarded as soon as Bernini returned to Rome; the project was assigned to Claude Perrault (1613-1688), assisted by Charles LeBrun the painter and Louis LeVau, who had been in charge of the final stages in the enlargement of Lescot's court.

In the *Colonnade of the Louvre* (Fig. 157), the eastern façade of the palace, which was built between 1667 and 1670, there are even fewer traditional French elements than at Blois, and an even more academic and monumental ideal. The high pointed roof, formerly traditional for climatic reasons, is no longer a factor; the flat roof is masked by a balustrade in the best Italian manner. This detail Perrault may have adapted from Bernini's rejected design, as well as the giant order that rises above the ground-story base which is the chief feature of the façade. But he retained the traditionally French five-part division of the façade by making the end and center pavilions project slightly and placing a pediment over the latter. Moreover, he

FIG. 158.   Versailles.   The Palace (1624-1708).

FIG. 159. Versailles. The Palace. Louis LeVau and
J. H. Mansart, Garden Front (1669-1685).

enriched his classic style by using an order of coupled free-standing Corinthian columns instead of engaged columns or pilasters. The design is not uniformly effective in all details. The relationship of the central pediment to the cornice balustrade is confused, and springing the arch of the main entrance on the ground level from the stringcourse of the first story makes it break into the one above, producing a rather ambiguous effect. But these are minor defects in a well-proportioned and unified design that is characterized by the effective use of light and shade to create relief in the colonnades and thus provide a just balance of voids against the solids of the projecting pavilions at the center and ends. Great scale is also achieved by these means and the whole ranks with the most impressive architectural embodiments of the spirit of the *Grand Siècle*, for the building's majestic dignity is eloquent testimonial to the absolute power of the monarch who had it built. This quality has made its design the basis of a formula for monumental buildings in France which has been almost standard from the closing years of the seventeenth century until very recently.

In a sense, the completion of the Louvre was a matter of state; it was done for political reasons. The enlargement of the château at *Versailles* (Figs. 158-161) was undertaken because Louis XIV preferred it to all his other residences. The scope of his purpose is indicated by his expressed desire to provide accommodation at Versailles for his entire court; the extent to which it was realized was so colossal that the national treasury of France was almost entirely depleted. The building was on a scale unapproached before or unequaled since in comparable structures, but this was achieved only at the cost of the national social and economic equilibrium. Size and effect are out of all proportion to function. Moreover, the total lack of relationship between the formal ideal embodied in the palace and the life of seventeenth-century France makes it the most eloquent architectural symbol of absolutism the world has seen, for the unbelievable sacrifices its construction involved were decreed by the unquestionable whim of one individual.

As seen today, the *Palace of Versailles* (Fig. 158) is laid out along the traditional lines of a French country house with an open court

its roof is visible from the garden above the palace roof (Fig. 159)—was begun in 1699 though it had not been completed by Mansart's death in 1708.

The *Garden Front* (Fig. 159) is in three levels —a heavy rusticated basement, a somewhat taller second story with arched openings and an Ionic order of pilasters and columns, and a low attic with rectangular windows divided by paneled pilasters. A balustrade surmounts the whole, ornamented with urns and sculptured groups. Projecting pavilions—a large one in the center, smaller ones near the ends of the central block, and three of equal size distributed symmetrically on the wing façades—give relief to the planes of the front as a whole. A rhythm of threes is carried through the entire design. It begins with the grouping of the openings by doubling the pilasters in the central block and extends to the elements in the total length being disposed in such a way that the visual angles subtended by each of the three blocks are seen as equal by an observer standing on the axis of the design at the top of the first terrace (Fig. 161).

The exterior of the garden front is characterized by purity of detail and sober, monumental effect, but this is far from true of the interior. On the second story almost the entire length of the central block is taken up by the *Galerie des Glaces* (Fig. 160), which was designed by Charles LeBrun and executed between 1678 and 1684. The measured rhythm of the windows opening on the garden is repeated by the arched mirrors on the opposite wall which give the hall its name; but where the external effect is monumental austerity, the painted and stucco ornament on wall panels and vault in the interior are altogether baroque in their exuberence. This is the nature of the compromise between Palladian purity on the one hand and dynamic baroque on the other achieved in France by investing a mathematically unified basic pattern with movement by means of surface decoration.

Gigantic as the Palace at Versailles is—the garden façade is more than a quarter of a mile long—its full effect cannot be grasped without taking into account the *Gardens* (Fig. 161) designed to complement and to be complemented

flanked by projecting wings. At the rear of this court is the façade of the brick and stone hunting lodge built for Louis XIII in 1624 which was the nucleus of the present gigantic building. It was first enlarged between 1661 and 1671 under Louis LeVau (1612-1670), who was also engaged in completing the court of the Louvre. He designed what amounted to an envelope enclosing the brick and stone château of Louis XIII on three sides; the side toward the rear was developed as an element in the gardens which were also laid out at this time (cf. Fig. 161). After LeVau's death in 1670, little was done on the exterior of the palace for some time; but the appointment in 1678 of Jules Hardouin Mansart (1645-1708), nephew of François Mansart who designed the Gaston d'Orléans wing at Blois (Fig. 156), marked the beginning of an extraordinary amplification of the structure. After some modifications in LeVau's garden elevation and a rearrangement of the rooms on that side of the building, Mansart extended the south wing in 1682 and the north wing in 1684. The Orangerie below the south end of the garden terrace was built between 1684 and 1687 and the chapel—

FIG. 160.   Versailles.   The Palace.   J. H. Mansart and Charles Lebrun,
Galerie des Glaces (begun 1678).

by it. These were the creation of André LeNôtre (1613-1700), one of the most distinguished names in landscape architecture. Begun in 1662 when LeVau undertook the remodeling of the château, they were completed in 1684. LeNôtre's layout called for two gardens, a smaller one on an upper terrace beside the palace and a larger one beyond and below. The terraces made the entire arrangement visible from the palace itself; its central axis is continued in the median line of the grounds, thus relating them to the building. Water is important in the composition. In the

small upper garden, reflecting pools and spurting fountains are the nuclei of carefully laid out clipped masses of shrubbery, growing from grassy lawns and accented by trees, which form varied geometrical patterns within a rigid framework of clearly indicated alleys. The shrubbery in the large garden is in simpler forms; but two intersecting canals—one on the principal axis of the composition and a smaller one at right angles—dominate this portion of the ensemble in which boldly indicated diagonal alleys radiate from focal points at each end. As in the

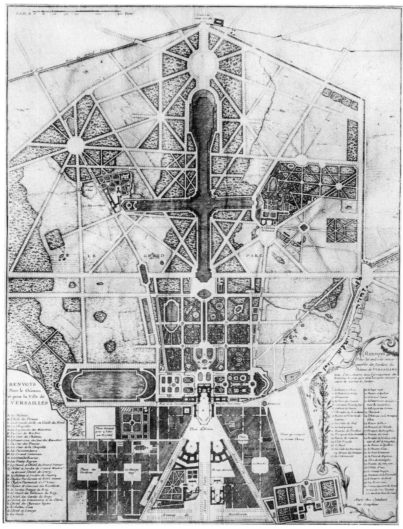

FIG. 161. Versailles. A. LeNôtre, Plan of the City
and Gardens (1662-1684).

Galerie des Glaces, the basic principle of the design is a logical and geometrical disciplined framework and unlimited variety in the details. Other than obviously enhancing the effect of the palace, these gardens stimulated artistic creation in the abundant opportunity they offered for decorative sculpture (cf. Fig. 159), both as accents on the terraces and in the innumerable fountains.

A glance at the plan of the gardens and at the aerial view of the ensemble (Fig. 158) makes it clear that everything in the setting of the Palace at Versailles was considered in its relationship to the central structure. Three wide avenues lead to the Place d'Armes, the great court in front of the building, in such fashion that there is no movement that does not focus upon or radiate from it. Within the angles thus created the city of Versailles was built. Thus on one side of the Palace there is a completely architectural vista and on the other a prospect of nature directed and controlled by human thought. Thus was completed the most overwhelming structural project of the seventeenth century in which form and space, the work of man and the symbol of nature, are wrought into a single and unified scheme contrived for the sole purpose of creating by its focus upon the central structure a symbol of the unquestioned and absolute power of its master. This scheme of radiating and focusing avenues dominated by a single building had far-reaching influence in the eighteenth century. Mannheim and Karlsruhe in Germany were laid out along similar lines, and Pierre Charles de l'Enfant stated his intention of planning Washington, D.C., the capital city of the newly created United States, after the pattern of Versailles.

Even more significant than its formal influence is the insight the plan of Versailles provides into the working of absolutism as a principle of government. The arbitrary creation of an entire city from the ground up in accordance with a preconceived notion of what it should be rather than as the result of organic growth is no more than the application in architectural thinking of the principle of absolutism on a scale seldom even remotely approached in earlier times. The design itself is similarly based on arbitrary rule and regulation. Mathematical in principle—and it should not be forgotten that one of the most far-reaching systems of seventeenth-century philosophy was formulated by a mathematician and Frenchman, René Descartes —it is the most comprehensive example of the tyranny of the axis in the architectural thinking of the time. This is graphically illustrated by the irresistible desire of every spectator viewing the building from the gardens to place himself where the symmetry of the façade will be clearest—in the center of the steps leading from the upper terrace to the garden below (Fig. 161). There his angle of vision is exactly filled by the palace as a whole; nothing else intrudes to detract from its overwhelming dominance—a symbol of the rigorous subjection of the individual to the impersonal order of the state that is the unfailing consequence of absolutism as a political and social principle.

The trend in French architectural evolution from the beginning of the sixteenth century to the close of the seventeenth is graphic evidence of the altered function of art in European culture with the passing of the mediaeval point of view. Classic forms introduced by kings and nobles as exotic and decorative adjuncts to structural elements still mediaeval in character were divorced from them and became the material of a rigidly enforced canon of design from which there could be no departure. The training of artists was taken from the trade guilds which held that prerogative in the Middle Ages and given to the Academies. The artist was thus detached from his environment of communal experience and his inspiration there was cut off from its rightful resources of life and vitality. Art was no longer the literature of the people but a source of entertainment for the elect, who forthwith imposed upon it an ideal of formal unity and artificial perfection similar to the political ideal forced upon a populace which had no part in its formulation. The social order that resulted from the arbitrarily created political institutions was made up of two classes—the aristocracy and the common people—separated by a spiritual abyss that could not be spanned. In this order, art was the plaything of the former and had no function for the latter. The Palace at Versailles is an overpowering monument to this state of affairs in its swallowing up of the taxes of decades for initial construction and the exhaustive drain upon the state that its subsequent maintenance has involved. Reaction was inevitable. The immediate one was away from the severe formality of seventeenth-century art and social usage toward frivolity and license in both manners and artistic style. The boudoir replaced the salon as the locale of social intercourse, and the minutely scaled forms of the rococo appear instead of the more massive baroque. But this reaction was superficial at best. It served only to emphasize the social disparity created earlier and in some measure to hasten the revolt which took place toward the close of the eighteenth century in the French Revolution. It will be seen later that, as the result of social and economic upheavals attendant upon the Revolution, expressive style in the eighteenth and nineteenth centuries involves different values than those that have been discussed.

ENGLISH ARCHITECTURE OF THE SEVENTEENTH CENTURY

During the greater part of James I's reign as king of England (1603-1625), English architecture followed the pattern of buildings like Wollaton Hall (Figs. 144, 145) and Hatfield House (Fig. 146). The symmetry of a plan like that of Wollaton has little expression in the external effect, for this is largely determined by the massing of the angle towers, the gabled pavilions, and the steeply pitched roof. Although the decorative details are derived from classic and Italian sources, they are treated in such a way as to seem far from classic. But toward the end of James' reign, a very different conception of architectural style makes its appearance in England; in it classic forms are used as correctly as any in current European design. This change in English architectural thinking is the more surprising because it was the almost single-handed achievement of one man, Inigo Jones (1573-1652).

Little is known of Jones' early life, but from 1605 until 1613, he designed settings for masques and other theatrical entertainments for the Court. In 1613, he was granted the reversion of the Office of Surveyor of the King's Works, the title then given the official architect of the realm. With this in mind, he traveled in Italy in 1613-1614 where he met and talked with men like Carlo Maderno in Rome and Vincenzo Scamozzi, a follower of and assistant to Palladio, in Vicenza in northern Italy. But he spent most of his time studying buildings, particularly those that remained from classical times, and those done by Palladio. So impressed was he by the latter that he purchased Palladio's great treatise, the *Four Books on Architecture*. Palladio's influence was almost immediately apparent in the buildings he designed as the King's Surveyor, a post to which he was appointed in 1615. In general, these buildings—one of the first was the Queen's House at Greenwich, begun in 1515-1516—reveal almost none of the forms currently used in England but follow Italian and specifically Palladian models with remarkable faithfulness. In so doing, Jones set a precedent for seventeenth-century English archi-tecture that makes it almost unique in European building; even in France with its firmly en-trenched academicism, the most puristic designs are still characterized by specifically French inter-pretations of Italian Renaissance idioms.

The *Banqueting House of Whitehall Palace* (Fig. 162) in London, which Jones designed for James I, was built between 1619 and 1622. The main façade is more Italian than that of any con-temporary European building outside Italy, and might well have been designed by Palladio him-self, so faithfully did Jones follow the precepts of the Italian master. Although the interior is a single high room, the elevation is in three levels, with a rusticated basement, an Ionic order for the first story, and a Corinthian one above, the whole crowned by a balustrade. The orders consist of applied columns in the three central bays and pilasters doubled at the ends of the façade—a device which creates a central axis and subordinates the framing ends in importance as Palladio had done in the Palazzo Valmarana at Vicenza (Fig. 136). Triangular and curvilinear pediments on brackets alternate above the win-dows of the first level, and swags of foliage form the frieze of the second; both follow Italian High Renaissance precedents (cf. Figs. 125, 147). Other buildings by Jones, notably some of his country houses, show a similar respect for the Italian High Renaissance theorists, along with the considerable refinement that is his own out-standing quality and that did much to establish the taste for Palladianism that is a major factor in English architectural design in the later seventeenth and eighteenth centuries.

Once the authority of Italian precedent was established in England, it was inevitable that other than academic models should be studied. The period of the Restoration with its incipient absolutism is marked architecturally by infusion of baroque exuberance into the generally sober and restrained manner of Jones and his immediate followers. The chief representative of the baroque in seventeenth-century English architecture is Sir Christopher Wren (1632-1723), whose

FIG. 162. London. Inigo Jones, The Banqueting House
(1619-1622).

professional career began with his interest in science and mathematics of which he was an instructor at Oxford. He came to the attention of Charles II through his ingenious solution of the structural problem presented by the roofing of the Sheldonian Theatre in Oxford and was appointed Surveyor in 1662. In this capacity he traveled on the Continent, where he studied architectural activity. He was particularly impressed by the ideas of Mansart and Bernini whom he met in Paris in 1665, Bernini having come there in connection with the Louvre project. The Great Fire of London the following year gave Wren his great opportunity. As architect in charge of rebuilding the city, he drew up a plan that would have surpassed even Versailles in magnitude had it been carried through. Typically baroque, it called for a radial distribution of buildings around certain key structures, notably the cathedral of St. Paul, with the composition focused through the spires of the small parish churches many of

which also had to be rebuilt. The project failed of execution because of the unwillingness of many landowners to wait for their stores and houses to be rebuilt in accordance with the new plans. As the city grew up in the late seventeenth and eighteenth centuries, it owed little or nothing to Wren's ideas.

Wren's original design for *St. Paul's Cathedral* (Fig. 163), one of the major focal points in his plan for the rebuilding of London, called for a domed structure of the central type, that is, with a radial rather than a horizontal base. A genuinely baroque conception, it embodied a vast centralized space and many subordinate spaces that provided many fine effects. However, it failed to be realized because of a conservative clergy's insistence on the traditional long nave and side aisles, transepts and deep choir. Hence the present structure was built along these general lines between 1675 and 1710. Wren managed to keep the dome as the dominant exterior element, although the interior spatial relationships are rather confused. The cupola rests on a drum with a free-standing peristyle apparently suggested by drawings of Bramante's unexecuted project for St. Peter's at Rome, although the cupola itself is quite different from that in Bramante's design. Italian influence is also apparent in the façade; the twin towers are not unlike those on a church by Borromini—Sant' Agnese in Piazza Navona—with corner colonnettes and entablatures at an angle to the plane of the façade (cf. Fig. 150). Here Wren's taste for the baroque is apparent. He combined it, however, with equal appreciation of the monumental and restrained qualities of French contemporary design, for the superposed coupled Corinthian columns in the portico are similar to the single order of Perrault's eastern Colonnade of the Louvre (Fig. 157). The upper order continues in pilasters along the sides of the church, applied to a wall that masks flying buttresses which sustain the small domes over the nave.

Throughout the entire building there is evidence of Wren's structural ingenuity, not the least striking example being the way the great dome is built. It is in two shells, like those of the cathedral in Florence (Fig. 113) and St. Peter's in Rome (Fig. 131), but the inner shell is relatively much lower and supports the outer one by a heavy intermediate cone of brick and metal. This cone rests also upon the drum wall; it functions actually as a point on which the outer dome of lead-covered timber beams is hung and so has little or no lateral thrust. The effect is striking, for the dome and its lantern tower rise more than 350 feet from the ground; the dominance of the city for which Wren had hoped is almost achieved. That this is done by suppressing the expression of structural facts—the actual means of support cannot be seen from either the interior or the exterior—in the interests of achieving a more spectacular effect than would have been possible if the dome design were more straightforward in indicating its means of support is a typical illustration of Renaissance interest in formal qualities rather than structural problems. In point of fact, Wren allowed so small a margin of safety that modern traffic vibrations have caused more than a few fissures in the dome and its supports; hence the building is in a more or less constant state of repair.

Of the small parish churches designed by Wren as part of the rebuilding of London, fifty-three were completed. Only thirty-three were standing in 1939, and seventeen of these were almost completely destroyed in World War II. But even the few that survived reveal his ingenuity and inventiveness. Built for the most part on sites that are awkwardly shaped and limited in size, these structures are planned internally to obtain maximum spatial effectiveness.

FIG. 163.   London.   Wren, St. Paul's (1675-1710).

Limitations of site usually restricted external effects to treating the bell tower as impressively as possible; these towers embody some of Wren's most attractive designs. In that of *Saint Mary-le-Bow* (Fig. 164), one of the first to be built—between 1671 and 1680—the transition from the square base of the tower to the circular spire showed such skillful adaptation of classic forms that it became at once a model and an inspiration for such buildings. Many of the churches built in the English colonies in North America during the eighteenth century, such as Old North in Boston and Christ Church in Philadelphia (Fig. 185), trace their formal ancestry back to the type created by Wren in the parish churches of London.

Baroque exuberance in some details and academic sobriety in others are characteristic of buildings designed by Sir John Vanbrugh (1666-1726), who was among the last to attempt a compromise between the contrasting tastes in seventeenth-century English architecture. Vanbrugh is an interesting example of the amateur architect then beginning to appear in England; he had a brilliant career as a writer of comedies before he took up architecture. *Blenheim Palace* (Fig. 165) was built by him for the Duke of Marlborough between 1705 and 1724. The general baroque effect is created by the contrasting masses of the central block with its outlying wings, and its great size—a quality of most of Vanbrugh's buildings that won for him the dubious distinction of being the butt of a satiric epigram by Pope—but the ordinance of the principal portico, the character of the Doric colonnades over a basement for the curving side wings, and the balustrades surmounting them are in the best academic style. In the plan, a central mass is preceded by a court flanked by wings around smaller courts; symmetry is the aim rather than convenience. The whole is a rather unusual example of overemphasis in the general picture of restraint in English architecture of the late seventeenth and early eighteenth centuries.

The Palladian principles Inigo Jones introduced in English design in the early seventeenth century continued without serious challenge from the baroque in at least one type of structure the average town or small country house. *Swan House* (Fig. 166) at Chichester, built in 1711, has been attributed to Sir Christopher Wren. The arrangement is typical of middle-class houses of the later seventeenth century and the Georgian period of the eighteenth, the source of the term Georgian that is applied to the type. There is a basement story for service quarters, and the rectangular block of the brick or stone-walled house rises two or two and a half stories above. The external character is established by the simple treatment of the symmetrically placed openings, the angles reinforced by quoins, and the central axis emphasized by the projecting bay and ordered entrance portico with its academically correct curvilinear pediment. Internally, the plan is relatively simple, a common arrangement being a central stair hall with rooms symmetrically placed on either side. These are given no small charm by well-designed paneling

FIG. 164. London. Wren, St. Mary-le-Bow (1671-1680).

FIG. 165.   Vanbrugh, Blenheim Palace (1705-1724).

and mouldings and by the furniture of the anonymous cabinetmakers who paved the way for the great masters of the mid-eighteenth century like Chippendale and Hepplewhite (cf. Figs. 624, 629). Like Wren's parish churches, it was these houses, built for prosperous and quiet citizens, that served as models for the emigrants to colonies in the New World (Fig. 182), rather than the more grandiloquent mansions like Blenheim Palace.

Even in its most Palladian aspects, English architecture of the late seventeenth and early eighteenth centuries was not sponsored by an official academy as in France but expressed a well-educated general taste. This was in large measure created by the noble amateurs (such as Sir John Vanbrugh, though his personal preference was for baroque effects), whose education invariably included the "grand tour" of Italy. They were prepared for this by the most readily available documentation; architecturally, this was the writings of Palladio and other Italian academic theorists. The many handbooks of architecture that were published in England in this period were both a consequence of this interest and a stimulus to its continuation; the

result was a well-grounded tradition of upper middle-class building in the Palladian manner represented by Swan House and many others of the same period. But it is interesting and significant that at the same time there was also a considerable amount of building in the older

FIG. 166.   Chichester. Wren (?), Swan House (1711).

mediaeval fashion—modest half-timbered houses (cf. Fig. 142) that represent architecturally the substratum of belief in the tradition of local self-determination that still prevailed in England in spite of all efforts to raise a superstructure of absolutism upon it.

This temper was indicated by other events, both political and artistic. Charles I's attempt to erect a governmental structure comparable in its absolutism to that of Louis XIV in France came to an end on the scaffold in 1649. The popular appeal to the democratic William of Orange in 1689 to replace James II was a no less emphatic statement of England's insistence upon retaining political forms that were the result of growth by accretion and adjustment to popular needs rather than the result of arbitrary creation in accordance with a reasoned and symmetrical plan. Popular reaction against Wren's plan for rebuilding London that would admittedly have made it a more reasonable and effectively laid out city but would have violated long-established rights is another indication of the same feeling—a feeling that still exists, as the planners of a new London after the destruction wrought in World War II have discovered. And if the modest Palladian town houses or the unassuming half-timbered dwelling was preferred by their builders because they had made a place for themselves in the English pattern of life and thought, it is because they won an echoing response in people like Samuel Pepys and John Evelyn, whose instinctive reactions against the ostentatious and grandiloquent were more characteristic of the temper of their times than the artificial glories of a court inspired by alien values.

Detail of Fig. 178.

CHAPTER ELEVEN

European Architecture from 1700 to 1870

Architectural style in France and England in the seventeenth century was essentially a compromise between baroque freedom on the one hand and puristic restraint on the other in the use of classic forms. In France, the baroque element is apparent in the great scale of buildings lavishly decorated with sculpture and painting, though the architectural features are treated with considerable sobriety (cf. Figs. 159, 160). In England, apart from churches and a few exceptionally large country houses, the prevailing mode is more restrained, more Palladian. The eighteenth century brought significant changes in architectural style to both countries, and the development

FIG. 167. Paris. Aubert and Gabriel, Hôtel de Biron (1728).

of quite individual styles in others, notably Germany and Austria.

Life was organized on a grand scale in France under Louis XIV. Society was dominated by the court at Versailles, and social usage was keyed to the great salons in the Palace (Fig. 160)—formal and stately, with rules to cover every conceivable situation. With Louis XIV's death in 1715, the artificial social structure held together by his autocratic personality began to disintegrate. Many changes took place almost immediately early in the reign of his successor, Louis XV, who ruled from 1715 until 1774, changes that are clearly reflected in the architectural style of the day. For example, few private houses were built in France during the later seventeenth century, for the entire court was expected to be at Versailles. But as its importance as the country's social center decreased in the early eighteenth century, considerable numbers of *hôtels particuliers* or private dwellings were built, especially in Paris. An example is the *Hôtel de Biron* (Fig. 167), now the Musée Rodin; the architects were Jean Aubert and Jules Jacques Gabriel. Noteworthy features of the exterior are the horizontal drafting or beveling of the masonry walls and omission of the orders, and the pitched roofs instead of the flat type with balustrade cornice used at Versailles (Fig. 159). The scale is modest; and though the rooms are

generally symmetrical, convenience and comfort are the controlling consideration, rather than a desire for formal display.

It is the interior decoration, in fact, that distinguishes the architecture of the Louis XV style most clearly from that of the preceding century. The *Oval Room* (Fig. 168) of the Hôtel de Soubise in Paris built about 1740 after the designs of Germain Boffrand, is one of the most comprehensive examples of rococo style, as this particular manner is called. The name is derived from the French *rocaille* and *coquille*, meaning rock work and shell respectively, and refers to the fluid and irregular curves in the ornament and also in the plan of the room; this is quite different from the formal rectangularity of Louis XIV interiors and consequently has an entirely different character. Formalism has given way to intimacy and the setting is keyed to the *conversations à deux* that supply the motive for so much painting of the period (cf. Fig. 481), rather than to the solemn *tableaux* of the court at

FIG. 168. Paris. Hôtel de Soubise (*ca.* 1740). Boffrand, The Oval Room.

Versailles. A similar contrast in the furniture of the two styles (cf. Fig. 623) is pointed out elsewhere. A point of historic interest is raised by the Oriental motives in the painted ornament of many rococo rooms like this one—*chinoiseries* and *singeries* they are called—an exotic element in the still prevailingly classical decorative repertory that is a direct result of newly established commercial relationships between Europe and the Far East in the early eighteenth century and anticipates tastes that had even more profound influence on later eighteenth-century style.

Space as a vital, fluid element of architectural form is a concept shared by the rococo with the baroque. The difference between them, although not easy to define in words, is quite positive in effect. It is evident in many eighteenth-century buildings—palaces and churches for the most part —in Germany and Austria. One is the pilgrimage church in Franconia called the *Vierzehnheiligen* (Fig. 169), so named because it is the burial shrine of fourteen saints. It was built between 1743 and 1772. As in the Oval Salon of the Hôtel de Soubise (Fig. 168), there is hardly a straight line or a flat plane. Every shape is curved or ovoid, as if the space were enclosed by a fluid or plastic substance instead of by stone and brick and stucco. Traditional distinctions between different parts of the church have almost lost their meaning. In the illustration, the main altar is in the nave, the choir behind it, and transepts to left and right. The implications in these conventional terms of clearly distinguishable parts is not borne out by what can be seen. Instead, the subtle interrelations of curving shapes, combined with the light, almost gay color scheme of gold, pink, and white, create an ethereal, almost intangible milieu, the essence of spiritual experience. The effect is undeniably theatrical, but for that very reason it is a persuasive statement of the fervent faith it stimulates and also embodies.

About the middle of the eighteenth century, the supremacy of earlier Palladian and rococo ideas was challenged by other concepts of style, which reflect more or less directly changes in the prevailing thought of the time. These, in general, extended the principles of free inquiry established in the Renaissance and the Reformation.

Then it was in the fields of art and letters and religion, now it is in history, politics, and science that the frontiers of human knowledge were pushed back. The character of eighteenth-century thought was largely determined by the new outlook attained in the process. A period of seeming confusion and chaos, it was nonetheless from the spiritual turmoil of the eighteenth century that modern thought was born, for then were developed the concepts of history, nature, and ethics that prevailed until comparatively recently.

The new concept of history in eighteenth-century thought is evident almost immediately in the architecture, in attempts to revive more or less directly the practice and idioms of past periods in western civilization, notably the classic of ancient times, and the mediaeval. The revival of classic forms is not hard to understand, for the Italian Renaissance was motivated in part by a desire to regenerate the beauties of classic art, and the whole structure of academicism was raised on a foundation of respect for antique usage. But up to the middle of the eighteenth century, firsthand knowledge of classic buildings was limited; the most general source of ideas for academic designers was not existing classic structures but the books of theorists like Palladio and Vignola. Although the ostensible ideal of the academicians was the classic, in actual practice they varied greatly from the models which in theory guided them.

About 1750, however, there occurred a series of developments that changed this theoretical concept of classic building and opened up different vistas for investigation. These were largely in the field of archaeology, the science of history, itself one of the most characteristic products of the new historical orientation of western thought in that century. In 1738, for example, the Roman city of Herculaneum, buried in 79 A.D. by lava and ashes erupting from Mount Vesuvius near Naples, was partially excavated; a similar project was begun at Pompeii in 1763. In 1750-1751, the Greek temples at Paestum (cf. Fig. 35) were studied and measured by official representatives of the French Academy of Architecture. These observations of certain

FIG. 169. Franconia, near Bamberg. Neumann, Vierzehnheiligen
(begun 1743), Interior.

FIG. 170.   Paris.   J.-A. Gabriel, Place de la Concorde
(1753-1763).

aspects of classic art of which the academic theorists had been largely unaware were made available in publications like *The Antiquities of Athens* by Stuart and Revett (1762), *Paestum* by Howard Major (1768), and those by Cochin and Soufflot, to mention but a few. To eyes surfeited with the pompous and extravagant forms affected by the academicians, the clarity and logic of Greek design and the graceful delicacy of the previously unknown styles of Pompeii were a welcome relief. Furthermore, the spirit of the time was critical, rebelling against artificial and synthetic formulas; and the restraint and straightforwardness of the ancient styles were thoroughly congenial to temperaments to whom J. J. Winckelmann's exhortation to aspire for "noble simplicity and quiet grandeur" (*History of Ancient Art*, 1764) was the definition of ideal formal character.

The initial consequence of the more archaeological understanding of antique art was a reaction away from the rococo minutiae of the Louis XV style toward greater simplicity and restraint in the Louis XVI manner. *The Place de la Concorde* (Fig. 170) in Paris by Jacques-Anges Gabriel (1698-1782) was created between 1753 and 1763; the two buildings, also by Gabriel, that flank the Rue Royale on the side of the Place opposite the river were built between 1762

and 1770. Known originally as the Place Louis Quinze from an equestrian statue of that monarch on the site now occupied by an Egyptian obelisk —this was also where the guillotine stood during the Revolution—it is west of the gardens of the Tuileries; its long axis extends to the east toward the Louvre and westward along the Champs Elysées to the Arc de Triomphe de l'Étoile. In the considerable size and great formality of the plan, and the careful relationship of architectural and natural elements, it is in the tradition of a planned and monumental environment initiated in the great ensembles of the seventeenth century (cf. Fig. 161). A similar continuation of Louis XIV concepts is seen in the façades of the buildings flanking the Rue Royale; the free-standing Corinthian columns over a rusticated basement story derive from Perrault's design for the East Colonnade of the Louvre (Fig. 157), but the effect is somewhat lightened by treating the lower story as an arcade.

The greater simplicity of Louis XVI classicism is apparent on the smaller scale of a single building in the palace called the *Petit Trianon* (Fig. 171) by Gabriel which was built at Versailles between 1762 and 1768 for the pleasure of Mme. de Pompadour. It is almost square in plan, and the façades are composed with notable reticence; there is an order of Corinthian columns

FIG. 171. Versailles. J.-A. Gabriel,
Petit Trianon (1762-1768).

or pilasters over a rusticated basement and mouldings of great delicacy around the openings, the monumentality of the design resulting from the well-studied proportions. The interiors of the Petit Trianon are in both the rococo of Louis XV and the more pronounced classicism of Louis XVI, for the building was much favored by Marie Antoinette, who had some parts of it redecorated. Instead of picturesquely irregular mouldings and panels and colorful paintings as in the Hôtel de Soubise (Fig. 168), there is geometrical regularity and simplicity in motives and details alike; the color is subdued and quiet in accordance with prevailing concepts of classicism.

The new classicism appeared in eighteenth-century English architecture at about the same time as it did in France. An example is the town house at 15 St. James Square (Fig. 172) in London, designed by James Stuart (1713-1788), and built in 1760. A pioneer in archaeological study in the period, Stuart collaborated with Nicholas Revett in publishing The Antiquities of Athens in 1762 and other books on previously little-known aspects of ancient art. The order that rises above a rusticated basement story at 15 St. James Square follows Palladian precedent, but his treatment of the upper stories as a classic temple façade is an innovation and the authenticity of the detail is likewise new. The Ionic order of

applied columns reproduces that on the north porch of the Erechtheum in Athens (Fig. 32), and the details of the mouldings as well as the proportions of the entablature and pediment are equally faithful to ancient models. As a result, the design more closely approximates a true classic ensemble in effect than in any other building as yet considered.

Even more influential than Stuart in shaping English taste in the third quarter of the eighteenth-century was Robert Adam (1728-1792), who worked in partnership with his brother James (1730-1794). In large measure this was a consequence of their interest and effectiveness in designing not only the exteriors of their buildings but the interiors and furniture as well. The Drawing Room from Lansdowne House (Fig. 173) was designed for a great town house on Berkeley Square in London between 1762 and 1765. The ceiling paintings are the work of Cipriani, an Italian, much in vogue at the time. Another Italian, Antonio Zucchi, decorated the pilasters and frieze with lively arabesques in delicate colors and gold, using as his model the type of ornament in the houses that had only recently been unearthed in excavating the city of Pompeii in southern Italy (Fig. 60). Similar prototypes were drawn upon for the details of the marble fireplace with its engaging frieze supported on Corinthian colonettes. The armchairs and fire screens (cf. Fig. 627) were also designed by Adam, though for another house, Moor Park. The colors of their Gobelin tapestry covers harmonize with those of the painted ceiling and pilasters and are set off by the gold of the silk damask that covered the walls before the room was moved from Lansdowne House to the Philadelphia Museum of Art. The result is an ensemble of the greatest dignity and distinction.

At the same time that one aspect, architecturally speaking, of the historical point of view in the eighteenth century was being developed by the new classicism of the Louis XVI style in France and the Adam style in England, a somewhat comparable Gothic Revival was also taking form. It is most apparent in England and Germany, where the growing awareness of historic traditions created an interest in the

FIG. 172.   London.   Stuart, 15 St. James Square (1760).

mediaeval past that was stimulated in no small degree by an increasingly self-conscious nationalism to which the art of the Middle Ages was as important a heritage of northern culture as the classic of Greece and Rome. Another element that contributed to the Gothic Revival was the romantic interest in far-off and exotic things; this also explains the already mentioned introduction, earlier in the eighteenth century, of Chinese motives in some rococo art. In another form, but still an expression of emotional re-action, the same taste is apparent in the cult of mediaevalism. Men like Horace Walpole in England and Goethe in Germany may not have had a well-informed comprehension of Gothic art, but they felt its expressiveness and saw in it an outlet for the feeling of their own age. This in turn was closely allied to the cult of nature in the writings, also basically romantic and sentimental, of men like Richardson and Gray in England and Jean-Jacques Rousseau in France. It was for such reasons as these that in architecture,

FIG. 173. Philadelphia. Robert Adam, Drawing Room from Lansdowne House in London (1762-1765).

the picturesqueness of organic and therefore "natural" Gothic forms recommended them as symbols of what was felt to be truly northern and emotively significant in the art, religion, and philosophy of the eighteenth and early nine-teenth centuries.

Gothic style was never completely forgotten in England. Wren designed Gothic spires for some of his London parish churches, and William Kent (1685-1748) is credited with a number of Gothic studies in the early eighteenth century. But the early impetus to imitate mediaeval his-torical monuments came from literary dilettantes and amateurs of architecture, chiefly because of real or imagined sentimental associations of the Gothic style. Foremost among these men was

Horace Walpole (1717-1797), wealthy, well educated, and much traveled, who pretended to some interest in writing. It is this last which perhaps most clearly reveals Walpole's en-thusiasm for Gothic style, for his house—*Straw-berry Hill* (Fig. 174)—was built between 1748 and 1772 just when he was writing one of his best-known romances, *The Castle of Otranto*, subtitled *A Gothic Tale*, which appeared in 1764. Although his builder, William Robinson, was profession-ally trained, his architects were amateurs—Richard Bentley, John Chute, and Thomas Pitt, later Lord Camelford, among others—and their designs are more superficially mediaeval than indicative of authentic understanding. At first the exterior embodied a simple symmetrical scheme. Its later irregularity was the result of self-conscious efforts to achieve greater picturesqueness by adding towers, gables, battlements, and whatnot—dictated "by literary dilettantism rather than by architectural feeling," as John Summerson has so aptly pointed out (*Architecture in Britain:* 1530-1830, p. 243). Others have characterized the sentiment evoked by such forms as agreeable melancholy. What is important for this in architecture is that the structure did not have to be soundly and well built to achieve this end. The symbol was more important than the fact. This completely overlooks that in mediaeval architecture of the Middle Ages, fact and symbol are one and the same. The most revealing indication of eighteenth-century Gothic taste for sentimental or associative rather than architectural values is the popularity of the imitation ruin or "fabrick," great numbers of which were built in the

studiedly "natural" and romantic English gardens of that time.

The turn of the century brought knowledge of mediaeval forms that archaelogically was more correct. In the *Houses of Parliament* (Fig. 175), erected in London between 1840 and 1865, there is better understanding of the idioms. The general plan was Sir Charles Barry's (1795-1860), but the detail was supervised by Augustus Welby Pugin (1813-1852), one of the first nineteenth-century students of mediaeval architecture to realize and apply the idea that it is the essential unity of construction and design that gives true Gothic building its expressive character. Although his workmen had the best available training in mediaeval craftsmanship methods, their understanding was academic at best; and the forms they created, while accurate enough as studies in the Gothic manner, are dry and lifeless in comparison with mediaeval work. Even in

Country Life

FIG. 174.   Twickenham.   Robinson, Strawberry Hill
(begun 1748).

Photograph by Pan American.

FIG. 175.　London.　Barry, Houses of Parliament
(1840-1865).

Pugin's work, the primary justification of the Gothic manner lay not so much in its plastic character as in associative values. These were no longer sentimental and literary but moral—a manifestation of his whole-hearted participation in the religious revivalism that was one of the significant phenomena in English nineteenth-century history. It was his sincere and frequently expressed belief that only by returning to mediaeval thinking and a deliberate and purposeful regeneration of its forms of expression could the social and economic evils attendant upon the growth of industrialism be cured. The same spirit animated others, among them John Ruskin, whose fluent prose was largely responsible for the widespread popularity of the style called Victorian Gothic in England and the United States during the later nineteenth century. Of greater importance than either, however, was the work of William Morris (1834-1896). Motivated at the outset by a similar moralizing purpose, his later writings reveal a concept of creative crafts-

manship that inspired some of the innovators of modern style in the closing years of that century (cf. pages 716 ff.).

In the revival tendencies that dominated European architecture in the first half of the nineteenth century, there was no perception of the basic principle that architectural style is expressive only when the three fundamentals—plan, construction, and design—are taken into account. The purpose of the majority of buildings then erected, either classic or mediaeval, was primarily the creation of symbols that were effective through association and sentimental identification rather than through formal qualities of mass and proportion and line and texture. This attitude was fostered by the then prevailing historical point of view and also, in a sense, by the increasingly obvious consequences of industrial expansion which tended more and more to isolate the arts from the main stream of social expression, thus reducing them to the level of a means of escaping the tawdry and debasing circumstances of everyday existence. Not all the architects of the period accepted these standards. Some realized the necessity of new architectural forms and methods to give appropriate expression to the new social order then developing; notable among them were Sir John Soane (1753-1837), an Englishman, and the German, Karl Friedrich von Schinkel (1781-1841). As a group that had no conscious homogeneity—indeed, it consisted of men whose individual achievement was varied and uneven—these architects stood for a rational rather than a sentimental principle in building, and developed forms that expressed the fundamental structural elements of plan and material as directly as any the time produced.

An example of this rational point of view in architecture is the *Bibliothèque Sainte-Geneviève* (Figs. 176, 177) in Paris by Henri Labrouste

FIG. 176. Paris. Labrouste, Bibliothèque Sainte-Geneviève (1843-1850).

FIG. 177. Paris. Bibliothèque Sainte-Geneviève, The Reading Room.

FIG. 178. Paris Garnier, Opéra. (1861–1874).

veals the same dualism of structural rationalism and decorative revivalism. The internal supports are of cast iron; from them a series of transverse arched girders of the same material are sprung to form the armature of two barrel vaults running the length of the reading room. The use of iron, whose strength under compression is much greater than an equivalent mass of masonry, permitted maximum space and light, and the objective function of the structure was effectively realized. But the supports have the shape of slender Corinthian colonnettes, strangely attenuated in translation into metal; and the transverse girders are pierced with a stylized foliate pattern derived from the classic acanthus *rinceau*—neither motive inherently suitable to the medium in which it is used here. Thus while Labrouste the builder and engineer handled his material so as to realize its structural potentialities very effectively, Labrouste the architect had to consider the resultant forms in terms of decorative principles entirely alien to them; consequently their expressive potentialities are scarcely realized.

The conflict in the nineteenth century between the architect as a builder and as a designer of "pure form" was hardly recognized at that time, and the importance of the few rationalistic buildings such as the Bibliothèque Sainte-Geneviève in showing this dualism was unnoticed. Instead, even the lesson of rationalism was not learned and the revival principle was carried to far greater extremes later in the century than was the case before 1850. Eclecticism was the guiding principle, and the architect was allowed complete freedom of choice in the historical styles, the only criteria being the designer's taste and the supposed appropriateness of certain forms to particular purposes. Thus religious structures were usually mediaeval, public buildings Renaissance, and monumental or commemorative edifices in the classic modes. The *Opera House* (Fig. 178) in Paris is one of literally thousands of examples of this. Designed by Charles Garnier (1825-1898) and finished in 1874, it has exerted strong influence in theatre design since it was built, owing in part to the prestige it enjoys as the seat of the French

(1801-1875), erected between 1843 and 1850. One of the first structures designed and built as a public library, it illustrates the new architectural demands created by the changing social fabric of the century. The exterior gives reasonable expression to the internal division between stack space for storage below and the more open reading room above (Fig. 177), amply lighted by the long unbroken row of arched windows. It is also an example of the tendency of even the rational architect of the early nineteenth century to think of his problems in historical terms, for the proportions of the window arcade and its general spacing and rhythm were suggested by Alberti's treatment of the niches on the side of the church of San Francesco at Rimini (Fig. 119). The decorative mouldings that enliven the somewhat severe masses and surfaces are profiled with a delicacy suggestive of Greek work, possibly from Labrouste's study of the temples at Paestum (cf. Fig. 35) while a *pensionnaire* of the French Academy at Rome. The interior (Fig. 177) re-

National Academy of Music and in part to the apparent appropriateness of baroque architectural forms to opera, the most baroque of all the arts. In designing it, Garnier followed late Venetian Renaissance models for the most part, although the applied order of doubled pilasters between projecting end bays with pediments and over an arcaded basement story reverts directly to the French academic formula established by Perrault (Fig. 157) and continued by Gabriel (Fig. 170).

The state of affairs in European architecture of the late nineteenth century has been called a "Battle of Styles," an eloquent indication of the chaos and confusion of architectural purpose at that time. But this was no more than a reflection of the instability of thought in general in a period which saw the reorientation of western culture in the rise and spread of industrialism, and the consequent weakening and ultimate disruption of most of the traditional values of post-Renaissance civilization. Furthermore, as long as the western world was committed to a historical vocabulary of form in attempting to express its ideas, there was of necessity an emphasis upon purely formal considerations to compensate for the lack of genuine and vital inspiration in the ideas themselves. Thus in spite of the ever-increasing resources of historical vocabulary and the growing sophistication with which it was used, the sterility of eclecticism as a guiding principle of design is obvious and explains the unmitigated dullness of most European architecture in the later nineteenth century.

Detail of Fig. 184.

CHAPTER TWELVE

American Architecture from Its Origins to 1870

Architecture in Colonial North America was based on the styles of the countries in which the settlers originated. The houses and churches of Colonial New England differ in no important respect from middle-class English structures of the seventeenth and eighteenth centuries. In New York, Dutch types appear. The polyglot colonies in Pennsylvania and Delaware produced a mixture of Welsh, German, and Swedish styles. To Florida, Mexico, and the Southwest, the Jesuit missionaries carried the baroque of Italy and Spain, though it was unavoidably modified

FIG. 179. Ipswich. John Whipple House (before 1669).

by the conditions under which the buildings were erected. The settlers' dependence upon the styles of their mother countries is obvious in descriptions of the first shelters they erected which have long since vanished. The terms in which Captain John Smith wrote of the huts built by the early colonists in Virginia imply that they were much like the rude shacks of the poorest laboring classes in England. By the end of the seventeenth century, more extensive settlement and greater security from attack gave the inhabitants of the New World more time to consider architectural problems. Houses of some pretension that were well adapted to their surroundings began to appear; and even though many of them were built of wood, so solidly were they constructed that a considerable number are still preserved.

One of these was the *John Whipple House* (Fig. 179) at Ipswich, Mass., erected some time before 1669. Its plan is simple, consisting of two rooms on each floor that run the entire width of the building and are separated by a hall containing the main entrance and a staircase to the second floor. The house is of the wooden frame type which the English settlers in Massachusetts brought from the Old World. Great corner posts support a rectangular framework of smaller beams on which the floors rest. The walls are a mixture of clay and straw that fills the openings between the wooden members of the frame and the stiffening studs or angle beams

FIG. 180.   Topsfield.   Capen House (1683), The Parlor.

connecting the vertical posts and the horizontal joists. This is the construction used in English mediaeval half-timbered houses (Fig. 142); the American version differs from it principally in having an outer sheath of overlapping clapboards made necessary by the severe New England climate, for the unmodified English half-timber construction had proved insufficient to protect against the cold. If the clapboards were removed, the Whipple House would look like its English prototypes.

Protection from the bitter cold is the reason for many construction details in buildings like the Whipple House. The brick chimney rises through the center so that the heat radiating from it could be retained. The central chimney also makes it possible to have one stack for all the fireplaces, of which there are four, one in each room. As the chimney is a salient feature of the exterior, so the fireplaces are focal points in each room. An example is the parlor of the *Capen House* (Fig. 180), built at Topsfield in Essex County in Massachusetts in 1683. Other notable and characteristic features are the wooden

paneling or wainscot on the fireplace wall, the plastering of the other walls—although this was apparently not a general practice in earlier Colonial houses—and the straightforward acceptance of the structural beams and posts of the frame as elements in the interior. The furniture in the illustration is of the same general period as the house itself and, like it, follows models currently used in comparable English structures.

Frank revelation of structure and little concern for formal design are the outstanding qualities of this first or Colonial style of American architecture. A possible exception to the prevalent structuralism of the design might be the overhang, the slight projection of the attic of the Whipple House over the second story which in turn projects beyond the lowest level. But even this is a structural reminiscence, for in the houses of English tradesmen which also served them as stores, the overhang protected the wares for sale shown on outdoor counters. Since the New England settlers came principally from the middle classes in England, this was the type of house they were most familiar with and they adapted it to the different circumstances of the New World. Although the overhang had no such function in the Massachusetts wilderness, it remained as a decorative feature just as the guttae and triglyphs of the Greek Doric order persisted as ornamental details long after their original structural function was forgotten. The ends of the overhang were sometimes carved as they are in the Whipple House, but this is usually the only evidence of a conscious attempt to relieve the unpretentiousness of the exterior.

It is hardly necessary to point out that the colonial builder was not primarily concerned with problems of formal design that affected the appearance of his structures. His main consideration was a practical and comfortable arrangement of the interior. If, as frequently happened, the house became too small for a growing family, it was enlarged by a lean-to usually added to the rear as another room whose slanting roof continued the pitch of the house roof. The Whipple House has a lean-to, the clapboards having been replaced to conceal the point between earlier and later parts. Though this made the ends of the house unsymmetrical, this was no more of a disadvantage in the builder's eyes than the irregular spacing of the windows, for they were placed in accordance with interior requirements rather than for external decorative effect.

It is for such reasons as these that the architecture of the Colonial period from 1620 to 1720 is often referred to as the mediaeval style in America. As was true of European mediaeval architecture, its character was determined by the constructive principles by which its forms were created. The parallel goes even further, for Colonial architecture is essentially organic, distinguished by striking appropriateness to its setting and the conditions in which it developed. In New England, the Colonial style involves the use of wood because the inevitable preliminary to settlement was the clearing of the forests, resulting in a large supply of lumber. In New York and Pennsylvania, stone was easily obtained; consequently the Colonial houses there are stone and are different in character from those in New England. In the South, brick was commonly used and the less rigorous climate allowed

more open building than was possible in the North. A specific difference between the northern and southern types is the placing of the chimneys at the ends of the houses in the South because it was not so essential to conserve the radiated heat. Another contrast was due to the difference in antecedents of the settlers in the two regions. In the North, the colonists were of the middle class, whereas many southern settlers were of the aristocracy. Large numbers of servants were required to maintain the southern establishments and they were housed in outlying structures which might or might not be connected with the main building but were subordinate to it. Thus in all the colonies regional styles were developed, represented by functional buildings that were comparatively unpretentious in appearance yet admirably adapted to their surroundings and purpose.

Even older than the buildings in the English colonies were many erected in the areas settled by the Spanish in the southwestern desert of North America. At Acoma, N. Mex., a little over fifty miles west of Albuquerque, the church of *San Estevan* (Fig. 181) was built about 1642. As in most of these Spanish settlements, the church was the most impressive building in the community, the result to a considerable extent of the way it was built. The church is adobe, desert clay formed into flat, slablike bricks dried in the sun, mortared and plastered with the clay. This building method had been native to the Indians of the region for ages before. It is reminiscent of the processes used in pre-Christian Mesopotamian architecture in the Near East (cf. pages 30 ff.), and the resultant forms have the same monumental massive simplicity. The spaces are not vaulted, however, but are spanned by closely set timbers supporting a flat roof. To the right of the church façade is the *convento* in which the friar-priests and lay brothers lived. The façade proper, although without ornament, is impressive in its simple, dignified shape; only the symmetrical towers suggest the baroque prototype its Jesuit designers followed in the handiwork of their Indian helpers. There is no more convincing example of the transformation of European style by immediate conditions and

FIG. 181. Acoma. San Estevan (*ca.* 1642).

circumstances than San Estevan at Acoma and the many comparable structures in other Spanish settlements of the Southwest.

By the early eighteenth century, political and social conditions in the English colonies were relatively stabilized, and the colonists could turn to matters which the earlier struggle to keep soul and body together had forced them to disregard. A more involved social order made its appearance, based on that in England and marked by clearer class distinctions. In architecture, this was reflected in a more pretentious style than the Colonial. Known as Georgian, it was used largely from 1720 to about 1790, the period during which the first representatives of the House of Hanover were on the English throne; from them the name of the style and the period is derived (cf. page 703). In general, the Georgian style in the colonies corresponds to that of the Renaissance in Europe, just as the Colonial style has many mediaeval qualities. The Georgian

shows a growing preoccupation with formal design similar to that in European Renaissance styles. The Georgian house is larger than the Colonial. Usually there are four rooms on each floor—that is, the house is two rooms deep—and the hall and its staircase are more important than in the Colonial style. Methods of construction in the two periods are much the same and there are the same regional variations in the materials. The greatest contrast between the two styles is in the appearance of the buildings.

The majority of Georgian house designs originated in the textbooks of architecture which were written in ever-increasing numbers by English architects early in the eighteenth century. At that time, English architecture was essentially classic and academic (cf. Fig. 166); and the theories elaborated in the writings of such men as Colin Campbell, James Gibbs, and Batty Langley were ultimately based on those of Palladio. Numerous books by these men were brought to the colonies. In the hands of journeymen masons and carpenters, they gave rise to a flowering of classic details on the buildings of the New World that was altogether comparable in spirit to that in fifteenth-century Italy, even though the two differed in the character of the forms employed.

The academic quality of Georgian architecture is exemplified by the façade of the Craigie or *Longfellow House* (Fig. 182) in Cambridge, Mass., built about 1759. Details that reveal this quality are the giant order of Ionic pilasters on bases, the continuous frieze of dentils, and the central pediment with horizontal and raking cornices both decorated with mouldings that closely follow the rules of academic design. The symmetry of the façade and the balustrade of the flat walk surmounting the hipped roof are other academic features. The hipped roof rising from all four sides of the house is an attempt to achieve a compromise between the flat roof dictated by

academic formulas and the pitched form made necessary by the rain and snow of a New England winter. That the builder of the house had no real understanding of classic style is evident in his treatment of the Ionic pilasters. The base is not continuous as in Roman and Renaissance examples (Figs. 50, 126) but appears only under the pilasters. Similarly, above each pilaster is a small section of an entablature as well as the complete one that circles the house. The architect was led into these errors because he was copying a diagram of the order that consisted of a single column with partial base and entablature, whose true functions he did not realize.

The Georgian interior is no less academic than the exterior. Typical is that from the Charles Steadman or *Powel House* in Philadelphia (Fig. 183), dating from about 1768 and now in the American Wing of the Metropolitan Museum in New York. The bareness of the

FIG. 182. Cambridge. Longfellow House (*ca.* 1759).

The Metropolitan Museum of Art.

FIG. 183. New York. Room from the Powel House
in Philadelphia (*ca.* 1768).

Colonial interior with its exposed ceiling beams and undecorated walls has given way to a more decorative effect. The fireplace wall is paneled in wood, with an elaborate mantel and over-mantel crowned by a typically academic broken pediment. The other walls are covered with elaborate painted paper showing pagodas, trees, birds, and mountains. This type of wallpaper was very popular in the Colonies during the third quarter of the eighteenth century, when much of it was imported from China. Around the top of the walls is a classic meander moulding, and the plaster ceiling is decorated with a delicate foliate design. The Chippendale furniture, of the same period as the architecture (cf. Fig. 634), completes a design of great dignity and formality.

In the South, the different environment pro-duced a type of house that differed from nor-thern houses but was no less academic in quality. *Mount Vernon* (Fig. 184) is typical of the southern Georgian style. It was given its present form by George Washington between 1758 and 1788, in several reconstructions of an earlier building. The fact that he was his own architect is evidence that some architectural knowledge was then an indispensable adjunct to a gentleman's education. The square paneled columns of the portico are a variation of the usual round type. Charac-teristically southern are the open portico and the outlying servants' quarters joined to the main building by arcaded passageways. An academic detail is seen in the Palladian window in the end of the house. The heavy pine boards of the sheathing are cut and painted to resemble jointed blocks of stone. Such attempts to give a wooden structure the more monumental effect of stone are frequent in the Georgian period, in contrast with the straightforwardness of the Colonial period.

A glance at a middle-class Georgian house in England like the Swan House (Fig. 166) shows how similar were the results of working with comparable materials and for similar purposes in the domestic architecture of mother country and colony. There is also a resemblance between the churches of the two. The designing of *Christ Church* (Fig. 185) in Philadelphia was supervised by Dr. John Kearsley, and the greater part was built between 1727 and 1744. The design follows that for the type of church erected by Sir Christopher Wren in London for the smaller parishes (cf. Fig. 164), although the immediate prototype of the spire appears to have been St.

Martin's-in-the-Fields in London done by James Gibbs; the Christ Church spire was completed by Robert Smith in 1754. There are various classic motives in the tower, which is well designed to achieve the transition from the square base to the octagonal spire. The superposed orders of the side walls express the two-part elevation of the interior. The white sashes and divisions in the windows are an effective decorative contrast with the red brick walls, which are themselves given variety by the use of slightly contrasting tones in adjacent courses. The balustrade with its urns is possibly too heavy in proportion to the rest of the building and the lack of agreement between the frieze of the side and that of the end wall reveals the hand of the amateur designer. The Palladian window in the end wall, however, is a masterpiece in its admirable proportions, its relationship to the wall, and the restrained decorative quality of the details.

FIG. 184.   Mount Vernon (1758-1788).

It deserves admiration in its own right as well as being historically interesting as the first appearance of the Palladian motive in American Georgian architecture. Christ Church is closely associated with the pre-Revolutionary history of Philadelphia; this gives it an importance in addition to that of its excellent design. The latter has led many critics to pronounce it the finest example of Georgian church architecture in the United States.

American architecture of the Early Republican period immediately following the Revolution continues the classic tradition of the Georgian, but with characteristic modifications. On the one hand there develops a style with unmistakable similarities to that of the Adam brothers in England (cf. Fig. 173); on the other is a style, going even farther in adaptation of antique forms than the Adams did, known as the

Classic Revival. Samuel McIntire (1757-1811) of Salem, Mass., is a representative of the first; however, its most distinguished adherent was Charles Bulfinch (1763-1844). Well educated and widely traveled, Bulfinch was content to be an amateur and dilettante of architecture until he was a little over thirty years; he then became a professional, one of the first in the United States. About 1796, he designed the first of several houses for the Bostonian, Harrison Gray Otis; today it is the headquarters of the Society for the Preservation of New England Antiquities. The dining room of this house (Fig. 186) reveals its Adamesque parentage in a number of details. The pilasters of the mantelpiece are carved with delicately scaled arabesques much like those in the Lansdowne Room (Fig. 173), and there are comparable similarities between the gracefully curved swags of foliage flanking the central

Pennsylvania Historical Society, Philadelphia.

FIG. 185.   Philadelphia.   Christ Church (1727-1744);
Spire (1754), from the painting by W. Strickland.

FIG. 186. Boston. First Harrison Gray Otis House (1796).
Bulfinch, The Dining Room.

panel and those in the Lansdowne Room frieze. The cornice of Bulfinch's room is of similar character, like all elements in the Adam classic repertory distinguished from earlier use of the same details by its greater lightness and smallness of scale. Although color does not have as varied a role in the New World version of the Adam style as in the London room, the soft green of the walls adds a harmonious note to the overall effect. Since it is known that Bulfinch had a rather extensive library of architectural books, there can be no doubt as to the source of his ideas—the publications of the Adam Brothers' work.

Thomas Jefferson was the outstanding figure in the early Classic Revival in the United States; the distinction of his political accomplishments is paralleled by his architectural achievements. His technical knowledge of architecture was equaled by his profound appreciation of its cultural value and philosophical implications. He approached the problem of an American style from the latter point of view, and it was that which finally led him to conclude that the forms of Roman architecture in the republican period were best fitted for adaptation to the buildings of the new republic in the West. It was therefore the similarity in theory of

FIG. 187. Richmond. Virginia
State Capitol. Jefferson, Original
Model (1785-1790).

government that was Jefferson's justification for believing that Roman architectural forms were the most appropriate for use in America whether they were really suitable to its needs or not.

Jefferson was a practical as well as a theoretical architect, and he supported his thesis with actual designs. These he derived from direct observation of Roman buildings instead of seeing them "as through a glass darkly" in the writings of Palladio and the other theorists. In part this was due to nationalistic opposition to the English academists whose works had exercised such a powerful influence on the American Georgian style. Thus when Jefferson was asked to draw up plans for the Virginia State Capitol in Richmond, he designed a modified form of the Maison Carrée in Nîmes (Fig. 50). This was one of the first actual examples of Roman architecture that he saw during a visit to Europe from 1784 to 1789 and its effect on him can be gathered from his statement that he gazed "whole hours at the *Maison Quarrée*, like a lover at his mistress." The model he submitted as part of his specifications for the *Virginia State Capitol* (Fig. 187) shows some variations from the original. One of these was the substitution of Ionic capitals for the original Corinthian to reduce the expense of carving. The solution of the problem of doors and windows also involved some deviation from classic prototypes. In solving it, Jefferson followed the practice of French classicists like Charles Louis Clérisseau. Still further

changes were unavoidable when the building was being erected; but for all this, it marked an epoch in architectural history. For one thing, it was the first building to be designed specifically to meet the needs of modern republican government, not only in this country but in the world. It was also the first time that the unmodified temple form was employed in a building that was intended for practical purposes, although the form had been used in memorial and decorative structures. In this adaptation of exact classic forms to modern ends, the American Classic Revival anticipated that in Europe by many years.

As soon as the classic temple motive appeared in American architecture, enthusiasm for it swept all other forms aside. Jefferson himself employed it for many buildings, notably those of the University of Virginia in which he

FIG. 188. Philadelphia.
Strickland, Second Bank of the
United States (1814-1824).

FIG. 189.   Hamilton.   Spencer House (*ca.* 1820).

reproduced the Roman orders with great accuracy. The professors' houses saw the temple form used for the first time in domestic buildings. As the popularity of the style grew, Greek as well as Roman forms were employed. The *Second Bank of the United States* (Fig. 188) in Philadelphia, designed by William Strickland (1788-1854) and built between 1818 and 1824, reproduces the general proportions and order of the Parthenon, although space made it necessary to limit the colonnades to the ends. In it Strickland expressed the ultra-classic principles which prevailed in American architecture in a form that won favor from many European commentators at the time. It antedates by at least ten years any foreign adaptation of the Parthenon design to modern needs; and the employment of the design in a utilitarian structure indicates a degree of classicism unparalleled in any other country.

The "Republican style," as it was currently known, soon spread over the entire United States. The geographical distinctions apparent in the Colonial and Georgian periods were wiped away and the pure classic style prevailed from Maine to Georgia and from New York to California. Buildings of all kinds were designed in the form of Greek and Roman temples. In houses, a classic portico was the touchstone of social position even in regions which were then the backwoods. The *Spencer House* (Fig. 189) in Hamilton, N.Y., is an example of such a "temple," erected with its Doric porch some time after 1820. In all parts of the nation the same phenomenon appeared; classic porticoes were the order of the day.

That the style of the Classic Revival was artificial in some ways needs hardly be said. The pioneers in central New York and the wilds of Ohio and Michigan could not be expected to express themselves naturally through the antique orders or to adapt the programs of their buildings to the restrictions of the temple form.

Copyright C.O. Buckingham, Washington, D.C.

FIG. 190.   Washington, D.C.   Thornton and others,
United States Capitol (1792-1865).

Accordingly, the form itself was soon subjected to many changes. In the Spencer House, the Doric order is far from pure, with its crushed echinus and a base under the shaft. The doorway is set at one side, breaking the symmetry that is the chief characteristic of classic form. To gain additional interior space, a wing is added to one side of the main "temple," modifying the symmetry of the structure even more. Still further changes were made so that the upper rooms in the front of the house could have some natural illumination. A full entablature would cut off almost all the light from those rooms. Sometimes this was remedied by inserting open grills in the frieze; in other cases, as here, the entablature is practically eliminated. In either case, the purity of the classic form is destroyed. It is evident that the function of the house is actually hampered by its classic temple form instead of determining the form. Attempts to arrive at a satisfactory compromise between them were never successful. Obviously one basic form could not serve for private homes, banks, churches, and statehouses. The classic builders themselves did not expect the temple form to be used for every architectural function. The Classic Revival attempts to use it for all kinds of buildings only emphasize the impossibility of achieving effective results when exterior appearance is held to be the most important factor in architectural design.

With all the limitations of the Classic Revival style, it cannot be denied that it contributed much-needed dignity to American building. The best effects of the Georgian style are the result of skillfully executed detail. In the hands of workmen with little taste or ability, it is often dry and monotonous. The Colonial style is that of a craftsman, attaining effectiveness by sound construction and an unconscious feeling for good proportions on the part of the builders. The buildings of the Classic Revival, on the other hand, have intrinsic solidity, sometimes in spite of inexperienced designers. A few well-turned Doric or Ionic columns lend distinction to many a house of the early nineteenth century which would otherwise be only mediocre. Furthermore, the style admirably indicates the growing sense of national importance which colored all American thought at that time.

The best-known example of the American Classic Revival is the *United States Capitol* (Fig. 190) in Washington, D.C. It is located on one of the focal points of a vast plan for the entire city drawn up by Major Pierre Charles L'Enfant

(1754-1825) after the model of Versailles (cf. Fig. 161). The original plan of the Capitol was made by an amateur architect, Dr. William Thornton (1759-1828) of Philadelphia. As first constructed, a low central dome modeled after that of the Roman Pantheon (Fig. 57) rose from a base formed by the chambers of the Senate and of the House of Representatives. The building attained its present form after various subsequent alterations, the most extensive by Thomas U. Walter (1804-1887), beginning in 1851. This involved extending the flanking wings by large blocks with pediments over their entrance fronts and free-standing colonnades along the side, and the construction of the present dome over Thornton's lower dome. Of cast iron painted to resemble stone, it was completed in 1865. Its design is somewhat like that of Saint Paul's dome in London (Fig. 163) with a free-standing peristyle around the drum. The details are rather stereotyped, and mechanical in execution; but the cupola dominates the masses of the wings in an overall effect of considerable impressiveness, its dignity well suited to its key part in the plan of the city as a whole. Its widespread influence is seen in the many state capitols that were built after the same general pattern.

As in Europe, there was a Gothic Revival in nineteenth-century American architecture. It was not without precedent here, for the Gothic style had been used before the Revolution—in the first building erected on the site of Trinity

FIG. 191.   Kennebunkport.   "Wedding-Cake" House
(*ca.* 1850).

so-called *"Wedding-Cake" House* (Fig. 191) at Kennebunkport, Maine, given its present form about 1850. The Gothic details are superficial; for underneath the pinnacles, pointed arches, and other decorative incrustations, the house is little more than a box. Upon its rectangular form Gothic motives were festooned just as classic details would have been applied a hundred years earlier. The extensive use of mediaeval motives was due to the fact that they were fashionable; however, their popularity was also due to a sincere if unformulated and unconscious desire for beauty that led those who used them to seize upon anything that would relieve the drab monotony of their structures. The naïve awkwardness of the results can be attributed to lack of the background of taste which imposed some restraint upon the use of revived historical forms in Europe. This fact too was unconsciously felt; and the fumbling attempts to acquire such background by arbitrarily creating its forms of expression without really understanding them left its mark on American architecture during the years immediately before the Civil War.

The closest approximation to authentic Gothic effects is found in religious architecture. The use in churches of mediaeval forms as known to the nineteenth century did not require the fundamental alteration of their character that was involved when they were adapted to types with which they had never had any structural relationship. For this reason, such buildings as Trinity Church by Richard Upjohn, Grace Church, and *St. Patrick's Cathedral* (Fig. 192) by James Renwick, all in New York, show less deviation from mediaeval models than do the Gothic houses built at the same time. Without the possibility of immediate comparison with mediaeval originals, St. Patrick's (1859-1879) seems very convincing. Its Gothic characteristics are only superficial, however; the nave vaults, for example, are of papier-mâché painted to look like stone. Throughout, the effects were planned to conform to a preconceived idea of appearance instead of resulting from the logical integration of structural details.

The pre-Civil War tendency toward superficial stylistic effects in American architecture is

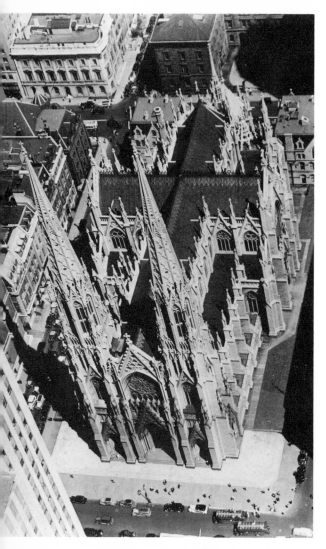

FIG. 192. New York. Renwick, St. Patrick's Cathedral (1859-1879).

Church in New York, for example. This slender connection with the Middle Ages was reinforced in the early nineteenth century by the romantic novels of Sir Walter Scott and Washington Irving, the latter having gone so far in his mediaevalism as to rebuild his home, "Sunnyside," in a pseudo-Gothic style somewhat as Walpole had done in England. From 1835 until about 1860, the Gothic style was as popular as the classic was a few years before. An example is the

even more pronounced thereafter. Several considerations affected architectural style during the "Brown Decades," as Lewis Mumford aptly termed the period from immediately after the Civil War until about 1890. One was patronage. Most buildings of the time were commissioned by people of wealth but little taste who preferred ostentation to the distinction of well-proportioned shapes and effective plans. Another was the development of mechanical processes for making the ornament such tastes preferred—the power jigsaw for wood, and cheaper methods of casting iron for metal. Influencing both of these was the persuasive prose of John Ruskin and his fellow writers, who expounded a return to mediaeval ideals and expressive forms as a cure for the evils they believed were being brought on by increasing industrialization.

Yet even during this time when taste was at such a low point in American architecture, there was imagination and intelligence in planning and the use of materials. Many of the small and stylistically negligible houses, for example, are well laid out for comfortable living. And as early as the 1830's, a new method of construction for wood buildings, the balloon frame, was developed in the Middle West; it took advantage of mechanical methods of processing wood and making nails. It soon displaced the traditional hand-work mortice and tenon jointing and the like, because it reduced both the amount of material needed and the costs of assembling, for the work could be done by relatively unskilled laborers.

Combining such realism in the matter of materials and building with a true sense of style was the achievement of Henry Hobson Richardson (1838-1886). Richardson was one of the increasing number of Americans to go abroad for artistic training in the nineteenth century. He studied at the École des Beaux-Arts in Paris, but his genius did not suffer from the academic atmosphere for which that school is noted. His first buildings in this country were in the current Victorian Gothic mode, but the structure which brought him general recognition was not one of these. *Trinity Church* (Fig. 193) in Boston, which was built between 1872 and

FIG. 193. Boston. Richardson, Trinity Church (1872-1877).

1877, is one of the first buildings to have the quality that distinguished Richardson's architectural thinking from that of the great majority of his contemporaries, a feeling for style in terms of material and construction, rather than decoration.

At first glance, Trinity Church may seem to be simply an example of the same historical revivalism that had produced St. Patrick's in New York a few years earlier, but Romanesque instead of Gothic; it is true that its most prominent feature—the great square tower—was admittedly copied after that of the twelfth-century cathedral at Salamanca in Spain. But the tower was not the individual work of Richardson but the idea of one of his assistant draftsmen, Stanford White, to whom Richardson entrusted developing a suitable design for that part of the building when earlier plans proved incapable of construction. In the lower portion, which was designed by Richardson, it is possible to see a resemblance in character to Romanesque structures too; but a distinction must be drawn between Romanesque character in construction, which involves the use of material, and Romanesque ornament, which involves only decorative detail. In the tower which was drawn up by Stanford White, it is the ornament that is Romanesque—in actual form as well as in general feeling since it follows closely that of the Spanish original; in the lower part of the structure, in the walls of the apse and transepts, there is no such copying. There the forms are the result of Richardson's being inspired by Romanesque buildings to work in the same way as the Romanesque builders did—in heavy blocks of stone, vigorously rusticated and massively proportioned (cf. Fig. 88), that are eloquent of the architect's knowledge of his material and his sense of the way it should be used. In thus working as a builder in terms of material instead of as a decorator in terms of ornament, Richardson restored to architecture the quality of structural integrity that, as has been said, is lacking in so much earlier nineteenth-century work in America. That the period in which he worked was incapable of realizing the importance of this and chose instead to see only superficial details that were identified by historical association as an attempt to revive Romanesque idioms as the Gothic had been revived by an earlier generation is no fault of Richardson's. The so-called Romanesque Revival was not his achievement but that of men who thought to see in his work precisely what he had not taken from the forms that inspired him, namely, another system of historical ornament.

Sense of material and a corollary insistence upon sound construction were the qualities of Richardson's architectural thinking that more than any others were invaluable potential antidotes to the superficial concepts prevalent in building styles of his time. They are present to a notable degree in the *Stoughton House* (Fig. 194) in Cambridge, Mass., which was built in 1882. The plan provides intelligently for comfortable living, with problems of orientation and circulation well solved. This is the basis for the L pattern of the two wings joined by the circular stair tower; the mass of the house as a whole is held together visually by the long and even roof line. Coherence is given the wall which defines

and encloses the spatial volume of the structure by its uniform surface of wood—beautiful in texture and a soft, silvery gray in color—a building material indigenous to New England which Richardson might well be said to have rediscovered following the long lapse from the straightforward and craftsmanlike use made of it by the Colonial builders of the seventeenth century (cf. Fig. 179). The clarity and realism with which Richardson approached domestic architectural style are readily apparent if the simple but beautifully proportioned Stoughton House is compared with the pseudo-monumental façade of the average Victorian house of the time, with its meaningless confusion of applied ornament and would-be picturesqueness.

Other than in technical and structural reforms in the use of material and emphasis on sound construction that Richardson contributed to American architecture in the late nineteenth century, the breadth of his imagination is evident in the great variety of building types to which he gave character and distinction. One is seen in the stations he designed for the Boston and Albany Railroad in the suburbs of Boston, and another in the small libraries erected in many of the same towns. Both appealed to him as forms characteristically of the time in providing for needs that stemmed from the social and economic conditions created by increasing industrialism and concentration of population around large manufacturing centers. Related to these in principle, since it too was designed to meet a characteristic and contemporary need, was the *Marshall Field Wholesale Building* (Fig. 195) in Chicago. Built in 1885-1887 but later torn down, it was seven stories high and built around a central court covered by a skylight. The internal piers and floor beams were of metal; the outer walls, the major weight-bearing elements of the building, were of stone. Maximum interior illumination was desirable; hence the relatively large proportion of window space to solid wall. It was from these features of the design that Richardson developed its character; there is no applied ornament and very little carving, the contrasting texture of smooth and rusticated stone giving character to the surfaces and the rhythmic pattern of the openings providing the basic formal unity. The result is masonry construction raised to the highest degree of architectural distinction by its realistic but inspired employment in a timely and significantly contemporary structural problem. The greatness of Richardson's achievement is attested to by the statement about the building made by Louis Sullivan, one of the few men of the later nineteenth century who really comprehended it: "Four-square and brown it stands, in physical fact a monument to trade, to the organized commercial spirit, to the power and progress of the age, to the strength and resource of individuality

FIG. 194.   Cambridge.   Richardson, Stoughton House
(1882).

⮞ 225 ⮜

FIG. 195. Chicago. Richardson, Marshall Field Wholesale Building
(1885-1887).

and force of character; spiritually it stands as the index of a mind large enough to cope with these things, taste them, absorb them and give them forth impressed with the stamp of a large and forceful personality; artistically it stands as the creation of one who knows well how to choose his words, who has somewhat to say and says it as the outpouring of a copious, direct, large and simple mind."

"Well-building hath three conditions: Commodity, Firmness and Delight." So wrote Sir Henry Wotton, a seventeenth-century English humanist in an essay on architecture. If the expressions good planning, sound construction, and expressive character are substituted for the more terse terms in Sir Henry's definition, it will apply as well to a later time as to his own, and, indeed, to all times. It is in this sense that Richardson's achievement can be most accurately evaluated, for he realized—as did none of his predecessors and few of his contemporaries and followers—that creative architecture does not result from copying or adapting the styles of the past. Only when a building's function and its relationship to its time in the broadest social sense are expressed in formal terms of distinction and character can genuinely original building forms be expected. This idea is implicit in the wish Richardson once expressed that he might design a grain elevator and the interior of a river steamboat—both characteristically American, and American of the nineteenth century. His death at forty-eight, in 1886, deprived the United States of its first great modern architect at a crucial moment, when his influence could have been of inestimable value. For it was about this time that the structural use of metal became general in this country.

Detail of Fig. 199.

CHAPTER THIRTEEN

Architecture of the Late Nineteenth and Early Twentieth Centuries

Richardson's architecture illustrates the same principle of rationalism that is embodied in Henri Labrouste's Bibliothèque Ste.-Geneviève in Paris (Fig. 177). It is an attempt to express structural functions by means of design; and like Labrouste's work, that of Richardson was misunderstood in its own time by being considered nothing more than another historical revival. So long as architecture was evaluated in terms of sentimental and literary associative ideas and conceived in historical patterns, there could be no understanding of it as an art involving formal values. This was realized by the German Karl Friedrich von Schinkel (1781-1841), one of the few sound architectural theorists of the early nineteenth century, when he wrote in 1824: "It would be a sorry thing for architecture and it would not deserve its rank in the circle of the other arts, if all the individual parts developed in ancient times—such as the orders of columns and the kinds of mouldings—were filed away, and nothing were left to imagination but to make some new combination of these ready-made forms. A scanty matter for reason!" And he continues further to state that only by using the "new technical inventions" of the Industrial Revolution which was reorienting the whole trend of western culture could the architect gain for himself a place as the interpreter of that culture by creating a style appropriate to it. Not the least significant implication of this statement is its recognition of the principle that style must grow from structural rather than aesthetic considerations. The soundness of Schinkel's reasoning is proved by the fact that when a new and modern mode of architectural thinking ultimately appeared, it came after glass and metal, industrialism's typical contributions to construction, had finally been understood and mastered by architects.

In many ways, the more efficient production of iron was the foundation of modern industrial manufacturing methods, and from early in the nineteenth century its use as a structural medium was common. Between 1843 and 1850, Labrouste covered the reading room of the Bibliothèque Ste.-Geneviève with barrel vaults resting on cast-iron columns and arches (Fig. 177), and a few years later used similar domes over the reading room of the Bibliothèque Nationale, also in Paris. In the United States, the dome Thomas U. Walter designed for the enlarged National Capitol in Washington, D.C. (Fig. 190), was built of this material. In 1848 James Bogardus developed a method of prefabricating cast-iron columns and arches for use as an adjunct to or instead of masonry walls. It was extensively employed in commercial structures between 1850 and 1880, particularly important examples being the A. T. Stewart Store, later Wanamaker's, and Harper &

Brothers' first building, both in New York though no longer standing. In all these cases, iron was used simply as a substitute for masonry, with no realization of its inherent formal characteristics and potentialities; Labrouste's structural columns have Corinthian shafts and capitals, the front of the Harper building was in the "Venetian Renaissance" style, and the Capitol dome was given the texture and color of stone by artificial means.

In contrast to the tendency of architects to think of the iron forms they designed only in historical patterns, men in other fields used iron in a more straightforward way; to some degree, the later path of architecture was prepared by engineers and builders whose work made no pretense to conscious formal character. An example is the *Crystal Palace* (Fig. 196), built in London for the Great Exhibition of 1851 by Joseph Paxton (1801-1865); originally in Hyde Park, it was taken down after the Exhibition and rebuilt at

FIG. 196. London. Paxton, Crystal Palace (1850-1851).

Sydenham in 1854, where it stood until its destruction by fire in 1936. Paxton, a greenhouse designer, had had considerable experience in using iron and glass for greenhouses before he built the Crystal Palace; it resembled a gigantic nursery more than anything else. A framework of cast-iron beams and columns in the form of a long barrel-vaulted rectangle with transepts at the ends and in the center furnished the support for an enclosing membrane of glass constituting the

FIG. 197.   New York.   Washington Roebling,
Brooklyn Bridge (1871-1883).

side walls and the fabric of the vaults above. No applied decoration marred the simple clarity of the external surfaces; and even though the interior iron beams were decked out with classical decorative motives, the scale of the structure was such that these counted for only little in the effect. The effect was essentially that of a great volume of space, defined by flat and curving planes of glass that were effectively weightless in character and whose sole function was to define the space they enclosed. This ideal became conscious in architectural thought after the First World War but in the Crystal Palace it was only incidental to an inexpensive yet spectacular way of using materials whose potential was unperceived by most architects of the time.

The bridge-building engineers of the nineteenth century were others who recognized the structural possibilities of iron and used it effectively. A cast-iron bridge with a span of 100 feet was built across the Severn River at Coalbrook-

dale in Wales in 1779, and even longer suspension bridges of iron chains and cables were built in the United States and Europe in the early nineteenth century. The perfection of cheap processes of producing steel—the Bessemer in 1855, and the Siemens open-hearth in 1862—was particularly important in this field, for the greater structural flexibility of steel over iron was a valuable asset in the construction of such a masterpiece of engineering as the *Brooklyn Bridge* (Fig. 197). Designed by Washington Roebling (1837-1926)—his father John had been a pioneer in the field earlier in the century—and built between 1871 and 1883, the Brooklyn Bridge is an outstanding example of an edifice with considerable formal character but built for inherently practical reasons and in such a way that they would be most effectively realized. The roadway is supported by great steel cables which hang from the granite piers in curves that are planned to realize the tensile strength of the metal to the utmost. Upon this the stability of the bridge depends and this is what gives character to the design; the form of the bridge was arrived at by solving the functional and structural problems involved with maximum efficiency, the only concession to contemporary "Gothic" ideals of architectural beauty being the pointed arches of the granite piers. These piers are necessarily massive and the contrast between their solid bulk and the delicate tracery of the steel webs they support is another factor that contributes to the formal distinction of the structure. The steelwork itself is devoid of ornament; nothing detracts from the straightforward simplicity of its logical and rational forms. This is the quality that most sharply distinguishes the products of late nineteenth-century engineering from architecture contemporary with it (cf. Fig. 178).

Practical necessity and the structural flexibility of iron and steel explain the rapid adoption and successful use of these new mediums by nineteenth-century engineers long before their architectural contemporaries used them. Eventually, however, preoccupation with formal design alone and obliviousness to structural considerations were no longer possible for architects; the pressure of practical needs forced them to make more than superficial use of the new structural materials. This was one of the consequences of the great demand for commercial buildings in the United States created by the industrial expansion after the Civil War. Chicago was the laboratory for the building experiments that eventually led to the first use of steel in formally creative design. The fire of 1871 had destroyed practically the entire commercial district and created a situation in which the general trend toward expansion was given particular emphasis by the immediate need for new buildings. Practical necessity and supposedly greater convenience in communication were also factors in the concentration of these new buildings in a relatively limited area—the Loop in Chicago, and, although the immediate necessity was not so great, in New York as well, in the financial district in lower Manhattan. One consequence of this concentration in rather limited areas was

an immediate and considerable increase in land costs which made it highly desirable commercially that the buildings erected there should have maximum space. This is why tall commercial buildings or skyscrapers came into existence, for lateral expansion of low buildings to gain needed space was of course not feasible because of the cost of the land required for this purpose. These circumstances were peculiarly American. It was in solving the problems, both structural and formal, created by the skyscraper, that steel played its first important part in architecture, giving to developments in this country a quite different character from that of contemporary work in Europe where none of these conditions were present.

Some of the first tall commercial buildings in the United States were of masonry, but stone and brick could not be used as efficiently as steel in the skyscraper for reasons that are indicated graphically in the comparative models in Fig. 198. In a masonry building, shown in the model at the right of the illustration, the walls support the internal structure of the floors and their own weight as well. In order to make the building taller, the walls would have to be made thicker at the base; for the increase in their weight attendant upon their increased height would place the lower parts under greater compression, and they would tend to buckle outward unless made thicker. This thickening gives the walls the shape of a rather tall and thin pyramid in section; it also reduces the useful space on the ground floors quite considerably and also raises the problem of natural illumination, because windows in such a wall cannot admit as much light as openings of the same size in a thinner one. A combination of masonry and metal supporting members, shown in the center model, removes these disadvantages to some extent and permits a somewhat greater height, but many of the drawbacks of all masonry construction still remain.

The model at the left represents a building supported entirely by a steel framework. In such a building, the total area in the plan is available for use from the ground floor to the top, except for the negligible space taken up by the relatively slight supporting members. These are vertical

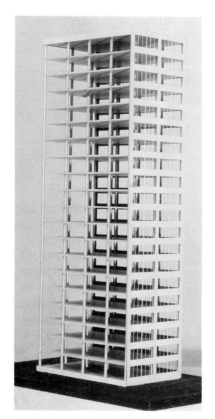

FIG. 198.   Structural Skyscraper Models.

steel beams which sustain the entire weight of the structure, including the walls which do not have to be even self-supporting because they are suspended from the outer ends of the horizontal floor beams (cf. Fig. 3). In principle, the walls serve only as a screen or membrane to define the enclosed space that is the building and separate it from that outside. This method of construction for a commercial building has many advantages. There is practically no limit to its height. The floor area from bottom to top is uniform. Interior illumination by natural light is much facilitated because the entire space between the supporting members can be opened out if desired, whereas in a masonry building the size of the windows must depend upon the relative importance of the wall as a means of support at a given place.

Steel was not used only in the structural beams of the skyscraper. As long cables, it was employed in the elevators so essential to the skyscraper. Obviously even a ten-story building requires some means of vertical locomotion other than human legs and flights of steps. The first office building with an elevator in the United States was built in 1871; from then on, the development of the elevator coincided with that of the skyscraper. Another problem of skyscraper construction that had to be solved was protecting the metal skeleton from deterioration by the elements and destruction by fire. Such early skyscrapers as the Home Life Insurance Building in Chicago, built by William LeBaron Jenney in 1884, and the Tacoma Building, built in 1887 by Holabird and Roche, also in Chicago, had steel skeletons sheathed with masonry in

forms reminiscent of Richardson's Romanesque. Later, terra cotta and concrete were used
for this purpose; the latter material, reinforced
with steel beams, was also used for floors. These
and similar materials are the structural elements
in modern architecture; to them should be
added plate glass which like steel first came into
commercial production in the last half of the
nineteenth century.

New constructive principles and materials
required an appropriate style. The importance
of this factor in architectural design will be made
clear by reference to some of the nineteenth-
century buildings already considered. The Marshall Field Building (Fig. 195) is obviously a
stone structure. Everything in the design points
to that fact—proportions, wall and window
membering, relation of solids to voids. The
Brooklyn Bridge (Fig. 197), on the other hand,
would be impossible in any medium other than
one with the tensile strength of steel, for the
outstanding element in its design is the great
catenary curve of the cables. In each case, the
design is functional as expressing the medium of
construction. This is not true of a building like
the Bibliothèque Ste.-Geneviève, whose exterior (Fig. 176) gives no hint of the iron and
glass vaults of the interior (Fig. 177). It stands to
reason that the historical styles are fundamentally inappropriate to buildings of steel, for their
forms are stone, wood, plaster, or simple concrete as distinguished from modern ferro-
concrete. This fact was apparently not realized
by most of the architects of the period.

The name of one man stands out in the
history of late nineteenth-century American
architecture as an exception to the last statement
in the preceding paragraph. Louis Henry Sullivan (1856-1924) was the first American architect
to undertake consciously the development of an
architectural style based on modern methods and
materials of construction. His aims are summed
up in the phrase "Form follows Function." This
principle was the result of Sullivan's observation that the great styles of the past were developed by giving expression to the purpose for
which a building was intended, the construction
method involved, and the material of which it

was built. Sullivan planned to apply the same
principle to the design of the tall, steel-framed
modern office building. Since obviously a
prototype for such a building did not exist in the
past, its style had to be developed according to a
rule which would be, in the words of Sullivan's
teacher, "so broad as to admit of no exceptions."

The realization of Sullivan's ideal was the
Wainwright Building (Fig. 199) in St. Louis,
built in 1890-1891. As a modern structure it
has no relationship to the past, in either function
or form; hence there is no suggestion of any
historical style. Its stability lies in its steel skeleton;
this is indicated by the protective vertical strips
so slender that they are obviously incapable of
supporting anything. The walls are reduced to
mere panels under the windows; they bear no
weight, for they are only screens separating interior from exterior space. Their nonstructural
function is indicated by delicate ornament of a
type individual to Sullivan and bearing no resemblance to that of any other architect or style.
The slender brick piers serve not only the practical
function of protecting the steel frame of the
building but the visual one of creating a vertical
effect which accentuates the loftiness of the
structure. This is the embodiment of another
element of Sullivan's architectural creed. Since
the modern office building is necessarily tall,
everything in the design should further the
impression of tallness. According to Sullivan,
the basic idea of masonry construction, the
superimposition of masses, is replaced in steel
construction by the principle of vertical continuity in consequence of which the building
becomes "a proud and soaring thing" and
possesses in its own way Sir Henry Wotton's
"condition" of "Delight."

Sullivan's formula was not limited to tall
office buildings. The *Schlesinger-Mayer Building*
(Fig. 200) in Chicago, now the Carson, Pirie,
Scott store, was built between 1899 and 1904,
with an addition in 1906. An unhappy alteration of
the top story was made in 1948 but is not shown
in the illustration. Instead of being vertical like the
Wainwright Building, the Schlesinger-Mayer
Building is predominantly horizontal, more in
keeping with the function of a department

FIG. 199. St. Louis. Adler and Sullivan, Wainwright Building
(1890–1891).

store, which requires large flat areas rather than the cubical volumes of an office building. The wide windows separated by narrow terra-cotta strips are admirably expressive of the open steel framework and also directly contribute to the efficiency of the building. Only in the lower stories is the clean-cut simplicity of the design somewhat obscured by the florid ornament that was at once Sullivan's personal delight and architectural weakness. In many of his buildings, particularly the later ones, the applied decoration is overinsistent. Although undeniably beautiful in itself, it tends to detract from the architectonic character of the designs. In this respect, Sullivan yielded to the idea so dear to the romantic mind, the expression of individuality, even though by so doing he violated the principles of an art which should be abstractly impersonal above all else.

It was this characteristic of his temperament the prevented Sullivan from having an influence on American architecture proportionate to his achievement. He did not give a full account of the social stewardship which is part of the architect's duty. That he realized this obligation and its importance is obvious in his writings. But his romantic background made him believe that the right to express his own individuality was even more important, and as a result, he was denied the recognition due a comprehensive architectural expression of the realities of modern life. In this respect he differed from Richardson who, had he lived longer, would undoubtedly have succeeded in making his style intelligible to the country at large. Sullivan, on the other hand, attempted to break finally and conclusively with all that had gone before. In refusing to accept anything of the past he deprived his own artistic creed of foundation. The conflict in Sullivan's nature is reflected in his realization that the tall office building is an anti-social form, creating congestion and chaos, a realization which he attempted to rationalize in his statement that a skyscraper should be a "proud and soaring thing." This was a romantic concept which even his own broad formula could not justify. The purpose of height in a skyscraper is not spiritual as it is in a Gothic

cathedral. Rather it is to increase commercial value, as an advertisement in structures like the Woolworth and Empire State Buildings, by providing more rentable space, or in the augmented efficiency resulting from centralizing many diverse activities under a single roof. In Sullivan's own buildings, the vertical idea he championed is not carried through consistently; witness the cornice of the Wainwright Building and the contradiction between the horizontal lines of the first two stories and the vertical ones above.

Sullivan's greatness is not to be found entirely in his buildings or his expressed theories. Rather it lies in his exemplification of the architect's obligation to consider his art as a

FIG. 200. Chicago. Sullivan, Schlesinger-Mayer Building (now Carson, Pirie, Scott & Co.), (1899-1904).

social manifestation, expressing the forces at work in society with the same clarity that characterized the work of Roebling and his fellow engineers. Sullivan stated that the architect should approach his work with the directness, simplicity, and singleness of purpose that unwittingly made contemporary engineering projects a source of aesthetic delight. To achieve this, the whole meaningless panoply of the forms of older cultures must be discarded, since they were the creation of social complexes wholly unlike existent ones; the problem of architectural style must be worked out anew. That Sullivan did not fully attain this goal himself detracts nothing either from its significance or from his own. His temperamental incapacity to give convincing form to his lofty conceptions was responsible for his personal tragedy in seeing the very principles he condemned exalted in the buildings of the eclectic movement, but the ideals for which he strove were destined to live in the works of his student and one-time assistant, Frank Lloyd Wright.

Before considering Wright's contribution to American architecture, the fate of Sullivan's idea must be discussed. His kinship with Richardson has already been pointed out. The greatness of both lies in their thesis that architecture is an art of ideas, not of formulas. Its forms must be not symbols of past cultures but expressive of the civilization that creates them. In the last decade of the nineteenth century, this truth which both Richardson and Sullivan had proclaimed was completely obscured by the wave of eclecticism that swept over the United States following the popular success of the principal buildings of the Columbian Exposition of 1893 in Chicago. They were designed, with one exception, by architects trained at the École des Beaux-Arts in Paris; the structures themselves were in the classic tradition as interpreted by the academic French school.

The effect of the gleaming white façades that embodied the classic formulas was immediate and powerful. Their plaster columns and arches had an obvious attractiveness quite different from the austere dignity of the Marshall Field Building and the early steel buildings in

Chicago. That this charm was superficial in contrast to the sturdy honesty of Richardson's work and the other functional buildings was not appreciated. The one exception to the spurious stucco and plaster façades with their semblance of stone was Louis Sullivan's Transportation Building. Its design was a frank statement of the impermanent materials of which it was constructed, in contrast to the seemingly permanent classic and Renaissance façades on every side. The immediate and popular reaction to these architectural pretensions is further evidence of the lack of artistic tradition in the background of America in the '90's. Many European critics perceived at once the strength and vitality of Sullivan's building at the Exposition and of many commercial buildings erected in Chicago and elsewhere in the preceding decade, but were disappointed with the majority of the structures at the Exposition which they rightly observed were the sort of thing being done better in Europe. Popular American judgment was then incapable of following them. The architects who influenced and catered to public taste in the early decades of the twentieth century in this country overlooked entirely the creative reintegration of construction and design in the work of Richardson and Sullivan, and continued the sterile tradition of historical eclecticism with its emphasis on superficial attractiveness at the cost of sound architectonic quality.

In the eclectic movement of the late nineteenth and early twentieth centuries in the United States, all the historical styles were considered available to the architect in designing a cloak for the steel frames that were in common use by that time. There are two general categories, the classic including Renaissance styles, and the mediaeval. The classic is best represented by the work of McKim, Mead, and White. Both McKim and White had been trained at the Beaux-Arts and in Richardson's office in Boston. Their first works date from about 1880 and have something of Richardson's sturdy ruggedness, but a break with this style appeared in 1888 in the design for the Boston Public Library. It was based on Labrouste's Bibliothèque Ste.-Geneviève (Fig. 176), with some modifications suggested by Early Renaissance Italian types. Largely because of the influence of this firm, the classic idiom was chosen for the buildings of the Columbian Exposition. The fame achieved by their own designs brought them commissions for many important buildings in the East during the first decade of the twentieth century. These include the New York Municipal Building, many of the Columbia University

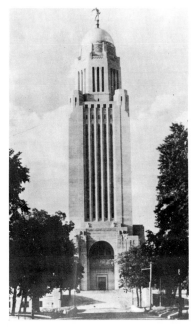

FIG. 201. Lincoln. Goodhue, Nebraska State Capitol (1922-1926).

buildings, and the Pennsylvania Railroad Station in New York City, whose Grand Concourse, originally an almost verbatim transcription of the great hall of the Baths of Caracalla in Rome (cf. Fig. 56), is considered their finest work.

Foremost among the adherents of the mediaeval style in the eclectic movement was the firm of Cram, Goodhue and Ferguson. Their output consisted principally of churches and college buildings—St. Thomas in New York and the First Baptist Church in Pittsburgh, the buildings at West Point and a number at

Princeton among others. The firm was dissolved in 1914, Cram and Ferguson continuing to produce mediaeval designs. Goodhue developed a much more individual style that reached its climax in the magnificent *Nebraska State Capitol* (Fig. 201) in Lincoln, which, finished in 1926, broke with the classic form used for such structures ever since the erection of the National Capitol.

The lack of connection between form and function that is an inevitable corollary of eclecticism appears in its most exaggerated form in the skyscraper. When the classic eclectics attempted to adapt their chosen forms to the tall building, they apparently overlooked the fact that the classic styles are essentially horizontal in effect. To solve this paradox, they generally regarded the skyscraper as comparable to a column with base, shaft, and capital. The chief objection is the unsatisfactory proportions that usually result. Thus in the New York Municipal Building by McKim, Mead, and White, for all the undeniable beauty of the details, the final effect is superimposed masonry forms with little or no expression of the steel skeleton.

For an obvious reason, the Gothic style seems more appropriate to the skyscraper than the classic. Vertical accents predominate in both. This coincidence was responsible for the immediate success of the *Woolworth Building* (Fig. 202) in New York by Cass Gilbert (1859-1934), erected between 1910 and 1913. From a distance it is not unimpressive. The mass is imposing and the relationship of tower and base well conceived. Furthermore, the steel framework is clearly expressed by the long, unbroken lines of the terra-cotta sheath, particularly from the rear. But even in the "Gothic" Woolworth Building, there is a paradox in the blossoming-out of the hard metallic vertical lines into a frosting of pinnacles, pointed arches, and flying buttresses. These are all intrinsically stone forms, employed by the Gothic builder to emphasize the vertical elements in his design to be sure, but primarily for structural reasons. In the Woolworth Building, they are not used for structural reasons at all; the strains in the steel framework are not lateral thrusts but forces of

FIG. 202. New York. Gilbert,
Woolworth Building
(1910-1913).

tension and compression. Furthermore, the Gothic quality of the Woolworth Building, in addition to involving superficial ornament without structural justification, not only does not express the function of the structure but interferes with it, because the arched cornices cut off practically all the exterior illumination of the offices immediately behind them.

The limitation of eclecticism as a guiding principle lies in the failure of its exponents to realize that architecture is an art of ideas and not merely of forms. Their methods bespeak their inability to give adequate expression to the many-sided character of modern life. Their concept of life was fundamentally static, for there can be no organic growth in an art which deliberately turns to the dead symbols of past cultures instead of creating its own forms of expression. Eclecticism is merely another aspect

of the romantic desire, in minds overwhelmed by the complexity of contemporary thought, to escape from the reality of the living present into a world of moribund beauty. Its popularity early in the twentieth century emphasizes the lack of tradition in the American background. Eclectic forms were stamped with academic approval and thereby gained a certain authority which was reinforced by their undeniably sensational qualities. To minds as yet uneducated to the more abstract elements of articulated mass, beauty of proportion, and the like by which Richardson and Sullivan expressed their ideas, these forms passed muster as great architecture.

The Roman temples, Italian campaniles, and Gothic cathedrals with which eclecticism clothed the American scene are only one aspect of early twentieth-century architecture in this country. The reverse of these polished façades is the slums which grew up in cities that expanded without plan or motive other than financial profit. Only recently has any attempt been made to relieve the shocking conditions in these regions. The majority of the flats were of the "dumbbell" type, so called from their shape; their plan made no provision for privacy, light, and air, but was highly successful in producing maximum income from the smallest possible amount of real estate. It is a devastating commentary on the lack of interest in low-cost housing in the United States that "old-law" tenements of this type were permitted to operate until very recently. Like the congestion in the modern urban commercial districts which they rivaled and often surpassed, slum conditions were a direct outcome of approaching human shelter solely from the point of view of maximum financial return on investment. To Sullivan's credit, he was concious in some measure of the consequences of such a point of view.

Even in more self-conciously pretentious examples, there is little distinction in the domestic architecture of the United States in the early twentieth century. The carefully polished façades of eclectically styled houses whose interiors were calculated to make the most impressive display of furniture and accessories differ from the tall, spiky exteriors of the earlier Victorian style with its badly planned and gloomy rooms only in being more sophisticated. A significant exception to this concept of the house, however, is provided in the designs of Frank Lloyd Wright (1867-1959), which as mentioned before, continued Louis Sullivan's fundamental ideas and principles. It was in Sullivan's office, in fact, that Wright was prepared to achieve what he did in domestic design, for otherwise his training consisted of little but two years in the engineering school of the University of Wisconsin. But it was Sullivan's logical and reasoned understanding of the commercial building as an architectural symbol of one aspect of modern life, combined with an inherently romantic antagonism to the lack of organic relationship between the Victorian house, with its artificially contrived and false monumentality, and the low-lying landscape of the midwestern prairies, that was the underlying factor in shaping the style that embodied Wright's expressive aim. This aim was to achieve a fusion of house and setting, to weld architecture and landscape into an organically integrated whole that symbolized man's inherent oneness with nature. The "Prairie House" was the result.

The *Robie House* (Figs. 203, 204) built on Woodlawn Avenue in Chicago, in 1909, represents the highest development of the "Prairie House." It is long and low, the horizontal lines echoing the level surroundings; vertical accents in the chimney and window frames give the necessary sense of support. The eaves and porches are wide; the porch roofs are cantilevered from

FIG. 203. Chicago. Wright, Robie House (1909).

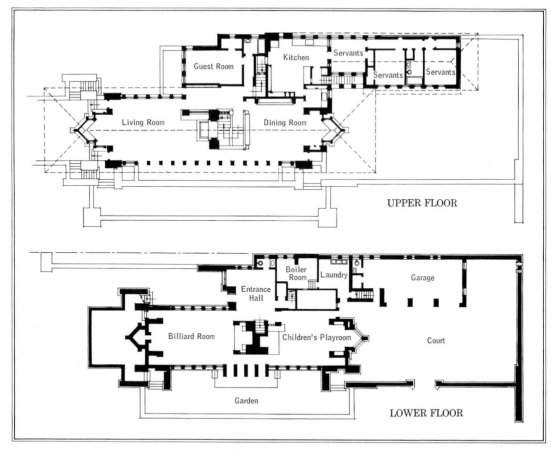

Guest Room — Kitchen — Servants — Servants — Servants

Living Room — Dining Room

UPPER FLOOR

Boiler Room — Laundry — Garage

Entrance Hall

Billiard Room — Children's Playroom — Court

Garden

LOWER FLOOR

FIG. 204.   Chicago.   Robie House, Plan.

the frame of the house to afford the openness so essential to comfort in the summer with the minimum of obstruction. The windows are grouped in long rows instead of being treated as isolated units, thus establishing an organic relationship between exterior and interior space. The plan (Fig. 204) reveals the most original treatment of enclosed space since the Gothic. Instead of considering the interior as a series of blocks isolated by walls, Wright treats it as a single elastic volume. One space flows into another, unobstructed by walls or doors and focused around deep fireplaces, thus integrating the interior and the exterior, where the design centers around the chimney stack. The living room and dining room merge into each other, separated only by the chimney stack and the staircase. The service quarters are isolated and the privacy of the bedrooms is assured by walls that separate them from the rest of the house. The banded windows and broad openings leading to the courts and terraces emphasize the integral unity of interior and exterior. Decorative effects come from contrasting structural materials and the fine proportions of the building, there being practically no applied ornament. In designing the "Prairie House," Wright faced squarely the problem of modern living and solved it with imagination and intelligence. The result is another demonstration of the basic soundness of Sullivan's creed that Form follows Function. Without concession to previous styles. Wright developed a style of his own that could be applied to many different types of buildings.

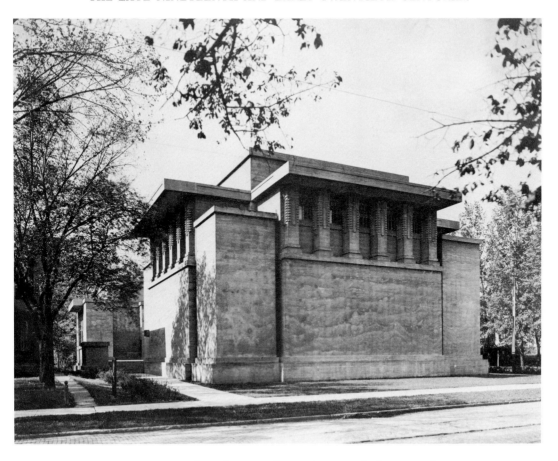

FIG. 205.   Oak Park.   Wright, Unity Temple (1905-1906).

Incidentally, although his approach to the problem of the modern house was primarily artistic, his solution of it revealed a thorough awareness of the social significance of good architecture. In providing for the necessities of modern life by insisting upon adequate light and air and free movement from interior to exterior, Wright incorporated in his designs the things which are the right of every human being.

In these early years of his career, Wright designed other types of buildings than houses. In the Administration Building of the Larkin Soap Factory in Buffalo, built in 1904, he created an architectural embodiment of the modern commercial spirit utterly different from any earlier structure. *Unity Temple* (Fig. 205) in Oak Park, Ill., built in 1905-1906, was an in-novation in construction as well as in design. It is of concrete poured in moulds and the structure is thus a huge articulated monolith. The flat roof is supported by four hollow piers which also serve as heating ducts. As befits a building for a modern sect, the form of the church is unrelated to any past style, yet its provision for the needs of the spirit is manifest in the solid outside walls that protect the interior from all disturbance. Entirely different in purpose and form were Wright's designs for the Midway Gardens, an enormous recreation center in Chicago, and for the Imperial Hotel in Tokyo. The latter was a triumph of modern construction. It is supported by piles of reinforced concrete that almost literally float in and on the soft mud that underlies the entire city. These piles were so designed

FIG. 206. Pasadena. Greene and Greene, Gamble House (1908-1909).

as to give the building a flexible and elastic foundation. Because of this the Imperial Hotel survived the earthquake of 1923 in Tokyo, which destroyed practically all other buildings by foreign architects in the city.

Apart from the work of Frank Lloyd Wright, the only considerable amount of significant nontraditional design in the United States during the first quarter of the twentieth century is that of the Greene brothers, Charles S. (1868-1957) and Henry M. (1870-1958). Having neither variety in type, since it is entirely domestic, nor the geographical distribution, since it is all in California, principally in Pasadena, their work has not been given the attention it deserves until comparatively recently. The *Gamble House* (Fig. 206), built in 1908-1909, is one of their most individual and characteristic conceptions. Constructed of timber, it continues the late nineteenth-century tradition of the imaginative handling of wood seen in such earlier buildings as Richardson's Stoughton House (Fig. 194). The low-pitched roofs and extended eaves are not unlike those of Wright's "Prairie Houses" in some ways (Fig. 203), but the organization in plan and the distribution of mass are less formal and the effect as a whole is quite individual in its picturesque openness. These architects also shared Wright's feeling about the necessity for fine craftsmanship; hence their interiors often have an elegance that even Wright's seldom match.

In Europe, progressive architecture of the late nineteenth and early twentieth centuries follows lines comparable in general to those in the United States, but the sharp clash of ideals in the American scene is missing in Europe. There no architect attempted to break sharply with the past as Sullivan and Wright did in America. The rationalism of certain architects, notably Karl Friedrich von Schinkel and Henri Labrouste, in the early nineteenth century has been mentioned. This rationalism, based on traditional forms, continued through the century as a latent force that produced significant results toward its close. Iron and steel were employed in engineering projects as in America, notably in the buildings of the Paris Exposition in 1889. A sharp line was drawn between the use of these materials in such works and their use in the more consciously aesthetic manner of men like Labrouste. In the purely architectural examples of iron and steel construction, eclectic methods persist; at the same time, however, there are occasional efforts to establish new styles by developing new ornamental motives, as in the short-lived *Art Nouveau* (cf. Fig. 644). A more essentially modern and functional style begins to develop early in the twentieth century, based on the use of steel and reinforced concrete. Its most significant examples are in Holland, France, Germany, and the Scandinavian countries.

The *Wertheim Store* (Fig. 207), in Berlin is an early example of functional design in Europe. Completed by Alfred Messel in 1904, it is a large, irregularly rectangular structure of blocks around a number of courts. Some of these courts are open to provide light for the interior; others are roofed over and have several levels of galleries. There are many Gothic reminiscences in the exterior design, evidence of a strong regional tradition. The mediaeval forms are a decorative sheath for the steel framework, which they express rather effectively in the long vistas of the unbroken street façades. In their compliance with mediaeval usage of detail, proportion, and effect, they contrast with the more arbitrary methods used in the Woolworth Building. Within, the steel construction is exposed and unobscured by decoration as in the somewhat earlier Bon Marché and Printemps stores in Paris.

The similarity in purpose of Messel's store and Sullivan's Schlesinger-Mayer Building in Chicago (Fig. 200) suggests a comparison between them. Of the two, that by the American is more direct in its statement of function and construction. Even today it is a modern building, whereas the Wertheim Store is a typical example

of a past style. This does not detract from its importance. Had Sullivan revealed more sympathy for tradition, his design would doubtless have had greater influence. As it is, it stood alone in the American development; its significance was not appreciated until much later. In contrast, Messel's building became a model almost at once; its influence is evident during the entire decade after its construction. The Tietz Store by Olbrich, built in Düsseldorf in 1908, is an example.

In contrast to Messel, who used traditional forms in the Wertheim Store as decorative adjuncts to modern construction, Peter Behrens (1868-1940) evolved a style based on the use of steel, glass, and concrete. In 1909 he was appointed architect of the A. E. G., the General Electric Company in Germany, and the many buildings he designed for it constitute the most important single body of modern construction in Europe before the First World War. Almost all are factories and power plants; hence practical

FIG. 207. Berlin. Messel, Wertheim Store (1896-1904).

243

efficiency was understandably a major consideration (Fig. 208). Being utilitarian, applied decoration would have been not only costly but inappropriate. The materials are steel, glass, and poured concrete. Color is important in the effect—gray-green in the slate roofs and windows, with purplish accents in the stone trim of the doors. The construction is frankly expressed throughout and is as modern as the purpose of the building, which attains monumentality through its proportions and vigorous outlines. Perhaps the most striking feature is the way the texture and color of the materials are utilized for decoration. Not only the expense of applied ornament is thus avoided but also the diluting effect of such ornament on the clean-cut lines and masses. It is not without significance that in Europe such utilitarian buildings as these were designed by architects. In America, the nearest approach to them is the great grain elevators of the Middle West, whose anonymous designers created better than they knew. Prosaic as they are in function and appearance, the elevators have an element of honesty that is all too often lacking in the more pretentious houses and offices of their owners.

One point that might be raised against Behrens' work is his use of modern building materials to achieve rather traditionalistic effects. The legitimate effect of glass and steel in construction is openness, volumes of space enclosed by a weightless membrane. In Behren's designs, however, these materials are employed to secure effects of mass through the treatment of surface and outline. In this type of effect, none of Behrens' buildings can compete with the *Stuttgart Railway Station* (Fig. 209) by Paul Bonatz (1877-1951), begun in 1913 and finished in 1927. There is a Romanesque air about it that is due entirely to the material employed and the way it is used, rather than to any specifically Romanesque ornament. In this, it is not unlike Richardson's Marshall Field Building in Chicago (Fig. 195). The use of stone is traditional and, in regions where it is abundant, more rational than the use of steel and concrete. Because the building is stone, the predominant effect is of masses, well related to each other in form, outline, and surface texture. These qualities make the Stuttgart Station one of the finest European examples of traditionalistic architectural style in the early twentieth century. Its effects are perfectly logical for the material employed and owe nothing to past styles; in this it contrasts noticeably with the Wertheim Store. At the same time, it reveals, as does the Marshall Field Building, the possibility of applying traditional structural methods to modern problems without subsiding into sterile eclecticism.

The late nineteenth and early twentieth centuries are the period in which modern architecture was born. New ways of living, new building programs, new methods and materials of construction—all made their appearance at this time and stimulated the development of a new architectural style. Its nature is first suggested by the steel-framed skyscrapers of the '80's in Chicago from which it might be concluded that the most fundamental developments in modern building should be looked for in American architecture. Actually, the style that developed in Europe during this period had more significant immediate results. There the weight of tradition exercised a certain restraint; and while European architects were not so quick to seize upon the new methods and materials as the unencumbered Americans, that tradition also enabled them to avoid the difficulties that beset Sullivan and Wright. For the same reason, the eclecticism predominant in American architecture of the early

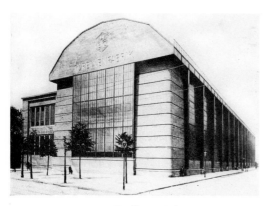

FIG. 208. Berlin. Behrens,
A. E. G. Turbine Factory (1909).

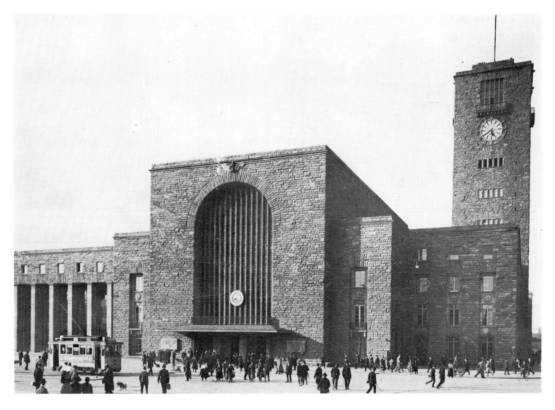

FIG. 209.   Stuttgart.   Bonatz, Railway Station (1913–1927).

twentieth century is present to a lesser degree in Europe. As pioneers, Sullivan and Wright paid the penalty of all innovators; only within the last decades has American architecture in general caught up to them. Thus although in the period under consideration no finer buildings were erected in Europe than Sullivan's Schlesinger-Mayer Building, the number of distinguished buildings was far less in America than in Germany, Holland, and France.

Detail of Fig. 227.

CHAPTER FOURTEEN

Architecture in the Twentieth Century

Architecture in the United States during the 1920's was predominantly eclectic, and the skyscraper attracted the most attention. When designed in classic style, it was treated according to the concept of a column, with base, shaft, and capital. When interpreted in mediaeval forms, the vertical accents of the steel frame were translated into Gothic idioms, as a rule, although other mediaeval styles were occasionally used. Of the 263 projects submitted in the competition sponsored in 1922 by the *Chicago Tribune*, 129 were classic and 74 mediaeval; the remainder were in a variety of nonspecific styles. First prize was awarded Hood and Howells' Gothic scheme, a tasteful adaptation of the Tour de Beurre of Rouen Cathedral (cf. Fig. 102).

Although the result of the competition seemingly indicated the unquestioned supremacy of eclecticism in American architecture after World War I, it is interesting to note that the most immediate influence of the ideas submitted was exerted not by the Hood and Howells building but by the design that won the second-place award for the Finnish architect, Eliel Saarinen (1873-1950). His design, a straight-forward statement of the tall steel-framed structure, had a few mediaeval overtones but was nonstylistic in comparison with the Gothic first-place award. One of the last articles Louis Sullivan wrote was an appreciation of this design as a lineal descendent of his own ideas, a relationship Saarinen acknowledged. That it was persuasive in proving the possibility of designing skyscrapers in nonhistorical style is clear in view of a number of later buildings—some by the same firm of Hood and Howells—like the American Radiator Building and the Daily News Building, both in New York City. The most publicized skyscrapers of the late '20's and early '30's are similarly indebted to Saarinen's Tribune Tower design—the Chrysler and Empire State Buildings, and the first buildings in the Rockefeller Center complex in New York (cf. Fig. 225).

Yet even as they were being built, a sky-scraper was rising in Philadelphia that proved to be a significant turning point in the history of the tall commercial building. The *Philadelphia Saving Fund Society Building* (Fig. 210) was designed by the American, George Howe (1886-1954), in collaboration with the Swiss, William Lescaze (b. 1896), and was finished in 1932. As Henry-Russell Hitchcock has pointed out, it represents a return to Sullivan's concept of the tall building as a great slab in comparison with the shaped towers in historical or non-historical forms that had risen in the '20's. But it departs from Sullivan's aesthetic in having horizontal rather than vertical accents. The aluminum strips on the sides and the elevator shaft do express the vertical elements in the structural frame, but the internal volumes are horizontal layers of space between the canti-

levered floors and these are expressed in the continuous banded windows. The exterior is thus a plane that defines a volume of organized and articulated space—a screen wall, rather than a massive bulk with penetrations. There is no applied ornament on the exterior, decorative effects being achieved by contrasting materials. The base is faced with polished granite slabs, the two stories above with limestone; the horizontal strips or spandrels between the windows are gray brick.

In comparison with the average American skyscraper, the Philadelphia Saving Fund Society Building exemplifies architecture as an art rather than as mere building. From the raw material of functional necessity, the architect developed a design having beauty of form and material that also effectively expresses the function and purpose of the structure. In contrast, the form of the traditional American skyscraper of the early twentieth century either has little to do with its function or, going to the other extreme, is determined by utilitarian considerations alone, with no concern for aesthetic character. In either case, the result is less than architecture.

The Philadelphia Saving Fund Society Building reflects an architectural style, developed in Europe in the '20's, that is often referred to as the International Style because of its general diffusion during that period. Its conception may be traced back to attempts of men like Behrens to develop an architectural vocabulary in terms of the new structural materials and in connection with new building types of the century. Among the earliest examples of the style, if not actually the first, is the factory designed by Walter Gropius for the Fagus Shoe Company at Alfeld a.d. Leine in Germany and built in 1909-1910; the character of this building is a direct consequence of the use of steel and glass and concrete as materials of construction.

It was after the First World War that the formal potentialities of these materials came to be generally realized in the characteristic qualities of the International Style, which are threefold. The first is emphasis on volume of space rather than on volume of mass as a basic principle.

FIG. 210.   Philadelphia.   Howe and Lescaze, Philadelphia Saving Fund
Society Building (1930–1932).

The second is regularity in spacing the elements of the design rather than spacing them symmetrically on either side of a principal axis as in most historical styles. The third is dependence of decorative effect on good proportion and the intrinsic qualities of the materials rather than on applied ornament. Each of these characteristics is a direct result of the new methods and materials of construction developed in the late nineteenth century. The first is a logical corollary of the steel framework that supports sheets of glass or opaque curtain walls whose primary function is the delimitation of space; an effect of mass or solidness would not be appropriate in a form having such a function. The second is also a result of the steel frame construction, for the vertical supports and the horizontal girders are spaced at equal distances in order to distribute the strains equally. In consequence, the skeleton has a basic and regular rhythm which should be expressed in the design of its sheath. The legitimacy of these two characteristics being admitted, the avoidance of applied ornament in the traditional sense is mandatory, for it would create an impression of mass and obscure the regular rhythm of the design. From this it follows that decoration must be intrinsic in the building itself—its general proportions, the elegance of its materials, and the technical perfection of the construction.

In the *Bauhaus* (Fig. 211) Walter Gropius (b. 1883), one of the creators and foremost exponents of the International Style, demonstrated the possibilities of a style based on modern structural methods and materials. The building was erected at Dessau in Germany in 1926 as the workshop of an art school that was organized to develop architectural forms and furnishings appropriate to the Machine Age (cf. Figs. 645, 646). The workshop was one of a group of buildings which also included a studio, classrooms, and an administrative office. In the design of the group as a whole, Gropius achieved an effective integration of the various units by means of fine proportions and appropriate treatment of materials. His thorough grasp of the nature of those materials made the design one of volumes of space rather than mass, for if the screening function of a wall is performed by a sheet of glass, an effect of mass will be not only inappropriate but a denial of the supporting function of the steel frame. The regularity characteristic of modern design is created on the long side by a rhythmic recurrence of accents indicating the piers, but is broken on the short side to express the different function of the entrance. As a form that is determined by functional requirement and attains aesthetic character in terms of the materials employed, the Bauhaus is as much an example of architectural style as the Parthenon or the Cathedral of Amiens. Furthermore, its avowed

FIG. 211. Dessau. The Bauhaus. Gropius, Machine Shop (1926).

purpose of applying Machine Age principles of efficiency to the house and its furnishings acknowledges the creative artist's obligation to society. The Bauhaus is not the only proof of Gropus' understanding of the sociological problems of modern architecture. In various low-cost housing projects he has applied his genius for organization to achieve results that are aesthetically fine as well as functionally efficient.

Another point of view than Gropius' but one that still embodies the principles of the International Style was held by the Franco-Swiss architect, Charles Édouard Jeanneret-Gris (b. 1888), known professionally as Le Corbusier. The formal element is dominant in his work; it takes precedence over construction, although he has made many contributions in that field as well. His most important early work was in the designing of houses and domestic architecture in general, and his concept of the house as a "machine for living" has been influential in establishing an ideological relationship between the idioms of the International Style and the machine culture of the twentieth century. But even in his own work this concept is subordinated to aesthetic considerations, for the structure is regarded as a work of art before it is anything else. The *Savoye Villa* (Fig. 212), built in 1929-1930 at Poissy-sur-Seine near Paris, is of

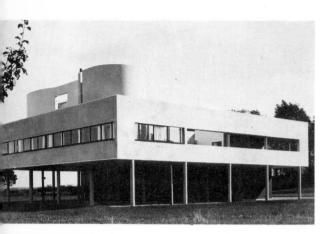

FIG. 212. Poissy-sur-Seine. Le Corbusier, Savoye Villa (1929-1930).

steel and concrete, the principal level being cantilevered out beyond the substructure and partially supported on unsheathed metal posts. Externally, this part of the house is symmetrical, but the regular spacing of the supporting members establishes the rhythm of the window openings. These are treated as continuous bands which stop short of the corners to state the function of the screen walls as planes defining the inner volume of space. Contrasting with the symmetrical and rectilinear form of this part of the house is the eccentric curvilinear pattern on the opposite side—a windshelter on the flat roof—a contrast heightened by the color scheme. The substructure, beneath the cantilevered projection, is dark green, the principal story is cream colored, and the windshelter is rose and blue. This color composition emphasizes functional distinctions between various parts of the structure, for the difference in the practical purpose of the main portion of the building and the accessory pleasantry of the windshelter on the terrace roof is clearly stated thereby; moreover, the patterns of form and color thus created are very similar in effect to those in much of the painting contemporary with the building. In this connection, it is significant that Le Corbusier is a painter as well as an architect, a fact which explains much of the character of his designs and his preoccupation with formal rather than structural matters.

Organization of interior space is as important architecturally as exterior design, and the concept of plan and furnishing developed in the International Style is closely allied to that observed in exteriors by Gropius and Le Corbusier. Concern for this aspect of architectural form is paramount in the works of Miës van der Rohe (b. 1888), who began his career in the office of Bruno Paul in Germany as a furniture designer, an experience that gave him the respect for fine craftsmanship and carefully wrought detail apparent in his treatment of the house as a whole. The living room and library of the *Tugendhat House* (Fig. 213) at Brno in Czechoslovakia, built in 1930, embody his concept of an interior. The two rooms are part of a single space volume, articulated but not divided by a

FIG. 213. Brno. Miës van der Rohe,
Tugendhat House (1930).

great slab of polished onyx that rises from floor to ceiling. The ceiling is supported by regularly spaced chromium steel beams, whose gleaming surfaces are part of a decorative scheme of contrasting colors and textures. What would ordinarily be walls are great sheets of plate glass that can be lowered below the floor level, thus permitting completely unobstructed passage from the room to the terrace overlooking the garden, This striking and effective relating of interior and exterior space expresses Miës' feeling that the outside of a building is really part of the interior and its design should be determined by internal arrangement rather than for external effect. It follows from this that he is aware of the necessity of defining and giving character to the inner space, which he does by emphasizing the quality and texture of luxurious materials. The windows can be screened, for example, by curtains of velvet woven in single pieces that extend their entire length. Polished surfaces of glass, metal,

and rare woods also contribute to an ensemble of great decorative distinction involving both structural elements and furniture. The chairs and tables were designed by Miës after long and careful experiments to determine maximum comfort combined with the finest aesthetic effect, an expression of his conviction that the artistic ideals essential to successful creative activity must be developed while the artist is learning good building.

"Without succumbing to an arid rationalism, the new architecture will be essentially utilitarian; but utilitarian without excluding aspirations of a superior order." Thus J. J. P. Oud (b. 1890), the outstanding figure in Dutch architecture after the the First World War, expressed his concept of modern architectural forms. The concept has peculiar validity coming from him, for it is based on his extensive experience and success in one of the most important and challenging fields of contemporary

FIG. 214. Hook of Holland. Oud, Workers' Houses
(1926).

architectecture—large-scale and low-cost housing. Appointed in 1918 as architect to the city of
Rotterdam, Oud worked largely in this field;
an outstanding example is the *Workers' Houses*
(Fig. 214) at the Hook of Holland, built in 1926.
They are of concrete and steel; and their design,
of great distinction, is possible only in those
materials. Regularity of accent comes from the
windows in long blocks with balconies and flat
roofs, giving the ensemble a horizontal effect.
The round pavilions at the ends of the principal
blocks have a functionally justified different
effect, for they are shops through whose plate-
glass walls can be seen the structural steel
members supporting the upper floor. Color is
skillfully used as a decorative adjunct to the well-
proportioned planes and solids of the exterior.

The distinction of Oud's Workers' Houses
is due not solely to well-organized plans, as is
true of much of Gropius' work, nor to formal
and decorative refinements, as is that of Le
Corbusier and Miës van der Rohe (Figs. 212,
213). Rather it derives from Oud's accepting a
program which provided little opportunity for
anything but plan and construction and subject-
ing it to a realistic and imaginative aesthetic
discipline. Thus the "aspirations of a superior
order" in the above quotation led to his achieving
an apparently simple yet eminently satisfactory
effect. What this meant for architecture in the

practical sense was shown in an exhibition of
low-cost housing at Stuttgart in 1927. Of the
many buildings submitted by leading architects
of the day, including Gropius, Le Corbusier,
and Miës van der Rohe, only two complied with
technical requirements within stipulated cost
limits without sacrificing formal character, one
being by Oud. What it meant for architecture as
an art is evident from the fact that in all European
low-cost housing in the '20's, no work is superior
to Oud's best work, little approaches it in quality,
and none better illustrates the architect's potential contribution to integrating the disparate
social forces of modern society.

The four architects just discussed were the
pioneers of the International Style as a coherent
architectural idiom in buildings of the '20's
largely in France, Germany, and Holland. Its
geographical diffusion was rapid, however; by
the end of the decade, the Scandinavian countries and Russia and even more distant regions
—the Orient, South America, and the United
States—had examples of it. The Philadelphia
Saving Fund Society Building (Fig. 210), for
instance, was an early International Style structure in America, and remains one of its most
successful skyscrapers. There were also important developments in England during the '30's.
Apart from a few isolated buildings of rather
indifferent character in the preceding decade,

there was nothing prophetic of the solid and constructive achievements following the formation in 1931 of the MARS Group (the initials stand for Modern Architectural Research) by some of the younger British architects for collective study and exchange of ideas. Of great significance, too, was the migration to England of a number of outstanding continental architects forced to leave their native countries for political reasons. Walter Gropius, Erich Mendelsohn, and Marcel Breuer all left Nazi-dominated Germany and went to England after 1933, where they continued work in the styles they had developed earlier.

Two examples of the International Style in English architecture in the '30's indicate both the extent to which the principles developed by the continental pioneers in the preceding decade were continued and the variations that were made by English protagonists. The *Penguin Pool* (Fig. 215) in Regent's Park Zoo in London was designed by a group of architects who practiced under the name Tecton; it was built in 1933-1935. Frankly intended to provide a setting for greater enjoyment of the birds' comical movements, the pool is an elongated oval, with curving ramps in the center on which the penguins solemnly parade. Having a relatively simple function, it has therefore been treated

FIG. 215. London. Regent's Park Zoo. Tecton, Penguin Pool (1933-1935).

more like a piece of abstract sculpture than anything else, an idea for which the concrete construction is admirably suited. Other buildings in the same zoo and also in the Dudley Zoo in London, the latter built in 1938, reveal a similar comprehension by the Tecton group of the possibilities of making the buildings expressive of the character of their exhibits, and have created a new tradition for this type of design and exhibition. Mention should also be made of the middle-class suburban apartment building called Highpoint on Highgate Hill, London, built by Tecton in 1935. The concrete building solves a difficult problem in urban housing and has considerable formal distinction.

An important contribution made by English architects to the International Style is the enlargement of the repertory of building materials. On the Continent glass and steel and concrete were used for the most part in the '20's. Although admirably suited to the abstract patterns of plane and surface and texture basic to the style, they also presented a problem of maintenance. The precise, machinelike forms of a design by Le Corbusier are seriously marred by ordinary and inevitable weathering; a building like the Savoye Villa (Fig. 212) must be kept in immaculate condition if its full effect is to be realized. The more traditional materials—stone and brick and wood—on the other hand, are often mellowed and made more interesting by weathering. A *House at Welwyn* (Fig. 216), designed by Eugen C. Kauffmann in 1939, shows how these materials can be used with the flexibility of plan and simplicity of form of the International Style. But the brick surfaces of the structure are in harmony with its simple natural setting, and the passage of time adds to rather than detracts from its character.

In 1936, the Minister of Education invited Le Corbusier to Brazil to advise on plans for the University of Rio de Janeiro. At the same time, he served as consultant for the building of the *Ministry of Education and Public Health* (Fig. 217), designed in 1937 by a group of architects led by Oscar Niemeyer, an associate of Corbusier's in earlier days; it was completed in 1943. Built of concrete, glass, and steel, the building is of

FIG. 216. Welwyn. Kauffmann, House (1939).

considerable size. One of its most striking features is the *brise-soleil* or projecting sunbreak on the west. It functions somewhat like a great Venetian blind, with movable slats or louvers that can be adjusted to give maximum protection from the heat and glare of the sun at all times. The sunbreak was developed by Le Corbusier for an office building in Algiers in 1933, and it has since been used extensively in tropical countries everywhere. Conceived originally as a practical device, it is no less effective in providing new varieties of pattern, texture, and even plasticity of form, contrasted with but related to the rhythmic order of the structural skeleton and the enclosing screen wall behind it.

Although the decade of the '30's was a depression period in the United States, there was a considerable amount of building in the International Style. Initially the work of Europeans or Americans using the style in a superficial way, by 1940 there was fairly consistent distinction. The acceptance of the style in the United States was in no small measure the result of the effective education of the public and architects alike. An exhibition of modern architecture, largely by the European pioneers of the International Style, was sponsored by the Museum of Modern Art in New York in 1932. Carefully organized and intelligently presented,

it was the first serious attempt to provide the American public with a critical analysis and evaluation of the style. Its immediate and pervasive influence made it a turning point in the history of American taste and of the understanding of architectural style.

No less important were the changes in architectural training and education that occurred in the latter part of the decade. Walter Gropius and Marcel Breuer were appointed to the Architecture Department of Harvard University in 1937, and Miës van der Rohe was made director of the Architectural Department at Illinois Institute of Technology in Chicago in 1939. Other contributions to a significant reorientation in American architectural education were made at Massachusetts Institute of Technology, and at Yale University under George Howe.

Growing public appreciation and increasing professional competence encouraged the innovations of the '30's in American architecture in spite of some obstacles. Obsolete building codes in the larger cities, for example, frequently made impossible the open plans and screen-wall enclosures basic to the style, a fact which accounts for the predominance of country houses, seaside summer homes, and the like as examples of the style during that decade. Another factor was the high cost of building methods which were unfamiliar to the average workman or discouraged by labor regulations. Moreover, the widely varying climatic conditions in the United States understandably led to regional variations rather than a single mode. Nonetheless, there is a consistent and frequently distinguished body of work in the International Style of the 1930's in this country.

California was the locale of developments that were of considerable interest, architecturally speaking, in the years preceding World War II. Several factors contributed to this, not the least important being the fact that for many years innovations were accepted there that would not have been accepted in other parts of the country. Even before World War I, as was said earlier, Charles S. Greene (1868-1957) and his brother Henry M. (1870-1958) were working in the Los Angeles area. Bernhard Maybeck

FIG. 217. Rio de Janeiro. Niemeyer and others, Ministry of Education and Health (1937-1943).

(1862-1957) worked in Fransciso. All three used local materials, notably redwood, in non-traditional designs that showed great freedom and considerable distinction (cf. Fig. 206). Irving Gill (1870-1936) and the Vienna-born R. M. Schindler (1890-1953) developed from different premises styles that invite comparison with the pioneering efforts of Europeans like Adolf Loos in the first decade of the twentieth century. The Lovell House built in Los Angeles by

Richard Neutra (b. 1892), an Austrian who came to the United States to work with Frank Lloyd Wright, was one of the first consistent examples of the International Style in this country, dating as it does from 1929.

It was more than novelty, however, which gave the principles of this style particular effectiveness in its development in California during the 1930's. The *Dunsmuir Flats* (Fig. 218), built in Los Angeles in 1939 by Gregory

FIG. 218.   Los Angeles.   Ain, Dunsmuir Flats (1939).

Ain (b. 1906), are a case in point. The lot on which the four units are built is restricted in size and has a pronounced slope, requiring a staggered plan. This the architect turned to good advantage in obtaining exposure on three sides, effectively secluded garden courts, and balconies from the bedrooms on the upper level that are completely screened from the adjoining units. All this is made possible by the use of wooden posts into which the glass is set directly. The plain, simple surfaces thus created emphasize volume of space rather than mass. Although the

Dunsmuir Flats are hardly suitable for any but the southern California climate, they well demonstrate the flexibility inherent in the concept of design they so successfully embody.

No less striking than the diffusion of the International Style in the United States after 1930, and possibly of even more artistic significance, is the work Frank Lloyd Wright continued to do. His "Prairie House" of the early twentieth century (cf. Figs. 203, 204) was a pioneer statement of basic architectural principles that was widely influential, particularly in planning; this is immediately apparent in the

International Style, which owes much to him in this respect. Unaccepted for the most part in his own country, in the little actual building he did immediately after the First World War Wright reveals a degree of creative imagination and sound thinking comparable to that in his earlier work. The *Millard House* (Fig. 219) in Pasadena Calif., built in 1923, differs in form from his earlier houses because it was planned for another climate and environment. The terrace roof and relatively small windows are as appropriate in California as the low gables and large openings of the Robie House are in its midwestern

FIG. 219.   Pasadena.   Wright, Millard House (1923).

FIG. 220.   Racine.   Wright, Johnson Wax Co.
Administration Building (1936-1939).

setting. There is still an effective relationship between house and site, however, and the same forthright treatment of structural material, concrete in this cases. Used in precast blocks whose surface patterns are formed by the moulds, the resulting ornament is integral in the material; a fine sense of texture, plastic form, and scale results from the play of light and shade. Although this medium is used in the majority of the International Style buildings of the same period in Europe (cf. Fig. 212), the basic concept of the forms is quite different. To Le Corbusier, concrete is a flexible material used to form a plane that defines and delimits the space volume of the house; Wright thinks of it as having inherent weight and bulk, to be handled almost sculpturally in walls that support as well as enclose. Different too is the concept of the structure in its surroundings. Le Corbusier's is inorganic—an artfully contrived entity isolated from its environment, existing for itself and to be understood in its own terms; Wright's is organic—one with its surroundings, moulding nature to human pur-

pose without sacrificing the character of either.

The caliber of Wright's architectural imagination and creativeness is shown most clearly by the great variety of building types he designed from 1934 on, when his greatness and the soundness of his ideas appeared at last to have been realized. Factories and offices, houses and apartments, churches and school buildings—he designed them all with perceptive understanding coupled with the ability to translate that understanding into extremely individual and distinguished forms. The *Administration Building of the Johnson Wax Co.* (Fig. 220) at Racine, Wis., completed in 1939, illustrates Wright's distinctive feeling for materials. The external walls are of specially made red brick with stone trim at the bases that provides a contrast of color and texture. There are no cornices in the traditional sense, for the angles where walls and covering meet are marked by horizontal bands of clustered Pyrex glass tubes; this material is also used for the ceiling. The volume of space thus defined is bathed in light, softly diffused yet colorful in its silvery gray, enclosed by the warm brick hue of the walls. Spaced at regular intervals in this interior are hollow columns of reinforced concrete, their delicately poised shafts rising to suddenly expanding capitals that have been compared to the floating leaves of a water lily. These columns have little of the orthodox function of support; apart from sustaining the light load of the glass tube ceiling, almost their only duty is to provide electric and telephone outlets. But their formal importance in the design is great. The ever-varying rhythms of the shafts and circular capital slabs seen in perspective are directly responsible for the sense

of enclosure in a space that has a vitality and life of its own that even the most casual visitor experiences.

To the problem of designing *Falling Water* (Fig. 221) for Edgar S. Kaufmann at Bear Run, Pa., Wright brought an almost romantic feeling for site and materials, expressed in forms as freely imaginative as those of the Johnson Co. Building, yet in quite a different vein. The house illustrated was finished in 1937; a guest house higher up the hill was added in 1938. It was the owner's wish that one should be aware of the waterfall everywhere in the house. Accordingly, Wright built massive cantilevers

FIG. 221. Bear Run. Wright, Falling Water (1936-1937).

FIG. 222. Okemos. Wright, Goetsch-Winckler House (1940),
Living Room.

from the rocky banks of the stream to provide support for the floors that hover in space above the cascade. This skeleton is clothed in concrete and glass and the native rock of the region; space and form interpenetrate, in contrast to the opaque enclosure of the Johnson Building. The materials and the horizontality may suggest comparison with a house in the International Style (Fig. 212), but only to emphasize the difference in effect and purpose. Where Le Corbusier turned his back to nature and isolated his building from its environment, Wright's crystalline forms bring the setting into focus just as do those of a Greek temple (Fig. 41), in a dramatic symbol of the significance that constructively controlled imagination may find in the interpretation of man's experience of the world he lives in.

At the same time Wright was designing these poetically beautiful but extravagantly luxurious buildings, he was also concerned with less spec-

tacular and economically more modest ideas. His Suntop Houses, built at Ardmore, Pa., in 1939, were an attempt to provide housing for middle-class families of limited means. Less revolutionary than they in plan and form are Wright's so-called "Usonian" houses of this period like the *Goetsch-Winckler House* (Fig. 222) at Okemos near East Lansing, Mich., which was finished in 1940. The exterior consists of long low forms of brick and wood in warm colors that blend with the surrounding greenery. The openness of these forms—the proportion of void to solid is high—directly expresses the character of the interior (Fig. 222). This is organized around a large space that is the living room, with subordinate alcoves for kitchen and a small studio, the private rooms of the house being reached by a corridor opening from another side. A characteristic device is the row of small rectangular windows at the top of the side walls, providing softly diffused yet abundant illumination, and also contributing to a sense of space that is at the same time enclosed and yet correlated with that surrounding the house. The materials are inexpensive and homely, yet the decorative effect of color and texture is eminently satisfying —proof of the possibility of achieving distinction without using applied superficial ornament or resorting to costly and luxurious textiles and woods and metals (cf. Fig. 213).

Wright's last building of major importance is the *Guggenheim Museum* (Fig. 223) completed only a short time before his death in 1959, although it had been planned some time before. Its function is specialized, even for a museum, for it houses a considerable collection of largely nonrepresentational or abstract art which, in the opinion of its administrators, required other means of presentation than those used for more conventional paintings and sculptures. Another factor which undoubtedly entered into Wright's conception of the structure was that it was the first commission he had ever received for a building in New York City. The exterior rises in a series of ever-widening circles of massive, seemingly windowless concrete, devoid of ornament, an implacable monolith in appearance. The interior of the museum proper, apart from administrative and service areas, is a single vast space enclosed from the ground up by outward-slanting walls around which a single continuous spiral ramp leads in front of the objects on display. Illumination comes principally from the opening at the top, which Wright intended to be covered by a single unbroken domelike expanse of transparent or translucent material. However, New York City building restrictions made this impossible, to the detriment of the planned effect, for the supporting metal armature introduces a distracting pattern in the intended impression of elemental simplicity. In spite of this, the interior design creates a feeling, unprecedented in its terms, of controlled, dynamic, integrated space. In the period in which the Museum was built, only interiors designed by the Italian engineer Pier Luigi Nervi, like that of the Palazetto dello Sport of the Olympic Games buildings in Rome in 1960, can be effectively

compared to it; and even they do not communicate, as Wright's does, in the language of ultimate architectonic abstraction. Only in one of the first creatively planned and still one of the greatest architectural interiors, the Roman Pantheon (Fig. 58), is vital space experienced in a comparable way.

An important factor in the contemporary architectural scene is the large-scale plan for entire communities designed and controlled by some unity of purpose. Ever since the seventeenth century when the expanding horizons of man's intellectual and emotional experience sought an adequate symbol in the planned city (cf. Figs. 153, 158, 161), the problem of achieving a coherent pattern in such symbols has confronted the architect and in their solution is reflected the character of the particular time. The Hemicycle at Nancy built in 1755, for example, is intimate in scale and refined in effect as befits the rococo eighteenth century. Georges-Eugène Haussmann's monumental pattern for the city of Paris between 1853 and 1869 was the most ambitious project of its sort in the nineteenth century. It was the outcome of a paradoxical desire to control popular uprisings that had wrought great damage in 1848 and 1852 when the narrow crooked streets complicated the task of the military in putting them down, and also to make the city conform to the ideals of splendid regularity characteristic of the industrial age against whose abuses the Parisians had revolted.

Also in the late nineteenth century, renewed appreciation of the landscape appears in community planning. Parks and tree-lined boulevards are part of Haussmann's plan for Paris; Central Park in New York City was laid out by Frederick Law Olmsted, the foremost landscape architect in the United States, between 1857 and 1861; and Philadelphia's Fairmount Park acquired much of its present character then. Inherently romantic in purpose, these bits of "controlled nature" within urban communities might be considered attempts to compensate for the consequences of the uncontrolled industrialism of the age. Of greater significance were the English "Garden Cities" of Letchworth and Welwyn,

FIG. 223.　New York.　Wright, Solomon R. Guggenheim Museum (1959).

FIG. 224. Philadelphia. Stonorov, Kastner, and Barney,
Carl Mackley Houses (1933-1934).

laid out in 1904 after the plans of Sir Ebenezer
Howard. In them a positive attempt was made
for the first time to create a community in
accordance with the need and function of modern
industrial life on a human scale rather than for
financial profit. But more than individual enter-
prise was required to achieve the planned community. Not until after the First World War did
political and economic circumstances make
possible a solution of the problem on a scale
of more than individual significance.

The character of a planned community is of
course dependent upon its purpose, and its
design must take this into account as it does in
the individual building. The problem is more
than architectural, however, because legal and
financial and sociological factors must all be
weighed. One of the most important contemporary categories of the planned community is
the one that provides low-cost housing. The
development of such communities in Holland
and Germany and the Scandinavian countries in
the '20's enlisted the services of leading architects
in those countries. Oud's Houses at the Hook of
Holland (Fig. 214) are a case in point. The
Bauhaus at Dessau (Fig. 211) is part of a planned
community; although it was not primarily
designed for the low-cost housing category,

FIG. 225. New York.
Rockefeller Center (1931-1939).

FIG. 226.   Rome.   Montuori and others, Termini Railway Station
(1947-1951).

its architect, Gropius did some of his most distinguished work in Germany as director of housing for the city of Berlin following his tenure as director of the Bauhaus School. Le Corbusier, too, has designed a number of such communities. He has also given much thought to complete urban developments and the modernization of entire cities which he has brilliantly presented in his theoretical treatises on urbanism, of which one of the most significant—*La Ville Radieuse*—was published in 1934. Since World War II he has had the responsibility of designing the new capital city of Chandigarh in the State of Punjab in India. In these cases and in many of the literally hundreds of such projects in Europe, the architect's obligation to create forms that are at the same time distinguished in character and effective in function has been realized.

Until the early '30's, low-cost housing in the United States was limited to a few planned communities like Radburn in New Jersey and Sunnyside Gardens on Long Island in New York. These were individually sponsored and financed, differing in this respect from the government-sponsored projects for low-cost housing communities in various parts of the country after 1933. Developed concurrently at first by the Public Works Administration and the Resettlement Administration, after 1937 the program was carried on by the United States Housing Authority. One of the first large projects of the Public Works Administration in the field of low-cost housing was the *Carl Mackley Houses* (Fig. 224), built in Juniata Park in Philadelphia in 1933-1934, with Stonorov, Kastner, and Barney, Associated Architects, as designers, for a cooperative organization of workers in a hosiery mill. It illustrates quite well the possibility of attaining architectural distinction in spite of the inexorable limitations of minimum-cost construction basic to all such projects. The material is concrete stone faced with terra cotta; the variegated buff-brown with blue trim creates a pleasing effect of color and texture in the absence of applied ornament. Within the rigid rectangular framework of the Philadelphia street system, the buildings are well placed to obtain maximum sunlight and air—

also basic problems in community plans of this type. There is adequate room space, and community facilities for sports and entertainments are also available. The design is sober and restrained, the simply treated walls being broken by well-proportioned ample windows and balconies that provide sufficient variety in the horizontal mass defined by their surfaces.

The most widely publicized community plan in the United States is not a low-cost housing project, but the complex of commercial buildings known as *Rockefeller Center* (Fig. 225) or Radio City in New York. The initial design

FIG. 227. New York.
Miës van der Rohe and Philip Johnson,
Seagram Building (1958).

was the work of three architectural firms in collaboration—Hood and Fouilloux, Reinhard and Hofmeister, and Corbett, Harrison and MacMurray. The Center was begun in 1931 in the area bounded by Fifth and Sixth Avenues and Forty-eighth and Fifty-first Streets. This initial unit was substantially completed by 1939, but subsequent extensions have been made. Buildings of various heights and sizes are grouped around and dominated by the 850-foot-high slab of the R.C.A. Building in an ensemble that fits into the rectangular grid pattern of the Manhattan street system. The form of the R.C.A. Building was determined primarily by technical considerations of circulation and illumination. The considerable number of elevators required in a building of this size are grouped with the service rooms in a central core. Around it is a volume of space whose proportions are determined by the maximum area that can be lighted by the vertical ribbonlike windows. These and the slender piers of the curtain wall establish the rhythm of the external design, the latter being cut back at levels corresponding to the heights of the various elevator shafts. The whole represents an extension of Sullivan's concept of the tall commercial structure into the larger area of the urban scheme instead of into a single, ever-taller building. Not until after World War II was this idea taken up elsewhere. The plan for the United Nations buildings owes something to it. The Secretariat—it was completed in 1950 by Harrison and Abramovitz but incorporates the ideas of an international group including Le Corbusier and Oscar Niemeyer—continues the concept of the dominant slab, but varies it in the almost completely glazed east and west sides whose surface treatment depends largely on the texture of the curtain-wall armature. During the '50's, the idea of the large-scale urban group was further developed in the United States. Pittsburgh's Golden Triangle is particularly noteworthy as an imaginative solution of the problem of rehabilitating an urban area. Comparable projects have been initiated in Philadelphia, Detroit, and Denver, and others are under study in Boston and Fort Worth.

Three points stand out in an overview of

FIG. 228. Philadelphia. University of Pennsylvania. Kahn, Alfred Newton
Richards Medical Research Building (1958-1960).

architecture since the Second World War—the great amount of building that is going on, its truly international scope, and, as Hitchcock makes clear (*Architecture: Nineteenth and Twentieth Centuries*, p. 383), the continuing and stimulating influence of the ideas and practices of the pioneering figures of the '20's and '30's.

Already mentioned is the part Wright played in the creation of new forms until his death in 1959 (cf. Fig. 223). Among the most striking churches of the mid-twentieth century is Notre-Dame-du-Haut, built between 1950 and 1955 at Ronchamp, Hte.-Saone, in France. It was designed by Le Corbusier in a style that owes almost nothing to his earlier manner (cf. Fig. 212). If the term "International Style" must now be applied to a group of buildings somewhat limited in style and restricted in time and area, it is nonetheless true that much of the most distinguished contemporary architecture represents an enrichment of its canon rather a contradiction.

The *Termini Railway Station* (Fig. 226) in Rome, left unfinished after 1941, was completed by a group of architects headed by Eugenio Montuori. They added the façade on the Piazza dei Cinquecento between 1947 and 1951. A cantilevered marquee over 400 feet long gives access to the ticket office which in turn leads to a gallery or concourse that opens on the train platforms. Characteristic of Italian building at its best is the craftsmanship that utilizes in effective harmony materials as traditional as marble and as contemporary as glass, steel, and concrete. It is the ease with which the concrete is shaped in moulds that makes possible the rhythmic arching profile of the principal gallery, expressing the imaginatively conceived volume of space with equal effectiveness both externally and internally. Most striking of all, perhaps, is the harmony, thus achieved, between this form so completely of the twentieth century and the fragment of the Servian wall of the fourth century B.C. at the left in the illustration. The fortuitous curve of the top suggests that of the steel and concrete forms of the gallery; it is hard to imagine a more distinguished expression of the relationship of old and new, of the vital continuity that is Rome.

The *Seagram Building* (Fig. 227) on Park Avenue in New York City was designed by Miës van der Rohe and Philip Johnson working in collaboration. At the moment of its completion in 1958, it represented what might well be considered the ultimate development and statement of the International Style. Raised above the ample plaza that enables it to exist in its own space (cf. Fig. 212), the forms of glass and bronze carry to an extreme the concept of a building as weightless volume given character by decorative harmonies of texture and tone. The same idea has been used by both architects in private houses. So far as it seems possible to believe that a quality can be common in the complex and varied architecture of the Occident in mid-twentieth century, this appears to be it.

Because the *Alfred Newton Richards Medical Research Building* (Fig. 228) of the University of Pennsylvania represents an obviously different conception of significant architectural form than the Seagram Building, it has been hailed, with reason, as marking the beginning of a new era in twentieth-century architecture. Designed by Louis I. Kahn (b. 1901) to house the complex functions of modern medical scientific research, it was begun in 1958 and in use by 1960. It consists of three lofty tower units of laboratory "studios" placed around a fourth service tower. Work areas on cantilevered slabs are the horizontal elements in the design; the verticals are stacks for ventilation. The materials are brick, precast concrete, and glass. Although the influence of other designers has been noted and acknowledged by the architect, the form of the building owes little to previous or current styles. Instead it is his concept of "served and servant" spaces as the essential elements of significant architectonic design that shapes it; this involves an exceedingly comprehensive understanding of the purpose of the building, including what it means as well as what it is and does. To accept this is to acknowledge ethical as well as aesthetic and practical values as being fundamental and essential in creative architecture. The forms of Kahn's Medical Research Building may be new, but the principle which they express visually is as old as eternity.

❧ SCULPTURE ❧

Detail of Fig. 230.

CHAPTER FIFTEEN

Sculpture: Methods, Terminology, and Early Styles

To the average person, the word sculpture evokes an image of a human figure in stone or metal. Sculpture is not limited to these materials, however, for any substance may be used which has sufficient density to retain the form given it by the artist. Some of the earliest sculpture is in bone or wood, and modern sculptors have been much interested in rare stones of the less expensive varieties as their materials. There is, in fact, no limit to the substances that can be used for sculpture, ranging all the way from soap and butter to solid silver. Obviously similar methods are not suitable for all materials. A medium that is soft, such as clay, lends itself to a modeling technique that consists of squeezing and shaping the material and adding to it as the artist's conception of the figure grows. In contrast with this, working with a hard medium like stone or wood involves taking away from the original block. The sculptor cuts the figure out of the substance, shaping it with a chisel or file.

A metal statue is produced by a method different from either of the above; in general it is as follows. The figure is first modeled in clay or wax and then a mould is made from it by enclosing it, after it is well covered with a lubricant, with liquid plaster of Paris, gelatin, or any fluid substance that becomes solid after exposure to the air. After the mould has hardened, it is removed in pieces and reassembled; the hollow formed by the original figure is filled with melted metal which flows into the cracks and crevices on the inside. When the metal cools and hardens, the mould is removed, leaving a metal replica of the original clay or plaster figure. This method of casting a metal figure has two disadvantages. If the figure is large, its weight is considerable. Moreover, the metal in the center cools less rapidly than that near the outer surface, setting up strains in the statue which might cause it to crack. Both these disadvantages can be avoided by making the metal figure hollow. A core is inserted in the hollow mould; it has the general form of the original clay or plaster figure but is somewhat smaller. This core is usually covered with soft wax which takes the exact shape of the original figure when the mould is squeezed around the core. The hot, liquefied metal is then poured into the space occupied by the wax, which melts and runs out of small openings or vents provided for the purpose. When the metal hardens, the outer mould is removed and the inner core raked out. The result is a metal shell whose outer surface reproduces that of the original clay or plaster figure. This is the principle of the *cire perdue* or "lost-wax" process of casting which has been employed in one form or another for metal statues from the earliest times to the present. Recently, metal statues have been made by an electrolytic pro-

cess which deposits the metal on a plaster core covered with plumbago or black lead, but this method has not replaced the *cire perdue* process in general favour.

A metal statue is usually of the modeled type since it reproduces a clay original, rather than the chiseled type of the stone or wooden figure cut out of a block. Until the Renaissance, stone figures were nearly always carved directly (cf. Fig. 294, B), the sculptor using, at the most, only a small model as a guide. Since the beginning of the sixteenth century, a mechanical method known as pointing has been in general use. On the original clay or plaster figure a number of points are marked. These are transferred mechanically to a block of stone by drills which bore into it to depths determined by the points on the original figure. When all the points have been transferred, the stone is cut away to the depths of the holes. The result is a reasonably exact reproduction of the general form of the model, which the sculptor then finishes with chisels and rasps. The pointing method is practically the only one in general use today. It has largely supplanted the practice of cutting directly in the stone block, for by indicating the depths beyond which the sculptor must not carve, the possibilities of ruining an expensive piece of material are considerably lessened.

Sculpture in general may be divided into types according to whether the figures are in relief or free-standing. The first term refers to figures attached to a background; a free-standing figure can be seen from all sides. The general category of relief is subdivided into high and low. In high relief the objects project considerably from the background (cf. Fig. 264) and appear to be almost in the round, whereas in low relief, the forms have relatively little projection (cf. Fig. 265). The difference between them is one of proportion, for a large figure in low relief may actually project farther from its background than one a quarter its size in high relief.

A still further general distinction in sculpture is between decorative and free figures. Decorative sculpture is planned as part of a larger whole; that is, it is not independent and self-sufficient but depends for its effect upon its relationship to something else, usually a building. The greater part of relief sculpture is in this category. A form of decorative free-standing sculpture is shown in the illustration of the Gardens of Versailles (Fig. 159); here the figures are accents in a planned landscape. Free sculpture is not necessarily free-standing sculpture; it has no relationship to a larger scheme or ensemble, like the well-known Aphrodite of Melos (Fig. 276). It is usually in the round, although free relief is not unknown, as on a coin or medal, for example (cf. Figs. 571, 608).

There is a fundamental reason for this. Whatever it may be, sculpture is not merely a three-dimensional imitation of the appearance of a person or object, an illusion of actuality. Representation has been a significant element in sculpture, it is true—a major one until the mid-twentieth century. Yet it has always been incidental to other qualities in examples of sculpture considered great, never an end in itself. A sculptured figure is always something more than a facsimile of the human form in stone or metal.

If the naturalistic ideal is ruled out, what qualities should be looked for in sculpture? The answer is much the same in its way as that to the question "What constitutes great architecture?" Possibly because in very early times sculpture had a practical purpose, it often seems more meaningful than sculpture today. In prehistoric times, the caveman carved his weapons with images of animals (cf. Fig. 548), thus supposedly making them more effective in killing the prey upon which he depended for food. In Egypt and Greece, one of the chief duties of sculptors was to create statues of the gods in human form (cf. Figs. 234, 261) for the early religions held the reverse of Christian belief to be true and made their gods in man's image. Although this religious function of sculpture is almost nonexistent today in the Occidental world, a curious instinctive feeling persists that forms portrayed in indestructible stone or metal should be intrinsically worthy of the permanence thus acquired. As a result, complete sculptural satisfaction is rarely found except in representations of the human form. Some sculptors

have attained distinction for their animal figures, but even the best of their works lack the significance of the greatest sculptural interpretations of the human figure. This fact also gives a clue to the inappropriateness in sculpture of many effects that are quite acceptable in painting. A picture of a man walking through a forest is perfectly legitimate, whereas it would be ridiculous in sculpture, as the displays in waxworks museums so painfully reveal. This is less true of relief than of free-standing sculpture. Nonetheless, the sculptor who strives for the varied naturalistic details, even in relief, that a painter can use without question, usually sacrifices some quality which is appropriate to his art.

The human figure is the raw material the sculptor works with, just as the purpose of the building is the point of departure for the architect. The sculptor so treats this raw material that the statue expresses what he feels or thinks about his subject, adding order and arrangement to it. The greatness of the artist depends upon his ability to create a form in which harmony of line, mass, and surface reveals the significance of his subject matter. The ideal of the sculptor is a formal order, based upon natural forms, perhaps, but with all accidental and temporal characteristics eliminated so that in the end his order is more perfect than that of nature. For the observer, the value of a work of art lies in its clarification of his own experience or understanding of those forms, and the heightened sense it gives him of their fundamental meaning as forms resulting from their being placed in a logical and coherent pattern. This suggests a reason why naturalism is not enough to make a painting or a piece of sculpture a great work of art. The inclusion of all the accidental details only obscures the characteristic pattern of which they are a part. This is well illustrated by the soldiers on the average Civil War monument. The most prominent features are the buttons and insignia, the wrinkles of the coat, the saber straps and the boot laces. The statue as a whole has no meaning other than symbolic, because the sculptor was so concerned with superficial details that he made no attempt to give them any formal meaning by establishing them as essential parts of a well-ordered pattern. The beauty of representational sculpture does not lie in its record of observation, but rather in the organization the sculptor perceives in or imposes upon the things he has observed. Where this organization is absent, as in the soldier on the Civil War monument, there is no beauty and no work of art.

Thus to the sculptor, the form of his model is not as significant or as real as the form he evolves in his statue. Just as merely fulfilling the immediate function in architecture is not enough to produce a great building, so merely representing form in sculpture is not sufficient to produce a great statue. It is the organization of the figure that is significant, a pattern of volumes indicated by planes and outlines, a pattern by means of which the interrelationship of those volumes is emphasized and the sculptor's ideal made tangible and apparent. Sculpture is primarily an art of form and mass, just as architecture is primarily an art of space. To the element of related forms, all other elements in sculpture are subservient and contributory.

Sculpture was one of the earliest arts practiced by man. Excavation of sites known to have been occupied in prehistoric times has revealed small figures like the *Nude Woman* (Fig. 229) of the late palaeolithic age found near Menton in France. It was probably a charm or fetish symbolizing its creator's elemental belief in the power of his deity to bestow the gift of fertility. The motivation of all early sculpture was religious or magical—to create a tangible symbol of an idea or concept. The idea underlying the figure from Menton is clear, for the breasts and thighs are exaggerated to emphasize the importance of those parts of the feminine body in the bearing and rearing of children. Otherwise, representation had no great importance for the primitive sculptor; the legs are shown only to the knees, the arms are included in the mass of the torso, and the head is a featureless oval. The sculptor has selected from the facts of the female form's appearance only those pertinent to his basic idea and has subordinated all those that have no bearing upon it. He has thus arrived at an organized pattern of sculptured masses whose symbolic function is made clear by the organization that emphasizes the significant elements of the form as a whole. The stone is a yellowish steatite, slightly translucent, and the figure is hardly two inches high; but so effectively is the material handled and so thoroughly are the volumes of form integrated in an organized pattern that its meaning could be no clearer if its height were as many feet instead of inches.

Religious belief is the motivation and convention is the predominant formal characteristic of the first great monumental style to develop in historic times in the western world—that of Egypt. In figures that are sometimes as much as sixty-five feet high (cf. Fig. 19) and that embody the fundamental and memorable qualities of the forms portrayed in conventions—i.e., patterns that have traditional significance because of established usage—the Egyptian reveals the same passionate desire for immortality that is evident in his tombs and temples. It was in the house of the god or the house of the dead, in fact, that the greater part of Egyptian sculpture was placed —in the serdab of the mastaba (Fig. 8) where it provided the spirit of the dead with an acceptable substitute if the original mummified body were destroyed, or in the temple where it was a visible symbol of king or god (Fig. 12).

Among the earliest examples of Egyptian sculpture for which a date can be suggested is a ceremonial slate tablet called the *Palette of*

Museum, Saint-Germain.

FIG. 229. Nude Woman
(Aurignacian).

Museum, Cairo.

FIG. 230.   Palette of Narmer (*ca.* 3200 B.C.).

Narmer (Fig. 230), made for one of the first dynastic rulers of Egypt between 3200 and 3000 B.C. A decorated slab of stone a little over two feet in its greatest dimension, it carried the pigment used to paint the king's face before religious rituals; the pigment was put in the circular hollow enclosed by the necks of the two animals toward the center of the side at the left in the figure. The theme of the ornament is consistent with this ceremonial purpose. Above the intertwined animals the king—much larger than his companions and wearing the crown of Lower Egypt—is shown viewing the headless bodies of enemies slain in battle; below he is shown symbolically as a bull destroying the wall of a hostile city. On the other side—at the right in the illustration—he wears the crown of Upper Egypt and grasps the hair of his kneeling foe before a hawk symbolizing the god Horus; below lie two defeated enemies. At the top on both sides the cow-headed goddess Hathor appears, flanking hieroglyphs of the king's name enclosed in a symbol of his royal palace. Early though the Palette of Narmer is in the definable chronology of Egyptian sculpture, it shows many

established conventions of Egyptian formal expression. Thus the monarch is always larger than anyone else; this stated a fact obvious to any Egyptian—namely, the king was more important than anyone else—that could not be obscured by portraying him in any fashion however naturalistic that would suggest a different idea. For a similar reason the ten headless bodies of his slain enemies are placed in two rows with one seemingly on top of the other so that each will be clearly visible as an unmistakable symbol of a stated number of victims, for the sculptor was concerned not with representing things as they may have appeared to him but with representing objective and immutable facts.

A similar concept is apparent in the portrayal of individual figures. The king about to strike his helpless foe with the scepter is shown with his head in profile, although the eye appears as if seen from directly in front. Equally inconsistent as naturalistic representation is the body with full-face shoulders and torso and the striding legs in profile. But as a description in formal terms of the various parts of the human body that make up a figure it is completely adequate to the sculptor's purpose of stating ideas that were objective and unchanging; to show them in that light, the forms must be presented in their most characteristic and memorable aspects. The concept which the Egyptian expressed is not the result of direct and immediate physical participation on his part, but one of communal value rendered significant by traditional acceptance throughout the memory of generations. It is this memory concept or picture which the Egyptian artist portrays; and every element therein must be a formal as well as conceptual whole contributing to a unity that is ideological and ideographic rather than organic. This is why the various symbols on the Palette are organized as they are—in clearly defined registers and spaced in a decorative and coherent pattern. Yet it is doubtful if this resulted from conscious desire on the part of the sculptor; his intention seems to have been merely an arrangement that would make clear and unmistakable the concepts he was dealing with.

Other conventions in portraying the human form appear in early Egyptian statuary in the round, an example being the double statue of *Menkaura and His Queen* (Fig. 231) in the Museum of Fine Arts in Boston. Menkaura was the builder of the third and latest of the Pyramids at Gizeh and this statute was probably carved about 2600 B.C. The material is exceedingly hard gray-green slate selected for its durability to symbolize the eternal greatness of the Pharaoh. Corresponding to the memory-picture convention in Egyptian two-dimensional representation is the law of frontality in the figure in the round; the body stands rigidly so that an axial plane cutting the figure vertically would pass through the nose, mouth, chin, torso, and crotch, dividing it into symmetrical halves. All movement is kept parallel to this plane; it is limited in general to the forward stride of the left leg, although in this statue the queen places her right arm around the king's waist and touches his left arm with her own left hand in gestures symbolic of her relationship to him. These again are descriptive conventions and do not affect the general impression of immobility resulting from the frontal poses, the king's clenched fists, and the arms held

Museum of Fine Arts, Boston.

FIG. 231.　Menkaura and His Queen
(*ca.* 2600 B.C.).

tightly to his sides. A technical detail is the web of stone between the two figures (there is a similar web between the king's legs) and between the arms and the sides; this is a mechanical device to stiffen the figures and as far as possible prevent essential parts from breaking off.

Unfinished Egyptian statutes have been found that show how such forms as these were made. Frontal and profile views of the traditional memory-picture type were drawn on the faces of the block from which the figure was to be carved. These outlines were then cut into the block until they intersected to define the general form; this was then rounded off and modeled, and surface details were indicated. The result is a solid bulk organized in three dimensions that complies in every respect with the definition of sculpture as a pattern of organized masses. Usually modern observers also find much attractiveness in the medium; however, to the Egyptian such values were only incidental, and, indeed, unnecessary. Since his purpose was to describe visually a traditional concept, pattern and surface texture and all aesthetic qualities were factors only insofar as they might contribute to the completeness and clarity of his description.

Menkaura and his Queen are shown as royal types; the symbols of their rank, like the Pharaoh's beard and headdress, were among the ideographic conventions of regal figures. They are not characterized as individuals beyond the most cursory personal traits, for the figures are identified by hieroglyphic inscriptions on the side of the base. Furthermore, it would have been inconsistent with the divine conception of royalty to preserve individual peculiarities of appearance which suggested mortal flesh rather than the divine principle.

Statues of commoners, on the other hand, were frequently remarkably individualized. An instance is the wooden figure called the *Sheikh el-Beled* (Fig. 232) in the museum at Cairo. Of the Fifth Dynasty, *ca.* 2550 B.C., it represents a man named Ka-aper; the workmen who found it in a tomb near Saqqara rechristened it because it resembled the headman of their village. Head, legs, and torso were carved from a single block of wood, the arms being fastened on. Originally the whole figure was coated with stucco on which details were painted. The stucco has flaked off, and the wig that presumably once covered the head has also disappeared. These would amplify but could hardly make more striking the realism of the head with its thick lips, flat nose, and heavy jowls and chin, to which the eyes of colored paste, inset in metal frames, added a strongly individualized note. These are essential details in a complete statement of the identity and social rank of the man and thus are appropriate to the object which records and preserves such

facts. Yet for all its individuality, the figure is as immobile and expressionless as its royal counterparts, for its function as a potential body for Ka-aper's spirit was also a social fact; hence the rigid frontal stance with left leg advanced, the right arm held tightly to the side, and the mask-like, imperturbable face.

The term naturalism means a complete and objective visual statement about a form or object. To the extent that the figure of Ka-aper is such

Museum, Cairo.

FIG. 232.   Sheikh el-Beled
(*ca.* 2550 B.C.).

Mastaba of Ti, Saqqara.

FIG. 233.   Hunting the Hippopotamus (*ca.* 2300 B.C.).

a statement, it may be said to be naturalistic in intention. But it is a primitive naturalism—"not an affair of the eyes [alone] but of the whole man and his spiritual attitude towards his experience of nature," as Wilhelm Worringer said (*Egyptian Art*, 1928, English translation). It was in seeking to define the whole man that the Egyptian carved the elaborate pictographs on the walls of tombs (cf. Fig. 9) that recorded riches in this life and provided nourishment for the soul in the next. For the modern observer they are also an invaluable source of information about everyday life in ancient Egypt.

In *Hunting the Hippopotamus* (Fig. 233), in relief on a wall in the mastaba of Ti at Saqqara, the master stands in a small boat directing his slaves' activities. He is larger than they, as King Narmer was larger than his companions (Fig. 230), and his pose is like that of the Sheikh el-Beled, combining the frontal and profile aspects of the two-dimensional memory-picture convention. The band of wavy lines at the bottom represents the Nile River, with fishes and hippopotami. The regular vertical ribbed pattern of papyrus stems above is the background for the human figures and supports flowers and buds that are thronged with birds and hunting foxes. The flattened forms and orderly bands give the whole a remarkably decorative effect to modern eyes. But they are only a part of the Egyptian's conventionalized descriptive vocabulary for defining objects in their most characteristic aspect. The overall scheme accords well with the flatness of the wall, but the intention behind it was no more than to make the clearest and most inclusive statement possible about the idea involved.

Once the methods of the Egyptian sculptor were developed and the types defined, there was relatively little change in conceptions and forms throughout the history of the country—a direct parallel to the persistence of basic forms in its architecture which was pointed out earlier. Thus the Sphinx of the Old Kingdom period (Fig. 11) was a type symbolizing the power of the king by associating his head with the body of a lion; the same type recurs in the *Sphinx of Sesostris III* (Fig. 234) of the Twelfth Dynasty in the Middle Kingdom, *ca.* 1800 B.C., even to the framing of the ruler's features by the royal headdress (cf. Fig. 231). The Middle Kingdom example is much smaller than the Sphinx at

Ny-Carlsberg Museum, Copenhagen.

FIG. 235. Amenemhet III
(*ca.* 1800 B.C.).

Gizeh, being only a little over three feet high, but it is carved from granite and has the same formal conventionalism noted in the earlier sculptures. In the face, however, there is an individualistic quality to be noted in the puffy forms, the broad nose, and thick lips that are unlike the more impersonal features of Menkaura and, indeed, are apparently of a different racial type. A head possibly of *Amenemhet III* (Fig. 235) in the Ny-Carlsberg Museum of Sculpture in Copenhagen is more clearly individualized. The material is very hard black-green slate that made it difficult to render minute detail; in addition, the accepted conventions of form led to generalization in the masklike expression. In spite of these, there is specific character in the shape of the lips, the lines slanting down from the nose, and the bulges underneath the eyes; all create the impression of a definite personality. As in the Old Kingdom examples, the craftsmanship

*The Metropolitan Museum of Art,
Gift of Edward S. Harkness, 1916-1917.*

FIG. 234. Sphinx of Sesostris III
(*ca.* 1800 B.C.).

is excellent, the most scrupulous attention being paid to the minutest details.

Egypt's greatest power as a nation was reached in the Empire or New Kingdom period between 1580 and 1100 B.C., a fact reflected in the great amount of sculpture then executed and in the great size of much of it. A life-size basalt statue of *Thutmose III* (Fig. 236) in the museum at Cairo continues the centuries-old type— rigidly frontal pose, with individualistic details generalized in accordance with the concept of royalty as above the specific qualities of ordinary human beings. Thutmose III was the half-brother of Hatshepsut, the famous queen of the Eighteenth Dynasty who built the temple at Deir el-bahari (Fig. 15); he first shared the throne of Egypt with her but later occupied it alone from about 1480 B.C. until his death in 1447 B.C. During that time he extended Egypt's power as far as Syria in the north and Nubia in the south and established himself as one of the most capable rulers the country ever had. The basalt statue came from Karnak where he had built a great festival hall as part of a complex of structures dedicated to Amon, the sun god. He is shown wearing the crown of upper Egypt, with the uraeus, the snake symbol of royalty, resting upon his brow. The details of the face are stylized in accordance with traditional formulas. The eyebrows are flat ribbonlike bands and the expression is impassive, but the vigor and energy of the powerful ruler are clearly expressed. The statue is an excellent example of the primitive naturalism referred to earlier, in which traditional symbols define not merely the appearance and individuality of the man but his spiritual attitude toward his experience of nature as well.

Egyptian representational conventions were developed to communicate as clearly as possible the concept of experience which had evolved through centuries; their acceptance by succeeding generations reflects both their validity and the continuing significance of their motivating concepts. Only briefly in the Eighteenth Dynasty, between 1375 and 1358 B.C., was there any serious attempt to depart from traditional modes of thought and expression. This occurred when Amenhotep IV, also called Akhenaten, tried to reform long-standing abuses in the nation's religion. The traditional sun god, Amon-Re, was replaced by Aten, whose name the ruler took as part of his own instead of the one he inherited. The capital was moved from Thebes to a newly built city on the site of modern Tell el-Amarna. The statues of himself and his queen Nofretete in its buildings and the reliefs on the walls reveal an intention as revolutionary as his religious reforms. In a relief in the Ägyptisches Museum in Berlin, *Akhenaten and Nofretete* (Fig. 237) face each other in casual and easy poses; the king, legs crossed, leans on a staff and looks at the queen, who holds out a bouquet of flowers. Both are lightly clothed, and their bodies are portrayed with unprecedented naturalism. The necks are thin and long, the abdomens swollen, the thighs and hips inordinately large, and the back of the queen's skull is almost monstrous in its projection.

Museum, Cairo.

FIG. 236. Thutmose III
(*ca.* 1450 B.C.).

These are no conventions but deliberate attempts to produce individual likenesses. The same characteristics are present in a number of plaster masks found at Tell el-Amarna in a building that was probably a sculptor's studio; the well-known painted limestone bust of Nofretete with its tall blue crown and inset eyes, which is also in the Berlin museum, was found at the same time. Like the incisive individualism of these forms and faces compared with the stark immobility of traditional types (cf. Fig. 236), their negligent attitudes contrast with the hieratic rigidity of King Narmer (Fig. 230) or of the later Seti I from his temple at Abydos (Fig. 239), a rigidness which is an interpretive convention just as the memory picture was a formal one. Interestingly enough, this last was something that even the obviously naturalistic intention of the Tell el-Amarna sculptor could not transcend; the eyes in the Akhenaten and Nofretete relief are full-front in profile heads, and the frontal shoulders are related to torsos seen from the side.

Akhenaten's religious reforms and the parallel modifications of artistic tradition died with their instigator; under his successors in the Eighteenth Dynasty, the old forms returned in religion and art alike. Tutankhamen, Akhenaten's son-in-law, and Haremhab, one of his successors, restored the cult of Amon-Re to its traditional primacy, and the artistic style that appears in the prolific years after the middle of the fourteenth century B.C. also harks back to older ideals. A relief of *Negro Captives* (Fig. 238) from Haremhab's tomb shows four Egyptians in charge of nine Nubian captives taken in one of the Pharaoh's many successful military campaigns. The distinction between the Egyptians and the Nubians with their Negroid features is made clear in spite of the conventionalized formulas by which they are portrayed. Such details and the comparable naturalism of the animals and fishes in the Old Kingdom mastaba relief (Fig. 233) indicate the accuracy of the Egyptian's observation. It follows that his use of formula was required by tradition for Egyptian figures, not because he could not see and portray accurately individual facts of appear-

Ägyptisches Museum, Berlin.

FIG. 237.   Akhenaten and Nofretete
(1375-1358 B.C.).

ance; for other peoples were shown with all their distinctive racial characteristics.

In the examples of relief sculpture that have been discussed, the figures have been cut into the stone. This "sunken relief" is characteristically Egyptian and is seldom encountered in other styles. Since such reliefs were almost invariably painted as well—the background of the relief of Akhenaten and Nofretete (Fig. 237) from Tell el-Amarna is yellow and the figures are gaily colored—it seems probable that the sunken relief technique may have been employed to keep the pigment from being rubbed off. This type of relief carving was utilized most extensively on the façades of buildings (cf. Fig. 18) in figures glorifying the achievements of the

Museo Civico, Bologna.

FIG. 238.   Negro Captives, Relief from the Tomb of Haremhab
(*ca.* 1325 B.C.).

Pharaohs, on the shafts of columns, and on the walls of tombs. The Egyptians also employed the other variety of relief sculpture—with projecting forms—on their buildings, an example being *Seti I Offering an Image of Truth to Osiris* (Fig. 239) from the temple he built at Abydos in honor of seven deities including himself. Seti I ascended the throne of Egypt in 1313 B.C. and was one of the first great rulers of the Nineteenth Dynasty in the Empire period. He was notable alike for the vigor with which he enforced Egyptian rule in conquered lands and the vast building program he undertook at home, which included the construction of the Hypostyle Hall in the great temple of Amon-Re at Karnak. The relief from Abydos is outstanding for its color and the fine execution of the delicately carved forms. Such refinement of line and surface would have been lost in the glaring sunlight on an external wall but appears to excellent advantage in its more somber interior setting. There are the

same formal conventions noted before, and if the vigor and austerity of Old Kingdom examples are lacking (cf. Figs. 230, 233), there is a compensating grace of line and refinement of form. The accessory color is as conventionalized as the drawing of the figures—a dark tone for male figures, a light one for females—the purpose being neither representational nor decorative but to make the forms clearer and more distinct in the ensemble.

Rameses II, who began his reign of sixty-seven years in 1292 B.C., was the son of Seti I and the longest-lived of the Nineteenth Dynasty rulers. Like his father, Rameses was a great warrior, and also like him he was indefatigable in erecting and decorating temples in honor of the gods and himself. The life-size seated figure of granite (Fig. 240), carved about 1250 B.C. and now in the museum at Turin, was intended for one of his many temples and shows another standard Egyptian royal type. Small figures on the sides of the statue, behind the legs, and below the thighs, represent his queen and one of his sons. As in the majority of Egyptian statues, working in the intractable stone appears to have presented no problem whatsoever; finely cut grooves represent the royal garment, the head-dress is covered with minute medallions, and there is the same delicacy of line and contour that was noted in the relief of Seti I, the characteristic in which these examples of Empire or New Kingdom sculpture differ most from the rugged and powerful forms of the Old and Middle Kingdom statues (cf. Figs. 231, 235).

An antithesis to the graceful delicacy of this figure is to be found in the same period in which this one was executed, for the colossal figures more than sixty-five feet high on the façade of the temple of Abu-Simbel (Fig. 19) are also of Rameses II and were begun about the same time, in 1257 B.C. These enormous figures would be impressive for their sheer bulk if for no other reason, the bulk which connoted the eternal for the Egyptian in a form, supposedly impervious to any normal process of decay, that recorded the communal belief in regal power and divinity. Possibly the grandiose proportions of the figures led to the very considerable generalization of the features and expression—quite different in effect from the delicate surfaces of the statue at Turin and with something of the imperturbable aloofness of figures carved in earlier times.

Rameses II was the last of the great Egyptian rulers; the power of his successors in the Twentieth Dynasty was not even remotely comparable to his. The Empire or New Kingdom period in Egyptian history comes to a close about 1100 B.C. after a succession of weak kings, many of whom bore Rameses' name but had none of his power. The series of minor monarchs—Libyan, Ethiopian, and Assyrian—in the Twenty-first to Twenty-fifth Dynasties (1100-663 B.C.) show all too clearly the disintegration of the centralized power and the glory of the once mighty kingdom. Only in the Twenty-sixth Dynasty (663-525 B.C.) during the Saïtic Restoration does a vestige of the old power reappear, and it is in this period that a few examples of sculpture comparable in quality if not in character to

Louvre, Paris.

FIG. 239.   Seti I Offering
(*ca.* 1300 B.C.).

Museo di Antichità, Turin.

FIG. 240.   Rameses II
(*ca.* 1250 B.C.)

older work can be found. The basalt head of a *Saïtic Dignitary* (Fig. 241) in the Museum of Fine Arts in Boston reveals craftsmanship of a quality equal to anything in the great periods. It is employed, however, for different purposes than producing conventionalized symbols of royal and divine power. The Saïtic heads are individual in detail, portraying every blemish, like the wart under the left eye in Fig. 241, and specifically personal in character. The greater freedom the sculptor had in these matters results in forms of more immediate appeal; the best examples are impressive in their perception of character and its direct statement in sculptural terms. But the grandeur of Menkaura (Fig. 231) and Amenemhet III (Fig. 235) is lacking, and even the vital alertness of Rameses II (Fig. 240) has no counterpart here. In such forms as these the centuries-old tradition of Egyptian sculpture comes to an end. Under the Persians,

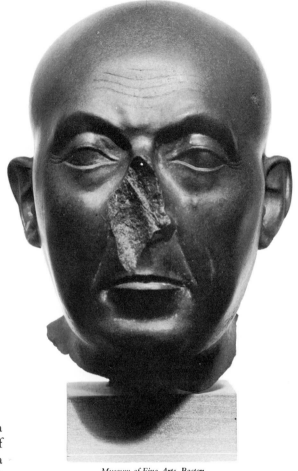

Museum of Fine Arts, Boston.

FIG. 241.   Saïtic Dignitary
(*ca.* 600 B.C.).

Greeks, and Romans, it is increasingly diluted and modified by alien concepts and methods to the extent that whatever there remains of truly Egyptian character is at most only one of numerous traits that are present.

Sculpture in Mesopotamia in the fourth and third millennia before the Christian era was similar in function to that of Egypt; it was of similar formal character as well, once allowance is made for differences between the two regions in culture and material resources. Mesopotamia had nothing like the abundant supply of stone available in Egypt, and as characteristic an

University Museum, Philadelphia.

FIG. 242. Sumerian Noble
(*ca.* 2700 B.C.).

of the same shaven head, beaklike nose and staring eyes, the same costume and stance, in many other statuettes of the period makes it clear that this engaging little form is a conventional type which evolved as a traditional symbol similar in basic character to the Old Kingdom figures of ancient Egypt.

Early relief sculpture in Mesopotamia also employs conventions similar to those of Egypt. The *Stele of Naram-Sin* (Fig. 243) in the Louvre in Paris was erected originally at Susa in Babylonia about 2300 B.C. to commemorate a victory

early example as the *Sumerian Noble* (Fig. 242) is very small—only nine inches high. The figure was carved between 3000 and 2500 B.C. and was found at Khafaje in excavations conducted by the University of Pennsylvania Museum, where it now is. The material is white limestone with inset eyes of shell and lapis lazuli. The figure is nude to the waist; the legs are covered by a ceremonial skirt that leaves the bare feet exposed. The pose is frontal, with the left leg advanced as in Egyptian standing figures; the hands were originally clasped over the breast. The torso consists of a few broadly modeled planes with the nipples of the breast indicated. The round head has prominent ears; the eyebrows are incised curved lines above the widely staring eyes and the strongly protruding nose. These characteristics at first appear to be individual and personal and the initial impression is of a rather summarily rendered portrait; but the recurrence

Louvre, Paris.

FIG. 243. Stele of Naram-Sin
(*ca.* 2300 B.C.).

Louvre, Paris.

FIG. 244. Gudea of Telloh
(*ca.* 2100 B.C.).

than built up as organic and articulated entities. At the same time, an elementary rendering of space has been attempted; the king is not only above but also behind his troops; the mountain stronghold he approaches is outlined against the sky with its two stars; the soldiers are obviously thought of as moving in several planes in depth, in contrast to the completely flat pattern of those similarly engaged in the Egyptian commemorative relief of Narmer.

Among the most characteristic examples of early Mesopotamian sculpture are the numerous figures found at Telloh, known in older times as Lagash, in southern Babylonia. These refer by inscription to a certain Gudea, a powerful lord in Asia Minor about 2100 B.C., and the statuette of green diorite in the Louvre (Fig. 244) is believed to represent him. About a foot and a half high, the figure is carved from stone that was probably imported, ·a circumstance that accounts for its relatively small size although others found at the same time are considerably larger. The pose is frontal and the traditional clasping of the hands noted in the earlier figure from Khafaje (Fig. 242) suggests that it was devotional. This may also explain the rather heavy and squat proportions of the body, like that of a dwarf, with the thighs and legs compressed in a rectangular block, and the thick torso. These characteristics seem inconsistent with the accurate details of the muscles and the modeling of lips and chin, but they confirm the conceptual and symbolic purpose of the form that is comparable to Egyptian figures of similar function. The face is blank and impassive, without even as much indication of personal character as there is in the Sheikh el-Beled (Fig. 232). From this it is clear that the naturalism of the Mesopotamian figure has the same expressive purpose as that of the Egyptian, however different the details of the forms.

It is difficult to discern a line of development in Mesopotamian sculpture like that of Egypt. The involved political and military history of the region in the second millennium before Christ was no more conducive to such activities there than was the case in the interim between the Middle and New Kingdoms in Egypt. About

won by the grandson of Sargon I, one of the most important Mesopotamian rulers. Cuneiform inscriptions in wedge-shaped characters describe the episode, represented in relief on a stone slab a little over six feet high; it shows Naram-Sin leading his troops in victorious battle through a mountainous country like that around Susa itself. As in comparable Egyptian reliefs (cf. Fig. 230), the figures are in profile and the king is much larger than his followers. The same memory-picture principle is evident in the way the bodies are organized as a group of elements shown in their most characteristics aspects rather

the tenth century B.C., however, a strong centralized power was established in the northern or Assyrian region, and from then until the destruction of this empire in 612 B.C., there are numerous examples of sculpture. An alabaster relief of *Assurnasirpal II Drinking* (Fig. 245) came from the palace built at Kalher by that ruler in the early ninth century B.C. and is now in the Metropolitan Museum in New York. The monarch stands with a bow in his left hand and a shallow drinking cup in his right, confronted by his attendant who extends another cup to him as he raises the ceremonial whisk that was his badge of office. All the primitive conventions are present —the striding stance, profile head with fullfront eye, shoulders distorted into both frontal and side views; details like the fringes of garments and hair and beards are indicated by schematized patterns of wavy lines and ringlets. Specifically Mesopotamian are the heavy, massive proportions of the figures, the strongly emphasized muscles of the arms, and the cuneiform inscriptions incised in a continuous band that takes no account of the figures, in contrast to the way hieroglyphs are used in an Egyptian relief (Fig. 239); there the writing and the carved forms complement each other in stating their common theme.

Typical too is the mundane subject of the Assurnasirpal relief. The Egyptian king-god is doing honor to his fellow deities; the Mesopotamian priest-king is recording his fondness for battle and the hunt. As was said elsewhere, the cult of the dead which was responsible for nearly all Egyptian artistic concepts had no counterpart in Mesopotamia. There the divinity of royalty was expressed by glorifying material achievement. This concept underlay the ziggurat (Figs. 20, 21), which was a palace-temple, and it explains the conventions emphasizing bodily strength and power in the Mesopotamian figures. And it is this concept which gives the *Wounded Lioness* (Fig. 246) its vigor and force in portraying the futile rage of the crippled beast as she drags her paralyzed hind legs over the ground in a final effort to attack her slayer. The relief is from a series depicting Assurbanipal hunting lions that originally decorated his palace which

was built at Nineveh between 668 and 626 B.C. Much detail has been omitted, and there are stylizations of more details, as in the wavy pattern of blood flowing from the arrow holes and the long curving line of the outstretched front leg merging into the throat and the muzzle; but the accurately rendered snarl, the laid-back ears, and the loosened tendons and muscles of the dragging hind legs are proof of the sculptor's ability to see and record the essentials of an episode in which he clearly had more than casual interest.

The scarcity of good building stone in Mesopotamia was mentioned earlier as a factor in the architectural style of the region; and it also affected sculptural style, for there is little statuary in the round as compared with that of Egypt. A form developed in the later period that has some characteristics of free-standing sculpture is the *Winged Man-Headed Lion* (Fig. 247) in

The Metropolitan Museum of Art,
Gift of John D. Rockefeller Jr., 1932.

FIG. 245.   Assurnasirpal II Drinking
(*ca.* 900 B.C.).

British Museum, London.

FIG. 246. Wounded Lioness (*ca.* 650 B.C.).

the British Museum in London; it was carved for the palace of Assurnasirpal II at Nimrud between 885 and 860 B.C. These monsters, conceptually similar to the sphinxes of Egypt (cf. Fig. 234), were the guardian genii of the Mesopotamian palace that scrutinized all persons and things that passed through its portals. As expressive concepts they belong to a culture that still conceived its gods in zoomorphic form. Formally they illustrate the inorganic and descriptive conventionalism noted in the human figures; a detail in point is the representation of the monster with five legs so that it will have four legs when seen from the side and also be properly supported when viewed from the front. Otherwise there are the same stylized details of hair and feathers and the strongly emphasized muscles noted in the

human figures, as well as a notable heaviness of proportion and massiveness of form in patterns of rectilinear severity and bulk.

Sculpture was a major art in both Egypt and Mesopotamia, a medium for expressing the most significant concepts developed by their respective cultures in preclassical times. This is not true of the third cultural area of that period, the Aegean. In Crete, for example, no stone sculpture of monumental size or content has been found. The plastered rubble walls of the palaces at Phaistos and Knossos (cf. Fig. 25) lent themselves well to painted decoration, and there are some traces of modeled stucco relief in the house of Minos. Relief modeling is found on some utilitarian objects such as vases, but sculpture in the round is limited almost entirely to very small images. One of the most striking of these is the ivory and gold statuette of the *Snake Goddess* (Fig. 248) in the Museum of Fine Arts at Boston. Executed in all likelihood about 1500 B.C. and some six and a half inches high, it represents a woman wearing a flounced skirt and open bodice, with a crown on her head and two gold snakes coiled about her outstretched arms. The theme is fairly common in the art of Crete, where the snake was worshiped as an earth deity. For all its diminutive size, the statuette is remarkably expressive; its vigorous tension is quite unlike the impassiveness of Egyptian and Mesopotamian cult figures. This comes from the

Museum of Fine Arts, Boston.

FIG. 248.   The Snake Goddess
(*ca.* 1500 B.C.).

British Museum, London.

FIG. 247.   Winged Man-Headed Lion
(*ca.* 875 B.C.).

poised stance in which the backward-curving torso balances the forward thrust of the arms, and from the interlocking curves of the gold serpents twining around the bent forearms. The prominent breasts suggest that this image was the goddess of a fertility cult, with much the same meaning as the prehistoric figure from Menton (Fig. 229).

As distinguished in its way as the Snake Goddess and unique in being a reasonably well-preserved example of large-scale stone sculpture from Aegean times is the triangular slab of the Lion Gate (Fig. 26) at Mycenae on the mainland of Greece. The gate was built about 1350 B.C. in all probability, and the relief slab is the earliest known monumental carving on the mainland of Greece. The symbolism is much the same as in the Mesopotamian guardian monsters in Fig. 247. The two lions stand with their forepaws on a stereobate from which rises a downward-tapering column surmounted by a bulbous capital of semicircular profile, and a schematic entablature of horizontal members separated by four disks representing roof beams. This column is a symbol of the house that is defended by the flanking lions. They once had heads that were carved from separate blocks attached to the bodies by wooden dowels in the square holes which are still visible. The relief slab is nine and one-half feet high, and the lions are thus of consderable size; the modeling, well adapted to the limestone, emphasizes their size and power. It is possible that comparable works elsewhere in the Aegean world have been entirely destroyed, but it is hardly likely that there could have been more distinguished examples of monumental

relief sculpture in stone than the Lion Gate.

The very nature of sculpture makes it peculiarly effective in expressing the ideals of preclassical cultures. It speaks most impressively in generalized terms, for its materials do not immediately lend themselves to minute and subtle effects and corresponding distinctions of meaning and significance. But perhaps because of these material characteristics, it seeks to define its forms with clarity and precision, qualities that are realized only when the expressed content itself involves clear and precise understanding. Such was the nature of primitive thought, developed in efforts to comprehend and evaluate natural phenomena and shape them to creative ends in symbolic forms that had certain and comprehensible meaning. In preclassical times forms of such significance are sculptural more frequently than architectural or pictorial. If the power of the Egyptian Pharaoh is perceived more directly in his carved portrait than in his temple, it is in part at least because the massive simplicity of the statue expresses that idea more directly than the inorganic sequence of courts and halls in the temple.

Detail of Fig. 255.

CHAPTER SIXTEEN

Greek Sculpture

Of all the visual arts, sculpture was most congenial to the Greek temperament. There are a number of reasons for this, but two are preeminent. The particular appropriateness of the human form as sculptural subject matter corresponds directly to the primarily anthropocentric philosophy of the Greek which is summed up in the epigram that man is the measure of all things. And since experience is judged on the basis of human values that are determined by sensory response, it follows that reality is what is tangible and concrete, capable of being apprehended by the senses. The terms tangible and concrete imply form— and sculpture is above all an art of form. These facts explain why, for example, Greek architecture is little concerned with space. Space is intangible; it becomes real only through intuitive interpretation of direct sensory experience. The objective and self-explanatory forms that give Greek architecture its serenely ideal quality are actually more sculpturesque than architectonic; the Parthenon is no more pervaded by surrounding space than are the sculptured figures that decorate it (Fig. 29).

Greek sculpture was primarily religious. The instinctive feeling that the gods can be approached best through images representing them finds expression in this, as it does in all anthropomorphic cultures. In the preclassical

Aegean civilization of Crete and Mycenae, for instance, there was little monumental sculpture; in the primitive religion of the time, trees and rocks—the "stocks and stones" of the Old Testament—were worshiped. In all the vast labyrinth of King Minos' palace at Knossos (Fig. 24), the major religious symbol other than the building itself was a stone pillar with a mystic symbol carved on its side. Invading northern tribes between about 1000 and 700 B.C. brought changes —infusing new blood into the native Mediterranean stock and with it an anthropomorphic religion in which gods were represented in human form. This is the immediate background of the Greek or classical style in sculpture.

THE ARCHAIC PERIOD

During the archaic period, from about 625 to 480 B.C., the foundation was laid for Greek art in every field. In sculpture, basic types were created which continue through the greater part of the Greek development of the art. Of these types, two of outstanding importance were the draped standing female figure and the nude standing male. An example of the first is the *Hera of Samos* (Fig. 249), so called from its dedication to the goddess in her temple in Samos, about 550 B.C. At first glance, the statue seems more like a tree trunk than anything else, evidence of the persisting primitive "stocks and stones" concept of deity. But a more human ideal is implied by the toes at the bottom, the suggestion of a torso, and the portrayal of the arms. Naturalistic representation was not the artist's intention, however. It was rather to effect a formal pattern of firm and sweeping curves in the silhouette and the edge of the overgarment. The draperies also are part of this design. They are stylized; that is, the folds are represented not as they might actually appear but in a pattern of parallel lines which are a visual foil to the curves of the outline. At the same time, the sculptor took note of the more significant naturalistic details of the figure. This led to the contrasted textures of the heavy overgarment and the lighter one underneath, the toes, and the suggestion of breasts under the draperies.

The standing male nude type in Greek archaic sculpture is seen in an *Apollo* (Fig. 250),

Louvre, Paris.

FIG. 249.   Hera of Samos
(*ca.* 550 B.C.).

The Metropolitan Museum of Art, Fletcher Fund, 1932.

FIG. 250.   Apollo (*ca.* 600 B.C.).

in the Metropolitan Museum in New York, which was carved about 600 B.C. Typical of the largest single category of archaic sculpture, figures like this are usually known as "Apollos," although the type was used for other gods as well as for mortals. All have some characteristics observed in Egyptian sculpture (Fig. 236)—rigid frontality with the left leg slightly advanced, broad shoulders, narrow waists, and clenched fists. These similarities imply actual connection between the two styles, the Egyptian having influenced the Greek. The most obvious differences are the complete nudity of the Greek figure, and the absence of the supporting back slab and the web of stone between the legs. Instead of the surface pattern of parallel drapery lines in the Hera of Samos (Fig. 249), the body itself is made into a pattern. The chest, abdomen, and groin are indicated by stylized planes suggesting the rounded surfaces. The muscles of the lower abdomen are indicated by a projecting ridge from the hip to the genitals. The head is conventionalized, the muscles of the cheeks and lips being reduced to smooth planes; the eyes bulge from their shallow sockets and the lips form a straight line, though in some Apollos they are turned up at the corners in the curious "archaic smile." The hair is also conventionalized in a mass of regular curls that falls down the back, its bulk giving needed strength to the neck. The net result is a figure decoratively unified by simplification of the body's large complex forms.

∾ **293** ∾

National Museum, Athens.

FIG. 251.   Victory of Delos
(*ca.* 560 B.C.).

plete in its way as that of the model. He thus created a unity or reality analogous to the human body but differing from it in being ordered and arranged. From his knowledge of the human figure, limited though it was, he evolved a conception that had life and vigor in its own right.

The rapid development of Greek sculpture was due to a far-reaching and lively curiosity about the human figure that extended to all its aspects and attributes. For instance, in the *Victory of Delos* (Fig. 251), carved about 560 B.C., movement is suggested by a conventionalized pose with the bent legs in profile and the upper body and outstretched arms full-face. As in the Hera and the Apollo just discussed, the form of the figure is determined by decorative considerations. It is an akroterion, a figure to be placed on the peak of a temple gable. The incised lines indicating the folds of the skirt are curved to suggest movement. The torso is stylized, reduced to the principal volumes of shoulders, breasts, and abdomen, as is the face with its projecting cheek bones, bulging eyes, and archaic smile. As in the Apollo, the hair is a mass of long curls hanging over the shoulders and reinforcing the neck.

Archaic relief sculpture was employed chiefly as architectural decoration. About 550 B.C., the metopes of a temple at Selinunte in Sicily were carved with mythological subjects, one of them being *Perseus Slaying the Medusa* (Fig. 252) while Athena looks on. As in the Egyptian relief of Seti I (Fig. 239), the lower part of each figure is in profile and the upper part full-face. The figures themselves are rather heavy and squat; the dull faces lack even the animation of the conventional archaic smile. Naturalistic details are stylized, notably the muscles of the calves and the hair. The problem in decorative sculpture of this type is to integrate its pattern with the architecture. Here the principal accents of the design are vertical to agree with the flanking triglyphs. To fit the figures into the available space, Perseus' right arm and the Medusa's left leg had to be made shorter than their counterparts. The kneeling Medusa follows the type of the Delos Victory (Fig. 251).

Its stiffness reveals the sculptor's limited knowledge of the complex mechanism of the human body. Nonetheless, he realized its organic unity, for he indicated the joints of knees and ankles and wrists and elbows, as the Egyptian sculptor did not, and thus achieved the articulation that gives the figure the spark of life. He did not relate those parts in the statue exactly as in a living model, but imposed a relationship upon them as com-

The average observer accustomed to naturalistic representation may not be much attracted by archaic sculpture. Nonetheless, there is considerable beauty. From a historic point of view, this sculpture is significant as the beginning of a sculptural tradition that, with some justification, is often considered the greatest that ever existed. On the broadest aesthetic grounds, it reveals the vital characteristic of artistic creation, the imposition of rhythm and order on the chaotic material of human experience. Furthermore, it has to a high degree the essentially sculptural quality of form. It is impossible to view a good archaic statue without sensing this; its bulk and weight, the articulation of limbs and torso, the texture of the material are all impressed upon the observer. The statue stimulates a desire on his part to feel and handle it, to experience tactually the modeling and the planes of the surface. As an art of form, this is a test of sculptural quality in any style or period and one which proves the intrinsic greatness of much archaic art.

Acropolis Museum, Athens.

FIG. 253. Statue Dedicated by Euthydikos (490-480 B.C.).

Museum, Palermo.

FIG. 252. Perseus Slaying the Medusa
(*ca.* 550 B.C.),
Metope from Temple C in Selinus.

Toward the end of the archaic period, a more naturalistic style begins to appear. The *Statue Dedicated by Euthydikos* (Fig. 253) was excavated from the debris used to level off some parts of the Athenian Acropolis (cf. Fig. 36) after the city had been sacked by the Persians in 480 B.C. Carved between 490 and 480 B.C., it was probably dedicated to Athena. The advances in naturalistic observation made since the time when the Delian Victory (Fig. 251) was carved are evident, especially in the head. The eye socket is deeper; the upper lid has definite thickness and seems to cover the eyeball instead of being an incised line on its surface. The lips curve down at the ends, giving the face an almost sullen wilful expression. Certain archaic conventions still persist. The hair falls over the shoulders in stylized waves, and the drapery is indicated by parallel lines. The upper arm is attached to the body in the same arbitrary way as in earlier work. Even in the head, which is more naturalistic in the rendition of the planes of the face,

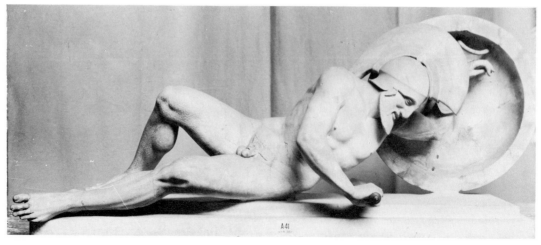

Glyptothek, Munich.

FIG. 254. Dying Warrior (*ca.* 480 B.C.), from the East Pediment of
the Temple at Aegina.

the contours of mouth and eyes are unbroken and the sides of the nose continue upward in a well-defined line that turns outward to indicate the intersection of brow and eye socket. All these details are traditional conventions that were retained in spite of the close observation of natural appearance evident in the treatment of the lips and eyes. Doubtless they were less obtrusive when the Euthydikos figure had its original coloring, for it was painted as were the majority of Greek statues. Traces of polychrome ornament are still visible on it and on the metope from Selinunte (Fig. 252).

The climax of the archaic style in Greek sculpture is reached in two groups of figures dating from about 480 B.C. which once stood in the pediments of the temple of Aphaia at Aegina. Each group represented a battle, probably an incident in the Trojan War. A *Dying Warrior* (Fig. 254) from the east pediment reveals even more than the Euthydikos figure the considerable knowledge of the human body at the end of the archaic period. No longer are hips and shoulders parallel, for the law of frontality has been discarded. The body can twist on its axis and free movement in either direction is possible. The muscles are accurately observed

though they appear rather hard, as they would be in the athletic type of figure which was apparently the sculptor's ideal. The greatest degree of naturalism in the statue is seen in the proportions of the body and the details of muscular and bony structure. In the head a number of archaic conventions persist. The rounded planes of the brow and nose are flattened, intersecting in a sharp ridge. The beard is a sharp angular mass with wavy incisions to indicate the hair. The archaic smile also persists, but it is modified by the shadow of the short mustache into an appropriate grimace of pain. Naturalistic though many of the details are, the figure is well unified formally. The sweeping curves of the lower side of the body create this unity; they establish a rhythm that begins slowly in the slight curve of the left leg, becomes more rapid in the body to culminate in the half circle of the helmet, and comes to a final close in the disk of the shield. The decorative rhythm of this progression of curves is counterpointed by the straight lines and angular silhouette of the upper edge of the body.

The archaic statues thus far considered all demonstrate the tendency in Greek art to disregard space. In the earliest statues like the

Victory of Delos (Fig. 251) the thickness of the figure is conditioned by the block it was carved from. Thus restricted in the depth dimension, the sculptor practically eliminated it and designed his figure to be seen only from the front. In later figures, like the Apollo in Fig. 250 and the Dying Warrior (Fig. 254) the sculptor used the more naturalistic rounding off of legs and arms to create a sense of the third dimension but only insofar as it emphasizes the mass of the figures. Furthermore, this effect is apparent only when the figures are viewed directly from the front or side; it is hardly perceptible from an angle. This indicates how similar the methods of sculpture and architecture were in the Greek world. Both were based on a two-dimensional conception of form that involved simplifying space to the point of eliminating it. By this sim-

plification the Greek sculptor emphasized the mass and volume of his figures and thus invested them with the grandeur and impressiveness apparent even in the earliest works.

By the end of the archaic period, the ideal of Greek sculpture was characterized by considerable naturalism, even though it was still expressed by many inflexible conventions. Later these conventions disappeared to some extent, being replaced by others based on closer observation of nature, but nonetheless conventional. In the Aegina sculptures, the change has already begun as far as the body is concerned, even though the general impression is overhardness. In the period subsequent to the archaic, known as the transitional, this change extends to the face and head as well as to the general proportions of the entire figure.

THE TRANSITIONAL PERIOD

The transitional period in Greek sculpture began about 480 B.C. and is generally considered to have lasted until 450 B.C. The term transitional has no implication that the art in that period is important only as a connecting link between archaic style and that of the Golden Age. On the contrary, transitional sculpture is as original in conception and as distinguished in quality as the work of any other period in Greek sculpture.

A notable example of transitional style is the bronze *Delphi Charioteer* (Fig. 255), which dates from about 475 B.C. The life-size statue was part of a group consisting of chariot, driver, and horses which commemorated a chariot race victory. Although erected to honor an individual, it is not a portrait in the exact sense. Rather it embodies the typical aristocratic youth who took part in the athletic contests of the day. It is also typical rather than specific in showing the figure not in the rapid movement of the race but standing calmly in the chariot holding the reins. In the head there is a closer approximation to actuality than there has been hitherto, the realism being heightened by the colored eyeballs and by the silver teeth visible between the slightly opened lips. The feet and the arm are

also portrayed very naturalistically, as compared with archaic works. This naturalism does not detract, however, from the unified design of the figure as a whole embodied in the organically related volumes of the body and the decorative pattern of hair and draperies. Although at first glance the latter seem to fall in regular folds, actually they are varied subtly to give interest to the pattern without complicating its simplicity. There is still no effort to reveal the body underneath the draperies. Both exist as separate entities, although the long robe seems to envelop the body, unlike the tightly stretched sheaths that represent garments in the archaic style (Fig. 251).

The largest single body of transitional sculpture now existent once decorated the temple of Zeus at Olympia, which was completed about 460 B.C.; it includes a number of figures from the pediments and several metopes. In the *Pediments* (Fig. 256) there was a problem of arrangement, namely, to relate the figures so that the groups would fit naturally in the flat triangular space. The Olympia sculptors solved this problem by making a god the central figure in each pediment—Zeus in the eastern one, which is above in the illustration, and Apollo in the western one. As divinities, they are larger than

FIG. 255. Charioteer (*ca.* 475 B.C.).

for Hippodamia, the latter's daughter; the western one shows the legendary battle between the Lapiths and the Centaurs. At the extreme ends of both pediments are reclining figures. Those in the eastern pediment symbolize two rivers, Alpheios and Kladeos, which bounded the area where the chariot race was run; those in the western pediment are figures of feminine spectators. The contrast between quiet and animated scenes becomes standard in subsequent pediment compositions. The design of each of the Olympia pediments is rather obviously symmetrical, with a central figure and others on the sides balancing in pose and action. Nonetheless, the individual groups are well related to each other and form a unified whole, particularly in the western pediment where the calm Apollo in the center and the passively reclining figures at the ends effectively stabilize the struggling groups.

The *Apollo* (Fig. 257) from the western pediment continues the standing nude male type of the archaic period (Fig. 250), but with certain changes. Where the pose of the archaic figure is mechanically balanced, there are variety and elasticity in the transitional figure; the weight rests on the right leg, the left one is partially relaxed. The Olympian Apollo also indicates greater observation of muscular structure than was apparent even in the most advanced archaic work (Fig. 254). It is an athletic ideal in both the Aeginetan and Olympian figures, but the Olympian sculptor avoided the exaggerated hardness which makes the skin of the earlier figure resemble tanned hide over strips of leather instead of firm flesh over well-developed muscles. This is the effect the sculptor of the Apollo obtained, particularly in the arms, the breast, and the horizontal bands of muscle across the upper abdomen. It is also evident in the head in spite of archaic formalisms in the ringlets of hair, the protruding eyeballs, and the unbroken contour of the eyelids. The planes of the cheeks and mouth merge into each other; and the hard intersection of the forehead and eye socket, characteristic of archaic work, is softened. The draperies over the right shoulder and left forearm lie in naturalistic folds, although the broad planes and sharp edges may suggest earlier, more stylized methods.

the mortals around them and are appropriately placed in the middle of the pediment from the viewpoint of both design and subject matter. They are the judges of the contests represented. The eastern pediment shows the preparation for the chariot race between Pelops and Oenomaus that was to decide the former's fate as a suitor

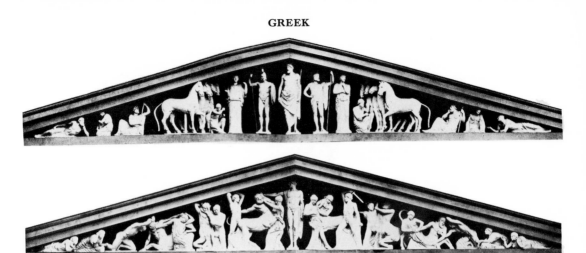

FIG. 256.   Temples of Zeus (*ca.* 460 B.C.) at Olympia: Pediment Groups,
Restored.

There is still some rigidness, but it is due here to the architectonic function of the figure; it is an important element in the pattern that welds the details with their incidental naturalism into integral parts of a larger scheme. There are certain conventions in addition to the above, notably the emphasis on the band marking the lower edge of the abdomen and the continuation of the forehead line in the nose. The band is characteristic of well-developed athletic figures and hence is a naturalistic convention; the forehead line was adopted quite early by the Greeks as an arbitrary feature of beauty.

The figure symbolizing the river *Alpheois* (Fig. 258) from the east pediment at Olympia also illustrates the increasing naturalism of transitional style. It is almost identical in pose with the Dying Warrior from Aegina (Fig. 254) but the details reveal differences. The breast muscles are soft and pliant masses in the Olympia figure rather than dry, hard lumps. There is a suggestion that the muscles of the left side are more strained than those of the right, a characteristic not found in the earlier figure. In both, the long curves of the lower side of the body are set off by the angular contours of the upper side, but this contrast is not as obvious in the transitional work. The sculptor's ideal was more naturalistic than that of the earlier period, and formal abstraction is not so emphasized.

There were twelve carved metopes in the temple of Zeus at Olympia, six over each end of the cella. They represented the twelve labors of Heracles and were similar in style to the pediment sculptures, although probably a little earlier in date. One of those labors involved obtaining the golden apples of the Hesperides; this could be done only with the aid of Atlas, the giant who supported the firmament on his shoulders according to Greek mythology. The metope sculpture represents *Heracles, Atlas, and Athena* (Fig. 259); Heracles bows under the weight of the world symbolized by the architectural entablature above the frieze, taking Atlas' place while the latter obtains the golden apples which he holds out to the hero. Athena stands behind Heracles and relieves the weight on his shoulders. As in the pediment groups, the design is architectonic, the paramount consideration being its decorative relationship to the architecture. The three figures repeat the vertical accents of the colonnade below and of the flanking triglyphs. The modeling is direct and straightforward with few details, for most of these were painted on the figures. Again comparison with an archaic work like the metope from Selinunte (Fig. 252) reveals the more extensive observation of naturalistic details in transitional sculpture. The male figures are in full profile, even to the eyes which are no longer frontal but foreshortened almost correctly. The male heads are angular and somewhat archaic in form, but Athena's has a rounded

Museum, Olympia.

FIG. 257.   Apollo (*ca.* 460 B.C.), from the West Pediment
of the Temple of Zeus at Olympia.

softness that anticipates the later style of the Golden Age. Notable is the masterly design of the bodies, in which broad planes and sharp contours articulate the masses of torso, limbs, and head in a unified whole. The drapery of the female figure seems almost naturalistic, yet its straight ordered folds are marvelously simple in arrangement, the realistic effect being due to subtle variations in the details.

The most immediately apparent difference between archaic and transitional sculpture is the latter's increased naturalism. Less obvious but equally important is the difference in content. In the archaic period, the sculptor was chiefly concerned with bodily structure and appearance; the content of his figures is born of his effort to express his ideas with a relatively limited technique. In the transitional period, the technical problems the earlier sculptor faced were less puzzling; many of them were solved as a result of more extended and closer observation of the human figure. But this increased knowledge brought a need for more than a mere approximation of the body's appearance. To satisfy this need, the transitional sculptor attempted to suggest personality. The elevation of the Olympian Apollo above the struggling groups around him conveys the superiority of the god to mortal beings. The Delphi Charioteer is likewise oblivious to the excitement and turmoil of the race just run. The ideal unity of personality thus suggested is reinforced by the ideal unity of environment which makes each figure complete in itself even though part of a group, and by the ideal unity of time achieved by representing action at a moment immediately before or after that of greatest activity—in the Charioteer, just after the race; in the east pediment group at Olympia, just before the race. Even in subjects entirely in terms of movement such as the Discus Thrower, a well-known example of transitional sculpture, the instant portrayed is the moment when opposing forces are balanced. In each case, the artist's aim was to suggest both previous and subsequent action and thus attain an ideal unity of time.

The attainment of an ideally unified time, environment, and personality in transitional sculpture resulted in a new seriousness of expression and bearing. The Olympian Apollo is aloof and dignified, above the petty dissensions of humanity yet conscious of his importance as arbiter. This realization of profound inner meaning is the most vital point of difference between archaic and transitional figures. The archaic (Fig. 250) are brisk and sprightly, their faces often animated by the archaic smile; the transitional are heavier and almost somber in expression. The prevailing tenseness of the archaic figure gives the impression of an organism that is almost mechanical in function; in the transitional figure, the balance of contracted and relaxed muscles suggests an inner will that controls the organism. The more naturalistic details of the body thus acquire greater meaning because they are the instruments of personality. The entire statue em-

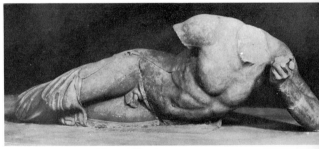

Museum, Olympia.

FIG. 258.   The River Alpheios
(*ca.* 460 B.C.), from the East Pediment
of the Temple of Zeus at Olympia.

bodies a conception which attains monumental effect in the large, simple, well-ordered pattern of volumes that makes the conception objective and tangible. It remained only for the Golden Age to give it even greater power by making it abstract.

Museum, Olympia.

FIG. 259.   Heracles, Atlas and Athena
(*ca.* 460 B.C.), Metope from the
Temple of Zeus at Olympia.

THE GOLDEN AGE

During the Golden Age of Greece from 450 to 400 B.C., the ideals outlined and suggested in the art and thought of the archaic and transitional periods were completely stated. The architectural ideal is embodied in the Propylaea, the Parthenon, and the Erechtheum (Figs. 38, 39, 41), all on the Acropolis of Athens. In literature, the great tragedies of Sophocles and Euripides were written then. In sculpture, Polykleitos and Pheidias produced their masterpieces. Architecture, drama, and sculpture all reveal a matured concept of life, a philosophy that had been formulated and tested. In the Golden Age, the Athenian Greek was sure of himself; the traditions of his race had been firmly established as valid and significant, and their artistic expression was completely integrated. That integration is the explanation of its greatness.

The transformation of archaic into transitional sculpture shows a trend toward an ideal at once naturalistic and abstract. That ideal was attained in the Golden Age. It is suggested in a Roman copy of a statue by Polykleitos, dating between 450 and 440 B.C., of an athlete carrying a spear known as the *Doryphoros* (Fig. 260) or Spearbearer. This statue indicates that the sculptor of the Golden Age has gone far toward mastering the representation of the human figure. The pose is that of taking a forward step; the weight rests on the right leg and the left one is relaxed, emphasizing the slight variation between the two legs apparent in the Olympian Apollo (Fig. 257). The arms are also differentiated; the right one is inactive and the left one held a spear. The head is turned slightly to the right; the tight, closely adhering ringlets of hair reveal the contour of the skull, the deep eye sockets enclose the eyeballs, and the upper lids overlap the lower ones at the outer end instead of forming an unbroken contour. These details and others like the indication of the muscles and veins show rather accurate knowledge of human anatomy.

The muscles are well developed, as would be expected in a statue of an athlete, though they may have been exaggerated in this Roman copy

of the original. Such copies tell most of what is known today about the work of the great Greek sculptors, for the originals have long since disappeared. These copies vary in quality, depending upon the skill of the copyist; at best they are only approximations of the originals. According to contemporary descriptions, this copy of the Doryphoros, which was found in the palaestra or athletic field at Pompeii and is now in the

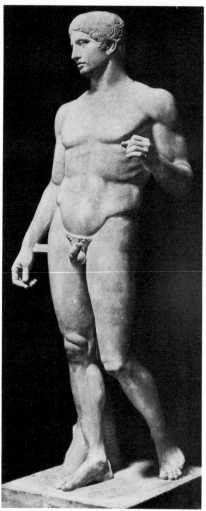

Museum, Naples.

FIG. 260.   The Doryphoros, after Polykleitos (*ca.* 450 B.C.).

Naples Museum, indicates the principal characteristics of Polykleitos' bronze original, though some details, like the muscles, show traces of Roman style. The conventional heavy band below the abdomen is very prominent, as are also the breast muscles. Throughout, the forms are well observed and well related to the movement of the body. To this relationship is due, in part at least, the impression of life in the statue, but it comes even more from the design as a whole. The right leg and arm are both straight, but the arm is relaxed, the leg sustaining the weight of the body. Both arm and leg on the left side are bent, but the arm is functional. The rhythm of this balanced cross relationship of tense and relaxed muscles is emphasized by the shoulder on the right side being lowered and the left one raised, creating the impression that the figure has perfect freedom of movement. At the same time, it is perfectly poised, for its center of balance lies within its own mass, the vertical axis touching the inner side of the right leg. It is evident from the Doryphoros that many problems of portraying the human figure naturalistically have been solved. The increased knowledge of bodily structure that made this greater realism possible was accompanied by greater awareness of the ideal requirements of a work of art. These were set forth by Polykleitos in a book called *The Canon*, meaning a rule, in which he gave the proportions of the Doryphoros as those of the ideal male figure. Characteristically, these proportions are based on mathematical relationships, just as in the Doric temple. Thus in addition to the organic connection between various parts of the body and the general solidness and sense of weight, the bodily elements are commensurates of a mathematical ratio. The head is one-seventh the height of the whole body, a heavier proportion than in either archaic or transitional figures, in which the ratio is one to ten and one to eight respectively. Similarly, the size of all the details is determined by a fixed ratio, the unit being one of those details, such as a finger or a hand.

The main characteristics of fifth-century sculpture of the Golden Age are present in the Doryphoros; but since it is a Roman copy, it obviously differs to some extent from the original. One thing the copyist introduced is the tree stump beside the right leg. He did this to strengthen the marble copy of the bronze original; for without it the brittle stone legs would have broken under the weight of the body. This also accounts for the bar between the right arm and the hip. The heavy muscles have already been mentioned as a possible exaggeration by the copyist. It is manifestly impossible to judge the full effect of the style of the Golden Age on the basis of such figures; for this, originals must be had.

The most impressive Greek originals of the Golden Age are the sculptures that were once on the Parthenon in Athens (Figs. 39, 40). There were free-standing groups in both pediments (Fig. 29), a continuous frieze in low relief around the outside of the cella wall, and figures in high relief on each metope. The pediment figures were probably carved between 438 and 433 B.C., the others a little earlier. The subjects of all the sculptures were related in some way to Athena, to whom the Parthenon was dedicated. The east pediment represented her birth; the western one, her contest with Poseidon for the sponsorship of the city of Athens. The frieze portrayed the Panathenaic Procession which ascended the rocky slopes of the Acropolis once every four years during ceremonies involving the renewal of the sacred peplos or robe woven by the maidens of the city which enshrouded the ancient wooden image of Athena in the temple treasury. The metopes concern various mythological subjects —combats between gods and giants, Greeks and Amazons and Lapiths and Centaurs. As related to each other on the Parthenon, the three categories of sculpture symbolize the Greek cosmos. The metopes show men's achievements in legendary times; the frieze shows human beings in relationship to their gods; the pediments show the world of the gods themselves. Very little of this sculpture remains on the Parthenon, for much of it was placed in the British Museum by Lord Elgin. A great deal of it was badly damaged by an explosion in 1687 that nearly demolished the building, and attempts prior to Lord Elgin's to lower the pediment sculptures caused irreparable damage to them.

British Museum, London.

FIG. 261.   Mount Olympus (438-433 B.C.), from the East Pediment of
the Parthenon in Athens.

The decoration of the Parthenon was conceived by Pheidias, an artist whose genius was recognized by nearly all writers of ancient times. Under his direction, the embellishment of Athens took place between 449 and 434 B.C., with funds diverted from the Delian Confederacy by Pericles. His was the ruling spirit among the multitude of artists including Iktinos and Kallikrates, the architects of the Parthenon, and the numerous sculptors who carved its figures. A noted sculptor himself, Pheidias' individual contribution to the Parthenon was the ivory and gold statue of Athena in the cella (cf. Fig. 40), but there can be no doubt that the conception of every figure on the building was his even if he did not execute them with his own hands.

A group of free-standing figures in the east pediment represented the birth of Athena. As in the Olympia group of the chariot race, the setting and time were indicated by symbolic figures; the event took place at dawn on Mount Olympus. At the left, the horses of the sun rise from the ocean as those of the setting moon sink below the waves at the right. Immediately beside the horses of the sun is a reclining male figure (Fig. 261); once thought to be Theseus, the Athenian hero, it is more plausibly identified as a symbol of Mount Olympus, the dwelling place of the gods, lighted by the rays of the rising sun. This figure sums up all that had been achieved in earlier periods in representing the male body. Polykleitan muscular conventions are evident in the three bands across the breast, stomach, and abdomen. However, the muscles of Polykleitos' figures are somewhat dry and exaggerated as is natural in an athletic type. In the *Mount Olympus* the muscles are clearly indicated and their function is well understood, but the overstatement of earlier styles is avoided. They are pliant and flexible; the skin and the firm, resilient flesh have elastic thickness instead of being hard and thin like a tanned hide. The ideal is a perfectly developed man in contrast to the Polykleitan concept of a perfectly trained athlete. The figure is seated on a stone covered with drapery that falls in complicated folds; its well-suggested texture contrasts effectively with the smooth firm flesh of the man. In spite of its damaged condition, the head reveals many of the characteristics of the Doryphoros. Its proportion to the total height of the body is about one to seven. The hair clings closely to the skull, revealing its contour and emphasizing its mass. The nose continues the line of the brow according to the Greek concept of beauty. The eye is recessed in its socket and the upper lid overlaps the lower one slightly at the outer end. As in the body, the modeling of the cheek and mouth is realistic without being merely representative. Again the carefully studied

balance of movement results in perfect poise. The facial expression is quiet and impersonal; in fifth-century Greek art the face and head were not emphasized as expressive elements but were contributory to the effect created by the entire body. The serene repose of the Mount Olympus is inherent in the figure as a whole and would be no less powerful even if the head were missing.

The three female figures at the right of the east pediment of the Parthenon bear out this generalization concerning the Mount Olympus. They represent the *Three Fates* (Fig. 262), believed by the Greeks to be present at every birth. Although all the heads are missing, it is doubtful if their presence would have made the figures any more impressive for, as in most Greek art, the concept of the whole is implied in the rhythms of the parts. There is carefully related movement in the group; the figure at the left is about to rise; the middle one turns toward her, and the third is in complete repose. This movement is a factor in the composition of the pediment group as a whole, a movement which extends from the outer figures to the central group of Zeus and Athena. It does not detract in the slightest from the compactness of the group

British Museum, London.

FIG. 262. The Three Fates (438–433 B.C.), from the East Pediment of the Parthenon in Athens.

Museo Civico, Bologna.

FIG. 263.   Head of the Athena Lemnia,
after Pheidias (*ca.* 450 B.C.).

of great interest in its own right but is nonetheless subordinated to the bodies underneath. Thus the simplicity or complexity of the folds is determined by the functional importance of the part of the body they cover. The folds over the legs are broad, giving way to smooth planes over the knees and becoming complex over the thighs and abdomen. The breasts are indicated by plain surfaces in contrast to the swirls between them. The forms are never obscured by the drapery but rather are made clearer, just as the major theme in a Bach fugue is enriched by a minor motive in counterpoint. In addition to clarifying the structure of the figures, the draperies also establish the three-dimensional volumes of the bodies, their curved lines conveying a sense of definite and solid mass beneath. The whole group is a masterpiece of effective details that give character and weight to a broad and comprehensive idea without losing their own individuality.

And what of the bodies themselves? A famous sculptor is reported to have said, when he first saw the Three Fates, "They look as if they were modeled on human bodies, but where is one to find such bodies?" This was just the impression the sculptor wished to give—beings in human form but without the individual and accidental imperfections of mortal bodies. If the gods can be represented as humans, it must be in forms of surpassing beauty, idealized. This the Parthenon sculptor realized; hence his statues of the gods represent a human ideal which could exist only in the minds of men, never in mortal flesh. This is why the writers of antiquity called Polykleitos the sculptor of men and Pheidias the sculptor of gods; in Pheidias' figures they beheld the epitome of the perfect physical beauty which they imagined the gods possessed.

Even in their imperfect condition, the Three Fates convey the impression of sublime repose that characterizes the Golden Age. No doubt the heads also contributed to this impression originally. Although there is no original by Pheidias that proves this, a marble head, copied from a bronze statue by Pheidias known as the *Athena Lemnia* (Fig. 263), gives weight to this supposition. The beauty for which the original figure was celebrated in classic antiquity is indicated in

itself or the unity of the individual figures. This unity is due to two factors, the lofty conception of the bodies and the complete harmony between them and the draperies, which fall in many folds. At first glance the draperies seem very naturalistic, but closer examination discloses a very subtle pattern, formed by the numerous folds, that is

a passage by Lucian in which he praises it particularly for the outline of the head, the delicate modeling of the cheeks, and the finely proportioned nose. All these characteristics are present in the marble head in the Municipal Museum at Bologna, even though it is a Roman copy. In structure and proportions it resembles the head of the Mount Olympus from the east pediment of the Parthenon. The austere expression is an integral part of the classic ideal embodied in the figure. Its impersonality bespeaks the same powerful abstract force that is evident in the Parthenon and informs the lines of Sophocles' *Oedipus Rex* with such awful meaning.

To return to the sculpture of the Parthenon, the metopes are in a somewhat less advanced style than the pediment figures. They were executed earlier, probably when the building was started in 447 B.C. The metope shown in Fig. 264 is from the south side and represents a *Lapith Battling a Centaur*. The figures are rather dry and hard, the style suggesting that of the transitional period. These characteristics are evident chiefly in the muscles, for the head of the Lapith is not unlike that of the Mount Olympus (Fig. 261) in the east pediment. The designs of the best metopes represent a considerable advance over the somewhat inelastic formulas of earlier periods. The violent action is kept within the space of the metope by the strong vertical accent of the Lapith's body and the emphatic curve of the Centaur's rump. The figures are arranged in balanced geometrical patterns which clarify the relationship between them. Note the recurring and contrasted curves of the outstretched arms, and the arc that rises at the lower left, extends through the Centaur's belly, and comes to an emphatic stop in the Lapith's left leg. The relief is high so that the figures would not be overwhelmed by the massive architectural setting and could also be seen more easily from the ground.

The frieze on the outside of the cella was probably carved between 442 and 438 B.C. Much of it was removed by Lord Elgin when the pediment figures were taken down and is now in the British Museum in London. The frieze represented the Panathenaic Procession; it begins over the west end of the cella with a group of horse-men and charioteers, victors in the Panathenaic Games that were part of the ceremony. The procession moves eastward along the sides. The rulers of the city, priests and musicians, and sacrificial animals appear; it culminates over the east end of the cella with the maidens who wove the peplos, the magistrates, and seated figures of the gods.

The frieze is carved in low relief (Fig. 265), the figures projecting a little more at the top of the band than at the bottom. This difference in relief was necessary because they were illuminated from below by light coming through the peristyle; therefore the lower part of the frieze had to project less than the upper part in order not to cast obscuring shadows. The lighting in the illustration is incorrect because it comes from above and creates a different effect from the one intended, for it makes certain details overprominent, like the veins in the horse's belly. The maximum projection is not more than about two and one-quarter inches, yet there is a pronounced effect of depth. It is sufficient, for example, to make the spatial relationship of the

British Museum, London.

FIG. 264. Lapith Battling a Centaur
(*ca.* 445 B.C.),
Metope from the Parthenon in Athens.

FIG. 265.   Horseman (442-438 B.C.), from the Frieze
of the Parthenon in Athens.

horse and the man behind it quite plausible. This was achieved by carving the relief in a series of receding planes which are not parallel but at slight angles. This refinement is hardly perceptible, but combined with the extraordinarily delicate modeling of the figures it establishes them as three-dimensional forms that seem to have much greater depth than their actual few inches.

Another characteristic of the frieze is the uniform level of the heads, whether the figures are standing or seated. This principle of design, known as isocephalism, is invoked in the interests of architectural effect. The figures on horseback are smaller than those on foot; but so well is the frieze as a whole composed and so convincing is each figure in itself that the disparities in size are unnoticed. In the same way, the smallness of the horses in relation to the human figures is not perceived in the effect of the frieze as a whole.

The date of the frieze midway between that of the metopes and the pediment figures explains the style, which is somewhat more advanced than the former and less so than the latter. Nor is it uniform throughout, suggesting that a number

of sculptors worked on it. They probably had less talent than those who executed the more prominent pediment figures, and the style is definitely related to that of the preceding period. The pose of the figure at the left in Fig. 265 suggests the Polykleitan Canon (Fig. 260), but the muscles are rather hard and the abdominal convention quite prominent. The somewhat exaggerated swing of the hips reveals the hand of an imitator of Polykleitos rather than of a sculptor who was his equal in originality. The two figures at the right show persistence of the archaic in the full-front eye in a profile head. There are, however, some very naturalistic details such as the rough beard stubble on the older man's face, the veins on the belly and legs of the horse, and the leg muscles of the figure at the left.

Although the naturalistic details in the frieze might imply an intention to achieve a photographically realistic portrayal of the procession, this could not be so, for there is no reference anywhere in it to the impressive setting of the event. The background is plain, although it would seem appropriate to represent the Acropolis and its various buildings to identify the procession. But the designer's intention was to create an ideal representation of the city's homage to its divine patroness, rather than a concrete and specific illustration.

Even in portraiture, usually considered an art in which the specific and real should dominate, the Greek did not vary from the impersonal idealism of the Parthenon sculptures. When Kresilas made a portrait of *Pericles* (Fig. 266) in bronze, he did not record the way the great Athenian statesman actually looked, even though certain personal traits are suggested, like the slight tilt of the head and the full sensuous lips. The statue is rather an ideal embodiment of the powerful personality who made Athens the foremost Greek city for more than forty years in the fifth century. The original bronze no longer exists but there are several copies in stone. Although Pericles was well past middle age when it was made, about 440 B.C., the creases and wrinkles that would normally appear in the face are absent. Such individual accidents of appearance were omitted in order to emphasize the ideal— not Pericles the man but Pericles the statesman. The idea for which he stood was more important to the sculptor than the incidental facts of how he looked.

The impersonal idealism of the Parthenon sculptures and the portrait of Pericles is the outstanding characteristic of sculpture in the Golden Age. The nature of this ideal is suggested in the sixth book of Plato's *Republic:* "Painters must fix their eyes on perfect truth as a perpetual standard of reference, to be contemplated with the minutest care, before they proceed to deal with earthly canons about things beautiful." This conception of the artist's aims accounts for many characteristics of fifth-century art. The background is omitted from the Parthenon frieze to avoid suggesting the specific setting in time and space which would rob it of ideal unity. Similarly the free figures of the pediments, and such works as the Lemnian Athena, are impersonal and self-contained, because the implication of any relationship between them and their surroundings or the observer would destroy the sense of integrated, self-sufficient personality that gives them ideal significance. The reason the

British Museum, London.

FIG. 266.   Pericles, after Kresilas,
(*ca.* 440 B.C.).

unity of frieze and free-standing figures alike would be destroyed by any reference to background and surroundings is that the reference would introduce an element of the specific which by its very presence would imply the existence of its opposite, namely, the indefinite. In discussing Greek architecture and in the opening paragraphs about Greek sculpture, it was pointed out that one of the fundamental characteristics of the Greek temperament was its abhorrence of the indefinite. Reality consisted only in what could be grasped by the senses—the concrete and the tangible. But even what could be seen was not real if it implied something that could not be seen. Thus the neutral background of the Parthenon frieze does not suggest setting but it also avoids suggesting space, for it exists as stone rather than as a portrayal of environment. The result is a unity which is ideal because it did not exist and never could have, but is nonetheless expressed in terms of concrete experience.

National Museum, Athens.

FIG. 267.　The Hegeso Stele
(*ca.* 400 B.C.).

full-front rather than profile. The draperies, of a thin and clinging material that falls in minute folds and indicates the bodies underneath, are more characteristic of the later fifth century. The design with its broad and sweeping curves is particularly fine in the mistress' beautiful chair and the subtle line of the robe hanging from the maid's shoulders. The figure of Hegeso is not a portrait but an ideal type not unlike the Athena Lemnia (Fig. 263).

The stele gives no suggestion that death means the end of mortal life. In fact, there is no suggestion of death at all. Hegeso is represented in an act normal to her everyday life; there is no reference to the fact that life is ended. This conception makes objective the statement that the philosophy of the Greek carried him to the mouth of the tomb but no farther. Reality for him was what could be grasped by the senses; he was powerless before the indefinite void of death. Thus in the eleventh book of the *Odyssey*, when Odysseus attempts to comfort the shade of Achilles by telling him that he is a prince among the dead, the latter replies, "Nay, speak not comfortably to me of death, oh great Odysseus. Rather would I live on ground as the hireling of another, with a landless man who had no great livelihood, than bear sway among all the dead that be departed." Occasionally the idea of death is symbolized as the departure on a journey with friends saying farewell, but the subject is treated with great restraint. There is never the bitter grief or cloying sentimentality that appears so often in the funereal art of later periods.

The value the Greek placed on the tangible and concrete is also apparent in the concept of death revealed in the gravestones or funereal stelae of the fifth and fourth centuries. One of the finest, the *Hegeso Stele* (Fig. 267), named for the woman it commemorates, is in the National Museum in Athens. She is looking at her jewels in a box held by the maid standing before her. The style is of the fifth century, though somewhat later than the Parthenon figures. That the execution is less sophisticated than in the Parthenon sculptures is evident from the somewhat awkward articulation of the wrists and the summary modeling of the arms. The bodies have something of the maturity of the more monumental works of the period, but the eyes are

In the Golden Age, the development that began in the archaic and continued through the transitional period reached its climax. The inflexible sixth-century figures acquired greater weight and the ability to move in the early years of the fifth, and then became supple and quietly relaxed in the Golden Age. With the changes in appearance, there went a corresponding change in mien and bearing. The rigid tension of the archaic Apollo in New York (Fig. 250) gives way to stern force in the Olympian Apollo (Fig. 257), which in turn is replaced in the Mount Olympus (Fig. 261) by quiet repose that makes the strength of the figure seem greater for not being explicit. This is the greatness of the sculpture of the Golden Age, that it gives final and definitive form to ideals only suggested in previous periods. Where archaic and transitional sculptors could portray only in part the beauty they dreamed of, the sculptor of the Golden Age revealed it in all its glory. Of Pheidias' great ivory and gold statue of Zeus in his temple at Olympia, Dio Chrysostom said, "No one, having seen it, will conceive him otherwise thereafter." This is true of all great art and is the secret of the consistent greatness of the sculpture of the Golden Age. The subjects represented are given ideal form, and they cannot be conceived in any other.

The lofty idealism of the Golden Age could not last indefinitely. Before the close of the fifth century, the spiritual fabric of Greek thought, based on belief in an established order revealed from time to time by the gods, was being weakened. Two factors were responsible, the materialistic thought of the Sophists on the one hand, and the abstraction of deity into moral order by Plato on the other. Coupled with these was the influence of naturalistic thought culminating in the scientific method of Aristotle. Moreover, the self-assurance of the Athenians, a vital factor in the cultural and political supremacy of the city, had been badly shaken by the defeat of their armies at Syracuse in 413 B.C. and the destruction of the fleet in 407 B.C.; it was completely broken by the final victory of Sparta at the close of the Peloponnesian War in 404 B.C.

The net result of all these influences was the invasion of the isolated Athenian civilization of the Golden Age by new and previously unconsidered ideas. The old culture had been founded on belief in divine authority, and that authority had been questioned; it was no longer valid in interpreting life and experience. It was replaced by the mode of thought embodied in the philosophy of Euripides, Plato, and Aristotle, potentially world-wide in scope rather than arbitrarily restricted to Athenians or even to Greeks, a mode of thought that shattered the complacent isolation in which the Golden Age had taken form. Its basis was not divine revelation but the study of man and nature. Obviously the art of the older culture could not adequately express such ideas, and modifications of it appear even before the end of the fifth century. Instead of Sophocles' austere impersonality, there is Euripedes' pathos and sympathy for human suffering which interprets the myths of the old beliefs in the light of human nature revealed by experience. There is a similar change in sculpture. The marvelous technique of the Parthenon figures is no longer

Muséum, Olympia.

FIG. 268.   Paionios, Victory
(*ca.* 421 B.C.).

utilized to define ideal physical and moral beauty; it is an end in itself. The figures are still ideal, it is true, but the ideal is on a less elevated plane.

An example of late fifth-century sculpture which indicates the beginning of many of these changes is the Nike or *Victory of Paionios* (Fig. 268), erected at Olympia about 421 B.C. A winged feminine figure is borne down from the sky on the back of an eagle, the bird of Zeus, and comes to rest upon a tall pedestal. The advances in realistic representation during the century and a quarter that separates this figure from the archaic Victory of Delos (Fig. 251) are obvious. But the Victory of Paionios also represents a change from the methods of the mid-fifth century, particularly in the treatment of drapery. In the Three Fates (Fig. 262), the robes are thick and heavy; they fall in carefully arranged folds independently of the bodies they cover even though contributory to their effect. In the later figure, the drapery is thin and transparent, hardly concealing the body. The covered right leg is as carefully modeled as the exposed left one; only an occasional ridge indicates the garment.

A little later than the Victory of Paionios are the reliefs from a balustrade around the small Ionic temple of Wingless Victory on the Athenian Acropolis, carved about 410 B.C. The one illustrated shows an attendant *Victory Loosing Her Sandal* (Fig. 269). As in the free-standing figure by Paionios, the drapery is thin and transparent. It clings to the body, revealing it in every detail, but without the motivation of rapid movement which explains the similar effect in the other statue. This is not realistic art any more than that of the Parthenon pediments; the sheerest material will not reveal the form it covers as it does in this relief where the effect is as arbitrarily planned as in the draperies of the Three Fates. The difference between the Nike relief and the Parthenon figures is in the ideal the sculptor sought to express. In place of majestic repose, there is the act of loosing the sandal. Such a subject is not appropriate to monumental treatment and the sculptor wisely refrained from attempting it. Instead, he gave full expression to his delight in mastering the technique which makes solid stone more ephem-

Acropolis Museum, Athens.

FIG. 269. Victory Loosing Her Sandal (*ca.* 410 B.C.), from the Temple of Athena Nike in Athens.

eral than the finest silk, completely revealing the charming, gracefully poised figure. No longer does the observer breathe the rarefied atmosphere of Olympus, for here is no goddess but a human being. The Victory loosing her sandal is not an ideal of divinity but rather a divinely beautiful mortal.

THE FOURTH CENTURY

During the fourth century, the ideals expressed in Greek sculpture continue to change along the lines suggested by the Victory of Paionios and the Victory loosing her sandal when they are compared with earlier works. The ideal and abstract beauty of the fifth century is succeeded by a beauty which is nearer to physical reality. Gracefulness of form and the expression of emotion are among the sculptor's aims. In achieving them, the human model is followed more closely and the figures become more naturalistic and less formalized. As one critic has remarked, "In the fourth century, the gods descend a little from Olympus and become more like human beings."

Two sculptors are outstanding in the first half of the fourth century, Praxiteles and Skopas. Both were celebrated in their own time for figures which, although widely divergent in character, exemplify the two tendencies in fourth-century art noted above. It is easier to form a definite opinion of Praxiteles' work from existing monuments, because a statue of *Hermes* (Fig. 270) by him was found in the ruins of the temple of Hera at Olympia. It was carved about 325 B.C. The Hermes is unique as the only existent statue known to be by one of the great Greek sculptors; it was identified as Praxiteles' work by a chance reference in the guidebook Pausanias wrote about his travels in Greece in the second century A.D. It is of marble and represents the god Hermes carrying the infant Dionysos on his left arm. The child is reaching for some object, probably a bunch of grapes which Hermes held in the missing right hand. Both legs were broken below the knee and have been restored, but the right foot is original.

The pose resembles that of fifth-century standing figures (Fig. 260), but the right hip is thrown out, giving the body a broad S-curve sometimes referred to as the curve of Praxiteles. The figure is not as heavy as the fifth-century type, the proportions of limbs, torso, and head being considerably lighter. With this change in general proportions, a method of modeling appears which is also different from fifth-century practice.

In both styles the flesh is represented by planes that merge into each other, creating an effect of roundness. In fifth-century figures (Fig. 261) these planes are relatively few in number and contrasted in direction. In the fourth century they are more numerous and merge almost

Museum, Olympia.

FIG. 270. Praxiteles, Hermes
(*ca.* 325 B.C.).

Museum of Fine Arts, Boston.

FIG. 271.   Girl's Head
(late 4th cent. B.C.).

extraordinarily delicate and complex, creating an arresting impression of physical reality. The nose continues the line of the brow which is divided horizontally by a deep crease, both conventions of the classic ideal of beauty. The sense of texture which makes the figure so convincingly real is also evident in the drapery over the tree trunk. It has an individuality of its own yet does not detract from the human figure; the smooth flesh acquires greater effectiveness by contrast with its involved folds.

All these details combine to create an impression of objective reality which more nearly approximates that of the living model than any figure hitherto considered. It is as if a body of transcendent physical beauty had been transmuted into an imperishable medium while retaining all its qualities. In the serene detachment of the figure there is almost the majestic repose the Parthenon figures, but the lofty remoteness of the fifth century has gone. Austerity is replaced by a more immediately appealing bodily comeliness, vigor by graceful languor. The Praxitelean ideal is not an inner spirit that informs the body with meaning but physical gracefulness.

The Hermes is one of Praxiteles' minor works. It is not mentioned by any of his contemporaries, although a number of his other statues are highly praised. Of these, only the vaguest impression can be gained from copies which convey little but the most general features of the originals. One is a Satyr in the Capitoline Museum in Rome, celebrated by Hawthorne as the Marble Faun; it is only a dim reflection of the work which Praxiteles himself considered his best. His most famous statue was the Aphrodite of Knidos, renowned for its success in suggesting the graceful softness of the feminine form. The goddess is nude, the first time a female divinity was thus portrayed in monumental Greek sculpture, although such treatment was forecast in the lightly clothed Nikes of the late fifth century. The Aphrodite is known today only through copies. The pose was similar to that of the Hermes, the indolent posture creating the same languorous, dreamy air.

A *Girl's Head* (Fig. 271) in the Boston Museum of Fine Arts, an original Greek work, in

imperceptibly. The result is an impression of flesh translated into stone, rather than an abstraction of that impression as in the earlier style. In other words, the sculptured figure is beginning to approximate the appearance of the model instead of being a self-sufficient identity. Where the older sculptors caused flesh to become marble, Praxiteles caused marble to become flesh.

The head reveals other characteristics of Praxiteles' style. Among these is the oval skull tapering toward the chin. The hair is a series of rough, irregular masses giving the effect of short curly locks, their texture contrasting with that of the smooth lustrous skin. The eyes are narrow; the upper lid projects so that the glance seems to fall, although it is clearly not directed toward any definite object. There is no specific emotion in the resulting effect of dreamy contemplation. The modeling of the lips and cheeks is

marble, from the island of Chios, may provide an inkling of the characteristics of Praxiteles' work that were so much admired. The sculptor is unknown, but the style has much in common with Praxiteles' and it was probably carved toward the end of the fourth century. As in the Hermes, the surfaces are modeled with great delicacy, creating a remarkable sense of life yet doing full justice to the structure of the forms. Contemporary praise of the Knidian Aphrodite suggests that this was the quality that made it Praxiteles' most renowned achievement. Its influence upon contemporary and subsequent sculpture was very great, for in it Praxiteles created the ideal form of the Goddess of Love just as Pheidias made the Greek conception of Zeus objective for all time. So true was this that for many years after the fourth century no statue of Aphrodite differed significantly from that created by Praxiteles.

Writers of antiquity linked Skopas with Praxiteles as the greatest sculptors of their time. However, the graceful and languid charm of Praxiteles' figures is replaced by powerful emotion in Skopas'. Unfortunately no existing statues can be positively identified as his, and even those that reflect his style are not well preserved. One is a *Warrior's Head* (Fig. 272) from Tegea, where, according to Pausanias, Skopas was in charge of rebuilding the temple of Athena Alea; the same source credits him with some of the pediment sculpture. Although there is no proof that the Warrior's Head was actually carved by Skopas, the style corresponds to descriptions of his in contemporary writings. It probably came from a battle scene in the western pediment. Comparison with the Lapith's head in the Parthenon metope (Fig. 264) reveals how far the fourth-century sculptor goes beyond the earlier artist in suggesting emotion. The effect is obtained by a different treatment of details than has been the case hitherto. The head is turned to the left and tilted back. The eyes are opened wide, in contrast to Hermes' half-closed eyes (Fig. 270), and are deeply sunken under oblique brows that cast a shadow over them. The glance is intent, focused upon some definite object. The mouth is open and the upper lip drawn back,

reinforcing the effect created by the eyes. The head is almost square, compared with the ovoid Praxitelean type; its massiveness accentuates the emotion conveyed by the general pose and the eyes and mouth.

These characteristics appear in copies of other works by Skopas, notably a statuette in Dresden which is a reduction of a *Raving Maenad* (Fig. 273) originally in Byzantium. The Maenads were female followers of Dionysos, and the statue by Skopas represents one of them rushing through the woods in an ecstatic frenzy generated by the orgiastic rites of the cult. The head is bent back, and the body, revealed by the Doric chiton held in place only by a girdle, is strongly twisted. The details of the head correspond to those of the one from Tegea; the entire pose expresses the girl's frantic ecstasy. Other works by Skopas celebrated in antiquity include sculptures for the tomb of King Mausolos at Halikarnassos and the temple of Diana at Ephesos, but none of the existing fragments from these buildings can be safely attributed to his own hand.

Praxiteles and Skopas date around the middle

National Museum, Athens.

FIG. 272.   Warrior's Head (*ca.* 350 B.C.), from the Temple of Athena Alea in Tegea.

Museum, Dresden.

FIG. 273.   Raving Maenad, after Skopas
(*ca.* 340 B.C.).

of the fourth century. Later in that century the outstanding artist was Lysippos, the last of the great original Greek sculptors. Although he was incredibly prolific—he made nearly fifteen hundred statues—not a single known original by him exists, and even the best available copies are not entirely adequate reproductions. The most accurate impression of his style as described by classic writers is obtained from a statue in the Vatican Museum in Rome known as the *Apoxyomenos* (Fig. 274), meaning The Scraper. It portrays an athlete cleaning oil and dust from his body with a strigil after exercising in the stadium. The figure is lighter and more agile than the fifth-century athletic type (Fig. 260). The lithe body resembles the Praxitelean type in proportions, the head being about one-eighth the total height, but the muscles are dry and hard as compared with the softer form of the Hermes. Lysippos was called a realist in his own time; according to his contempoaries, he made figures

as they were rather than as they ideally ought to be. This may seem incompatible with the fact that, like Polykleitos, Lysippos developed an ideal canon of proportions; but if the Roman copy of the Apoxyomenos can be trusted, this canon was based on a series of conventions much more naturalistic than previous ones.

The greatest difference between Lysippos' statue and earlier figures is the conception of the figure as a whole. Polykleitos' Doryphoros (Fig. 260) is in the act of taking a step; the contrasted tense and relaxed muscles suggest that the figure is capable of moving but is stabilized by the functional balance of arms and legs. In the Apoxyomenos (Fig. 274) the movement is actually represented, for the figure is in the act of shifting its weight from one leg to the other, in contrast with the Doryphoros which is capable of moving but does not. This introduces an element of time, an intangibility quite foreign to the ideally unified concepts of the fifth century. The impression of movement is made even stronger by the tenseness of the body and the excited awareness of environment in the face. This characteristic involves a consciousness of setting that is also foreign to the fifth-century ideal; it is emphasized in the Apoxyomenos by the three-dimensional spatial concept of the figure. As was said earlier, the prevailing concept of the statue in earlier styles was a two-dimensional unity which could be grasped from a single point of view and from no other. Even in the Three Fates (Fig. 262), the impression of three-dimensional solidness essential to its unity can be felt only from a specific standpoint. But the Apoxyomenos is so designed that its full effect can be grasped only from several points of view successively assumed. From the angle at which the motion of the left arm and its relationship to the right arm is clear, the movement of the lower body is less intelligible. It is thus necessary for the observer to move *around* the statue to obtain the full effect of its action, an implicit acknowledgment that it is surrounded by space with which it is definitely related.

These characteristics of fourth-century style in the sculpture of Praxiteles, Skopas, and Lysippos are not significant solely because of the changes in appearance from fifth-century types. They are indicative of a different philosophy of life. For the self-sufficient impersonality of the earlier figures, the fourth century substituted the languorous grace of Praxiteles, the passion of Skopas, and the space-implying three-dimensional concepts of Lysippos. Any or all of these qualities in a statue make it no longer an isolated entity, for its full significance can be grasped only by recognizing the existence of things other than the statue itself. In the Hermes, the suggestion of elements outside the figure is negative, implied by the air of dreamy reverie quite different from the comprehensive assurance and impersonal poise of a fifth-century figure. In Skopas' work the suggestion is positive, for the fixed glance of the eyes carries the observer from the figures. In Lysippos' figure, the suggestion becomes objective in the three-dimensional conception that establishes a definite relationship between statue and environment and in the awareness of environment expressed in the face.

All these details reveal clearly that every artist is the child of his age, no matter how original or how great his creative genius. It would have been impossible for the fourth-century artist to work in the style of the fifth because his background of thought was different. By the close of the fourth century man was becoming increasingly aware of his surroundings, and the earlier anthropocentric philosophy based on consciousness of himself alone was inadequate to evaluate experiences hitherto disregarded. The sublime self-sufficiency of the Golden Age was born of an imaginative simplification of life. The relative complexity of experience in the fourth century required a more elastic philosophical scheme of interpretation and a more naturalistic artistic style to express it. The Aristotelian code replaced the Socratic; the art of Praxiteles, Skopas, and Lysippos succeeded that of Polykleitos and Pheidias.

Vatican Museum, Vatican City.

FIG. 274. The Apoxyomenos, after Lysippos (*ca.* 320 B.C.).

Detail of Fig. 278.

CHAPTER SEVENTEEN

Hellenistic Sculpture

For all the greatness of its achievement, the culture of the Golden Age was primitive. Its philosophical method was restrictive, concerned with interpreting human experience within a limited scope. In its most comprehensive aspect the culture was Hellenic, that is, it pertained to Hellas or the peninsula of Greece; in its narrowest aspect it was Athenian. There are similar limitations in the art of the Golden Age as well, as has been pointed out. The political dominance of Athens in the Greek world ended with the fifth century, coincident with the appearance of new modes of thought that shattered the intellectual isolation of the Golden Age. The fourth century was a period of expanding artistic productivity in Greece, geographically as well as in variety of expressive aims. When the various Greek city-states were subjugated by Macedonia and incorporated in the empire of Alexander the Great between 336 and 323 B.C., it became possible to speak of a general Hellenic art. The great military leader's appreciation of the intellectual and artistic achievements of the people he had conquered is well known; it is illustrated by his patronage of Aristotle, whose pupil he was, and of Lysippos, the only sculptor permitted to make his portrait. The encouragement he gave Greek artists and the spreading of the principles of Greek art over the entire known world by his military conquests were instrumental in finally destroying the isolation in which fifth-century art had been born, and which the fourth century had modified. This is the immediate background of the style called Hellenistic.

Hellenistic is the term applied to the culture and art of the whole Mediterranean world from the death of Alexander the Great in 323 B.C. to the conquest of Greece by Rome in 146 B.C. During that time, the productive centers of art were no longer on the Greek mainland but in the new states that arose in the Alexandrian empire. Their prosperity drew the successors of the great fourth-century artists away from Athens, which sank rapidly in power and prestige in the subordinate political role to which it was reduced. Pergamon, Rhodes, and Alexandria were the chief artistic centers, with minor ones in Antioch and Corinth. The sculpture in these centers continues the tendencies of fourth-century art; its style is Hellenistic, the product of the geographical diffusion of Hellenic ideals and their artistic transmutation by influences from other traditions.

A deservedly famous example of Hellenistic sculpture is the Nike or *Victory of Samothrace* in the Louvre (Fig. 275), carved by a sculptor of Rhodes. Its date is uncertain. Some critics think it to be of the early third century B.C., whereas others place it in the middle of the second. The fact that important naval victories were won by the Rhodians in 191 and 190 B.C. may bear on this, for the Victory stands on a base shaped like the prow of a ship and could well commemorate

Louvre, Paris.

FIG. 275.   Victory of Samothrace
(*ca.* 190 B.C.).

such an event (the complete base is not shown in the figure). It is the culmination, formally speaking, of a long series of flying figures, beginning with the Victory of Delos (Fig. 251) and continuing through the Victory by Paionios at Olympia (Fig. 268). The head and arms are missing, but a fragment of a hand discovered fairly recently is thought to be part of the figure; the hand is so disposed that it may have held a wreath. The draperies fall in folds that are heavy here and light elsewhere, revealing the form beneath and suggesting its sweeping forward movement in the patterns of line. Winged figures such as the Victory always posed a problem in logical articulation of wings and body. Here it is solved by balancing the wings against the forward thrusting breasts and massive torso; this contributes

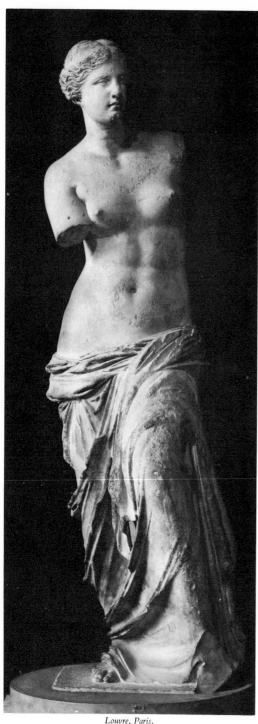

FIG. 276. Aphrodite of Melos
(*ca.* 150 B.C.).

directly to the appropriately dramatic character of the figure, and makes it a particularly successful embodiment of the violent emotions of conflict and victory.

No less famous than the Nike of Samothrace is the *Aphrodite of Melos* (Fig. 276) in the Louvre in Paris. More generally known as the Venus de Milo, it is probably the best-known classic statue in the world, its popularity resulting, in part at least, from its discovery in the early nineteenth century, the period of the Classic Revival, when enthusiasm for things classic was at its height. Its exact place and date of origin are unknown, but it was probably carved in the late third or early second century B.C. The action of the missing arms can only be guessed; one suggestion is that the right hand held the draperies and the left rested on a column supporting the figure. The hair is conventionalized not unlike that of the Lemnian Athena (Fig. 263), but the expressiveness of the face is closer to the Praxitelean than the Phedian ideal. The head is small, too, in proportion to the body, which has the slightness of the Lysippic canon and its twisted stance. The flesh is modeled in broad, simplified planes and has the softness of Praxiteles' work but lacks the sensuality seen in that of many of his followers. Its texture contrasts with the draperies which are at the same time naturalistically rendered and arbitrarily arranged to display the figure to best advantage. Some critics feel that this gives the statue a touch of affectation; but even so, the figure nonetheless embodies a noble and dignified conception of humanity. In the fifth century the sculptor's ideal was divine; in the fourth century it became semidivine, and in the Hellenistic period it became human. This is the ideal embodied in the Aphrodite of Melos—an earthly rather than supernatural beauty, befitting a worldy age and civilization.

The Nike of Samothrace and the Aphrodite of Melos are Hellenistic interpretations of traditional forms or types. The *Dying Gaul* (Fig. 277), in the Capitoline Museum in Rome, is a subject not known to fifth- and fourth-century art. The bronze original, here copied in marble, was one of a group of statues erected at Pergamon shortly after 241 B.C. to celebrate the victory of

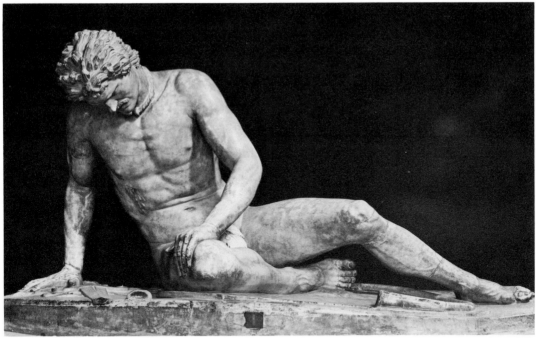

Capitoline Museum, Rome.

FIG. 277.　Dying Gaul (*ca.* 240 B.C.).

Attalus I over northern barbarians who invaded Asia Minor. The wounded warrior, at the point of death, supports himself on an arm which yields as his strength ebbs. The realistic details of the mustache, matted hair, and twisted gold collar around the neck identify the figure as a barbarian or non-Greek by contrast with the ideal type of Hellenes. Other touches of Hellenistic realism are the hard dry skin, heavy muscles, and the drops of blood oozing from the open wound. The proportions of the figure follow the canon of Lysippos but the strong emotional content is Skopaic. Such naturalism in portraying a subject like the Dying Gaul might easily have been highly disagreeable had not the sculptor exercised great restraint. The naturalism is used not as a tour de force of technique but to make concrete the idea the figure represents, the anguish of defeat that shatters the spirit rather than the physical pain that destroys the flesh.

A related aspect of Hellenistic art is shown in a relief, *Athena Slaying a Giant* (Fig. 278), from the Altar of Zeus at Pergamon, erected between 180 and 160 B.C. It is part of a frieze nearly four hundred feet long that represents the mythical battle between the gods of Olympus and the giants of the earth, the legendary conflict between light and order and darkness and chaos. This was a favorite subject for architectural sculpture from the beginning of Greek art, but its treatment here has little resemblance to earlier examples. Struggling serpent-legged giants and gods fill the entire frieze, the design being unified by the violent action that pervades the ensemble. Action is suggested by knotted muscles and contorted faces and also, more abstractly, by the diagonal accents of the composition as a whole. The animation of the figures is carried to the point of exaggeration, for there is hardly a single body in repose in the entire frieze. Skopas' influence is apparent in the heads, both in the shapes and in the impassioned expressions. The great technical skill of the sculptors is evident throughout the entire frieze in the accurately rendered anatomical details, the textures of draperies and flesh, and the powerful wings of the gods, no less than in the masterful achievement of the unified design.

In striking contrast with the violent unrestrained emotion of the Pergamon frieze is the gentle sentiment in reliefs like the *Peasant Driving a Cow to Market* (Fig. 279) in the Sculpture Museum at Munich. Called Alexandrian—for early examples apparently originated in Alexandria during the Hellenistic period—the one shown here was probably carved about 50 A.D. The pastoral subject embodies the same idyllic concept of rural life that motivates the poems of Theocritus. In contrast to fifth-century reliefs (Fig. 264), the background is naturalistic. The figures also differ from those of fifth-century sculpture, for they are suggested by the play of

light and shade rather than by modeling. This means that the details are not carved to reproduce the model but that the stone is worked in hollows and projections to create a pattern of shadows and highlights suggesting the form of the original. The resulting visual simulation of reality justifies designating the style as illusionistic. There is an illusion of space as well as of form, created by varying the degree with which different objects project. The peasant and cow are almost detached from the background, whereas the temple and the statue base stand out only slightly. The tree growing through the temple portal also contributes to the illusion of depth, serving as it does to connect the foreground and the background. This illusionism implies an optical rather than a tactile point of view as in earlier styles. A fifth-century relief would be

Pergamon Museum, Berlin.

FIG. 278.   Athena Slaying a Giant (180–160 B.C.), from the Frieze of the
Altar of Zeus in Pergamon.

Glyptothek, Munich.

FIG. 279. Peasant Driving a Cow to Market (*ca.* 50 A.D.).

reasonably intelligible to the touch without being seen; a Hellenistic relief like this one is intended primarily to be seen and makes hardly any appeal to the sense of touch. Still another point differentiates the pastoral Hellenistic relief from that of the fifth century. It begins to take on the quality of a picture in stone, independent of its surroundings, whereas fifth-century relief is almost entirely architectonic, subordinate to the scheme of the building it ornaments. To some extent, this new conception of relief may reflect a similar tendency in painting, with easel pictures to be hung as wall ornaments replacing the earlier architectural murals painted directly on walls.

The dates of the Hellenistic period, 323 to 146 B.C., given at the beginning of this chapter might be somewhat amended, for in the broadest sense the Hellenistic period did not close until several centuries after the beginning of the Christian era; the Hellenistic influence is perceptible in much of the art of the first millennium. Nonetheless, after 146 B.C. the Greek strain in Hellenistic art is more diluted and other influences are correspondingly more pronounced. Thus sculpture from 146 to 27 B.C. is usually called Graeco-Roman. Although much of it was created in Greece or by Greek artists, it was done for Roman patrons. Many of the copies of

Vatican Museum, Vatican City.

FIG. 280.   Laocoön and His Sons (*ca.* 50 B.C.).

fourth- and fifth-century statues that are now almost the only source of objective information about the sculpture of those periods were made at this time. But Roman taste is also evident in the original work, in the subject matter and the striving for ultra-realistic effects that is one of the main characteristics of certain types of Graeco-Roman sculpture.

One of the most famous statues of classic antiquity, the group showing *Laocoön and His Sons* (Fig. 280), is an example of Hellenistic sculpture produced about 50 B.C., during the Graeco-Roman period. It is now in the Vatican Museum in Rome. Its fame is due in part to the circumstances of its discovery in 1506, when it was hailed as a masterpiece of the finest period of Greek sculpture. Its popularity was enhanced by the renown achieved by the book of the same name by the German aesthetician Lessing which set forth one of the most widely accepted theories of art in the eighteenth century. The general arrangement follows Vergil's account of the punishment of Laocoön and his sons in the second book of the *Aeneid*. The bodies are composed in a compact pyramidal mass. The father's right arm and that of the son to his right have been incorrectly restored; they should be lower, which would make the compactness of the group even more marked. The naturalistic modeling of the bodies, characteristic of the period, establishes effective contrasts such as that between the adult and the adolescent bodies. Another contrast is evident in the muscles of the figures, the father's strained in an almost superhuman effort to free himself and his sons from the entwining snakes, those of the son to his left likewise tense, while the other youth has collapsed. The expression of agony on the father's face, created by the downward-sloping brows, the drooping eyes, the contorted forehead, and the parted lips, is very convincing. The group was the work of three Rhodian sculptors. It may not be easy to admire the ideal upon which their skill was lavished, for the extent to which they dwelt on details of physical pain and suffering is almost pathological. The statue should be compared with the Dying Gaul (Fig. 277), which portrays mental anguish rather than bodily torture. The sympathy aroused in the spectator by the earlier work may not be felt in the presence of the Laocoön group, but its technical bravado cannot fail to impress.

The realism of the Laocoön is an outstanding characteristic of certain phases of Graeco-Roman art. In this particular case, it cannot be said to express Roman taste, for the sculptors were Greeks and the entire concept may be rightly considered a continuation of the style of the Pergamon Altar (Fig. 278). A more direct Roman influence upon a Greek artist is apparent in the *Boxer* (Fig. 281) in the Terme Museum in Rome, for it is signed by Apollonios, the son of Nestor, an Athenian who was active about 50 B.C. It is probably a free copy of a third-century Pergamene original made more naturalistic to suit Roman tastes. It is of bronze, the color of the metal suggesting the weather-beaten hide stretched taut by the enormously developed muscles. The professional fighter is identified by the gnarled fingers of the stubby, powerful hands, the cestus or gloves of metal knuckles and strips of leather, the broken nose and thick

Terme Museum, Rome.

FIG. 281.   Apollonios, Boxer
(*ca.* 50 B.C.).

cauliflower ears. Other veracious details are the hairy chest and legs and the beetling brows. The realism of the face was originally accentuated by colored paste eyeballs. The sense of actuality these characteristics give the figure is heightened by its momentary pose, the head turned to one side as if in response to a question whose answer the jolted brain painfully seeks.

Hellenistic sculpture is noteworthy for its great variety—of methods, forms, and subjects. The Nike of Samothrace and the Aphrodite of

Melos are themes from earlier periods and there is also precedent for the sculptural methods used. The Pergamon Frieze, on the other hand, is an old theme treated in a new way; the Dying Gaul and the Peasant Driving a Cow to Market are new motives in classical sculpture, the latter involving a new technique. So great is the variety of Hellenistic sculpture, indeed, that it may seem to tend toward confusion; yet even this is a truthful reflection of the spirit of the times. The prevailing mode of thought in the fifth century was logical and well integrated within its self-established limits; the art of the time was correspondingly homogeneous as an evaluation of the limited experience within which significance could be found. In the Hellenistic period, the scope of experience was tremendously enlarged. Old philosophical systems and artistic styles were no longer adequate for its interpretation. The variety in Hellenistic sculpture is a direct consequence of attempts to solve new problems, both by adapting old forms and by development of new ones.

Hellenistic sculpture is often called decadent, a judgment manifestly unfair to a style with such vitality and technical virtuosity. The qualities considered decadent are rather evidence of its lack of significance in the traditional sense, in not embodying an ideal that could be effectively expressed in sculpture. Fifth-century thought lent itself well to this end, involving as it did the isolation of the individual form or concept, an ideal that could be stated with relative ease by an art dealing with specific and tangible shapes.

Even in the fourth century when the individual began to be conscious of his environment, an art of form could still be valid. But in the Hellenistic period, the individual was no longer isolated from his environment or merely conscious of it; he was conditioned by it. In an art which seeks to portray man as part of his surroundings, some means of suggesting space as a significant concept is essential. Hellenistic man lived in a world of space and light and shade; his fifth- and fourth-century ancestors lived in one of form and expressive outline and surface. In a word, the Hellenistic world was that of a painter rather than a sculptor, and Hellenistic art is most significant when it deals with space and light and shade in paintings (cf. Fig. 363). What seems to be decadence in Hellenistic sculpture is a consequence of its technical virtuosity and its expressive limitations. The inherited methods of expression had been perfected, but the ideals which gave them meaning were no longer valid. When a means of expression exists but there is nothing to express, the result is inevitable. Without new problems to solve or new subjects to interpret, sculpture could only turn back on itself or attempt to follow the path of painting. There was little to be gained in either case. The latter, as in the Peasant and Cow (Fig. 279), only points up the representational limitations of the art. In the former, a brilliant eclecticism emphasizes the limited content, as in the Aphrodite of Melos (Fig. 276); only an occasional new theme (Fig. 277) achieves ideal meaning through superb technique.

Detail of Fig. 287.

CHAPTER EIGHTEEN

Roman Sculpture

Italy, the land of the Romans, had been partially colonized by the Greeks as early as the seventh century B.C.; in some parts of the country, notably the south, remains of Greek temples still stand (Fig. 35), and Greek sculptures and vases have been found in abundance. At the same time, in other parts of Italy, the central area in particular, there is evidence of a culture at least as old as the Greek if not older—that of the Etruscans. Their temples were usually of wood (Fig. 47), with lavish use of terra cotta for revetments and decorative figures, both in relief and in the round. One of the latter is the grandiose *Apollo from Veii* (Fig. 282), named from its discovery on the site of a major Etruscan city a

Museo Nazionale di Villa Giulia, Rome.

FIG. 282.   Vulca (?), Apollo from Veii
(*ca.* 500 B.C.).

Vase (Fig. 564), was found in an Etruscan tomb. The massive proportions and dynamic movement of the figure are unlike contemporary Greek work, however, and the entire spirit suggests little that is Hellenic. Therefore the Apollo from Veii is best understood as an example of the indigenous Italic style, but already subjected to certain Greek influences which became even more of a factor from about 150 until 27 B.C. Sculpture produced in Italy during this latter period should be considered one of the many regional Hellenistic styles (cf. Fig. 281).

With the establishment of the Roman Empire, the character of Latin sculpture changes. This change is explained by the need which then arose to express ideas that were specifically Roman and, as such, could not be effectively embodied in earlier forms. This is why the mannerism and artificiality of much Hellenistic sculpture is not so apparent in the Roman. New subjects required new forms. The need to praise the grandeur of Rome and glorify the deeds of the emperor was a stimulus which again led to the creation of genuinely expressive figures. The sculptures in which these ideas were embodied fall into two classes, portraits and historical reliefs. Both may be considered specifically Roman contributions to the art of sculpture, for the highly developed Roman taste for realism is evident in both. The two forms have Hellenistic precedents, it is true, but in Roman hands they are treated in a way that makes them genuinely original.

The Roman fondness for realistic portraiture may have originated in the Etruscan practice of making wax death masks to serve as models for portrait statues. Obviously, such a procedure involved no idealization, nor was any desired. Perfection was the "speaking likeness" and any departure from the exact appearance of the model was considered a defect. Thus in the marble bust of *Caracalla* (Fig. 283) in the Art Museum of Princeton University, no detail is missing that might contribute to an exact likeness of the man who was emperor from 211 until 217 A.D. This is in striking contrast to the idealization in Kresilas' portrait of Pericles (Fig. 266). The shaggy hair and beetling brows over sharply

short distance north of Rome; its probable date is the late sixth or early fifth century B.C. It has been suggested that it may be the work of a certain Vulca, celebrated as a sculptor in the region. Apart from the missing arms, the figure is well preserved, retaining much of its original painted color. Certain characteristics—the archaic smile and slanting almond-shaped eyes, the stylized ringlets of the elaborately arranged hair, and the drapery patterns in particular—suggest comparison with Greek archaic figures. This is not surprising, for it is known that Greek art was greatly valued by the Etruscans; one of the most important early Greek vases, the François

peering eyes, the massive jowls and full sensual lips are not merely a record of how Caracalla looked; they also tell something of the man who built one of the most extravagantly pretentious of all the great Roman public baths (Fig. 56). In contrast to the portrait of Pericles, this bust defines the individual characteristics of Caracalla as a person rather than symbolizing the idea of him as a statesman or emperor.

An attempt to combine traditional Roman realism with Greek idealism is seen in the statue of *Augustus Addressing His Troops* (Fig. 284) found in the villa of his wife Livia near one of the ancient gates of Rome called Prima Porta. Executed about 15 B.C., it shows the emperor exhorting his army before going into battle. The head shows every known individual trait of the man; the tapering chin, the high cheek bones, the deeply recessed eyes, and the arrangement of the hair can all be observed in other portraits of Augustus. Realistic touches are evident in the elaborately carved breastplate, the numerous folds of the drapery, and the tunic fringe. The

literal treatment of these details contrasts strangely with the idealizing tendency in others. The feet are bare in the Greek tradition of the heroic figure, and the expression of the face is calm and self-contained. The pose and proportions are based on the Polykleitan canon (Fig. 260) and furnish evidence of the renewed influence of Greek sculpture on that of Augustan Rome. This was due in large measure to the taste of Augustus himself, whose appreciation of Greek art was quite genuine. The combination of naturalistic and generalized details in the Prima Porta statue that resulted from the more or less conscious efforts of the Roman sculptor to create a figure with ideal significance is not entirely successful. In trying to rise the concept to that level, he introduced Cupid astride a dolphin at the emperor's feet, a symbolic reference to the divine ancestry of the Julian family which claimed descent from Aeneas, the son of Venus and a half-brother of Cupid. The relief on the breastplate also has symbolic meaning; it refers to the peace and harmony that prevailed throughout the Roman Empire under Augustus' wise and benevolent reign. Such efforts to invest a concretely conceived figure with ideal meaning by allegoric attributes are typical of an art of naturalism that is attempting to transcend its innate materialism.

A combination of naturalism and allegory somewhat similar in purpose to that of the Augustus from Prima Porta is found in the greatest sculptural monument of Augustus' reign, the *Ara Pacis Augustae* or the Altar of Augustan Peace which stood on the Via Flaminia in Rome. The altar was a rectangular building about thirty-five feet square; its inner and outer walls were covered with relief sculptures representing state officials and the emperor with his family making a sacrifice of thanksgiving to the Earth for peace and prosperity. It was ordered by the Senate in 13 B.C. to commemorate the final pacification of Gaul and Spain by Augustus. The Earth or *Tellus* (Fig. 285), happy and productive under Roman rule, is personified by a feminine figure. On her lap are two children typifying Humanity which thrives upon the Earth's bounty symbolized by animals and the life-giving elements of Air and

Art Museum, Princeton University.

FIG. 283.   Caracalla (*ca.* 215).

Vatican Museum, Vatican City.

FIG. 284.   Augustus Addressing His Troops (*ca.* 15 B.C.).

Water. This relief was the goal of a procession formed by the royal family and a retinue of officials. The ideal type of the Tellus figure contrasts strongly with the naturalism of the animals and the garlands. The technique is not unlike that of the Hellenistic pictorial reliefs (Fig. 279), the figures being built up in many planes of varying depths. The relative nearness of the seated figures is indicated by pronounced projection, whereas the foliage is barely raised from the relief background. By this means the neutral background is identified with real space, an illusion that is furthered by the extremely naturalistic treatment of the draperies and the modeling of the figures which seem to merge into the stone.

The illusionistic relief style of the *Ara Pacis* reaches its climax in the *Reliefs on the Arch of Titus* (Fig. 286), which was erected near the Roman Forum to commemorate the conquest of Jerusalem in 70 A.D. (cf. Fig. 49). These reliefs portray the triumphal procession in which the spoils of the Temple of Solomon in Jerusalem were displayed to the Roman populace. In the upper panel the emperor in his chariot is accompanied by a symbolic figure of Victory; others personifying Rome and the Roman people appear elsewhere. In the lower panel a group of soldiers carrying the table of the showbread, the long trumpets that called the Jews to prayer or battle, and the seven-branched candlestick, are about to pass through a triumphal arch. In both panels the sculptor attempted to portray the scene as it would appear to a spectator looking through a window represented by the frame of the panel. To give the scenes reality, an illusion of space is created by subtle variations in the depth of the relief, the foreground figures standing out very clearly, objects in the background being almost imperceptible. The resulting effect of light and shade gives the impression of real air circulating between the figures. Only the absence of a systematic effect of perspective prevented the sculptor from attaining the complete illusion of concrete reality that was his intention. Because of this, for example, the figures in the lower panel do not march through the arch, and the chariot horses in the upper one are represented as if they were one in front of the other instead of abreast.

Composition and arrangement do not exist in the Arch of Titus reliefs. The figures are not subordinated either to an architectural scheme or to order that is formal in its own right. Instead, they are placed in the relief space with a casualness that is entirely naturalistic, moving about in real space as if seen through an opening in the side of the arch. They are therefore mainly descriptive in purpose, without the ideal unities of time, of space, and of plastic form that a Greek sculptor would have etablished (Fig. 265). The lack of chronological unity in the reliefs is apparent in their arrangement parallel to each other across the central passage of the arch, although their actual relationship to each other was consecutive.

Yet there is coherence in these reliefs, in the life and vitality that seem to animate each figure. This liveliness is produced by the play of

FIG. 285.   Ara Pacis, in Rome, Tellus
(13 B.C.).

light and shade, creating patterns that conform to the actual appearance of the objects represented. A considerable degree of technical skill was essential to such an effect, for the artist had to understand completely the modeling of the figures in order to create the effects of light and shade which this modeling would produce. When that understanding disappeared, as it did in the late years of the Roman Empire, the illusionistic style was no longer capable of producing intelligible results. This is clearly demonstrated by the *Reliefs on the Arch of Constantine* (Fig. 287), erected in Rome in 315 A.D. The reliefs under consideration are those in the long rectangular band which are later in date than those in the round medallions; the latter came from an earlier monument. Instead of being united in a common action, the figures are arranged in monotonous rows, each one isolated from those around it. In them, the descriptive tendency of the earlier reliefs is carried to excess; the sculptor felt it necessary to portray each figure and every detail of each figure very clearly, neglecting entirely the dramatic and spatial relationships that unify the earlier works. It is as if one of the animated scenes in the earlier style had been crystallized; the separate components are carefully depicted, but there is no element to establish a connection between them, whether dramatic and spatial as

FIG. 286. Arch of Titus, in Rome, The Triumph of Titus (*ca.* 82 A.D.).

FIG. 287. Arch of Constantine in Rome, Commemorative Reliefs:
(Upper (161-180 A.D.); Lower (315).

in the Arch of Titus reliefs or formal and rhythmic as in Greek relief.

The squat and unprepossessing figures that people the reliefs on the Arch of Constantine represent the final stage of the classic tradition of sculpture in the West. Superficially they bear some resemblance to the archaic figures with which the tradition began (Fig. 252), for in them also each part of the body is represented in its most characteristic aspect. In both styles, the figures are portrayed by conventions, but there is a significant difference in the conventions. Those of the archaic method are conventions of form, whereas those of the crystallized illusionistic style are conventions of light and shade. The result in

either case is not naturalistic. This is a minor consideration in the archaic figure, for its strongly developed plasticity gives it character; it is a very important consideration in the late Latin figure, for without naturalism it is nothing, inasmuch as the basis of illusionism was disregard of plastic values in favor of dramatic or spatial values. When the ability to represent things in naturalistic fashion no longer existed, there was no longer anything in the figure, for it had never had formal plastic values but only an illusion of them.

Roman sculpture, and Roman art in general, continues Hellenistic tradition. In one sense, it is a step toward evaluating the varied experiences which were part of the universal and comprehensive Hellenistic thought. The initial bewilderment of the Hellenistic mind in the face of such complexity is evident in the diffuse character of Hellenistic sculpture. In the Roman period there is an effort to resolve this complexity into order in terms that are still classic because they are factual and concrete. As was said earlier, the Roman architect sought to make space an objective thing in the interior of the Pantheon (Fig. 58). A similar motive animated the Roman sculptor when, as in the Arch of Titus reliefs, he attempted to make both time and space objective by portraying definite persons in a specific setting at a definite moment. The difference between the Greek and the Roman point of view is the fact that the Greek sought to establish ideal unities of time and space whereas the Roman sought to make these unities specific and concrete. In architecture this attempt was successful; in sculpture it was only relatively so, for the Roman sculptor could create spatial values only at the expense of formal ones by virtue of his illusionistic technique of light and shade.

As was said at the beginning of this chapter, Roman sculpture attained an individual and characteristic style by infusing Hellenistic forms with new meaning to express ideals that were specifically Roman. The decadence of Roman art set in when there were no longer valid ideals to stimulate creation. Furthermore, even here there is a difference from the Hellenistic period. For all the emptiness of many brilliant tours de force of Hellenistic style, there still remained something of the classic tradition of expressive form, as well as the obvious delight many Hellenistic sculptors had in displaying their technical skill. A period thus characterized can hardly be called decadent. By contrast, the Roman period from about 200 A.D. to 330 can hardly be called anything else. Neither abstract ideals nor technical skill is apparent in the sculpture of that period, the final stage of the classic tradition. New ideals had to be evolved and a new technique developed before a new sculptural tradition could take form. This occurred in the first millennium of the Christian era.

Detail of Fig. 303.

CHAPTER NINETEEN

Mediaeval Sculpture

THE EARLY MIDDLE AGES

During the first millennium of the Christian era, sculpture, like the other arts, became a handmaiden of the Church in spite of the Biblical injunction against the creation of images that was an essential feature of the Jewish faith among Semitic peoples. When Christianity spread to western Europe, this interdiction like many others, was more or less disregarded. The whole concept of Christianity in the Occident was based on compromises involving the adaptation of many pagan beliefs and their incorporation in the new faith. One aspect of this adaptation is seen in Early Christian sculpture, which consists almost entirely of forms

Lateran Museum, Rome.

FIG. 288.   Sarcophagus of the Two Brothers (late 4th cent.).

derived from current Latin and pagan practice to which new meaning was given by symbolic devices. An outstanding example is the new significance in Christian art of a subject found in classic art from earliest Greek times, a shepherd carrying a lamb on his shoulders. It was not difficult for the Christian to see the Good Shepherd in this subject and it was carried over almost unchanged into Early Christian art.

As the Latin Church passed through the earliest stages of its development and outgrew the primitive beliefs that had sufficed in the beginning, the comparatively simple way of expressing those beliefs as exemplified in the adaptation of the Good Shepherd was no longer adequate. By the middle of the fourth century there is a more complicated symbolism in Early Christian art. Most of the sculptural examples are sarcophagi like the one in the Lateran Museum in Rome known as the *Sarcophagus of the Two Brothers* (Fig. 288), from the portraits of the deceased in the conch shell. The friezes show Old and New Testament scenes that express symbolically a belief in life after death, the element in Christian faith that appealed most strongly to the early adherents of the Church. The figures are in the decadent illusionistic style of the frieze on the Arch of Constantine (Fig. 287). The nude figure of Daniel in the lions' den below and to the left of the conch shell is vaguely reminiscent of the fourth-century Lysippic canon. There is some attempt to distinguish the heads of the two brothers, but the sculptors' inadequate technique falls short of investing them with the life and vigor found in earlier Roman portraits. The decay of the Hellenistic and Roman illusionistic style is even more evident in the dull formulas of the heads and draperies and the monotonous repetition of the figures. Scenes are neither separated from each other nor related in this art which can achieve neither decorative nor dramatic unity. The classic tradition in the West was worn out; even the powerful stimulus of new beliefs could no longer invest its decadent forms with significance or beauty.

While sculptors in the service of the western Church were fruitlessly endeavoring to fill the old bottle of decadent and crystallized illusionism with the new wine of Christian symbolism, a process also apparent in the related art of ivory carving (cf. Fig. 579), their contemporaries in Byzantium and the Near East were developing a style which also had its roots in classic art. *Christ and Two Disciples* (Fig. 289), a fragment of a sarcophagus dated *ca.* 400 A.D. in the Kaiser Friedrich Museum in Berlin, is carved with a figure of Christ standing between two apostles in an architectural setting of columns and a gable. As in the Latin sarcophagus (Fig. 288), the figures are direct adaptations of classic models in posture and movement. They are the type that Greek and Roman sculptors used in representing philosophers, but with a new and Christian meaning given by symbols like the cruciform nimbus behind the head of Christ. Changes also were made in the formal character of figures and objects. The Corinthianesque capitals of the colonnettes resemble those in Byzantine architecture (cf. Fig. 70) in that they are defined by planes in which the designs are incised in patterns of contrasting accents of light and shade instead of being plastic in form. A comparable effect is seen in the figures; they are flattened, in contrast to antique prototypes, and tend to become two-dimensional areas of linear patterns of grooves cut with a running drill.

In using light and dark contrasts as major compositional elements, the Byzantine sculptor followed Hellenistic precedent (cf. Fig. 279), but he departed from it in creating patterns that are not plastic and three-dimensional but are organized in a single plane and unified by rhythmic accents. The figures are dematerialized in the process, losing the organic articulation that made the prototypes effective embodiments of the objective evaluation of experience for which the classic mind was ever striving. But their very immateriality makes them more suitable for communicating the transcendental content of Christianity. This is the initial result of the impact of Oriental prepossession with the indefinite and the immaterial upon ways of thinking which retained much classic character, comparable in its way to the architectural compromise between the same principles in the Hagia Sophia (Fig. 68). In varying degrees, depending

Kaiser Friedrich Museum, Berlin.

FIG. 289.   Christ and Two Apostles (*ca.* 400), Fragment of Sarcophagus.

upon whether Hellenic or Oriental ideas predominate, Byzantine ivories like the leaf of a diptych in the British Museum (Fig. 580) or the Throne of Maximianus at Ravenna (Fig. 581) illustrate the same transformation of classic forms in the service of the Church.

It was the nature of Christian thought that it should express itself in symbolic rather than representational terms; and inasmuch as such forms are particularly suitable for decorative treatment, it is not surprising that Byzantine artists should have so used them very often. The *Sarcophagus of Theodorus* (Fig. 290) was made for a fifth-century archibishop of the Byzantine city of Ravenna in Italy and is in the church of Sant' Apollinare in that city (Figs. 71, 72). Classic decorative elements are still present—the simplified pilasters at the ends and the mouldings across the top and on the lid—but Christian symbols are the most important features. The cross is shown in two forms. In one the Greek letters alpha and omega hang from the horizontal arm and the vertical arm is rounded to form the letter rho. The other has a superimposed X, the

Sant' Apollinare in Classe, Ravenna.

FIG. 290.   Sarcophagus of Theodorus
(1st half of 5th cent.).

Greek letter chi; it with the rho forms the initials of Christ's name. The alpha and omega have the same meaning (Rev. i, 11), as does the vine (John xv, 1-5) on the long side. The vine also refers to the wine as the blood of Christ, one of the most frequent symbols of the Savior in Christian thought. The heraldic peacocks are another popular motive in religious art of the first millennium; they are of even greater antiquity as a symbol of eternal life. Clarity and simplicity are the outstanding characteristics of the pattern created by these forms defined in two planes against a neutral background. The arrangement is symmetrical, but the rhythmic recurrence of circular motives—in the branches of the vine and the medallion with the monogram of Christ—is the major unifying element in this design, which in both expressive and formal character is one of the most characteristic examples of Byzantine stone sculpture.

The amount of large-scale Byzantine sculpture in stone was probably never very great. Oriental distaste for such forms, expressed in the prohibition of graven images in the Second Commandment of the Decalogue, was a constant element in Byzantine feeling, conflicting with the classic concepts inherited by the Eastern Empire. This element, coming to the fore in the iconoclasm of the eighth century, resulted in the extensive destruction of images which gave the movement its name. It is unlikely that the Moslem conquerors of Byzantium in the fifteenth century were more appreciative of the figures they saw than the earlier image-breakers were. This is why the most comprehensive understanding of Byzantine plastic art from the ninth to the fourteenth centuries is gained from ivories like the Harbaville Triptych in the Louvre (Fig. 582). Some examples of late Byzantine stone sculpture, however, are still in existence, among them the *Madonna Orans* (Fig. 291), so called from the arms raised in prayer. It is in the church of Santa Maria in Porto in Ravenna and was carved in the eleventh century. The figure, in low relief, stands in a frontal pose with the right leg slightly relaxed. The schematized draperies reflect the antique formula, but reduce it to flat planes and incised lines that reveal little of the form beneath. In this it resembles the figures in the Triptych; and if the effect in each is far from that of the world of nature created by the sculptors of Greece and Rome, there is an

Sta. Maria in Porto, Ravenna.

FIG. 291. Madonna Orans (11th cent.).

been assimilated into the Roman world and had maintained a degree of independence from its political order. But as these barbarians overran the land, they were themselves subjected to the influences of the Hellenistic-Christian culture of the Empire. The period from the end of the sixth century on is as much that of the rise of the Church as of the decay and fall of Rome. Western Christian art in the latter half of the first millennium was a product of these conditions. Its development from the formal traditions of the dissolving Empire and the Teutonic barbarians parallels the emergence of Byzantine art from the fusion of Hellenistic style with that of the Oriental cultures of the Near East.

The art of the Teutonic tribes in its native purity is best exemplified in the manuscript illustrations which were executed for a Gospel book written in an Irish monastery at Kells toward the close of the eighth century (Fig. 367). It can be characterized essentially by two words—linear and dynamic. These are the dominant qualities in all the art forms of the northern races. Their impact upon the already weakened Latin tradition in which the western Church expressed its concepts (cf. Fig. 288) led to its further disintegration, as is evident in the style of the *Sigwald Relief* (Fig. 292) in the Baptistery of Cividale, a small town in northern Italy. Its execution between 762 and 776 as part of a canopy built over the baptismal font by the

impression of nobly hieratic and supernatural beings standing immobile in a solemn and impressive rite. Thus the Byzantine artist sought to convey, in forms of classic self-sufficiency but Oriental in their unworldliness, the profound significance of Christian dogma.

At the same time that classic style was being transformed into the Byzantine under the influence of Oriental cultures impinging upon the east Mediterranean areas, it was also being modified in the West. There the weakening Empire was subjected to recurrent infiltrations of non-Mediterranean Teutonic tribes which had never

Baptistery, Cividale.

FIG. 292. The Sigwald Relief (762-776).

Patriarch Sigwald is recorded in the inscription below the cross. The cross is flanked by stylized palmettes and rosettes and two forms that suggest candelabra; below is a tree with some of its branches ending in animal heads and with birds sitting in it; it is flanked by two grotesques, part animal and part bird. Four medallions complete the panel, each enclosing a winged figure symbolizing one of the Four Evangelists, the compilers of the Four Gospels. In the upper left is an eagle representing John and in the upper right is the winged man of Matthew; below to the left is a winged bull, the symbol of Luke; the winged lion of Mark at the right completes the quartet. It is in the symbolism in the relief that its Christian character is clearest. The cross is an obvious detail of this, and the Four Evangelist symbols are an interpretation of the Vision of Ezekiel (Ezekiel i, 5-11) in accordance with mediaeval theology. They constitute a motive that is one of the most important in mediaeval art, for it occurs in almost all representations of the Last Judgment.

The style is the linear one of the Teutonic tribes; it attains some distinction in purely decorative motives like the interlace on the cross and the tree in the lower center, but is weak and unconvincing in the Evangelist symbols whose form was dictated by Christian iconography; the model was probably in the plastic late antique style which the barbarian sculptor with his linear and two-dimensional prepossession could not understand. Yet it is this way of seeing things in terms of line and movement which gives the ornamental elements in this style their vitality and unity and at the same time reduces forms probably portrayed with some naturalism in the model to awkward ideographs. Certain motives in the Sigwald Relief are primarily northern—the interlace, the grotesque animals, and the animal-headed branches of the tree; there is nothing of classic character, other than the presumptive nature of the model, unless the symmetrical arrangement can be considered a faint reflection of the splendid order achieved by the artists of the Hellenic past.

The Sigwald Relief is hardly sculpture at all in the sense of organized plastic elements, for it is executed in only two planes—the background, and the face of the slab on which the forms appear to have been drawn before cutting them straight in to the desired depth. Its ineptitude is due to the fact that neither the classic nor the northern component in the style is sufficiently forceful to give point and positiveness to the forms. These characteristics appear only when there is certainty of meaning and conviction of the significance of experience—creative factors that were supplied in mediaeval culture in some measure in the time of Charlemagne (742-814) and immediately thereafter in his attempt to re-create in his Holy Roman Empire something of the grandeur that had been Rome. The limited success of Carolingian efforts to contrive a monumental architectural style (cf. Fig. 74) was mentioned earlier, and there is a similar paucity of large-scale sculpture. The story is different in the more limited category of ivory relief carving (cf. Fig. 584), for the small panels made to decorate the covers of manuscript books or adorn reliquary caskets often have the individuality and unity of style so lacking in the Sigwald Relief.

On a larger scale than the ivory book-cover panel, the same quality is evident in the bronze reliefs of a pair of doors made for the church of St. Michael at Hildesheim in Germany between 1007 and 1015, and later moved to the cathedral in the same city. A gift of Bernward, the Bishop of Hildesheim, they were probably inspired by his admiration for the elaborately carved fifth-century wooden doors of the church of Santa Sabina in Rome (Fig. 65). There are two sets of eight panels each, those on the left relating the story of Genesis from the Creation of Man through the Murder of Abel, and those on the right depicting the life of Christ. The immediate impression of these panels like that showing the *Judgment of Adam and Eve* (Fig. 293) is the amazing forcefulness and vitality of the figures. Compared with the heavy and stolid ones of the Latin sarcophagus (Fig. 288), the dignified Byzantine forms (Fig. 289), or the ugly and formless creatures on the Sigwald Relief (Fig. 292), those on the Hildesheim Doors are alive, instinct with a vigor that seems almost to tear them free of their

FIG. 293.   Hildesheim.   Judgment of Adam and Eve, Detail of
Bronze Doors (1007-1015) of Cathedral.

relief backing. The theme is rendered with a naïve sense of the dramatic that makes the observer forget the crudely shaped bodies with their overlarge heads and unarticulated limbs. The unknown sculptor's power of characterization transcends his lack of anatomical knowledge, for there is no mistaking the significance of the threatening head and denunciatory finger of the Deity whose accusation is promptly passed on by the apprehensive Adam to Eve who in her turn shifts the blame by gesturing at the dragon Tempter on the ground. The sense of a powerful force animating the figures is present even in the twisted tree and the wiry foliage of the panel border. It is this abstract, prevalent force that unifies the composition. There is obviously none of the formal architectonic unity of Greek relief, the spatial unity of Hellenistic or Roman relief, or the rhythmic, decorative unity of the Byzantine. Instead, the sense of movement

arising from the sheer vitality of the figures themselves unites them in common submission to some unseen but irresistible power. Technically, this effect is brought about by the sculptor's linear method of representing the various objects in the relief, as compared with the classic tradition of modeling and the Hellenistic-Byzantine dependence on light and shade. This linear method is the barbarian contribution to the artistic synthesis initiated in the first millennium and maturing in the Romanesque period.

Of the three principal sculptural styles of the early Middle Ages, that in the Hildesheim Doors was the most vital. The decadence of the Latin or west Christian mode has been commented upon. In the last years of the Byzantine Empire, a falling-off from the level attained in the earlier works is evident, although a certain stiff and hieratic dignity, nearly always present even in the least accomplished examples of the

Byzantine style, saves them from the ineptitude of late Latin sculpture. But it was the northern or barbarian style with its dramatic intensity and windy movement that galvanized these outworn modes into life and produced the monumental art of the Romanesque and Gothic periods, just as the fusion of the vigorous northern tribes with the exhausted Roman stock brought about the renewed spiritual and intellectual activity of the twelfth and thirteenth centuries.

ROMANESQUE SCULPTURE

The renewed vitality of western thought in the eleventh and twelfth centuries is apparent in sculpture as in all fields of human activity. In general, it is evident in the search for a style capable of giving full expression to the synthesis of thought then taking place. Throughout all the period, however, and through the entire Middle Ages, sculpture did not develop as a free and independent art but was subordinated to architecture. From the beginning of the Romanesque period until the end of the Gothic, little sculpture was produced that was not related in some way to architecture; and even free-standing figures imply an architectural setting. The period of Romanesque sculpture corresponds rather closely to that of Romanesque architecture but begins a little later, the first important works coming in the last quarter of the eleventh century. This was a natural consequence of its subordination to architecture, for the structural problems of building had to be solved before the resultant forms could be decorated. The period comes to a close about 1200.

Romanesque sculpture has something in common with the Greek archaic in that both result from attempts to express ideas with a limited technique. The archaic sculptors' lack of extensive knowledge of the human body was mentioned elsewhere. The Romanesque sculptor was hardly better off at the beginning of the twelfth century, for no tradition of comparable authority had replaced the classic in the years following its exhaustion. Thus when he attempted to express his ideas through the medium of the human form, he had no formulas to guide him and had to develop new ones. To aid him, there was his unconscious heritage from the past, comprising the triple influence of the Roman, Byzantine, and barbarian traditions embodied in illuminated illustrations of manuscripts (Figs. 368, 369) and carved ivory panels (Figs. 580, 585). In various proportions these determine the individual character of the various schools of Romanesque sculpture which correspond in general to those of Romanesque architecture.

Limitation of technique is thus common to both Greek archaic and Romanesque sculpture. What makes them so different in effect is the difference between the ideals they express. The archaic sculptor—and all Greek sculptors, for that matter—conceived their gods in the image of man; for them divinity became concrete and real in the human form and perfection was attained in its complete understanding. "Know thyself" was the aim of the Greek, for in knowing himself he also knew all that his world could mean to him. But in the Middle Ages, God was a completely abstract principle, a spirit, incapable of representation. He could not be comprehended intellectually but only sensed intuitively because He existed as a supernatural principle, manifest in all things that have being and constituting the element that gives them reality. This explains the naturalism of some later mediaeval art, for since all objects are a reflection to some extent of the all-embracing divine principle, it follows that they are beautiful and worthy of portrayal. At the same time, the greatest value of the objects portrayed is symbolic because they stand for rather than represent the divine principle. As will be noted later, Romanesque and Gothic figures differ in that the Romanesque are emotional symbols of reality, whereas the Gothic are intellectual in being part of an ordered system by which the spirit could begin its ascent from earthly to heavenly things. But in both cases, complete realization of their significance can only be intuitive. Herein lies the essential

FIG. 294. Vézelay. La Madeleine,
Capitals (*ca.* 1110).
Top, Moses. Bottom, An Execution.

difference between the classic point of view and that of the Middle Ages; in the former, reality was understood by knowing; in the latter, it could be understood only by feeling.

Monumental sculpture in the Romanesque world of the late eleventh and twelfth centuries had a twofold function. It was a means of instructing those who could not read, and it was an accessory to architectural form, i.e., it was decorative. Thus its subject matter deals almost entirely with Christian beliefs—stories from the Bible, the lives of the saints, etc.—and the forms interpreting this subject matter are also a factor in the architectural style of the period. Of these, two types are preeminent—the historiated capital with figures to illustrate a story (Fig. 294) and the wall relief (Figs. 297, 298). The *Capitals* are in the church of the Madeleine at Vézelay in Burgundy in France, a monastery that dates from the late eleventh century; however, the capitals were probably not carved until about 1110. The one on the bottom is particularly interesting because it is unfinished; the roughly shaped block of stone was put in place to support an arch and carved later. Although this may not have been invariable Romanesque practice, it was fairly general and it illustrates the prevailing architectonic concept of the sculptured capital. This also explains the way the subjects are treated. The subject of the unfinished capital has not been identified, but the capital above shows Moses breaking the tablets of the law while a demon escapes from the open mouth of the Golden Calf. The human figures have overlarge heads, judged by a naturalistic standard, and there is only the most summary suggestion of bodies beneath the fluttering draperies. But if these details are regarded not as parts of a physiologically articulated human figure but rather as a pattern of accents in an architectural scheme, it will be seen that they stress the portions of the capital where a sense of support is needed and that the flow of line unites these into a coherent whole. The capital form is basically classic Corinthian, suggested in the angle volutes, the foliate background, and the moulded impost-block; but the linear style of the figures is based on the manuscript illuminations which served the sculptor as models.

There is considerable variety in Romanesque wall relief, ranging from examples apparently carved directly on the surface as at Modena (Fig. 298) to the more complex relationships of the *Façade of St.-Trophime* (Fig. 295) at Arles in southern France. Here the wall seems to have been hollowed out in niches for the figures. From the stylistic point of view, they are

FIG. 295. Arles. St.-Trophime.
Sts. James, Trophime, and John,
Detail of Main Portal
(2nd half, 12th cent.).

examples of the Roman contribution to Romanesque art; this is not surprising, because Arles was the center of a flourishing school of sculpture in Roman times and many monuments are still preserved there. These undoubtedly served as models for the mediaeval sculptor at St.-Trophime who attempted as best he could to reproduce their forms. The subject of the portal as a whole is the Last Judgment. Above and to the right, not shown in the illustration, Christ is seated in the semicircular tympanum; the twelve apostles are below on the lintel. A frieze of figures on the same level as the lintel at the top of the illustration represents the souls of the saved going to paradise; a corresponding one on the other side shows the damned on their way to hell. In the niches below are large figures of the

apostles and one figure representing the saint who established Christianity at Arles. In carving these figures, the sculptor was clearly influenced by Roman models. The bodies resemble those on the Lateran sarcophagus (Fig. 288) in pose and proportions. Similar conventions for hair, eyes, and drapery are evident in both, and the garments of the Arlesian figures are not unlike the Roman toga. Another classic principle is isocephalism; the heads of the standing figures of the saved and those of the seated apostles on the lintel are all on the same level. There are other evidences of Roman influence in the foliage carved on the pilasters separating the large figures, and in the colonnette capitals, some of which approximate the classic Corinthian type rather closely.

Byzantine influences, on the other hand, predominate in the sculpture on the *Main Portal of San Niccola* (Fig. 296) at Bari in southern Italy. The Corinthianesque capitals, for example, are the type found in Byzantine architecture (Fig. 72) and sculpture (Fig. 289) of the fifth and sixth centuries. The leaf pattern is suggested by a play of light and shade created by incisions in the surface of the stone rather than being modeled to project outward. The foliate design in the arch similarly involves an arrangement of flat bright surfaces marked off by lines of shadow. The acanthus leaves on the stilt-block are the sharp-pointed, weedy Byzantine type, although the egg-and-dart above follows classic prototypes. At the left in the illustration is an angel whose draperies are suggested by patterns of incised lines like those of the Byzantine Madonna Orans (Fig. 291). Byzantine models had a direct influence on Bari sculpture, for the entire southern part of Italy was colonized by the Greeks and it had remained in close touch with the eastern Mediterranean. In other parts of Europe, the Byzantine style affected Romanesque sculpture less directly, largely through illuminated manuscripts and ivory carvings imported from the Orient.

The third component of Romanesque style, the barbarian, is dominant in much of the northern and western work, particularly the French (cf. Fig. 294). It is apparent in the complex linear patterns of figures like the prophet *Isaiah* (Fig. 297) in the church of Souillac, dating from the first half of the twelfth century. As in the figures on the Hildesheim Doors (Fig. 293), the sense of movement in these arabesques of line seems to express a powerful force that animates the swirling draperies and motivates the twisted posture. The source of this linear style seen at Hildesheim and Souillac apparently was the pen-and-ink miniatures with which the Reims school of Carolingian manuscript illuminators decorated their books, such as those in a Psalter in the University Library in Utrecht (Fig. 368).

FIG. 297. Souillac. Isaiah (*ca.* 1135), on Inner West Wall of Church.

It is easy to understand from looking at the miniature why this technique was peculiarly appropriate as a medium of expression for the emotional Teutonic barbarian temperament. It must have been such a miniature that the sculptor of the Souillac Isaiah had before him as a guide. The folds of drapery suggested in the drawing by heavy pen strokes are rendered in the figure by meticulously chiseled parallel lines. The hollow under the sweeping curve of the skirt is a painful transcription into stone of an effect easily secured in the drawing by shading. Nonetheless, with an entirely linear technique, the sculptor achieved definite plasticity of form, making even stronger the general emotional effect created by the ceaseless flow of the outlines and the impression of unrest in the flying draperies for which a supernatural motive must be imagined.

The nervous, animated figures of the Utrecht

FIG. 296. Bari. San Niccola, Detail of Main Portal (early 12th cent.).

Psalter and the Hildesheim Doors express the ideal of effective force which was the northern or barbarian contribution to the mediaeval cultural synthesis, an ideal given monumental form in the Isaiah at Souillac. The same ideal is expressed in figures, quite different in character, that represent the *Sin of Adam and Eve* (Fig. 298) on the façade of Modena Cathedral, carved about 1100 by a sculptor named Guglielmus. This figure style also derived from manuscript illumination of the pre-Romanesque period (Fig. 369), but it differed from that in the Utrecht Psalter. The figures in the Resurrection of Lazarus have a static solidness that is vastly different from the dynamic liveliness of those in the Utrecht Psalter; they are plastic forms rather than linear patterns. They represent a still further modification of classic concepts than that in the Arles sculpture; a type originally developed to express physical or moral beauty is made to express the northern ideal of effective force by giving it a racial Teutonic appearance. The head and shoulders jut forward and the gestures are clumsy and awkward but fraught with a certain power by that very awkwardness.

These characteristics are also present in Guglielmus' figures of Adam and Eve at Modena. Obviously the sculptor had little knowledge of human anatomy, but this is overshadowed by his rediscovery of the plastic form which gave the carved figures of classic antiquity such impressiveness. However awkward these great hulking bodies may be with their clumsy hands and peasant heads, they reveal the sculptor's sense of the significance of the human body. And nowhere in Romanesque art, even in examples of comparable style and character like the episcopal chair in San Niccola at Bari (Fig. 599) of about the same period, is this idea conveyed more forcefully than in these reliefs. Handicapped as the sculptor may have been by his limited technique, and naïve and unsophisticated though these figures may be, they are instinct with a primal power that gives life to them and significance to the sculptor's simple yet expressive conception of the human form.

Guglielmus' method of attaining this end is comparable to the classic sculptor's, although he

Cathedral, Modena.

FIG. 298.   Guglielmus, Sin of Adam and Eve (*ca.* 1100).

did not copy classic originals in any sense. The background is neutral, with all but the essential features of the landscape eliminated; the story is told by the human forms alone. There is classic precedent also for subordinating the figures to the architectural design, standing as they do under a series of pendant arches with an occasional colonnette and a foliate cornice. The term classic is used advisedly, without any suggestion that a direct classical influence is to be seen in these figures. It means rather that Guglielmus discovered for himself the principles that also govern classic sculpture. For his expressive vocabulary he uses the human form, creating a rhythmic pattern of its masses which he then subordinates to the larger scheme of the architecture.

A glance back at the example of Romanesque art thus far discussed leaves two impressions. The first is the absence of homogeneity in the style as a whole. On the one hand there are the figures at Arles and Modena, heavy and solid, with something of classic sobriety in pose and restrained movement. On the other there is the agitated figure of the Souillac Isaiah. The apparent lack of similarity in these figures makes the second impression clear—that a synthesis of content and expression has not yet been achieved in mediaeval art. The Arles and Modena figures are attempts to embody the emotionalism of the northern temperament in forms that still smack of classical, intellectually attained unity. In the Isaiah, the emotional content of the figure overflows, swamping the form with linear movement to the extent that its plasticity is almost lost. In both, the effect is obviously due to superficial characteristics—the movement of the drapery, the physical bulk of the bodies—and not to an inner, spiritual significance intrinsic in the forms. In other words, the content or meaning of these figures is still symbolic rather than being stated directly in terms of human experience.

The synthesis of form and content lacking in the earlier Romanesque sculpture is attained in the *Ancestors of Christ* (Fig. 299) in the west portal of Chartres Cathedral (cf. Fig. 99). This part of the cathedral dates from around 1150, about fifty years earlier than the rest of the building. An important distinction from earlier Romanesque figures is the closer relationship of the Chartres statues to the architecture; they appear to be part of the building itself, not just attached to its surface. From a naturalistic standard the bodies are "deformed," a quality often incorrectly ascribed to the sculptor's lack of skill. Actually, it is the result of modifying superficial facts of appearance in the interests of a definite pattern that will make the ideal embodied in the figures tangible and intelligible. As was pointed out in the discussion of Greek sculpture, this is the sculptor's purpose at all times. The difference between the patterns of Greek and of mediaeval sculpture is explained by the different ideals they express—the Greek, concrete and physical; the mediaeval, abstract and spiritual.

FIG. 299.   Chartres.   Ancestors of Christ, West Portal (*ca.* 1150) of the Cathedral.

There is another characteristic of the Chartres figures which seems at first sight to be directly antithetical to their architectonic quality and the resultant abstraction of forms. This is a new interest in nature, evident in the treatment of the faces; the features are decidedly French and are differentiated in an extraordinarily realistic way. Notice, for example, the distinction between the heads of the two queens of Judah on the outermost columns in Fig. 299. In spite of the fact that the bodies are abstract patterns in stone, the faces are so expressive that these figures have a real and human existence instead of being symbols of an abstract theological idea. It is interesting to compare the mediaeval and the Greek sculptor's method of making figures meaningful. The Greek ideal is expressed in the entire body; the head is only a part of it and hence is not emphasized in any way, as can be seen in the Three Fates (Fig. 262), where the absence of the heads does not detract materially from the meaning of the group. The logical and organic structure of the bodies gives them significance, as does also the emphasis on their existence as independent and self-sufficient entities. In contrast, the Chartres sculptor makes the body an abstract pattern, the embodiment of a spiritual concept which is made concrete by the remarkable expressiveness of the face and which attains ideal significance in its relationship to the architectural background.

The sculpture at Chartres represents the final harmonization of the various elements of Romanesque style. Two characteristics stand out. The first is the more ordered arrangement of the figures, not only with respect to the architectural setting but in themselves. This is a characteristic illustration of the later mediaeval concept that the significance of all things is determined by their place in a preconceived system. The larger implication of this fact is its indication of an intellectual rather than an emotional point of view; and since mediaeval thought was essentially and almost exclusively religious, it indicates a rational and analytical rather than an intuitive faith. The effect of this change on Romanesque art is evident in the difference between the Souillac Isaiah and the figures at Chartres. As long as Christian thought was based on emotional fervor, its ideals could be embodied in an art of linear movement. When an intellectual leaven was added, a greater degree of form and static strength was essential.

The second characteristic that distinguishes the Chartres sculpture from the earlier Romanesque is its intensely human quality. There is a world of difference between the ideally youthful kings and queens of Judah and the meager saints or brutal peasants that embodied earlier ideals. Again the change in art reflects one in the tenets of the Church. Until the middle of the twelfth century, mediaeval theology was to all intents and purposes the highly intellectualized and abstract code of the Early Church fathers. The literal and objective Middle Ages could interpret such a theology only with the aid of an emotional fervor that swept away all the obstacles placed in the way of its being accepted by naïve minds, an emotional fervor powerful to such a point of fanaticism that it would inspire the incredible undertaking of the early crusades. In the latter part of the Romanesque period, a more human spirit transformed Church doctrines, a development contemporary with the decline of the monasteries and the rise of the communes. From that time on, however much the ideas of art may have been determined by the Church, the forms which expressed them came from the minds of the people. The figures became more human, subject to the same laws of order as the people who carved them, and expressive of a point of view that found significance in intellectually contrived systems rather than emotionally felt abstractions. It was this that brought about the more realistic art of Chartres as well as its higher degree of organization and formal discipline.

GOTHIC SCULPTURE

The sculpture on the west portal of Chartres occupies a pivotal position in French mediaeval art, for it is at once the culmination of the Romanesque style and the beginning of the Gothic. Characteristic of the latter style are the cheerful gravity of the figures, replacing the earlier ecstasy or the stolid reserve, the greater naturalism, and the heightened significance of physical as well as decorative integration with architectural setting. All these changes are direct consequences of the shift from the Romanesque emotional approach to spiritual reality to the intellectual Gothic approach. In this respect, Gothic sculpture is one with the other manifestations of the human creative instinct in Europe during the thirteenth century. In every field of activity, intellectual interpretations of experience as the preliminary to intuitive perception of its ultimate significance took form in complex systems in which every detail of every aspect of human knowledge was wrought into a comprehensive and well-articulated scheme. In philosophy, it was the scholasticism of Thomas Aquinas' *Summa Theologiae;* in literature, the *Divine Comedy* of Dante; in architecture, the cathedral, of which the sculptured ornament was an integral part. Even in the sculpture, this passion for system and order is apparent in the complex iconography or scheme that governs its arrangement. The ornament is often naturalistic, reflecting the Gothic conception of the universe as the revelation of God's will whence every detail is beautiful and each individual form is worthy of representation. In consequence, Gothic sculpture is organic and varied as nature itself in its seeming lack of coherence, but it is rendered significant by the iconography or arrangement and by its relationship to the architectural background with which it is indissolubly wedded.

Just as the transitional sculptures of the temple of Zeus at Olympia suggest the ideal fully attained in the Parthenon figures, so those at Chartres forecast the culminating Gothic style of the early thirteenth century as seen in the west portal of Amiens Cathedral (Fig. 100). Here in a monument dating between 1220 and 1230, the idea of a structural union of sculpture and architecture appears in its most developed form. The subject matter and the way it is represented are typical of Gothic iconography, the term for the rule or tradition in such matters, even to indicating where it should be on the cathedral. Thus the north portal at Amiens is devoted to the story of Saint Firmin, the patron of the city of Amiens; the south portal relates the story of the Virgin to whom the building is dedicated (Fig. 301); and the *Central Portal* (Fig. 300) represents the Last Judgment. This is shown in the tympanum, the arched relief above the doors, which is divided into three registers or levels; the Resurrection and Judgment of the Souls are in the lowest, the Separation of the Elect and the Damned in the middle, and Christ as Judge at the top. The theme is carried over into the voussoirs, or arches of the splayed vaulted porch, on which are carved, proceeding outward from the tympanum, angels with the Elect, Martyrs and Confessors, the Wise and Foolish Virgins, the Elders of the Apocalypse, the Tree of Jesse with the Genealogy of Christ, and the Patriarchs of the Old Law. In the embrasures on both sides below, on the level of the doors, are larger than life-size figures representing the Apostles of the New Testament and some of the Prophets of the Old; they are identified by the instruments of their martyrdom or by other means. Below the Prophets, quatrefoil medallions in the wall have carved illustrations of their prophecies; below the Apostles are the Virtues and their opposite Vices, one of the most ancient themes in Christian art.

On the *trumeau* or central pier is a standing figure of Christ (Fig. 302). The other portals are decorated in the same way, differing only in subject matter. The large figures in the north portal of St. Firmin represent the Church Fathers and Saints; those in the south portal are the Queen of Sheba, Solomon, Herod, and the Three Magi on one side, and the *Annunciation, Visitation, and Presentation in the Temple* (Fig. 301) on the other, with *trumeau* figures of Saint Firmin and the Virgin respectively. The choice and arrangement of these figures and their subjects were not left to chance or to the individual preference of the sculptors, but were determined in accordance with the most authoritative theological opinion of the time, the source in this case being Vincent of Beauvais' encyclopaedia called the *Four Mirrors of Human Knowledge.* The sculpture at Amiens has been called "the Bible in stone," and its instructive function for those who could not read is clearly indicated.

In considering the style of the sculpture, it must always be remembered that it is architectural. The size of the figures, for example, is determined by their part in the design of the building regardless of any inconsistency with those adjoining them. Within these limits, however, there are certain changes from the similarly conceived figures at Chartres (Fig. 299) which are evident in the New Testament scenes on the south portal at Amiens (Fig. 301). There is still very little movement in the bodies, but the draperies are heavier than at Chartres and they fall in more plastic folds, evidence of the naturalistic trend of Gothic development. This is also true of the way the heads are turned to relate the

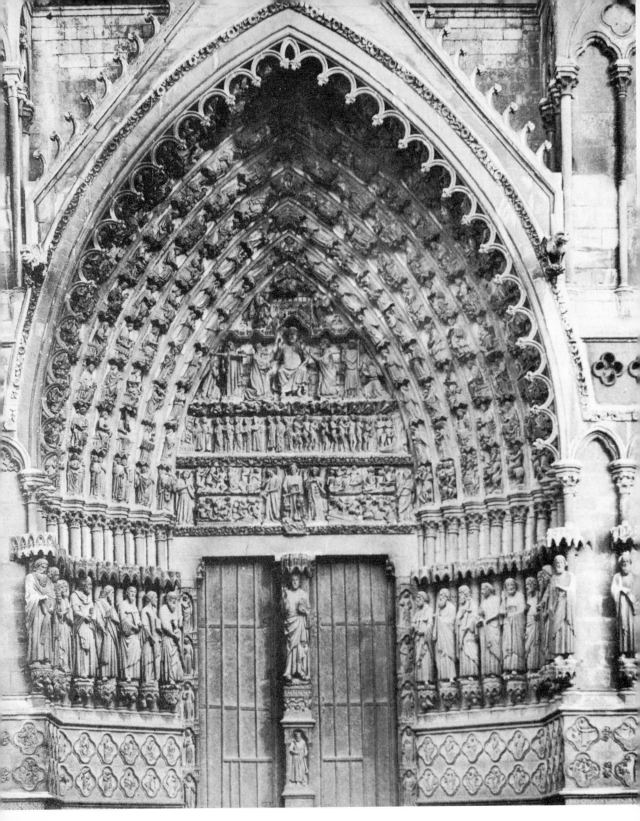

FIG. 300. Amiens. Last Judgment, Central Portal (1220–1230) of
Cathedral Façade.

FIG. 301. Amiens. Annunciation, Visitation,
Presentation in the Temple, South Portal (1220-1230)
of Cathedral Façade.

figures in three groups—the Annunciation, the
Visitation, and the Presentation in the Temple,
reading from left to right. This treatment of the
heads and the loosening of the draperies modify
the rigidness of the Chartres figures, but the
canopies over the heads integrate them with the
architectural setting. The heads are somewhat
larger in proportion to the bodies than at Chartres
but are less sharply differentiated; they are types
rather than portraits.

The *Beau-Dieu of Amiens* (Fig. 302) might

well be considered the complete embodiment
of the thirteenth-century ideal. Occupying the
trumeau or central post of the Last Judgment portal
(Fig. 300), it represents Christ with the Book of
the Law in His left hand, and the right raised in
benediction. Under His feet are the adder and
the basilisk, symbolic of the forces of evil He
overcomes. The full draperies are arranged according to the High Gothic formula, vertical
folds on one side and a horizontal cascade on the
other. The heavy band around the hips was the

Gothic sculptor's favorite device to mask the faulty articulation of legs and torso. Also evident is the absence of any suggestion of a body underneath the draperies. The face is modeled in large simple planes whose broad surfaces create the effect of firm and youthful roundness which was an integral part of the robust High Gothic ideal. Gothic too is the calm, cheerful dignity of the figure, very different from the tortured stance of the Romanesque prophet (Fig. 297). Here is no fanatic threatening sinners with the tortures of hell but a just and benevolent ruler who deals with each according to his deserts. No single figure could better reveal Gothic theology's emphasis on the joys of earth and heaven in contrast to the Romanesque preoccupation with the punishments in the next life for him who sinned in this.

French Gothic sculpture, like the architecture of which it is a part, can be considered the stylistic norm of the period. Though it was occasionally influenced by other traditions, the reverse was more often true. Thus about the middle of the thirteenth century the figures of the *Margrave Ekkehard and the Margravine Uta* (Fig. 303) in the Cathedral at Naumburg in Germany were carved out of the pier they adorn much in the French fashion of that period. But the Germanic ideal they exemplify is much closer to nature than that of their French contemporaries. Ekkehard and Uta were among the traditional benefactors of the cathedral at Naumburg, and the statues commemorate their generosity some two centuries earlier. The figures are therefore not contemporary likenesses, but are nonetheless extraordinarily individualized. In this they share the liking for the concrete and specific that distinguishes German from French Gothic style. Ekkehard is the personification of the coarsegrained yet forceful Teutonic noble; Uta is one of the most engagingly feminine figures in mediaeval art. There are still some traces of the color that made them even more personalized originally but did not detract from the emphatically sculpturesque masses of broad planes of drapery and strongly modeled surfaces.

The fine balance between concrete naturalism and abstract decoration in the figures on the

FIG. 302. Amiens. The Beau-Dieu, Central Portal (1220-1230) of Cathedral Façade.

west front of Amiens Cathedral is characteristic of French sculpture through the first half of the thireenth century and is the outstanding trait of High Gothic style. During the second half of the century, the latent naturalism of the style comes to the fore as in the *Vierge Dorée* (Fig. 304), of Amiens, on the *trumeau* of the south transept portal. It dates from about 1265, the name deriving from the gold leaf that originally decorated it. The sculptor's close observation of simpler natural forms in the hawthorn borders of the lintel contributes to a realistic effect but without sacrificing decorative unity. The human figures show a similar disposition toward naturalism, but the admirable synthesis that achieves an ordered whole out of infinite variety in the foliate borders is lacking. Two factors are responsible for this. The first was the sculptor's indifferent knowledge of anatomy which made it impossible for him to make the figures convincing in themselves. The second is the less architectural character of the figures, the result of attempting to make them more naturalistic. To give them more realism, the sculptor, resorted to mannerisms of gesture and conventions of form, hoping thus to compensate for their unconvincing construction. This is apparent in the Apostles on the lintel, debonair figures far different from the sturdy burghers who were the Apostles on the west portals (Fig. 300). They stand rather casually under canopies which have lost their architectural significance by being merged in a continuous border; the sole factor that relates the figures is the light-hearted conversation which only partially occupies their attention. The effect is not convincing, for the sculptor still conceives the forms in architectural conventions, as in the fall and cascade of draperies of the Beau-Dieu. But the significance the earlier figure derived from its architectural setting is not so great in the later figures and their naturalism is not sufficient to make them convincing in other ways.

The disintegration of High Gothic architectonic style that accompanied the more naturalistic ideal and the attendant weakening of content is also apparent in the Madonna. In contrast with the bourgeois ladies on the western portals (Fig. 301), the Vierge Dorée is given the form that humble minds believed to be aristocratic. Instead of the noble gravity of the earlier figures, there is gracefulness; the concept of the Virgin as the Queen of Heaven, given dignity by the severely architectonic form, is replaced by that of an altogether human mother. The youthful freshness of High Gothic faces is exaggerated and the attempt to attain greater expressiveness without adequate anatomical knowledge produces mannerisms like the slanted eyes and the smile.

The "hip-shot" effect in the body, with the weight of the swaying figure resting on one leg, was the result of an effort to create a more graceful pose. The contrast between the lines of the figure and the rigid verticals of the pillar marks the first step in the separation of sculpture from the architecture that had given it stability and significance in the High Gothic period.

The mannerisms of the Vierge Dorée are exaggerated in fourteenth-century French sculptural style. It has already been pointed out that

FIG. 303. Naumburg. Margrave Ekkehard and Margravine Uta (*ca.* 1250), Western Choir of Cathedral.

FIG. 304. Amiens. The Vierge Dorée,
South Transept Portal (*ca.* 1265)
of Cathedral.

contrast with the strongly architectural lines in High Gothic figures, have become a major interest; the robes are an end in themselves, an entity independent of the body which is not even suggested. The human sentiment of the Vierge Dorée is here carried to the point of artificiality in the exaggerated hip-shot pose and the childish head with its almond eyes and thin mouth whose immaturity is emphasized by the overlarge crown. This affectation of pose and sentiment expresses an ideal that is devoid of any very profound meaning, but the figure retains the saving grace of a certain distinction or elegance. However artificial the concept, the figure has style, a quality characterizing French art ever since the Middle Ages even in its most uncreative and sterile phases. It was this distinctiveness that made French fourteenth-century style a powerful influence on late mediaeval sculpture in all parts of Europe, particularly Italy.

The mannered grace and delicacy of the Virgin of Paris indicate one trend in French fourteenth-century sculpture. Another one, greater naturalism, is apparent in statues like those of Charles V and Jeanne de Bourbon in the Louvre, which are among the first true portraits in mediaeval art. This tendency in fourteenth-century sculpture had its roots in the latent naturalism of High Gothic style; it was stimulated by a desire for greater realism in sepulchral figures, a cause and effect analogous to the similar phenomena in Roman sculpture. The realism of fourteenth-century art indicates the relaxation of High Gothic idealism better than words. Although it had always been an element in native French style, the immediate source of this realism was the art of the Netherlands where it dominated the High Gothic manner, as it did in Germany (cf. Fig. 303). Transferred to France by Flemish artists working in Paris, this realistic mode soon became popular. It appears in monumental form in the art produced in Dijon toward the end of the fourteenth century and early in the fifteenth by Flemish artists serving the Dukes of Burgundy.

The outstanding sculptural example of this Franco-Flemish style is the *Well of Moses* (Fig. 306) in the erstwhile monastery of Champmol

the spiritual content of late thirteenth-century sculpture was weakened by greater naturalism on the one hand and a conception of beauty intrinsic in the figures on the other. The effect of substituting an aesthetic ideal for one of religious significance becomes apparent in *Notre-Dame la Blanche* (Fig. 305) in the Cathedral of Paris. There is no pretense at relating the figure to an architectural setting. The drapery folds, in discreet

Chartreuse de Champmol, near Dijon.

FIG. 306.   Claus Sluter, Moses
(1395-1403),
Detail of The Well of Moses.

FIG. 305.   Notre-Dame la Blanche
(*ca.* 1330),
Choir of the Cathedral in Paris.

near Dijon. The illustration shows one of six figures representing Old Testament prophets that were carved as decorations for a well-head by the Netherlandish sculptor Claus Sluter (d.1405) between 1395 and 1403. The motivation is interesting. The well-head was originally the base of a carved group of the Crucifixion. The idea of relating the Old Testament prophets to this scene came from one of the mystery plays that were so popular during the Middle Ages. The source of this particular idea was the prologue to a passion play, like that recurrently celebrated at Oberammergau, in which Christ is condemned to die for humanity by a tribunal of patriarchs and prophets who pass sentence upon Him. In the sculptured figures, the pronouncement

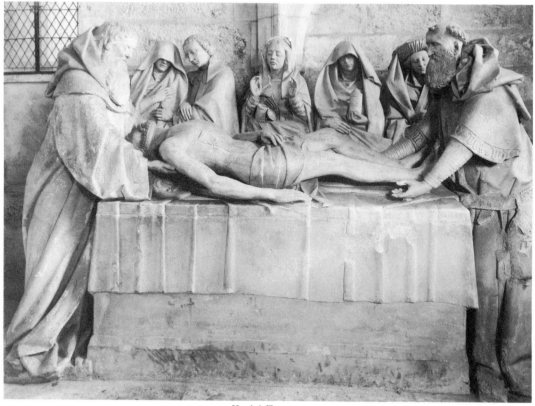

Hospital, Tonnerre.

FIG. 307. Holy Sepulcher (1454).

of each judge was inscribed upon the long scroll he holds. Moses (Fig. 306) speaks in words from the book of Exodus xii, 6: "The whole assembly of the congregation of Israel shall kill it [the Paschal lamb] in the evening." In creating this figure, from which the well is named, Sluter omitted no detail of appearance, but it is no mere study in realism. The venerable patriarch seems to bear the weight of centuries upon his shoulders in the realistically draped folds of the robe. The ease with which he supports them is translated in the observer's mind into an indication of intellectual as well as physical power, an impression furthered by the sense of superhuman vision in the piercing eyes. The architectural background is reminiscent of the High Gothic method of investing the figures with authority, but the poses are not motivated by it. Originally, the realism of the figures was intensified by color,

a tradition in Flanders where sculpture was usually little more than painting in high relief. At the same time, the group is characteristically French in the powerful impression of definite form and bulk, for the figures are conceived as sculptural masses rather than painted images.

In Sluter's works, objective realism is transfigured and ennobled by the epic poetry of lofty conceptions. His less gifted followers could seldom do more than record the facts of appearance, confounding the truth of his figures with mere ugliness. As a result, only rarely were their works genuinely expressive. In parts of France outside Burgundy—in the Loire region, for example—the crude realism of Sluter's followers was never popular and the prevailing style was only mildly naturalistic. A characteristic example is the *Holy Sepulcher* (Fig. 307) in the Hospital at Tonnerre in Burgundy, which dates from 1454.

FIG. 308.   Head of a Saint (early 16th cent.).

Flemish realism that is forceful to the point of harshness in the Well of Moses is considerably tempered here. Again the idea is derived from the mysteries. The grouping of the figures around the tomb is naturalistic, based on a scene from a passion play. The carefully studied contemporary costumes, as well as the faces, also reveal a dependence on actual models. This is particularly true of the Virgin, the figure in the center, a frequent type in contemporary Flemish painting. Naturalism does not detract from the emotional content of the group, however, but adds poignancy by making it individual and specific. The sense of bitter grief and depression in these figures is conveyed by the heavy draperies whose broad folds weigh down their wearers so oppressively. Each person's emotion is focused on the dead Christ, Who thus unites the group spiritually, just as the various figures are wrought into a plastic unit by the strong horizontal accent of the corpse (cf. Fig. 382).

The Tonnerre Holy Sepulcher represents the initial step in the final phase of French mediaeval art. The culmination of this phase, and in many ways its most captivating forms, appear in the Champagne region to the east and south of Paris. Its inhabitants were of the bourgeoisie; and a deep spirituality, almost High Gothic, is apparent in their art for some time after aristocratic French society had adopted the more fashionable and consciously aesthetic style imported from Italy by royal order. It is this sense of the reality of spiritual experience that animated the style known as the *détente*, meaning a relaxation of the unsparing naturalism of the fifteenth-century Franco-Flemish manner; it apparently had its center in the city of Troyes. The *détente* ideal is beautifully portrayed in a limestone statue of a *Feminine Saint* (Fig. 308) in the Princeton University Art Museum, Princeton, N.J. It was a realistic ideal, for the face is characteristically French and the drapery is obviously studied from nature. At the same time, these realistic elements are generalized; they exist not as ends in themselves but to give point to the emotional content of the figure. This in turn is expressed in a quiet and restrained fashion, very different from the unfettered manifestations

of grief in the Franco-Flemish style, and indicative of profoundly felt inner experience. The figure was originally part of an Entombment group similar to that at Tonnerre although later in date, probably the first quarter of the sixteenth century. Since the group was to stand in a niche, the modeling of the features is broad and summary, in sharply intersecting planes. Such treatment was required for a proper effect in the relatively subdued light of a secluded interior, for overrefined details would escape observation under such conditions. The generalized effect of the summary modeling invests the figure with lofty idealism, a characteristic of all *détente* art. In this quality, it is not unlike the art of the thirteenth century but with this significant difference, that High Gothic idealism was impersonal and abstract, based on theological interpretation of experience, whereas sixteenth-century idealism is individual and concrete and has its roots in human emotion. In giving form to this ideal in the last years of the sixteenth century, sculpture once more became a self-sufficient art that had inherent significance. It thus recovered the individuality it had yielded when it was subordinated to architecture in the all-embracing Gothic synthesis of the thirteenth century.

Détente art was the final manifestation of the French mediaeval spirit and in many ways it was the most complete and effective expression of the humanizing tendency that characterized Gothic art from the outset. The lyric grace of its forms was peculiarly appropriate to the pathos of its favorite subjects, but the style lacked intrinsic vigor. This vigor it might have developed had it not been overwhelmed by the powerful Italianizing style propagated by the school of art established by royal decree at Fontainebleau. The French *détente* was contemporary with the Italian High Renaissance, and the winsome saints of the Troyes school gave way to athletic figures embodying the more virile but alien concepts of the southern country. Their ultimate supremacy in French art spelled the doom of the mediaeval tradition. Henceforward French artists were concerned no longer with giving form to spiritual ideals but to aesthetic ideals. The mediaeval spirit was dead.

Detail of Fig. 323.

CHAPTER TWENTY

Renaissance Sculpture in Italy

The disintegration of the High Gothic system in the fourteenth century was in its way a reflection of the declining authority of the Church. In French sculpture, this disintegration is apparent in the loosening of figures from the architectural setting which had given them significance in the High Gothic period and in a growing mannerism of pose, gesture, and expression. At the same time, the naturalism in mediaeval style continued with unabated vigor, forceful and masculine in Claus Sluter's Moses (Fig. 306), delicate and feminine and transfigured by profoundly felt emotion in the figures of the *détente* (cf. Fig. 308). Both reveal an interest in the individual that is diametrically opposed to

Baptistery, Pisa.

FIG. 309.   Niccolo Pisano, Nativity (1260), Detail of Pulpit.

thirteenth-century collectivism. The fifteenth century no longer viewed nature as a symbolic manifestation of the mystic order conceived in the minds of theologians and interpreted by scholastic thought. Instead, it was a revelation of life itself, experienced directly by the individual with a poignancy reflected in all fifteenth-century art; this was seen in the French *détente* and will be observed in Italian figures as well. To give ideal meaning to the expression of this idea, the northern painters had recourse to the infinite vistas of landscape (Fig. 373). In Italy, stronghold of the classic tradition, that end was attained in the classic manner by giving the figures significant form, i.e., form which has inherent meaning and character.

At first glance, it might seem that this concept of giving concrete form to ideas would result in reproducing classic figures. Actually this was not the case. The goal of classic thought and art was the determination of universal types; individual manifestations of those types were accidental aberrations. Owing to its immediate heritage of mediaeval thought with its recognition of specific and individual qualities, the fifteenth century started at the other end and conceived the universal in terms of the particular. As a result, Renaissance art is dynamic, even in its most classic aspects; it has an air quite different from the calm and ideal self-sufficiency of classic antiquity. Thought was much more complex in the fifteenth century than in the fifth century B.C.;

it could not be fully expressed in forms whose very existence depended upon generalized concepts and processes of simplification.

This is clearly revealed by an attempt to employ classic forms in Italy in the thirteenth century. The design Niccolo Pisano (*ca.* 1205?-1278?) made for a monumental pulpit for the Baptistery of Pisa in 1260 includes a series of panels showing episodes in the Life of Christ. The pulpit was a hexagonal box on Corinthian colonnettes; it was reached by a flight of steps leading to one side which was left open. On the first of the five other sides is the *Nativity* (Fig. 309). Niccolo employed classic types in the figures. The Virgin reclines on her couch like a dignified Roman matron. The angel of the Annunciation at the left is a youth clad in a Roman toga, reproducing a type often found on late Latin sarcophagi. The formulas of hair and drapery have the same source; Joseph's beard is a series of tight curls with a drill hole in the center of each, and the broad angular folds of the robes are of similar derivation. The generalized figures and the simple composition of quiet vertical and horizontal accents both contribute to a classic sense of repose. At the same time, the intense expression on the face of the announcing angel betrays the artist's discontent with his classicizing forms as conveyors of the emotional content of the subject. It is clear from this that he was no precursor of the Renaissance, as he has sometimes been called. The content of his Nativity is still mediaeval and its forms are only incidentally cast in a classic mould.

Less obviously classic in form yet paradoxically more faithful to classic expressive tradition is a *Madonna with the Christ Child* (Fig. 310) by Niccolo's son, Giovanni Pisano (*ca.* 1250-*ca.* 1317). It was made for the Arena Chapel in Padua about 1305, when Giotto was painting its walls with scenes from the New Testament (cf. Fig. 389). Superficially, Giovanni's Madonna seems French (cf. Fig. 305), and there is evidence that he was familiar with contemporary northern art. The draperies are disposed in the familiar horizontals and verticals of the Gothic "fall and cascade," the finely chiseled facial details include the quasi-Oriental almond eyes, and the hip-

shot stance also contributes to the Gallic effect. But by comparison, the Virgin of Paris is artificial and mannered, its gestures quaint and ingenuous. The Italian figure shows profound intent and tragic sensibility, a protagonist in a profoundly moving drama. Beneath the draperies is a tangible and articulate form whose movement supplies a comprehensible motive for their agitation. And where the French Virgin has the air and charm of an elegantly dressed mannequin, "Giovanni's Madonna looks with tragic intensity at the Child, who peers into her eyes as if to discover the secret of his impending Passion," as Charles Rufus Morey has stated it (*Mediaeval Art*, p. 318). Herein is the revelation of the Italian's classic inheritance of form

Arena Chapel, Padua.

FIG. 310. Giovanni Pisano, Madonna with the Christ Child (*ca.* 1305).

inherently significant. The Virgin of Paris is a mannered and sophisticated statement of an elegant and graceful conception of feminity. Giovanni's Madonna is an expression of sincerely felt emotion.

Italian sculpture of the fourteenth century followed, in general, the path indicated by Giovanni's work. In Italian hands, the modish figures of late French Gothic derivation acquired ideal significance by virtue of the Italian heritage of the classic tradition of expressive form. The meaningless gestures of the French figures were invested with geniune meaning by making them indicative of deeply felt emotion. Thus in Italy of the fourteenth century as in France, sculpture was developing a style that would adequately express the concepts of personal and individual interpretation of experience that evolved from and contributed to the breakdown of the High Gothic synthesis.

THE EARLY RENAISSANCE

By the beginning of the fifteenth century, the mediaevalism of Italian sculpture begins to be modified by one or both of two concepts previously not present—a renewed interest in classic forms and a more positive realism. Both tendencies are quite pronounced in Early Renaissance sculpture. The interest in classic art may be traced to the affinity between Renaissance humanism and the antique preoccupation with human values. At the same time, Renaissance humanism also involved genuine scientific curiosity which found much to intrigue it in the naturalism of later mediaeval art. However, the fifteenth-century approach to nature was very different from that of the Middle Ages in being analytical rather than synthetic, leading to the study of observed facts for their own sake rather than as symbols of a divine order. Not the least important result of this was the reappearance in sculpture of the nude human figure as a subject for monumental treatment. Its use had been limited to a very few themes in the theological art of the Middle Ages and it rarely if ever appeared in statutes in the round (cf. Fig. 298).

The work of Lorenzo Ghiberti (1378-1455), one of the three outstanding sculptors of the Early Renaissance in Italy, illustrates the new interest in classic forms. Ghiberti first gained distinction in 1401 by winning a competition in his native city of Florence for the honor of creating a pair of bronze doors for the Baptistery of San Giovanni. In this competition his chief opponent was Brunellesco, whose failure to win it was instrumental in turning his attention to architecture (cf. Figs. 113-115). All participants in the competition were required to interpret the same subject, Abraham's Sacrifice of Isaac; the panels by Brunellesco and Ghiberti are preserved today in the Bargello in Florence. Of the two, Brunellesco's is the more mediaeval in the diffusion of interest in the composition, the lack of spatial effects, and the dramatic intensity of the protagonists. In contrast, Ghiberti's panel is effectively unified by well-suggested space and by modification of dramatic content in the interest of greater decorativeness. The subject of the bronze doors was the life of Christ. Some critics feel that they are less inventive than the competitive panel, for they are still quite mediaeval in some ways. Whatever the judgment of posterity, they were enthusiastically acclaimed when Ghiberti finished them in 1423; they were placed in the eastern portal of the Baptistery.

The following year, another pair of doors for the same building was commissioned from Ghiberti. Completed in 1447, they replaced the first set in the eastern portal of the Baptistery, the earlier ones being moved to the southern entrance. In the second doors, called worthy of being the *Gates of Paradise* (Fig. 311) by Michelangelo, Ghiberti created a masterpiece of relief sculpture; unsurpassed for sheer technical skill, it has been a model of its kind ever since. The theme originally assigned was a symbolic parallel of Old and New Testament subjects, a typically mediaeval concept. With characteristic Renaissance individualism, Ghiberti rejected this scheme and persuaded the sponsoring guild to accept his own. Ten large panels tell the Old Testament story from the Creation of Man to the Meeting of

Baptistery, Florence.

FIG. 311.   Ghiberti, The Gates of Paradise (1425-1447), the East Portal.

FIG. 312. Ghiberti, Story of Abraham, Detail of Fig. 311.

Solomon and the Queen of Sheba, beginning in the upper left corner and reading across both valves. Each relief is devoted to one character or group of characters, although a number depict more than one incident. Thus there are two episodes in the *Story of Abraham* (Fig. 312) in the second panel from the top on the right side—the visit of the three angels and the sacrifice of Isaac (cf. Fig. 365). To unify these subjects which were unrelated in time, Ghiberti placed them in a magnificently wrought landscape background, bringing the two incidents together in a single volume of space. This sense of space in the panel is created by varying the depth of the relief planes, from great projection in the almost free-standing foreground figures to hardly perceptible lines in those more distant. The result is an impression of air circulating around the figures, an effect like that obtained similarly in the Arch of Titus reliefs (Fig. 286). The greater realism of Ghiberti's relief compared with the Roman came from his knowledge of the laws of perspective that had been codified by his rival Brunellesco and developed by Alberti (cf. pages 134, 469). His rather naïve pride in this knowledge is apparent in the way the donkey stands with his rump pointing toward the observer, providing the artist with an opportunity to demonstrate his skill in fore-shortening.

The style of the human figures is a compromise between the mediaeval and classic traditions. The feminine figure in the small niche at the left of the Abraham panel represents one of the pagan sibyls who foretold the coming of Christ. She has the fourteenth-century Gothic hip-shot pose (cf. Fig. 304), and there is no effective correlation of body and drapery. Again, the anatomical construction in the lovely group of the three angels is far from accurate, but this can be overlooked in view of the stately rhythm of their progress toward the kneeling patriarch, a rhythm repeated in the row of trees in the middle distance. Such is Ghiberti's assimilation of the decorative component of classic style. His use of classic prototypes is even more apparent in the nude male figure in the niche at the right of the panel. It represents Samson in the guise of a Hercules of Praxitelean pose and Roman muscularity. In spite of such antique overtones, Ghiberti's mediaeval background is betrayed in Samson's bushy hair and small skull, traits of thirteenth- and fourteenth-century Gothic figures. The mixture of floral and animal motives in the border of the portal is also mediaeval rather than classic, conceived in linear, not plastic terms.

In the final analysis, Ghiberti's classicism was more or less incidental to a style still fundamentally mediaeval. In nothing is this shown more clearly than in his use of landscape and architectural backgrounds, depending upon their heroic breadth to invest the Old Testament legends with the significance the figures lack. How little Ghiberti was capable of giving his figures significance is evident in the meaningless and rhetorical gestures used in dramatic scenes like the Expulsion of Adam and Eve from the Garden of Eden. Instead of attempting to make his figures other than decorative, he creates a sense of awe by the epic grandeur of the deep backgrounds which his incomparable command of relief made so convincingly real. Thus the panels are effective as ensembles rather than be-cause of the intrinsic character of the individual figures, a conception as mediaeval as the decorative scheme of a Gothic cathedral.

Jacopo della Quercia (1371-1438) had a different concept of the human form from Ghiberti's decorative approach. In the Sin of Adam and Eve (Fig. 313) on the main portal of S. Petronio at Bologna, done between 1425 and 1438, Jacopo reverted directly to classic method by suppressing the background almost entirely, telling the story by the figures alone. As a result, they acquire heroic importance, just as do Guglielmus' crudely powerful figures on the façade of Modena Cathedral (Fig. 298). The dramatic import of the scene is thus conveyed directly to the observer instead of indirectly and vaguely as it is in Ghiberti's landscape backgrounds. The hip-shot pose is a mediaeval reminiscence but it is motivated by Adam's horror and Eve's seductive pleading. The proportions of the figures and the treatment of the muscles show the influence of antique models, but the personal and dramatic note is Renaissance in spirit.

Jacopo's figures are impressive despite their limitations. His knowledge of anatomy and sense of form were inadequate to suggest weight or convincing movement. That his technique of relief carving was not the equal of Ghiberti's is apparent in his failure to suggest the distance between near and distant legs, or to achieve a satisfactory spatial relationship between Adam's right arm, his body, and the tree around which the snake is entwined. But the concept of life these figures reveal is lofty and dignified, and Jacopo's limited technique does not obscure it any more than the restricted methods of the Romanesque sculptor could stifle the emotion he sought to express. In regarding backgrounds and accessories as so many hindrances to clear expression and in giving form to his ideas by the human figure alone, Jacopo is closer in spirit to Greek than Roman methods. Whence he derived this manner, unique in the early fifteenth century, it is impossible to say. But his contemporaries and immediate successors failed to realize its potentialities; not until Michelangelo early in the sixteenth century was it developed to the fullest possible extent.

S. Petronio, Bologna.

FIG. 313.   Jacopo della Quercia, Sin of Adam and Eve
(1425-1438), Detail of Main Portal.

The influence of classic art upon Ghiberti and Jacopo della Quercia is quite evident; each reacted to it in his own way. Ghiberti, the decorator, saw the formal beauty of its rhythmic pattern; Jacopo, its expressiveness. Neither man was wholly successful, however, in developing forms having these qualities that were also capable of fully expressing the thought of his own age. This is explained by the fact that neither was technically equipped to give his figures the con-creteness that has ever been the ideal of scientific-ally-minded ages such as the Renaissance. We have seen that Ghiberti was unable to make his figures move and act convincingly and that Jacopo's did not have weight commensurate with their physical size. Both sculptors lacked the knowledge of human anatomy necessary to shape a human body that would be convincing to the observer. It was the acquisition of this knowledge that made Donatello (1386-1466) one of the most important figures in Early Renaissance art. During his long career he posed nearly every problem involved in portraying the human body objectively, and he solved a great many of them. His study of the mechanics of the body enabled him to do this; and with this knowledge he adapted the classic idiom to forms capable of adequately expressing the complicated involutions of modern Christian thought. In so doing, Donatello established himself as the outstanding sculptor of the early fifteenth century, his only equal as an artistic personality being the painter Masaccio, a contemporary who was carrying on similar investigations (cf. Figs. 398, 399). These two men completely dominated Italian art of their time.

Donatello's journey to Rome with the disgruntled Brunellesco in 1403 is one of the early recorded incidents in his life. The many examples of Roman art he must have seen there seem not to have affected his own style, for the earliest work attributable to him is still in the Gothic manner. A series of experiments with classic forms around 1410 did not produce any very important results; but about 1416 several works of the most intense realism appeared. The figure called *Lo Zuccone* (Fig. 314) or Pumpkin-head from its bald pate is one of the statues carved for niches in the Cathedral Campanile in Florence (Fig. 113). The highly individualized head and draperies show Donatello's impatience with meaningless generalization and are characteristic of the ugliness almost invariably present in the early stages of a realistic art. Donatello did not hesitate to portray all details of the powerful figure however lacking they were in conventional beauty. But the tensed muscles of the neck, the bent right wrist, the huge hands instinct with power, and the crumpled folds of the drapery create an impression of vital force that transfigures the repellent face, with the note of abstraction in the shaded eyes. The resultant effect of a spirit within the figure is the quality which distinguishes its Italian and Renaissance realism from that of Sluter's Franco-Flemish Moses (Fig. 306), whose meaning is conveyed in the mediaeval way by the accessory draperies. Along with its realism, the Zuccone shows Donatello's familiarity with classic formulas in the lowered shoulder above the leg supporting the weight of the body, a formula he employs to heighten the sense of power in the figure by the *contrapposto* or twist that it creates.

Opera del Duomo, Florence.

FIG. 314.   Donatello, Lo Zuccone
(*ca.* 1416),
from the Cathedral Campanile.

S. Croce, Florence.

FIG. 315.   Donatello, The Annunciation
(1428-1433).

Bargello, Florence.

FIG. 316.   Donatello, David
(ca. 1430).

During the later 1420's, Donatello worked in various parts of Italy and it seems probable that his travels brought him once more in contact with classic art. In any event, in *The Annunciation* (Fig. 315), made between 1428 and 1433 for the church of Santa Croce in Florence, the extravagant realism of the Zuccone has been tempered by a degree of antique idealism. The background and the architecture of the niche have many classic motives. The Virgin's head is almost Greek in its purity of line and the modeling of the features, but invested, by virtue of Donatello's sense of the concrete, with a humanness of expression that is rarely absent even from his most decorative works. The drapery treatment is also classic, the robes revealing the forms they cover, but having an existence of their own. The nude cherubs or *putti* at the ends of the entablature are a favorite Renaissance subject, providing ample opportunity for realistic treatment of the chubby childish bodies and their abandoned movement.

These two examples of Donatello's sculpture illustrate two outstanding traits of Italian Renaissance humanistic thought, an interest in classic art and a realistic conception of the human form. Continuing along these lines as he did, it was inevitable that Donatello should come to realize that the highest achievement in sculpture is the portrayal of the undraped human figure. One of his earliest nude figures, a Crucified Christ in wood dating about 1420, is notable for the relentless realism that led the outspoken Brunellesco to characterize it as a peasant's conception of the Savior. As a figure to be viewed from only a single point the Crucifixion is still in the mediaeval tradition which almost invariably limited the nude to treatment in relief. The bronze nude *David* (Fig. 316), *ca.* 1430, breaks sharply with that tradition by being in the round; and in representing the youthful figure unclothed, Donatello created the first free-standing nude statue of monumental character since classic antiquity. His debt to antique concepts is apparent in the relaxed quietness of the figure as well as in the pose, with the body supported mainly on one leg. The modeling is generalized, but there are specific and individual details such as the thin arms and the bony right hip that makes an awkward angle in the outline of the figure. Both of these are features of the undeveloped adolescent body observed by Donatello's realistic eye. The hat, similar to those worn by Tuscan shepherd lads, is another specific detail that is rather disquieting in the predominant generalization. It casts a shadow over the face which again is unclassic in effect, creating as it does an impression of pensiveness that is personal and individual. The mixture of concreteness and generalization in the figure contributes directly to its impression of extraordinary nudity.

Donatello's best-known work is the statue of the Venetian general *Gattamelata* (Fig. 317) he began in 1444 in Padua. In it he revived another sculptural type that had disappeared in the Middle Ages—the equestrian figure. It is based on a classic prototype, probably the statue of Marcus Aurelius now on the Capitoline Hill in Rome (Fig. 133), which Donatello had doubtless seen. Its quietness and repose are classic, an effect

Piazza del Santo, Padua.

FIG. 317.   Donatello, Gattemelata (1444).

attained by the broad planes of the massive volumes and the balanced design of the group as a whole. The triangles formed by the horse's legs support the heavy horizontal accent of the body, contrasting with the vertical of the rider and the sharp diagonal of the sword and the general's baton. The ball under the left front hoof stabilizes the group, decoratively and actually, for it prevents the horse from seeming to march off the pedestal in addition to maintaining its physical equilibrium. In solving the problem of

Bargello, Florence

FIG. 318. A. Rossellino,
Matteo Palmieri
(1468).

the equestrian statue, one of the most difficult in sculpture, Donatello studied the anatomy of the horse with the same scientific spirit of realism as he did the human figure. The veins of the legs and nose are specifically represented, as well as the bony structure of the skull. Equally realistic is the contrast in texture of the horse's hide, saddle blanket, and armor. The horse, a heavy draft animal, seems somewhat overlarge in proportion to the rider; but this too is a realistic detail because a smaller horse could not support the weight of a grown man in full armor. The apparent disproportion in the group partially explains the rider's failure to dominate the composition as he should. Seeking to compensate for this, the sculptor attempted to emphasize his importance by a wealth of minute detail on the armor and by the *putti* playing on the saddle behind him, details which tend to draw the observer's attention away from the more broadly modeled charger. The *putti* are a classic motive, as are also the winged genii on the relief decorating the pedestal.

As was stated above, Donatello followed classic prototypes in the Gattamelata; but, as in his other works, he used classic forms to express quite different concepts from those of antiquity. Thus in the Gattamelata, something of the mentality of the successful military strategist is suggested by introducing in the prevailing generalization a concrete and personal note in the fixed, steady glance of the eyes. The greatness of the figure lies in its transcendence of specific details; it is a type rather than an individual. The statue represents Erasmo da Narni, but it does more than represent him, for it suggests his subtle and crafty mind as well.

Donatello towers head and shoulders above his contemporaries because his work is the complete embodiment of the Early Renaissance spirit. His achievements cannot be summed up in a phrase, as can Ghiberti's by graceful decoration, or Jacopo della Quercia's by robust power; his genius was too great to be restricted to a single mode. He found sculpture still pervaded by mediaeval thought and restricted by mediaeval technique. He left it a powerful instrument, capable of expressing the widely varied ideals of the Renaissance—its apprehension of the antique, its realism which is so concrete and modern in its intellectuality, and above all, the enthusiasm with which it regarded the drama of life with its joy and pain, the drama so long obscured by the veil of mediaeval theological symbolism.

In the second half of the fifteenth century, two trends can be distinguished in Florentine sculpture, both originating in Donatello's style. One is a search for lyric beauty, the other a tendency toward drastic realism that developed from the scientific aspect of Donatello's art. Exemplifying the latter is a portrait bust of the Florentine philosopher *Matteo Palmieri* (Fig. 318), modeled in 1468 by Antonio Rossellino (1427-1478). There was no attempt to idealize the homely features, which were probably reproduced, as in Roman portraits, from a death mask. Moreover, there was no wish to modify specific qualities, for the Early Renaissance still took keen pleasure in its newly realized interest in the actual appearance of things. Not until the end of the century was there an effort—in Leonardo da

Philadelphia Museum of Art.

FIG. 319.   Desiderio da Settignano, Madonna and Child
(*ca.* 1460).

Vinci's painting—to idealize the aged face; until that time, in the hands of the realists, it was merely ugly.

The other trend in Florentine sculpture, toward lyric beauty, is apparent in youthful or feminine forms that contrast sharply with the aged male portraits preferred by the realists. One of the most ingratiating examples of this lyric style is a relief of the *Madonna and Child* (Fig. 319) by Desiderio da Settignano (1428-1464). A

pupil of Donatello, Desiderio inherited something of his master's honesty of observation, and acquired from him too the technical skill that makes his linear low relief a remarkably expressive vehicle of tender sentiment. The aristocratic elegance of Desiderio's figures is a personal characteristic in which he differs from the best-known fifteenth-century Florentine lyric sculptor, Luca della Robbia (1400-1482). Luca's career fell chiefly in the early years of the cen-

Bargello, Florence.

FIG. 320.   A. Pollaiuolo, Hercules and Antaeus (*ca.* 1470).

tury, but his sturdy, almost rustic types anticipate the gentle charm so pervasive later in the century. His favorite subject was the Madonna and Child, and his preferred medium was the glazed terra cotta with which his name is associated. The technique lent itself to broad generalization rather than to the specific and concrete effects more readily achieved in bronze or marble and was thus particularly appropriate to an ideal of tenderness and grace.

In contrast with the lyric beauty in the work of men like Desiderio da Settignano, the unsparing realism of their more scientific contemporaries is all the more striking. A logical continuation of Donatello's tradition of scientific curiosity led to research in the structure of the human body. Thus in the statuette of *Hercules and Antaeus* (Fig. 320) Antonio Pollaiuolo (1432-1498) attempted to solve the problem of convincing movement. Like most of the scientific realists, he preferred to work in bronze for greater accuracy in detail, and in the statuette he rendered the muscular organization of the struggling giants with great faithfulness. In the hands of a lesser man, this might have had the dryness of an academic study, but Pollaiuolo succeeded in giving the figures character by endowing them with tremendous energy; they should be compared with those in his equally vigorous engraving of the Ten Fighting Nudes (Fig. 408). Although the group is only a few inches high, it radiates an energy that makes it far more than a mere tour de force of representation.

Contemporary with Pollaiuolo and like him a representative of the scientific trend in late fifteenth-century Florentine sculpture was Andrea Verrocchio (1435-1488). He is like Pollaiuolo too in making the human form more than a factual portrayal of anatomical structure. This interest is apparent in his bronze *David* (Fig. 321), modeled about 1465 for the Medici family. In it the bony cage of the spare adolescent figure is so strongly emphasized that the ribs show through the leather corselet in a pattern of bumps and hollows that should be compared with the smoothly rounded planes of Donatello's David (Fig. 316). The impression of muscular tension is quite different from the quiet relaxation of the earlier statue. The staccato effect of such details is accentuated in the body as a whole; the angularity of the left arm, for instance, recalls that of the Donatello figure, but adds harshness instead of balancing in classic rhythm the movement of the right arm supporting the sword. The head is uncovered, and the minutely rendered planes of the face contribute to the subtle and baffling expression which reminds us that Verrocchio was the master of Leonardo da Vinci (cf. Fig. 415). These details are all anatomically accurate and well composed in an organically structural pattern; in addition, they contribute to the impression of nervous vitality that keys the figure up and is the most significant difference between it and the earlier one by Donatello. For it shows that the late fifteenth-century artist was becoming aware of the limited expressive resources of the unmodulated naturalism which had been his predecessors' almost exclusive interest. He is

Bargello, Florence.

FIG. 321.   Verrocchio, David (*ca.* 1465).

trying to use creatively, as it were, the vocabulary of form compiled by earlier artists who exhausted their inspiration in merely assembling it.

Similar characteristics appear in Verrocchio's equestrian statue of *Colleoni* (Fig. 322) in Venice. Comparison with Donatello's Gattamelata (Fig. 317) shows even more clearly than the two Davids the changes that occurred in sculpture during the fifteenth century. Under the spell of the classic, Donatello gave his figure the form of a Roman general and endowed it with potential and intellectual force. Verrocchio, on the other hand, has at his command all that the fifteenth century learned about emotional

Campo dei SS. Giovanni e Paolo, Venice.

FIG. 322.   Verrocchio, Colleoni
(1488).

expression; his figure seems alive with nervous energy arising from the sense of general movement created by the innumerable planes of the modeling. The rider's pose also contributes to this effect. In contrast with Gattamelata's easy relaxation, Colleoni stands in the stirrups, his body turned to his right; he glares at something to his left. The horse is high-spirited, quite different from Donatello's ambling nag, yet it is dominated by its rider. Its forward movement is controlled by the backward pull on the reins indicated by the creases in the neck; thus Verrocchio attained directly the balance of opposed forces and decorative stability that Donatello achieved indirectly by the ball under the horse's front hoof. Psychologically, Donatello's work is superior. It conveys the shrewd personality of the mercenary soldier more effectively than Verrocchio's figure does. But as an embodiment of the warrior's fiery passion, the theatrical pose and defiant expression of the Colleoni undoubtedly make it surpass the more restrained Gattamelata. Colleoni's savage spirit, very different from Gattamelata's cool passionless intellectualism, is conveyed directly to the observer by the grim face whose features are so strongly emphasized as to be almost caricatured, the rider's control over his mount, and the suggestion of tremendous power in the twist of his body.

Verrocchio was the last great sculptor of the Early Italian Renaissance. His work retains much of the indiscriminate love of life that characterizes the period and explains the intense interest of its artists in natural forms. In the early fifteenth century, the expression of this interest was somewhat tempered by the feeling, unconciously inherited from the Middle Ages, of a need for universal significance. It was this that led Ghiberti to place his Old Testament scenes in heroic landscapes from which his decorative figures might indirectly acquire an authority they did not have in themselves. It is apparent too in the lofty conception of the human figure that transcends the technical limitations of Jacopo della Quercia's work, and in the personal, intellectual note in Donatello's style. But the deep undertones of mediaeval thought became fainter with the passing of time; even in Donatello's last works, the classic balance of the Annunciation and the Gattamelata gives way to unrestrained emotion. Furthermore, his work stimulated a technical interest in the exact portrayal of the human body; this, combined with the fascination intrinsic in representing things as they appear to be, caused later sculptors to have an increasing fondness for natural forms for their own sake that is seen most characteristically in the male portraits (Fig. 318). Implicit in such an attitude is the idea that all that is natural is for that reason good in its own right. This cult of the natural was not limited to fifteenth-century sculpture; it is evident in painting (cf. pages 467-469) and underlies Lorenzo de' Medici's *Canzoni*. Its connotation of personal and individual values as criteria is present even in what political theory there was, the only principle of which called for achieving personal ambition without regard for the good of community or state. The consequence, moral decay, was inevitable with a philosophy whose ideals are couched in materialistic terms. In Florence, it led to the wanton festivals which alternated with periods of bitter armed strife, both so weakening the city that it fell an easy prey to Charles VIII of France when he invaded Italy in 1494 after the Medici had been exiled. Florence's eminence in fifteenth-century European art, attained under the benevolent tyranny of the Medici, was lost and never recovered. The increasing power of the papacy made Rome the most important center of creative artistic activity in Italy in the early sixteenth century, the period of the High Renaissance.

THE HIGH RENAISSANCE

The second phase of the Renaissance in Italy falls in the first half of the sixteenth century and is differentiated from the earlier phase by the term High Renaissance. It is distinguished by a reaction against the extremes to which fifteenth-century naturalistic thought had led. This reaction, which had set in even before the sixteenth century, appears in the temporary transformation

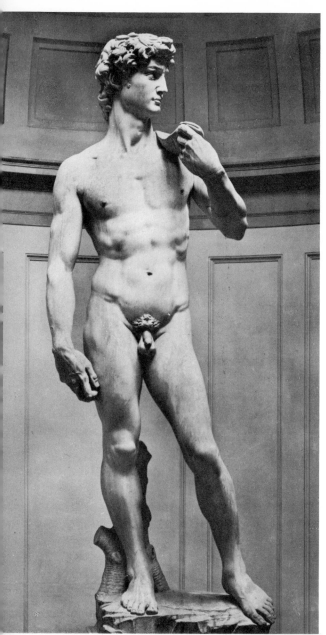

Accademia, Florence.

FIG. 323. Michelangelo, David (1504).

of the libertine morals of Florence into a puritanically austere mode of conduct as a result of Savonarola's wrathful fulminations. In painting, it is evident in the discontent with fifteenth-century formulas implicit in the wistful sadness of Botticelli's Virgins and pagan goddesses (cf. Fig. 413) and in the simplification of forms and composition that characterizes Leonardo's work (cf. Fig. 416). In sculpture, it is apparent in the more pointedly expressive qualities of Verrocchio's Colleoni in comparison with the earlier Gattamelata.

This reaction is a significant indication of the growing feeling that modes of conduct and forms of artistic expression should have greater authority than that of a personal or individual point of view. This feeling led to the High Renaissance search for ideals of universal meaning, and to its artists' evolving forms capable of giving those ideals concrete expression. Some sought this in a closer reproduction of antique forms which seemed appropriate to this purpose because of their generalized character, but this proved unfruitful, for the heritage of Early Renaissance individualism was inescapable. Because of it, the path to universal truth had to lead through the individual, whereas classic thought attained it through generalization. The artistic forms of antiquity were thus fundamentally incapable of expressing Renaissance thought. As the Renaissance could conceive the universal only in terms of the particular, the universal had to be attained by means intrinsic in the particular. This explains the restlessness that characterizes the art of the period, for the straining away from life on an ordinary plane to the higher one where universal truths are realized left its mark on the style. Greek art, with which High Renaissance art is often compared, acts on the observer like like a soothing anodyne descending from heights of ethereal beauty (cf. Fig. 263). Sixteenth-century art arrests him by its concreteness while transmuting the base material of his experience into golden beauty by the intense fire of sheer physical and intellectual force.

The dominant personality in High Renaissance sculpture is Michelangelo Buonarroti (1475-1564). He was a man of amazing versatility —architect, sculptor, painter, poet, and engineer —but of all the fields in which he worked, sculpture was the most congenial. In his earliest figures, a relationship to fifteenth-century art is apparent. The *David* (Fig. 323), done in 1504, shows unmistakable traces of Donatello's style—the hooked wrist of the right hand, for example, that was noted in the Zuccone (Fig. 314). The detailed anatomy and the fixed glance of the eyes are also fifteenth-century characteristics. But for all its concrete expression, the face is an idealized type which reappears in later works. The great size of the figure (it is eighteen feet high) is another High Renaissance device to attain ideality, the magnification of physical proportions. A third High Renaissance characteristic is the sense of strain created by exaggerating the difference in shoulder level and the tension in the neck muscles that results from turning the head toward the left or raised side of the body. The impression of unrest thus created is emphasized by the two opposed structural axes of the figure, the torso and head against the legs. A classic statue (Fig. 270) has three axes—head, torso, and legs—and thus achieves formal stability; this the Renaissance sculptor deliberately avoided. To be sure, the generalizations of Michelangelo's figure make it seem almost classic when compared with Donatello's romantic shepherd lad (Fig. 316) or Verrocchio's more realistic young warrior (Fig. 321). But at the same time, its concreteness is such that his David seems capable of performing the deeds attributed to the Biblical hero; this cannot be said for the fifteenth-century examples, for Michelangelo did not attempt either a symphony of classic grace or a specific portrayal of an individual youth. His aim was to create a form that would typify the unbounded energy and confidence of youth in all its physical strength; the beauty of the statue lies in the completeness of his interpretation of that idea.

Of about the same period as the David is the *Madonna and Child* (Fig. 324) in the church of Notre-Dame at Bruges in Belgium. Michelangelo's conception of the subject differs in several important characteristics from the fifteenth-century idea embodied in Desiderio's relief (Fig. 319), particularly in its treatment as a free-standing group. Different too is the relationship between the two figures. In Desiderio's relief, the Child is on His mother's lap, whereas in Michelangelo's group He stands between her knees, His figure outlined against the shadowy

drapery folds. The tender playfulness that is such a human element in the fifteenth-century relief gives way to grave solemnity. The Virgin's face is turned away from the Child, whose mien is as thoughtful as her own. The impersonal dignity of the expressions is given authority by the treatment of the bodies. In the twisting of the torso, the *contrapposto* which is an effective instrument of emotional expression in Michelangelo's later

Notre-Dame, Bruges.

FIG. 324.   Michelangelo, Madonna and Child (1501-1505).

Louvre, Paris.

FIG. 325. Michelangelo, Bound Slave
(1513-1516).

the drapery; at the same time, the subordination of accessories to the body forecasts Michelangelo's later style in which the human figure alone is the vehicle of expression. Another detail that recurs in later works is the ideal sexless mask of the face which is deliberately subordinated as an expressive factor.

Michelangelo's later style appears first in the tomb that Pope Julius II commissioned about 1506. It was partly to provide a suitable setting for this tomb that the Old Basilica of St. Peter in Rome was destroyed, to be replaced by the half-Renaissance, half-baroque structure that now bears that name (cf. Figs. 130-132). Much of the bitterness that clouded the sculptor's last years can be traced to the many interruptions that constantly militated against the completion of this project. The tomb, now in the church of S. Pietro in Vincoli in Rome, is a sorry compromise between Michelangelo's ambition and the niggardliness of Julius' heirs; it gives only a meager idea of the original conception. Only the colossal Moses is Michelangelo's, but a number of figures elsewhere are known to have been planned for it. Two of these are the so-called *Bound Slaves* in the Louvre in Paris, one of which is shown in Fig. 325. It was probably meant to symbolize one of the liberal arts freed by the munificence of Julius but fettered again after his death. Whatever the symbolic meaning, its larger significance lies in its embodiment of tremendous power, conveyed objectively by the great muscles and the body twisted in the *contrapposto* noted in the Christ Child in the Bruges group. To this extent the sculptor works as he did in the David; but here he goes further, adding abstract poignancy to the physical potential of the figure by the constricting band around the chest against which the figure has struggled in vain. This motive for its exhaustion may seem insufficient, just as the snakes in the Laocoön group (Fig. 280), discovered in Rome in 1506, apparently do not fully explain the agony of the dying father and his sons. But by representing not the moment when the figure exerts its strength to the utmost but the collapse after its energy is spent, the artist raises the concept from the physical to the abstract. The futility of the magnificent physique

works makes its appearance. The body is perfectly expressed by the arrangement of the draperies to emphasize the important structural facts of the anatomy—for example, the heavy folds at the juncture of arm and shoulder. The entire statue is marvelously compact in mass, achieving unity in spite of the variety of movement in the two figures. Carved between 1501 and 1505, the statue shows a trace of the sculptor's fifteenth-century background in the detailed treatment of

before a power that is all the greater because it is not represented but suggested is the essence of tragedy.

In the Bound Slave, Michelangelo approaches his ideal of the plastic expression of ideas through the human form. His progress toward this goal can be measured by comparing the Madonna and Child of Bruges (Fig. 324) with the *Madonna and Child* (Fig. 326) in the Medici Chapel in S. Lorenzo in Florence, probably executed between 1525 and 1533. The comparatively simple movement of the figures in the earlier group has become more complex, with increased expressive poignancy. Notice, for example, the torsion in the Virgin's body resulting from forcing the right shoulder back as the head turns to the left. The crossed legs create more involved patterns of form in that part of the body also than in the Bruges group where the only movement is the placing of the left foot above the right. The compactness of the earlier composition is retained by placing the Child astride the Madonna's knee, the *contrapposto* motivated by the search for His mother's breast. The Virgin's face, almost masculine, is subordinated as an expressive element; this is characteristic of the artist's ever-increasing intolerance of details that might detract from the concept as a whole. This is true also of the way the drapery is treated. In the earlier group it was represented in some detail and with a suggestion of intrinsic texture, but now it has become a neutral substance whose primary function is to clarify the articulation of the powerful body underneath. Thus although there is hardly any contrast between the left foot and the drapery covering the leg, the three folds radiating from a point immediately below the knee emphasize the organic function of the joint, accenting a detail essential to understanding the structural unity of the pattern of volumes that make up the figure.

The Medici Tombs in the New Sacristy of S. Lorenzo in Florence (Fig. 147) are the climax of Michelangelo's plastic style. He was both architect and sculptor; although the chapel was never completed, the consistency of the whole forecasts the synthesis that took place in the baroque period. Planned as a commemorative

Medici Chapel, San Lorenzo, Florence.

FIG. 326.   Michelangelo, Madonna and Child (1525-1533).

mausoleum for the Medici family, the original scheme included four tombs, one each for Giuliano de' Medici and Lorenzo, the Duke of Urbino, and a double tomb for Lorenzo the Magnificent and his brother Giuliano; but only the two single monuments were completed. A symbolic statue of the deceased is seated in the architectural niche above the sarcophagus on which are two reclining nude figures, one male and one female. These represent Night and Day

Medici Chapel, San Lorenzo, Florence.

FIG. 327. Michelangelo, Tomb of
Guiliano de' Medici (1525-1533).

FIG. 328. Michelangelo, Night,
Detail of Fig. 327.

on Giuliano's tomb (Fig. 327); those on Lorenzo's sarcophagus are Morning and Evening (Fig. 147). There is no pretense at portraiture in the statues of the deceased, for each has the sexless mask seen also in the Madonna and Child in the same chapel (Fig. 326). Only in the postures is there any differentiation, Giuliano as the alert symbol of an active life balanced against the contemplative Lorenzo. The shadow over the latter's face heightens the impression of an abstract and impersonal entity, an expressive device that anticipates baroque methods.

In the figures on the sarcophagi, Michelangelo realized his ideal of making the human form the sole means of expressing abstract ideas. The figures are nude, for drapery would have detracted from the fullest realization of this ideal. Even the faces are expressively unimportant, drowned in shadow in the figure of *Night* (Fig. 328) and left unfinished in the figure of Day (Fig. 327). In the bodies, characteristics noted in Michelangelo's earlier figures are emphasized. In the Night (Fig. 328), a powerful *contrapposto* results from the left leg being forced back against the forward twist of the right arm and shoulder, creating violently contrasted movements within the body. The pose seems humanly impossible, but Michelangelo makes it plausible by investing the figure with all the concreteness that Renaissance naturalism could achieve. Another expressive contrast is between the delicately profiled face and the heavy torso of brutally masculine proportions, with hanging breasts and wrinkled abdomen. These physical discordances are poignant details in the general impression of superhuman strength sapped by deadly weariness to which the precarious poise on the sarcophagus also contributes. The figure becomes thereby an element in the greater dissonance of the whole design, born of the conflict between sculpture and architectural setting.

The spectator viewing these powerful bodies wracked and exhausted by superhuman forces experiences an indescribably tragic emotion. In their presence he has much the same sense of human futility that invests the Bound Slave with such pathetic meaning, yet it is achieved more subtly than in the earlier work—by the languor and weariness of the figures instead of the bonds —and is consequently more powerful. Michelangelo thus evolved a method of expression comparable to that of the fifth-century Greek sculptor, namely, a formal arrangement of the human body; but nothing could be less classic in effect than these tremendous figures. The difference between the beauty of the Mount Olympus of the Parthenon (Fig. 261) and that of Day on the tomb of Giuliano de' Medici (Fig. 327) is inherent in the different ideals they embody—intellectual and impersonal in the Greek figure, individual and emotional in the Renaissance figure. In these statues Michelangelo gave concrete form to the disillusionment and sense of frustration in his own soul. A sincere Christian, he lived in an age notable for its disbelief. A champion of municipal and national political freedom, he saw his beloved Florence crushed under the heel of anarchy, and Italy enslaved by foreign powers. A consummate artist, he was prevented from completing every one of the projects that were dearest to him. In light of all this, it is scant wonder that below the personifications of the Active and the Contemplative Life over the sarcophagi of the Medici scions, he placed these gigantic beings, of superhuman power but overcome by lassitude and exhaustion, a withering commentary upon the futility of human endeavor before the forces of ignorance and evil. The superlative thing about them is that the alchemy of genius transmutes personal feeling into universal symbols, providing an investiture of beauty for human suffering in all ages.

Detail of Fig. 333.

CHAPTER TWENTY-ONE

European Sculpture from 1550 to 1800

Michelangelo's influence upon scuplture was great and not invariably beneficial. So authoritative were his gigantic forms that,
by comparison, the work of his predecessors and contemporaries
who still employed fifteenth-century methods seemed pallid and
feeble, and there was little demand for it after Michelangelo's
time. But the taste for the extraordinary and the striking he had
created was catered to by his successors, who imitated his forms
but failed signally to match their profound meaning. In this
respect, Michelangelo's relationship to sculpture of the late
sixteenth century is much like Donatello's to that of the fifteenth;
the technical problems he posed were understood, but the content

that gave his figures significance was not perceived. This is apparent in the three main tendencies in Italian sculpture after 1550. The first was to reproduce the colossal size of Michelangelo's figures and trust to physical bulk to attain monumentality. The second was to utilize his forms for decorative purposes. The third sought to transform the suppressed power implicit in his figures into explicit movement.

The first of these tendencies needs no detailed discussion. The technical proficiency sometimes evident in the work of the exponents of the colossal like Bartolommeo Ammanati is never sufficient to offset the ineptitude of their ideas. The best-known exemplar of the second or decorative tendency is Benvenuto Cellini (1500-1571). His intriguing personality still lives in his *Autobiography*, whose lively prose invests his sculpture with a literary and anecdotal interest greater than that of its plastic patterns. His fascinating account of casting the bronze *Perseus with Medusa's Head* (Fig. 329) in the Loggia dei Lanzi before the Palazzo Vecchio in Florence (Fig. 111) has much greater vitality than the figure itself. Executed in 1548, the statue is an excellent example of the technique of bronze-casting by the lost-wax process. It is in two parts, one the body of Medusa and the other the hero holding her severed head. The drama of the subject is entirely lost in the mannered Michelangelesque form which combines overemphasis on muscular structure with the minute rendering of detail that reveals Cellini's training as a goldsmith. In the contrasted horizontal and vertical accents of the two figures, there was a possibility of diffusing the interest of the group, a danger the sculptor sought to avoid by the somewhat ludicrous device of having Medusa's leg pulled around the base by her left arm. The same subordination of dramatic considerations to decorative ends is evident in the blood spurting from the severed neck and head. The irrepressible egotism of the sculptor, present in every line of his *Autobiography*, is equally apparent in the prominent inscription of his name on the diagonal strap across Perseus' shoulder and in the mask with his own features placed on top of the helmet, its invisibility protecting him from the jeers it

Loggia dei Lanzi, Florence.

FIG. 329.   Cellini, Perseus (1548).

would certainly have evoked from his contemporaries.

The third tendency in Italian sculpture of the late sixteenth century is seen in the work of Giovanni da Bologna (*ca.* 1524-1608), who attempted by highly animated poses to impart to his figures something of the power latent in Michelangelo's. The three bodies in the *Rape of the Sabine Woman* (Fig. 330), executed in 1583, resemble those created by the great Florentine in their *contrapposto*. But it is a decorative device rather than a means of emotional expression, the twist of each figure combining with that of the others to achieve balanced spiral upward movement in the contours. The same static movement appears in Giovanni's best-known work, the bronze Flying Mercury. The effectiveness from all points of view thus attained anticipates the formal conceptions of seventeenth-century baroque art.

Loggia dei Lanzi, Florence.

FIG. 330. Giovanni da Bologna, Rape of the Sabine Woman (1583).

The discussion of late sixteenth-century architecture in Italy pointed out that the taste of the time was decidedly academic. This is no less true in sculpture. In the Rape of the Sabine Woman, for example, the faces of the three figures are ideal generalized classic types. The old man is clearly related to Laocoön (Fig. 280) in both expression and the gesture of the hand; and the body of the woman, for all its distinction of sex, was evidently modeled on that of the youth at the left in that group. As was said earlier, the Hellenistic statue was discovered in 1506 and conceivably inspired Michelangelo; its immediate popularity was doubtless considerably increased by the taste for violent movement created by Michelangelo's works. Its notable influence on the late sixteenth-century sculptors who were attempting similar effects is not surprising. No less academic than the style was the formal problem that Giovanni set for himself: to portray and contrast in a single statue three different nudes, the feminine, the youthful masculine, and the aged masculine. He was interested only in technicalities, but the humanist critics of the time gave it the classic title by which it has been known ever since. In such circumstances, it could hardly be expected to have any profound meaning, nor does it have. It is highly decorative, however, a fact which explains its considerable influence on later sculpture, not only in Italy but elsewhere in Europe.

Outside of Italy, France produced the most important sculpture in the last half of the sixteenth century. As in architecture, early Renaissance sculpture in France is only superficially Italianate, evident in attempts to modify the concrete and realistic native style along more consciously aesthetic and decorative lines. Italian sculptural modes were introduced into France as were the architectural—by men whose eyes had been opened to the novel beauty of Italian art during military expeditions into Italy. As a result of the interest thus aroused, Italian artists were encouraged to come to France; among the sculptors was Benvenuto Cellini, whose accounts of his experiences in the French court constitute some of the most entertaining pages of his *Autobiography*. The decoration of the palace begun at Fontainebleau by Francis I and continued by his successors from about 1530 on was done almost entirely by Italians, and their *atelier* at Fontainebleau soon became a school where many French artists were trained. There, too, first appeared the enthusiasm for classic ideas that led to the importation from Rome of bronze replicas of antique statues. The ingredients of the late sixteenth-century French sculptural style were thus threefold—the native and realistic mediaeval tradition, the classic, and the Italian High Renaissance interpretation of the antique.

As French sculpture developed, the classic-Italian manner soon became dominant, thanks to the prestige given it by its aristocratic patronage. There is an important difference, however, between classicism in sixteenth-century France and that of fifteenth-century Italy. Italy turned naturally to the antique when the Gothic yoke was thrown off, for it was a rightful inheritance from the past. But in France, the classic mode was more an imitation, based on the concept of *a priori* perfection. Hence it was incapable of such development as that in fifteenth-century Italian art or the earlier French Gothic for that matter, both of which fulfilled an intuitively felt need and changed with the ideals of the civilizations that produced them. In contrast to this, the sixteenth-century French classic ideal was realized not intuitively but by intellectual process; once attained, there could be no further development. A style thus contrived can have nothing of the vitality derived from a connection with contemporary thought, for it is entirely a matter of theory. The corollary of this was the appearance during the sixteenth and seventeenth centuries of many theories of art and the emergence of the "science" of aesthetics in the eighteenth. From this, it is only a step to the idea of art as a thing apart from life, capable of theoretical exposition, intelligible only to the favored few, and similarly restricted as a medium of expression. The authority this conception of art attained later was a result of the logical and typically French synthesis achieved in the style developed by the end of the seventeenth century which bore the stamp of formal approval by the Academies. It was thenceforward accepted as the basis of artistic judgment throughout the western world.

Attempts by French sculptors to apply preconceived principles based on classic art are evident as early as 1549. In that year, Jean Goujon (*ca.* 1510-*ca.* 1568) produced his masterpiece, the *Water Nymphs* (Fig. 331), for the Fountain of the Innocents in Paris. The transparent draperies which reveal the bodies beneath suggest comparison with the Greek reliefs of the late fifth-century B.C. Nike Balustrade (Fig. 269). The technique is very similar in both, the upper surfaces of the drapery folds kept quite narrow and the lower planes broadened. In the French example,

Fountain of the Innocents, Paris.

FIG. 331.   Goujon, Water Nymphs
(1549).

Louvre, Paris.

FIG. 332.   Pilon, René Birague (1584).

the clinging effect is motivated by water pouring from the jars. It should not be inferred from this comparison that Goujon was actually inspired by the Nike reliefs, but only that he was undoubtedly influenced by classical ideas. He was well acquainted with these, for he made the illustrations for the first French edition of Vitruvius. His style is saved from dryness by his lively sense of beauty and his feeling for graceful design. That the mediaeval tradition was not completely dead is indicated by the fact that Goujon was most effective in architectonic sculpture like the Water Nymphs and the reliefs on the mid-sixteenth-century portion of the Louvre (Fig. 139). Also mediaeval is the concrete differentiation in the faces of the nymphs and the modish coiffures, a persistence of late Gothic

realism. Here it is combined with the Italian decorative ideal to produce a somewhat artificial type that is characterized as "aristocratic genre" for lack of a better term. To this same concreteness, never wholly absent from French art, is due the remarkable naturalism of the sinuous bodies revealed by the clinging draperies.

Even more striking than the realism of Goujon's Nymphs is that of the bronze portrait statue of *René Birague* (Fig. 332), made in 1584 as an adjunct to his tomb by Germain Pilon (1535-1590). So powerful is the characterization of this head that all the numerous and insistent details of the naturalistic draperies and other accessories cannot distract attention from it. This intrinsic realism was originally still more pronounced because the figure was painted. But

even Pilon, confirmed realist that he was, suc-
cumbed to a movement that spread through the
Catholic countries of Europe in the last years of
the sixteenth century, the reaction against the
Protestant Reformation in the north. Evidences
of this reaction appear in all phases of sixteenth-
century life—the Jesuit movement and the bloody
Massacre of St. Bartholomew's Day in Paris in
1572, to mention only two. In Pilon's sculpture it
is apparent in the emotion that practically overwhelms the content of his figures, as in the case
of a statue of St. Francis of Assisi which had to
be removed from the Louvre and placed in a
church because the great number of votary gifts
heaped about it in the museum inconvenienced
the officials. But Pilon's figures are only minor
examples of the emotional art in which the
Catholic reaction is manifest. This is the baroque,
and its greatest exponent was the Italian, Bernini.

As was said earlier, the outstanding characteristic of baroque art is its intensely emotional
quality. In sculpture, this was achieved by investing the animated but cold forms of the late
sixteenth century (Fig. 330) with a new content
involving a definite modification of the style.
Just how this was done can be seen in the statue
of *St. Theresa in Ecstasy* (Fig. 333), executed in
1646 by Gian Lorenzo Bernini (1598-1680). The
subject is a typical illustration of the emotional
fervor that accompanied the Counter-Reformation. The statue shows the saint in a dream, described in her writings, in which an angel
appeared before her holding a dart, symbolic of
divine love, with which he pierced her heart.
The static movement of Giovanni da Bologna's
group has become dynamic in Bernini's, an effect
achieved by opening out the closed contours of
the earlier work into broken and indeterminate
ones. Thus the movement generated in the animated draperies is not restrained by a firm silhouette but seems to extend beyond the figure, an
effect which is heightened by the hanging foot
and the inclination of the saint's head. The composition involves not only the carved forms but
also the surrounding space with which they are
related, a sculptural concept similar in principle
to that of seventeenth-century architecture. The
closed contours that emphasize the bulk and

weight of sixteenth-century figures (Figs. 328,
330) are abandoned. The definiteness of High
Renaissance style gives way to indefiniteness in
the baroque, and the method of portraying the
figures is more suggestive than representational.
Light and shade and color also are important.
Michelangelo's chiaroscuro affirms the plastic
values of his figures, whereas Bernini's emphasizes
movement of surface and contour, and the specific light source creates a more positive relationship between the group and its enveloping
space.

In all these characteristics, the baroque nature
of Bernini's style is apparent. The term baroque
applies to an art in which an arbitrary handling
of material to produce striking effects causes it to
pass beyond its proper limits into those of another
art whose medium allows more fluent expression.
Thus the fluid surfaces of baroque architecture
create effects that are intrinsically sculptural (Fig.
150). The term might be applied to the Laocoön
group (Fig. 280) or the Souillac Prophet (Fig.
297), for each transcends its medium to attain
emotional effects. It might even be used to
describe Ghiberti's Old Testament panels (Fig.
311) in their approximation of painting. But the
meaning of the term is most fully realized in
Bernini's sculpture. In the impression of space
around the figures and their relationship to it,
in the play of chiaroscuro created by a light
source within the composition, Bernini employed pictorial effects at the expense of sculptural
weight and volume. That this was his aim he
admitted when he said he was trying to "paint
in marble." More fundamental than this, however, is the idea underlying all baroque art—to
astonish the observer and thus stimulate a positive
emotional reaction. It is for this reason, rather
than to demonstrate the artist's skill, that the
tons of marble in the St. Theresa group seem to
float in the air, the very form of the material
denying its essential weight.

The St. Theresa is characteristic of the art of
the Counter-Reformation in its attempt to express spiritual emotion in terms of material
experience. The rapture in the saint's soul takes
form in a physical transport approaching the
sensual, as, in fact, she described it in her writings.

Sta. Maria della Vittoria, Rome.

FIG. 333. Bernini, St. Theresa in Ecstasy (1646).

In this respect, the statue makes objective the Counter-Reformation's end purpose—to re-establish the authority of the Church by appealing to the emotions. The mediaeval way to the spirit through the intellect was no longer possible, for the seventeenth century was separated from the thirteenth by the Renaissance, with its awakening to the reality of physical experience, a reality never to be forgotten. As a result, the message of the Church had to be cast in a dif-ferent form, attained abstractly in the doctrines of the Jesuit movement and concretely in baroque art.

The pervasive movement that contributes so materially to the emotional expressiveness of the St. Theresa is characteristically baroque. In Bernini's portraits, like that of his mistress *Costanza Buonarelli* (Fig. 334), it is utilized to create an impression of highly realistic expres-siveness. Here is the same irregularity of contour seen in the religious group, and the restlessness of the broken contours pervades the whole, in the flowing lines of the tossed hair and the play of light and shade on the crumpled folds of the garment. To this is added the momentary pose—the open bodice partially revealing the breast, the slight turn of the head, the flicker of light in the eye from the drilled hole of the pupil, and the partly opened mouth.

The movement that contributes so much to the emotional effect of baroque religious sculpture and the naturalism of its portraiture achieves most ingratiating results in decorative works like fountains which ornamented many of the Roman piazzas or open squares, like the one in the Piazza de Spagna (Fig. 153), in the seventeenth century. In them, the actual movement of water over the fluid surfaces of the figures adds to their animation. One in front of the Pantheon in Rome (Fig. 57) is made up of writhing tritons spurting water from their mouths and grouped around a base surmounted by an Egyptian obelisk, a great number of which had been brought to Rome in the Roman period. An obelisk is also the crowning motive of Bernini's *Fountain of the Four Rivers* (Fig. 335) in the Piazza Navona in Rome, executed between 1647 and 1651. The four figures representing the Rhine, Ganges, Nile, and de la Plata Rivers are allegorical symbols of the four parts of the world; all acknowledge their allegiance to the spiritual rule of the Church symbolized by the papal tiara and keys. The symbolism is not over-prominent, however, since the sculptor's chief aim was to produce a decorative ensemble unified by the flow of water over the irregular natural rock forms. Fountains were also used by baroque architects for other than urban ornament, particularly in the extensive gardens of great country estates like the Villa Torlonia at Frascati near Rome (Fig. 154).

In France, baroque style like Bernini's is reflected in the exaggerated groups in which Pierre Puget (1622–1694) tried vainly to reconcile his own stormy nature with seventeenth-century classic taste, but his case is isolated. Baroque sculpture in the Italian sense had little more currency in seventeenth-century France

than its parallel architectural style. This fact can be explained in some measure by the relatively secondary role of the Church in the French state under the absolute rule of Louis XIV. Baroque art, primarily the instrument of the Counter-Reformation, expressed a religious absolutism in the Church comparable to the political absolutism established by the French monarch. But the royal style in France was essentially classic; hence no encouragement was given the baroque, with its emphasis upon qualities alien to a classic point of view.

Bargello, Florence.

FIG. 334. Bernini,
Costanza Buonarelli (*ca.* 1635).

The founding in 1648 of the French Academy of Sculpture, following the creation of the Academy of Letters in 1635, and of the Academy at Rome in 1677 confirmed the classic taste initiated by the school at Fountainebleau. More than this, it extended to sculpture the principle of absolutism already established politically in the government of Louis XIV. The ideal this absolutism imposed on French sculptors is stated concisely in a letter from Colbert, Louis XIV's Minister, to the director of the French Academy at Rome. "Take good care that the sculptors copy purely the antique, but without adding anything," he wrote; and again, "See that there is no change from the originals, i.e., that the copies which you have them make are of the same measurements." With such restrictions as these, it is small wonder that there is no first-rank French sculptor from 1661, when Louis XIV assumed power, until the close of the eighteenth century. That this is not as true of seventeenth-century painters and architects is due only to the relative sparseness of classic models for painters and the persistence of an indigenous architectural tradition for architects.

Just as French classic sculpture was born and spent its childhood in the decoration of Fontainebleau, so its early maturity was reached in the ornamentation of the palace and gardens at Versailles (Fig. 159). A relief of *Bathing Nymphs* (Fig. 336), executed by François Girardon (1628-1715) around 1670 for the Fountain of Diana, shows the style. Girardon had studied in Italy where he was not so much impressed by Bernini's baroque genuis as by Giovanni da Bologna's more academic concepts. The latter influence is apparent in the greater substance of Girardon's Nymphs in comparison with Bernini's pictorial marble visions (Fig. 333). But their robustness derives from the baroque canon rather than

Piazza Navona, Rome.

FIG. 335.   Bernini and others, Fountain of the Four Rivers (1647-1651).

Bain de Diane, Gardens of the Palace, Versailles.

FIG. 336.   Girardon, Bathing Nymphs (*ca.* 1670).

from Giovanni's more slender and muscular type (Fig. 330), and is suggestive of the fleshy ideal Rubens had popularized in northern countries (Fig. 457). Other features of seventeenth-century French style are the elegance that is never completely absent from French concepts, and the concreteness of the carefully delineated reeds as well as the disquietingly individual and personal note in the Nymphs which, for all the classic generalization of the faces, makes them appear like a group of buxom French *demoiselles* in an unsuspecting moment of idle sport. The relief is an excellent example of all that is meant by the Louis XIV style, for even in the supposedly abandoned movement of the figures there is a correctness which becomes stiff pomposity in more formal subjects. This correctness, an element of the norm of perfection to which the academic sculptors were forced to conform, made all of their work competent and none of it interesting. The dull vistas of the Louvre galleries of seventeenth-century sculpture sometimes make one feel that it would be a pleasure to see an incorrectly drawn figure because of the note of vitality it might sound in the soporific symphony of all-prevailing exactitude. Only in an occasional portrait does the native French

sense of the concrete thrust through the conventions the Academy forced upon the country's creative genius.

The eighteenth century brought a reaction against the formality and correctness of the seventeenth. The stately decorum of Louis XIV society relaxes under Louis XV and becomes licentiousness in Louis XVI's reign in the last part of the century. The change is more immediately apparent in architecture and painting than in sculpture. The formal halls of Versailles (Fig. 160) give way to intimate boudoirs like that in the Hotel de Soubise (Fig. 168), ornamented with light and graceful forms that represent an application of baroque principles of design to surfaces rather than outlines, producing the style known as rococo. The movement and vivacity of rococo architecture also appear in the painting of Watteau (Fig. 479), only to lapse into calculated voluptuousness in Boucher and Fragonard (Fig. 481).

The eighteenth century in France is often decried as a period of unbounded licentiousness and condemned as decadent. That the latter criticism at least is not unqualifiedly merited is evident in the vitality of a group like the *Cupid and Psyche* (Fig. 337) by Claude Michel

FIG. 337.   Clodion, Cupid and Psyche
(*ca.* 1775).

century French sculptors. Judged by his work, he apparently was particularly sensitive to the intellectual currents of the time, although his assimilation of their ideas must have been intuitive rather than conscious. The Bathing Nymph in the Altman Collection in New York's Metropolitan Museum is rococo in technique but the sentiment is that of Rousseau's cult of nature. In other works he followed the generally classic trend of contemporary taste, but always with a measure of concrete and objective realism. It was this characteristic of his style that finally brought him to portraiture, the sphere of activity in which he achieved his greatest distinction. He executed busts of the most prominent personalities of the day, among them *Voltaire* (Fig. 338), the example illustrated being one of many that he made of the illustrious dramatist and poet. The rococo

(1738-1814), who is usually known as Clodion. Here the old French sense of the actual wells up once more, to invest the academic seventeenth-century formulas with new life. That Clodion's conceptions were no loftier is the fault of his time rather than of his temperament. Most of his works are small statuettes like the Cupid and Psyche, designed for interior ornament (Fig. 623) and as appropriate to the boudoir as the heroic seventeenth-century figures were to formal gardens. The brisk if artificial gaiety of the eighteenth century is well suggested in the animation of Clodion's figures, both in the poses and the highly naturalistic modeling. His facility was due in part at least to his use of terra cotta which lends itself readily to rendering the flowing surfaces of rounded limbs, mobile lips, and expressive nostrils that embodied his sensual ideal.

In many ways, Jean Antoine Houdon (1741-1828) is the most interesting of the late eighteenth-

FIG. 338.   Houdon, Voltaire (1788).

technique is seen in the curling line of the hair and in details like the deliberately roughened edge of the hole representing the pupil of the eye to give it a glint. Houdon's naturalism is apparent in the scrupulous exactness with which the features are represented, but the bust is more than a translation of the model into marble. By emphasizing the essential traits and subordinating the irrelevant, the sculptor made his work not only a record of individual appearance but the embodiment of a type. The glint in the eye, for example, is the sparkle of half-cynical, half-benevolent amusement, the spirit of Voltaire's poems and plays. By such means, Houdon tells not only how Voltaire looked but also the way his personality affected those who came in contact with him; thus he created a telling and powerful portrait.

For Americans, Houdon has more than usual interest from his association with the United States immediately after the Revolution. He crossed the Atlantic to make a portrait statue of Washington, now in the Capitol at Richmond, Va., which flatters the subject somewhat less than many of his painted likenesses. While in the United States Houdon also made busts of several leading citizens of the Republic, notably Franklin, Jefferson, John Paul Jones, and Robert Fulton. Probably his best-known work is the full-length seated portrait of Voltaire in the Comédie Française in Paris, in which neo-classic draperies contrast most strangely with the characteristically realistic head. Apart from their intrinsic value as works of art, Houdon's sculptures are of great interest in reflecting the changing thought in the late eighteenth and early nineteenth centuries. It is this quality of his work that makes it more or less independent of any school or movement and invests it with a peculiarly timeless character.

Detail of Fig. 348.

CHAPTER TWENTY-TWO

Sculpture Since 1800

The neo-classic movement in early nineteenth-century art was the first and intellectual phase of the revolt against the old absolutism, a revolt which had already taken place politically and socially in the American and French Revolutions. The academic and rococo styles of the old regime had been swept away with its political and religious paraphernalia, to be replaced by the neo-classic. Since the intellectual and social background of the neo-classic movement was discussed in connection with architecture (cf. pages 197; 216), here we add only that the conscious attempts to re-create the artistic forms of classic antiquity are apparent to a greater degree in sculpture than in either painting or architecture for a more or less self-evident reason. The antique mode in painting could not be effectively recovered because few monumental examples existed. Practical considerations obstructed the use of reproductions of classic buildings for modern purposes. Neither limitation applied to sculpture, for it had no generally practical purpose and there were many genuine classic statutes that could be used as models.

The neo-classic movement was partly a result of popular enthusiasm for antique art stimulated in the eighteenth century by the discoveries at Pompeii and Herculaneum. This enthusiasm underlies the writings of the German scholar Winckelmann, who has been called the father of modern archaeology. His writings develop the theory that the purpose of all good art is the attainment of "pure beauty," i.e., beauty of form, with no consideration of content. This "pure beauty," according to Winckelmann, was realized only by the Greeks and by the moderns who approached nature as he imagined the Greeks did, by striving for effects of "noble simplicity" and "quiet grandeur." These terms reveal the moral tone in his artistic theories, a tone which was undoubtedly a reaction against the sensual mode of the time, for Winckelmann

preached his gospel of the beautiful to regenerate Europe spiritually as well as artistically. His formal ideal was based on classic sculpture whose beauty of line and contour he recognized; but he failed to perceive the important function of modeling. It seems strange today that the most popular dissemination of Winckelmann's theories —through the writings of his pupil Lessing— should have centered around a discussion of the Laocoön group (Fig. 280), the very antithesis of his ideal in content as well as technique.

The extent to which Winckelmann's aesthetic pervaded early nineteenth-century sculpture is evident in the work of the Italian, Antonio Canova (1757-1822). His Cupid and Psyche, his best-known piece, reveals a scrupulous observance of the Winckelmann formula in its formal design and total lack of content. His portraits can be similarly characterized. That of Napoleon's sister, *Pauline Borghese* (Fig. 339), is typical in attempting a compromise between the generalization thought to be the primary quality of classicism and the realism essential to a portrait. This compromise was achieved by placing the stamp of individuality upon the face alone; the body followed classic models. As a result, the features of the Corsican princess surmount the

Villa Borghese Rome.

FIG. 339. Canova, Pauline Borghese (1805).

half-nude body of a Roman goddess, the lower part of the figure having been modeled after a late Hellenistic Venus. Even the effort to generalize the torso does not disguise the sculptor's contemporaneity with the rococo revealed by the rippling flesh surfaces. But the drapery is in linear folds and the hard contours are typically neo-classic.

The popularity of the neo-classic ideal is attested by its geographical diffusion. The Danish sculptor Thorwaldsen (1770-1844) was probably a better exponent of Winckelmann's theories than Canova, for he was less affected by the rococo than his Italian contemporary. As a result, his figures are even more frigid. That he had no real appreciation of classic sculpture is apparent from the fact that after he restored the figures from Aegina (cf. Fig. 254) his own style showed no influence of the Greek work. The neo-classic style was also popular in England, its linear quality appealing to a taste apparent in English art ever since the Middle Ages. Its outstanding English protagonist was John Flaxman (1755-1826), of whom no more need be said than that he considered the British Museum's acquisition of the Parthenon sculptures to be of "doubtful value." Sculpture in France and Germany during the early nineteenth century was likewise dominated by neo-classic concepts.

This is also true of the first attempts at sculpture in the United States. Of all the visual arts, sculpture was the last to appear in the young republic, a fact explained by the complete lack of any need for it. Even as late as 1820, the painter John Trumbull discouraged a young stonecutter who came to him for advice by saying that "nothing in sculpture would be wanted in this country for yet a hundred years." Men who persisted in pursuing their interest in sculpture in the face of such an attitude had only one course, namely, to study in Europe. In the early nineteenth century, Europe meant Italy to a sculptor, and there the neo-classic style was firmly entrenched. The effect of the training early American sculptors received in such circumstances is evident in the work of Hiram Powers (1805-1873). There is little to distinguish the *Greek Slave* (Fig. 340), his best-known piece, from the rank and file of

neo-classic work except possibly the characteristically American factualness of inanimate details like the chain and the shawl. The pose is derived from the so-called Medici Venus, a late Hellenistic statue based on the Aphrodite of Knidos. The overgeneralized modeling of the figure makes it

In the Collection of The Corcoran Gallery of Art, Washington, D.C.

FIG. 340.   Powers, Greek Slave, 1843.

lifeless and cold; but in spite of this, its nudity would hardly have been tolerated in puritan America had it not been for the title which appealed to sympathies aroused by the Greek fight for freedom from Turkish rule. For example, this sentimental and entirely unsculptural consideration allowed a group of clergymen in Cincinnati to pronounce the statue unsubversive of public morals when they examined it prior to exhibition in that city. The same reason must account for the popularity that made a reproduction of it an indispensable adjunct to any American household with pretensions to culture in the mid-nineteenth century.

The consequences attendant upon the birth of American sculpture when neo-classic ideals dominated taste are evident even today. The feeling that an ideal figure must be treated in the classic manner is one, as well as the dependence on abstract symbols to invest such figures with meaning. The persistence of these ideas in American sculpture long after they had disappeared in Europe is directly traceable to the lack of artistic background in the United States and the consequent absence of any but the most elementary critical sense. American sculptors clung to pseudo-classic Italianate ideals long after their inanities were realized in Europe and artistic leadership had passed once more from Italy to France where the romantic movement was in full swing.

In the romantic movement, the revolt against seventeenth-century absolutism enters its second phase. It is distinguished from the earlier intellectual neo-classic stage by its emotionalism and its insistence upon the artist's complete freedom to express his emotions according to his own desires. This personal point of view naturally resulted in a subjective and individual criterion of taste; the test of a work of art is whether it "grips you," rather than its formal quality, i.e., design. Such a point of view holds that feeling is the proper content of artistic expression, rather than thought; *vide* Wordsworth's definition of poetry as "the spontaneous overflow of overpowering feelings." This concept has been encountered before; it is the very essence of the baroque. But between baroque and romantic art there is this significant difference: the feeling expressed in baroque forms is impersonal and abstract, whereas the feeling that animates those of the romantic period is individual, and concrete too, at least as far as the artist is concerned. Here is the genesis of an attitude toward art that has

not been unqualifiedly constructive. The academic point of view was limited but at least it stressed the need to learn the methods of formal communication and thus made possible some understanding on the part of observer and public. But the romanticist places everything in the artist's hands. The form his creations take depends upon his own feeling; if the result is art for him, its significance to anyone else is of no importance. Thus the effect of the separation of art from environment brought about by the Academies was intensified by the separation of the artist from his public that took place in the nineteenth century.

Sculpture is not the best adapted of the arts to express fully a content so lyric in character; its material limitations turn it toward general rather than personal expression. The effect of romanticism is discerned more immediately in literature and painting. In sculpture it is marked first by preference for inherently emotional or dramatic subjects and subsequently by the development of a style of surface movement and chiaroscuro that conveys emotive or dramatic values somewhat more abstractly. In the first category is the group by François Rude (1784-1855) known as *Le Départ pour la Guerre* or, more popularly, *The Marseillaise* (Fig. 341), carved for the Arc de Triomphe de l'Étoile in Paris in 1835. The theme is the spontaneous response of all Frenchmen, young and old, to their country's call voiced by the shouting figure flying above them. Rude remains traditionalist in some respects; the costumes of the volunteers are those of Roman warriors, and the modeling of the figures has some neo-classic hardness of surface, but the group as a whole is so instinct with movement that the soldiers seem actually to be filing past, and the shrieking Bellona above is a furiously animated personification of the violently clashing emotions of physical combat. The popular name of the group proves its effective interpretation of French patriotism, for its forms arouse the same sentiment as the stirring song of the same title. Its romanticism lies in the fact that it is so directly addressed to the emotions rather than symbolically to reason and intellect.

Less profound but equally romantic is

Arc de Triomphe, Paris.

FIG. 341. Rude, The Marseillaise
(1835).

Flora (Fig. 342), crouching among rollicking *putti*, that was carved by Jean Baptiste Carpeaux (1827-1875) to decorate the Pavillon de Flore of the Louvre in Paris. The forms are almost baroque, but a baroque closer to the pictorial style of Rubens (cf. Fig. 457) than to Bernini's sculptural idioms. The impression created by the kneeling woman's form is frankly carnal, achieved by the extraordinarily skillful rendering of the flesh in movement, and heightened by the contrast between its flickering highlights and the deep background shadow. In using a device which anticipates Rodin a little later in the century, Carpeaux reveals himself as a pictorial sculptor who depends upon effects of chiaroscuro rather than on form and mass as means of expression. It is these effects, however, that invest his figures with the *joie de vivre* that links his work to

the romantic movement, although it is an abstract and general quality rather than one inherent in individual figures.

The entire achievement of nineteenth-century French sculpture is summed up in the work of Auguste Rodin (1840-1917). This is tantamount to saying the achievement of all Occidental sculpture, for at no time, not even in the Middle Ages, was French art so universally dominant as in this period. Technically, Rodin's sculpture continues Carpeaux' expressive modeling which gives the figures abstract vitality. He thus takes his place in the long line of French artists extending back through Clodion to the Flemish painter Rubens. But where his predecessors were content to achieve a sense of movement in their figures, Rodin attempted to make that movement expressive of psychological function and, in so doing, to give his figures character. In this respect, he is akin to Houdon and, going back to seventeenth-century painting, to Rembrant, both of whom, primarily interested in their subjects, concentrated on expressing character and were more or less contemptuous of formal or absolute beauty in their figures. Thus Rodin's sculptures are at the same time astonishingly real and psychologically valid as a result of the play of light and shade created by the expressive modeling of the surfaces.

All this is apparent in *The Kiss* (Fig. 343), inspired by the tragic story of Paolo and Francesca,

Pavillon de Flore, Louvre, Paris.

FIG. 342. Carpeaux, Flora
(1863-1868).

Musée Rodin, Paris.

FIG. 343.   Rodin, The Kiss (1898).

the ill-fated lovers in the fifth canto of the Inferno in Dante's *Divine Comedy*. It illustrates admirably Rodin's frequent statement that sculpture consists of successive hollows and projections; by their means, the effect of actual flesh is strikingly simulated. This simulation was not an end in itself, however, for Rodin emphasized many details to achieve a clearer expression of the inner meaning of the group. Notice, for example, the contrast between the tenseness of the man's hand and its light contact with the woman's thigh, and the convulsive contraction of the toes of his right foot. These and other similar contrasts eloquently convey the passion animating the figures. But where the effect would be sensual and suggestive had the artist intended only to represent the entwined nude forms, Rodin made it abstract by veiling the heads in shadow and thereby achieved a more powerful expression.

Rock Creek Cemetery, Washington, D.C.

FIG. 344. Saint-Gaudens, Adams
Memorial (1887).

In using light and shade to create an impression of actuality, Rodin's methods were comparable to those of contemporary Impressionist painters (cf. Fig. 507). The movement of surface resulting from the play of light and shade on the figure is part of the general movement of the entire body, a movement that is real to a degree never approached by any of Rodin's predecessors. In The Kiss, for example, there is no sense of artificially posed figures, for the artist's analysis

of their movements was so complete that he could give them every appearance of naturalness. Such use of light and shade is pictorial rather than sculptural, but the closed contour Rodin employed with it gives the figures sculptural mass and weight. Their energy and life come from the movement of line and surface within the contour; pictorial chiaroscuro is employed only to the extent that it contributes to that effect, and creates the sense of environment demanded by modern taste.

The spontaneity evident in The Kiss disappears in Rodin's later pieces, and with it the beauty of the figures, a consequence, it would seem, of his theorizing about sculpture and then creating forms to illustrate the theories. Instead of embodying abstract ideas, as in The Kiss, his figures tend to become projections of his own temperament which, a combination of bitter pessimism and extreme eroticism, was bizarre even in a time when the unusual was deliberately sought out. Thus he created a female centaur with outstretched arms, seeking to objectify the soul's struggle to raise itself above the level to which it is restrained by mortal flesh. Rodin failed to give significant expression to this idea, because he was unable to clothe it with formal beauty. Michelangelo, inspired by a similar concept, produced a symphony of volumes in the Medici Tombs (cf. Fig. 328). It is this essential of sculptural beauty, form in arranged and related masses—or, in other words, the organization that means style—that Rodin's later work lacks. In The Kiss, the emotional content of the group acquires meaning by virtue of a formal arrangement to which the naturalism of the figures gives power and intensity. It thus becomes a moving symbol of the tragedy inherent in modern life, the soul attempting to find surcease from its besetting fears and uncertainties in the purging emotion of love.

At first glance, the *Adams Memorial* (Fig. 344) by Augustus Saint-Gaudens (1848-1907) might seem to have little in common with Rodin's Kiss, yet both reveal the doubt that besets the modern mind. The figure was commissioned by Henry Adams in memory of his wife; he asked only that it suggest his sense of loss in her death, the form it took being left to the sculptor. This idea Saint-Gaudens conveyed in the overwhelming depression of the figure, an effect attained by the broad simplified folds of the ponderous draperies, made abstract by the simple setting and the sexless face of the bronze figure, and given poignancy by the single visible arm and the listless fold between the knees. The result is a sense of spiritual exhaustion, its repose one of weariness rather than of quiet and serene faith. The various names that have been applied to the statue—"Grief," "Death," "The Peace of God"—all show the breadth of the sculptor's concept and the universal meaning attained in the abstractions of figure and setting. To everyone it gives according to his spiritual need, whether cynic or believer. Thus it stands for all that modern man feels about life in the hereafter, just as the Hegeso Stele (Fig. 267) reveals the calm objectiveness of the Greek and the Saint of the French *détente* (Fig. 308) the serene and trusting faith that was the finest flower of the Middle Ages.

Saint-Gaudens' position in American sculpture of the late nineteenth century is comparable to Rodin's in France in that both summed up their respective technical and interpretive traditions. Saint-Gaudens expanded the technical resources of American sculpture by introducing the delicate low relief of fifteenth-century Italian work (cf. Fig. 319) and a new appreciation of the mutual enhancement of sculpture and architecture. At the same time, his figures are American in their sense of fact and broad, vague idealism, both characteristics of American thought from pioneer days. This apparently irreconcilable dualism appears in American sculpture of the early nineteenth century which consists of vapid generalizations in the Italian manner on the one hand, and mere translations of fact into stone and bronze on the other. Saint-Gaudens' great contribution to American sculpture was to unite fact and generalization in a rugged and poetic harmony. Thus his sense of actuality gives poignance to the figure of the Adams Memorial, just as his lofty idealism makes the standing Lincoln in Lincoln Park, Chicago, the embodiment of all that the martyred President means to

the American people, much as the Pheidian Zeus summed up all that could be thought of him by the fifth-century Greek.

European sculpture in the closing years of the nineteenth century and the first decade of the twentieth was dominated by Rodin. His influence is seen in the vast number of figures done by his pupils and followers in which impressionistic technique expresses vague metaphysical ideas. In America, the outstanding protagonist of this mode was George Gray Barnard (1863-1938), at least in his earlier figures. Rodin's example was a powerful stimulus that awoke European sculpture from the academic torpor

Reinhart Collection, Winterthur.

FIG. 345. Maillol, The Mediterranean (1902).

into which it had sunk, but it also opened the way for all manner of technical and expressive exaggerations by less gifted followers and imitators. The most striking and distinctive reaction was the emphasis on sculptural form in the work of Aristide Maillol (1861-1944). In *The Mediterranean* (Fig. 345), executed about 1902, Maillol conceived the sculptured human figure as a pattern of volumes almost Hellenic in character. It is perhaps significant that when he was in

Private Collection.

FIG. 346.   Meštrović, Portrait of a Lady
(1925).

sensuality of Rodin's figures and emphasizing the relationship between the masses of the figure as a whole, Maillol achieves the necessary balance between abstraction and realism.

Sculpture of the western world in the first half of the twentieth century has presented an overall impression of great variety and individuality of style. New materials have come into use, and the traditional mediums have been used in forms that often have little relationship to established ideas of sculptural expression. In many instances, indeed, the term sculpture has apparently been redefined in applying it to conceptions which often contradict the historical notion that it means a composition of organized volumes of mass. Yet two categories can be recognized which include at least a majority of the work done up to the middle of the century. In one, content or explicit meaning is an important consideration. In the other, sculptors are almost exclusively preoccupied with abstract form.

Ivan Meštrović (1883-1962) is representative of the first category. A native of Yugoslavia, though he lived and worked for many years in the United States, his early work is intensely nationalistic in spirit. There is something of this in his bronze *Portrait of a Lady* (Fig. 346), done in 1925, but it has been generalized in the formal design. The draperies are simplified, reduced to a pattern of broad folds which effectively express the volumes of the form beneath. The system of planes by which this is attained is a feature of Meštrović's relief sculpture too, a category in which he has achieved considerable distinction. The Portrait of a Lady, in fact, is more a conception in relief than in the round, although it has no background plane. The head is a fine portrait, realistic yet formalized, with an expression of calm serenity. It is objective, but has an almost Hellenic impersonality quite unlike the impassiveness of Maillol's Mediterranean (Fig. 345). Its direct impact upon the viewer comes from its intense humanity, comparable to that which ennobles Rodin's most distinguished ideas, but communicated by essentially sculptural means. Inherent in Meštrović's mastery of form and apparent in his treatment of plane and

Greece he was most interested by the Olympia sculptures (cf. Fig. 257), but Maillol's Hellenism is in no way an archaistic reversion to older styles. It is rather a matter of figures that are powerful, rugged, and self-contained. To the realization of this classic rather than classical conception Maillol adds a fine feeling for materials; if Rodin's ideal was to translate marble and bronze into flesh, Maillol's was to transform flesh into stone, terra cotta, or bronze. There is also an obvious delight in the robustness and animal vigor of the body quite foreign to the classic point of view. But by avoiding the romantic interpretive overtones and

volume is his sense of material; the bronze of the figure seems to have melted and flowed instead of being changed by some mysterious alchemy from clay or plaster. In this, as in the sculptor's most distinguished work, there is a harmony of realism, formal design, and content that makes him an outstanding figure in twentieth-century sculpture.

Where emotional content is implicit in Meštrović's Lady, it is explicit in the *Sorrowing Woman* (Fig. 347) by Ernst Barlach (1870-1938), a German sculptor. The medium is wood, which Barlach was particularly fond of using in quite strongly simplified figures that are nonetheless vividly expressive. As a young man, Barlach was greatly moved by the furious intensity of Van Gogh's painting (cf. Fig. 516). The same quality of poignant expressionism attracted him to the arts of primitive peoples (Fig. 229) and of the Middle Ages (Fig. 297), with their purposeful and significant distortions. The strongly drawn silhouettes and effective surface textures of his figures are the elements of planes that define solid and massive volumes. In the Sorrowing

FIG. 347.   Barlach, Sorrowing Woman (1909).

Woman, these planes are organized to suggest deep anguish and the unconcious rocking movement intuitively expressive of such emotion, and they also create the stable and three-dimensional pattern that is forcefully expressive in a characteristically plastic way. The color and texture of the wood are also important in achieving this effect.

As has been mentioned, Rodin's influence, either interpretive or technical, was a significant element in twentieth-century sculptural style, apparent either in direct emulation by his followers or in a contrary reaction, as in the work of Maillol. Carl Milles (1875-1955) was Swedish by birth but lived almost continuously in the United States after 1933. He studied in Paris and learned much from Rodin whose influence is apparent in his early works. From the outset, however, his sculptural conceptions were quite individual—a quality that derives from his craftsman's feeling for material, from his rhythmically abstract patterns, and from his realization of the need for expressive content in sculptured forms. Thus his monuments to the great heroes of Swedish history, Folke Filbyter and Gustav Vasa, are imbued with a sentiment of patriotism that makes them symbols of moving pathos. No less expressive but more abstractly significant is *The Orpheus Fountain* (Fig. 348), done in 1936, which stands before the Hall of Music designed by Ragnar Ostberg in Stockholm. Orpheus, of heroic proportions, rises in the center of the fountain from which other figures emerge in response to the music of his lyre. The play of water contributes in no small degree to the effect of upward-surging movement in this lower group.

In comparison with a figure by Rodin, Maillol's work is rather impersonal and abstract, an organization of neutral masses that suggests the human form but does not depend on its representational quality to communicate its meaning. Some of the later sculptors in the early twentieth century carried this idea further, Constantin Brancusi (b. 1876) for one. His *Mlle. Pogany* (Fig. 349) is only little concerned with the individual and personal characteristics of the subject's appearance, for it consists of ovoid shapes

Stockholm.

FIG. 348. Milles, The Orpheus
Fountain (1936).

and elliptical ridges with an occasional line precisely incised in the silver surface. The underlying concept has little to do with conventional sculptural notions but might be characterized as form for form's sake. Form that means something else is the more usual and accepted thing; one form may mean "horse," another may mean "apple," yet another may mean "woman." Brancusi poses the possibility that form may mean "form," and nothing more—and still be meaningful. His own feeling has led to a particular preoccupation with ovoid shapes, like those in the Mlle. Pogany, among others. For him, this shape of primal simplicity overshadows in importance any reference to the personal characteristics of the woman whose name it happens to share. In other words, the sculpture

is an abstraction, for it was created by abstracting what the sculptor considered the significant elements of form from the initial concept or experience which happened in this case to be Mlle. Pogany.

Figure (Fig. 350) by Jacques Lipchitz (b. 1891) is no less abstract than Brancusi's Mlle. Pogany. Beginning in 1913, Lipchitz was associated with the painters and other artists of the Cubist movement, and some of his early work seems like three-dimensional developments of contemporary paintings (cf. Fig. 522). Figure, done between 1926 and 1930, is a symmetrical arrangement of curving and elliptical shapes in bronze that refer even less than the ovoids in the Mlle. Pogany to the physiological form of the human figure. As an abstraction, it also differs in being composed of voids as well as solids. Here the underlying conception is that if form may be inherently meaningful, may not "unform" or "non-form" or void be equally so in an organized context? The sculptor has added shapes of air to the solid masses that are his traditional vocabulary.

The idea that solid and void are coequal sculptural values is specifically of the twentieth century. "A hole can itself have as much shape —meaning—as a solid mass. The mystery of the hole—the mysterious fascination of caves in hillsides and cliffs" is the way Henry Moore (b. 1898) expressed it. An Englishman, he has been particularly interested in the nature of materials; he works with equal imaginativeness in bronze, wood, and stone, in all of which he perceives, almost mystically, inherent expressive forces. It is the release of these forces he strives for, working toward forms which are curiously biological in character without being anatomical in any sense. He has studied and written perceptively about a wide variety of subjects, ranging from Mexican and African Negro sculpture to Masaccio's frescoes in the Brancacci Chapel in Florence (cf. Figs. 398, 399). This is not meant to suggest that his *Reclining Figure* (Fig. 351) is an archaistic study or a pictorial conception; one of Moore's most creative qualities is his ability to sense the essential principle of what he sees as an aid to suggest determining what is essential for himself. His feeling for material is well suggested in the wooden Reclining Figure. Although the composition is horizontal, the extended contour lines and the wood graining are related to suggest the upward twisting movement of the tree, the ideal for wood sculpture in Moore's opinion.

Moore's conception of sculpture is based on the abstract notion of shapes intrinsically significant because of their inherent formal vitality. The plastic masses of the Reclining Figure exist in a relationship that invites little comparison with forms of nature but offers experiences of surface and texture and color that acquire new meaning in the organic relationship of solid to void. In a word, space becomes positive in Moore's work; this may suggest comparison with baroque sculpture of the seventeenth century in which the idea is somewhat similar but

Collection, The Museum of Modern Art, New York, Van Gogh Purchase Fund.

FIG. 350. Lipchitz, Figure
(1926–1930).

the expressive purpose is obviously quite different.

Once void or space was established as a primary sculptural value, it was logical to make it the principal or only value as far as possible. The idea seems closer to architecture, perhaps, than sculpture, and it is interesting that some of the first efforts to realize this idea were made by artists calling themselves Constructivists. The movement, of Russian origin, arose in the 1920's and fell victim in its homeland to the Communist purge during that decade. But its ideas were spread in the 1930's and underlie a considerable amount of experimenting with new sculptural materials, among other things. The very idea of space as a major sculptural value implies the absence of material solidness. Transparent sheets of plastic are easily shaped to give

Private Collection.

FIG. 349. Brancusi, Mlle. Pogany
(1913).

Buchholz Gallery, N.Y.

FIG. 351. Moore, Reclining Figure (1946).

visually weightless definition to a volume of space; threads of nylon can be stretched in paraboloid planes for the same purpose. There is similar preoccupation with space as the major element in constructed form in Ibram Lassaw's *Kwannon* (Fig. 352), done in 1952. It also illustrates one of the technical procedures that has been added to the sculptor's repertory in recent times—welding. The form, which is six feet high, is built up of silvered bronze wire into a cage which envelopes space as it is pervaded by it. Its balanced poise refers to the sculptor's concern, as he was working on the form, with Kwannon, the Japanese god of compassion and pity, according to his own account.

Lassaw's Kwannon makes it clear that the term sculpture may be used in the twentieth century to refer to forms which have little if anything in common with earlier examples of the art. The catalogue of an exhibition of sculpture of the mid-twentieth century at the Museum of Modern Art in New York makes a distinction between statuary and sculpture, suggesting that

the former be used in referring to solid forms that occupy space, and the latter for those in the round but penetrated or pervaded by space. In either case, representation need play no part, for all that is significant is the experience of form in the round. That Lassaw's Kwannon has this quality is apparent even in the illustration; it is even more so when the form is actually seen. Once this notion is accepted, it is legitimate to ask what such an experience can convey beyond objective characteristics of patterned form in space. Lassaw, for example felt he was suggesting the concept of tranquillity, an attribute of the Japanese god; but even if the precise nature of the artist's private experience that resulted in this form is not described its essential meaning should be sensed.

However far the trend toward abstraction in the mid-twentieth century may have limited sculpture in communicating content of communal significance, it has opened the way to its reattaining its one-time vitality as an architectural adjunct. The spare, elemental forms of much

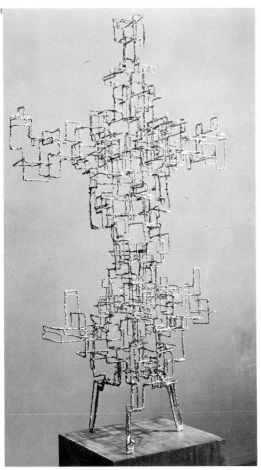

Collection, The Museum of Modern Art, New York,
Catherine Cornell Fund.

FIG. 352. Lassaw, Kwannon (1952).

De Byenkorf Store, Rotterdam.

FIG. 353. Gabo, Construction (1956).

building in the second and third quarters of the century (Figs. 211-218) provide no opportunities for the sculptor's art in any way comparable to those of classic antiquity (Fig. 29) and the Middle Ages (Fig. 300). But in 1956, Naum Gabo (b. 1890) created a monumental *Construction* (Fig. 353) of metal and concrete as an adjunct to the *Byenkorf,* a contemporary modern department store in Rotterdam, Holland. Its shapes of concrete and steel with weblike patterns in the voids are completely abstract in that they have no resemblance to identifiable forms. Its total impression is of angular metallic elements, others of concrete that are straight and curving, and the

immaterial planes of the webbing between. Although the form stands free of the building, its shapes seem intimately associated with the severe planes of the structure which are pierced with but few openings (some of them narrow slits in a pattern suggesting a painting by Mondrian; the surface texture of hexagons on the main façade refers to the building's name, which means "beehive" in Dutch. The monumental dimensions of the form make it a significant element in the organized space of the building and its surroundings; on a smaller scale, it would have little more character than a pleasantly decorative pattern.

 PAINTING ❧

Detail of Fig. 422.

CHAPTER TWENTY-THREE

Painting: Principles and Techniques

In common understanding, the word art almost invariably means painting. Architecture is popularly thought of as the science of construction rather than art. Sculpture, as we have seen, plays a relatively small part in our lives today and so does not receive much consideration as an art. But painting in one or another of its various forms is an everyday experience—advertisements, magazine illustrations, and wall decorations, to mention only a few. In the general mind, the term artist has the connotation of *painter*; usually it means something else only if it is specifically stated. What is the reason for this, and why is painting the most widely practiced of the visual arts today?

To begin with, painting is a more flexible medium of expression than either architecture or sculpture, and thus is capable of great variety of effects. In this respect, it can be compared with the piano which can produce both harmony and melody, either many-voiced polyphony or a single melodic line. So in painting it is possible to convey effects of space, which we have seen to be in the domain of architecture, and also of plastic form which is in the province of sculpture. The painter, whose medium is more fluent than either architecture or sculpture, can make expressive use of effects legitimate in both the other arts. Nor is he as liable as architect and sculptor to the risks involved in going beyond the limits of their respective arts. Iktinos, for example, in designing the Parthenon (Fig. 39), treated it as a sculptural form; space was a subordinate consideration. Bernini, on the other hand, in his St. Theresa in Ecstasy (Fig. 333), employed every available means to suggest space, not only that in which the figures are placed but also that which extends far beyond; in consequence the group lacks something of the sense of plastic volume we look for in sculpture. In contrast, painting can suggest both space and plastic form and produce cumulative effects of realistic appearance that are both more immediately and more powerfully appealing than the abstract ones of the other visual arts. To this is due in great part the more general interest in painting than in either architecture or sculpture in our own time.

In view of this greater fluency of painting, it may seem a paradox to say that in some ways it is also more limited than either architecture or sculpture. To revert to our earlier simile, the piano, capable of the massive harmonies of the orchestra as well as the melodic line of vocal and solo instrumental music, is incapable of their contrasted tonal colors and textures. Instead of the shimmering tone of flutes, harps, and violins, the piano produces a cascade of notes all more or less alike in quality. The continuous melodic line of the voice or violin becomes a series of isolated tones to which even the greatest pianist can give only an approximation of the organic flow that characterizes the products of the others. In other words, effects possible in other forms of musical expression can be rendered on the piano, but in an abstract form that has only a suggestive resemblance to them. In like fashion, the painter does not organize actual space like the architect, nor does he have to do with tangible three-dimensional form like the sculptor. Those qualities can only be *suggested* in a painting, for the painter seeking to create a synthesis of analyzed experience is limited to the two physical dimensions of length and width. He can no more compose his picture in actual depth than the pianist can recreate the variegated tonal color of a symphony orchestra. Nor can he paint a figure, house, or tree so that it is actually round to the touch any more than Rachmaninoff could make his piano produce an unbroken line of melody that sounds like the human voice or the violin. The painter can evolve only abstractions in pictorial idioms of the qualities of form and space and so suggest them to the observer.

The first step the painter must take, then, is to subject his three-dimensional experience to a process of abstraction in order to express it in terms that involve only two dimensions. The extent to which this is true can be observed in an example of two-dimensional representation which violates this principle, the Gates of Paradise by Lorenzo Ghiberti (Figs. 311, 312). In these panels, Ghiberti was working two-dimensionally to all intents and purposes. Space is suggested by skillfully varied planes in the backgrounds that create an almost endless vista behind the figures. But the figures, at least those in the foreground, stand free of the relief in an actual third dimension, and at times cast shadows on parts of the background supposedly an infinite distance away. This incongruity is a consequence of attempting to combine unrelated effects. Ghiberti was working partly as a sculptor and partly as a painter, employing figures that had an actual third dimension in a two-dimensional scheme. Idioms of both arts are mixed together and unalloyed realism is impossible. The effect is much the same as that often observed in the theatre when an actor's shadow falls on the painted backdrop and seems to extend miles away. In both cases, failure to attain a consistently real effect is the result of attempting to be realistic using terms which have no basic relationship to each other.

On the two-dimensional plane of canvas, wall, or paper, the painter organizes a pattern of forms defined by lines or colors, or a combination of the two. These are the basic elements in pictorial expression, whatever the period or style or subject may be, and the means of attaining all the complex effects avilable to the painter are ultimately reducible to these fundamental devices. In the work of a painter like Ingres (cf. Fig. 490), the line may be dominant to the almost total exclusion of color, whereas other painters use color so extensively that lines as such hardly appear. The painter may suggest solid form by juxtaposing lines to create areas of dark or light or by varying the tonal value of an area of color; in either case, the effect is attained in terms of the basic pictorial element. For line and color, with dimension only in a flat plane, are of necessity the means by which the painter, limited as he is to two physical dimensions, must achieve the patterns of his picture. The relative importance of line and color as pictorial elements varies in different times and styles. In some of the earliest known pictures, the line is used exclusively, whereas the significant trends in painting since the late nineteenth century have stressed color as the important element. Whatever the character of an individual style or period may be in respect to these devices, it can always be analyzed in terms of one or the other or a combination of the two.

Painting in the western world has been concerned for the greater part of its history with portraying by line and color, effects of three-dimensional form in space. In creating such effects, painters have used two principles of visual representation—perspective and modeling. Two perspective methods are generally employed, linear and aerial. Linear perspective is based on the fact that parallel lines receding into space from the observer seem to converge on the horizon. This is readily observed on a long straight road or railroad track; the sides or rails and telegraph wire apparently meet at a single point on the horizon. Another quality of linear perspective is that objects of the same size seem smaller the farther they are from the observer. This involves the idea of scale, that is, the measuring of objects by each other, which is also an integral part of the two-dimensional portrayal of three-dimensional space. Aerial perspective, the second of the two methods is based on the diffusing, softening effect which atmosphere has on the forms, outlines, and colors of distant objects. This can be observed by looking at a tree that is close at hand and comparing it with one far away. The nearer one will be seen to consist of many individual leaves and branches, each quite clearly distinguished from the others in form and color, whereas in the distant one the individual parts merge, the brilliant green of the leaves becomes less intense, and the whole outline is less sharp and clear. This effect in a painting suggests that the object portrayed is some distance away.

Both aerial and linear perspective were known to artists as early as the Hellenistic period (Figs. 363, 364), although then the aerial was more generally employed than the linear. Before the Renaissance, linear perspective was intuitively felt rather than intellectually understood; not until Brunellesco evolved a system that incorporated it to give his architectural drawings reality (cf. pages 364, 469) was it seen to depend on relationships that can be mathematically determined. The absence of such system is responsible for the curious distortions, mentioned earlier, in the architectural background of the reliefs of the Arch of Titus in Rome (Fig. 286).

Perspective is the device by which pictorial depth is suggested. The effect of plastic form in painting is produced by modeling, of which there are two general types: modeling by contrasts of light and shade, or chiaroscuro, and modeling by color. In either case, the result is an impression of objects with the roundness and solidity of form which our experience leads us to believe they have. Chiaroscuro modeling is based on the fact that an illuminated solid object casts a shadow and that one side will be more brightly lighted than the other unless the observer is directly in line with both object and light source. This effect in painting often involves the use of color, as when shadows are a darker value of the intrinsic color of the object itself. However, it can be suggested by using only varying intensities of black and white (Figs. 417, 491). Many of the monochrome reproductions of paintings in this book illustrate this point, because the photographic process reduces color modeling to values of gray. Chiaroscuro modeling has been employed by painters from comparatively early times (Fig. 363), but modeling in pure color was almost unknown before the end of the nineteenth century. Paul Cézanne, the great French Post-Impressionist painter, was among the first to realize that some colors seem to recede and others advance. He used these characteristics to give roundness and solidity to the objects in his paintings and to secure effects of depth. It is the absence of color values that makes Cézanne's pictures so hard to comprehend in photographic reproductions (Figs. 512, 513,) although in their actual presence the sense of solid forms existing in space is very powerful.

The discussion up to this point has centered around the generally held idea that painting is the art of portraying in two dimensions the appearance of objects that actually exist in three. This idea has been an important element in painting since the Renaissance and is still important. We must not forget, however, that there have been times when it was *not* the purpose of painting to produce realistic two-dimensional abstractions of a three-dimensional world. In the Middle Ages, for example, painters strove for didactic, expressive, and decorative effects rather than representational illusionism. Comparison of the stained glass window of the Madonna and Child in Chartres Cathedral (Fig. 371) with Filippo Lippi's matter-of-fact representation of the same subject (Fig. 404) shows how greatly the aim of the mediaeval craftsman differed from that of the Renaissance painter. The latter considered his panel an area upon which to record the lineaments of his mistress in a reasonably realistic fashion; to the former, the glass of the window was the means by which, to quote C. R. Morey, "the light of day became the Light Divine." The realism bestowed by perspective and modeling would have been not only superfluous but detrimental to the supernal glow of his image. For similar reasons, the spiritual ideal which Stephan

Lochner sought to express in his Adoration of the Magi (Fig. 383) appears disembodied of the incidentally realistic qualities that are popularly regarded as the end of the painter's art.

The extent to which the modern painter has been particularly preoccupied with representing the appearance of things is still further revealed by comparing the use of the line as a delineating device in mediaeval art and in postmediaeval examples. The figures in the illustration from the Utrecht Psalter in Fig. 368 consist entirely of lines. Similarly, the figures in drawings by Watteau (Fig. 480) and Van Gogh (Fig. 517) are represented by combinations of lines. The mediaeval line and the modern line have this important difference. The mediaeval line is a thing in itself; the artist conceives his subject in terms of line and the line alone is real. Space and plastic form are disregarded, or suggested only insofar as the *idea* of those qualities seem real to the artist. The opposite is true of the modern line. This line has meaning only as it contributes to realistic qualities of form and space, as a two-dimensional convention suggesting three-dimensional values. Thus in the Watteau, the roundness of the head is suggested by the curved contour. In the Van Gogh, the line is thick here and thin there, a fluent instrument in the drama of trees outlined against the sky. In both, the line has meaning in its relation to some material object and not as an independent, self-sufficient expression as in the illustration from the mediaeval psalter.

The basic styles in painting may be viewed as expressing two different attitudes toward physical reality. The most popularly accepted attitude is the one made familiar by the Renaissance masters. It is expressed in the imitation of nature effected by aerial and linear perspective and all the related devices that can provoke a sense of vicarious experience. For some five hundred years this type of realism has been the principal one acceptable to the western world. Through the frame of the picture the artist projects a view of concrete objects—of men, landscape, or still-life—contrived to produce a strong impression of actuality. The purpose of such painting was not so much to deceive the eye, however, as to persuade the sensibilities by means of a plausible presentation of objects in air, light, and space. This method, in practice, was employed to create a kind of agreed-upon fiction precisely as Thackeray or Shakespeare gave us fiction in novels or plays.

But to describe painting exclusively in such terms is to falsify its nature, since, as we have said, there are whole epochs in which artists used entirely different means and worked toward entirely different ends. For hundreds of years in mediaeval times, painting was nonillusionistic and symbolic. And much of the painting in our time has been largely of a similar nature, nonrepresentational.

The art of painting does not *necessarily* have to do with an accurate or correct rendering of nature. The long centuries of naturalism with its exalted masters like Leonardo, Rembrandt, and Goya have so accustomed our sensibilities to a representational style that any other style may seem alien, primitive, or eccentric. But this misreads the evidence of history which provides an abundance of nonillusionistic styles. The abstraction of contemporary art is only the latest instance of artists finding a new way to express new experience. We are accustomed to the most radical shifts in scientific or political thought, but are sometimes less alert to equally radical shifts in aesthetic thinking. Men's ideas about experience profoundly influence the artistic images they make. Men in a materialistic age like the twentieth century inevitably make very different images from those made by the Frenchman of the Middle Ages.

The materials of the painter are colored pigments applied to wet plaster, canvas, wood panel, or paper. The most familiar type of painting is done with oils on canvas, a method that has been employed since the fifteenth century. Pigments mixed with oil provide a medium that gives richness in opacity of light and depth of shadow. Great precision and infinite nuance of color are possible to the painter in oils, because corrections and retouching are relatively simple. On the other hand, oil paintings are subject to destruction by time. Unless the painter is highly skilled in the science of sizing the canvas, mixing his oils with pigments and varnishing the surface, he cannot expect his pictures to last more than a few years.

Before oils were in general use, a type of painting called tempera was popular. Egg was mixed with dry pigment, and resin or wax added for transparency. This substance was applied to prepared wood panels. Such painting sometimes produced flat dry effects like fresco and sometimes attained the richness of oil, depending upon the mixture. The most permanent type of painting is fresco, in which colors are mixed with water and applied to fresh plaster which absorbs the color. Since the pigment has been incorporated with the plaster, it lasts until the wall is destroyed. Fresco painting requires great skill and knowledge to be effective. Each day the painter must prepare a small area of fresh plaster which he must paint before it dries. Once dry, it cannot of course be altered or retouched, so the master must work with great speed and sureness of hand. Fresco painting flourished during the fifteenth and sixteenth centuries, when Masaccio, Michelangelo, Raphael, Tintoretto and many others covered the walls of Italian churches with their great masterpieces. The twentieth century has witnessed its revival in the work done by the Mexican nationalist painters and by some men in the United States.

Pastel is a more recently invented process than any of the foregoing. The pigment is bound so as to form a crayon which is applied directly to the surface, usually paper. Pastel is a delicate and seductive medium, but subject to damage; hence it is customary to spray it with a fixative lest the dry powdery color rub off. Water color is a process familiar to every school child. Colored powder is formed into cakes with gum arabic, then mixed with water. The transparency of the medium allows the paper to show through, adding its own color and luminosity to the finished effect. Though most popular with the amateur and dilettante, water color is a difficult medium. It was much used by the Old Masters for studies and preparatory sketches.

With painting we may group the *graphic arts*, the art of the black and white print. The woodcut, the etching, and the engraving were first developed so that many copies might be made of a single design. But instead of continuing to be merely a reproducing medium, these processes have become definitely established as techniques with laws of their own. For a woodcut, a drawing is made upon the plank or long-grain side of a block of wood. With a sharp instrument, the artist gouges out the areas that are to be white in the picture, leaving the parts that are to be black flush with the surface of the block. The block is then inked and pressed upon the paper which absorbs the ink. For etching and engraving the process is just the reverse. The engraver gouges out of his copper plate the parts that are to be black. His sharp graver digs grooves in the copper plate, which is then sponged with thick black ink. When the surface is wiped clean the ink remains in the grooves, and the pressure of the press forces the spongy paper into these, where it absorbs the ink. The result is a crisp definite linear impression. In etching, the metal is covered with a thin coat of gum. The artist then draws a picture in the gum with a pointed etching instrument, laying bare the metal beneath. He then places the plate in an acid bath. The acid acts upon the exposed metal, the part under the gum being unaffected. When sufficiently bitten, the plate is taken from the bath, and the gum removed. The plate is inked and wiped, the ink catching in the bitten places. Then it is pressed against the paper as in the engraving. The plates and blocks may be used again and again, though they deteriorate after many impressions have been made.

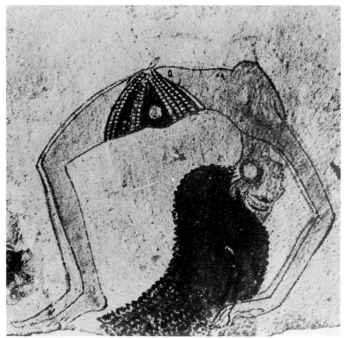

Detail of Fig. 358.

CHAPTER TWENTY-FOUR

Painting Before 1300 A.D.

Painting was one of man's earliest creative activities, vying with
sculpture in embodying the concepts and ideas of his primitive
experience of life. It is impossible to know which of the two
representational arts was first practiced in the distant ages of
prehistory. Some anthropologists have thought that sculpture is
an older art than painting, beginning with a chance observation
of a similarity between the shape of a rock or piece of bone
and that of some animal. Others feel that equally fortuitous
stains on the rock walls of a cave may have provided a similar
creative impulse, the primitive painter having only to heighten
the suggested effect with a few lines scratched with the end of a

charred stick or painted with a crude brush. In any event, the earliest known painted forms deal with basic and elemental concepts, largely concerned with preserving man's mortal existence and assuring a future life which he instinctively felt existed after this one.

PRECLASSIC AND CLASSIC PAINTING

The rock walls of a cave at Altamira in northern Spain were painted in the palaeolithic period, when much of Europe still lay under Ice Age glaciers, with likenesses of the *Bison* (Fig. 354) that were the cave man's food. In patterns of incised lines heightened by color, the two basic pictorial elements, the animals are portrayed with remarkable accuracy in spite of the simplified details. Two things contributed to this faithfulness to visual fact. One was the sharp eye of the artist-hunter whose life depended on his ability to see his prey under the most difficult conditions. The other was his interest in the animal as food, expressed in the emphasis on the parts of the beast that made it most desirable and useful. So guided and inspired, his hand recorded in sure strokes with sharp stick or crude brush the characteristic aspects of form and movement, and these salient visual facts are emphasized in his representation.

Like the fertility symbols he was carving at the same time (Fig. 229), the cave man's paintings were believed to have magic power that enabled him to control the forces of nature and turn them to his advantage. The drawing of the *Palaeolithic Paintings* (Fig. 355) at Altamira shows the helter-skelter relationship of the individual likenesses—varying sizes and positions, some

Frobenius Collection.

FIG. 354. Altamira. Cave (Magdalenian), A Bison Cow.

FIG. 355. Altamira. Cave, Palaeolithic Paintings.

painted over others, etc. To modern eyes, there seems little organization of any kind, decorative or narrative or whatever. Whatever the significance of these forms, it is not primarily aesthetic, the result of an urge to make something pleasing and attractive to the eye. These shapes were created as magic charms to assure success in the hunt. When these shapes no longer worked, they were painted over, or others added. Thus they are direct and convincing, i.e., realistic statements about something very important to the artist; this is equally true of the work of creative painters at all times, even in the mid-twentieth century (Fig. 545).

In Egypt, painting hardly existed as an independent art; it was generally an accessory to statues and relief carvings on the walls of tombs (cf. Figs. 9, 233) and temples (cf. Fig. 18), to accent the more durable stone forms. For permanence was essential to the objects the Eygptian created to record his experiential concepts, and painting alone was usually thought too fragile for this purpose. There are certain periods, however, and there were presumably always some places in which this was not a critical limitation. In a Middle Kingdom rock-cut tomb at Beni-Hasan (cf. Figs. 13, 14), the *Slaves Feeding Oryxes* (Fig. 356) is painted directly on the wall without preliminary relief carving. The forms are outlined, as are the contours of arms and legs inside the general silhouettes. These outlines are then filled with flat color, i.e., without modeling tones—terra-cotta red, yellow, green, brown, and white. It is hardly necessary to identify the conventions of drawing in the figures; they parallel those of Egyptian relief sculpture (Figs. 230, 233, 238), involving simultaneous presentation of frontal and profile views of the same form so that the most characteristic aspect of every part may be accurately described. This works quite well for animals—the profile view represents them very adequately—but does not make for organic consistency in the human figures. Even in them, however, there is rather more flexibility than in comparable relief sculptures; at least an attempt has been made to suggest the foreshortened shoulders and backs of the profiled forms. But there is no perspective, and

the figures' existence in depth is only descriptive, for their shapes are as flat as the wall on which they and the identifying hieroglyphs are painted.

A wall painting of a *Nobleman Hunting* (Fig. 357) from an Eighteenth Dynasty tomb at Thebes is similar in theme to the Old Kingdom relief from the Tomb of Ti (Fig. 233), and many of the same conventions are present, notably the greater size of the master and the familiar profile

FIG. 356. Beni-Hasan. Tomb of Khnumhotep (*ca.* 1900 B.C.), Slaves Feeding Oryxes.

views. In contrast with Ti's static pose, he gestures animatedly, however, holding three decoy birds by their legs in one hand and a boomerang in the other. In the painting of the birds, one problem of perspective depth is handled in a way that conveys ideas descriptively, for they appear simply as a series of overlapping profiles. But there are certain bits of naturalism of a high order; the birds and fishes are portrayed with great accuracy, and the hunting cat sitting in the bending lotus stems before its master with birds clutched in teeth and claws is a small masterpiece of feline characterization. Again we must point out that the values of Egyptian art are basically conceptual rather than sensuous. In representing the master's activities on the walls of his tomb, the

British Museum, London.

FIG. 357. Nobleman Hunting (*ca.* 1450 B.C.), from 18th-Dynasty
Theban Tomb.

artist was concerned with typical and universal qualities rather than momentarily naturalistic ones. This accounts for the clarity and order of the arrangement which to modern eyes may seem to be dictated by desire for decorative beauty but which is simply the Egyptian's way of defining his ideas with the greatest possible accuracy. The training of eye and hand required was selective and intense. Occasionally it is seen in more informal themes like the *Girl Acrobat* (Fig. 358), done in the Twentieth Dynasty, about 1180 B.C.; it was found on a flake of limestone in the remains of an artist's workshop and was presumably the pastime of an idle moment. Con-

Museo di Antichità, Turin.

FIG. 358.　Girl Acrobat
(*ca.* 1180 B.C.).

ventions are still present, notably the portrayal of the eye, and the feet are rather summarily indicated, but the precisely drawn lines of the arched body render the action with amazing vividness and accuracy.

Of the painting that decorated Aegean and Mesopotamian palaces, it is possible to speak with assurance only about the former. The colored glazed brick that faces the Tower of Ishtar in Babylon (Fig. 23) was employed as a ceramic rather than pictorial art. In Crete, on the other hand, the conglomerate walls of the Palace of Minos were ideal for a specifically pictorial medium; and a considerable number of fragments, some rather large, have been recovered and restored. The griffon on one of the flanking walls in the Room of the Throne at Knossos (Fig. 25) was pieced together from fragments found where they fell in the catastrophe that damaged the structure, in all probability about 1400 B.C.; the bare rubble of the other wall shows the necessity for the stucco finish upon which the decoration was painted. The colors are bright and varied, with yellow and red, blue and green in vigorous and highly decorative patterns. The wavy bands and the foliate forms are a stylized landscape setting for the animal which was probably a guardian, with its presumed counterpart on the other wall, sacred to the earth goddess served by the priest-king, in the manner of the heraldic lions on the fortified gate of the mainland Aegean city of Mycenae (Fig. 26).

Also of religious significance in all probability was the *Toreador* (Fig. 359), one of the most striking Cretan paintings found in the Palace of

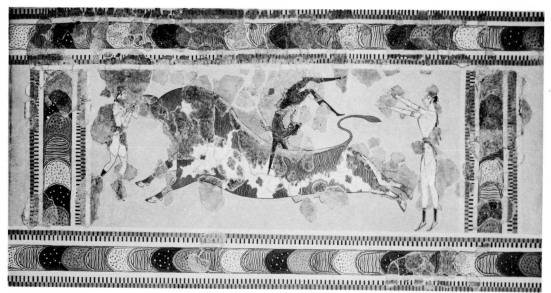

Museum, Candia.

FIG. 359.　Knossos.　Toreador (*ca.* 1500 B.C.), Restored.

National Museum, Athens.

FIG. 360.   Tiryns.   Departure for the
Hunt (*ca.* 1200 B.C.).

are white—a distinction of sex common in early representational art. The flying gallop of the bull is another convention often employed to suggest movement. The border of variegated patterns and colors suggesting different kinds of stones plays its part in the architectural function of the painting. The bull is a frequent motive in Aegean art, occurring also, for example, on the gold Vaphio Cups found in a pre-Hellenic mainland tomb (Fig. 560), and the figure style is likewise common to the Aegean area in general. The narrow-waisted girls with sharp noses, pointed chins, and curling strands of hair are like the ivory and gold Snake Goddess (Fig. 248); the same type appears in the two ladies in a chariot in *Departure for the Hunt* (Fig. 360) restored from fragments found in the ruins of the citadel at Tiryns (cf. Fig. 28). Dating probably around 1200 B.C., this fresco is somewhat later than those of the palace at Knossos. The color is strongly conventionalized, the trees being blue, gray, and terra cotta, with yellow borders; the leaves are outlined in black against their fanlike silhouettes. The chariot is crimson and the horses are red and white. The figures, in stiff profile, are white, with a blue and a violet robe; they have the same small pointed features noted in the Cretan girls. The Aegean artist's decorative sense which makes these architectural paintings so effective is also apparent in the naturalistic ornament of vases and jars from both island and mainland sites in the pre-Hellenic world (cf. Figs. 557, 558).

Writers of antiquity mention great paintings that once adorned the walls of many Greek buildings of the Hellenic age, but no trace of them remains. What little is known about them, other than from written descriptions, is based on mosaic copies (cf. Fig. 362) or the smaller versions on vases. But the art of vase painting seems to have developed independently of monumental style in Greece and to have followed its own line of evolution for some time. It is thus possible to speak with assurance about Greek painting, even though there is little that corresponds directly with popular concepts of the art today; the religious and mythological scenes from jars and cups of various shapes and sizes can be used as examples. The techniques em-

Minos, as to both subject and formal character. Much of the design has been restored, but enough original fragments were recovered to show the principal features. Against a blue background, a male figure, nude save for a loin cloth, is about to spring from his hands off the back of a charging bull. A girl, equally lightly clothed, reaches out her arms to catch him, and another girl is about to leap through the bull's horns after her male companion. The youth is dark red and the girls

ployed are discussed in detail under the Minor Arts (cf. pages 657-658); here we shall say only that there are three basic methods—one with dark figures on a relatively light background (Fig. 566), a second that reverses this relationship (Fig. 568), and a third with outline figures on a creamy white ground (Fig. 569). Areas that appear light in monochromatic illustrations like these are actually a reddish brown, the color of the clay vessel that was baked in an oven.

Greek vase painting, like Greek sculpture, was principally concerned with the human form, and the way it was treated paralleled those used in Greek sculpture. Thus the figures in a funeral procession on the great Dipylon Crater in the Metropolitan Museum in New York (Fig. 563), dating around 800 B.C., are combinations of geometrical shapes. The upper frieze shows the dead man on the bier being mourned by his family and women who tear their hair; the chariots and armed figures below represent the athletic games celebrated in his honor. The heads are circles with pointed beaks for noses and dots for eyes, the torsos are triangles, and the arms straight lines. The artist's descriptive intent is clear; each figure is defined as individually as possible with the conventions available to the painter, and the result, if childlike in its naïveté, is highly decorative. By the second quarter of the sixth century B.C. when the François Vase was painted by Klitias ca. 560 (Fig. 564), the artist is more ambitious and uses a more flexible figure style. There are still archaisms like profile legs joined to frontal torsos, and the forms are usually shown from directly in front or from the side; but lines scratched in the black silhouetted forms indicate surface modeling, drapery folds, and even some anatomical details. One of the high points in this black-figured style of Greek vase painting is the work of Exekias, whose kylix with Dionysos in a boat painted on its bottom (Fig. 565) and amphora with Achilles and Ajax playing draughts (Fig. 566) are among the most ingratiating examples of the art. Though still pervaded by conventions, Exekias' superb draftsmanship transcends the limitations of the medium, and the figures are not only well realized in a decorative sense but also characterized by a

sprightly grace akin to that of contemporary archaic sculpture (cf. Fig. 250).

Greek black-figured vase painting reached its high point in the third quarter of the sixth century B.C. when a new technique enabled further research in realistic portrayal of the human form. This so-called red-figured style appeared about 530 B.C. A vase in the University of Pennsylvania Museum (Fig. 567) done ca. 500 B.C. by the master called the Kleophrades Painter shows the style. The background is dark, for the figures were "reserved" when the vase was painted and are lighter in tone; the details of anatomy and drapery are painted on with a fine brush instead of being incised as in black-figured examples. With this greater ease of portrayal, this artist ventured effects that would have been very difficult in the earlier manner, like the foreshortened body of Herakles struggling with the lion and the torsion in the figure. Contributing to these effects is the construction of the forms in planes so they appear to be sculpturally round instead of flat, as is apparently the case in the black-figured examples. The painting from a kylix showing an old man and a girl (Fig. 561) is possibly a little later than the Kleophrades Vase but has many of the same qualities. Both represent the same stage in the vase painter's being freed from the limitations of the archaic technique as that seen in sculpture in the figure from the temple at Aegina (Fig. 254) and its contemporary, dedicated by Euthydikos (Fig. 253).

Popular Greek tradition credited Polygnotos of the mid-fifth century B.C. with the invention of painting, thus recognizing his achievement in perfecting a style of monumental mural decoration. Only descriptions and reduced adaptations of these paintings on vases are known, and whether it was the taste he created for more complex and involved effects that contributed to the decline of vase painting as an art can only be surmised. Vase painting of distinction continued in the late fifth century, to be sure; an example is the meeting of *Odysseus and the Ghost of Elpenor in the Underworld* (Fig. 361) dating about 440 B.C. on an amphora in the Museum of Fine Arts in Boston. The figure at the right is Hermes, who does not appear in Homer's

FIG. 361. Odysseus and the Ghost of Elpenor (*ca.* 440 B.C.),
Red-Figured Amphora.

account of this episode in the eleventh book of the *Odyssey* but is represented because he escorted the souls of the dead to the underworld. Elpenor stands in a trench filled with blood from the slaughtered sheep that magically gives him temporary substantiality, and Odysseus sits with drawn sword to fend off other spirits who wish to drink it. The style of the figures is comparable to that in contemporary relief sculpture; the proportions and muscular conventions of Elpenor's torso are very similar to those of figures in the Parthenon frieze (Fig. 265), and Odysseus' head resembles that of the man standing behind the horse on the frieze slab. More foreshortening is attempted, however, and the painter has ventured beyond the relief sculptor in suggesting the setting. Although this may have been in part because the Homeric poem mentions it, there can be no doubt that painters were increasingly

interested in such things as the fifth century progressed. In a scene showing Thamyris and the Muses on a hydria in the Metropolitan Museum in New York (Fig. 568), executed in the last quarter of the fifth century in the manner of the Meidias Painter, the figures are in the freest attitudes, with varied foreshortenings and perspective relationships that reveal the greatest skill in drawing, but are considerably less effective as decoration than in the earlier red-figured and black-figured examples. There is also more variety in color which, along with the greater complexity of effects, indicates the efforts of late fifth-century vase painters to vie with contemporary masters of monumental mural decoration like Polygnotos.

The art of mural painting continued to develop in fourth-century Greece, and at least one of its notable achievements—the *Battle of Alexan-*

der and Darius (Fig. 362)—has been preserved in a monumental copy; the original, painted by Philoxenos in all probability about 310 B.C., is known today through a later mosaic version of the Hellenistic period discovered in a house in Pompeii. It has been considerably damaged, but the upper part of the youthful conqueror's body is seen, and also the spear with which he slays the Persian general who sacrificed his life that Darius, at the right, might escape in his chariot. In spite of the awkward technique of building up forms with hundreds of thousands of small marble and glass cubes of different colors, many devices suggest three-dimensional forms in space. There are contrasted areas of bright and dark and highlight accents to model the figures, and those farther away are diminished in scale to create an effect of perspective depth; the horse in the foreground before the wheel of Darius'

chariot is accurately foreshortened. The spears outlined against the sky contribute to the effect of air surrounding the figures like those in the Arch of Titus reliefs (Fig. 286), as well as to the decorative pattern of the composition. The colors are sober—white, brown, gray, and black—but in a variety of tones. And the composition is dramatic too, in spite of being a copy in such a restrictive technique; the violent action of the battle is suggested, and the characterization of the protagonists—Alexander's impetuous daring and Darius' grief at the death of his friend—reveals the same expressive values in painting as those for which fourth-century sculptors also strove.

Painting in the Hellenistic period has already been partially described in pointing out the pictorial character of much of its sculpture (cf. pages 323, 326). Though more originals are available than is true of Hellenic painting, copies

Museum, Naples.

Fig. 362   Battle of Alexander and Darius, Mosaic, After a Painting by
Philoxenos (*ca.* 310 B.C.), from Pompeii.

Museum, Naples.

FIG. 363.   Herakles and Telephos, After a Pergamene
Original (2nd cent. B.C.), from Herculaneum.

of works famous in antiquity are still the principal source of knowledge. These have been found in considerable numbers in the houses of Herculaneum and Pompeii excavated from the ashes erupted by Mt. Vesuvius in 79 A.D. (cf. Fig. 60). An example from the former is *Herakles and Telephos* (Fig. 363), dealing with an incident in the legendary history of the strong man of antiquity and his son Telephos. The original it copies was probably painted in Pergamon (cf. page 321) in the second century B.C. It is clear

that the Hellenistic artist has observed many phenomena of light and space either unnoticed or disregarded by his Hellenic predecessors. In the Meeting of Odysseus and Elpenor (Fig. 361), there is little suggestion of either light or space; the figures are modeled by curving lines, the setting is similarly delineated, and the whole is reduced to a flat decorative pattern. But in the Hellenistic fresco, the background seems to be set in space by the contrasted areas of light and dark. The figure of Herakles may have been inspired by a sculptural original (cf. Fig. 281), but its three-dimensional form is created by the contrasting light and shade of its modeled surfaces. Distinctions in the sharpness of outlines, as if they were blurred by atmosphere, also contrast with the precise silhouettes of the figures on vases, but are paralleled in contemporary sculpture like the relief of the Peasant and Cow (Fig. 279).

The Hellenistic painter's methods of representing forms in space are fundamentally pictorial. In pre-Polygnotan vase painting (Fig. 567), the precise contours and planes of the figures are more sculptural than pictorial; in the fresco, on the other hand, the patterns of light and shade that create the illusion of form are the devices of a painter. Thus at a time when sculpture had almost exhausted the inspiration of a limited repertory of subjects and effects in brilliant but mannered and often meaningless technical show pieces, the generally unexplored possibilities of painting were only beginning to be realized. The point of view developed in working out the problems of rendering form and space in patterns of light and shade is primarily visual. This contrasts with the formal and sculptural concept that dominated earlier Greek art and reached its climax in the architecture and sculpture of the Golden Age in effects achieved in tactile terms of plane, volume, and mass.

The changes in the method and purpose of painting in the Hellenistic period reflect the changing point of view in Mediterranean culture of late antiquity. That of the fifth century was dominated by Athens, outstanding among the city-states of the time but still only a city-state. Its philosophy was purposely limited and the art that expressed it was equally restricted—an art of form. Hellenistic culture, by contrast, was geographically extensive and cosmopolitan in character. Its philosophy was broad and inclusive, attempting to evaluate man's experience in his environment as well as the limited anthropocentric concepts of Hellenic thought. It was a natural consequence that artists' eyes should open to many aspects of nature unobserved by the purposely restricted vision of the fifth century. The result of this in sculpture has already

been discussed. But the very nature of the expanding awareness of natural phenomena in the Hellenistic world made painting the logical means of its expression. Art moves from a world of form into one of space filled with depths of shadow and gleaming light, from a world of sculpture into one of painting.

The enthusiasm with which this illusionistic art of light and shade and spatial effects was received is indicated by the importance of such effects in Roman art. In the Arch of Titus reliefs (Fig. 286) in Rome, the artist's whole purpose was to force the recalcitrant stone to effects easily secured by contemporaneous painters. In architecture too, a sense of space achieved by light and shade is an important element (Fig. 58). In painting, it lends surprising naturalism to the extensive landscapes the Roman added to the repertory of painting, well illustrated in a fresco from Pompeii of *Paris on Mount Ida* (Fig. 364) in the museum at Naples, thus posing the final problem of realistic representation, the convincing relationship of objects to infinite space. The

Museum, Naples.

FIG. 364.   Paris on Mount Ida
(50–79 A.D.), fresco from Pompeii.

atmosphere-blurred forms of tree and shrine in the middle ground and of mountains in the distance anticipate nineteenth-century Impressionism, though the mood is lyric and Horatian. A characteristic background detail is the reclining figure symbolizing the mountain with typical classic anthropomorphism. Thus in the brief period of a few hundred years, classical painting passed from a stage in the sixth and fifth centuries B.C. which for all its distinction still bespeaks a primitive mode of thought, to these realistic Roman landscapes that at least forecast the comprehensive complexity of modern concepts.

PAINTING IN THE MIDDLE AGES

During the first millennium A.D. painting in the western world, like architecture and sculpture, was done in the service of the Church. Its principal functions were twofold—the monumental decoration of religious buildings, and the physically smaller but no less significant illustration of religious books. Its immediate and ostensible purpose, at least in the monumental examples, was didactic, to give instruction in the dogma of Christian faith to those who could not read. Church walls were decorated with fresco paintings or with mosaic (Fig. 72) made, like the classic Alexander Mosaic (Fig. 362), of small cubes of colored glass or marble set in the plaster of the wall while still soft and held firmly in place after it hardened. Because they were of relatively permanent materials, many mosaics have been preserved in much their original state, an example being the *Story of Abraham* (Fig. 365), in the choir of San Vitale at Ravenna (cf. Fig. 70). In

FIG. 365. Ravenna. San Vitale, Story of Abraham (526-547).

the center of the semicircular lunette are the three angels who came to visit Abraham in the plains of Mamre (Genesis xviii, 1-8) and to whom he served food while Sarah his wife stands in the door of their tent at the left; at the right is the Sacrifice of Isaac (Genesis xxii, 1-19). In the upper left spandrel above the arch is the prophet Jeremiah, and at the right is Moses receiving the Ten Commandments, with the murmuring children of Israel below. It is obvious that between the first century, when the Roman fresco of Paris (Fig. 364) was done, and the middle of the sixth century, the interest of artists in the appearance of things changed. This is especially true of spatial relationships. The grouping in the central lunette is reduced to a single plane even though the artist thought of the seated angels as being farther away than Abraham; the group of Jews at the right are in a similar relationship to Moses above. But in subordinating or even ignoring realism the artist emphasized decorative elements. The pictorial design is an adjunct to the architecture of the building, and its nonspatial character thus emphasizes and preserves the integrity of the flat wall surface. The background hills are a rhythmic sequence of cylindrical objects and the draperies are a series of lines radiating fanwise from a single point.

The meaning of the entire composition other than as a pictorial story is symbolic, all dramatic and representational values being subordinated. In themselves, the subjects have little dramatic unity, for two different incidents are shown in one composition. But both together represent the idea of Abraham, who stood in mediaeval theology for the old order of Judaism, transformed into the new one of Christianity by the death of Christ on the cross, symbolized here by the Sacrifice of Isaac. This symbolic idea is carried still further by the figures of Jeremiah and Moses who represent the Old Law just as Christ, symbolized by the Cross held by the flying angels, represents the New. This artist attempts no further interpretation as later ones might; he is content to present his subject for contemplation. The figures in the lunette could mean to a Christian only those in the story of Abraham; for the figures of the prophets where

identification might not be so easy, the artist has used inscriptions. But the effectiveness of mosaic ornament goes beyond its adaptation to the architectural setting or its exposition of an abstract theological point. Its greater purpose is emotional, achieved by the gleaming gold backgrounds and the luminous colors glowing softly in the dark interior which thereby becomes a pulsing spatial entity. In such circumstances, the figures take on a mystic significance that completely transcends their character as objective images.

Book illustration in the early years of Christianity is exemplified by the *Joshua and the Angel of the Lord* (Fig. 366), from the Rotulus of Joshua in the Vatican Library. The importance of these miniatures, in addition to their style, is that they once were part of a long scroll, the form in which books were first made; it was read by rolling the illustrated text sheet from one spindle to another. The relative importance of the pictures is clear, for the text is written into the spaces left in the landscape background of this pictorial epic of the Israelitish diaspora. Joshua is represented twice—once standing as he salutes the angel of God and once kneeling before him to receive the command to attack the city of Jericho in the background. There is good reason to believe that the Joshua Rotulus originated in the Egyptian Hellenistic city of Alexandria, whence came also the style at least of another masterpiece of Early Christian art, the ivory Episcopal Throne of Maximianus in Ravenna (Fig. 581), and that it was executed early in the eighth century. A Hellenistic prototype is reflected in the free movement of the figures and their somewhat casual placing in space, and in the illusionistic rendering of humans, trees, buildings, and mountains by accents of light and dark. The whole is a convincing illustration of how Christian content was infused into the forms of classic antiquity in the initial phases of their assimilation by the new faith.

The importance of the pictures that were drawn or painted on the pages of the handwritten books used in the service of the Church is out of all proportion to their physical size, because they are the largest body of evidence regarding paint-

FIG. 366. Joshua and the Angel of the Lord, from the Rotulus of Joshua
(early 8th cent.).

ing in the western world between the sixth and eleventh centuries. They served, moreover, in the revival of monumental painting and sculpture in the later Romanesque and Gothic periods, for, as was pointed out elsewhere, manuscript illuminations were often the models for artists who decorated churches in the eleventh and twelfth centuries. The character of early mediaeval art resulted, as was also noted earlier, from the fusion of the various styles developed in the three great pre-Christian cultures of the western world. One was the classic tradition with its embodiment of an ideal of physical or moral beauty that was expanded in Hellenistic and Roman times to include landscape and setting as well as the human form. The second was the Byzantine tradition, whose outstanding characteristic is its decorative unity. These two elements are represented by the Hellenistic and Roman frescoes in Figs. 363 and 364 and the Joshua miniature in Fig. 366, and by the Ravenna mosaic in Fig. 365 respectively.

The third element, the contribution of the barbarian tradition, is best described as the idea of effective force expressed in powerful abstract decorative patterns wholly unlike any others of the time. It appears in its purest form in the illuminated initial letters of the *Book of Kells* (Fig. 367), an Irish manuscript of the late eighth century, in linear patterns that are utterly unreal and unsymmetrical but have a unity that can result only from the sheer vitality and continuity of the line itself. In itself, this barbarian mode of expression did not develop a formula for the human figure because it achieved its effects chiefly by abstract linear patterns (Fig. 292). But when it was brought into contact with the classic and Byzantine concepts of Christian art in the late antique tradition, it galvanized their forms with new life and produced a style destined to have its climax in the monumental sculptures and paintings of the Romanesque and Gothic periods. The manifold aspect of this style is best seen in the ninth- and tenth-century manuscript illuminations which were the most significant artistic achievement of the short-lived Carolingian Renaissance that was initiated by Charlemagne's desire to recapture the glory that had been Rome and was continued sporadically under his successors (cf. pages 86-87).

Many different styles of Carolingian illumination developed in the various monasteries which were the centers of the Carolingian revival. They can be grouped together, however, in two main categories, the East Frankish and the West Frankish, according to their stylistic characteristics and the geographical distribution of the monasteries in which they originated. The East Frankish style included the output of a monastery at Reichenau which can be considered typical of the whole; the West Frankish manner characterizes the manuscripts of the Reims school, so called because most of them apparently were written and illustrated in monasteries near that city. Though the two styles differ greatly in details and effect, their basic intent is the same—to give expression to the ideal of vital force which was the Teutonic contribution to the art of the Middle Ages.

The outstanding example of the Reims style is the series of pen drawings in a Psalter in the library of the University at Utrecht in Holland. These drawings are naïvely objective in their references to the accompanying text, as in the *Illustration of the 74th Psalm* (Fig. 368) in the King James version. At the extreme upper right the figure of Christ on a high mountain representing Zion, described in the second verse, points a wand toward the sun, moon, and stars, and two figures symbolizing Summer and Winter, mentioned in the sixteenth and seventeenth verses. In the center the enemies of the Lord break down the carved work of the temple with axes and hammers. At the right is the Nativity, a symbolic reference to the twelfth verse, "For God is my King of old, working salvation in the midst of the earth." A figure in the left foreground smites the heads of the dragons in the waters as described in the thirteenth verse, and at the right are the people of the wilderness cutting up leviathan to be meat, as in the fourteenth verse. The artist who made this drawing was evidently trying to

copy with pen and ink a miniature in the illusionistic style (cf. Fig. 366) of late classic painting. The personifications of Summer and Winter continue an anthropomorphic symbolism that also had its origin in Hellenistic art. In the heads, the representation of the eye by a triangular dab suggesting the shadow in the eye socket carries over from an illusionistic original. But these are only details that indicate the source of the figure style in the Utrecht Psalter; the artist's purpose was not to suggest form in space but to express emotion and feeling by the intrinsic vivacity of linear movement. The Carolingian artist was probably attracted to the illusionistic style of his late Hellenistic model by the lively vividness of its patterns of light and shade, but that effect was translated into linear terms in his

Trinity College, Dublin.

FIG. 367.   Initial IN, from the
Book of Kells (*ca.* 800).

FIG. 368.   Illustration of the 74th Psalm from the Utrecht Psalter (*ca.* 830).

own work. The West Frankish style of the Reims school acquired great prestige and spread over most of western Europe, as far as England and Spain. Miniatures in comparable linear style were undoubtedly models for the scenes on the Hildesheim Doors (Fig. 293) and the Prophet Isaiah at Souillac (Fig. 297) where linear patterns achieve genuine monumentality.

The East Frankish style was also derived from the late antique, but instead of the vivacious illusionism that the Reims style translated into linear patterns, it took the solid and sculptural forms. Thus the figures in the *Resurrection of Lazarus* (Fig. 369) from the *Gospels of Otto III*, a manuscript in the State Library at Munich which dates from about 1000, retain something of the classic in their restrained gestures and bulky forms, quite different from the exaggerated

movements and wispy, wind-swept figures of the West Frankish style. The antique types are nonetheless transformed into one that embodies the Teutonic ideal of effective force in the heads jutting forward on the shoulders, the staring eyes, and the huge misshapen hands and feet. It is static rather than dynamic force, as in the Utrecht Psalter miniature; hence it lacked the emotional intensity of the linear style. But for all that, it is a northern concept, whose form of expression owes little to classic models. Like the West Frankish style, the East Frankish pronouncedly influenced later art in furnishing the direct inspiration for Guglielmus' bulky, crudely powerful figures on the façade of Modena Cathedral (Fig. 298). When the emotional fervor of the Romanesque which found expression in the contorted forms of the monumentalized Reims style

(Fig. 297) yielded to intellectual discipline in the Gothic period, the consequent need for static strength in its forms of expression was filled indirectly by the East Frankish style through the medium of north Italian Romanesque sculpture.

Manuscript illumination is one of the most characteristically mediaeval of the visual arts, for as long as the Word of God was held to be implicit in written symbols, the surface upon which it was inscribed was worthy of enhancement by line and color. Illuminations are found in books other than the Scriptures, however, an example being the *Flying Fish of Tyre* (Frontispiece) from a Bestiary in the Morgan Library in New York. The mediaeval Bestiary was a moralizing treatise on animals that interpreted them symbolically as allegories of Christian concepts; this particular example was written and illuminated about 1170 in a monastery near Lincoln in England. In mediaeval times the Flying Fish of Tyre was supposed to be huge and to fly after ships until its wings tired, when it would return to the place it came from, a symbol of those who willfully refused to abjure their sinful ways and believe in God. No one doubted that such a monster actually existed, although none had ever been seen, for mediaeval man trusted the evidence of his imagination before that of his senses. In any event, the reality of the concept symbolized by the fish was much more significant to him than any possible physical unreality. Words and picture compose an ensemble, the wings of the fish breaking through the frame that encloses the greater part of the miniature and intruding into the text. Both are also considered in relation to the page they are on, the forms being as two-dimensional as the letters of the handwritten script; the resulting decorative unity is an aesthetic "reality," the formal equivalent of the conceptual reality with which mediaeval man invested these imagined creatures. The figure style is comparable to that of contemporary Romanesque sculpture (cf. Figs. 294, 298); the gestures naïvely express fear and wonder at the baleful phenomenon in the sky. The heavy rhythmically swinging line that conveys these feelings also defines the color areas. These are quite simple for the most part, as is the

color composition which is limited to a few basic hues—red, yellow, blue, and green—but the effect as a whole is one of great vivacity and charm.

The complete history of mediaeval thought can be followed in manuscript pictures alone, but one further example will show the attitude revealed in the Gothic thirteenth century. The *Enthroned Virgin* (Fig. 370) is from a manuscript Psalter in the British Museum in London that was made for an Englishman named Robert de Lisle about 1285. It is generally contemporary with the Vierge Dorée at Amiens (Fig. 304) and quite similar to it in its mannered gracefulness. More significant, however, is the relationship of the figures to each other in an architectural setting; the Virgin is seated under a pointed and

Staatsbibliothek, Munich.

FIG. 369. Resurrection of Lazarus, from the Gospels of Otto III (*ca.* 1000).

British Museum, London.

FIG. 370.   Enthroned Virgin, from the
Psalter of Robert de Lisle
(*ca.* 1285).

Cathedral, Chartres.

FIG. 371.   Notre-Dame de la
Belle-Verrière (*ca.* 1150).

cusped arch, and the smaller figures of angels and
saints at the sides look like the statues in niches on
the flying buttresses of a cathedral. The background behind the Virgin is tooled and burnished
gold; above the central arch is an all-over
diaper pattern of brightly colored small medallions. The dominance of architecture in the Gothic
style has been mentioned elsewhere (pages 349-

352); it is characteristic that even the decoration
of a book page should employ forms originating
in that art.

Manuscript illumination is important because it gave expression to mediaeval ideals long
before they were sufficiently defined to be embodied in sculpture and architecture. In the
Romanesque and Gothic periods, as has been

seen, the need for monumental expression led to a tremendous development of these two arts; and painting was also involved, for in the form of stained glass it contributed to the emotional effect for which the Gothic builder strove. The elimination of walls in Gothic building obviously made it impossible to use the traditional methods of fresco or mosaic for painted decoration. But in the stained-glass window, the mediaeval painter created a way of glorifying God and the Church which has never been surpassed in its way.

The stained-glass window, *Notre-Dame de la Belle Verrière* (Fig. 371), was made in the twelfth century for the cathedral at Chartres (Fig. 99). It consists of innumerable pieces of glass impregnated with color which has been fixed by firing; these are fitted together and held in place by strips of lead. Thus the figure is made up of large colored areas consisting of many small pieces held together; details like the eyes and nose were painted on the glass after its original firing and then baked on to it in the oven. The effect of the window in place in the cathedral is one of pure and intense color. Curiously enough, this is partly the result of the black lines of the leading that separates the colors. Without them, the hues would blend in the eye; and instead of seeing pure blue and red side by side, the eye would see a violet less intense than either of the original colors.

Needless to say, the stained-glass maker of the Middle Ages did not strive for naturalism in his figures. Like the mediaeval sculptor, he was primarily concerned with fitting his panels to the architectural scheme rather than designing independent compositions. His ideal was a flat pattern of color, and representation was always subordinate to this consideration. This was essential not only for the decorative needs of the architecture but also as part of the moving effect that the whole interior produces, the sense of luminous darkness with its suggestion of infinite space.

Detail of Fig. 386.

CHAPTER TWENTY-FIVE

Painting of the Late Middle Ages

Manuscript illumination and stained glass are the most distinctively mediaeval forms of painting during the Romanesque and Gothic periods of the twelfth and thirteenth centuries, particularly in northern Europe. Fresco painting and mosaic, both practiced in classic antiquity, continued through the Middle Ages in the southern regions, notably Italy, but were less appropriate to the isolated supports and weightless walls of northern Gothic cathedrals (cf. Fig. 97) than stained glass, as has been seen. But painting as it is generally thought of today—compositions on canvas or wooden panels in frames to be hung on walls—was relatively uncommon. Such panel paintings, as they are sometimes called, are not entirely unknown before the fourteenth century, but whether because many have been destroyed or because they were never very numerous, very few exist today. One of the most distinctive and characteristic developments in late mediaeval painting was the greatly enhanced popularity of panel or easel painting, both in Italy and the Low Countries of the north. Almost all the examples to be considered in the following paragraphs are of this type, painted for the most part on carefully seasoned wood covered with *gesso*, a mixture of plaster and glue, to which the colors are applied.

THE FRANCO-FLEMISH TRADITION

As the Middle Ages drew to a close there appeared, as a symptom of a new world view, the most extraordinary changes in artistic thought and practice. The best way to see these changes is to place side by side two paintings, each representative of its period: the Enthroned Virgin (Fig. 370) of about 1285, and one, about two hundred years later, by Memling (Fig. 378). In the first example, the flat design, the severely formal attitudes of the figures, and the absence of sentiment are evident. But in the second, everything is changed. The Virgin now appears less a remote idea or austere symbol than a human and appealing embodiment of tenderness and warmth. We feel her presence and sense her emotion because Memling has invited those feelings and emotions by means of material, tangible properties. Mary is a recognizable mother with the affectionate attitude toward her child common to all mothers. This movement toward greater realism and deepening pathos in presenting the sacred images is found in all phases of art in the late Middle Ages— in music and literature as well as in the representational arts of sculpture and painting.

In this transformation two centers of art take the lead, one in Italy and one in Flanders, in what is now northern France and Belgium. In these regions painting came to surpass the arts of sculpture and architecture because it was so inherently appropriate for transmitting the doctrines of Christian charity taught by the saintly Bernard of Clairvaux (1091-1153) and Francis of Assisi (1182-1226), both of whom had an enormous effect upon the thought of their own and following generations. Like every form of human activity, art was almost wholly penetrated by Christian doctrine. Its very existence depended upon its answer to the all-embracing question of man's relation to God. The realistic painting of the late Middle Ages was created to enhance, by every means of sympathetic indentification, the sacred images, the Madonnas and the Saints, and to declare their reality in a more compelling and sympathetic manner by appealing to the feelings of those who beheld them. Thus a sacred picture was constructed in a new way that gave expression to the material structure of the Christ-Child's body, the construction of the chair upon which His mother sits, and the landscape seen through the window. But the new method of painting also implied a fatal split between spiritual and material reality, between the worldly and the other-worldly. The pleasure and satisfactions of the senses do not necessarily contribute to the revelations of Christian doctrine. Since illusionistic art as opposed to symbolic art speaks through the senses, a dualism developed in which the borderline between the religious function of painting and the secular intent of the artist became blurred at a time when the religious use of art was a paramount consideration. From this period on, secular and sacred elements are intermingled components of art. In the Middle Ages art was not regarded in the same light as it is today, as having relevance to every aspect of life and as a self-justifying activity. Only in rare instances was it revered for its own sake, collected by enthusiasts or exhibited. Its value and usefulness, however, were fully recognized by the Church, and even the most realistic details (cf. Fig. 375) were understood to signify spiritual values.

The historian Huizinga says of the late mediaeval times, "All life was saturated with religion to such an extent that the people were in constant danger of losing sight of the distinction between things spiritual and things temporal. If, on the one hand, all details of ordinary life may be raised to a sacred level, on the other hand, all that is holy sinks to the commonplace, by the fact of being blended with everyday life. In the Middle Ages the demarcation of the sphere of religious thought and that of worldly concerns was nearly obliterated."

At the end of the mediaeval period in fifteenth-century France and Flanders, there was a tremendous passion for pictorial images. Gorgeous pageants were contrived, and elaborate costumes; realistic pictures and statues abounded. As if to assure meaning to life, all activities were formalized—love into a fantastic code, honor into a ritual. The idea of the Trinity was conceived in tangible form and reduced to a mere plaything in statuettes of the Virgin which opened up to reveal the figures of the Godhead inside. Jean Fouquet, one of the greatest French artists even went so far as to paint the king's mistress as the Virgin, fashionably clothed and offering her bared breast to the Christ Child.

Though this symbol-making was a symptom of the decline of faith, it had positive results of great significance to art. At its best it produced the sculptures of Claus Sluter (cf. Fig. 306) and the paintings of the van Eycks. At its worst it produced tedious and vulgar literature, ingenious toys, and empty rituals. Although religion was in danger of becoming a travesty and public and private morals a scandal, the means had been found for the beginning of a realistic art. The painting of this period in northern Europe is sometimes called *primitive*, because it marks the beginning of realistic art; but it is primitive only in that it is a beginning. It has also been termed decadent, for it marks the end of the mediaeval epoch; but this ignores its amazing vigor in the hands of a few masters. Its significance lies in the fact that though the ages of faith were coming to an end, the northern culture had the vitality to establish firmly a tradition of naturalism which, fused with the Renaissance tradition of Italy, was to create an integrated style.

The impulse to seize the image of things and, by representation, make them part of the mind that perceived them came to a focus in the Burgundian court of the Duc de Berry. He surrounded himself in the early years of the fifteenth century with numerous artists, particularly the greatest book illuminators of his time. Among them was Pol de Limbourg, who with his brothers Herman and Jehannequin painted the illustrations for the *Trés Riches Heures du Duc de Berry*. The Book of Hours is a collection of prayers, psalms, and lessons for the layman's devotions and includes a calendar of church festivals, saints' days, and the like. The calendar pages of the Limbourg Book of Hours have vividly realistic landscapes such as the world had never seen. Never before had men recorded so faithfully and vigorously the spectacle of common things. Freed from abstract and traditionalized ecclesiastical subjects and rules, the artists pay abundant homage to the joy of sensual experience. The months are illustrated by scenes of common activity peculiar to the season. June, for example, shows men with scythes slashing wide paths through the tall grass and two barefoot girls with rake and fork piling the dried grass into small stacks. The windows of the Duke's castle look out toward Paris; through the distance winds the river Seine, with the Ile de la Cité and its edifices, some of which may still be seen after more than five hundred years.

With lively interest these painters represent *February* (Fig. 372) by a farmyard with deep snow covering the ground and the roof of the sheepfold that is full of huddling sheep. All creatures are cold: the sheep seek the communal warmth of their own wool, the girl blows on her frosty hands, the woman and the two children in the shelter lift their wet garments and warm their bare bodies at the fireside. The artists have missed nothing; they see the row of beehives, the crinkly branches of the barren tree, the woodsman, and the peasant plodding through the heavy snow driving a donkey laden with firewood. In spite of this great wealth of narrative detail, there is no crowding or confusion. And if proper perspective is slightly lacking, it is scarcely noticed in the vivid rendering of the details. Though done on a scale no larger than the page of this book, these landscapes are among the first in painting.

Musée Condé, Chantilly.

FIG. 372. Limbourg brothers, February, from the
Très Riches Heures du Duc de Berry (1413-1416).

St. Bavon's Church, Ghent.

FIG. 373. Hubert and Jan van Eyck, Adoration of the Lamb, part of
The Ghent Altarpiece (1432).

The symbol of active man shaping the physical character of the world he dominates by the strength of his hand has been achieved and will be echoed again and again in later art. In earlier illuminations the landscape was stylized (Fig. 369) or the figures were placed against a flat gold background. But the Limbourgs definitely abandoned that tradition in favor of greater naturalism.

The significance of this innovation was far-reaching. In the school of book illumination to which it belongs were educated the greatest Flemish masters of the fifteenth century—Hubert van Eyck (*ca.* 1370-1426) and his brother Jan (*ca.* 1385-1440). It is possible that Hubert van Eyck was the painter of miniatures which for knowledge of the effect of atmosphere on the

appearance of distant objects surpassed even those of the Limbourgs. It is certain that the van Eyck brothers painted the great Altarpiece in St. Bavon's Church in Ghent, Belgium, a framework of pictured panels that swing open like doors to reveal the central subject. Begun by Hubert, it was completed after his death by Jan in 1432.

Painting a large alterpiece for public display requires a method somewhat different from that used for tiny book pictures. The van Eycks could not simply enlarge the miniatures because tradition dictated an exacting formula for altar pictures. The subject was of prescribed religious character and had to be treated with appropriate dignity. In the Ghent Altarpiece it is apparent that the van Eycks departed from the usual manner of the book illuminators. The central part of it is the *Adoration of the Lamb* (Fig. 373); the subject is taken from the Apocalypse, "And I looked, and Lo, a Lamb stood on the Mount Sion" (Rev. xiv, 1). In a deep landscape, the Lamb, symbol of Christ's sacrifice for human salvation, stands upon an altar that is part of the Fountain of Life. Large groups of martyrs, prophets, sibyls, judges, and knights have come to witness this proof of God's love. The observer sees at once the richness of the painting and the great detail in the garments, individual faces, and even flowers in the grass. But the perspective is not arranged so that all things appear as if seen from a single point of view. It is rather as if van Eyck had placed several groups of spectators together and was not concerned about their being unified in atmosphere and perspective. This lack of unity results from the fact tht the mediaeval painter is interested chiefly in subject matter and less in how its forms are handled with regard to the atmosphere, landscape, and so on. As in the miniatures of the Limbourgs, the pictures are built up by the addition of thousands of details. Consequently the eye is somewhat bewildered by the profusion of objects, all of which are rendered with arresting distinctness in brilliant colors. The van Eycks employed a technique much like oil painting and with it produced effects never surpassed for luminous richness. It is the incredibly transparent greens, the lustrous reds, and the crystal whites which give authenticity and unity to the picture and compensate for the pinched uncorrelated space effects. To the mediaeval mind every object in the world had a peculiar significance and radiance by virtue of being a divine creation. The mediaeval artist declared this quality or content, sometimes at the expense of aesthetic coordination and unity. About twenty separate panels comprise the altar, some of which are related to adjoining scenes; the majority however, are treated as isolated parts. Although later ages aimed at a more logical and unified pictorial treatment, the still mediaeval painter of the Ghent Altarpiece remained content with an aggregate of kindred subjects symbolically held together by the enveloping landscape.

St. Bavon's Church, Ghent.

FIG. 374. Jan van Eyck, Adam and Eve, part of The Ghent Altarpiece.

The concept of space is implicit in the term landscape, whence it follows that in providing such a setting for the Adoration of the Lamb, Jan van Eyck must have had a specific sense of its significance. At first glance, the *Adam and Eve* (Fig. 374), also from the Ghent Altarpiece but in the upper row, might seem to contradict this. Nude and awkward, the figures symbolize humanity fallen from grace yet still hopeful of salvation through the mystery of the blood of the Lamb. The artist has spared no detail of appearance. The torsos and limbs are a pasty white, whereas the normally exposed hands and faces are weathered and brown. The toes of Adam's right foot, seen from below, curl up in unconscious reaction to the chill of the stone floor. Apart from this, the figures are starkly motionless, fixed in a scheme that derives its essential meaning from the effect of the whole rather than from details. These symbols of mankind are observed and described with the same emotionless detachment that characterizes the minutiae of flowers and stones and animals which are also part of the universe created by the Deity and so partake of the Divine.

But the figures are something more than inanimate and devoid of spirit. And characteristically, to suggest their increased significance in the late mediaeval scheme of things, Jan van Eyck had recourse to the idea of space surrounding them. It is not deep as in the landscape of the Mystic Lamb; it is only sufficient to give relief to the shadows cast on the curving surfaces of the niche-like recesses. But this is enough to establish the forms as three-dimensional. If they stand in rapt immobility, almost like stone figures on a Gothic portal (cf. Fig. 301) on the verge of becoming human, it is because they symbolize humanity that is still in a state of elemental simplicity.

In 1434, two years after the Ghent Altarpiece was dedicated, Jan van Eyck did another painting in which a man and a woman play an important part, the portrait of *Jan Arnolfini and His Wife* (Fig. 375). It is easy to understand from it why the portrait becomes a major pictorial type in van Eyck's hands. Earlier mediaeval artists had occasionally represented specific individuals, but they were usually so identified by symbols or inscriptions. Like his fellow Fleming, Claus Sluter (cf. Fig. 306), Jan van Eyck searches for and finds the telling characteristics of appearance that are the individual. The shrewd and calculating Arnolfini clasps the hand of his bride. A handsome chandelier above them contains a single lighted candle which symbolizes the presence of God, invoked in the oath that was part of the marriage vows. The ceremony is witnessed by the friend of the couple and the painter of their portrait, Jan van Eyck; we see him in the mirror behind the couple, and his name is written above on the wall in elaborate official script as a participant in the rites.

Everywhere is evidence of the painter's sharp eye for detail and his skill in recording it. The texture of the fur trimming and the heavy brocade, the gleam of the brass chandelier, and the dark grain of the carved wooden bed—all are more vivid than if they were actually before us. Even the ten scenes from the Passion of Our Lord in the tiny medallions of the mirror frame can be identified. To the interest always inherent in such faithful accuracy the man of the fifteenth century added a general understanding of many of these forms as symbols, allegorical concepts that have meaning beyond and above their intrinsic character. The little dog, for example, represents fidelity to the pledges made by the couple; and a figure carved on one of the bedposts is St. Margaret, invoked by brides. Not to be overlooked, either, is the importance of the oil technique with its nuances of tone, depth of color, and precision of texture and detail in enabling these effects to be realized.

The symbolism of the Arnolfini portrait may easily pass unnoticed and ununderstood today, and photography may equal its veracity of detail; yet its popularity in the National Gallery in London testifies to the spell it never fails to cast over the spectator. Neither arcane meaning nor verisimilitude of appearance is responsible for the feeling of light-filled space that envelops these forms. From the window at the left, the light falls on a piece of fruit on the sill, touches the rosary beads as it diffuses over the wall, is reflected from the mirror and strikes highlights from the chandelier, glows in the transparent green of the bride's gown, and is lost in the shadows of the tester bed. It pervades the whole room and gives life to its space—space which does more than merely provide room for the forms as in the Adam and Eve of the Ghent Altarpiece; it is the pictorial expression of the spiritual essence that gives significance to all things. The Gothic feeling for intangible space so powerfully exploited in cathedral architecture now finds further expression in painting, giving significance to isolated objects as the structure of the cathedral gave meaning to the carved figures adorning it.

Among the many artists that followed the van Eycks was Rogier van der Weyden (1400-1464). His *Descent from the Cross* (Fig. 376) done

FIG. 375. Jan van Eyck, Jan Arnolfini and His Wife (1434).

Prado, Madrid.

FIG. 376. Rogier van der Weyden, Descent from the Cross (*ca.* 1435).

about 1435 shows a command of minute detail comparable to Jan van Eyck's, and in giving the impression of a group of figures in a niche suggested by the Gothic tracery in the angles it shares the van Eyck impulse to modernize cathedral art. His figures, however, do not have the immobile objectivity of the Arnolfini portrait, but are moved by powerful emotion. Possibly the difference is indicated by the idea that Jan van Eyck's figures suggest their reality as spiritual entities by their impassivity, whereas Rogier's are emphasized as psychological entities. Their feelings are as real as their forms and are suggested in some measure by descriptive devices such as tearful faces and tortured expressions. But what might have been clinical definitions of emotional disturbance are generalized by the simple yet subtle color scheme and by the abstract stylization of the friezelike arrangement and the suggestion of architectural setting.

Rogier van der Weyden was the only great Flemish master of the mid-fifteenth century known to have visited Italy. It is significant that only an occasional compositional motive from his Italian experiences found its way into his personal style, apart from the restrained sweetness that characterizes his late paintings. A whole generation of younger artists, notably Hans Memling, exploited this for purposes quite different from Rogier's.

The northern masters painted small pictures for the most part because the Gothic style of architecture provided no large wall surfaces like those found in Italy. Of interest was the result when an Italian patron demanded of Hugo van der Goes (active 1465-1482) a large *Nativity* (Fig.

377) broad enough to fill the wall space of a good-sized living room. In comparison with Italian painting of its time, it appears to lack unity and order. We seem to see the Madonna from one distance, the angels from another. The eye is first engaged by the angels and the still-life of irises and columbine in the vases. Then, putting two and two together, we see that the people, the angels, the shepherds, and the Virgin form an adoring circle about the Holy Child lying naked upon the rude pavement. By conventional standards the picture is in truth a series of brilliant fragments, but fragments fraught with the most intense and poignant feeling. When the donor Tommaso Portinari presented it to a

Florentine hospital in 1476, it was the despair of all the Italian masters who flocked to see it, for they had never seen such vivid realism or delicacy in drawing combined with astonishingly brilliant colors. Their Madonnas had not been given such homely features alight with lyrical tenderness. And never had their art shown such uncouth, horny-handed fellows as the shepherds—these genuine peasants gaping with loutish adoration at the Babe.

The presence of this large and notable northern painting in Florence was one of many incidents of contact between northern Europe and Italy. The impact of Flemish art upon Italian and of Italian upon Flemish continued increasingly during and after the late fifteenth century.

Uffizi, Florence.

FIG. 377.   Hugo van der Goes, Nativity, part of The Portinari Altarpiece
(*ca.* 1475).

*National Gallery of Art, Washington, D.C.,
Mellon Collection.*

FIG. 378.   Memling, Virgin and Child
(*ca.* 1490).

The Italians profited from a demonstration of brilliant craftsmanship in color and drawing. In turn the Northerners benefited from the Italian's capacity to organize plastically and psychologically. A comparison of van der Goes' *Nativity ca.* 1475 with Leonardo's *Adoration* of 1481 (Fig. 416) suggests the divergent aims of the two schools as well as their common dedication to the concrete and specific.

Of all the early Flemish masters perhaps Hans Memling (*ca.* 1430-1494) is the most generally popular. He was no investigator or pioneer but, working in the latter half of the fifteenth century, he took advantage of the achievements of the age, and summed them up in a style that has considerable sweetness and

sentiment. The portrait of Barbara and Willem Moreel in Brussels and another in Bruges, with portraits of their numerous offspring suggest the quality of his painting. Unself-conscious sentiment delicately expressed, comparable to that of the *détente* in France (cf. Fig. 308), is the keynote of his most individual work. The requirements of theological exposition called for elaborate and complex narrative which often taxed his limited capacity, but in intimate portraiture and in the treatment of the Virgin and saints he attains a lyrical expression that has to a large degree become popularly identified with all of early Flemish art. The charm of his *Virgin and Child* (Fig. 378), done about 1490, is undeniable even when the simplified surfaces and rhythmic movement of line are recognized as a popularization of the work of more creative masters like Rogier van der Weyden. Memling's art poses no problems and creates no difficulties. His vision of saints and holy ones has something in common with Fra Angelico's, although lacking the Italian master's passion and sustained purity.

The final phase of the waning Middle Ages in the Netherlands is scarcely suggested by Memling's deliberate narratives or his lyrical portraits and Madonnas. There are depths of experiences yet to be recorded. Jerome Bosch (1450-1516) and Quentin Massys (*ca.* 1465-1530) did much to reveal the temper of their age and its culture. Both were cosmopolitan in their own way, Massys responding to the art forms that emanated from Italy and Bosch creating pictorial and psychological types that are as valid today as when he painted them in the late fifteenth and early sixteenth centuries.

Unlike Memling, Bosch presents spectacles of almost incredible horror. The Middle Ages produced minds of the most humane and balanced character but it also frequently inflicted a terrorism unrivaled in history. Bosch lifts the veil from the shadowy nether world of creeping, writhing, tortured beings. No misshapen monstrosity is loathsome enough to convey his conception of the seven deadly sins. He invents a thousand diabolical creatures combining features of man, beast, and bird to illustrate the psychological hell of man's depravity. We must not

The Art Museum, Princeton University.

FIG. 379.   Bosch, Christ Before Pilate (*ca.* 1505).

suppose that Bosch was merely a cataloguer of mediaeval superstitions, an illustrator of neurotic and psychotic personalities of his day. Although occasionally he masses vast amounts of material with studied disregard for continuity and cohesion, in most instances he proves himself a master of pictorial invention. Like that pioneer in the cinema, David W. Griffith, he employs the close-up to increase the effectiveness of his psychological study. He learned to relate small dramatic figures with a dominant landscape before anyone else did. His peculiar genius is for observing human behavior, without malice or condescension but with searing lucidity. The *Christ Before Pilate* (Fig. 379) in the Princeton University Art Museum, painted about 1505,

makes it clear that the horrors in Bosch's art are no inventions of a morbid mind but actualities based on man's ever-constant capacity for suffering torment and inflicting it. The greatest tortures are of the mind and the most excruciating are those inflicted for official expediency. The terrible complacence of the Pharisees and the dour habitual gesture of Pilate are manifestations of naked power more chilling than the overt brutality of the soldiers or the insane shrieks of the mob. Bosch makes no attempt to make Christ dominate; in fact, He cowers numbed before the torrent of malediction. What Bosch has given us, in this demonstration of the warping and perversion possible to human nature, is the spectacle of a Gestapo court, a lynching party.

Museum, Antwerp.

FIG. 380.   Massys, Deposition (1511).

Sometimes such scalding revelations by their very shock bring into focus moral issues too often left untouched in expressions of the noble and heroic. As a superb master of irony, as an analyst of man's basest and noblest impulses, as a landscapist and recorder of the common man, Bosch had wide influence. He became the spiritual guide to Bruegel later in the century.

Quentin Massys, who also worked at the turn of the century, is a more conventional artist in the tradition of Hugo van der Goes and Rogier van der Weyden which he broadens and heightens with close-knit patterns enriched with color that becomes strong, singing, and sustained with dramatic force. In pointing up the dramatic and integrating psychological elements of design, Massys parallels the mood of his Italian contemporaries, Leonardo and Botticelli. His *Deposition* (Fig. 380), part of an altarpiece done in 1511, owes much to Rogier's earlier version (Fig. 376).

But comparison with a similar subject painted about the same time in Italy—Perugino's Lamentation (Fig. 411)—provides a significant clue to the relation between these two dominant schools.

The rhythmic harmonious patterns of Perugino's Christ are opposed to Massys' painfully disposed figure. The poignant suffering of the others so deeply studied by Massys is handled more broadly by the Italian. The silhouette of landscape tellingly integrated with the figures in both paintings is characteristic of each. Yet for all the differences it is apparent that both masters are approaching the sustained psychological and formal equilibrium that is called classic. Massys with his heightened feeling for psychological phrasing goes beyond his Italian contemporaries in dramatic vigor and foreshadows the tumultuous art of Rubens and the psychological penetration of Rembrandt in the seventeenth century. But Massys' art is reticent even in sensational themes like Salome's Dance and the Martyrdom of St. John the Evangelist, two subjects treated in the wings of the altarpiece just mentioned. His faces somehow stay in the memory, haunting and deeply human.

Massys and Bosch together typify the tradition of artistic Flanders before that country was engulfed by a flood of Italian imitators. The authority and vitality of the Middle Ages were drawing to a close in all artistic spheres. The new age called for a more cosmopolitan, more systematic art language. From Italy came the impulse to new forms in music, literature, and the plastic arts. English poetry—that of Wyatt and Surrey —the great age of drama in Elizabeth's time, came to fruition through Italian influences. In painting, northern Gothic and classic Italian did not become reconciled in a day and the period of reconciliation was often painfully affected and barren, but in the seventeenth century Flemish art emerged, revivified with Rubens who made Flanders one of the most influential European art centers in that fertile age.

French art in the fifteenth century is so closely related to Flemish as to be almost indistinguishable from it at times. Jean Fouquet (*ca.* 1415-1482), one of the many gifted Frenchmen of this period, was a prolific illuminator of manuscripts in the Franco-Flemish tradition, and even more celebrated as a portraitist. The international character of his style foreshadowed the interaction between north Europe and Italy which became the rule in the sixteenth century. More sober and abstract than the Flemings, Fouquet readily absorbed the Italian influences for formalization and the subordination of details to large effects. The pinched and meager face of *Charles VII* (Fig. 381), finely modeled, emerges from the flat schematic drapery of the curtain and costume in an unforgettable pattern. He is Charles *Le Victorieux*, the unhappy weakling whom Joan of Arc made king of France.

The greatest single monument in French painting of the later fifteenth century is undoubtedly the *Avignon Pietà* (Fig. 382), painted by an anonymous master or masters about 1465. The often-repeated theme of the Virgin mourning her dead Son is here treated with sublime pathos.

The large figures and monumental effect of their arrangement indicate the influence of the formal and abstract contemporary Italian style. The main figures are characterized by a noble and ascetic restraint in their mute expressions of grief. The very human donor who kneels at the left plays a significant part both formally and expressively as he shares the grief of the sacred persons imaginatively in his devotion. That a layman should be portrayed so realistically and given such great prominence in a sacred picture indicates the growing importance of the individual in the social and religious thought of the times; in late Gothic sculpture (cf. Figs. 306, 307) there is the same exquisite blend of realism and religious sentiment. The picture is set in a barren landscape, brown and austere, illuminated only by the burnished gold background against which loom the towers of Jerusalem. The use of this gold background (for it can scarcely be called a sky) long after it had been displaced in other styles by realistic landscape is significant of the sophisticated and eclectic character of the painter, who used

Louvre, Paris.

FIG. 381.   Fouquet, Charles VII (*ca.* 1445).

every device he knew to express a mood of deep spirituality. It is thus a product of the various artistic influences current in fifteenth century France, and though stylistically a *tour de force* it is withal a creation of transcendent beauty.

In Germany, in the fifteenth century, the Gothic manner continued at first without being modified by the naturalistic and classic ideas sweeping across Europe. In the *Adoration of the Magi* (Fig. 383) Stephen Lochner (*ca.* 1390-1451) shows no effect of the vigorous Flemish art with which he must have been acquainted. He removes from his subject any concrete reference to a specific place and sets it in an imaginative realm of pure meditation. With sweetness and absorption his Madonna and Magi dwell apart from the intense psychological drama of Rogier

van der Weyden and beyond the passionate world of love and anguish of the Avignon Pietà. The mystical experience of the individual speaks as it does so frequently in German art. In Lochner the mystical vision does not obtain positive expression but lingers in an engaging borderland between myth and fairy tale. Other Germans of this age are bolder and more forthright in exploring the physical—men like Moser, Pacher, and Witz—and they, rather than Lochner, point the way to the emergence of a great school of art in Germany in the sixteenth century.

In many ways, however, the most important Germanic contribution to late mediaeval art was the development of the graphic processes of making prints on paper or textile. One of the earliest examples is the woodcut of *St. Christopher*

Louvre, Paris.

FIG. 382. The Avignon Pietà (*ca.* 1465).

Cathedral, Cologne.

FIG. 383. Lochner, Adoration of the Magi (*ca.* 1450).

(Fig. 384), dated 1423, in the John Rylands Library at Manchester, England. It was stamped with a wood block on whose surface the design was incised by cutting away the areas that were to print white, leaving ridges which caught the printing ink. The mechanical parallel with printing is obvious; and the woodcut process is indeed the counterpart, in the visual arts, of printing which was first developed in Germany around the middle of the fifteenth century. Like printed books, printed pictures involved the use of paper, another technological development of great importance in the fifteenth century.

Woodcuts were very popular from the outset. They were less expensive than paintings, they could be colored, and they served the same devotional purpose as their more costly counterparts. The St. Christopher, for example, is the patron guardian invoked by all who traveled away from home, such as pilgrims. This was apparently the purpose of the print in Fig. 384, for it was found in a prayer book. As a pictorial design, it may seem halting and naïve when compared with contemporary painting (Fig. 373). The perspective is inaccurate, and no attention seems to have been given the scale of the figures. But like

Oriltofon faam die quanumqz tiens ·:·   Millelimo ccc°
3lla nempe die more mala non moriuns ·:·   rr° nnno ·:·ĸ·

John Rylands Library, Manchester.

FIG. 384.   St. Christopher, Woodcut (1423).

the painting of the day, it speaks the language of symbolism rather than of visual fact; and as a design, its pattern of lines is well coordinated in a unified and decorative whole.

Northern fifteenth-century art is a seeming paradox. Reaching unsurpassed heights of spirituality in the Avignon Pietà (Fig. 382), it also expresses in Bosch's Christ Before Pilate (Fig. 379) the breaking down of traditional morality embodied in the teachings of the Church. The period was one of political chaos too—the disastrous Hundred Years' War between France and England, the conquest of the Netherlands by Spain, and the division of Germany into its many separate states. The transition from feudalism to nationalism was characterized by bloody wars and unbelievable violence that laid waste whole kingdoms. The wonder is that, with comparatively little stability of cultral tradition, art flourished at all. When it does appear, it is confined to local schools, sometimes highly abstract as in the German schools, and again surprisingly naturalistic as in Flanders. The provincial isolation of schools was somewhat relieved by the sporadic movement of painters to and from Italy. With the unification of France late in the fifteenth century and its subsequent invasions of Italy, the international trend became increasingly greater until, in the early sixteenth century, Francis I of France, a great patron of the arts, called to Fontainebleau a group of Italian painters, decorators, and craftsmen who formed a school that was a potent factor in unifying the European tradition. The nature of that fusion will be considered in the discussion of Renaissance art.

LATE MEDIAEVAL PAINTING IN ITALY

Painting during the early and high Middle Ages took a somewhat different course in Italy than it did north of the Alps. In those countries, as has been seen (cf. pages 107-108), occurred the remarkable synthesis of mediaeval thought of which the Gothic cathedral is the most monumental and comprehensive artistic statement, and whose expressive ideal pervades the arts of painting and sculpture to an equal extent. Italy witnessed no comparable dramatic climax in the visual arts. Gothic forms were regarded there with suspicion, a point of view ultimately expressed in Italy's invention of the term *Gothic* in the sixteenth century to suggest the barbaric. When the more obvious idioms of Gothic style like the pointed arch and window tracery were employed in mediaeval Italian buildings like the Florentine Palazzo Vecchio (Fig. 111) and the older parts of the Cathedral of Florence, it was rather superficially, without fully understanding their organic implications.

However, unlike its northern neighbors, Italy had inherited an expressive tradition even older than theirs, one that went back to the pagan world of classic antiquity. From top to toe of the peninsula there were countless fragments of Roman art—temples, aqueducts, carved statues. And Italian painters of the Middle Ages had before them the decorations on buildings erected by their Early Christian predecessors, like the mosaics of San Vitale at Ravenna (Fig. 365). As has been seen, the influence of Oriental thought on the stylistic traditions of late antiquity had transformed the inherent naturalism of that manner into the decorative formalism. known as Byzantine. As late as the middle of the

thirteenth century, Italian painters were utilizing the formulas of Byzantine style, as is apparent in a *Madonna and Child* (Fig. 385) by Coppo di Marcovaldo in the church of Santa Maria dei Servi at Orvieto. Painted about 1265, it is nearly eight feet high. The Madonna is seated and holds her Son with her right arm; her left hand supports one of His feet and her head inclines toward Him as she regards the spectator. Posed in this way, the Madonna is the Byzantine *Hodegetria*—"she who points the way." There is little feeling of depth in the painting, either in the figures or in any suggestion of space. Nor is there any immediate impression of feeling or emotion in the forms except for the hieratic dignity found in the earlier religious art of the Byzantine Near East (cf. Fig. 580). The color scheme is simple; the blue of the Virgin's robe is shot through with a weblike pattern in gold and stands out against a gold background enhancing the feeling of unworldly spiritualism created by the symmetrical composition and the gravely dignified expressions of the faces. These characteristics make the painting a *symbol* of her through whom God became man that the world might be saved, even though it tells little about the human feeling or emotion inherent in the concept.

Toward the end of the thirteenth century a significant change is perceptible in the expressive purposes and methods of Italian painting. It is evident in other fields too—in sculpture, for example, in the figures carved by Niccolo Pisano (Fig. 309), and notably in literature. Dante and, a little later, Petrarch and Boccaccio transformed the conventionalized phrases of earlier writing, giving up Latin, the scholar's international

Sta. Maria dei Servi, Orvieto.

FIG. 385. Coppo di Marcovaldo,
Madonna and Child (*ca.* 1265).

language, in the process and expressing their
ideas in the Italian spoken by the people. Something like this also occurred in painting. Forms of
tangible actuality, motivated by understandable
sentiment and feeling, find a place in Italian painting in the very late thirteenth and early fourteenth
centuries, just as they do in the robust naturalistic
narrative prose and lyric poetry of the literature
of the time—the *Divine Comedy*, the *Canzoniere*,
and the *Decameron*.

In his *Madonna Enthroned* (Fig. 386), painted
about 1285 for the church of Santa Trinità in
Florence, Cimabue (*ca.* 1240-1302) presented

a conception clearly dependent upon current
Italo-Byzantine tradition in some respects—for
example, in the plain gold background, the
decorative gold webbing of the Madonna's robe,
and the symmetrically frontal composition. But
the throne is drawn with some feeling for spatial
depth, and the four Old Testament prophets
underneath the arched base increase the monumental dignity of the group above. Even more
striking is the sentiment conveyed by the insistent
appeal to the spectator in the Madonna's eyes.
Her right hand points to her Son, but the inclination of her head and her sideward glance direct
the observer's attention to Him in a specific and
positive way that gives the whole composition
much more immediate meaning than the with-
drawn contemplativeness of the earlier conception (Fig. 385).

In the *Purgatorio* (xi, 94), the second part of
the *Divine Comedy*, Dante speaks of Cimabue as
having been the most distinguished painter of his
day, and then, in talking about the transience of
mortal fame, he says that in his (Dante's) day, it
was Giotto (*ca.* 1266-1336) who was acclaimed by
all. This he well knew, for they were contemporaries and friends. Although he came from a
small village near Florence, Giotto is as completely identified with the city itself, as was his
friend Dante; he attained the distinction of being
master of all its public works in his later years
when he designed the lovely campanile or bell
tower of the Cathedral (Fig. 113). It is primarily
as a painter that he is honored today, however,
and among the earliest works associated with his
name is the fresco, *St. Francis Renouncing His
Worldly Goods* (Fig. 387), in the Upper Church
of San Francesco at Assisi, a small town in the
hill country of central Italy.

The story of Francis of Assisi (1182-1226) is
eloquent testimony of the changing spirit of the
late Middle Ages in Italy. Son of a wealthy man
and profligate in his youth, he renounced all his
earthly possessions and gave himself to the service of God; he established in his native city the
community that became the Franciscan Order in
1223. Both his way of living and his doctrines
preached the brotherhood of man, and his sympathies embraced all nature, even animals and

FIG. 386.   Cimabue, Madonna Enthroned (*ca.* 1285).

San Francesco, Assisi.

FIG. 387.   Giotto, St. Francis Renouncing His Worldly Goods (*ca.* 1296).

trees and flowers. He so vitalized and dramatized the theological scholastic doctrines of the Church that he embodies as few other men do the truly living thought and feeling of the late Middle Ages. Many see in him the origins of the Renaissance itself. Saint Francis is the exemplar of passionate Christian love in practice. Teaching a way of life through the denial of earthly possessions and an affirmation of the kinship of all things, he asserted a pantheistic harmony of temporal and spiritual experience. Through a love focused on this world as Saint Bernard of Clairvaux's was not, he denied the traditional Christian dualism which separates body from soul. Love of birds and beasts, of fire and water, of sun and moon, of men and women, was for him the unifying and humanizing force in the world. It was in no small measure the thought of Saint Francis that swayed the poet Dante and the painter Giotto three-quarters of a century after his death. The vitality of the experience he revealed compelled these masters to explore their own hearts and the world about them, and in so doing to produce a world of images that would be models for centuries to come.

Saint Francis Renouncing His Worldly Goods is one of a series of paintings believed to have been executed by Giotto shortly before 1300 in the Upper Church of the basilica raised over the saint's tomb in the latter half of the thirteenth century. It is a fresco—i.e., painted in a medium something like water color on the wall plaster while it was still damp or fresh (*fresco* in Italian)—of monumental proportions. Planned as part of the decoration of the church nave, it was understandably conceived as an adjunct to the architectural design. But unlike the subordinate role of such architectonic pictorial designs in Early Christian mosaic (Fig. 365) and Gothic stained glass (Fig. 371), the Assisi fresco seems to open into a world of space peopled with actual beings. To be sure, there are still reminiscences of the decorative formalism of an older tradition. The buildings symbolizing the piazza or main square of Assisi where Saint Francis dramatically returned his earthly goods to his father are only symbols and do not pretend to be anything else. But even so, they accent the physical and spiritual separation of the two groups of figures that bulk large in the foreground. On the right is Saint Francis, nude save for the cloak given him by the bishop who stands, almost alone, beside his friend. The saint's gesture reveals the completeness of his renunciation of temporal wealth and power. His father and the other citizens of Assisi, on the left, can hardly believe what is taking place; two small boys in the lower left foreground stoop to pick up stones to hurl at Saint Francis. Such telling naturalistic details are not alone in convincing us that we are seeing an actual incident, for the figures of the protagonists seem to have tangible physical existence. They are bulky and have a notably three-dimensional mass quite unlike the flat forms painted by

Coppo di Marcovaldo (Fig. 385) and Cimabue (Fig. 386).

The remarkable change in the concept of expressive form and the means of establishing it is even more apparent when the *Madonna Enthroned* (Fig. 388) Giotto painted around 1305 for the church of Ognissanti in Florence is compared with the works done by his predecessors. He paints her not as a symbol but to dramatize her compassionate spirit, to make her moral qualities felt and understood by all who viewed his painting, and thereby to command their worship. To establish the reality of these qualities in men's minds, it was necessary to create images which in themselves were persuasively real. In other words, this was the problem: to translate the abstract

Uffizi, Florence.

FIG. 388.   Giotto, Madonna Enthroned
(*ca.* 1305).

ideas of the Middle Ages into readily understandable images of people and situations. The great intellectual refinement of the concepts of life by thirteenth-century scholasticism had placed the essentials of Christianity beyond the grasp of the mass of humanity. The formulas, fixed codes, and systems imposed upon the simple faith of the people had made them spiritually destitute. The appeal of original Christian doctrine lay in its humanizing and dramatizing of the abstract ethical and metaphysical ideas of antiquity; now the time had come when Christianity itself must undergo the same revivification.

Giotto makes his images of angels, Mother, and Child palpable and real by working out a scheme of light and shadow. He arranges the figures so there is space for each tangible form. The sides of the Gothic throne are foreshortened, and the heads of prophets are seen through the side frames. The steps leading to the throne project into space. In all these details, Giotto departs radically from the still Byzantine tradition of Cimabue (Fig. 386) which represents the Madonna as an object of adoration but makes no attempt to interpret what she means in terms of human mercy, love, and compassion. Cimabue could imbue his painting with fervor and express in powerful linear patterns some of the passion of the Romanesque sculptures of the north like the Prophet Isaiah at Souillac (Fig. 297), but his art is static in comparison with Giotto's. There is no life-giving gesture or expression; all the faces are almost exactly alike; the angels stare fixedly at the observer. In Giotto's painting there is great variety among the angels in gesture and feeling. They and the prophets direct their attention toward the Mother and Child as if they, like the spectators, were devotees. This device augments the illusion of spaciousness and vastly heightens the dramatic effect. Where the traditional Byzantinizing masters present static and abstract concepts, Giotto does the opposite. He defines the time, the place, and the circumstance, and thereby permits us to identify ourselves more completely with the figures he represents.

It is this feeling of sympathetic identification that invests his painting of the *Lamentation Over Christ* (Fig. 389) with overwhelmingly intense and profound emotion. It is part of the series of the life of Christ which Giotto painted in fresco about 1306 in the Arena Chapel at Padua in northern Italy, and, with the Avignon Pietà, it is one of the most affecting images of love and death ever created. The forms move in a slow and measured symphony of grief, borne down by the appalling spectacle of the dead Savior. Powerful as the sense of death is, the tragic reverberation of love among the mourners strikes a stronger note. Each responds according to his nature—the women with wailing and despair, the older men with quiet resignation. The Virgin's face is twisted by poignant anguish as she bends low over her Son's still body; she has realized to the full the foreboding expressed in Giovanni Pisano's statue (Fig. 310) on the altar nearby.

The awful intensity of the tragic drama results largely from the organization. The lower space is packed with figures, yet there is no crowding or irrelevant detail; only the elemental necessities of the drama are set forth. The mourners form two rectangular main groups linked by the figure of Christ and the barren ledge of rock sloping down from the right. The body of the Savior forms a unit with the seated women and joins the groups at left and right. We sense at once that these groupings conform to the emotional and psychological attitudes of the people involved. They are the elements of a plan that is perfectly organized to give visual clarity to the composition and articulation to the dramatic content. Christ is not only the psychological motivation for the action, drawing all eyes to Himself, but the plastic core of the formal scheme as well. Even the landscape bends to this universal grief. The descending movement of the sloping rocky ledge terminates in His head, relating the principal elements of the design and directing attention to Him. Through this large pattern of action that is logically and dramatically integrated, the story thus told attains the deep tragic pathos befitting the language of the Scriptures. These massive figures, these gestures and movements, have meaning only insofar as they are consciously organized and directed toward a definite end. Painters of the late Middle Ages in the north were far greater masters of nature than

Arena Chapel, Padua.

FIG. 389. Giotto, Lamentation Over Christ (*ca.* 1306).

Giotto, but never equaled his sense of the underlying rhythm of the emotions or his feeling for the unity of the theme as a whole. They lack the human understanding that gives his figures intrinsic rather than symbolic values.

An eye accustomed to the infinite variety of formal and spatial patterns and the complex colorism of later art may at first find Giotto's frescoes rigid and flat. But more likely the impression will be freshness and unaffected directness of intention. His economy of means is the despair of the would-be emulator. With disarming simplicity he sets forth an involved narrative in the *Raising of Lazarus* (Fig. 390) which is also in the series at the Arena Chapel in Padua. Comparing it with the miniature of the same subject in the manuscript of the Gospels of Otto III (Fig. 369) of about 1000 provides eloquent demonstration of Giotto's achievement as a narrative and dramatic painter. In the older work, the anonymous master presents suggestive symbols of the incident. His interpretation of the legend places the emphasis on Christ's supernatural power, who as if by magic stuns all who witness the feat. To verify the authenticity of the magical act, a spectator obtrusively holds his nose against the stench of the corpse. To Giotto the miracle is not as simple and naïve. His Christ is no performer of amazing feats but a teacher of the way of life. By a grave and authoritative gesture the Lord summons Lazarus from the dead, as He summons the world to a way of life through love. The folk myth has passed through the mind of a great seer to return fresh and revitalized, rational and human.

From the thirteenth century through the sixteenth, the significant centers of creative painting in Italy were Siena, Florence, Rome, and Venice. Of these, Siena was in many ways the most mediaeval. Both the style and the content of its painting refer back to Byzantine traditions of formalized abstraction. But a new quality becomes apparent about the beginning of the fourteenth century, characterized by a degree of naturalism that is consistent with the effective narration of Biblical tales and the expression of delicate feeling. For Siena was a city of almost mystical religious fervor, dedicated to the Madonna and her cult of lofty sentiment; what is new in Sienese painting is still in the service of these ideals.

Duccio di Buoninsega (ca. 1250-ca. 1318) is the Sienese painter in whose work this new quality first appears. In 1311, he completed the front of a great altarpiece for the cathedral in Siena; it represented the Madonna in Majesty, or *Maestà* (Fig. 391) as it has been known ever since. Our Lady holds the Child in a pose adapted from Byzantine models. Nimbed figures, standing or kneeling in rows on either side, are the angels and saints who attend her in Paradise. There is little indication of space; and the figures, which fill the surface to the point of crowding, seem to have no more bulk than silhouettes. But the placing of the golden nimbi and the accenting of the colors of the robes create a decorative rhythm that is almost musical in its gracefulness. The Madonna shares this graciousness, and the Child has a genuinely human quality quite different from the manikins of older art (Fig. 370). Sweetness and humility are positive qualities in Duccio's painting, and make him the effective interpreter of Sienese religious sentiment that he was.

A few years after completing the Maestà, Duccio painted a series of smaller panels to go with it. Some, originally in the frame around the Maestà itself, depict the life of Mary; others on the back recount the life of Christ. A number of these are now in museums elsewhere—the Frick Collection in New York and the National Gallery in Washington, D.C., among others. The *Betrayal of Christ* (Fig. 392) is still with the Maestà itself in the Opera del Duomo, the museum of the Sienese Cathedral. Here, abstract symbols are no longer sufficient, and fresh and sensitive interpretations are embodied in lively narrative. The

Arena Chapel, Padua.

FIG. 390.   Giotto, Raising of Lazarus
(*ca.* 1306).

Opera del Duomo, Siena.

FIG. 391. Duccio, Maestà (1311).

Christian epic not only must be recited, it must be vivified with sympathetic images that appeal to the beholders' hearts. The Betrayal of Christ shows Christ awaiting the kiss by which His friend Judas identifies Him among His disciples in the Garden of Gethsemane. Christ in the center turns toward the traitor as his followers flee. The sky is still a flat gold surface in the Byzantine manner. The landscape is a barren hill slope, dotted with trees; there is only enough of it to give the figures a general location. The trees are stylized shapes silhouetted against it, with little natural quality, but they are effective decorative accents in characterizing the drama—one above Peter who is cutting off the ear of the high priest's servant, one above the Savior, and a third that is an implacable barrier between Him and his faithless friends. The figures, although highly generalized, are characteristic in their gestures. Typical, too, is the sharp gold band that edges Christ's blue robe in a lively linear pattern that also sets off the dominant person

in the tableau. This decorative calligraphy of garment folds and contours is characteristically Sienese.

Duccio, the first master of the school, was followed by other superb artists, notably the brothers Ambrogio and Pietro Lorenzetti, and Simone Martini. Pietro Lorenzetti, active *ca.* 1320–*ca.* 1348 suggests the diversity of Sienese painting and its problems. The triptych done in 1342 representing the *Birth of the Virgin* (Fig. 393) indicates the current predilection for narrative. In a Gothic house with the front walls removed, he presents the domestic drama of the birth chamber and the adjoining room where Joachim eagerly awaits information. Here the artist is seeking an interior space commensurate with the figures. This planning of pictorial space is the same problem the Flemish masters faced in the next century; it was a major consideration of painters for centuries to come. The way the Sienese master meets the problem is indicative of the aesthetic approach of the whole school. The

Opera del Duomo, Siena.

FIG. 392.   Duccio, Betrayal of Christ (*ca.* 1318).

perspective construction of the rooms is only approximated. Our eyes, accustomed to later and more naturalistic examples, are conscious of discrepancies like the tilting floors and the over-large proportions of the mother. But there are exquisite patterns of color, not even suggested in a photograph, that make Pietro Lorenzetti's Birth of the Virgin a supremely beautiful painting. To find a parallel to the stimulating, self-sustained drama of small patterns alternating with broad surfaces, all enriched with interlocking hues in subtle and unexpected relationships, we would have to look to the work of Picasso and Matisse in the twentieth century. And we must recognize as these modern masters themselves have, that they found the inspiration for much of their art in the work of the fourteenth-century Sienese masters.

The achievements of these Sienese masters sometimes seem overshadowed by the more dramatic and naturalistic work of their Florentine counterparts. One of them, however, Pietro Lorenzetti's brother Ambrogio (*ca.* 1300–*ca.* 1348), went beyond any other painter of his time in developing a monumental style in which space is a vital and expressive element. There is reason to believe that he worked for a time in Florence and may have been influenced by Giotto, with whom he shared a particular fondness for fresco painting. This he employed in *The Peaceful City* (Fig. 394), part of a vast mural decoration done in the council chamber of Siena's town hall, the Palazzo Publico, between 1337 and 1340. In its entirety, the theme of the decoration is the contrast between the effects of good and bad government as seen in the life of town and country. Ambrogio's Peaceful City is Siena itself; its streets, squares, and buildings are shown in panorama as if viewed from the lofty bell tower of the Palazzo Publico. Many of the

Opera del Duomo, Siena.

FIG. 393.   P. Lorenzetti, Birth of the Virgin (1342).

buildings in the painting can be recognized today. Even if there are inconsistencies of scale and if systematic space relationships are lacking, there are compensating truths in the portrayal of light effects, and in the delightful genre touches in the many details of everyday life in a busy mediaeval city. Ambrogio's Peaceful City is, in fact, one of the first landscapes in the exact sense of the term. Though part of a work that has symbolic content, it is nonetheless a portrait of a place. But even beyond this, it is significant in indicating a new conception of the expressive function of space in art. In the thirteenth century, the Gothic architect made space a vital element in designing the cathedral. Now, whether in the intimacy of Pietro Lorenzetti's Birth of the Virgin (Fig. 393) or Ambrogio's vista of Siena and its countryside, the fourteenth-century painter senses the meaning of space as a correlating and unifying factor in interpreting experience. Much of what Jan van Eyck achieved in giving expressive power to his concept of nature (Fig. 373) can be traced back to the spatial interests of the Sienese masters.

There is no more convincing proof of the lasting significance of the painting done by the great innovators of the early fourteenth century in Italy—Giotto, Duccio, and the Lorenzetti brothers—than the relatively uninspired achievements of their successors in the latter half of the

Palazzo Publico, Siena.

FIG. 394.   A. Lorenzetti, The Peaceful City (1337–1340).

century. For the pioneers, each problem solved led inevitably to an awareness of more problems that demanded solution. Their followers seemingly exhausted their inspiration with variations, sometimes charming but seldom moving, on the patterns made by the preceding generation. But it was a period of consolidation in which the innovations of the earlier masters became the tradition of those who succeeded them. This is the immediate background of Renaissance painting as it developed in Italy in the fifteenth century.

Detail of Fig. 405.

CHAPTER TWENTY-SIX

Renaissance Painting in Italy

To understand the luxuriant flowering of Italian painting in the fifteenth and sixteenth centuries, the period known as the Renaissance, the influence of Giotto's work must be carefully gauged. He effected a revolution in modes of artistic thought that was echoed in every major work of pictorial art for hundreds of years, for the sober naturalism of his great designs stimulated the imagination of all who saw them. But the sweet color and flat, schematic decorativeness of older mediaeval styles did not disappear at once. Indeed, for more than a century after Giotto, some of the most attractive paintings were created in the old manner. As has been said, Giotto's immediate impact on Florentine painting was not revolutionary; for almost a century after his death it produced nothing comparable to his work. His pupils and disciples repeated again and again the new words and phrases he had given them, embroidering his themes with small essays in realism and perilously complicating his simple and direct space patterns. No one seemed able to use the new instrument of expression Giotto had created except to contrive novel and hollow narratives which at best were no more than ingenious and charming. Even his most competent assistant, Taddeo Gaddi (*ca.* 1300-1366), could take from his master only the lively and picturesque, for he was insensitive to what was central to the main thought. He frequently painted the same themes, and is as prolix, trivial, and confusing as Giotto is terse, pointed, and sober.

THE EARLY RENAISSANCE IN THE FIFTEENTH CENTURY

Well into the fifteenth century, the taste for the vivid hues and gold of older pictorial traditions was current to some extent in Florence. In 1423, when Gentile da Fabriano (*ca.* 1370-1427) painted the *Adoration of the Magi* (Fig. 395), an altarpiece for the church of Santa Trinità, he created a world more like that of the book illuminators of the Gothic north than the one conceived by Giotto. In some ways, the key to its sentiment is the elaborately decorated arches and pinnacles of its architectural frame, which remind us far more of the setting of a mediaeval pageant than the classical arcade of Brunellesco's contemporary Pazzi Chapel (Fig. 114). It encloses a scene crowded with pilgrims, servants, birds and dogs, and the whole retinue of the Wise Men. A thousand small details claim attention. Tucked into a corner, the Virgin, directly descended it would seem from her counterpart in Duccio's Maestà (Fig. 391), unobtrusively receives the homage of the magnificently arrayed Magi. Heedless of any need for logical spacing and rational motivation for the action, the painter tumbles a wealth of detail before our eyes, and endeavors to make evident the splendor of the homage the Christ Child commands. It is like an endless mediaeval romance in which an inexhaustible series of episodes takes the place of a carefully constructed plot. Yet some touches are indicative of a new outlook. The little scene of the Nativity in the predella (the base of the altarpiece as a whole) is a nocturne with gold stars in a deep blue sky, and the Flight into Egypt beside it is set in a landscape that is bathed in the cool clear light of dawn. Realisms like these reveal the period of this painting of Gentile's, even though its prevailing sentiment harks back to a chivalric past.

The religious mysticism and profound devotion of mediaeval forms whose decorative picturesqueness was continued by Gentile da Fabriano in the early Renaissance reechoes in the painting of his slightly younger contemporary Fra Angelico (1387-1455). Born in nearby Fiesole and a member of the Dominican order of San Marco in Florence, Fra Angelico expounded the spiritual values of Christian faith on panel and wall alike in his lifelong service to the Church. Between 1437 and 1445 he painted the *Descent from the Cross* (Fig. 396) for Santa Trinità in Florence, the church where Gentile de Fabriano's Adoration of the Magi was placed. In spite of such obvious similarities as the elaborate frame and the panoramic landscape, there is evidence that Fra Angelico belonged to another school of thought. Christ's body is given tangible and articulated mass, with more than a little indication of anatomical structure, and though this may not be as apparent in the draped figures, they too are forms with perceptible bulk and weight. Also indicative of the painter's interest in the immediate and tangible is the almost portraitlike quality of some of the faces (according to Vasari, the figure wearing a black cap at the extreme right is the architect Michelozzo), and the sensitive characterization of the light that fills the golden green landscape of the background.

For all his gentleness and sweetness, Fra Angelico is never soft or sentimental. His paintings are imbued with passion and strength. Although he may be considered one of the last

Uffizi, Florence.

FIG. 395.   Gentile da Fabriano, Adoration of the Magi
(1423).

mediaevalists because of the sincere religious content of his work, he was equally keenly aware of the reforming developments in the art of his time; it is characteristic that the changing details of Michelozzo's architecture (cf. Fig. 117) are recorded in many of the buildings in the landscapes of his paintings. In frescoes executed by Fra Angelico and his assistants in the monastery of San Marco itself, he shows himself a master of monumental design. In his last years he painted the chapel of Nicholas V in the Vatican Palace at Rome with scenes from the lives of Saints Stephen and Lawrence, an exemplary demonstration of his command of contemporary realistic style.

This contemporary style was an expression of the synthesis that took place in the early Renaissance in a very complex process. This involved, among other things, an almost complete revolution in the thought of the time; it moved toward a rational interpretation of experience as opposed to the intuitional mysticism of the Middle Ages, and called for a wholly new approach to reality. This implies a systematic investigation of the world man knows through his senses, and a correlation of sense impressions with the organized knowledge of science. The artist participated in this revolution. The mediaevalist could dispense with any profound analysis of the physical appearance of the external world

Museo di San Marco, Florence.

FIG. 396.   Fra Angelico, Descent from the Cross (*ca.* 1437–1445).

and, relying upon bright decorative colors and a lively sense of design, express his feelings and convictions without analytical investigation of the forms he saw around him. If he was to paint the kneeling Virgin of the Annunciation, he was satisfied with a credible symbol of the act of kneeling. But the Renaissance painter asked himself what exact physical arrangement of legs and torso was involved in the simple act of balancing the body upon the knees. The physical phenomenon has two coexistent and inseparable aspects, the will and the act. Unless he reveals this dual truth without ambiguity, the artist will fail to express the reality of the experience. This attitude is implicit in the naturalism of the early Renaissance.

The Renaissance study of nature was motivated by a desire to understand and thus control it, and to shape life in accordance with its laws. This is the great meaning that naturalism holds for modern man. Nature had been subordinated for a thousand years, in accordance with the belief that truth had been revealed once and for all in the body of ecclesiastical literature. In the Renaissance, man woke from his long, dogmatic slumber to explore the physical and psychological realities, to discover himself, and to accept the perilous way of a life based upon self-knowledge and science. We speak of the Renaissance world as the modern world because we today are still interpreting the world on the basis of concepts first articulated in fifteenth-century Italy.

Mastery of the physical world in realistic images was a long and difficult process. It was more than a matter of learning to *draw* and *compose* realistically. Images had to be reshaped and reorganized in relation to the artist's inner experience. To a creative artist, there is no such thing as *correct* drawing; it is correct only when the pictorial design is the means of externalizing some real experience. This means of externalizing was made possible in the fifteenth century by basing composition on nature.

Technically, much had to be learned—how to show forms in motion, how to indicate the organically functional structure of the human body, and how to suggest the interaction of atmosphere and color and the blending of colors in light and air. But the problem that seems first to have seized the Renaissance artists' imagination—architects and sculptors as well as painters—was perspective, the device by which a two-dimensional plane is transformed into a visual symbol of three-dimensional space. Although one of the first things taught in art instruction today, the diminution in size of objects the farther they are from the picture plane, and the system of parallel lines that apparently converge as they recede in space were not known, except in a tentative and half-understood way, until the fifteenth century.

In *Herod's Feast* (Fig. 397), a fresco by Masolino da Panicale (1838-*ca*. 1447) in the Baptistery of Castiglione d'Olona in northern Italy, this problem confronted the painter, as it did also his Flemish contemporary Jan van Eyck in the Adoration of the Lamb (Fig. 373). Masolino, a Florentine, benefited from the researches of Brunellesco (cf. page 364) and Alberti, and possibly Ghiberti, for this painting dates from about 1435. If the parallel lines receding in depth in this fresco are extended, they will intersect in a single point, an effect Giotto (Fig. 387) and Pietro Lorenzetti (Fig. 393) apparently sensed

without understanding, and Jan van Eyck was only vaguely aware of. There are other new realisms in Masolino's painting. Although the human forms are not too clearly articulated, they are in scale with the architectural setting which they are quite able to move around in, unlike Giotto's symbolic structures. The architecture is in the style currently in vogue in Florence, like Brunellesco's Pazzi Chapel (Fig. 114) and Michelozzo's Riccardi Palace (Fig. 117); the latter, indeed, may well be the source of Masolino's design for the loggia on the right side. Equally current are decorative details like the *putti* with swags of foliage above Herod's banquet loggia on the left; if not identical with those on the shrine of Donatello's contemporary Annunciation (Fig. 315) in the Florentine church of Santa Croce, they greatly resemble them. In fact, the painting is almost a categorical listing of what was novel and striking in Florentine art early in the fifteenth century. If the spectator is not moved by the horror of the theme that Oscar Wilde and Richard Strauss made into masterpieces of psychological pathology, his eye will be intrigued by space patterns and charmed by the delicate pinks and greens that prevail in the color scheme.

In introducing the more modern aspect of Florentine painting of the early fifteenth century by discussing one of its minor prophets, it is only to emphasize the stature of its giants, first and foremost of whom is Masaccio (1401-*ca*. 1428). Like Giotto he was one of the Florentines who made that city celebrated as the fountainhead of European art. His outstanding work is on the walls of the Brancacci Chapel in the Church of the Carmine in Florence which he decorated in fresco between 1422 and 1427. At first glance these paintings are modest in appearance, and even in Masaccio's own time there were few who fully understood the force of these somber murals. Giotto had all but been forgotten as masters like Masolino and Gentile da Fabriano (Fig. 395) contented themselves with the refinements of Gothic idioms. Not until more than two further generations of fifteenth-century painters had passed was the full force of Masaccio's originality realized.

Baptistery, Castiglione d'Olona.

FIG. 397.   Masolino, Herod's Feast (*ca.* 1435).

In the *Expulsion from Paradise* (Fig. 398) the new spirit in painting is abundantly evident in the spontaneous action, the feeling for actuality and, above all, the dramatic movement. Adam and Eve, thrust from Paradise by the angel with a flaming sword, are two common people with the emotions common to humanity. Eve's tearful lamentation and Adam's withering shame are integral parts of the design of their bodies, which move rhythmically through well-defined space. To understand the harmonious organization of this painting, its broad handling in chiaroscuro,

one should contrast it with the Adam and Eve by Jan van Eyck of Flanders (Fig. 374) painted about the same time. The northerner amazes us by his explicit naturalism; he seems to thrust us into the very room where two graceless Flemings have taken off their clothes in a bright light. The effect is startling but not deeply moving. The Italian master, on the other hand, shapes his figures with light and dark so they exist in deep space and the dramatic meaning becomes apparent without ambiguity. He expresses the feeling for the episode without striking an ingenious illusionism. Italian art is marked by a special talent for treating the human figure systematically by organizing it in broad and rhythmically decorative patterns, an inheritance from the ancient figure art of the Graeco-Roman tradition which was a constant force in the evolution of Italian painting and sculpture. This peculiar background gave these arts a special role in the Renaissance (cf. Fig. 313).

Masaccio demonstrates most compellingly the new outlook of his time in *The Tribute Money* (Fig. 399), the chief fresco in the Brancacci Chapel and the master's greatest single work. The subject, unusual in Christian art, is taken from Matthew xvii, 24-27. A Roman tax gatherer in a short tunic thrusts out his hand, demanding tribute for Caesar. The disciples turn in their dilemma to Christ, who directs Peter to go to the river's edge. At the extreme left Peter finds the money in the mouth of a fish, and at the right he gravely tenders it to the collector. One marvels at the simple ease with which the complex action is narrated. Beside even Giotto's art, that of Masaccio reveals a new freedom. His men seem to stand upon their own feet, to move about freely of their own volition. In Giotto's work men seem to be arranged and placed, and to act less in accord with their impulses than in response to some external compulsion. Technically, by 1427 painting had advanced far toward a rationally understood naturalism. For the first time the action takes place in a deep landscape. The figures, hills, trees, architecture are bathed in atmosphere. *Aerial perspective*, the effect of atmosphere in blurring distant objects, is now understood as well as *linear perspective*, the conducting of the eye into space through converging lines as shown here in the foreshortening of the architecture. In such ways Masaccio creates the effect of space and bulk, and by rounding figures by alternating areas of light and shadow he blends forms together so that they reveal structure and mass. The disciples radiate in a circle about Christ, producing an ample space pattern. Yet with all these innovations, the artist retains Giotto's monumental effects, his dignity and his coherence. All the great Florentine artists —Leonardo, Michelangelo, and Raphael—went

to this little chapel to learn from Masaccio how to gain dignity and simplicity for their own paintings and sculptures.

If Giotto is the father of modern painting, it may be said that the seed of his genius came to a rich harvest in Masaccio and others who followed in the fifteenth century—masters like him in having a rare sense for fixing the ever-fluid surface of nature. By simplification, condensation, and coordination they drew their figures in unforgettable patterns of fine amplitude and force. Among these masters are Paolo Uccello and Piero della Francesca, and, in a later generation, Andrea del Castagno, Andrea Mantegna, and Pietro Perugino. The clean force and simple grandeur of

Brancacci Chapel, Church of the Carmine, Florence.

FIG. 398. Masaccio, Expulsion from Paradise (*ca.* 1427).

Brancacci Chapel, Church of the Carmine, Florence.

FIG. 399.   Masaccio, The Tribute Money (*ca.* 1427).

their work justify the accepted designation of these men as monumentalists. All were students of the new realism, but they are even more significant for their boldness and originality as pictorial designers. Their aim was not so much novelty or accuracy as the life-giving disposition of line and color and mass.

Paolo Uccello (1397-1475) is of the same generation as Masaccio and shared his passionate curiosity about the visible facts of the world around him. His interests were more specialized, however, and ultimately came to focus on the idea mentioned above—perspective. The *Battle of San Romano* (Fig. 400) is one of a series of panel paintings in which he sought to demonstrate his skill in this art, for it was held to be an art in the fifteenth century. A few clashing riders stand out in the foreground on a stage made spacious by foreshortened pikes and weapons pointing inward on the ground, leading the eye back to the hedges and roads slanting up to an apex at the top of the picture. Certain details are acutely observed and faithfully represented—the fencing warriors in the background and the oranges on the trees. Others are somewhat less convincing, like the pawing and prancing horses. But they are here as elements in the organized spatial

volume of the pictorial design rather than as studies in equine anatomy. Regarded as such and not as contributing to a dramatic incident, they are seen to be part of a beautifully integrated decorative scheme drawn directly from observation of the natural world, particularly its limitless space.

Florentine leadership in Italian art of the early fifteenth century has been discussed elsewhere in connection with architecture and sculpture (pages 140, 375); it is equally apparent in painting. Illustrative of this is the distinction achieved in Florence by Domenico Veneziano (*ca.* 1400-1461) whose work before he came there from northern Italy is of only nominal interest but whose inspiration was greatly stimulated in the Tuscan city. The *Madonna with Saints* (Fig. 401), painted about 1445 for the church of Santa Lucia de' Magnoli, shows how understandingly he assimilated the innovations of his adopted environment. John the Baptist might have been taken directly from a figure by Donatello, and the architectural setting is replete with references to current developments in Florence by men like Brunellesco and Michelozzo. His own greatest contribution was an extraordinarily sensitive feeling for nuances of light made possible by his competence in a medium of oil or varnish glazes over tempera that had not been much used before in Florence. The softly luminous pinks and greens created in this medium contribute directly to the mood of quiet contemplation that is the expressive end of the composition.

Another non-Florentine destined to make a definitive contribution to its expressive tradition was Piero della Francesca (1416-1492). At one time he was an assistant to Domenico Veneziano in Florence and shared his feeling for light and color. But his natural gift for pictorial expression was as great as that of any man of the century, and this more than anything else places him in the front rank of the fifteenth-century monumentalists. His knowledge was profound—his treatise on perspective became the standard work—and his taste unfaltering. His frescoes of the Story of the True Cross in the church of San Francesco at Arezzo are notable for their cool reserve and sus-

tained energy and rank among the finest in the world. Portraits, landscapes, battle scenes, and Biblical subjects are handled with deliberation and a very rare feeling for rationally articulated design. His paintings reveal a world in which all action seems suspended in contemplation, peopled by superhuman beings subject to an order that transcends all earthly power. Among the later painters Picasso, who has realized his strength, is most like him. Each is a *natural* painter in the sense that whatever he touches attains some arresting and meaningful character.

The rarefied sphere of Piero's world is defined with monumental impressiveness in the *Resurrection of Christ* (Fig. 402) which he painted about 1465. The risen Savior stands bolt upright in the thin pale light of early dawn, the stark energy of the figure dramatically set forth by the contrasting languor of the slumbering guards. Mystery and passion illumine a face that seems to

National Gallery, London.

FIG. 400.   Uccello, Battle of San Romano (*ca.* 1457).

search a world beyond any known to man. Seldom if ever has an artist so completely expressed the union of the physical and spiritual. Piero was perhaps the most learned and articulate painter of his day. He wrote a number of mathematical treatises in addition to the one on perspective, and during his entire life investigated theories of space forms. The night scene in the Dream of Constantine in the Arezzo frescoes is hardly surpassed for its mastery of mood and illumination. No other Italian painter is so reserved, so deliberate and discriminating, or so deserving of study. Making no concessions to the growing taste for entertaining illustration and picturesque narrative seen in the work of many of his contemporaries who made their art catchalls for random sentimentality and graphic memoranda, Piero ennobled and clarified his art, lifting it to sublime levels of thought and passion.

If Andrea del Castagno (1423-1457) lacks the universality of Piero della Francesca's vision, he nonetheless shares the austere temper of Masaccio and the searching analytical curiosity of the sculptor Donatello (Figs. 314, 316). His *Crucifixion* (Fig. 403), a fresco done about 1450, shows him without Masaccio's native instinct for composition and the handling of light; but his very harshness becomes a virtue when, with peasant-like directness, he shapes the statuesque pillars of saints beneath the awful reality of the slain Christ. In the somber intensity with which the protagonists are characterized, Castagno's Last Supper in the museum (formerly a church) of Sant' Apollonia is one of the most powerful treatments of the theme before that by Leonardo da Vinci.

From Masaccio and Piero della Francesca and Castagno come noble and austere statements of the truths perceived in the analytic and the-

Uffizi, Florence.

FIG. 401. Domenico Veneziano, Madonna with Saints
(*ca.* 1445), part of The Santa Lucia Altarpiece.

Palazzo Communale, Borgo San Sepolcro.

FIG. 402.   Piero della Francesca, Resurrection of Christ (*ca.* 1465).

oretical investigations by which they uncovered the external world. Another and no less important aspect of the process was that stimulated by changing taste and feeling rather than impersonal scientific impulse. The rich industrial and commercial life of Florence bred a worldly leisure class that was keen for the attractiveness of charming faces and picturesque views. As their fortunes became secure, the Florentine patrons of art wanted to enjoy the fruits of their toil. Hence the artist assumed a different role as he indulged that taste for worldly, mundane pleasure. Fra Filippo Lippi (1406-1469) took considerable pleasure in seeing a handsome face. A

Museo di Sant' Apollonia, Florence.

FIG. 403. Andrea del Castagno, Crucifixion (*ca.* 1450).

pretty girl was something intrinsically charming; it was not necessary that she suggest the exalted loveliness of the Mother of Sorrows. Conventions still restricted him; that is to say, like other painters he was commissioned to paint altarpieces and wall decorations for churches. But in these paintings he gave free reign to his own spontaneous feelings and sentiment. His *Madonna and Child* (Fig. 404) in the Uffizi Gallery which dates about 1450 is not a Saint and the Holy Infant, not even an abstract symbol of maternity—none of these; it is no more than a portrait group of an attractive girl, a robust bambino, and a ragamuffin pertly masquerading as an angel, with a nod to convention in the almost invisible nimbus above the mother's head. In spite of its ostensible subject, this is no

religious painting but a naturalistic and mundane rendering of the way such people looked in Florence shortly before the middle of the fifteenth century. As if to underscore his interest in optical veracity, Filippo Lippi placed the group in front of a window that opens on to a landscape in which recognizable features of Florence's River Arno are clearly portrayed.

Such art is a reminder that the Church itself was beginning to hold more secular views as well as that there was a growing society rich enough to bid against it for the talents of artists. But more important still, it indicates the breadth of the humanistic base upon which the thought of the century was developing. The lively, prosaic imagery of Filippo Lippi deeply colored the

FIG. 404.   Filippo Lippi, Madonna and Child (*ca.* 1450).

Medici-Riccardi Palace, Florence.

FIG. 405. Benozzo Gozzoli, Journey of the Magi (1459),
Detail of the Chapel.

stream of Italian painting. He was one of the first artists to make his religious figures wholly realistic, presenting them in the current fashions of dress and coiffure. Common they may be, but they are never shallowly conceived or carelessly drawn. The artist's wife was the model for his Madonna, their son for the infant Savior. This son, Filippino Lippi, became popular as a painter in the latter half of the century, carrying on his father's style of painting with increasing sentiment and overembellishment of detail and dramatic incident. The floodgates of secular narration flew open after the middle of the century.

Much of the art of this period is popular, descriptive, and often superficial. An elaborate parade is the theme used by Benozzo Gozzoli (1430-1497), a one-time pupil of Fra Angelico, in the *Journey of the Magi* (Fig. 405), a fresco on one wall of the chapel in the Medici-Riccardi Palace in Florence (Figs. 116, 117). Painted in 1459, it is really a souvenir of a splendid procession honoring a visiting Oriental potentate which Gozzoli had seen in his youth; the religious subject is only a pretext for celebrating the faces, wealth, and power of the Medici family, the ruling Florentine dynasty and his patrons. Obviously the worldly mood of this new culture had little in common with the soul-searching of the earlier masters. Charmingly illustrative as it is, and decorative and popular, this art reflects the knowledge gained by more original minds but adds little to it.

After the middle of the century, new interests mark the work of the imaginatively creative artists of major caliber, notably a different understanding of the art of classic antiquity. This too is not limited to painting; Leon Battista Alberti's architecture (cf. Fig. 119) is characterized by the same spirit. It is particularly evident in the painting of Andrea Mantegna (1431–1506), who obtained his artistic training in the north Italian city of Padua. There he must have seen frescoes by Giotto in the Arena Chapel (Figs. 389, 390) and sculptures by Donatello in and near the church of Sant' Antonio (Fig. 317). Indeed, it may well have been his study of such earlier art that gave rise to Mantegna's enthusiasm for classic forms. In the *Judgment of St. James* (Fig. 406, one of a series of frescoes he painted between 1448 and 1457 in the Ovetari Chapel of the Church of the Eremitani in Padua, he dwells

Ovetari Chapel, Church of the Eremitani, Padua.

FIG. 406.   Mantegna, Judgment of St. James (1448–1457).

Gonzaga Palace, Mantua.

FIG. 407. Mantegna, Ceiling of the
Camera degli Sposi (1474).

upon ancient themes—classical architecture and statuesque figures. The precise definition of forms and the marvelously crisp and intricate details remind us of those in an imperial Roman relief like the Tellus from the Ara Pacis (Fig. 285), and the triumphal arch in the background could hardly have been conceived without knowledge of some such monument as Constantine's arch in Rome (Fig. 287). Even the figures, including himself as a Roman soldier at the extreme left, are sharply drawn as to costume, yet the details are so rigorously subordinated in the stable composition that no confusion results. The story or drama is indeed directed and articulated by the architectural setting.

Although the pronounced classicism of Mantegna's art may seem an academic trait to the twentieth century, it was a significant and imaginative innovation in its own time. His venturesome experimentation led him into still other fields, notably the study of perspective. Certain of the frescoes in the Ovetari Chapel series employ what is known as "frog's-eye"

perspective because everything seems to be high above the observer's head. Much the same conception underlies the novel decorations Mantegna painted in 1474 for the bridal chamber in the ducal palace of the Gonzaga family in Mantua, the *Ceiling of the Camera degli Sposi* (Fig. 407), as it is called. The flat surface has been painted away, and we have the illusion of looking through an actual opening at sky and clouds and birds and people, even mischievous children climbing over and through the open-work balustrade. The effect anticipates Correggio (Fig. 438) and the baroque masters of the seventeenth century. This ceiling and the great Dead Christ in the Brera Galley in Milan, in which the body is drawn extremely foreshortened as if looking from between the feet toward the head, only begin to suggest the range and depth of Mantegna's genius. Except for Piero della Francesca, there is scarcely a more penetrating intellect or a surer hand in the fifteenth century. He was one of the first and greatest Italian engravers; the wide circulation of his prints did much to disseminate the Renaissance spirit, notably north of the Alps where Albrecht Dürer's study of them gave him his first impressions of the intellectual and artistic ferment that was the Italian Renaissance.

It is impossible to overstate the importance of the graphic arts of woodcut printing and metal engraving as a means of communicating ideas in the fifteenth century. One of the most important examples is the *Ten Fighting Nudes* (Fig. 408), a print made from a metal engraving by the Florentine Antonio Pollaiuolo (1429-1498) about 1475. It is certain that Dürer knew this print, for he adapted many of its details to his own expressive ends. In its own right, it indicates that the later fifteenth-century masters continued the interest shown by their predecessors like Masaccio and Donatello in the anatomy of the human and other natural forms. Pollaiuolo himself, it will be recalled, was also a sculptor. His statuette of Hercules and Antaeus (Fig. 320) reveals the same interest in the dramatic nude in action as the engraving does. The well-defined muscular structure of the figures is the creation of a systematic investigator of anatomy, but their pattern

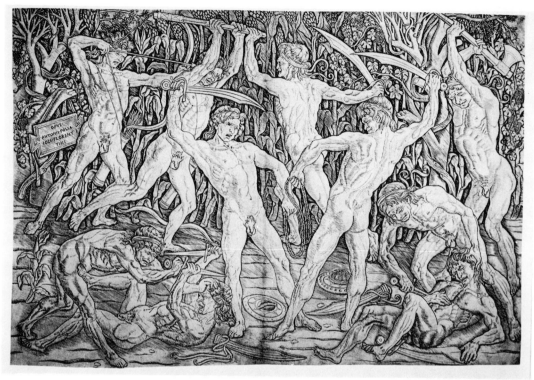

FIG. 408.   A. Pollaiuolo, Ten Fighting Nudes, Engraving (*ca.* 1475).

against the interwoven trees and foliage of the background is equally the manifestation of the artist's instinctive sense of decorative design.

Domenico Ghirlandaio (1449-1497) is the most accomplished exemplar in Florentine painting of the later fifteenth century of the descriptive naturalism given currency earlier by Filippo Lippi and Benozzo Gozzoli. He was a remarkably prolific artist—he is said to have expressed the wish that the entire city wall of Florence could be given him to decorate! The quality of his art is well brought out in a Biblical series he painted in the choir of Santa Maria Novella; ostensibly episodes from the New Testament, they are in reality elaborately gossipy accounts of life and manners in Florence late in the century. In one scene, supposedly the Visitation, Mary and Elizabeth are given the likeness of two ladies of a well-known Florentine family; they meet and embrace in a still identifiable place overlooking

the Arno, with the Palazzo Vecchio and other buildings in the background that can still be seen in Florence. The lively Flemish naturalism of Hugo van der Goes' great Adoration of the Shepherds (Fig. 377) which Tommaso Portinari brought to Florence for the Hospital Church of Santa Maria Nuova only stimulated Ghirlandaio's natural predilection for copious illustration. The current flair for enumeration of casual detail is evident in the *Last Supper* (Fig. 409) he painted for the church of Ognissanti in Florence in 1480. The theme did not inspire him to an unusual design; instead he used the traditional arrangement of a long table with Christ and eleven disciples on one side and the betrayer Judas alone on the other, merely embroidering it with casually selected naturalistic details. He gives a good deal of attention to the monastery garden outside with birds sweeping through the air—but the tragic quality of the theme entirely escapes him.

Ognissanti, Florence.

FIG. 409. Ghirlandaio, Last Supper (1480).

The disciples sit like stolid guests at a boring banquet, seemingly unaware of the Savior's fateful words.

At first glance, the *Miracle of the True Cross* (Fig. 410) by Gentile Bellini may seem no more than the Venetian equivalent of the descriptive naturalism that pervades Ghirlandaio's Florentine chronicles. Signed and dated 1500, it represents a legendary incident that occurred during one of the picturesque festivals so much loved by Venetians, when a heavy reliquary was dropped by its bearers while crossing a canal bridge but miraculously floated until it was recovered. Gentile does not ask us to take this seriously any more than Filippo wishes us to believe that his Madonna (Fig. 404) is anything but an engaging Florentine damsel. Many of Gentile's Venetian contemporaries are represented in the guise of spectators, and the architecture of the buildings is as carefully studied as in Ghirlandaio's frescoes in Santa Maria Novella. The composition is beautifully organized in terms of space, and thanks to the softly vibrant colors used in the painting, its atmosphere is flooded with luminous light like that seen in Venice occasionally even today. Where Ghirlandaio was content with prosaically listing the things that might be seen in a given context, Gentile Bellini conveys something of the wonder and charm of life in the city that was the queen of the Adriatic.

Italian painting at the end of the fifteenth century and the beginning of the sixteenth reveals in a number of ways the appearance of a new spirit or sentiment. A *Pietà* or *Lamentation over Christ* (Fig. 411) painted in 1495 by Pietro Perugino (1446-1523) illustrates one aspect. The theme had been treated earlier by Giotto (Fig. 389), and Perugino's conception understandably contains many of the same elements as the older artist's. But the landscape setting is expanded in scope by the feathery trees and softly outlined hills so like those in the painter's native Umbria, and its tender mood softens to a scene of brooding contemplation the tragedy that Giotto stated so powerfully. Figures and setting are interrelated even more than in Giotto's version. The inclination of a head, the outline of a figure, conform to the slope of a hillside. Each figure is so placed in relation to the group as to create a world in which all is lawful and harmonious, and nothing unessential has any place in it. If what was a solemn dirge in the Trecento artist's conception has become a plaintive threnody in Perugino's, the flawless consonance of its statement cannot be denied.

Also from Umbria but a man of very different temperament was Luca Signorelli (1441-1523). His early work reflects the ideas of Piero della Francesca and Pollaiuolo with whom he shared the interest in the nude figure that is so apparent in the *Torments of the Damned* (Fig. 412), one of a series of frescoes he painted between 1500 and 1504 in the Chapel of San Brizio in the cathedral at Orvieto. Not content with observing the superficial appearance of things, he set about investigating their underlying physical construction the better to represent their bulk and texture.

Through patient dissection of cadavers, he studied the structure of the body—the skeleton, and the muscles that interact with it through tendons and ligaments—for he knew that only accurate knowledge could develop the skill necessary to render the organic movement of the body convincingly. As no painter before him had done, he correlated emotion with physical action, a commonplace today but novel in the Renaissance. In the Torments of the Damned, the writhing of men and women in intense agony is realistically portrayed, for Signorelli measures the psychological and emotional in terms of its physical manifestation. The compressed joints, the line of a swelling muscle, the highlights of

Accademia, Venice.

FIG. 410.   Gentile Bellini, Miracle of the True Cross (1500).

Pitti, Florence.

FIG. 411.   Perugino, Pietà (1495).

the skin painted in colors that shift in bizarre fashion from purple and blue to green, red, and orange—all are set forth with a powerful and resolute hand.

A more reflective attitude is apparent in the painting of Sandro Botticelli (1444-1510) at the end of the fifteenth century. But he courted not so much the glories of the fresh landscape, like Perugino, or the physical vigor of the athletic nude, like Signorelli, as the moods they may arouse. His eye turns inward from sensuous experience to reflecting upon it, from material tangibility to thought and feeling about it, and his style makes this abstract thought objective. Thus his *Birth of Venus* (Fig. 413), dating *ca.* 1488,

may seem artificial at first glance, as it is in the sense that subject and arrangement do not come spontaneously from familiar experience. The figures of Venus, the nymph receiving her on the shore, and those symbolizing the winds wafting the goddess to the shore are drawn close to the frontal plane, producing a continuous sequence of movement from one side to the other of the foreground. Sea and shore line are conventionalized, the waves reduced to V-shaped lines and the shore to a sharp zigzag that gives no real impression of depth. The Venus, in a pose of self-conscious modesty inspired—like the Aphrodite of Melos (Fig. 276)—by Hellenistic copies of Praxiteles' renowned fourth-century statue of the goddess, is sharp in contour; her long coiling hair seems of spun metallic strands. She approaches the shore sadly, as if reluctant to encounter the hostility of the modern world. The artist's mood is nostalgic, a longing for the imagined happier times of long ago.

Botticelli's choice of a theme from antiquity reflects the current enthusiasm for classical learning already noted in Mantegna (Fig. 406) and is another indication of the tendency of Renaissance artists to search beyond the Christian legend for subject matter. Though an avid pursuer of realism in his earlier years, Botticelli turned from its methods and the popular taste of his times to dream of the past. Despite his vast talents for poetic expression, his art was so

Cathedral, Orvieto.

FIG. 412.   Signorelli, Torments of the Damned (1500–1504).

Uffizi, Florence.

FIG. 413.   Botticelli, Birth of Venus (*ca.* 1488).

personal that his immediate influence was inconsiderable. His distinctively individual manner, exemplified in the Birth of Venus, makes the fullest use of animated linear patterns. Atmosphere is almost wholly excluded; the emphasis is on a lashlike line that is inexpressibly nervous and vital.

A similar tendency to formal lyricism is present in Venetian painting at the end of the fifteenth century. If Botticelli is compared with his Venetian contemporary, Giovanni Bellini (1430-1516)—the brother of Gentile who painted the Miracle of the True Cross (Fig. 410)—we find expressive parallels. In Giovanni's *Madonna with Four Saints* (Fig. 414) painted in 1505, the figures are grouped as formally and harmoniously as in the Birth of Venus. In both pictures the subject is no longer familiar or plebeian, though Domenico Veneziano had painted such a gravely contemplative group a half-century before (Fig. 401). The saints comport themselves in a way neither commonplace nor intimate,

but studiedly formal. Botticelli evokes a mood of melancholy, Bellini one of religious revery, brooding yet intense and sustained. The Italians call a mute gathering of saints such as this *Sacra Conversazione*, "Sacred Conversation." Both masters exclude irrelevant details, subordinating and suppressing the trivial and accidental to the grandeur of the principal theme. But there are interesting and significant differences too. Botticelli, typically Florentine, obtains his effects by precision of line and astringent color, and the painted forms are often closely akin to sculptured forms. Bellini's work, on the other hand, is rich in softening atmospheric effects, and the figures are delicately modeled in warmly sensuous flesh tones.

With the turn of the century, elaborate detail and complicated narrative were abandoned for a style that is grand and formal and continues the process of consolidating and integrating the discoveries of the pioneers in naturalism that began with Perugino, Botticelli, and Giovanni

FIG. 414.   Giovanni Bellini, Madonna with Four Saints (1505).

Bellini. Bellini in particular reveals the trend toward a new monumentalism that culminated in the High Renaissance. The change is apparent when the Madonna with Four Saints is compared with Domenico Veneziano's earlier treatment of a similar theme (Fig. 401). The saints on either side of the elevated Madonna produce a stable balance in both paintings, but the architectural background in Bellini's limits the dramatic action like a stage setting that permits the eye to see only what is important. The setting does not attract undue attention as it tends to in the earlier painting but acts as a sounding board reinforcing the dominant melody. Everything in Giovanni Bellini's picture contributes to a new grandeur of style that is manifest in the more monumental architectural setting and in the increased order and more stately rhythm of the forms and draperies.

Leonardo da Vinci summed up the accomplishments of the age before the end of the fifteenth century. However, his art was so radical and the style he created so influential upon the art of the next century that it is better to consider him in the context of the High Renaissance, for he is the one figure who overlaps and links the two main periods of Italian Renaissance painting.

THE HIGH RENAISSANCE IN FLORENCE AND ROME

The early years of the sixteenth century have been called the Golden Age of Italian Renaissance painting, and with reason, for the names of the masters of this period—Leonardo, Michelangelo, Raphael—have become household words. Through their minds and in their works, Italian art acquired the discipline that gave it the status of classic authority. The fifteenth-century local schools were overshadowed by the prestige of a cosmopolitan expression originating in Florentine style. It would be a mistake to consider men like Masaccio, Piero della Francesca, and Mantegna only as minor steppingstones to the achievements of the High Renaissance, for they created sublime concepts of the world of their time. But they were the pioneers; those who followed refined and systematized what to a very large degree they had established.

The work of Leonardo da Vinci (1452-1519), whose life spanned the last half of the fifteenth century and the first two decades of the sixteenth, reveals the nature of the transformation that took place. He was tutored in the artistic lore of the fifteenth century by Andrea Verrocchio (1436-1488), a distinguished sculptor (cf. Figs. 321, 322), craftsman, and painter. In his workshop, when he was thirteen, Leonardo began his ten-year study of the most advanced art of the early Renaissance and made himself master of its traditions. As Verrocchio's assistant, he painted part of the Baptism of Christ (Fig. 415) for the church of San Salvi in Florence about 1472. The detail shows two kneeling angels from the lower left of the composition, and a glimpse of the river landscape behind them. This landscape and the angel at the left whose head is almost in profile were Leonardo's work. The difference between the two angels in style and content is the difference between the early and the High Renaissance.

Like other fifteenth-century masters, Verrocchio was primarily concerned with translating the centuries-old religious themes into naturalistic terms. This involved giving substance and fiber to the stark symbols of the Middle Ages, a method generally called humanistic because it expressed in human terms the abstractions of love, sacrifice, and divinity which past ages had formulated in a language of symbols. But the early Renaissance cult of naturalism had run its course by the end of the fifteenth century and painting appeared to have reached the limits of representation and dramatization. The works of Perugino (Fig. 411) and Botticelli (Fig. 413) show two ways in which new expressive methods were sought—one in a simpler and more stately language, the other in a wistfully nostalgic sentiment.

Characteristically, the different quality of Leonardo's figure and the landscape behind it is twofold, technical and expressive. Verrocchio's

FIG. 415.   Verrocchio-Leonardo da Vinci, Two Angels,
Detail of The Baptism of Christ
(*ca.* 1472).

angel, competently naturalistic as it is, was done in the traditional medium, tempera. Leonardo's was executed in oil glazes, giving a soft roundness to the flesh and fluffiness to the curly hair, and a sense of light and movement in the atmospheric space of the background. Where Verrocchio was content to describe form accurately, Leonardo sought to give it character and meaning.

The twentieth century considers Leonardo a scientist quite as much as an artist, for his notebooks are filled with his observations of nature, with projects for engines of war like the submarine, tank, and airplane, and with anatomical, geological, and astronomical studies of bewildering diversity. But because he lived in an age when art was a universal medium of expression, his greatest influence came through his artistic activity. Directed toward the problems of art, his scientific mind early mastered all the learning of the fifteenth century, and added further observations regarding perspective, movement, and anatomy. He recognized the conflicts and limitations of fifteenth-century naturalism. He witnessed the secularization of sacred themes and the effort to dramatize nature. The reconciliation of naturalistic art with spiritual expression was the problem of one of Leonardo's first and most important paintings, *The Adoration of the Magi* (Fig. 416). He interprets the often-repeated legend in a new light, making it a pilgrimage of the heart, the world paying homage to the Holy Child as a symbol of love.

Instead of confining the Virgin to a cramped throne or a narrow space before a window, Leonardo shows her seated graciously upon a bank in the open air. The throng which has gathered can only be guessed from the small print shown here, but some sixty figures are represented. Earlier interpretations of the theme also contained many figures (cf. Fig. 395), sometimes so many, indeed, that it was difficult to identify the principal persons. One of the outstanding achievements of the sixteenth-century masters was to restore to painting the clarity, monumentality, and dignity appropriate to the sacred theme which had been lost in the exuberant and indiscriminate naturalism of the late fifteenth century. Through chiaroscuro effects, Leonardo creates the illusion of deep space by atmospheric suggestion. Furthermore, by modeling in light and shade he accents the significant figures and subordinates the minor ones. In the illustration the three or four main actors are made dominant by being light against a dark background. Lesser pilgrims are also present, but only the flash of a face or a hand is seen; the body is obscured in shadow. The principal figures are welded into a firm pyramidal design rendered stable by the dark statuesque figures at the extreme right and left. In this carefully planned structure, Leonardo introduces the richest variety of human types. For back in the space near the architectural ruins are tilting knights, a memory of the mediaeval past. In the foreground, the holy pair is encircled by young, passionate faces; old, ascetic, religious faces; men and women from the corners of the earth, all under the spell of love for the young Savior.

Leonardo left the Adoration unfinished in 1481. It is, then, essentially a drawing with the chiaroscuro developed in the monochrome underpainting. But he worked on it for years, making many experimental drawings, turning over in his mind the complex problems of perspective; he weighed again and again the psychological significance of the whole and of the details. Where others relied on rule-of-thumb, he planned and tested, evolving a pictorial scheme so sound, so balanced and organically effective that this picture served a whole generation as a veritable reservoir of artistic lore. There are echoes of this painting in scores of Renaissance pictures, including the most majestic works of Raphael and Michelangelo.

Leonardo gave human personality the same intense study he gave to relatively formalistic problems of space and design, not to mention his purely scientific problems. All his paintings and notably his Mona Lisa reveal his absorption in this problem. If *St. Anne and the Virgin* (Fig. 417), a drawing that is called a cartoon, is placed beside Fra Filippo Lippi's Madonna (Fig. 404), Leonardo's figures appear suddenly to live as vivid active forms in tangible space, but they also live in a new psychological dimension.

Uffizi, Florence.

FIG. 416.   Leonardo da Vinci, Adoration of the Magi (1481).

This is a psychic world of persons existing in the most highly articulated relation to each other. With the wisdom of age, Anne contemplates the rapt devotion of the Madonna for the infant Christ who in turn blesses the enthralled St. John. The physical interaction of bodies finds its psychological equivalent in the wordless dialogue of earthly and heavenly love. The awkward theme of Mary being seated in her mother's lap was dictated by tradition. Leonardo's solution of the problem through chiaroscuro and by accentuation of the psychological drama leaves one almost unaware of the physical incongruity. As in so many of the master's works, this massing of figures in a compact monumental pyramid served as a guide to almost all his contemporaries, especially Raphael, whose Madonnas and Holy Families seldom fail to reflect some phase of Leonardo's work.

Many see in this drawing the epitome of Leonardo's art, the master work of the age. The personal character of this psychological study is

FIG. 417. Leonardo da Vinci, St. Anne and the Virgin (*ca.* 1498).

Refectory, Sta. Maria delle Grazie, Milan.

FIG. 418. Leonardo da Vinci, The Last Supper (*ca.* 1495–1498).

not something that could be *learned* or *practiced* by others. The wordless dialogue, the inscrutable passion of Saint Anne, the loveliness of the Virgin, the mother lost in joyous tenderness for her babe—all this drama of love is the culmination, the classic statement, of what men had been striving to say for generations. Leonardo's statement is at once supremely human and supremely spiritual.

In one epochal work Leonardo gave a definitive exposition of the Renaissance science and art of painting. *The Last Supper* (Fig. 418) is a ruined masterwork, an unsuccessful experiment in painting on a dry wall. Aside from the grand scheme, its original quality can be imagined only from some of the rare drawings, such as the *Head of Judas* (Fig. 419), made as studies. How completely Leonardo revolutionized the casually discursive style of the late fifteenth century may be seen by comparing his Last Supper with Ghirlandaio's (Fig. 409). Where the latter is prolix and discursive, Leonardo is brief and dramatic. In Ghirlandaio's picture, the disciples sit placidly at the table, almost as if unaware of Christ's words. The incidentals are as interesting as the main subject; the eye is caught by the

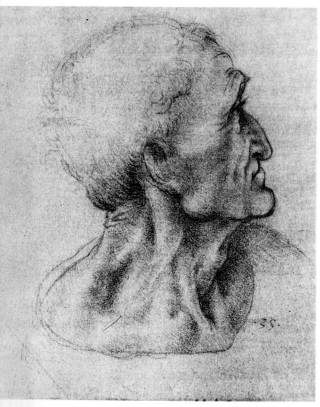

Windsor Castle.

FIG. 419. Leonardo da Vinci,
Head of Judas (*ca.* 1495).

birds sailing over the garden. Leonardo banishes all such trivialities. He directs attention to what is happening as Christ says, "One of you shall betray me." His disciples are electrified with sudden protestation, horror, despair. Each responds according to his nature in a torrent of released emotion. Pictorially a highly complex problem has been solved *in the design*. Every gesture and accent is clearly defined and contributes to the total effect. We may well ask how Leonardo, while preserving a closely coordinated and monumental design, still manages to tell so much about the thirteen characters and at the same time sustain the dramatic unity. The answer is found in an analysis of his design. A room, bare but for the tapestried walls, is the setting for the long table. The disciples with Christ in the exact center are grouped on one side

of the table with Judas, who in earlier pictures had been awkwardly isolated on the other side. These thirteen figures are divided into five groups, the disciples in units of three, with Christ occupying the middle space alone, isolated psychologically as well as physically from the others. To give Him further emphasis, His head is silhouetted against the sky in the natural halo of light from the window in the end wall. If the lines of the architecture, the tapestry edges, the beams of the ceiling and the pavement lines are projected, they converge at Christ's head, making Him the point of optical concentration. The system of grouping makes the disciples integral units of the design; even those who are standing are related in the rhythmic horizontal movement toward Christ created by the gestures that are also a psychologically unifying element in articulating their emotion. Only Judas, his dark face in the shadow, recoils in hate and fear. As in the Adoration of the Magi, Leonardo has given a universal image of man. The disciples are not literal renderings of chance models but typical men, abstractions condensed and generalized from thousands of studies of humanity made by the painter. Strictly speaking, this celebrated religious painting is not fundamentally religious in character. It represents the psychological observations of the profoundest scientist of his time as he synthesizes his investigations through the medium of pictorial design.

In the Last Supper, Leonardo was faced with the problem of achieving psychological unity in his expressive treatment of the thirteen protagonists in the Christian drama, and he did this by placing them in a definite situation to which they responded as individuals, each in accordance with his own temperament. The grip that the great painting has maintained on the imagination of its viewers from its creation down to the present results in no small degree from the directness with which such human values are transformed into and expressed by the formal elements in the design. The same thing is true on an even more abstract level in the no less famous *Mona Lisa* (Fig. 420), which Leonardo began to paint in 1503 and which he considered still unfinished when he died in 1519. Mona Lisa was

Louvre, Paris.

FIG. 420.   Leonardo da Vinci, Mona Lisa (1503).

the wife of a Florentine citizen, Francesco del Giocondo; we know little of her otherwise save that she was saddened by the loss of a child when Leonardo was painting her portrait and that music was played to distract her as she posed. Although these circumstances may account for the actual painting, they are of little importance in suggesting its character, for there is no reason to think that Mona Lisa was of more than average intelligence and personality, hardly the self-sufficient and worldly-wise woman Leonardo painted under her name. The portrait is, in fact, an ideal one, like those another great Florentine carved for the tombs of the Medici scions two decades later (cf. Fig. 327). And also like them, it tells more about the creator than about the relatively undistinguished person portrayed. The painting has been changed somewhat since Leonardo's time, for it was originally a little wider and columns at the sides framed the figure with its landscape background. It has also darkened very considerably because Leonardo, always the scientific experimentalist, used chemically unstable pigments which have deteriorated. Such deterioration is frequent in old paintings and in modern ones too. The freshness and vital coloring mentioned by early writers are no longer evident. But even in the somber hues of the crackled pigment it is still possible to discern the amazingly minute modeling of the hands and face—the almost imperceptible planes by which the forms are built up.

In this most celebrated of portraits Leonardo gave new breadth and new content to this particular branch of painting. The character of the High Renaissance style, shown here, comes to light in comparing this portrait with another celebrated earlier one—Piero della Francesca's Duchess of Urbino. The latter portrait, painted some forty years before Leonardo's, is like a legal document soberly recording the characteristic profile, the royal costume, the jewels, and the domain of the duchy in the landscape, with almost artless directness. Here the portrait serves a purpose different from Leonardo's; it is more a record than an intuitive re-creation, a statement of fact rather than a poetic interpretation. This infusion of subjective overtones into pictorial expression characterized the art of the High Renaissance.

By contrast, Leonardo's picture is extraordinarily artful as he consciously composed the figure, accenting the hands and turning the shoulders slightly. The delicate scarf falling from the head effects a fluid, uninterrupted silhouette with no angles or sudden transitions. No jewels or striking elements of costume provide individual or personal notes. The half-length likeness with hands displayed—an additional enrichment to the accent of the face—was made

current by this portrait. So, likewise, was the method of giving alertness and intimacy through the action of the eyes and the mobile features. With the play of light, and the undulating curves suggesting the round and solid structure of head and arms, the master has given physical and spiritual substantiality to the image unrealized before this time. The qualities which make this portrait above all others an object of admiration are just those that illuminate the self-awareness of the Renaissance personality. It tells much about the age and its efforts to measure the capacity of mankind to meet the dilemmas of the world with reason and fortitude.

Through his continuous study of nature, which he viewed as the artist's only true guide, Leonardo fertilized European art with profound spirituality. Everything he touched he endowed with grace and loveliness, dignity and grandeur. He is a living reminder that the artist with intelligence and sensitivity may shape the symbols of love and faith by which men live. More than any other person he closed the gap in men's minds that separates mankind from nature. Through comprehension and love he translated science into poetry and harmonized the two worlds of outer and inner experience.

Like Leonardo, Michelangelo (1475-1564) belongs among the Titans of the sixteenth century. As sculptor (cf. Figs. 323-328), architect (cf. Figs. 131, 133, 147), painter, and poet he embraces all the arts. But it was as a sculptor that he revealed himself and his age even when he painted. As a youth he learned the painter's craft with Ghirlandaio, but he soon devoted himself exclusively to sculpture until the pope demanded that he leave his chisel and marble to decorate the ceiling of the Sistine Chapel in Rome, upon which he worked from 1509 to 1512. Given a free hand, he conceived a tremendous decorative scheme, using the nude human figure as a basis for the huge fabric. Down the center of the ceiling in nine rectangular panels is recorded the epic of mankind from the Creation to the Deluge. In the *Fall of Man and Expulsion* (Fig. 421) the two heroic parents receive the forbidden fruit from the serpent. Many artists have treated this theme from the Middle Ages

Sistine Chapel, Vatican City.

FIG. 421. Michelangelo, Fall of Man and Expulsion (1509–1512).

on (Figs. 293, 298, 313, 398), but none with Michelangelo's stark, concentrated power. The Garden of Eden is a desolate rocky spot in the wilderness, but Adam and Even themselves are instinct with colossal power. Eagerly they accept the fruit of knowledge and with bitter reluctance they leave Paradise, thrust out into a world of pain and labor by an angel with flaming sword, Adam overwhelmed by an awful sense of guilt, Eve bitterly bewailing her unhappy fate. As Leonardo illuminated the Biblical subjects with profound insight, so Michelangelo passed beyond a conventional narration of an ancient legend. To him, man's fall from his first innocence was the beginning of his endless conflict with evil, a conflict that forces him to labor with sweat and pain to attain peace which is denied by an inexorable world, a strife that strains every nerve and fiber of his intellectual and moral nature. All Michelangelo says is conveyed through the action of the figure. Impelled by the dramatic force he sensed in Jacopo della Quercia's sculpture (Fig. 313) and the frescoes of Masaccio (Fig. 398) and Signorelli, and guided by exhaustive knowledge of the body gained from intensive study of cadavers, he made the human form more expressive than it had ever been before.

The last panel in the Sistine Ceiling series represents *God Separating Day from Night* (Fig. 422). How vain to attempt the rendering of so colossal an idea in pictorial language! But Michelangelo overwhelms us by the thought he embodies here. From the outer darkness of un-created chaos a supernatural and cosmic being

Sistine Chapel, Vatican City.

FIG. 422. Michelangelo, God Separating Day from Night
(1509–1512).

emerges, so mighty that the imagination can hardly conceive it. With a powerful movement involving the whole body, the Almighty thrusts back the clouds of darkness and performs the miracle that rendered the universe intelligible. As if the painter realized that the imagination must be deeply engaged to grasp the meaning of the idea portrayed, the sharply defined sculpturesque figures employed elsewhere in the series are renounced for a half-obscured image engulfed in the receding shadow of the heavens. The effects produced suggest the rhythm of cosmic forces convulsed in creation.

The main panels of the Sistine Ceiling appear as if they were rectangular openings in the vault of the chapel, framed by painted mouldings. These mouldings are in turn supported by painted cornices with heavy blocks at the corner of the panels, each with the seated figure of a nude *Athlete* (Fig. 423). Of the same heroic race as their sculptural counterparts for the tombs of Julius I (Fig. 325) and of the Medici (Fig. 328), their ostensible purpose is to support the heavy garlands and ribbons connecting the decorative medallions; actually they perform a kind of plastic dance to accompany the figures on the main panels. Varying spiritual moods are expressed in movements and actions impossible of human attainment in many cases but rendered plausible by the painter's utter command of design. Some of the youths are weighted down by their burden, their joints and muscles compressed under the crushing weight. Others seem so light and volatile that they all but spring from their places. Depression and exaltation, lassitude and vitality all appear in these figures as attributes of the human spirit and the human body which are not considered by Michelangelo as a duality but as one and the same.

There are similar psychological concepts in the heroic Prophets and Sibyls. The *Jeremiah* (Fig. 424), most melancholy of the prophets, is thought to be a portrait of Michelangelo himself because it is clothed in a sculptor's smock. Crouched on a low throne, the massive figure assumes an almost global form. Heavy falling lines define the ponderous bulk of the body. The head inclining heavily upon the arm supported by the knee, the muscular inert left hand, bespeak a colossal power made impotent by frustration. For a parallel to such tragic brooding, one must look, other than to the master's sculpture (cf. Fig. 328), to the Book of Job or the Melencolia I (cf. Fig. 446) of Dürer, Michelangelo's great German contemporary. A contrasting mood is that of the *Delphic Sibyl* (Fig. 425). The seeress, holding the scroll that contains her prophecy, is buoyantly elevated by a voice toward which she suddenly turns. The spirit and the flesh respond with sustained free energy in action. The erect head, the strong serenity of the clear glance, the lifted arm, and the triumphant sweep of the mantle all speak of a will to life that is denied to the Jeremiah.

In his frescoes Michelangelo expressed himself much as he did in sculpture. By eliminating

Sistine Chapel, Vatican City.

FIG. 423. Michelangelo, Athlete (1509–1512).

Sistine Chapel, Vatican City.

FIG. 424.   Michelangelo, Jeremiah
(1509–1512).

Sistine Chapel, Vatican City.

FIG. 425.   Michelangelo, Delphic Sibyl
(1509–1512).

or severely subordinating accessories and incidentals of setting, he focused attention upon the
large monumental figures which he painted with
the same clarity and titanic vigor seen in his
sculpture. Through bodily movements that in
themselves may be trivial or unnatural, they
communicate the life-giving impulse of the
spirit that created them. Our own muscles and
joints respond to the kinaesthetic sensations so
powerfully suggested by statue and painted
image. Michelangelo has translated the language
of the sculptor to the flat walls in symbols so
deeply charged with meaning that they cannot
be called beautiful in the ordinary sense. The
sweet graciousness of Leonardo's lyric naturalism
is denied them, for Michelangelo swept it aside
in a thunderous language of plastic form. Nor
are the forms realistic in the sense of being representations of actual or even typical living men
and women. Rather through abstractions of his
models based upon enormous knowledge of the

physical body, he constructs heroic, convincingly
powerful symbols of humanity.

The mysteries of birth and death, of exaltation and suffering, lie tragically in the master's
every artistic thought. With pen, crayon, chisel,
and brush he expounded those mysteries. The
drawing, *The Resurrection* (Fig. 426), becomes,
through the human form viewed in relation to
the supple ripples of cloth and the rigid structure
of the tomb, an embodiment of man's will and
spiritual fortitude. As in Piero della Francesca's
interpretation of the same theme two generations
earlier (Fig. 402), the factual statement of a
Christ emerging from the grave is translated into
a universal drama vaster than any religion of any
time or place. We are presented with the unfathomable miracle of life. That it is couched in
terms of Christianity is incidental.

Raphael (1483–1520), the third of the great
High Renaissance painters, was the opposite of
Michelangelo in temperament and personality.

Taught in Perugino's studio in Perugia (cf. Fig. 411), he came to Florence but discovered that the serene and deliberate style he had faithfully absorbed from his master was now old-fashioned. Leonardo and Michelangelo were the popular gods in Florence, and Raphael was quick to perceive the validity of their unquestioned leadership. It was clear that the small delicate landscapes, the dreamy-eyed saints, and the quiet rhythms of his compositions in Perugino's style would not suffice in a city that was becoming accustomed to the heady outpourings of Michelangelo's art. His first attempts to combine his natural lyric grace with the dramatic force of the current style were almost grotesque. But it was his peculiar genius to absorb the artistic gifts of those about him. With extraordinary intuition he was able to grasp the architectural concepts of Bramante, the sculptural impulses of Michelangelo, and the pictorial subtleties of Leonardo; he chose from them with intelligence and tact and formed a style that was his own.

Like Michelangelo and many others, Raphael was called to Rome to the service of the pope in 1508. Between early 1509 and November, 1511, he painted four rooms of the Vatican palace. One of his large decorations, the *School of Athens* (Fig. 427), is an allegory of philosophy. Under the spreading vaults of an imagined temple are gathered all the celebrated scholars, scientists, and philosophers of the ancient world. With the Last Supper by Leonardo in mind, Raphael composed a lucid and integrated mural decoration in a monumental scheme. In the center are the two great philosophers of ancient Greece, Aristotle and Plato. Lest they be lost in the throng, a compelling triple accent of soaring arches rises immediately above them. The actual shape of the wall is echoed in these painted architectural vaults which were inspired by those Bramante designed only a short time before for the rebuilding of St. Peter's Church (Fig. 132); through these spreading arches the multitude is unified in articulated space. The figures in the middle ground, flanking Aristotle and Plato, are arranged in a continuous horizontal band. The two smaller groups balanced one against the other in the foreground, right and left, further

articulate the pictorial space. It is an almost perfect solution of the problem of mural decoration. Stated simply, this problem involves decorating a wall pictorially without destroying its space-defining function as part of the actual architecture. The effect Raphael produces is not that of a hole broken through the wall and revealing depth, the result achieved inadvertently by too many overzealous fifteenth-century masters. By organizing the individual figures of the coordinated groups into surface patterns horizontally

British Museum, London.

FIG. 426. Michelangelo,
The Resurrection (*ca.* 1532).

oriented, he preserves the wall plane inviolate. Its surface is perfectly integrated with the abstract space representation. The inborn feeling for space organized by articulate rhythms that Raphael inherited from his Umbrian master Perugino is raised in the School of Athens to its highest capabilities of expression. For sheer intelligence combined with a sense of the harmonious and rational, it is one of the finest decorative murals ever conceived.

The most widely known works of Raphael are his various paintings of the Madonna and Child. Usually these consist of some variation of the scheme evolved by Leonardo, who with fine condensation arranged his figures in pyramidal groups, as in the Adoration of the Magi (Fig. 416) and the Cartoon of St. Anne (Fig. 417). Raphael achieved his most sublime treatment of the theme in the *Sistine Madonna* (Fig. 428), painted about 1515. Characteristic of the High Renaissance style is the monumental treatment of the figures to which the background has been subordinated. The Virgin, silhouetted against a cloud of tiny cherub heads, is balanced symmetrically by the figures of Pope Sixtus and Saint Barbara. The design is unified by the flowing line rising in the garment folds of the Pope and continuing through the silhouette of the Virgin, attaining the apex of her head. From this point it falls slowly and gracefully, descending

Stanza della Segnatura, Vatican Palace, Vatican City.

FIG. 427. Raphael, School of Athens (1509–1511).

Museum, Dresden.

FIG. 428.   Raphael, Sistine Madonna (*ca.* 1515).

through the curtain and the billowing mantle. The double accent of the wind-blown drapery arrests the downward movement, which comes to a full pause in Saint Barbara, only to continue through her lowered glance. The elfish cherubs on the lower frame halt the movement once more and then deflect it upward again to complete the wonderfully rhythmic and continuous flow of line and surface that gives movement to figures which in themselves are motionless. Through the melodious cadence of the forms, Raphael attains the grandiose dignity befitting his theme. Although lacking the penetrating observation and vast originality of Leonardo and Michelangelo, he has contrived a classic harmony of forms that recalls certain phases of Greek and Roman art.

One of the finest of Raphael's earlier

FIG. 429. Raphael, Alba Madonna (1509–1510).

Madonnas, the *Alba Madonna* (Fig. 429), painted 1509–1510, is in the National Gallery at Washington. In an expansive landscape Mary rests in pensive contemplation of the child Jesus and Saint John, the notable plastic patterns of the group both complementing and being emphasized by the circular shape. All that is individual, accidental, or casual is suppressed for what is noble and restrained. The ideal and aristocratic Madonna is a far cry from the pretty snub-nosed girl Madonnas of the fifteenth century (cf. Fig. 404). In the High Renaissance there is no place for the random aspects of nature, however fresh and gay; every form must be rendered in terms of a deliberate and stately harmony.

The peculiar requirements of decorative frescoes and religious themes demanded broad and generalized treatment, but in his portraits

Raphael expounded values that are concrete and specific. The power and intelligence of many Renaissance personalities were unforgettably recorded by his brush in a number of celebrated portraits, among them that of *Baldassare Castiglione* (Fig. 430), painted about 1515. The flowing outlines of the torso and shoulders merge with the contours of the face and cap, and create a movement that continues in the arms and hands. Yet the characteristic physical appearance of the individual has not been sacrificed to an abstraction of moral and intellectual qualities.

In seeking clarity through order and consistency Raphael pursued a dominant principle of Italian art. Whereas lesser men following his path often lapsed into sentimentality, misunderstanding the nature of his felicitous harmony, others like Poussin and Ingres were enriched by his example. Michelangelo lived to see his mighty cadences evoke contrived mannerism among his uninspired followers in both

Louvre, Paris.

FIG. 430.   Raphael, Baldassare Castiglione (*ca.* 1515).

painting and sculpture. Raphael's death in 1520, a year after that of Leonardo, brought to a close the brief golden day of the High Renaissance. Except for Michelangelo, painters in Florence and Rome evolved either an affected and studiedly artificial style known as mannerism or an eclectic vocabulary that imitated the departed giants.

THE HIGH RENAISSANCE IN VENICE

Intellectual and spiritual leadership belonged to Florence in the early Renaissance; Rome had by turns taken Florentine art and deepened, urbanized, or diluted it. In a very real sense it remained for Venice to endow the art of Italy with the attributes that ultimately enabled it to become effective in the wider European world. Historically this implementing role was made possible by a number of factors including its wealth and accessibility to the maritime world, especially the East, its background in Byzantine culture, and particularly its contacts with the mature art of Florence. The closest collaboration was realized between Venice and the mainland for generations. In the neighboring city of Padua Giotto and Donatello had left monumental works (cf. Figs. 317, 389), and it was here that Mantegna taught the brothers Bellini (cf. Figs. 410, 414), founders of a great age of painting in Venice.

From the first the painters of Venice reflect the buoyant and worldly character of a city of dazzling splendor. Its citizens must have resembled the Chinese or the French in their prudent worldly good sense. They were lovers of pleasure and good living. Proud of their independence and secure in their wealth, they were quick to respond to a natural craving for ornament and luxury. The color and light of the sea and canals may have bred a sensitivity to color which is the prime characteristic of their painting, but these painters' love of warmly sensuous tones is consistent with the pagan worldliness of the Venetian way of life.

The first illustrious name in Venice of the High Renaissance is Giorgione (*ca.* 1475-1510). Only a few of the scores of paintings attributed to him are actually his, but during his own life and for a long time thereafter his art was reflected in that of many Venetian masters, making exact attribution in some cases almost impossible.

Under his brush the local forthright tones of his predecessors, the brothers Bellini and others, give way to colors of notable vitality organically related to each other. Line, light, and color are so treated that their interrelation creates a consummation of the form. We are no longer aware of linear areas enriched with color, for Giorgione's form is an equilibrium of interacting or interweaving contours, mass, light, and color. As Masaccio was the first painter to key his art to the habits of the eye with respect to mass in atmosphere and space (Fig. 399), so Giorgione was the first to apply the habits of the eye to color. As far as our direct perceptions go, an object like a human figure or a complex of drapery folds is a mass of color and not a series of lines with color between the lines. Giorgione never forgot this and through this he contributed to one of the fundamental traditions valid during centuries of painting.

Occasionally we encounter a work of art so perfectly made that nothing intervenes between the thing itself and our complete grasp of it. In other words, we do not think or feel anything except the miracle of the artist's experience which he passes on to us in its nascent state. The world the artist lives in is completely ours, with no reservations in our mind as to time or place or means of accomplishment. Like the sudden harmony wrought from the melodies of a Bach chorale, or the perfect timing of a dancer's movement, the result is a completely satisfying resolution of all the values involved. The equation balances. With the recognition of the part played by color in our optical perceptions, Giorgione closes the first great epoch of naturalistic art and opens the second one leading to the phase dominated by Titian, Tintoretto, the Spaniards, and the Dutch.

Never in all painting had there been seen anything like the opulent splendor of his *Sleeping*

Museum, Dresden.

FIG. 431.   Giorgione, Sleeping Venus (*ca.* 1508).

Venus (Fig. 431). Only the Greek sculptors had envisioned such exalted loveliness, but the sphere of sensuous reality which sculpture could not reach Giorgione attains in color and the amplitude of the enveloping world of landscape. The Venus becomes identified with the landscape, her melting contours merge with the hills and the silver satin of her couch. The painting, begun about 1508, was left unfinished at the master's early death; the landscape was painted by Titian, who momentarily understood and shared Giorgione's transcendent poetry.

The brief span of Giorgione's life—about thirty-five years—was so fruitful that though only a few of his works are known, these will always live as almost ultimate values of their kind in the painter's art. Uncounted masters in his time and since have felt the sustained drama of his paintings. We would like to know more

about him than the few scraps legend gives us. He may have come under the spell of Leonardo, who was in Venice in 1500. As a youth he worked with Giovanni Bellini and later paid him homage in *Christ Bearing the Cross* (Fig. 432) now in Boston; it follows almost exactly a painting by Bellini. Giorgione's Christ, once seen, can never be forgotten. Not even Leonardo ever conceived the features of the Savior at once so compassionate and tragic as this. Titian in his early work often attempted to recapture Giorgione's mood as in his Tribute Money (Fig. 434), and El Greco a hundred years later essayed the mood, but the quality of Giorgione's panel is inimitable.

The great artist has a peculiar sixth sense for the genius of his medium. With Giorgione and Piero della Francesca this sense is an awareness of the mute, arrested world of painted forms which because of their fixed character must always

FIG. 432.   Giorgione, Christ Bearing
the Cross (*ca.* 1504).

vibrate with enigmatic overtones. Few masters have had the ability to seize upon this apparent limitation and translate it into sustained musical reality. In the painting called *The Three Philosophers* (Fig. 433), dated about 1510, Giorgione does just this. Taking as he often does an obscure theme from myth or legend he submits it to his own interpretation, bringing forth a passionately felt drama of man and nature which requires no literary explanation or reference. Three ages of man, three temperaments, establish their identity in a mysterious and haunting landscape. It is vain to probe for fugitive literal explanations of this completely realized world of imagination. The wisdom of pagan antiquity lives again in this appeal to our deepest feelings through sensuous perceptions, half-forgotten slumbering sensations stored ages ago in the memory of the individual and the race. The mute harmony of spirits called the Sacred Conversation of Giovanni Bellini (Fig. 414) is enriched and broadened by

his pupil Giorgione to encompass the Platonic concepts then flowing in Renaissance thought.

But it remained for another to bring Venetian art to its fulfillment. Titian (1477-1576), schooled under Gentile Bellini in his early years, is first known in a style like that of Giorgione, who was Titian's own age but more precocious. Some of Titian's early works can scarcely be distinguished from Giorgione's, so much are they in the latter's poetic vein. *The Tribute Money* (Fig. 434) is one of these. Masaccio painted the same theme more than seventy-five years earlier with epic breadth (Fig. 399), placing Christ and His disciples with the Roman tax gatherer in a landscape of profound space filled with atmospheric light and dark. There are lights and shadows in Titian's version, too, but they are charged with the color Giorgione had sensed even in patterns of chiaroscuro. There is even something Giorgionesque in the subtle characterization of the two who together act the drama for which Masaccio used a full cast of characters. But it is not a mood of reverie or reflection that Titian creates; a more exact sense of structure and a more tangible feeling for surface plane results in forms that have concrete and physical actuality (cf. Fig. 432).

The moist air of Venice was not sympathetic to the medium of fresco painting. Nor did the rather restrained hues of fresco appeal to the exotic taste of a city which had known the brilliance of Byzantine mosaics for centuries. Now in the sixteenth century, with oil pigments on canvas, Titian wrote a new and magnificent chapter of European art. Sustained by Raphael and Michelangelo, the masters of central Italy, and deepened through Dürer's feeling for nature, he created a forthright sensuous and decorative style. Under Titian the trenchant line of the Florentines yields something of its precision and definition to values more earthly and human, values of immediate sensation inherent in color. This he uses with enormous energy and subtlety. He thinks with color where others used it largely as a supplement to linear design. Thus Titian took the final step in Renaissance painting—the step that was once and for all (for better or worse) to disengage painting from its role as illustrator of ideas. In other words, art attained with Titian a new and sensuous independence, a new cultural authority, as the artist more and more created the content of his pictures, becoming thereby less dependent upon literary, religious, and philosophical sources. Our contemporary idea that the painter may create an imaginative world of form, independent of illusionism, stems from him. Along with other Venetian masters Titian had a very individual feeling for landscape, linking it with the figure in establishing a union of man and nature. In this respect he stands between Michelangelo and Rembrandt, modifying the sculptural austerity of the one and foreshadowing the spatial ideal of the other.

To follow through the development of Titian's art is to examine the evolution not of one man's art but a whole epoch. It leads from his early enthusiasm for Giorgione's lyricism to the inventive and strenuous period of his middle years and finally to the full glory of his last conceptions. Between 1516 and 1518, about the time he emerged from Giorgione's spell, he painted *The Assumption of the Virgin* (Fig. 435). The poetry of Giorgione is modified by the dramatic gusto that characterizes so many of Titian's works. This painting may be profitably compared with Raphael's Sistine Madonna (Fig. 428), which was painted in Rome only a couple of years earlier. Instead of the sublime tranquillity of Raphael's picture, there is a splendid pageant, the grandiose culmination of an opera. Superb movement, deeply human emotion, sustain the moment of Mary's greatest glory. This splendor of color and drama was what the Venetians loved, and Titian brings to the theme a supreme mastery of sensuous experience. The types are Venetian, full-bodied and vigorous. Renaissance worldliness and ecclesiastical symbol are reconciled here as far as that reconciliation was possible. Frequently in Venice the Christian themes are treated in a more frankly pagan manner; Titian's Fall of Man is an example.

In the entire history of painting nothing is comparable to the phenomenon of Titian, strong and ever-creative even under the weight of three generations but ceaselessly exploring with matchless taste and incredible originality the fields of myth and legend, drama, sacred history, portraiture. He was past eighty in 1559, when he painted the *Rape of Europa* (Fig. 436), celebrating as he so often had before the cosmic power of natural law. Zeus disguised as a bull carries the nominally protesting girl across the Hellespont to the consummation of their union in the Dictaean Cave on the island of Crete. Here is a case, frequent in the history of art, in which a master transforms a subject of popular appeal into sheer symbolism. With imagination and passion he elevates. the theme from the realm of the decorative or erotic into the sphere of allegory.

The most profound creations of Titian's mind and imagination were produced at the very end of his career, after his ninetieth year. Outstanding among them is the great *Pietà* (Fig. 437), revealing a tragic conception of life shared by only the greatest spirits. Titian was working on

Kunsthistorisches Museum, Vienna.

FIG. 433. Giorgione, The Three Philosophers (*ca.* 1510).

FIG. 434.   Titian, The Tribute Money (*ca.* 1510).

this painting when the plague brought his life to an end in 1576; for many years it marked his tomb in the church of the Frari in Venice where the earlier Assumption (Fig. 435) hangs above the high altar. In contrast with its frankly sensuous colorism, the Pietà seems restrained and sober, with only a gleam here and there of hues shining through the silver and russet overpainting. Color is too transitory and uncertain, the artist

seems to feel, to expound this drama of life and death—only silver across deep shadows—light and dark, figures grouped compactly in space that dilates and murmurs. The painter portrays himself in the kneeling Joseph of Arimathea who seeks grace in the touch of the Savior's hand.

The treatment of space has a primary and peculiar place in Renaissance art. In painting we may trace its development from the severely

Church of the Frari, Venice.

FIG. 435. Titian, The Assumption of the Virgin (1516–1518).

restricted patterns of Giotto (Fig. 387), who was content with the skillful manipulation of the narrow span of a stage. Following him, Taddeo Gaddi made bold and disastrous experiments without adequate knowledge of how to control and organize his spaces. In the fifteenth century, with Brunellesco and Masaccio (Fig. 399), the beginning of a rationally constructed space pattern appears which is brought to a climax in the scientifically controlled designs of Leonardo in the High Renaissance (Fig. 418). The painters of the Renaissance are distinguished from those of the ancient and mediaeval worlds by their invention of a cage of space to measure and articulate physical phenomena.

Men of northern Italy, Mantegna (Fig. 406) and the Venetians (Fig. 431) had long shown a predilection for bolder and more experimental treatment of space. In Venice the employment of oil as a medium encouraged even more intricate

space patterns, and in the provincial schools of Parma and Padua near Venice the traditions of art were more flexible. In Parma, Correggio (1489-1534) continued Mantegna's earlier experiments. In painting the *Ascension of Christ* (Fig. 438) on the dome of the church of S. Giovanni Evangelista at Parma in 1520, he opened out the cupola in a breath-taking expanse of boundless space; the heavens open and the Savior ascends. In comparison with Raphael's School of Athens (Fig. 427) or Michelangelo's God Separating Day from Night (Fig. 422), the unorthodoxy of Correggio's conception links him with the seventeenth-century baroque masters rather than with his own generation, although he could hardly have painted this and other similar works without knowledge of Mantegna's pioneering ventures (Fig. 407). Not used to viewing figures floating in clouds as Correggio's do, some of his critics called the dome of the cathedral in

FIG. 436.   Titian, Rape of Europa (1559).

Accademia, Venice.

FIG. 437.   Titian, Pietà (1573–1576).

Parma a frog pond; but Titian praised it highly, saying that gold pieces filling the cupola would not represent its full worth.

A similar taste for the lyrical and exotic, fundamentally at variance with the sober Renaissance humanism of Florence and Rome, is apparent in other works by Correggio. In his *Madonna of St. Jerome* (Fig. 439), the expressions on the face of the Magdalene as she embraces the Christ Child's foot and of the angel who holds the Madonna's book are perhaps more indicative of physical than spiritual experience. Imitators and admirers seized upon this note of exoticism or eroticism with results both less ambiguous and less effective. As for Correggio himself, although not a Venetian in the literal sense, his close kinship to that city's expressive traditions and his painterly style link him to the developments stemming from it.

A story told about Titian illuminates the last important phase of Venetian painting. One day the master entered his studio and chanced to see some drawings by one of his numerous helpers. He asked who had made them and thereupon told his assistant to have the young apprentice expelled from the studio. The legend has been interpreted rather naïvely as a sign of Titian's jealousy of a gifted potential rival; if the tale is true, it is more likely that the master saw substantial evidence that the apprentice, Tintoretto (1518-1594), a youth more than a generation younger than his teacher, could learn nothing of value from him. Certain it is that Tintoretto's brilliant intuitive art was to violate the essential pattern that Titian had set.

The older man thought of his canvas as a kind of stage. He drew a sharp line excluding the spectator from the stage or spectacle—the Pietà (Fig. 437) is an example. The opposite is true

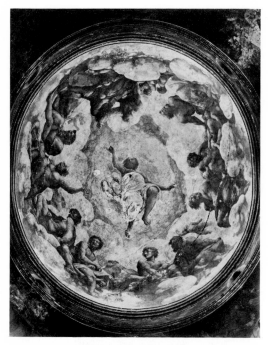

S. Giovanni Evangelista, Parma.

FIG. 438. Correggio, Ascension
of Christ (1520).

and thus emphasize the drama of the scene. Even if we could not see a single face clearly, the force of his colors, the crackling and splashing light, the thrusts of the space pattern, would be adequate to arouse powerful emotion. Although not so bold, Titian late in his life worked in much the same manner, for his color and light became increasingly powerful as a means of expression. However, the late years of Tintoretto's art found him even further advanced in abstract and expressive design. His sketch for *Paradise* (Fig. 441), made in 1587 for the Ducal Palace in Venice, shows how bold and inventive and "modern"

Museum, Parma.

FIG. 439. Correggio, Madonna
of St. Jerome (1523).

of Tintoretto who (to maintain the analogy) figuratively places a ramp from the stage to the audience so that the old barrier of footlights is removed. Flashing diagonals lead the eye directly into deep space, figures are always in action or poised for movement. He abolishes the basic conception of the figure set *against* a background; for him there is no such thing as background. Walls, banks of trees, horizon lines are handled so as to make them as dramatically potent as the figures. He thus achieves an all-over pattern with broken lines, curved lines, light that bursts and dies. His *Last Supper* (Fig. 440), painted in 1594, illustrates his method. Where Leonardo constructed a clearly designed and neutral boxlike room for his painting (Fig. 418), Tintoretto made his whole canvas dramatic. Leonardo's treatment is illustrative and descriptive of psychological values, depending as it does upon facial expression and movement of hands and arms. Tintoretto uses line, color, light and dark, and space to make the surface of his canvas surge and flow

S. Giorgio Maggiore, Venice.

FIG. 440.   Tintoretto, Last Supper (1594).

he had become. El Greco and Rubens felt the impact of Tintoretto's dramatic language and adapted it to their painting, and the art of many moderns is based upon just such a conception of painting. The individual figures become part of the "landscape" in this view of heaven. They coalesce with clouds of light to form vast concentric swirls. Light, color, space merge in a tremendous cosmic drama to which individual figures as actors are subordinated. The closest analogy with other arts is found in music, for in it sheer sound becomes a vehicle for incalculable shades of emotion. The world is configured by the painter as by the musician in an untranslatable idiom of sensuous stuff. Tintoretto does not go as far as Kandinsky and Picasso do in the twentieth century, but there is ample evidence that he clearly understood the revolutionary principles implied by his art.

In literature such devices as figures of speech (irony, hyperbole, metaphor) are so common that we are almost unaware of them until they are pointed out and explained. Because most people are relatively unfamiliar with the language of the pictorial arts they are frequently puzzled when a painter employs similar devices. Men like Tintoretto seem on the surface to be violating inherent rules of art when in reality they are using established principles of design in a new manner that is more appropriate and more effective for their own generation. Inheriting the freer and more casual arrangements of space and forms that had long prevailed in Venetian painting, Tintoretto developed his art further in that direction. The Venetian colorists always composed on the basis of color spotting as opposed to the linear designs of central Italy (Raphael, Michelangelo). Tintoretto carried this practice to what, for his time, was a daring conclusion, plunging the spectator into active imaginative participation in his dramas. This practice can be observed a hundred years earlier in the frescoes

Louvre, Paris.

FIG. 441.   Tintoretto, Paradise, Sketch (1587).

of Mantegna (cf. Fig. 406), but it was Correggio and particularly Tintoretto who gave currency to the idiom which prevailed even into our own day.

Paolo Veronese (1528-1588) was a slightly younger contemporary of Tintoretto, and his career in painting parallels the latter part of Titian's life. To say that he has neither Titian's monumental versatility nor Tintoretto's drama but is as Venetian in his way as they are may seem paradoxical. Nonetheless, in such a painting as the *Triumph of Venice* (Fig. 442) in the Great Council Hall of the Doges' Palace, he adds his tribute to their praises of the Queen of the Adriatic. An allegory of materialism it might be termed, for this pictorial celebration shows the confident worldliness with which Venice and her sons and daughters viewed themselves and their possessions. Unrivaled in richness and harmony of color, the oil pigments spread on canvas a magnificent pageant of human bodies clothed in sumptuous fabrics and set off by opulent architectural forms. Very characteristic too is the reasonable compromise with more exacting conceptions of space achieved by Veronese. Although it is painted on the ceiling, the picture plane is at a forty-five-degree angle to that of the

ceiling so it does not force the observer to view it from immediately beneath its center, as comparable designs often do (Figs. 402, 438) but allows him to see it more comfortably from one end.

Although Veronese maintained a high level of Venetian style in such splendid decorations, he remained a local Venetian spirit, whereas Giorgione, Titian, and Tintoretto belong to a larger world. And of these three it was Tintoretto who kindled the imagination of later men. Actually he belongs not to the High Renaissance but to the Baroque. The path he took leads specifically to El Greco, Rubens, Rembrandt and other masters of the seventeenth century.

Moreover, while Tintoretto (with other painters) was drastically modifying the rigid cage-like space of the Renaissance, comparable and related changes were occurring in other fields like religion, architectural, and music. Italian architects (Fig. 148) were evolving an epochal style in response to the requirement of the Counter-Reformation. The Church in its militant reaction to the threat of Protestantism welcomed the dramatic flights of the baroque masters and the city of Rome was becoming transformed by the new style.

Grand Council Chamber, Doges' Palace, Venice.

FIG. 442. Veronese, Triumph of Venice
(1578–1585).

Detail of Fig. 447.

CHAPTER TWENTY-SEVEN

Renaissance Painting in the North

The transformation of art and life in Italy during the fifteenth century did not materially affect the contemporary art of northern countries beyond the Alps, for the Gothic pattern persisted there for a century or more after the sensuous and individualistic ideas basic to the Renaissance had permeated Italian art. The mediaeval painters of France, Flanders, and Germany had before them highly naturalistic models in the cathedral sculptures. Had Renaissance art been simply a matter of imitating nature, we might hold that the northern peoples were well in advance of the Italians; but the classical ideas that also shaped the cultural pattern of Renaissance Italy were relatively scattered in the north or appeared there only sporadically before the sixteenth century. Then, largely through Albrecht Dürer, classical art became integrated with the native Gothic style, effecting a synthesis comparable to the new art of Italy.

When Italy was producing the robust art of Filippo Lippi (Fig. 404) and Pollaiuolo (Fig. 408), German artists were still adhering to the late Gothic style. Its essential features are present in the *Virgin in a Courtyard* (Fig. 443), done about 1480 by Martin Schongauer (*ca.* 1430-1491). The Virgin Mary is no aristocratic lady elevated to a queenly throne but a bourgeois woman adoring her child, an example of the folk character in German art which was a strong and healthy heritage of the Middle Ages. Schongauer illuminates the theme with delicacy of line and sensitivity to space patterns. His Virgin rests in a veritable sea of crisply breaking folds, one of

those late mediaeval mannerisms of pattern that also appear in the sculpture and architecture of the time. Richness of decoration for its own sake had become an aesthetic burden which was to disappear with the influx of classical thought. There is, moreover, a conflict between the tortured drapery and the sensitively felt silhouette of the tree. The inconsistency between this sympathetic observation of the nuances of nature's forms and the deliberate artificial pattern of the draperies is only one of the many manifestations of internal conflict in this transitional art.

In addition to these differences in style and content there is also a difference in medium, for Schongauer's Virgin in a Courtyard is in another medium than the tempera or oil in which the Italian Renaissance paintings discussed thus far were done. Schongauer's Virgin is an engraving, printed from a copper plate in which the line pattern was incised and then filled with ink and stamped on paper. Pollaiuolo (Fig. 408) and Mantegna were masters of the art in Italy, but in its early stages it appealed particularly to northern artists. For Schongauer lived in the fifteenth-century Germany that saw the beginning of printing in the western world. Moreover, from about 1400, Europeans had been using carved blocks of wood to stamp designs on cloth and paper (Fig. 384), a practice known to the Chinese at least as early as the ninth century. The mechanical parallel between the printing of words and images (whether from wood blocks carved in relief or from incised copper plates) is obvious. Just as printing gave widespread knowledge of new ideas, so the *printed picture* made for the dissemination of knowledge. The Flemish and Germans in particular were quick to adopt print-making. Cultural ideas received the fullest dissemination in local areas and over an international field. The exchange of prints from town to town and country to country might bring local and provincial schools within the orbit of larger and more cosmopolitan thought. Something comparable has occurred in our own day in the perfection of color reproduction processes. The collotype perfected only a few years ago makes it possible for the design of a painting to be reproduced in full color and pass into the

The Metropolitan Museum of Art,
Gift of Felix M. Warburg, 1925.

FIG. 443. Schongauer, Virgin in a Courtyard, Engraving (*ca.* 1480).

hands of millions where formerly the single painting might go into the almost total obscurity of a private collector's living room or storeroom.

Albrecht Dürer (1471-1528), the German artist, saw the great potentialities of the printed picture. Although he was also a painter, it was through the graphic arts—woodcut, engraving, etching—that he made his greatest contribution to European thought. In his hands the woodcut and copper engraving became major vehicles of expression. Beginning in his youth in the tradition of the mediaeval Schongauer, he lived to raise German art to world-wide importance in the Renaissance tradition.

The affinity of verbal and pictorial printing is a significant factor in Dürer's artistic personality. Apprenticed as a youth to one of the leading book illustrators in Germany in the late fifteenth century, he used literary subjects for his own first distinctive projects, notably the Apocalypse, the Revelation of St. John the Divine. *The Four Horsemen of the Apocalypse* (Fig. 444) is the most widely known of the fifteen woodcuts in the series; these are not illustrations in the usual sense of the term but pictorial interpretations of the text. Thus each horseman is described serially in the Revelation vi, 2-8, but Dürer combines all of them in one design, intensifying the dramatic fury of the verbal images by concentrating the forms. By skillfully massing black lines far beyond the simple contours of earlier woodcuts like the St. Christopher of 1423 (Fig. 384), he suggests convincingly not only the terrified human beings in all their actuality but also the threatening personifications of death, famine, pestilence, and hell that ride them down, no less real for being also a vision. The Apocalyptic Vision was not new in western art; scores of illuminated manuscripts interpret its themes in notable designs. But it is significant that from the appearance in 1498 of Dürer's conception of the end of the world, it has been accepted as the classic definition, as that which having once been seen cannot be otherwise imagined.

Dürer had been in Italy for a short time before he made the woodcuts of the Apocalypse series, and he was also familiar with the work of many Italian artists through the medium of prints

like Pollaiuolo's Ten Nudes (Fig. 408). He seems particularly indebted to Mantegna for many significant details in the series. Even so, Dürer still thought largely in mediaeval terms in this and his woodcuts of the Large Passion, and the difference between his rather harshly angular figures and those of his Italian contemporaries was not lost upon him. For some years around 1500, he strove conscientiously to grasp the principles of classic beauty which guided the Italians. He studied the writings of Vitruvius, the Roman theorist, and the later Renaissance writers like Alberti (cf. pages 138-139), particularly Leonardo da Vinci; he even began to develop an artistic theory of his own.

The *Fall of Man* (Fig. 445) sums up Dürer's interests that resulted from these studies. A metal engraving, signed and dated 1504, it is universally recognized as one of his most distinguished works. Going far beyond Schongauer in the technique of the burin, the pointed metal instrument used to gouge the lines in the plate, Dürer achieved the means of representing in this difficult medium practically any quality of surface or substance he chose. In the Fall of Man he uses it to establish the individual characteristics of different materials like fur, flesh, the bark of the tree trunks, thus making them convincing and real in graphic terms. All of this is to make the symbolism more meaningful. Adam and Eve are humanity in its perfect and ideal state before sin came into the world. It is significant that both are modeled on classic forms that Dürer knew from drawings or prints. Adam, for instance, has the proportions, pose, and gestures of the Hellenistic statue called the Apollo Belvedere which had been found in Rome only a short time before. Dürer was also indebted to Pollaiuolo for the idea of the dark forest background, and the tablet with his name and the date suspended above his right shoulder; both appear in the Ten Fighting Nudes (Fig. 408).

Yet for all Dürer's familiarity with classic forms and understanding of the concepts they embody, the Fall of Man is the work of a northerner. It was much admired in Italy, but it could never be taken for an Italian achievement. He seems to have sensed this himself, for when he

Collection of Mr. Lessing J. Rosenwald.

FIG. 444.   Dürer.   The Four Horsemen of the
Apocalypse, Woodcut (1497–1498).

went again to Italy in 1505, he was much less
impressed by the things he saw on his first
visit. He went to paint an altarpiece for the
chapel of the German colony in Venice, and for
some time was more active in painting than in
the graphic arts. But on his return to Germany in
1507, he reverted to the art of the print in works
which make evident his realization of the

impossibility of translating his own northern
concepts into the formal idioms of Renaissance
Italy. Woodcuts, some of which were issued in
book form, were usually cut by specially trained
craftsmen after his drawings; but the metal engravings were done by his own hand. Three of
these, made in 1513 and 1514, are Dürer's most
celebrated works—Knight, Death, and the Devil;

National Gallery of Art, Washington, D.C., Rosenwald Collection.

FIG. 445.   Dürer, Fall of Man, Engraving (1504).

St. Jerome in his Cell; and *Melencolia I* (Fig. 446) —revealing as they do his ultimate compromise between the fundamentally emotional values of his northern inheritance and the rational beauty of Italian Renaissance forms. Technically these prints have never been surpassed in the craftsmanship by which lines laboriously gouged in the copper plate record and characterize such minute details as difference in texture between glass and polished metal. Expressively, the woman sitting in the immobility of mental inertia

rather than physical weariness, surrounded by the symbols of fruitless learning, is filled with a pessimism of almost Faustian profundity.

The clarity with which these ideas are set forth was achieved in part from Dürer's study of Italian art. He came to recognize the necessity for couching even the most subjective concepts in organized formal patterns if their nature was to be fully perceived. If the Melencolia I is comparable in content to Michelangelo's Jeremiah (Fig. 424), it is likewise a northern counterpart

National Gallery of Art, Washington, D.C., Rosenwald Collection.

FIG. 446. Dürer, Melencolia I, Engraving (1514).

National Gallery of Art, Washington D.C., Rosenwald Collection.

FIG. 447. Dürer, St. Anthony Before the Walls of Nuremburg, Engraving
(1519).

of Leonardo's Mona Lisa (Fig. 420). In the engraving, Dürer ponders (even as does his winged woman) the dilemma of faith and science, of reason (the measuring instrument of science) and religion. The positive evaluation of such experience is evident in another of Dürer's great prints of 1513-1514, the St. Jerome in His Cell, and also in the somewhat later one showing *St. Anthony Before the Walls of Nuremberg* (Fig. 447), which was engraved in 1519. Here the forms of nature fall into lucid and orderly patterns, the buildings in the town mounting up in a pyramid that reinforces the form of the saint profoundly absorbed in his meditations in the foreground; the composition is as forceful in its embodiment of finally realized truths as the Melencolia I is of doubt and despair. Dürer thus remains true to his inheritance of significant spiritual experience, but embodies it in patterns that effectively

represent the first creative fusion of northern content with the formal concepts of Renaissance Italy.

There are three major voices in German painting—Dürer, Grünewald, and Holbein. The brief span of fifty years, 1500-1550, saw the beginning and the end of their heroic effort. If Dürer is the supreme master of line, Matthias Grünewald (*ca.* 1465-1528) is no less distinguished as a master of color. His greatest achievement is the Isenheim Altarpiece painted in 1515. It is a series of panels that fold over each other like the one painted by the van Eycks in Ghent (Figs. 373, 374), with scenes of the Passion and the lives of saints. The *Crucifixion* (Fig. 448) is the central and climactic act in a series of epochal transformations. As the Gothic artists symbolized in the cathedral all heaven and the shadows of earth, and as Michelangelo undertook in the Sistine Ceiling to create a mighty all-inclusive cosmos, so Grünewald's colossal imagination embraces pictorially the entirety of human experience. Like Bosch he explored the nether world of dreams in the Temptation of St. Anthony; the *Angelic Serenade and Nativity* (Fig. 449) is a paean to creation. The Incarnation is the divine mystery set forth in the Annunciation. The Crucifixion is the climax followed by the pathos of Entombment and the fearful consuming light of the Resurrection. This awful pageant of man and salvation can be compared only with the supreme creations in art; it is like the *Divine Comedy* in scope and force, or the Greek tragedies. As the masses of Palestrina and Bach unfold the drama of life step by step so also does this altar with its successively unfolding panels.

In German art generally, color is subordinate to linear design, but Grünewald uses it with extraordinary force, less for its structural function, as in Venetian painting, than to effect a psychological impact. The Virgin is a beaming German girl radiantly maternal in the Nativity (Fig. 449), the Magdalene of the Crucifixion a study in morbidity. The model for the Christ crucified is the festering corpse of one pitifully racked with frightful disease. The altar was painted in 1515 for the chapel in the monastery of St. Anthony at Isenheim where contagious diseases were treated. The artist has taken a broken and diseased body such as might be seen there to symbolize the agony of the Redemption.

If Grünewald is mediaeval in his utterly religious purpose and in the intensity of his psychology, he is modern in his persistent use of nature in homely intimacy and in the grand scale of his drama. But in another sense he rises to expressive heights beyond any art tradition or local school. There has been no one else like him in the Germany of his day or since.

The third great German master, Hans Holbein (1497-1543), came a full generation after

Museum, Colmar.

FIG. 448.   Grünewald, Crucifixion, part of
The Isenheim Altarpiece (1515).

Museum,.Colmar.

FIG. 449. Grünewald, Angelic
Serenade and Nativity, part of
The Isenheim Altarpiece.

detached. In his portrait of *Henry VIII* (Fig. 450), painted about 1539, the king is crafty and intelligent. Bravely arrayed in the pompous trappings of his office, he stands full-face in a frame which seems too small to contain his overbearing presence. The bull neck, beady eyes, tight sensuous mouth, and small puffy hands are displayed against the elaborately detailed costume. The richness of fabric and jewels emphasizes the florid personality reveling in barbaric splendor. Though the portrait is extraordinarily analytical, the details are united in a lucid and coherent pattern. This design differs markedly from that of the humanist *Erasmus* (Fig. 451), painted in 1523, just as the personalities of the two men differed. The figure of Erasmus is smaller, the room space more ample. There is none of the tightness and tension of the king's portrait. The scholar sits at ease in his quiet study, his attention directed to his writing. The warm blended colors and the apparently casual composition of the forms characterize the mood and activity of an observant and

his illustrious compatriots. His father was a painter in the mediaeval tradition, but the son's cultural world had experienced the impact of Renaissance humanism. The moral fervor and passionate convictions of Grünewald and Dürer were scarcely shared by Holbein, for he was a man of the world both as an artist and as a personality. As a graphic artist, he executed a brilliant series of woodcuts called The Dance of Death, a common theme in the northern art of the time, but his religious paintings are relatively perfunctory and it is only natural that in an age of increasing secularism he should have done his principal work in portraiture.

Seeking patronage, he found it in England where he became court painter to Henry VIII; as a result, that monarch's court circle is probably the most thoroughly documented pictorially of any in history. Scores of portraits—among them Anne of Cleves, Sir Thomas More, Jane Seymour —come from him in oil and drawings. In every instance Holbein is a rationalist, cool and

Corsini Gallery, Rome.

FIG. 450. Holbein, Henry VIII
(*ca.* 1539).

contemplative spirit. With an eye quick to contrive a flat decorative pattern that would summarize the solid bulk of his subject, Holbein always achieved a design that was harmonious in itself, even if little in his portraits recalls the charged linear patterns of Dürer. Holbein was the last pictorial genius to emerge from Germany. The Thirty Years' War, in which a great part of the population of Germanic countries was annihilated, brought to an end any further important development in the arts for a century.

In Flanders, painting had a rich heritage in the van Eycks, Hugo van der Goes, and others of the fifteenth century. In the sixteenth century, it attained fresh vitality in the hands of Peter Bruegel the Elder (1525-1569). Where Leonardo and Michelangelo in the south studied the human figure to make it a vehicle for the expression of thought, Bruegel in Flanders expressed his profoundest convictions through landscape. Landscape painting had been important in the miniatures of late Gothic manuscripts (Fig. 372), and the fifteenth-century masters had continuously been occupied with its interpretation in the backgrounds of their paintings (Fig. 378); but it remained for Bruegel to explore its deepest implications. In a series of paintings representing the four seasons executed in 1565, he gave an exhaustive account of the peasant's activity, the intimate experience of man in closest contact with the freezing air of winter, the harvest of summer and bronzed autumn. The picture representing *Summer* (Fig. 452) hangs in the Metropolitan Museum in New York. Peasants heavy with fatigue and the lassitude of noonday heat sit eating or sprawl asleep beneath a tree in a harvest feld. Bruegel sees everything—the peasants' greedy feeding habits, the precise method of harvesting grain, the jug of water in the shade, the birds in the trees, the village in the distance with children at play. For the first time in art, the anonymous and inarticulate aspects of man's communal activity and the familiar life of the countryside are recorded on a monumental pictorial scale. Yet the hundreds of observations, the almost countless birds and people, the buildings that sprinkle the hills and valleys are so skillfully distributed and controlled in the large

Louvre, Paris.

FIG. 451.   Holbein, Erasmus (1523).

pattern of space that the landscape is seen as a unit, as logically constructed and lucidly articulated as a figure composition by Leonardo. By means of a large pattern in which the details are integrated structurally and psychologically, scenery becomes landscape expressive of profound spiritual implications. For here, man is conceived as an integral part of nature; the landscape results from his labors and has significance only in terms of the form he gives it. This is the identical truth that Leonardo expounded in Florence earlier in the century; it is the same truth that gives such great authority to Titian's art.

The Reformation sweeping the northern countries was implicitly expounded by Bruegel. When he painted the Crucifixion it became a veiled comment on the ravages of the Spanish Inquisition which at that time was crucifying Flanders. In a deep landscape with hundreds of tiny figures the peasants come trooping out of the town toward a distant Calvary. A ring of curious sensation-seekers collects around the cross almost invisible in the distance. The implication is clear, for the setting is the Flemish countryside and the soldiers are obviously Spanish. By the same token, his Slaughter of the Innocents is portrayed as a savage searching party of the Inquisition brutally seizing its victims in a Flemish village. Bruegel's love of the uncouth peasant celebrations, recorded in weddings, dances, and drinking bouts, earned him the name of Droll Peter and Peasant Bruegel.

There are good reasons for considering him the first great modern master in the sense that his unself-conscious portrayal of common things—children at play, peasants dancing, farmers at work—indicates a mind that saw in the customary routine of humanity the meaning of life. Thus the landscape is no more only a picturesque sight, but a pattern of man's life activity. The *Wedding Dance* (Fig. 453), now in Detroit, is more than a quaint record of folk customs. One may see all manner of things in a Bruegel painting—the obvious narrative, the picturesque customs, the lively recorded anecdote. But beyond this is the clear statement of a man who recognized the underlying implications of a civilization. A peasant wedding dance is a drama of human forces no less than the Dionysiac revels of Greek times and as revealing of spiritual implications as the ceremony of an eighteenth-century minuet or a twentieth-century jam session. The seasonal ritual—the celebration of the harvest, the planting time, the marriage—are focal points revealing the zest for life common to all peoples. No artist graphs these life

The Metropolitan Museum of Art, Rogers Fund, 1919.

FIG. 452.   Bruegel, Summer (1565).

The Detroit Institute of Arts.

FIG. 453. Bruegel, Wedding Dance (1566).

impulses more explicitly and with greater assurance than Bruegel. His art is deeply religious, though it does not always use the symbolism of Christianity. It celebrates a drama older than Christianity itself, one that will be manifest in the art of Rembrandt, Goya, and Daumier in ages to come.

As the tide of Gothic thought receded and humanism replaced it as the dominant way of life, the process that was in full tide in fifteenth-century Italy did not reach its height in the north, until the next century. Although the new synthesis of thought was undoubtedly taking place spontaneously in Germany and Flanders, it was immeasurably accelerated by the continuous contact of the northerners with the more advanced thought of the Italians. Dürer and Bruegel visited Italy and Holbein knew its art; all were deeply influenced by that contact. And Italy in turn was impregnated with the vital energies of the Gothic spirit that lay behind the northern Renaissance. In the following century there was a complete fusion of European art and thought; but Italy's vitality waned, and the leadership was assumed by France, the Netherlands, and Spain.

Detail of Fig. 464.

CHAPTER TWENTY-EIGHT

Painting in the Seventeenth Century

It is difficult to generalize about the new painting of the seventeenth century, for art had a larger and more extended audience in that period than in the sixteenth century in either Italy or the north. Painting still served the Church by appealing to the emotions of the faithful; in other instances it catered to the more popular interest in representational naturalism. But to a large degree the symbolic function which gave it direction and purpose during the Renaissance was relaxed. In the waning sixteenth century in Italy, the grand, formal, and expressive discipline of the older masters was not renewed by their successors. There were those who paid lip service to the earlier masters, to be sure, and confidently expected to acquire by easy imitation the energy and nobility they recognized in Raphael, Michelangelo, and Titian; the result all too often was only facility, superficiality, and eclecticism.

The basis of eclecticism was emulation of the Renaissance masters, including the exotic Correggio. Without recourse to the emotional and intellectual forces of an earlier day the Italian eclectics sought to sustain the lofty style by learned imitation. Two cousins, Lodovico Carracci (1556-1619) and Annibale Carracci (1560-1609) of Bologna, were the leading exponents of the movement. Annibale's principal work is the painting of the great hall of the Farnese Palace in Rome (Fig. 125). Here he followed the grand decorative scheme of Michelangelo's Sistine Ceiling, but now the decorative borders dominate the scheme. The enframed pictures are scarcely more than medallions about which the decorative nudes revolve.

The showmanship and sensationalism of the eclectics were encouraged by the Church, which, after the schism resulting from the Reformation, found itself in a perilously weakened position (cf. pages 170-171). To fortify itself, the Society of Jesus had been organized to compel allegiance and faith. Begun by Ignatius Loyola in 1534, the Society encouraged architects, sculptors, and painters to dramatize Church doctrines to the point of sensationalism. The results are apparent in the work of the masters who came specifically within the orbit of the Catholic Church, notably Bernini in sculpture (Fig. 333) and architecture (Fig. 130), Rubens and El Greco in painting.

While the eclectic masters were exploiting movement and melodrama to persuade men of wavering faith, another assault upon the sensibilities was being made by the realists. In reaching out for a wider public, the eclectics made practical efforts to sway its thinking through emotional appeal. The realists made their appeal through the senses too. With Caravaggio (1573-1610) comes a change in European art that has been felt to our own time. His subjects have a lively and immediate appeal; they are often taken from everyday life, like the Card Players

and Fortune Tellers. His realism is simple and pragmatic, being based upon the look of things. In the *Entombment of Christ* (Fig. 454) which he painted for the Roman church of Santa Maria in Vallicella between 1602 and 1604, the protagonists do not move in the stately rhythm of a solemn ritual as in Titian's Pietà (Fig. 437), painted only a few years earlier. Instead they weep and moan and gesticulate with the emotional fervor that marks similar occasions in the Roman slums near the church even today. Compare the wildly waving tavern wench, who is Mary Magdalene in Caravaggio's painting with her counterpart in Perugino's (Fig. 411), or the plebeian Nicodemus who bears the weight of Christ's legs with such grievous effort and the urbane aristocrat who kneels at the Savior's feet in the earlier picture. It is true that Perugino's Pietà is not a deeply felt interpretation, and Caravaggio's is melodramatic by contrast. Some, including the authorities of the church it was painted for, have felt it to be an overstatement; the painting no longer is in the place planned for it but hangs in the Vatican Museum.

Yet though Caravaggio's Entombment has neither the lyric charm that is the anodyne of grief in Perugino's painting, nor the austere monumentality that invests Titian's version with lofty tragedy, it is powerfully moving. By means of the light that plays over the forms and gives them the immediacy of sculptured figures, the design involves the spectator in the drama to an extent not achieved by any earlier painting. Even Tintoretto, using light in seemingly the same way (Fig. 440), still creates a world which the observer enters if he wishes; but when he looks at Caravaggio's, he is caught up and swept along, perhaps against his volition. By sheer intensity of vision and the powerful light that makes visible the truth perceived by that vision, the painter speaks of fundamental experiences.

This vivid and arresting art made a great impression on the German and Flemish artists living in Italy at the turn of the century. By direct or indirect means the method also reached Spanish, Dutch, and Flemish masters, who found it consistent with the increasingly democratic function

FIG. 454. Caravaggio, Entombment of Christ
(1602–1604).

of their art. Rubens will modify it with the power of Venetian color. Rembrant will refine it into mystery of space, and Velasquez into the lucid rhythms of his extraordinary perception. For in this Italian world at the turn of the century were formed the styles of the northern artists who are the giants of the seventeenth century. El Greco had already gone to Spain after apprenticeship in Venice. But to Rome came the two Frenchmen, Claude le Lorrain and Poussin, and from Flanders came Peter Paul Rubens,

dissatisfied with the Italianate mannerists he had known at home who seemed to understand neither Italian nor Flemish art. Educated in their feebly imitative Italianizing ways in Flanders, Rubens (1577-1640) turned eagerly to a first-hand study of the work everyone seemed obsessed with copying. From 1600 to 1608 he was in Italy painting and intently observing everything, especially the great sixteenth-century masters. Rubens also gave his eclectic and realist contemporaries close attention, and with energy and above all intelligence he absorbed from them too what was useful to him, rejecting the artistic deadwood.

Almost everything he painted later indicates his contact with Michelangelo's heroic figures, the richness of Titian's structural color, and the drama of Tintoretto. Movement and energy pervade all his work, transforming the relatively stable plan of Renaissance figures, or designs. His vast knowledge and the fluency of his energetic style make the work of the Italian eclectics look dry and barren in comparison.

With deep and complex space patterns Rubens deliberately constructs grandiose plans or stage sets for the enactment of miracles or the narration of classic myths. One might say that he interprets life in terms of dynamic contrasts —in the active thrust and athletic movements of heroic giants reminiscent of Michelangelo. Those who seek an ideal and serene harmony in art will find little comfort in his swirling volcanoes of energy.

The style of the Counter-Reformation called for a crescendo of emotion. Rubens supplies it in plastic terms, finding richness of color, space, and line to suit the psychological tempo. The often-told account of the mourning for the dead Christ usually treated with reserve and reticence (cf. Fig. 389) is for Rubens (Fig. 455) an occasion for almost unbelievable drama. Christ's body is that of a Michelangelesque athlete. The Virgin pathetically closes the dead eyes. The Savior's death induces uncontrollable anguish bordering on the pathological among the witnesses. This torrent of feeling is reminiscent of the excesses of the later Middle Ages, but the heroic nude suggests a pagan ritual of death more than the ascetic resignation of Christianity.

As a classical scholar Rubens had a deep feeling for pagan attitudes. The religious themes are not wholly congenial to his temper and he handles them always frankly, with an eye to their pathetic and emotional implications. The depiction of miracles frequently requested by the Church is done with his inherent taste for energy and drama. Love is a recurring theme in his art and appears in his pagan legends like the

Three Graces, the Rescue of Andromeda, the Judgment of Paris. The selfless love of the Madonna for her Child is portrayed, but not with the confidence and lyrical outgoing splendor of the Venus, the Diana, the Andromeda. For Rubens the Venus is a symbol of earth's fertility, for all his themes are unerringly conceived in terms of their widest implication. The impulses of love are wild and orgiastic or restrained in bourgeois conventions, as the case may be. In the *Garden of Love* (Fig. 456) painted in 1632, he treats the theme as manifested in his own society. Courtly folk decorously disport themselves in a courtyard before a baroque palace. The fountain figure is an opulent Venus with flowing breasts who presides over a court of winged loves. The master and his wife, Helena Fourment, move in from the left while an ardent Cupid busies himself with his task of persuasion. Rubens used Helena's opulent charms as the model for many if not most of his later feminine characters. The type is most unclassical and even unattractive to many today. Whether it was a matter of personal idiosyncrasy or not, one may justly say that Rubens found in its buxom ripeness what he considered inherent characteristics of the Venus, the archetype of the mother of mankind, ample of hip and breast, a symbol of fertility.

More outspoken and characteristic of his gift for interpreting the subject of love is the

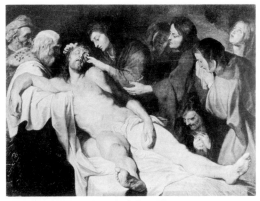

Lichtenstein Gallery, Vienna.

FIG. 455. Rubens, Lamentation over Christ (1614).

Rape of the Daughters of Leucippus (Fig. 457), painted about 1618. The broken shimmering surfaces in the Garden of Love and its rich space pattern are not so highly developed here; more stable and simpler patterns prevail. The pagan theme gave ample opportunuties to Rubens' enormous energies. No illusionism or naturalism is intended. The struggle is an elaborate and theatrical display of feminine loveliness and masculine ardor. In a fine tableau like an episode in grand opera, the bronzed brothers, Castor and Pollux, eagerly but with noble discretion seize their prize. The women, with appropriate rhetorical appeals to the gods, unreluctantly enact this ritual of love.

Many of Rubens' works were painted with the aid of assistants. The artist maintained a veritable picture factory, he furnishing designs and his assistants doing much of the preliminary painting; the whole was supervised and the finishing colored glazes were applied by the master. Some of his men were specialists in one field or another like still-life or animal figures. Van Dyck, his most gifted assistant and student, worked on the last-mentioned picture.

Rubens lived on a grand scale intellectually and socially. His art was enormously successful throughout Europe and he reaped a rich material reward for his incredible energy. To a very large degree he integrated the art traditions of the north with those of Italy. In his great Kermesse, or country dance, in the Louvre he proved how thoroughly he carried on the plastic and cultural concepts of the sixteenth-century giant Bruegel (Fig. 453), and in his late landscapes he continued a tradition extending back in Flemish art to Pol de Limbourg, Jan van Eyck, and Bosch. As he enriched Flemish art with the forms of Michelangelo, with the lyric and structural colorism of Tintoretto and Veronese, he passed these on

Prado, Madrid.

FIG. 456.   Rubens, Garden of Love (1632).

Alte Pinakothek, Munich.

FIG. 457.   Rubens, Rape of the Daughters of Leucippus
(*ca.* 1618).

transformed to the eighteenth-century masters, notably Watteau, and to the nineteenth-century romantics. His vital, decorative style became the stock-in-trade of lesser men who endlessly exploited his pictorial methods.

Rubens' disciple, Jordaens, popularized the method in superficial melodrama. Anthony van Dyck (1599-1641) is often only an extension of the master's talent, selecting from Rubens the softer, more feminine aspects to exploit. It was as a portraitist that van Dyck had his chief vogue. His work has a certain aestheticism, as though he looked upon a painting as a decorative design not necessarily having specific relation to any

serious interpretation of life. He is most congenially occupied in creating flattering and engaging portraits of aristocratic people. Many of these are out-and-out commercial jobs with no expressive merit. At his best, however, he sometimes penetrates deeply, reaching and illuminating intimate and personal life more completely than Rubens. Van Dyck's influence was very great and perhaps out of proportion to his intrinsic merit. As court painter to the English king, *Charles I* (Fig. 458), he followed in the path of Holbein a hundred years earlier (cf. pages 525-527). In his decorative brilliance he anticipates the rococo style of the eighteenth

Louvre, Paris.

FIG. 458. Van Dyck, Charles I
(*ca.* 1635).

appetite for all that was noble in the classic past, only indirectly affected neighboring Dutch artists. Flanders was Catholic, and Rubens shared the afflatus of the Counter-Reformation, which sought to revive the waning authority of the Church through the dazzling splendor of the spectacular and dramatic in architecture, sculpture, and painting. Furthermore, Rubens was a gentleman of wealth and aristocratic culture. As an ambassador of kings and a scholar of note, he belonged to the social world of the aristocrat and the intellectual.

The painters who were his Dutch contemporaries are quite different. Holland was Protestant and wealthy, its citizens good industrious merchants. The Protestant faith had no use for showy altarpieces nor was there any demand for religious painting in its churches. What the Dutch did want was small realistic paintings for interior decoration. They liked pictures of interiors, still-lifes of luscious fruit and vegetables, landscapes and genre studies of everyday scenes of home and street; especially they loved portraits, either singly or in groups. The Dutch painter did not try to express a subtle and abstract idea as the Italians had and as Rubens had under southern influence. Having won its centuries-long conflict, first with foreign powers and then against the encroaching sea, Holland set about enjoying freedom and prosperity. Secure within itself, the country asked only that its painters paint its likeness. There was nothing too trivial not to be of interest. Subjects unthought-of by Rubens and the Italians now became of first importance to Dutch painters. Adriaen Brouwer (1605-1638), a brawling tavern tippler, was fascinated by animated scenes like roisterers in a saloon. Typical is the *Company of Smokers* (Fig. 459), showing the painter with three of his convivial artist friends —Frans Hals, Adriaen van Ostade, and Adriaen de Vois—indulging in the new pastime of the day. The theme may seem far from the aristocratic garden party of Rubens' lords and ladies (Fig. 456), but the artist develops it with singular sensitiveness to subtle color patterns which do much to relieve the coarseness of the subject matter.

Brouwer, Adriaen von Ostade, and Jan

century, especially in the English school. In his work the English found exactly the model for their portraits and landscapes, but it is significant that the French masters of that century turned to Rubens rather than to the more superficial van Dyck.

It would be difficult to overstate the effect of Rubens' art in his own century and the following two centuries. His presence was felt wherever art flourished, and as a consummate master of color he was one of the most influential painters who ever lived.

The art of Italy, which fired Rubens with desire for the heroic and grandiose and fed his

FIG. 459.   A. Brouwer, Company
of Smokers (*ca.* 1631).

Steen are among the so-called Little Masters of
Holland. Together they explore from varying
vantage points the life of the peasantry, the city
and country slums, middle-class manners, and
folkways. Brouwer is almost obsessed with pain
and violence and brute passion, though his
paintings show exquisite sensitivity and high
technical discipline. Jan Steen (1626-1679) is an
inheritor of Pieter Bruegel's zest for folk drama,
which he makes more intimate and descriptive.
The Dutch masters painted with the frankest
literalness the free, pleasure-loving, pub-crawling
habits of their people. Their biographers often
present the artists themselves as abandoned, wife-
beating drunkards, but these legends of dissipa-
tion are little substantiated by the longevity of

many of these painters and above all by the vast
quantity and consistently high quality of their
craftsmanship, not to mention their unfailingly
individual styles.

That Jan Steen was a hearty liver, a robust,
genial, witty, and forthright spirit is indeed the
only conclusion to be drawn from much of his
painting. Especially in his early years, he was
particularly fond of the tavern scenes and other
convivial aspects of the day. Subsequently,
humor which often approaches satire makes its
appearance, as in the *Lovesick Girl* (Fig. 460),
painted probably about 1665. The doctor knows
that his remedies will not help the lady's afflic-
tion; hence his pose and gesture are all the more
solicitous. Almost lost in the shadow by the
girl's chair, a string burns in a cup to ward off
fainting spells. Steen is perhaps more concerned
with telling an anecdote than painting a picture.
He describes facts rather than composes in color
as Brouwer did with an inherently less preposes-
sing theme. But he brings the same point of
view to bear as did Molière, his contemporary

FIG. 460.   Jan Steen, Lovesick Girl
(*ca.* 1665).

Wallace Collection, London.

FIG. 461.   Hals, Laughing Cavalier (1624).

in the French drama; there is more than a time parallel between *Le médecin malgré lui* and Steen's Lovesick Girl. His is not the most profound sensibility among the Dutch, but no artist had a more lively eye. More than any painter of his generation, perhaps, Steen tells of the energy, the spirit, and the humor of a violent and lusty society.

While the scientists were analyzing the physical world in order to reduce it to categories and systems in the fields of astronomy, physics, and chemistry, the painters were likewise observing and making note of any and every bit of human experience. If some of this popular painting seems trivial, it must be remembered that from this self-observation, from this inquiry into the most intimate aspects of experience, was fashioned the greatest spirit of the age, Rembrandt. It must also be borne in mind that the Dutch were materialists with voracious appetites for hearty worldly pleasure, and as such they supported the painters who could best mirror themselves. Franz Hals (*ca.* 1580-1666) reflects them vividly in portraits of bubbling humor and contagious buoyancy such as the Gypsy Girl and the Laughing Cavalier, which are deservedly popular. In such works as these, Hals broke down for northern painters the formal barrier that remained in Ruben's art as a heritage of the Italian Renaissance, and showed the way to an art embodying profound human understanding based on sympathy for common mankind.

Protestant Holland was producing a culture in the seventeenth century which functioned outside the Church's orbit. Its middle-class citizens had no understanding or taste for the gods of Olympus, for they were engrossed in military affairs, in commerce and industry. Where Flemish Rubens had found patronage in the Church and in the rich and powerful English lords and Italian dukes who bought his pictures, the Dutch painters found patronage in the middle class. Caravaggio in Italy had also reached this

new market, but Hals' realism is different from the Italian's because it lies not so much in exploiting dramatic situations with an arresting spotlight illumination as in building a painterly form through structurally realized passages of light and color. Like that of every painter, his work varies in quality. Many of his paintings have surface showmanship in both technique and theatrical gestures, but the obvious bravura of the *Laughing Cavalier* (Fig. 461), painted in 1624, is carried off with provocative spirit and gayety. Yet at times Hals approached the heights attained by Rembrandt in penetrating the very essence of his sitter's personality. Such a painting is the *Lady Regents of the Haarlem Almshouse* (Fig. 462) of 1664, a group portrait in which the five personalities fuse into a natural harmonious pattern. Each individual is distinctly portrayed, yet each participates in the psychic interplay of personality that is the essence of a group. The

Halsmuseum, Haarlem.

FIG. 462.   Hals, Lady Regents of the Haarlem Almshouse (1664).

∽ 539 ∾

dexterity and facility of Hals' brushwork produced effects of refreshing spontaneity. A complex detail is rendered in its totality by a single broad stroke of his brush, and the whole is amplified in a few accents of color and light that suddenly reveal the complete character of the subject.

Dutch art in the seventeenth century flowered in profuse response to the needs of a rich and energetic middle-class Protestant society. With Rembrandt van Rijn (1606-1669) this art was crowned with a towering genius. His name belongs with the few very great names—Giotto, Leonardo, Michelangelo, Raphael, Titian, and El Greco. In his breadth of interest he spanned the century, revealing every phase of its spiritual and intellectual character; from the realism and materialism of its scientists, its Little Masters in painting, to the mysticism of its saints—everything can be found in this master's paintings and etchings. No artist ever turned his heart and hand to so great a diversity of subject matter. With the actuality that was born of the analytical and scientific spirit of his age, Rembrandt set about systematically to make himself master of reality in its smallest and least observed particles. Characteristically he took for analysis what was closest to him. With the aid of a mirror he sketched, painted, and etched his own face repeatedly, not from vanity, for his features were coarse, but to reduce the texture of flesh and hair and the complex pattern of light and color to a schematic arrangement on paper or canvas. Very early he realized that light was the binding medium that flowed over all visible things and united them as mortar holds together the bricks of a building. And he further observed that light was fluid; that it had a rhythm of movement and was endowed with a life of its own often more real than that of the objects it casually illuminated. Where Raphael had found the common unifying element of art in the line, Michelangelo in the sculptured mass and the Venetians in color, Rembrandt found it in light and atmosphere.

Early in life, while still intent upon capturing the exact appearance of things, fitting the details into the fabric of design, he was continually making essays in the rhythm and flow of light and color. The early landscapes are symphonies of luminous space, harmoniously orchestrated, Wagnerian in their sweeping emotional depths. At times he came close to the borderline of the abstract, to music, in his denial of the literal shape of trees and houses and streams, by abstracting from his subjects the flow and movement of light. The nature of his development is discernible in a series of group portraits. Commissioned to paint a group of Dr. Tulp's medical students in 1632, he faithfully rendered in the *Anatomy Lesson* (Fig. 463) the scene in the dissection room, with each of the auditors distinctly portrayed as they listen to the argument of the demonstration. A strong light strikes full upon the cadaver and illuminates the face and hands of Dr. Tulp, who is appropriately set off from his students. But the observer feels that the demands of a factual clearcut delineation of each face have resulted in a certain artificiality and coldness. The picture shows a series of juxtaposed individuals rather than a lucidly unified group. Ten years later Rembrandt painted another group portrait, the famous Night Watch in Amsterdam. By this time, he realized that the demands imposed by a merely descriptive realism conflicted with what was for him the greater function of his art: the production of a fully unified vision of light and color playing over the forms.

From a purely technical point of view the Anatomy Lesson is less inventive than several group portraits already done by Hals. In the Night Watch, painted in 1642, Rembrandt demonstrated that his genius belonged to an inestimably wider sphere. As a group portrait it was a compromise. The men are portrayed, to be sure, but individual identity is absorbed into the mysteriously poetic world of Rembrandt's invention—his luminous chiaroscuro. The greatest artists have always transformed their subjects in one way or another. The local, the topical, the isolated character of things and persons is absorbed in a universal order perceived by a superior intuition. A portrait by Titian or Raphael, a landscape by Bruegel or Claude le Lorrain bears the imprint less of the person or the scene represented than of the spirit of the artist who takes purely sensate impressions and gives

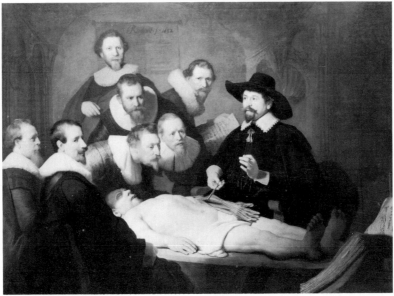

Mauritshuis, The Hague.

FIG. 463. Rembrandt, Dr. Tulp's Anatomy Lesson (1632).

them place and scale in the realm of expressive values.

Considered as an example of pictorial style, the Night Watch is a development of the "dark manner" which Rembrandt inherited from Caravaggio's school but developed into a method. Earlier he had made many small paintings like the Philosopher with the Winding Stairs in which chiaroscuro renders space almost musically eloquent in terms of movement unified in cadence and mood. The Night Watch is an adaptation of this peculiar art language to the exacting requirements of realism in portraiture. The results are mixed. Some twenty years later, in 1661-1662, he painted another group portrait called *The Syndics of the Amsterdam Cloth Guild* (Fig. 464). Here five Dutch businessmen with their clerk are engaged in a routine meeting. The unpromising and prosaic material is enlivened and dramatized by a trivial episode invented by Rembrandt: the conference is interrupted, the attention is shifted from the work in hand to an unseen visitor. The dark swirling chiaroscuro of the Night Watch has no place here. The darks are luminously transparent, the

space echoes and vibrates with the light. Above all, the artist has become aware of the controlled patterns he observed in Italian art. He draws the accents of the wainscoting, the horizontals and verticals of chair and table, even the tilt of a collar and hat into a design of the utmost lucidity. The sobriety of the Dutch merchants has its plastic equivalent in the severity of the structural pattern. But over all is the rich life-giving warmth of the chiaroscuro which glows in the smoldering spot of red on the near corner of the table covered with an Oriental rug and penetrates to the farthest reaches of the room. No individual represented is sacrificed to any formal or stylistic requirement. Each is a unique personality and acquires humanity by social relationship.

Although Rembrandt's art is Dutch from beginning to end, it was profoundly shaped by his intimate study of the Italian masters. Unlike most baroque painters he had not visited Italy but he knew Italian paintings in Holland and collected them. His drawings, a rich mine for the Rembrandt student, show how he studied the design of Leonardo's Last Supper for his own

FIG. 464.   Rembrandt, The Syndics of the Amsterdam Cloth Guild
(1661–1661).

Sampson's Wedding Feast and the Supper at Emmaus. Frequently these drawings give a keener insight into his intentions than formal paintings do. They are like kernels of thought reduced to a pithy phrase. Many of Rembrandt's drawings, like that of his wife *Saskia* (Fig. 465), are perfect plastic organizations. It is like some great line of Shakespeare. The complete crystallization of a pictorial idea, the absolute economy and felicity are proofs of its profound inspiration.

Pictorial reality meant much more to Rembrandt than the skillful organization of sense impressions found in the work of the Little Masters. More and more he looked upon objective reality as something to be translated into intrinsically expressive rhythms. His later paintings, drawings, and etchings offer less and less of illustration and description as he organizes his compositions from within to create drama in space, mass, and color; and as a result they have a peculiarly timeless character. In the *Bathsheba* (Fig. 466) done in 1654, the figure is no more specifically Dutch than Michelangelo's Jeremiah (Fig. 424) is Italian. In this woman of the Old Testament, Rembrandt suggests every impulse to which the image of woman has ever given expression—the Venus of olden times, the Eve, and the Virgin and Mother of the Middle Ages, the instrument through which the stream of life flows from generation to generation. In the sphere of religious painting Rembrandt produced hundreds of illustrations of Biblical texts, pictures that differ in purpose and nature from all the devotional altarpieces and decorative murals of the past. He presented with consummate understanding the human significance of each theme rather than its hieratic or symbolic implications. The story of the *Good Samaritan* (Fig. 467) is dramatized in concrete detail. The Samaritan is seen stopping at nightfall in the court of an inn. While the boys and servants attend to the wounded man, he confers with the keeper about the unfortunate traveler he has befriended. The story is told for the kernel of compassion that animates the simple Bible tale. Tenderness of the strong for the weak has never been so touchingly portrayed. A glance is sufficient to inform the observer of the whole complex movement. The head of the Samaritan turning to indicate his charge, the boy peering inquisitively toward him, the people looking out of the windows—all is so organized that the drama is more pathetically moving than it would be if we saw the event with our own eyes. The wellhead and the rope center attention upon the sick man; the very contours of the architecture assist in articulating the drama. It is mercy and compassion that are the subject of the painting, abstractions implicit in the behavior of the characters. Rembrandt's greatness lies in this capacity to reveal in terms of line and color the deepest human experience with authority and conviction.

As an etcher, Rembrandt is unrivaled, his prints sharing an equal place with his painting. Etching was an almost unexplored medium when he began, but he made it into a subtle and flexible instrument of expression. He recognized the peculiar scope of the abstract black and white print and never confused its technique with that of painting. It is notable that his drawings and etchings record some of his most intimate observations and experiences. The well over three hundred plates constitute a record not only of his artistic development but of his intimate life. Even more fully than his paintings, they give direct accounts of the artist's appearance,

particularly in his early years. His wife Saskia is shown, radiantly happy in the years before her early death in 1642, an occurrence which marks the beginning of tragic times for Rembrandt.

Though a considerable number of the etchings were produced for an art market, as were the majority of his fashionably finished oil portraits in the 1630's, to a large degree the prints are the artist's most personal works. Many of them have a primitive simplicity and directness in design, for Rembrandt used a kind of pictorial shorthand that suggested infinitely more

The Pierpont Morgan Library, N.Y.

FIG. 465. Rembrandt, Saskia and Rumbartus (*ca.* 1636).

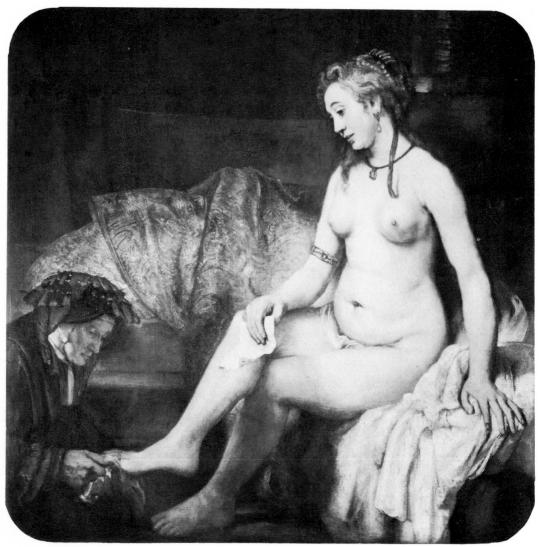

Louvre, Paris.

FIG. 466.   Rembrandt, Bathsheba (1654).

than was represented. It is no wonder that in the prime of his life few understood his work, for Rembrandt had left that comfortable and familiar ground of objective description expected from the Dutch artist, to explore the mysteries of the mind. Today this phase of his art is sometimes called *expressionistic* because the distortion of normal appearance aims at emotional expression beyond any tangibility portrayed. Yet Rem-

brandt was at the same time a supreme realist with the keenest relish for living things, and delight in the grotesque and the infinite vagaries of nature. In this respect he was in closest kinship with the whole northern tradition. Though he learned much from the Italians, he was never lured, even early in life, to adopt their art modes which he must instinctively have felt were foreign to his nature. The Italians, pursuing

Louvre, Paris.

FIG. 467.   Rembrandt, Good Samaritan (1648).

classical ideas, saw the human figure as an object of all beauty and perfection. Rembrandt saw it as a part of the larger world, one that included the borderlands of doubt, tragedy, and mystery.

An early etching, *The Fall of Man* (Fig. 468), done in 1638, suggests his imaginative range in this medium. The picture sparkles with contrasts of every shade from black to white. The two innocents are seen on a hill with a spacious

view in which, of all the animals of Paradise, only an elephant is visible. Framed by the trees and rocks, the human figures are the focal point of attention. Although the subject was expounded by many masters since mediaeval times, Rembrandt's treatment differed from any traditional interpretation. He saw in the theme not so much an episode of Christian mythology as a study of primitive mentality. The primeval parents of humanity are not godlike creatures, sole rulers of the world, as Jacopo della Quercia (Fig. 313) and Michelangelo (Fig. 421) conceived them; they are simple and childlike in their ignorance, knowing only their native impulses to the one forbidden act that makes them human. The psychological differences between man and woman the Italian masters suggested are here accentuated, Eve all eagerness to devour the fruit and Adam restraining her. This drama of the Fall is reminiscent of Milton's version in *Paradise Lost*, written about the same time, in its deep understanding of human nature.

It is interesting to compare this thoroughly naturalistic treatment of the legend with one done in the pre-Romanesque period (Fig. 293). Characteristically, the mediaeval sculptor at Hildesheim used a series of panels, all of which

National Gallery of Art, Washington, D.C.,
Rosenwald Collection.

FIG. 468.   Rembrandt, Fall of Man,
Etching (1638).

are required to tell the story fully. The modern artist, although no more graphic in representing typical action, can condense the episode into a single composition expressive of the complete drama. This condensation was made possible by the complexity of the realistically portrayed setting and the elaborate analysis of human behavior. We become aware imaginatively not only of the acts immediately presented but of those that preceded and those that inevitably followed them. This condensation of narrative is possible only when the eye has been disciplined to great subtlety of pictorial representation; it is impossible in pre-naturalistic art such as the Greek or the Romanesque.

The Fall of Man was made in 1638 when the artist's mode was descriptive and explicit. An etching done twenty years later, *Seated Woman* (Fig. 469), reveals another side of Rembrandt's personality and of his graphic technique. Linear forms have become solid masses, space is represented by movements of light and dark. There is no narrative or anecdote. The nude is in no way beautiful, but the etching is supremely moving and mysterious. The velvet tones of chiaroscuro give some precious relevance to every object. In the scale of tone between the white of the paper and almost total black, Rembrandt achieves a drama of wonder and beauty unsurpassed even in his own painting. The mystic dream of a complete and sufficient world is realized by interlocking patterns of light and shapes related in the figure to produce compactness, balance, and ultimate serenity.

The Dutchman Jan Vermeer (1632-1675) of Delft painted some of the most beautiful pictures of the century. In his whole career he produced only about forty known works, and these few are almost all alike in plan and subject matter. The *Young Woman with a Water Jug* (Fig. 470) of about 1665 is typical, a figure—usually a woman—doing some household task, reading or writing letters, or making lace. The figure is seen against a flat wall which is broken by a map or a picture frame and by silhouetted objects in the foreground. Certainly Vermeer did not seek novel or startling pictorial effects; but as no one else of his time and very few since, he gave the feel

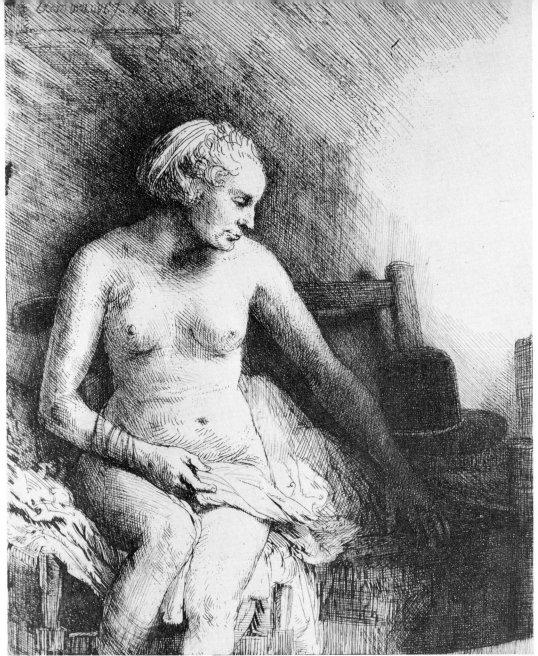

FIG. 469. Rembrandt, Seated Woman, Etching (1658).

of a spacious room flooded with light. Where Rembrandt invented his own mysterious light in his oils and a brooding shadowy world in his late etchings, Vermeer kept a clear palette to evoke the sparkling poetry of his light-flooded interiors.

His method is more linear than that of most baroque masters, but line interacts with color and light so harmoniously and structurally that there is no awareness of color or lines as such; they are wholly attributes of things. Like Giorgione he takes into account the normal process of seeing and in his paintings presents nothing that deviates from ordinary perception. The result is a high degree of reality. But he obtains this sense of realism by constructing his painting with an eye

The Metropolitan Museum of Art, Gift of Henry G. Marquand, 1889.

FIG. 470.   Vermeer, Young Woman with a Water Jug
(*ca.* 1665).

to the inner logic of light and space patterns, of color harmonies consistent with the space and the light. Vermeer anticipates the screening process of normal vision in subordinating details to the basic psychological theme. With structural handling of color the forms emerge logically and compellingly as having an inner life beyond the surface appearance. No peep-show illusionism is involved, for Vermeer creates a heightened reality not only of light and color but of textures, the weight and density of porcelain, of oriental fabrics, of cool linen, glass, and copper. A century later Chardin in France had the same unique

gift, but it is doubtful if he ever saw Vermeer's work.

Although Vermeer is extraordinarily conscious of the quiet moods of women seen in their unself-conscious household acts, he approaches their portrayal through the construction of the enveloping space. Like other baroque painters he finds in *space* an element that may be molded and shaped as earlier artists shaped the dense masses of tangible marble and bronze or simulated those stable masses in their painting. Renaissance artists of the fifteenth and sixteenth centuries seem scarcely aware of space in the sense in which

Vermeer or Rembrandt understood it. In Italy only the Venetians, particularly Tintoretto, sensed its incalculable possibilities in pictorial design. In the other arts—literature, music, architecture, and sculpture—parallel developments occur.

Although the Dutch school of painting was relatively free from any direct influence of the Italian Renaissance, El Greco (1541-1614), the first of the great painters in Spain, was greatly influenced by Italian art. Born a Greek on the island of Crete, he worked in Venice as a young man under the influence of Titian and Tintoretto. His early works are quite Venetian in character, being especially linked with Tintoretto's style. In his adopted Spain where he went in 1575 to spend the rest of his life, his manner of painting underwent a radical change. The breakup of the High Renaissance style of Raphael and Titian with its sculpturesque forms, its poise and equilibrium, its static space compositions, appears in Tintoretto's work; with El Greco, the transition to the baroque style is complete. As in Rubens and Rembrandt, the space patterns are infinitely complex and the dramatic play of light is a primary element in their composition. In the *Nativity* (Fig. 471), painted between 1606 and 1608, supernatural light emanating from the Holy Child flashes from object to object like quiet lightning. Its leaping movement is echoed in the ecstatic gestures of the shepherds, who rapturously express their wonder and adoration. There is nothing of the sober matter-of-factness of the Dutch, or of Rubens' grandiose spectacle. It is an imaginative translation of a miracle into the articulate language of color, space, and movement. The Church, seeking to maintain its authority through the Counter-Reformation, found in El Greco and other baroque artists a means of declaring the verities of the miracles that were being discredited by the humanists and the scientists. But a miracle that is merely described in color and design is a miracle that is explained in concrete and rationalized terms and therefore destroyed as an authentic manifestation of the supernatural. The significance of El Greco's art lies in his capacity to employ the rhythms of fluid light, the emotion-arousing color, the nervous tempo of moving lines. These

rhythms he combined in incredibly beautiful arabesques that to the highest degree are symbols of human emotional and spiritual experience.

Like all the baroque masters, El Greco was an acute observer of nature. The elongated forms and the distortions of his later art arose from a knowledge that things in themselves have no meaning until imagination plays upon them, until they are shaped into intelligible communicative patterns. Direct observation and analysis are evident in the portrait he painted *ca.* 1600 of *Cardinal Guevara* (Fig. 472), the prosecutor of the Spanish Inquisition. No master has ever excelled El Greco in the brilliant handling of the intricate lace against the rich luster of silk. But he goes beyond these incidental objective facts to observe the nervous gestures of the Cardinal seated on the edge of his chair, the febrile hands that are studiedly idle, the alert erect head. The face is a study in arrested energy. The wide hard mouth is devoid of pity or compassion of any kind; the cold eyes stare through thick lenses. Ruthless zeal and cruel fanaticism were never so pitilessly laid bare. More than a portrait of an individual, this is a portrait of the Inquisition. As an interpreter of the spiritual history of his time, El Greco is rivaled only by Rembrandt.

The portrait and the landscape are two forms of painting upon which the baroque masters lavished their greatest efforts. At a time when life was being reoriented toward a new naturalistic synthesis, the artist searchingly scanned the human face as though recognizing the active role the individual was assuming in shaping his own destiny. In the Middle Ages the portrait was all but unknown, because the individual was considered an insignificant unit in a hierarchy at whose head was the Deity. In the Renaissance the portrait made its appearance as soon as the individual asserted himself as a creative agent in moulding his world. In landscape there is an objectification of the portrait; that is, it is a portrait of the artist's personality. Though the minor Dutch painters described its physical features factually even as they rendered the pots and pans of their kitchens with simple directness, Rembrandt made it a vehicle for his waves of undulating color harmony. Rubens' fields and

FIG. 471. El Greco, Nativity (1606–1608).

forests are as sensuous and living as his female nudes. For each, the actual scene was transformed by the imagination according to what of his own consciousness the painter found reflected in it. Such a landscape is El Greco's *View of Toledo* (Fig. 473) painted late in his life, between 1600 and 1614. The flashing crest of buildings that follows the rolling hills is silver against deep green shot with black. The sky oppressed with ominous clouds seems bursting explosively with blinding light which transforms the world into nightmare. It is a scene pregnant with some awful foreboding. Actually Toledo is a city of dead gray stone lodged on bare granite hills, arid and drenched by the blazing sun; only a few olive trees relieve the stark monotony of its drabness. But through El Greco's eyes it becomes more than a dusty provincial hill town; it is the scene of mystery and passion, light and darkness, growth and decay.

In older accounts of painting, El Greco's name is often omitted or barely mentioned, because his concept of what is real does not coincide with the usual concept of painters. It has even been suggested that his strange visions were due to defective eyesight. But since the appearance of the Post-Impressionists late in the nineteenth century El Greco has been understood and appreciated for the mystic and seer that he was. Perhaps people failed to understand Greco's immensely stirring art for almost three hundred years because he was overshadowed by another Spanish master of the same century who recorded with consummate genius all the intricacies of light and color playing over the forms of nature, and achieved to an amazing degree the pictorial naturalism for so long the implicit aim of painting in the popular sense. Even if he did only this, no painter has ever shown a greater mastery of the technical means of his art than Diego de Silva y Velasquez (1599-1660).

Where El Greco saw miracles, the triumph of the Cross, the spiritual agony of hell, and the ecstatic visions of heaven, Velasquez' sober eye encompassed strolling musicians, beggars, peasants eating their noonday meal of cheese and wine. An aristocratic counterpart of the contemporary Dutch painters, he did not engage in

*The Metropolitan Museum of Art, Bequest of
Mrs. H. O. Havemeyer, 1929.
The H. O. Havemeyer Collection.*

FIG. 472.   El Greco, Cardinal Guevara
(*ca.* 1600).

moral, philosophical, or religious contemplation but followed Caravaggio's example (Fig. 454) in both technique (in his early works) and point of view. When he painted mythological subjects, such as Apollo appearing at the forge of Vulcan, only the theme belonged to antiquity; Velasquez attempted to paint realistically a semi-nude youth standing in a blacksmith's shop addressing a

FIG. 473. El Greco, View of Toledo (1600–1614).

muscular blacksmith. He did not search the literary past for an interpretation. His religious paintings are only nominally religious; he did not clothe legends with the imagination of El Greco or the tender humanism of Rembrandt. As empirical as the scientists of his time, he painted only the visible realities. But that is enough, for no painter ever had his sensibilities of vision, his capacity to see the nuances of color and light, and the fluid sequence of space that results from harmoniously blending forms in atmosphere.

On a visit to Rome in 1650, Velasquez painted a portrait of the pope, *Innocent X* (Fig. 474). Although he clearly had El Greco's Cardinal Guevara (Fig. 472) in mind, his approach was not

that of the older man, who set out to reveal the cardinal's innermost soul through analysis and interpretation. Instead, it is as though Velasquez had walked into the pope's presence, painted impersonally the figure he saw, and stopped. One feels that no judgment has been made, no conscious mind has intervened between the subject and the canvas, but that he is in the physical presence of the shrewd and crafty Innocent X. The story that the pope was displeased with so objective a scrutiny of his countenance may well be believed, for Velasquez recorded not the majesty of the head of Christendom, not the spiritual leader of the Church, but the lowering scowl on a face, and shimmering silk and lace. The texture of the moist skin, the vibrating whites and crimson of the silk, the hand casting a luminous shadow on the white fabric—these are the things Velasquez painted. Yet it is also apparent that he did not paint scrupulously minute details as the fifteenth-century Flemish masters did (Fig. 375). Fully aware that the eyes sees only salient accents, Velasquez painted these accents; he left the details blurred, rendering them as tone masses. The treatment of the lace is an example. A collar or sleeve is a spot of white that blends with other spots in the characteristic pattern of the ensemble. Such an impressionistic view can carry no suggestion of the sculpturesque and statuesque. Even the spacing within the frame differs from that employed by artists of the previous century. The casual placing of the figure off center, the seemingly accidental exclusion of the lower part of chair and figure, give an amplitude to the space and an informal effect that characterize all baroque art. From such compositional factors the freshness and reality of the subject are realized.

In Rome, Velasquez painted his first landscapes. They too are faithful records of sunlight filtering through trees, reducing architecture and figures to a spotty arabesque. For the first time direct observations of the effects of light and atmosphere were made and veraciously recorded in oil pigment. One might easily mistake them for the studies of those specialists in painting sunlight, the Impressionists of nineteenth-century France, but they were random and casual pictures, soon forgotten in Velasquez' absorption in interiors. Realizing the inability of pigment to attain the absolute scale of outdoor light, he turned to the half and quarter lights, the fugitive tones and silvery shadows in the indirect illumination of interiors. We have observed repeatedly the baroque painters' special predilection for the rendering of space, in Rembrandt, Vermeer, Rubens, El Greco. Velasquez sensed space as something that might be made dynamic and living through the blending of tonal values, i.e., the amount of light or dark in colors.

In the *Maids of Honor* (Fig. 475), painted in 1656, space becomes deeply expressive. The subject of the painting is so involved as to require some explanation. The king and queen, just visible in the mirror in the background, look into a room where Velasquez as the official court painter is standing before a huge easel whose straight accent sets the limit of the scene. In the foreground near the painter are various members of the court; a little princess in elaborate costume is attended by two maids from whom the title of the picture is oddly enough dervied. Among several others is a dwarf, a pathetic creature kept like a pet animal to amuse and flatter the vanities of the royal household. The room itself is described with mathematical exactness, the rapidly foreshortened wall at the right converging with the rear wall and the ceiling. The pictures, the mirror, and the door-frame break up the rear wall into a series of rectangles. The play of atmosphere, the uneven illumination, and the variety of colors blended through air and distance exclude any feeling of rigidity or hardness from this cubic frame. The figure of

Doria Gallery, Rome.

FIG. 474.   Velasquez, Innocent X (1650).

Velasquez himself looks outward into undefined space where imaginatively the spectator stands. The observers (in this case the king and queen) give reality to that space by being shown in the mirror, thus doubling the distance represented, a device Jan van Eyck had also used (Fig. 375). Further elaboration results when the eye, making a sudden leap from the figures close at hand, observes through the open door a series of steps upon which a courtier stands looking back through the tangible space toward the court scene. The spontaneous movement of the figures within this fluid space gives it final verification. The interrelation of lines converging in depth and varying hues of surface make for a closely integrated pattern of the greatest subtlety.

If there is such a thing, Velasquez is the painter's painter. For him the meaning of painting lay in making his scene articulate through continuous patterns of color and light and space. The identification of the object he painted seems almost a by-product of his observation of the continuity of a pattern that embraces all. In this respect he is close to Vermeer, at moments to Rembrandt and especially to Poussin. In certain of their canvases, the created world is all-sufficient, a microcosm closed and complete, like little worlds in which the tension, the drama and tumult of the actual universe are resolved into the harmonious music of form and color. A conception of unity and harmony, such as that Christianity gave the world spiritually in the thirteenth century, obsessed these baroque masters, who thought to realize a comprehensive unity through rationalistic and intellectual means. In spheres outside of art, it was sought in the moral and aesthetic Neo-Platonism of Shaftesbury in England, in the absolute monarchy of Louis XIV in France, in the philosophical systems of Leibnitz and Spinoza, and in the absolutism of the Counter-Reformation and the Jesuit movement. If, indeed, all ages have directly or indirectly searched for the basic harmonies, the ultimate unity of the world, the images of this harmony evolved in the seventeenth century are peculiarly articulate and complete. No artists thereafter succeeded in evolving a synthesis approaching them in universality, except the

musicians Bach (so close in spirit to the seventeenth century) and Beethoven.

All human activity is directed toward some satisfaction or other. A problem is stated so that its conflicts may be resolved. A dramatist creates complex situations so that he may untangle them to his audience's satisfaction. Classic art is based upon complete clarification and perfect satisfaction in solving moral and intellectual and emotional problems, whether in a Greek tragedy explaining the relation of the gods to men, or a Greek statue embodying the concept of the ideal man. From antiquity on, this concept in art has been a powerful shaping force. In Renaissance Italy, for example, the classic ideal was dominant, particularly in the sixteenth century when many artists consciously strove to regenerate its expressive idioms.

In the seventeenth-century baroque period, the classic conception of self-sufficient clarity was largely displaced by ideals of drama, energy, and mysticism, and by romantic or sensational naturalism. But there is one notable exception in the French master Nicholas Poussin (1593-1665). Of the few truly great creative painters, he has been one of the least known and least understood. Until recent decades, hardly any paintings by him were even to be seen in this country, but today many see his art as the cornerstone in the structure of modern painting. For the French school he has been, and is, a guiding star, a criterion of integrity. It was not his weakness but his greatness that caused the Academicians to misinterpret his meaning and degrade his principles to the dry rot of a school formula.

When in 1624 Poussin went to Rome, then the art capital of the world, he was thirty-one years old. Caravaggio was dead, but his style was enjoying an international vogue. Rubens was already a major artistic light. A young artist needed to make choices; there was the sensuous and turbulent drama of Rubens, the naturalism of Caravaggio, the classic severity of the Graeco-Renaissance style. It is an oversimplification to say that Poussin chose the last immediately, for his early work is both sensuous and romantic, but it becomes increasingly classic with the years. He accepted the classic view in its broadest

FIG. 475. Velasquez, Maids of Honor (1656).

terms, not by the easy adoption of formulas. He translated classic attitudes into the current idiom of baroque art, enriching the formal patterns of antiquity with the light, color, and space characteristic of the painting of his century. He revivifies Raphael's poised and serene system (Fig. 429), and from the Venetians (Fig. 436) he learns how to infuse sculpturesque figures with vitality and warmth.

As the Greeks and Romans and High Renaissance masters had rejected everything that was topical, momentary, and accidental, so Poussin dwelt more and more on the ideal, the beautiful, the harmonious. In his work the superficial qualities of the merely charming, picturesque, diverting, or sensational were rigorously excluded at a time when such values were the stock-in-trade of most painters. In this respect Poussin was in complete agreement with the principles then being expounded in the French classic drama. Corneille inaugurated an epoch in the theatre with *Le Cid* (1637), in which the

FIG. 476.   Poussin, Holy Family (1651).

unities of time, place, and action were strictly maintained. The force of his drama comes from the passionate assertion that a man is master of his own fate through exercising his intellect and controlling his emotions, a sentiment which is merely an elaboration of the implication of Greek tragedy.

Undoubtedly Poussin took this moral view for himself and his art. As an artist he severely subjected his work to the judgment of his intellect, leaving nothing to chance. Impulse and emotion are rigidly controlled. His work never reflects a fleeting impression or a transitory feeling, for he felt that behind the casual surface appearance there was some larger order, some reality that must be divined more by the mind than by the first impulsive response of emotion. This rationalistic attitude is the exact opposite of impressionism, romanticism, or realism. Poussin saw that these principles had been exemplified in the austere, orderly, and unified art of the High Renaissance. They are expressed in his *Holy Family* (Fig. 476) of 1651. To a casual observer the painting looks not unlike a Raphael or the work of some other Renaissance master, but closer observation brings to light a different scheme of plastic organization of space and line in the off-center wall fragment with the landscape that balances it. Above all, Poussin uses a rich and organically integrated space pattern in the arrangement of figures and in the landscape. Although organized internally in a left-to-right orientation (classic order), the group also has its regular space-in-depth movement (baroque order). The landscape has the measured cadence of the figures with a transparent film of air softening and enveloping its cubes and planes. Everything—to the remotest tower, the reflections in the water—has a specific and characteristic shape. Corot in the nineteenth century painted similar landscapes and Cézanne consciously undertook to give his paintings the structure and logic of Poussin.

Poussin's drawings provide insight into the formation of his grand formal periods. These animated preparatory sketches include realistic studies of emotion and drama reminiscent of Rembrandt and Daumier. But they are only observations of nature, useful studies in preparing for the formal structure of the paintings in which the incisive, direct, psychological thrust is sublimated to the level of deliberate rhetoric. An analogy may be made between Poussin's mode of painting and the style of an actor's delivery. An actor does not buy a Pullman ticket using the same studied voice and gesture as he does in speaking his lines on the stage. There he seeks to project himself and the content of his lines in a sustained *illusion* of reality that is not an imitation of actuality but a formal re-creation of a situation. Poussin consciously raised everything he painted to the level of the characteristic, the typical, as Corneille and Racine did in the French theatre.

The *Landscape with St. Matthew and the Angel* (Fig. 477) strikes a significantly different note than has yet been seen in any such interpretations of nature. Though peopled, it has none of the casual informality of Bruegel's Summer (Fig. 452), for the poses are grave and statuesque. Given over largely as it is to the proper elements of landscape—sky and hills, water and trees—yet there is no feeling of shattering drama as in El Greco's Toledo (Fig. 473). Instead, all is calm and peaceful. It would seem that if the subject or theme is meaningful, it would be entirely proper for the word of God to be communicated to man in such serenity. In part this expressive character is created by color—the blue of the sky, the greens and yellows and browns in trees and buildings, the white and russet red in the garments. But even more it is created by the integrated pattern of three-dimensional forms in space. Very subtly, by such devices as the parallel lines of the architectural forms, the verticals of the foreground figures reiterated in the ruined tower, a formal unity is achieved, a kind of visual music that in its way is like the complementing of a theme played by violins in counterpoint by the woodwinds. Poussin's landscape may at first seem dry and uninspired, too calculated to stir, too contrived to appeal. But the experience of finding one's way into and around the world he creates is to know a grandeur and impressiveness altogether akin to that of the classical temples Poussin so much admired.

This classic concept of art is as valid as any other as long as it is infused with the fire and passion of a great spirit. Like all significant ideas it was seized upon by men incapable of understanding it. Charles le Brun institutionalized it in establishing the French Academy of Painting in 1648. Rules were set up governing subject matter and ways of painting; exact methods were taught on the assumption that a painter need only follow prescribed methods to make himself an artist. For a couple of hundred years, the Academies dominated much of the art-thinking of Europe, particularly France; and to hundreds of painters art was only a skill, a vehicle for a pedantic display of learning, until finally the term *academic* became synonymous with sterility. At best the Academy produced a kind of pompous historical portrait and a grandiose scheme of decoration. But the history of art was made by the men who submitted to a discipline infinitely more exacting than the pedagogical rules of the classroom—the discipline of creation. Poussin was himself no academician even though the Academy deified him. The school saw only his outward conformity to the ideas of antiquity; they failed to observe that he was one

FIG. 477. Poussin, Landscape with St. Matthew and the Angel (*ca.* 1651).

of the great colorists and landscapists. They shut their eyes to the original and creative side of his art and slavishly confined themselves to its least significant aspects—classicizing allegorical subjects, interpreting them in a linear and colorless style of the utmost monotony.

Poussin's friend and fellow expatriate in Rome was Claude le Lorrain (1600-1682); together they constitute the background of French painting since the seventeenth century. Of the two, Poussin was the scholar, the intellectual, and philospher. Claude le Lorrain was none of these; rather he was the lyric poet of nature, with a rare gift for landscape. The tiniest fragment of a Roman sculpture, a broken Corinthian capital, was of the most vital interest to Poussin; but what caught Claude's eye were the direct experiences of nature, the light from the

river, the wan lemon hues of early dawn, and dissolving foliage against the light. Simple in taste, he was indifferent to heroic striving for absolutes. While Poussin was engrossed in the art and literature of antiquity, Claude was cultivating the friendship of certain Dutch and German landscape painters living in Rome, for landscape was the only subject that interested him. In certain externals, his pictures are like Poussin's in their largeness of view involving grand vistas, picturesque ancient ruins, and, incidentally, figures of Biblical or classical derivation. Claude himself cared nothing for the figures, but tradition demanded some element of narration or edifying drama, so he dutifully tucked into his compositions a few harmless shepherds or Biblical persons, calling this landscape a Flight into Egypt and that one the

Marriage of Isaac and Rebecca. He thought little of these incidentals; he used to say, "I give my figures away but I sell my landscapes." Often enough he permitted a hack assistant to paint them into his finished scene. For Poussin, such a procedure would have utterly destroyed the underlying significance of his grand architectonic design. Yet Claude's landscapes have something of the same balanced organization of Poussin's, and a formality that has given rise to the term *heroic landscape* to distinguish them

from the intimate landscapes representing fragments of meadow or forest such as the Barbizon school painted in nineteenth-century France.

Claude builds up his scene usually according to an established formula calling for a rather detailed foreground flanked at the sides by imposing masses of trees or buildings, beyond which one looks into deep luminous distance. The movement of the light emanating from the opaque sky, caressing the hills, gleaming from water, and piercing the foliage of the trees is the life

National Gallery, London.

FIG. 478.   Claude, Embarkation of the Queen of Sheba (1648).

of these landscapes. Where Poussin's are static and classical, Claude's are more romantic with their appeal to the emotions by movement and warm colors. He adhered only nominally to the classic principles of order and balance, but to the extent that he felt this discipline, it gives special point to the emotive elements of color and movement.

The theme he liked most to paint is shown in the harbor scene called the *Embarkation of the Queen of Sheba* (Fig. 478) done in 1648. A simple analysis indicates how greatly he was indebted to Poussin for the compositional elements of his pictures. If lines are drawn from opposite corners of this painting, it will be seen that the composition falls into four triangles. The triangles converge at a point far in the central distance, effecting a pyramid of space, whose apex is the source of illumination. The rising sun acts as a magnet toward which the trees turn and the very architecture inclines. When the lines of the cornice, the balustrade, and the pavement are projected, they terminate in the golden light that flows back, tipping the crest of the ripples

and rounding the smooth columns of the temples. Claude had no philosophical understanding of the classic tradition but he used it with tact and intelligence to express a pantheistic naturalism. Deriving his experience from a continuous contact with nature, he reduced his impressions to patterns so lyrically expressive of its inner life as to rival the subtlest design of the Chinese masters. His freest and most spontaneous statements are found in his drawings. In these he felt no need to repress the fleeting experience of the moment. The dense mass of foliage whitened by the sun, the movement of the wind circulating through the plumed branches—such observations will be cherished by the romantic landscape painters of the nineteenth century. In his finished paintings, Claude suppressed this dramatic activity of the landscape, searching as Poussin did for the larger, more inclusive architectonic pattern. As an intuitive poet of nature, he had no equal in European landscape painting of his time; and his influence upon Watteau and Corot in France, upon Turner in England, and nearly every subsequent landscapist is incalculable.

Detail of Fig. 481.

CHAPTER TWENTY-NINE

Painting in the Eighteenth Century

The establishment of the French Academy in the seventeenth century was an authoritarian act of a monarchical system. The monopoly of art education established by the state and maintained by subsidy fostered an official style that was correct and accomplished but spiritually bankrupt. In the following century, masters working outside the Academy or only on its borders were those ultimately recognized as the living spirits of the age, and a somewhat similar situation prevailed in the nineteenth century. For the Academy had promulgated a conception of the absolute validity of classic art; i.e., it had thought to find models in Greek, Roman, and Italian Renaissance styles that could guide the modern artist. In thus closing by precept the eyes and minds of its adherents to the vital springs of immediate experience, it condemned their work to polished sterility even before it was started.

But Antoine Watteau (1684-1721), the first great French painter to emerge in the eighteenth century, found the bases for his art in Rubens rather than the ancients or the Italian Renaissance masters or even Poussin. He came from a Flemish province that was annexed by France shortly after his birth; and because he was the first great French painter in modern times to develop within his own country, he is called the founder of the French school. Deprived of the benefits of official recognition, he lived in poverty, conscious of the artificial world of play-acting in the time of Louis XV to which he

did not belong. Polite society, constrained under the monarchy and regency to the ritual and routine of absolutism, based its pleasures, its fashions and manners on the artificial life established by the court. The masked ball, the company of Italian players, the garden party, appear again and again in Watteau's canvases as with detached air he observes the gay company making love and music as though these were the end of all desire. A society isolated by a government whose fixed mechanism reduced human intercourse to a game of intrigue and strategy found its expression in every form of graceful amorous play. Wealth and power, concentrated at the court and spreading to the thin layer of the privileged few who lived by its favors, created a society founded on leisure and elegance. The divertissement of this

Schloss Museum, Berlin.

FIG. 479.   Watteau, Embarkation for Cythera (*ca.* 1718).

aristocratic society Watteau took for his special subject.

The theme of festive love-making engaged the imagination of northern artists from mediaeval times. It appears in early German woodcuts and engravings. Dürer represented the peasant's lusty dance, Bruegel painted the wedding party (cf. Fig. 453), the Kermesse of village folk. Rubens particularly was often absorbed with the wild orgy of the Dionysiac revel through which he expressed the passions of men and women drunk with wine and lust. Even Poussin repeatedly painted the drunken feast of Bacchus with penetrating insight into its significance as a symbol of renewal. But Watteau, unlike the classicist Poussin, turned to the Fleming Rubens, to his dynamic life rhythms, his inexpressibly living orchestrations of color. He made dozens of drawings from Rubens' pictures and learned from them not only the secret of their vital patterns of movement but also something of the great seventeenth-century master's marvelously decorative color.

Watteau's greatest painting, the *Embarkation for Cythera* (Fig. 479), executed about 1718, was directly inspired by such paintings of Rubens as the Garden of Love (Fig. 456). The refinement of love in Rubens' treatment of the theme appealed to Watteau's sensibilities, for it more nearly approximated the languorous festivals of his age than the violent frenzy of the Bacchic dance usually portrayed by the Flemish painter. Rubens' robust types Watteau changed to slight graceful French forms and the mood is more wistful, but the fanciful setting is similar, with the scented atmosphere of the park opening into the depths of a misty expanse. The winged loves and the garden sculpture of Venus as the presiding deity of the festival appear in both. But Watteau refined the gleaming silks, made the passage from color to color more subtle, the movements more graceful and harmonious. His festival of love belongs wholly to the dream world of the imagination, whereas Rubens' touches actuality in the veracious portraits, the solid tangible baroque architecture, and the substantiality of a hundred realistic details. The episode Watteau painted— the departure of the felicitous ones for the island

Louvre, Paris.

FIG. 480.   Watteau, Figure Studies (*ca.* 1720).

of eternal love—is itself a fantasy, a dream. In a golden barque with gauzy sails lovers flee from the constraints of the real world into the pearly mists. The winged cherubs urge the reluctant or swing in flowery circles about the golden mast. All the movement is from the shady grove where lovers sit, toward the gleaming promise of bliss. They move as in a dance, through varying stages from reluctant hesitation in the seated figures to acquiescence in the rising ones, culminating in the languid anticipation of the pair strolling down the path. Though lovers, barque, and landscape are spun of the imagination, the mood of yearning evoked is nonetheless real.

No master in all eighteenth-century art painted with greater feeling for delicate nuances of color and line than Watteau. His drawings (Fig. 480) give clues to his introspective vision. The turn of a head, the resting arm, or the tilt of a hat sets in motion other forms as the break of still water creates a shimmering surface in a quiet pool. Every stroke of brush or crayon brings forms to life in liquid silver and light. Like Rubens before him he learns how every object implies movement. Most rococo art is far removed from the heroic mood of the seventeenth century, for where the baroque is epic, the rococo is lyric. A Poussin or a Rubens encompasses a vision of the vast world in which man is a heroic actor; Watteau constructs no such large drama

The Frick Collection, New York.

FIG. 481.   Fragonard, The Lover Crowned (*ca.* 1773).

but is content with a song, a melody at once witty, lovely, and melancholy.

Although the French Academy admitted Watteau to its ranks only in a special and inferior category, his style dominated the century. The superb decorative element in his painting, more particularly his use of color, set a precedent that prevailed among his successors such as Fragonard and Boucher. J. H. Fragonard (1732-1806) was a creature of his age and of a particular social stratum in eighteenth-century France; but be-cause he did not project himself beyond that era, he is all the more typical a representative of it. *The Lover Crowned* (Fig. 481) is one of four paintings commissioned by Mme. du Barry about 1773 to decorate her pavilion at Louve-ciennes; they are now in the Frick Collection in New York City. The theme of the series is the Romance of Young Love, the Lover Crowned being the consummation. Like the ladies and gallants of Watteau's Embarkation, these stylishly dressed persons enact an amusing ritual in a studiedly romantic setting. From Watteau came the color scheme too, though in a major key of reds, yellows, and greens rather than in his minor harmonies. The whole has the same qualities found in most eighteenth-century art—costumes, furniture (Fig. 623), architecture (Fig. 168), music, and literature. These qualities are grace, charm, wit, and a sprightly energy at once disciplined and wayward.

As might be assumed, Fragonard represented a hedonistic society dedicated to pleasure. The privileged few in a monarchical system (as in France) or a landed gentry (as in England) exercise their last perquisites before political and industrial revolutions. But in that interlude artists create exquisite things. Artificiality becomes a norm. The landscape in Fragonard's painting is the cultivated grounds of a palace with its ornamental sculptures and boxed orange trees; the light that glows among the trees is a theatrical glow of warm mixed colors; the air is perfumed. Even the drama of love is not real but play-acting, a tableau contrived ostensibly for the exquisitely costumed painter making a sketch. The swirling manner of Rubens (Fig. 456) and the color of Venice are transformed in gayety and brilliance. Such talent abounded in eighteenth-century Europe in the early work of Goya in Spain, of Gainsborough and Hogarth in England, and of Tiepolo and Canaletto in Italy. In its flexibility, its lightness and drama, this tradition of decorative art was an extension and a variation of basic elements in baroque art. Its influence has been felt in all decorative arts calling for fantasy and sheer ornament, and many modern painters, notably Renoir (Fig. 510), have found sources of enrichment in the tradition.

Watteau and Fragonard derived their styles from Flanders and Venice by modifying and gallicizing Rubens. J. B. Chardin (1699-1779) drew similarly from seventeenth-century Dutch genre painters. His bourgeois world knew nothing of Fragonard's cosmopolitan wit and sophistication. Following the Dutch example Chardin painted only the most familiar objects —bunches of vegetables on a table, intimate homely utensils in his own narrow kitchen. An honest craftsman, he painted slowly and with scrupulous application. For him, realities were the things he could touch and taste and smell—a bun beside a sugar bowl, a bottle of wine—and to these he brought a feeling for their familiar qualities and a sensibility quick to appreciate the moist flaky crust of pastry, the hard glaze of the porcelain bowl. With sober and naïve eye, he saw the texture of common things, the soft matte textile of the napkin, and the warm brown of the pepper grinder (Fig. 482). The atmosphere that surrounds his inanimate objects vibrates with reflected light so that at a distance a single unified vision arises giving the effect of a direct visual experience. Nor is any trick of illusionism involved, because no literal representation, however skillful, can make us feel the inner structure, the essential qualities of objects as Chardin does.

With the same powers of observation for people, he caught the intense absorption of children spinning their tops or making a house of cards; in *Saying Grace* (Fig. 483) the child speaks with scarcely restrained haste while the mother watches with tolerant humor. All these he painted with marvelous insight into the atmosphere of sentiment that gives each scene its special flavor. A painter who found such a wealth of intimate experience of people and things everywhere close at hand had no need for

Museum of Fine Arts, Boston.

FIG. 482.   Chardin, Kitchen Table, Still-Life
(1733).

Louvre, Paris.

FIG. 483. Chardin, Saying Grace
(1740).

posturing models. His subjects were the kitchen table with pots and bottles, and his wife and children; and they were enough because they were the known realities of his world of sense and sentiment. The market woman stepping into the kitchen with her newly baked bread with its powdery crust, the sack of provisions containing a chicken for the Sunday dinner, produced from him a design of space and light that becomes a coherent pattern of thought and feeling. Light enters into Chardin's color in somewhat the same way it does in that of Velasquez and Vermeer, giving buoyancy and body to his forms. The organization of his pictures, so subtle in the arrangement of balanced masses and the integration of space and color in an harmonious

design, proclaims him one of the greatest masters of pictorial art.

In a century characterized by the domination of the intellect over the total experience of mind and body, Chardin is one who integrated and oriented his life with sureness and finality. While philosophical and legalistic minds were desperately striving to attain a balanced and articulate conception of life by juggling abstractions about a religious life, the natural man, reason, and law, Chardin was unobtrusively attaining a synthesis without recourse to ponderous intellectualization. Unconsciously he expresses the spiritual forces of the submerged middle class that was soon to destroy the machinery of a monarchy that was inadequate to administer the nation's affairs; its fall in 1789 had profound reverberations in the development of French art.

Watteau's art is the subtlest expression of an age in which formal pictorial ideas inherited from the seventeenth century were employed with increasingly brilliant results for decorative purposes. In Spain, Italy, the Netherlands, wherever painting is found, there emerges a style notable for its charm and frequently of great beauty. In England the mode was that imported through van Dyck's painting (Fig. 458) a century before. Lacking a significant active native tradition in the plastic arts, the English had from time to time given patronage to foreign painters like Holbein, Rubens, and van Dyck; from the latter two Gainsborough and Reynolds developed in the eighteenth century. In this age English art becomes more and more the expression of a political and economic class, and Thomas Gainsborough (1727-1788) is shaped as a painter by his aristocratic patronage. Protesting his chief interest to be landscape, he nevertheless must be regarded primarily as a painter of portraits for the wealthy. In these he records with superb taste, if not notable originality, the elegance and loveliness of the noble folk. *The Honorable Mrs. Graham* (Fig. 484), painted in 1775, is characteristic of Gainsborough's peculiar skill in setting forth the pride and charm of woman in a still semi-feudal society. This type of decorative painting, well represented in America by his Blue Boy in the

Huntington Collection at San Marino in California, is particularly effective in the architectural settings of the day (cf. Fig. 173).

The costumes of the eighteenth century like its furniture (Fig. 623) reflected the attitude of the period. The powdered and elaborately arranged wig, the voluminous folds of lace and rich stuffs indicate a love of decoration, a frank acceptance of an aesthetic of form. Nature is something to arrange in tasteful patterns. A studied artificiality is the ideal. The landscape in the Graham portrait is a bit of stage property, as is the classic pedestal upon which her fragile arm rests. In painting, the piquant, the picturesque and poetic values are sought and, too often, the pretty and sentimental as well. But William Hogarth (1697-1764) preserves a more convincing contact with reality. He is the outstanding English painter of his time, and his art has something of the earthy vigor of English literature. Comparison of his Mary Edwards, in the Frick Collection in New York, with a Gainsborough portrait readily shows his greater mastery of structure, his deeper conception of human values.

National Gallery of Scotland, Edinburgh.

FIG. 484. Gainsborough,
The Honorable Mrs. Graham (1775).

In England as in France a great deal of art was watered down to the level of a luxury adornment for the rich, but the healthy vigor of Chardin's and Hogarth's art is indicative of the new forces developing in European society. The eighteenth-century English writer Richardson invented the novel as an art form in which to write sympathetically about common people; it marked an epoch in the history of English letters. In painting, Hogarth undertook to comment critically on the life and manners of English society from the point of view of the discreet common man. Where Gainsborough portrays the exotically beautiful and the picturesque, Hogarth forthrightly employs a humorous and didactic art to reveal the evils in the various social levels of English life. In Marriage à la Mode, a series of paintings that were reproduced in engraving and widely circulated, he tells a lively story of the degradation of marriage in the aristocracy. English life was split between the great landholding gentry and the degraded gin-drunking rabble, to the corruption of both classes. As a journalist, but one with immense talents, Hogarth reports the chaos in English society, using the copper engraving to broadcast his moral dramas, such as A Rake's Progress and A Harlot's Progress. From Marriage à la Mode, executed in 1745, comes *The Countess' Dressing Room* (Fig. 485), describing the distractions of a faithless wife seeking relief from the boredom of a loveless union. The vacuous faces of the characters indulging in the fashionable amusements of the day are recorded with explicit realism. The nature of Hogarth's moral fervor is revealed in his inclusion of two pictures by Italian mannerists on the walls, the implication being that such pictures are further manifestation of debased morals. Art is now taking on the function of criticism and becoming an instrument of social reform. Like a dramatist, the painter realistically proclaims the message of reformer and moralist. His method is frankly that of the theatre, to entertain with wit, satire, and irony while he preached. Bernard Shaw in the twentieth century does the same thing in his plays.

Hogarth's lusty use of art was so original and unprecedented that "right-thinking" people condemned him, but the English public took him to their hearts. The cheap engravings of his work made for great popularity, and in thus using the graphic processes he was reviving the means to reach a large public as Dürer and Rembrandt had done before him and as Goya and Daumier did later. Purists may cavil at his mixture of drama, illustration, and didacticism, but he proves again that the house of art has many mansions and that no narrow theory of art can long confine a vigorous spirit.

In France the sentimental philosophy of Jean Jacques Rousseau found a powerful champion in the critic Denis Diderot, who believed that painting should be a kind of graphic literature illustrating moral issues. If in addition the picture was beautiful, so much the better; but its chief value lay in the moral it contained. Diderot found his ideal painter in Jean Baptiste Greuze (1725-1805), the painter of the "picture that tells a story." With self-conscious sentimentality he extolled the natural goodness of rustics in detailed anecdotal pieces like *The Village Bride* (Fig. 486), painted in 1761. In Greuze's hands, Chardin's fine sentiment is broadened to obvious banality; the domestic virtues of the villagers are laid on with calculated bathos. But the overwhelming popularity of such mawkish painting is easily understood in view of the hunger of a public starved by the trivialities and insincerities of the fashionable painters who in their own way were as far removed from reality

National Gallery, London.

FIG. 485. Hogarth, The Countess' Dressing Room (1745).

Louvre, Paris.

FIG. 486.   Greuze, Village Bride (1761).

as Greuze. He appeared as a spokesman for the inarticulate mass of people whom the suggestive and titillating art of Fragonard and Boucher had never reached. In Greuze's languorous, half-depraved pretty milkmaids and shepherdesses there was just enough of the voluptuousness of the old art to make them acceptable to all, together with the flattering and obvious morality that met the demands of popular sentiment. The Revolution of 1789, however, brought recognition of his ambiguous position and with Fragonard and the other aristocratic artists he was discredited.

When the French Revolution liquidated the class that had dominated eighteenth-century culture, the style of art changed as radically as the form of government. At the beginning of the century Watteau had developed the baroque language of Rubens, giving greater expression to atmosphere and evolving a freer arrangement with figures more delicate in scale to produce a more expansive pattern of light and space. Fragonard had gone even further in his decorative treatment of color and forms. Chardin, Boucher, and Greuze had turned more and more toward the inspiration of the Dutch and Flemish masters of the preceding century. A tradition of landscape, deriving largely from the Netherlands, began among minor painters.

Just before the Revolution of 1789, there appeared a man, fresh from the Roman Academy, who ultimately became the art dictator of France. As a winner of the *Prix de Rome*, Jacques Louis David (1748-1825) submitted to the classical

Louvre, Paris.

FIG. 487.   David, Oath of the Horatii (1784).

training of the Academy. His style was formed on such models as Poussin, Florentine painting of the High Renaissance, and classical sculpture, for no influence of Chardin or Watteau was permitted to taint the students isolated by the Academy's iron-bound routine. David brought to Paris in 1785 one of those carefully contrived paintings promoted by the Academy, a monumental composition involving a classical subject with sculpturesque figures. Had the *Oath of the* *Horatii* (Fig. 487) come to light at some other time or place, it probably would have caused no particular stir; but coming into a revolutionary atmosphere it was hailed as a symbol fraught with iconoclastic implications of stalwart republican virtues. Horatius' three sons, in a triple accent of extended arms, swear to their father to come home with their shields or upon them. Here, it was felt, was a simple expressive style of stately forms dealing with heroic social qualities and free from the gauzy fripperies of the hated aristocratic art. As the art of antiquity had been closely integrated with the state, so now it became a servant of the Revolution and, under Napoleon's consulship, David became the official state painter.

The ordinary processes of development in painting came to a sudden halt in France when David's style was established as the dominant mode of expression. The Oath of the Horatii is cold to the point of frigidity, the color scheme coarse and mechanical; the light serves only to round the harshly sculpturesque contours. The arrangement of the figures against an architectural background and the planiform spacing in a monumental order are descriptively reminiscent of Florentine and Roman painting of the High Renaissance and were taken from the severely unified stage-sets of the classical French theatre. So intent was the painstaking David upon rhetorical anecdote that he disregarded the lessons he might have learned from the baroque painters about treating atmosphere, color, and movement. He designates each stone in the pavement, every sandal strap, with exactitude. The garment folds seem literal transcriptions of sculptural forms. This very minuteness and clarity made his art more acceptable to a nationalistic caste that required a symbol of itself dignified by history and legend. Similarly in our own country forms were borrowed at this time for public buildings and sculpture (cf. Fig. 187) to give official dignity to a government that had not yet developed its own organic symbol. As a propagandizing agency, art is unquestionably of great value. It was an instrument of the Church in early times and later of the Counter-Reformation, and now at the end of the eighteenth century and the beginning of the nineteenth it gave voice to the authority of the new French nation. But this use of art involves the dangerous risk of compromising its larger function of interpreting life as a whole. In our own time, too, totalitarian regimes have attempted to use art for political purposes, only to find that its creators are not notably stimulated to poetry or music by the activities, however ingenious, of the secret police.

David's best work was done when he was not constrained by the exacting requirements of his official duties of glorifying Napoleon's exploits. In the sphere of portraiture, he produced many fine character studies, among them the portrait of *Madame Hamelin* (Fig. 488), painted in 1800 and now in the Chester Dale collection in the National Gallery in Washington. The

National Gallery of Art, Washington, D.C., Chester Dale Collection.

FIG. 488.   David, Madame Hamelin (1800).

harsh and urgent rhetoric of the historical paintings is not invoked in this most harmonious study. With rarest discrimination David plays off the flowing lines of the figure and the drapery against the rectangular shapes of the picture frame and furniture. The theme is regarded as a problem in visual harmony to be solved through reconciling verticals and horizontals in an integrated structure. Although the effect is one of complete naturalness, it is clear that the master has subjugated every detail to creating harmonious interaction of lines and forms. Even the color David so often handles with scant regard is sympathetically related to the cool and deliberate pattern. In such works David justifies his method and his leadership.

In his severe simplicity, in his adherence to classical or Neo-classic ideals David is no isolated phenomenon. His age is that of the Greek Revival in architecture, and the Neo-classic ideal in sculpture, as seen in his Italian contemporary Canova (Fig. 339), whose marble portrait of Pauline Borghese is almost an exact counterpart of David's Madame Recamier in style. Europe and America respond to the same impulses as they seek once again to derive sustenance from the classic tradition. For the art of the new century, David broke with a single stroke the prestige of an art that had become soft and was expressive only of a decadent society, replacing it with one which although anachronistic was pregnant with moral idealism.

Detail of Fig. 503.

CHAPTER THIRTY

Painting in the Nineteenth Century

David's career parallels that of Napoleon, for he rose with the emperor and went into banishment when he did. The school of art which he fostered produced no great masters except Ingres, however; and the romantic impulse, of which Napoleon was the most universal expression, generated new and revolutionary tendencies even among David's immediate pupils. One figure of great talent was Prudhon, whose contact with Italian art differed from David's. Influenced by Correggio and Leonardo, he exhibited none of the hardness of the official school. His sensitive drawing and coloring fostered romantic feelings suppressed in the prevailing Neo-classic school, and he carried into the nineteenth century something of the warmth of the rococo age.

THE NEO-CLASSIC SCHOOL

David's real successor was his pupil Jean Auguste Dominique Ingres (1780-1867). Though both adhered to the classic tradition of noble sentiment and sculpturesque figures, Ingres revealed considerably more flexibility in his drawing. His enthusiasm for severe Roman types was equaled by his appreciation of the lucid rhythms of Greek art, particularly those in vase painting, and he admired and studied as well the Italian primitives, the work of Giotto, and the fifteenth-century masters. In accordance with the academic conception of the classical tradition known as Neo-classicism he conceived of painting in

The Metropolitan Museum of Art, Wolfe Fund, 1938.

FIG. 490.   Ingres, Odalisque en Grisaille (*ca.* 1814).

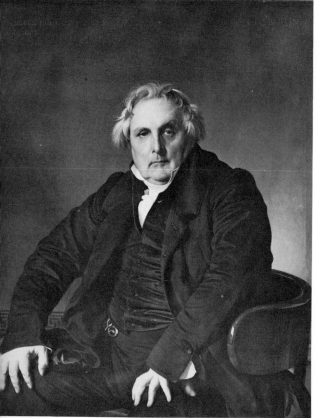

Louvre, Paris.

FIG. 489.   Ingres, Édouard Bertin (1832).

terms of drawing, maintaining that if a picture was well drawn it was well enough painted. His remarkable drawings are extremely sensitive and vigorous even though his color is indifferent, being often dry and lifeless. Like David, he conceived grand decorative compositions. A ceiling decoration in the Louvre is characteristic of his more ambitious style which he modeled after Raphael. The Apotheosis of Homer, one of his best-known works, is learned and cold, with its symbolism of the Parthenon before which is enthroned a heroic Homer accompanied by the great artists and writers of ancient and modern times. In spite of having little feeling for unifying large spaces, Ingres was a master of single figures; and several details—namely, the allegorical Iliad and some of the portraits—are vigorously executed.

But in his more intimate portraits Ingres exhibits a great sensitivity to personality and a fine feeling for the pattern of line with which the figure is created. His portrait of *Édouard Bertin* (Fig. 489) in the Louvre, painted in 1832, is one of the finest of the century. It is not only an arresting likeness but one that is typical of the whole class to which the model belongs. The precision of the Neo-classic linear style is admirably adapted to the requirements of portraiture. With it the likeness may be made gratifyingly concrete; forms may be given definition and finish. However much Ingres relied upon Raphael's discipline, the salient fact is that he could turn the method to his own creative ends in interpreting the personality of his epoch. His portrait of Bertin is a free variation of the scheme Raphael used in his portrait of Baldassare Castiglione (Fig. 430) in the firm and sensitive line and the geometrically massive forms. Though the Renaissance method is employed, the personality which emerges is that of the aggressive bourgeois man of affairs. Here is a romantic interpretation characteristic of a basically romantic age.

There are moments when Ingres' theories betray him beyond his capacities and there are figure compositions like his celebrated *La Source* which suggest vanity in his attempt to rival the sublimities of Greek art. His constant endeavor to "correct nature" at times leads him into a betrayal of nature. Thus *La Source* inclines to prettiness and suavity where nobility and drama of form

The Fogg Art Museum, Harvard University, The Grenville L. Winthrop Collection.

FIG. 491. Ingres, The Forestier Family, Drawing (1804).

are intended. In his best work, by which of course his talents must be judged, the austerity of a noble mind is evident. No oversweetness or sentimentality mars the *Odalisque en Grisaille* (Fig. 490) in the Metropolitan Museum, New York. The three-dimensional forms are presented in a tense and lyrical linear design that makes it one of the great modern studies of the nude. A discriminating musician, he raises the drama of his paintings to the level of tension called concert pitch. In his work one senses a musical strain in the flowing cadence of line.

To augment a less than modest income during his long residence in Italy, Ingres sometimes made rapid pencil portraits. Anyone but he might have regarded these casual commissions as boring commercial assignments to be got through with as painlessly as possible. One of them, *The Forestier Family* (Fig. 491), which is dated 1818, proves the integrity of his art. The deft silvery pattern with which he draws together the individual members of the family group indicates the art of a man who even in his smallest tasks regards his work as a sacred calling. Perhaps it is this all-absorbing seriousness, this fanatical dedication of his life, which accounts for the high level of his work and also for his occasional lapses in judgment. These lapses are great ones but they are not the failings of faintness or compromise.

THE ROMANTIC SCHOOL

No one who has experienced the art of Titian, Velasquez, Rembrandt, and Rubens can imagine that the theory behind Neo-classicism could long remain unchallenged. Only the die-hards of the Academy, men entrenched in the advantages of wealth and position, continued to take its dictates seriously. Ingres stood off the rising tide of individualism which he felt to be a destroyer of a true art. He lived to 1867, long enough to see many strong and able men dedicated to a principle called Romanticism. No pat definition of the term completely fits the ramifications of acknowledged Romantic art. In general, Romanticism is a renewal of Renaissance individualism. From late in the eighteenth century the Neo-classic masters held that the artist should subordinate his personal feelings to an ethical ideal expressed in classical forms. When Ingres and David portrayed the Emperor Napoleon, their paintings expressed the supreme ideal which in their eyes the emperor represented. He was serene, noble, godlike—in short, a hero. Likewise in their portraits of less exalted persons their objective was the *type* rather than the individual. For all their fidelity to appearance, none of their portraits can be described as naturalistic studies of character. Much of the validity of these two men as painters lies in their power to express universal humanity in the types they present.

The Romantics in the arts of literature and music—Victor Hugo, Wordsworth, Byron, Beethoven, Berlioz, Wagner, and, among painters, Delacroix, Corot, Constable—found the old rules of art inadequate. How could Beethoven have conveyed the feeling expressed in the Eroica in the musical idiom of Mozart? No more could Wordsworth have expressed his understanding of nature and freedom in the classical couplets of Pope.

Freedom was the battle cry of the young spirits of the early nineteenth century—Liberty, Equality, and Fraternity was the slogan of the French Revolution when the French middle class broke the antiquated political forms of the monarchy. In all phases of life European society was experiencing a demand for a fresh interpretation of man and nature, a new realization of itself. Neo-classicism was a belated attempt to apply reason and the authority of ancient art ideals to the modern scene. Jean Jacques Rousseau in the eighteenth century proclaimed the doctrine of nature, assuming, perhaps on faith, that man was good by birthright and was corrupted only by institutions—the Church, the schools, the laws. In the nineteenth century this attitude toward Nature with a capital N became dominant. In art, men should be free to give voice to their feelings—their passion, fear, love, and longing. They were to celebrate the *natural man*, to shake loose the restraint imposed on artists by an Academy or a bygone day.

Specifically this attitude meant for painting that all kinds of experiences previously suppressed were to find their way into art. The landscape is again a favored theme in France and England and America. The mysteries of love and death were to be explored. Drama and sentiment replace the decorum and reticence of the Neoclassic masters. The atypical as opposed to the typical fascinated the romantic artist because it was part of the unfathomed mystery of an inscrutable world. Violence and arresting or shocking contrasts permeate much of the literature and art of the peroid.

The nineteenth century saw philosophical, political, social, and scientific ideas formulated in earlier times become available to society at large. The Industrial Revolution tended to make science more than a cloistered disinterested study for scholars. The poverty of the industrial workers gave increased emphasis to social theory. Extensive urban life made men more acutely conscious of the landscape.

All phases of intellectual activity were to a great extent dominated by the scientific attitude. Science itself is based upon empiricism, the evidence of the senses. The art of the nineteenth century closely follows science in stemming from the individual's empirical experience. In art what the painter *feels* about his subject became roughly equivalent to what the scientist *knows* about his material. Thus the way an artist worked was conditioned by his imagination, his sensations, and his feelings. Hence there arose a great variety of style—Romantic, Realist, Impressionist, and Post-Impressionist. But in each the common denominator is nature. *Art is nature seen through a temperament* is the way one writer expressed it. Since there are as many temperaments as there are individuals one might suppose that such a theory would lead to undiscriminating chaos—a kind of artistic anarchy. And, indeed, the impression created by the untold thousands of imitative and feeble pictures made in the past hundred years is something much like anarchy. Certainly no period in history produced so much quantitatively both good and bad. The great

variety of expression in the Romantic age inevitably made it extremely difficult for a confused public to distinguish the sheep from the goats. But out of this welter of painting emerged men of great stature who gave an intelligible interpretation of their world.

Among the great individualists of the new epoch, the Spanish master, Francisco Goya (1746-1828), must be given the foremost place. There is no one who more fully embodies in his art so much that we consider peculiarly modern. There is scarcely a major pictorial development in the past two hundred years to which Goya did not contribute. His early works are in the rococo decorative tradition and are not unlike the paintings of Watteau and Fragonard, as gay and spirited, as witty and delightful as any in the eighteenth century. Elevated to the post of court painter, Goya increasingly shows his admiration for Velasquez. His royal appointment did not hamper his artistic development, however, for he was not wholly dependent upon court patronage. His considerable work for himself and members of the court and the wealthier middle class enabled him, as he said, "to make observations for which commissioned works generally give no room, and in which fantasy and invention have no limit."

Fantasy and invention were so far developed along psychological and technical lines by Goya that one may say that single-handed he anticipated and often directed the art of many European masters for a century. The position of court painter naturally called for large numbers of portraits; his supreme gift is in giving reality and drama to his persons. In the *Family of Charles IV* (Fig. 492), painted in 1800, he understandably followed Velasquez' solution of a similar problem in the Maids of Honor (Fig. 475). Both paintings are large, and both include self-portraits of the artist standing beside a tall canvas actually that of the painting itself. But where Velasquez produced a profound vision of luminous but static figures, Goya's have a kind of smoldering vitality. Instead of the quietly diffused light of Velasquez' studio, the illumination of Goya's is an arresting implement of psychological characterization. It falls on the coarsely

FIG. 492. Goya, Family of Charles IV (1800).

obese form of the king, the raddled features and gross neck of his queen, the depraved faces of children and courtiers—and sets off against them the pomp and circumstance of jeweled silks and satins. Like Hogarth before him in England, Goya uses his brush to point out the evil and corruption behind the glittering façade of wealth abused by power. He is a moral force in an age of incredible moral disintegration. Only the strongest, most ruthless, even brutal person could have survived the corruption of the Spanish scene in Goya's time with integrity.

Late in life he witnessed the horrors of the French invasion, recording the catastrophe in a series of prints made in etching and aquatint about 1810 called Disasters of War. With relentless and devastating literalness Goya describes the bloody terror of a mass execution, the heaps of slaughtered women and children being dumped into a pit. With scalding irony he names one of them Charity. In others dismembered bodies are hung from trees, Spanish men are mutilated, women raped. These prints call to mind the unspeakable slaughterhouse of Europe in Hitler's regime, so immediate and overwhelming is their power. If his paintings prove Goya a master of trenchant design, these prints reveal, if anything, an even greater genius for compression and economy. One to which he gave the terse inscription *Why?* (Fig. 493) reveals some measure of his method. The space of the print is broken by a single wedge-shaped pattern containing the two figures of the hanged Spaniard and the ironically quizzical French officer. A few vertical accents suggest the unending tragedy of torture and slaughter. Nothing is exactly described but everything is suggested. That is Goya's power: to suggest by appealing to the imagination with what is omitted. It is the method that is generally adopted in his painting and graphic art. Much of his graphic work dates from his last years when he was a virtual exile in Bordeaux. In France, removed from the constant dangers of reprisals by Church and state, he was free to speak candidly of the nightmare he had witnessed. Old, deaf, and embittered, he continued to lift his voice against the clouding miasma of man's calculated bestiality. In his exile at the age of seventy-three he mastered the newly invented process of lithography and recorded in a series of masterly designs upon stone the drama of blood and courage of the bull ring. The same incisive pattern, the same suggestion of action are evident in them. The French Romantic Delacroix met Goya and his own lithographs reflect Goya's methods. His influence was not felt fully, however, until some decades later when Manet discovered and adopted his technical pictorial ideas.

Goya's death in France in 1828 came when French art was experiencing many waves of the new Romantic feeling from within its borders and from abroad. Géricault and the young Delacroix were impressed by the English landscape painters—Turner, Bonington, and most of all Constable. The exhibition of Constable's Hay Wain at the Salon of 1824 prompted Delacroix to repaint passages in his own Massacre of Chios shown in the same exhibition. The English have always had a predilection for landscape and country life. John Constable (1776-1837), beginning as one of a minor school of English landscapists, found those abiding charms in nature common to most Romantic artists. The rain-drenched fields, the elms stirred by the wind aroused his imagination and sensibilities. He saw the Dutch and Flemish landscapes of the seventeenth century and found kinship in them. He discovered that their intimate mood had little in common with the heroic landscapes of Poussin (Fig. 477) and his followers. In his own painting he sought the infinite variety of nature —its random color and, above all, its mood. His landscapes were not conventional studio inventions but grew from fresh and affectionate first-hand observations. Like Goya he discovered that there are no lines in nature, but only areas or masses of color; this laid the foundation for Impressionism. *Salisbury Cathedral from the Bishop's Garden* (Fig. 494), painted in 1826, suggests how his light-swept landscape breathes and vibrates. His color is made fresh and alive in a mosaic of broken fragments. This method was not so much a device to increase brilliance, as it became for

FIG. 493. Goya, Why? Etching and Aquatint from The Disasters of War (*ca.* 1810).

the Impressionists, as the result of simple observation of visual realities. There are few solid color areas in nature; objects like a tree or field are actually vast complexes of color spots, though we may *think* of them as being brown or green. The older painters represented foliage as muddy brown or at the most a subdued olive hue; Constable met an objection to his bright colors by placing a violin against tree boughs to demonstrate that the foliage was not really brown.

In practice Constable anticipated some principles of French Impressionism by about forty years. This can also be said for J. M. W. Turner (1775-1851), who in painting the *Burning of the Houses of Parliament* (Fig. 495) also selected a famous Gothic building for his subject. But he obviously regarded it in a different way. For Turner, it was the drama of nature that was important, and his intention in painting was to induce or contribute to an excitement comparable to his own. To achieve this, he used color in a way unlike anything seen before. Applying it pure, as Constable had done, he so relates his shapes and surfaces that everything seems vaporized in light, figuratively as well as with the literalness implied in the example in Fig. 495. Sometimes it is a drama at sea, like the Slave Ship, in the Boston Museum of Fine Arts. Or it may be a railroad train crossing a viaduct in a rainstorm, like Rain, Steam, and Speed, in the National Gallery in London. Whatever the subject, his practice of painting light and atmosphere

The Frick Collection, New York.

FIG. 494. Constable, Salisbury Cathedral from the Bishop's Garden (1826).

Philadelphia Museum of Art.

FIG. 495.   Turner, Burning of the Houses of Parliament
(1835).

in patches of pure wispy color provided Monet a few years later with a clue to solving his problem of re-creating the effect of sunlight on his canvasses.

Although Goya and the English masters were well advanced in Romantic expression in the first decade of the nineteenth century, the French progressed more slowly because of the strong hold of Neo-classicism. Even professed disciples and students of David like Gros and Girodet found it difficult to reconcile their art to the school's rigid code. Romanticism as an attitude toward life had no single source; it was in the air of the western world.

In France the first articulate assertion of revolt from the French Neo-classicist camp appears in the painting of a brilliant young artist named Théodore Géricault (1791-1824). A man of means, he was not dependent upon the good will of the official custodians of art, and he went to Italy where he studied the frescoes of Michelangelo instead of the diluted formulas of the academic pedants. Too intelligent to copy Michelangelo literally, he did absorb his great plastic rhythms and the controlling designs into which they were cast. His studies in Italy, like the *Riderless Races at Rome* (Fig. 496) done in 1817, indicate his profound understanding of the athletic forms of the Sistine Ceiling. His jockeys and horsemen are only modern transcriptions of Michelangelo's nude athletes (Fig. 423). Where the athletes bend their enormous strength of sinew and mind to supporting slender garlands in an abstract allegory of strain and tension, Géricault's jockeys exert their energy to restrain the impetuous horses about to start a race. The contingencies of realistic action demanded less a concentration upon single figures than a weaving together of scores of figures in a coherent pattern of movement. The theme itself, a popular horse race along the Corso, a street in Rome, was utterly antagonistic to academic standards of what was considered legitimate subject matter for the artist of 1817. Horses might be painted,

Walters Art Gallery, Baltimore.

FIG. 496.   Géricault, Riderless Races at Rome (1817).

surely, but only as adjuncts to Greek or Roman heroes, and then they must be still and lifeless like cast-iron statues. From Rubens (Fig. 457), Géricault obtained an idea of how the horse might be treated as a plunging, pawing embodiment of energy, and also a concept of the expressive value of color. All his life he was an enthusiastic horseman, and like a sensible person he saw no reason for not painting the dramatic colorful spectacle of the races. Visits to England where he came in contact with popular sporting prints gave further impetus to his painting of horses.

In their training, the Academies insisted upon the minute representation of detail in clear sharp lines, with every buckle and strap and hair of the horses' manes exactly rendered. But Géricault knew, as Goya did, that at a race his eye saw not these details but the race as a whole—the flashing curve of a neck, the spot of white on a horse's head, the sudden gesture of a jockey bringing down his whip. The excitement and movement of the scene could not be expressed in the severe lines of the classic mode. Seeking a more appropriate style, he found it in baroque art, especially in Ruben's animated manner. The masters of the seventeenth and eighteenth centuries well understood the technique of painting by suggestive spots, with broken color and light accents merging. The Neo-classicists reverted to an archaic style, isolating each object through the decisive metallic contour line. Géricault too realized that the complex action of a group must be unified and given clarity or its pictorial effectiveness would be weakened. All the Renaissance masters taught him the necessity of simplification through order, and in the Riderless Races this simplification is achieved geometrically. The excited horses and the spectators are restrained by the rope and the pavilion. The diagonal accents they form create a movement in space terminated by the rectangle of the building in the background. Against the foil of straight lines and emphatic planes the dynamic action of the race itself holds the observer's undivided attention. The many spectators are portrayed by a single band of mottled light and shade in which no one person stands out. This method of subordinating details to the composition as a whole was not fully appreciated by Géricault's contemporaries and immediate followers. Not until later in the nineteenth century did painters fully realize its significance as a means of attaining unity from diversity.

When Géricault returned to Paris in 1818 he painted a huge picture that was condemned by the Academicians and lauded by the Romanticists. A short time before, the newspapers had carried an elaborate account of a disaster at sea when the French man-of-war *Medusa* had been wrecked and its survivors battered for three stormy weeks on its single life raft. In painting the Raft of the *Medusa*, Géricault expressed realistically the desperate agony of the survivors as they hail a ship seen on the horizon. Exhibited at the Salon of 1819, it at once set aflame the smoldering controversy between the Neo-classicists and Romanticists. It was called the worst of daubs by one group and acclaimed as a great modern masterpiece by the other. The recognition Géricault won as a result was so great that had he not died a few years later he would have become the undisputed leader of the Romantic movement in painting. He was its champion and his example profoundly influenced those who followed him. He established the precedent of painting the image of the world about him and he proved the independence of the artist to choose for himself the means of color and form needed to express that vision.

In the intelligent and cultured Eugene Delacroix (1798-1863), the Romantic school found its leader after Géricault's untimely death from an accident during a horse race. As a youth Delacroix had been swept off his feet by the expressive vitality revealed in Géricault's art, and his imagination had also been fired by the romantic poetry of Byron, Goethe, and Shakespeare which later provided the themes of many of his lithographs and paintings. His illustrations, whether inspired by contemporary literature or the classics, are never a pale transcription of or addition to the literary text. With free imagination and insight he rendered the inner psychological intensity and the spirit of the theme with such force that they are independent of any text. Technically the results are not illustrations in the ordinary sense, because they are self-contained concepts developed from the themes suggested by literature or taken from history.

An episode in the war between Greece and Turkey is the subject of *Scenes of the Massacres of Scio* (Fig. 497) which Delacroix exhibited in the Salon of 1824, achieving thereby the same quality of fame or notoriety which the Raft of the *Medusa* had won earlier for Géricault. One of the most horrifying incidents of its kind in the annals of human cruelty, the massacres of Scio revolted the entire civilized world. Delacroix interpreted this feeling on a large canvas nearly fourteen feet high, which left nothing unsaid about the suffering of the victims. Instead of presenting an ordered tableau which the spectator views as on a stage in the manner of David's Horatii (Fig. 487), Delacroix draws him into the composition by a series of jagged diagonal movements in depth and sweeps him through it with the suggestion that action begins and continues far beyond the compositional limits. Even more striking was Delacroix' use of color. While still a young student, he carefully examined Rubens' great decorative works in the Palais de Luxembourg (Fig. 155), and he saw Constable's famous landscape The Hay Wain just before it too was shown in the 1824 Salon. Struck by the freshness and vigor of Constable's color patterns, Delacroix repainted almost the entire background of his own composition, adding the emotional expressiveness of brilliant hues to the descriptive details of tragic suffering in the poses, gestures, and expressions of the figures. Although the Academy and critics of like mind called it "the

Louvre, Paris.

FIG. 497.   Delacroix, Scenes of the Massacres of Scio
(1824).

massacre of painting," the historic importance of Delacroix's recovery of color as a significant expressive factor in painting was not lost on generations of his successors.

Color, which the Neo-classicists David and Ingres had relegated to the role of a descriptive adjunct to drawing, was for Delacroix the essence of painting. From the Venetians and Rubens he found how to give depth and brilliance. His forms are built up in rich color volumes, as opposed to the traditional style of augmenting the drawing with color. In the Massacres of Scio, the tragedy of suffering is felt in the depth of pulsating color, rather than being described by a literal rendering of the scene. Like a musician who builds up a mood through abstract tonal qualities, Delacroix finds the psychological equivalents of emotions in terms of color. With color and light, space dilates and condenses dramatically, shapes appear and dissolve as color solidifies into substance.

To Delacroix the world was a place of danger, glamour, and exotic beauty. Like his literary counterparts Victor Hugo and Scott, he found material for his art in the remote in time and place. He traveled in Morocco and painted the picturesque and strange beauty of the tropics. His Lion Hunts are reminiscent of Rubens upon whom he constantly draws. Like the Romantic poets he is haunted by the sea, finding in it a kind of symbol of mortality. Death flits through many of his paintings as a heroic fulfillment or an inevitable conclusion of man's conflict with nature. The cloudy mysteries of life are pondered in his Bark of Don Juan, inspired by Byron's poem, and *Christ on the Sea of Galilee* (Fig. 498). While Christ sleeps, the storm rages with the fury of shrieking wind,

the pounding gray-green volumes of waves, the savagely snapping wind-ripped sail. These symbols describe man's place in the universe with passionate eloquence.

With Delacroix there enters into French painting elements that had long been absent: baroque design, the color of the Venetians and Rubens, and pictorial drama. He uses these elements with force and conviction, even though some feel that his art is too circumscribed by literary concepts; often the mood of his paintings springs from romantic episodes in literature and history. He relies, perhaps more than a painter should, upon an experience at secondhand. By

FIG. 498. Delacroix, Christ on the Sea of Galilee (1854).

FIG. 499.   Corot, The Harbor of La Rochelle (1851).

1863, the year of his death, his conflict with Neo-classicism had been won; but it was the men who gave their attention to specific contemplation of nature—the Barbizon masters, Courbet the Realist, and Daumier—who consummated the Romantic revolution.

One of the most characteristic and significant features of Romantic art is the return to the landscape as found in the poetry of Wordsworth and in the formal language of painting. Since the time of Poussin and Claude le Lorrain, the subject had been treated in French painting only by a few minor masters. Watteau's garden scenes were the nearest he came to it. David and Ingres with their absorption in classical themes involving figures alone were scarcely conscious of it. Constable was the artist who, early in the nineteenth century, opened Delacroix' eyes to the emotional and pictorial possibilities of landscape painting, and he gave the French painter a method of realizing its possibilities as well. Then, around 1830, a few painters living in Paris began to drift out to a small village near the city called Barbizon, where living was cheap and there

were woods and fields to paint. Corot, Rousseau, and Millet were among those who formed the Barbizon school.

As Chardin in the eighteenth century had painted still-lifes and interiors with an intimate feeling for the glowing warmth of fruit and vegetables and the atmosphere that surrounds them, so the Barbizon painters endowed their landscapes with a sentiment that finds in each meadow and forest path its peculiar intimate beauty. Théodore Rousseau paints the solitary oak dominating a flat patch of pastureland. He sees the peculiar rugged character of the gnarled branches, the coarse density of the oak foliage, the tufts and clods of the turf with pools of standing water like glass reflecting the sky. The grand compositions of Poussin's heroic landscapes are replaced by others that express the spontaneous and informal aspects of nature in the manner of the Dutch landscape painters. These nature lovers, Daubigny and Diaz among others, saw the landscape in its quiet moods with fresh naïve eyes. Seldom if ever did they bring to it the romantic passion of Delacroix nor did they view it as a background for narrative; they loved it for its own peculiar charm and painted it for its intrinsic delight.

This group of painters would have been of rather local interest, were it not for Camille Corot (1796-1875). Corot is Chardin out-of-doors. Everything he sees is instinct with visible charms. He has something of Claude's innocence. Taking no account of the heated controversies between Romanticists and classicists, he demanded of life only paint and canvas and adequate leisure for their use. An indulgent father gave him a small income and he never felt the necessity of modifying his style to suit critic or patron. As a result, his art has an indescribable charm of ease and casual simplicity. But this very simplicity is disarming, for Corot had a sure sense for composition and balance. His designs are so spontaneous and free from strain or artificiality that they seem like happy accidents. Like so many others he was drawn to Italy where he was enthralled by the clear light and the sharply defined hills of the Latin landscape. In this land of classic art he apparently absorbed the principles of structural logic in painting.

Although Corot's popular works are the semi-literary scenes of dancing nymphs in misty woodland glades, paintings reminiscent of haunting romantic music, the student of art finds greater satisfaction in the severe figure compositions and solidly designed landscapes. *The Harbor of La Rochelle* (Fig. 499) which Corot painted in mid-career, in 1852, fully reveals his felicity in organizing structural elements. What seems to be the most unpremeditated, even accidental, distribution of figures and objects is in fact a most astute ordering of them. The cluster of figures at the right is an anchoring base for the shapes of the distant towers just as the single lounger, at the extreme right, echoes the dome that pierces the horizon above. Similarly the squared objects in the foreground repeat the cubic structures of buildings beyond. The loose drift of gold-touched clouds gives their color to the earth and the reflections in the water. What to an ordinary observer is only a casual view Corot transformed into a vision of tenderness and human warmth.

National Gallery of Art, Washington, D.C., Chester Dale Collection.

FIG. 500.   Corot, Agostina (1866).

The implicit presence of the people who created the landscape is always felt in Corot's work, giving it texture and vitality. This human quality is in marked contrast to the romantic loneliness of the picturesque wilderness which American painters of the Hudson River school were discovering in the untrodden vastness of the New World at about the same time. In recent decades Corot's figure paintings have gained increased esteem as his art has been re-evaluated. His small nudes are among the finest of the century; they have none of the archaeological remoteness of the Neo-classic or the brutality of Courbet. A late figure painting *Agostina* (Fig. 500), although done in 1866 when the popular misty landscapes were being painted, is so solid and monumental as to bear comparison with the best of Goya or Titian. The warmth of the blues and the depth of the dark tones create an indescribable aura of mystery. Housed in the National Gallery in Washington, the romantic Agostina makes a striking contrast with David's Neo-classic Madame Hamelin (Fig. 488).

Although none of the Barbizon school and perhaps no other Romantic painter attains the stature of Corot, J. F. Millet (1814-1875) marks an important redirection of social attitudes of the nineteenth century and an extension of Romantic thought. As the Romantic revolution gave rise to a fresh contemplation of the landscape, so also there is a new interpretation of humanity. Millet's thought and feeling are for the *creator* of the landscape, the peasant. In turning to figure composition he returns to the great tradition of Mediterranean culture—Graeco-Roman and Renaissance. He views the gleaners of the field, the sower of grain, as monumental symbols of man's essential morality. They are endowed with mute dignity eloquent of the anonymous ritual of toil wherever men have husbanded the gifts of nature. His deep moral purpose is not unlike David's; but where the latter saw meaning only in grandiose historical personages like Napoleon or the Roman heroes, Millet found it in those who create a culture directly through the daily pattern of their lives. The worker, his relation to society, the sanctity of human life so eloquently implicit in Millet's pictures are dominant concepts in world thought, in art, in philosophy, and in politics.

Louvre, Paris.

FIG. 501.   Millet, The Gleaners (1851).

It is no accident that Millet once was the one French master to be popularly known in America. The somber eloquence of his pictures is universally understandable, especially to a people emerging from a pioneer life of hard work and little adornment. His pictures are strong and simple, like *The Gleaners* (Fig. 501), done in 1851, all elements being condensed in a few broad accents. The figures are disposed in a pattern that unifies them with the contours of the field and the haystacks so they become an integral part of the landscape. In the spontaneous design lurks no self-conscious bid for the Salon, no musty reminiscence of the Academies. Painted from memory without models, Millet's compositions are planned along large, ample lines reminiscent of Poussin. A reader of the Psalms and of Greek pastoral poetry, Millet reflects their ageless humanity.

THE REALISTS

No name like Romantic or Realist goes very far in describing the thought and feeling an artist may express in his work. The terms are convenient labels but often not very accurate, for any study of Millet or Corot will disclose representative works which have strong classical features though we apply the term Romantic to them. Ingres likewise, even in his own day, was charged with having Gothic and Romantic tendencies. Nevertheless, until about the middle of the nineteenth century we may say that modern painters were basically divided in attitude and technical procedure between the Neo-classic school of thought and the Romantic. The individualism of the Romantics achieved overwhelming authority as time passed, with only the Academies of art staging a last-ditch fight for the studio practices, if nothing more, of the classic tradition.

Gustave Courbet (1819-1877) added the term Realism to modern painting. Self-taught, arrogant and opinionated, he could not stomach what he felt were the affectations of both Romanticists and Classicists. The Romanticists saw the world through a veil of poetry and sentiment; the Neo-classicists scarcely saw it at all, preoccupied as they were with Greek and Roman ideals. Like Caravaggio two hundred and fifty years earlier (Fig. 454), Courbet would demonstrate once and for all that painting was a matter of physical realities. Why should any artist compose lyrical rhapsodies in painting a landscape or torture figures into sculptured perfection when no one had been able to paint even the bare facts of actuality? Courbet would show them. And he did. His landscapes lack the mystery of the fusing light Corot's searching eye deliberately sought. They are sober and harsh. Where Corot saw the picturesque poetic aspects commonly found by a city-bred man who goes into the country, Courbet avoided them. When he painted a nude he was careful not to betray his theories by making the figure suggest a Venus, a nymph, or a Danaë. His nude is a female model seated on the bank of a stream or resting on a studio couch. The detachment he sought often led to a cold and repellent brutality. But the human body is not a slab of meat nor the landscape a parcel of rocks and sticks as Courbet well knew; many of his paintings are deeply felt and expressive, though sometimes his theories made for self-conscious gestures. While shunning the attitudes which dominated the pictorial art of his time, he had the courage to re-examine nature and to expand the resources of his medium. He studied the methods of the Spaniards and the Dutch to learn how colors and texture and planes might be handled to produce effects of great strength and sober realities. The weight and mass of rocks, the heaviness of snow upon the fields and roofs, the rolling surf are recorded with feeling and conviction. Though

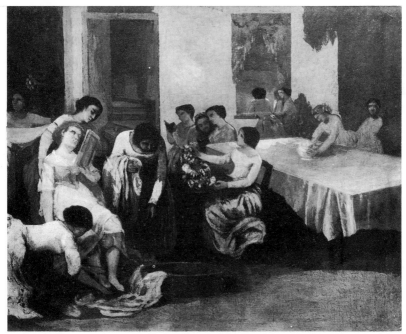

Smith College Museum, Northampton.

FIG. 502.   Courbet, Preparation for the Wedding (*ca.* 1865).

FIG. 503. Daumier, The Legislative Belly, Lithograph (1834).

his work has curious passages of a kind of awkwardly expressed sentiment and sometimes an overexplicit naturalism, his art is fresh and vigorous.

Some of Courbet's best works are in American collections, among them the *Preparation for the Wedding* (Fig. 502) at Smith College. With something of the skill of Velasquez (Fig. 475), Courbet uses an arrangement of space-creating planes that relate values of blue and gray to effect transitions from figure to figure and space to space. Purely illustrational details are subordinated to structural considerations. The canvas is unfinished, and hence provides a better view of Courbet's talents than other of his works which are burdened with factual details of irrelevant surface treatment. His claim of liberating art from the faked sentiment of "noble" themes

came when the representational potentialities of photography were first being realized. In literature, writers were following a similar path in a movement known as Naturalism. Balzac, Flaubert, Zola in the novel, and Ibsen in the drama are kindred spirits.

While Courbet was shocking French sensibilities with his pictorial iconoclasm, Honoré Daumier (1808-1879) was making himself felt in the field of journalism as a political cartoonist. No one of his time suspected that the man who did an almost daily illustration for the press would one day be considered a supreme master of modern painting. His cartoons were in the main routine, political editorials often weighted with enormous satire and irony. One of them directed at the king sent Daumier to prison for six months. No major artist has ever reached so wide and varied a public as he did in the thousands of published lithographs that made Parisains laugh at their own foibles and vanities.

Like Dürer, Rembrandt, and Goya, Daumier brought the graphic arts to a new status. Goya was the first major artist to use lithography; Daumier was the first to use it extensively and fully exploit its expressive possibilities. The picture is drawn in reverse with crayon on a prepared stone; copies can be made in any quantity in the printed text of a publication or as individual prints. In his drawings and lithographs, Daumier exhibits Rembrandt's humanity and Goya's satirical fire, as well as a profound interpretation of character peculiarly his own. A staunch republican, he loves his Paris and all its people even when he makes them the butt of his humor or irony. Stupidity, vanity, human frailties of all kinds are represented in his work no more often than courage, patience, and tenderness. A great-hearted humanity pervades Daumier's art. He reserves his most scalding comments for injustice and callous brutality; for common human frailty he has an indulgent but salty humor. The lithograph done in 1834 called *The Legislative Belly* (Fig. 503) is as devastating as any social comment by Goya. Although directed at a particular legislative assembly, it is in reality a passionate protest against all legal banditry. The theme of entrenched rapacity, the mockery of justice, is presented with equal force in his painting Christ Shown to the People. The tragicomedy of the law courts calls forth a long series of drawings, lithographs, and paintings dealing with lawyers and their peculiar comedy of manners. He explores their pomposity, their rhetorical behavior in court, their sly complacency, their thousand characteristic actions. They are, he observes, shrewd and calculating actors, opportunists performing before complacent judges, defenders of pretty blonde criminals, petty chiselers, or bewildered citizens.

But Daumier's art is rich in human warmth as well as in scorn for sham and hypocrisy. He scans the lives of all classes of men equally, with such capacity for seeing and understanding that he creates a kind of bourgeois mythology comparable in the world of formal art to the *Comédie*

Humaine of his great contemporary, the writer Balzac. No artist of any age has had his unique ability to compress in a few spare lines the temper, the character, the nerve, and the heartbeat of a society. When he paints a game of chess he cuts through to the essence of the game, seeing it as a life-and-death struggle. He draws a musician playing, and the line trembles and vibrates with the sound. Infallibly the inner laws operating to animate the theme find expression in a tense direct pattern. He paints or sketches the theatre and the circus, noting the performer's tension, the pathos, the specious gusto and thin tinsel of showmanship. Whatever grotesque attitudes men take, they are always human beings to Daumier. In *The Side Show* (Fig. 504) the weird trappings of the carnival of freaks meets the eye, but the artist sees the face of the drummer darkened by some private sorrow. In his own way Daumier was realizing the great ethical ideal

Esnault-Pelterie Collection, Paris.

FIG. 504. Daumier, The Side Show, Water Color (*ca.* 1845).

FIG. 505.   Daumier, Third-Class Carriage (*ca.* 1865).

of classic art: to portray essential humanity stripped of accidents and irrelevancies. Spontaneously his noble mind perceived what was noble in his world and laughed and makes us laugh at what is pretense and vanity.

Even more profound in content are Daumier's paintings like *Third-Class Carriage* (Fig. 505), where no particular situation is described, no action takes place; where the theme is simply humanity. A group of people on a journey—

just this and no more is his subject. Yet in it, as Giotto, Michelangelo, and Rembrandt had done earlier, Daumier expresses the deepest mysteries. In restrained and somber colors, a few dark tones here, a trenchant line there create shapes that convey the quality of mind and spirit, unconsciously revealing the essence of humanity. Daumier is a modern mystic who renders intelligible what is chaotic, broken, and obscure.

IMPRESSIONISM

The story of nineteenth-century French painting is one of a democratic and bourgeois society incubating individualistic artists or groups of artists. At first the new men were rejected, often being finally accepted only after death, a process that has continued into the middle of the twentieth century. One explanation for this lies partly in the romantic and individualistic foundations of nineteenth-century art and the growth of a relatively large public for it. The founding of public galleries, with newspapers carrying stories of exhibitions, gave the artist a wider art-

consuming public than in any previous period. Up to 1850, Daumier reached a really vast public to be sure, but only through the broad humor and satire of his lithographs; his paintings remained unknown except for a few of his fellow artists. But among that small group his influence was very great.

The emergence of each new "school" brought indignant protests not only from an irresponsible public of gallery visitors but from fellow artists, critics, and journalists. The Impressionists were attacked for being revolutionists, incompetents, anarchists, and perversely immoral, i.e., on aesthetic, political, moral, and social grounds. Perhaps a more valid reason for their rejection was the natural human reluctance to change established habits and opinions in a period of great cultural ferment. A man who brings a new idea to the court of public opinion invites the wrath of the complacent, the stupid, and the ignorant along with the considered judgment of his peers. Many conflicts are bound to occur because every individual is inclined to invest himself with authority, especially in matters involving aesthetic judgment.

The Realists and to a large degree the Romantics took nature as a model. They outlawed a threadbare classicism and a faded romanticism that was no longer valid in a socially dynamic materialistic age. They took themes from the familiar world about them, scrupulously avoiding anything that suggested the grand manner, the lofty sentiments of patriotism or piety. Daumier and Courbet were moved chiefly by visual sensations and kept their work relatively free of a literary or sentimental consideration. But for these visual experiences to have any significance as art, they of course needed to be organized into intelligently coherent and illuminating patterns. When the Realists achieved this, they did so by emphasizing direct visual experience and avoiding the stereotyped conventions of the Academies regarding composition and color treatment.

In the '60's there emerged a number of younger painters who in general shared the viewpoint of the Realists. In a few years, however, they evolved a radical art language which became known as Impressionism. Their early predilection for realism gave them a bad name with officials of the government and the traditional Academies and with the public. When protests at their exclusion from the Salon grew too strong, Napoleon III provided a special means of showing their work to the public in the famous Parisian *Salon des Refusés* of 1863, where were exhibited all the pictures rejected by the official Beaux Arts Salon. It seemed that at last the iconoclasts were to be given an opportunity to show their work, but this was not to be.

When Napoleon III and his empress Eugénie visited the *Salon des Refusés* they made no secret of their distaste for much of what they saw, particularly a painting officially labeled Le Bain (The Bath), but almost immediately titled *Le Déjeuner sur l'Herbe* (Fig. 506), only weakly translated into English as The Picnic or Luncheon on the Grass. It was the work of Édouard Manet (1832-1883). Critics and public were quick to follow their monarch in condemning it on both moral and technical grounds. Morally it was held indefensible to paint on so large a scale—the painting is about twelve by seven feet—a mixed group of recognizable people in which the men are clothed, one woman semi-nude, and one naked. Technically, academic critics held that the method of painting was abominable, that it lacked both the smoothly finished surfaces and impeccable contours of academic style and the smouldering colors of Romantic emotionalism. Neither criticism took into account Manet's explicit and implicit purpose in the painting—to make visual experience at its simplest and most unequivocal level the subject of the painting. What is seen is relatively unimportant, but the way it is seen is all-important. With Goya, Manet realized that the human eye is aware only of planes that are accepted as forms, without lines or modelling patterns of light and dark, but colored. It was quite literally to recreate this visual experience as completely as possible that Manet painted the way he did.

A couple of years later he exhibited a nude called Olympia, also painted in 1863, which raised another storm of abuse. The episode is of no special significance in the development of painting except that it sheds light on the increasing gulf between the artist and a public with mixed and contradictory opinions about art. Manet was developing his art from sources antagonistic to the Academy, going to the Dutch and especially to Goya and Spanish masters for ideas about handling light and color. He saw how, in contrast to everything he had been taught, they worked with broad areas of color instead of tight line drawing. These spots of color were made rich with light, and the shadows were frequently subordinated to keep the color

Louvre, Paris.

FIG. 506. Manet, Le Déjeuner sur l'Herbe (1863).

fresh and lively. Playing down the shadows or representing them as deeper color instead of gray produced a flat design which appears in his Olympia. In Japanese prints the Impressionists found out how Oriental artists made wonderfully expressive patterns "in the flat" by ignoring or telescoping space intervals and arranging figures in striking unbalanced poses. Photography may likewise have influenced the designs of this period. Manet was a painter of urban and cosmopolitan upbringing who was interested in good painting from an aesthetic standpoint. The observer is not moved by his work as by that of Daumier. If it lacks passionate human warmth, it has other qualities no less valid—discrimination, sensitivity, and intelligence.

Some of Manet's painter friends were a good deal more radical and original, though not necessarily superior to him. Camille Pissarro, Alfred Sisley, Claude Monet (1840-1926), and Pierre Auguste Renoir turned to the pragmatic task of finding means of making their paintings more

truly representative of visual reality. Landscape painting interested them particularly, not for the romantic moods and grand architecture Corot had found but for its color and light. Like scientists they inquired *with their eyes* what a particular landscape looked like, and they painted only from the visual sensations. Physically any landscape is no more than a series of color sensations. These colors are not flat and local, isolated from others, but extremely complex, fusing in atmosphere. The better to observe and record this dancing and ever-changing kaleidoscope, these men went out-of-doors to paint. Monet made a dozen paintings of the same strawstack because he saw that at different times of day the sunlight varied in intensity and direction and its colors consequently differed; the strawstack presented an entirely new appearance each hour. He and others cultivated rapid brushing to capture in a few minutes this fleeting show. The sketchy unfinished effect of their pictures gave the name Impressionist to the school. *The Seine at Argenteuil*

(Fig. 507), which Monet painted in 1874, is a study in flickering color in which a flat sheet of water is broken by several objects that happen to be boats. Nothing is allowed to obstruct the on-the-spot visual analysis; there is no narration or illustration. The method produced incredibly luminous and sparkling pictures of a character rarely found in the old masters. Where the latter painted in the cool even light of the studio from notes and drawings made at another time and place, the Impressionists worked directly in the presence of the thing they were painting, for no memory could adequately retain the sunlight and the colors as they changed continuously with the passing hours.

The science of color and light was studied in books on physics. Practical methods were examined such as the division of color. Green mixed on the palette produced only dead solid color, but a bright green could be made by spotting the canvas with greens of varying intensities. Short dabs of the color produced effects of movement and atmospheric vibration. Shadows were not darker tones but deeper purples or yellows. Most of these observations had been made by earlier masters, notably Titian, Watteau, Delacroix, Constable and Turner, but now they became the stock-in-trade of the school. Blacks and muddy browns disappeared from painting along with lines and small details.

Some have called Impressionism a kind of color photography, a type of painting in which all meaning is sacrificed to impersonal scientific observation. They argue that Monet's boats are not solid objects but areas of yellow and purple

Louvre, Paris.

FIG. 507.   Monet, The Seine at Argenteuil (1874).

Louvre, Paris.

FIG. 508.   Degas, Prima Ballerina
(*ca.* 1876).

longer calls forth any spiritual response, for the formula has little meaning without the informing spirit of its creators. The term Impressionist is convenient for designating a group of men who agreed more or less as to method and point of view. Claude Monet most completely utilized the method. Manet became an Impressionist only in the latter and perhaps lesser phase of his artistic career. Edgar Degas (1834-1917) scarcely qualifies for the name. His talent was for a disciplined draftsmanship and design at a time when most of his contemporaries in the Impressionist camp had their mind on other matters. He found in Ingres, if not an ideal, a great master of linear construction to emulate. When Degas was asked why he didn't go outdoors to paint as the others did he replied, "Painting is not a sport," a remark indicative of his pithy wit and revealing of his mode of working. He often used photographs with their chance relationships of forms, organizing his patterns in ways that owe something to his study of Japanese prints. Although he accepted the high palette and broken color of his friends and exhibited with them, he gave his attention to subjects involving the human figure. But his interest in the figure is limited. He brought it to nothing of Daumier's all-embracing humanity or Renoir's sympathetic intuition. He found in it material for a design of a peculiarly individual character. The nude figure is most often represented as a bather in a bathroom wholly unconcious of any spectator. His aim is to render the unself-conscious pose in a firm and logically coherent design. Portraits, for which he had a special gift, are likewise of people who are not posing but are caught at their accustomed tasks. One study of this was made in New Orleans when he visited his brothers who operated a cotton exchange there.

Ballet dancers, whether rehearsing in a studio or taking a curtain call as in *Prima Ballerina* (Fig. 508), called forth a great many paintings and pastels and lithographs. Not a profound colorist, Degas no less than the others in his group employs color with charm and spirit, especially in pastel. But fundamentally he is a draftsman, one of the best of his century. He is an enormously talented man who views his world in limited

and therefore the painting has no significance. But this partial truth is modified by other considerations. Although they excluded illustrative narration and moral and intellectual values, all of which may be and are found in painting, the Impressionists discovered an exhilarating beauty in nature. The splendor they found is communicated to us. Their discovery of light in color may be called the last great achievement in an analysis of nature that began in Giotto's time.

Tens of thousands of Impressionistic paintings have been made. Some belated individuals are still painting them after a formula which no

Gangnat Collection, Paris.

FIG. 509.   Renoir, Mother and Child (*ca.* 1885).

fragments. Certain personality traits deny him the possibility of complete understanding of life and consequently complete fulfillment as an artist. His biting and sardonic comments spring from the circumscribed mind of an anti-Semite, a rabid nationalist and royalist, and a bachelor. The deep and generous affirmations of Daumier, Renoir, and Cézanne are not to be found in his life or in his art.

But no artist can be evaluated by any means except his work. The breadth of his spirit is measured only in the humanity of his art. The impulses operative in artistic creation are obscure, and only the art object offers any effective measure of those impulses. Some masters bring to their art faltering and unsteady talent which at first appears of no account; Rembrandt's early work gave little or no indication of what was to come. Technical gifts are one thing and spiritual energy and magnitude another. The latter calls out and expands technical equipment. In a period which saw an astonishing outcropping of artistic talent, there was one man who was endowed with no supreme natural gifts for painting. Even to his friends, Auguste Renoir (1841-1919) at first seemed an unpromising painter. What they could not see were the hidden energies and the capacity for spiritual growth—the imponderables which made him one of the greatest single forces in a richly creative epoch.

To call Renoir an Impressionist is to name only one phase of his extraordinary career. His early work is in the dark firm manner of Courbet that stems from the tradition of Velasquez and Goya. With the use of pure pigments in broken patches, his great genius as a colorist emerges and Impressionism as a method blossoms into a style. He had a facility for invention in coloristic terms unprecedented in his century. Color assumes a primary role in the structure and form of his work and he handles it with strength and sensuous warmth. His own natural buoyancy and charm seem miraculously to flow into his pictures; joy in life is an inherent gift which finds spontaneous expression in all his work. This joyous warmth is not something occasionally observed in things or people but is the constant outflowing of a measureless vitality.

For all the iridescence and flowerlike delicacy of Renoir's pictures, in addition they have *reality*. Some artists have a very limited appeal because they speak of some peculiar experience to those who can reconstruct that experience imaginatively. Other artists have a broader more universal base and reach a correspondingly wider circle of humanity. By developing a highly sensuous colorism, Venetian masters of the Renaissance infinitely enriched and enlarged the appeal of European art. Modern painting does not fully employ this sensuous colorism until Renoir's time. Drawing on the Venetians and on Rubens and Watteau, Renoir became one of the few supreme colorists.

His common touch is like Daumier's and Rembrandt's. Searching always to expand the power and appeal of his work, he found the formula of Impressionism too restrictive though he had attained great artistic and material success

Schmitz Collection, Dresden.

FIG. 510. Renoir, Bather (1895).

through it. In common with other French masters he began to strengthen his designs and to compose figures with firmer linear accents. From this period of renewed concern for structural values comes his *Mother and Child* (Fig. 509), painted *ca.* 1885. Without sacrificing the sparkle and movement of color he draws the figures into a crisp lozenge-shaped pattern and poises them against the secure accents of the fence, the building, and the tree trunk. Such compositions are also found in Ingres' work, whose Forestier Family (Fig. 491) is similarly designed.

Mother and Child is a study of Madame Renoir and their son Pierre, but it is only incidentally a portrait. In its extraordinarily compact pattern in which all objects fall logically into interacting rectangles that fuse with repeated egg-shaped forms, the "Mother and Child" theme emerges with the utmost freshness and reality, like a happy incident of observation. The strong underlying formal structure present in the art of Corot, Daumier, and Renoir sets their art off from much work that is too largely illustrative and superficially descriptive. From this time on, Renoir's art becomes increasingly classical. He gives more thought to weight and mass, to the solid forms of Renaissance and baroque painting.

The line becomes an interweaving of light and color of remarkable strength.

In the latter phases of his career, color and line and light are magically combined in supremely symbolic works. As Rembrandt, Poussin, and Titian had reserved their full creative achievements for their latest years, so it is with Renoir. The *Bather* (Fig. 510), painted in 1895, demonstrates the incandescence of his color, the solidity of his vital figures. A lover of women and children, he paints them as though they were exquisite flowers, the jewels of creation. Flesh is the color of mother-of-pearl with the firmness of Praxitelean marble. A bather's dress or hat on the sand glows with the mystery of a precious jewel. Without leaving the knowable world Renoir carries us with him into a realm of wonder and exaltation.

THE POST-IMPRESSIONISTS

Renoir's search for an artistic language beyond Impressionism should be considered in the light of other masters who came to be known as Post-Impressionists. These men —Cézanne, Seurat, Gauguin, and Van Gogh— were engaged through the '80's in a quest comparable to Renoir's. Each in his own way found a method that was essentially personal, but despite a high degree of individuality some general characteristics emerge. All four painters evolve from Impressionism and employ its full rich light and color. But notably they all work toward solid structure and are more systematic in the way they paint, feeling that the Impressionists had relied too much on rule-of-thumb. The greatest of the Post-Impressionists was Paul Cézanne (1839-1906). In his own words, he "wished to make of Impressionism something as solid and durable as the old masters in the museums." He was thinking of the monumental Italian Renaissance art of Masaccio and Michelangelo, and of Titian and of Poussin. In the older art he recognized solidity and continuity of definite forms integrated in stable space rhythms. Cézanne particularly admired the work of Poussin, who created harmonious and lucid patterns in mass and space. The problem Cézanne set for himself was to take the luminous atmospheric colorism of Impressionism and with it construct images that would have the stability, the depth and solidity of the older pictures. He felt that the characteristic form of things had been dissolved into intangible and meaningless color spots by the painters of his day. He recognized the achievements of the Impressionists in restoring color to its place as a fundamental pictorial element, but he also saw that in doing so they neglected considerations of contour and form limits, rendering the forms themselves vague and without substantial reality.

In his long labors to evolve a method that would render nature more comprehensively and at the same time more expressively than Impressionism had done, Cézanne made many false starts. All his fumbling attempts met with extremely caustic and very cruel disparagement from nearly everyone who saw or even heard of his work. He was the ugly duckling of the Impressionists when he was working in their method. Apparently he had no gifts or talents. Nothing he did pleased anyone, least of all himself. Retiring from Paris to his birthplace, the provincial city of Aix-en-Provence in southern France, he isolated himself from all external influences to "remake Poussin after nature." No painter ever had so many failures or showed more courage in going on and on after countless abortive efforts. He worked much with still-life (Fig. 511), because a bowl of apples on a table never moves and can be studied at leisure. He investigated the architectonic relations of the round bowl and the spheres of the fruit, noting the movements in color and accent that established relationships between the essential shapes, coordinating them with the fold of a napkin and the table edge. He submitted the still-life to the same analysis that Raphael gave to a Holy Family, observing the formal relations that make for adhesion and unity. He would first view the subject as an abstract design, a pattern of shapes, in order to realize the dynamic relations of its component parts interacting. But his interest was not in a pleasing and unified design for its own sake. He was concerned with inner organization solely in order to effect a complete realization of every aspect of his subject. In short, he aimed at the most *telling* image of the apples and napkin that could be produced.

When Cézanne worked he took nothing for granted. He had no formula; each canvas was a new venture, a new problem whose solution tested all his resources to the limit. In this respect he was like Rembrandt, constantly studying the means to greater condensation, a shorter, more direct path to a fuller expression in his medium. He found that the problems in a still-life were the same as those in the portrait and landscape. There were the same elements of space, of surface texture, of density and mass to be reckoned with. No two of his paintings are alike because his eye profoundly tested the infinite variety of nature. To achieve the harmonious organization of color and line in design prompted him to distort the physical appearance of objects. In *Un Dessert* (Fig. 511), a still-life done in 1873-1877, the variety in oval and circular forms calls for the distortion of the jug and wine glass. All painters distort the shape of things to some degree or other; Cézanne's distortions are only a little more obvious. The spherical shapes are played off against two broad planes marked by the table edge and the wall. Within those areas there is an animated drama of shape, color, and space.

Cézanne's search for a means of expressing the depth of cubic form led him to make an exhaustive study of the continuous planes that make up a solid. He designated each plane by a certain color intensity, and by careful gradation in the planes he effected a powerful sensation of three-dimensional forms. No trick of deception was involved. Cézanne sought an image, related to but different from the model, having its own identity, a vitality independent of all but itself. Seeking such images, he found them not by imitating appearance, but by creating them.

The transformation of a subject from its everyday apperance to one conceived by the artist for greater monumental and expressive ends occurs in his later painting *The Great Bathers* (Fig. 512). Tree trunks are "distorted" into an enveloping Gothic arch above the figures. This is repeated in reverse below by the arms of the women. At the same time the figures are so arranged as to comprise stable pyramidal groupings at right and left. In forming an integrated structural pattern all kinds of distortions are made in familiar objects, especially the figures. In this work there is a kind of balance between traditional representation as found in Corot's canvases and twentieth-century abstraction; Poussin's architectural structure finds agreement here with the invented forms which the Cubists contrived a decade or so later. Such painting, devoid of anecdote, sentiment, and familiar beauty, was incomprehensible to Cézanne's generation. Few recognized the epoch-making innovation he brought into the stream of European art.

Cézanne had many failure for every success, but even his failures are magnificent fragmentary revelations of experience. He recognized better than anyone when he succeeded, or failed to "realize his sensations" as he put it. He thought of himself as a primitive working in the method he had discovered. And there is indeed something of primitive directness and instinct for essentials in his pictures. The *Card Players* (Fig. 513), one of his greatest figure pieces, brings complex plastic bodies into equilibrium with the fluid

Collection of Mrs. Carroll S. Tyson, Philadelphia.

FIG. 511.   Cézanne, Un Dessert,
Still-Life (1873-1877).

Philadelphia Museum of Art.

FIG. 512.   Cézanne, The Great Bathers (1898–1906).

space of the room. Everything essential has been rendered convincingly—the texture of cloth in the drapery, the flesh tones, the cards, and the atmosphere—and all are translated into an arresting pictorial reality. The picture gives the subject an immediacy and directness comparable to that of Jan van Eyck's Arnolfini portrait (Fig. 375), together with the monumental stability of Giotto and Masaccio.

A Post-Impressionist of the utmost originality was Georges Seurat (1859-1891), who, like Cézanne, was conscious of the looseness of Impressionist design. He composed his color areas by tiny disks of pigment (pointillism), sug-

gesting mass and receding space by variations of intensity. Where the Impressionists wished to show flickering light in restless motion, Seurat strove for monumental tranquillity, a repose of solemn grandeur that uncannily suggests the most momentary and casual movement. His *Sunday Afternoon on the Island of La Grande Jatte* (Fig. 514), in the Chicago Art Institute, his masterpiece, was painted between 1884 and 1886. The forms are disposed upon the canvas with such exact understanding of their relation to each other, their position is so justly established with respect to the total design that the strollers in the park seem crystallized in their most characteristic attitude as in timeless space. The most trivial forms—a plug hat, the silhouette of a bustle, the arc of an open parasol—are so subtly interwoven in the fabric of the design that they become permanent and signally revealing elements of a moment in time that has been forever fixed. A kind of super-reality attained by rigid adherence to rules of order and harmony places Seurat's work in the grand classic tradition in French art. But it is classic in feeling, as Cézanne's and Renoir's works are, with no mustiness of archaeological formulas. Even today, despite the curious styles in costume, the world he portrayed has the pictorial authority of the old masters.

While Cézanne and Seurat were finding the means of realizing solid forms and classically lucid patterns of space, Vincent Van Gogh (1853-1890), a Dutch painter working in France, was evolving a style the exact antithesis of theirs. His art cannot be dissociated from his intimate life, for no master has ever poured out his passionate being in his painting as he did. In his early years, Van Gogh was an evangelist in miserable mining towns. His passionate love for humanity and the excessive zeal with which his almost insane devotion manifested itself led him into all manner of tragic conflicts. People were revolted by his fanaticism and he was defeated at the very

The Metropolitan Museum of Art, Bequest of Stephen C. Clark, 1960.

FIG. 513. Cézanne, The Card Players (*ca.* 1890).

FIG. 514.   Seurat, Sunday Afternoon on the Island of la Grande Jatte
(1884–1886).

beginning of a career that absorbed him body and soul. He was a mature man when he devoted himself to the study of painting; and in a few years he mastered the technique and developed a personal style, whereas most artists take decades. Following now Millet or Delacroix, now Daumier, and now the Impressionists, he finally evolved a method that was entirely his own. In painting that has the most violent colorism he found symbols for the burning intensity of his visions. The sunflowers he paints writhe and twist, consumed by the heat of their own radiance. Forms take motion to correspond to the sensation of the painter who sees them as living embodiments of energy like himself. He paints cypress trees that bend to the wind, their foliage twisting in long darts like tongues of fire. Color excites him to a frenzy of activity, and he paints

FIG. 515.   Van Gogh, Peasant,
Drawing (1888).

the sun-drenched wheat fields as if they were caldrons of molten gold.

Every subject he essays is a search for the inner life. He cares nothing for the externals except as they offer a clue to some unseen reality. With tense linear patterns, with nervous staccato stipple, he constructs surfaces and masses into the unforgettable and haunting face of a *Peasant* (Fig. 515). He is attracted by Daumier's deep humanity and follows his methods in giving powerful movement to planes and lines.

In his work is found the greatest variety of expression from the most lyrical beauty to studies in morbid psychology. The interior called *The Night Café* (Fig. 516), painted in 1888, is not so much the portrayal of a place as the calculating analysis of a heightened emotional experience. He describes his picture in a letter to his brother Theo as representing a place of livid horror where one might go mad. To most eyes the café may not look different from a hundred others, but Van Gogh's extreme sensibilities to color and mood find in it an inferno of suspended horrors. In fact, it is no less than a nightmare of dilating space; shapes of chairs and tables assume tortured patterns; light coagulates about the lamps. The colors are ghastly in their power to shock and disturb and are harmonious only in that they are all calculated to flay the nerves. They are decaying purples, poisonous greens, and hard inflaming reds. Such lurid studies speak of the mind of a man who is tortured by suffering and

Yale University Art Gallery, Bequest of Stephen C. Clark, B.A., 1903.

FIG. 516. Van Gogh, The Night Café (1888).

Museum, Bremen.

FIG. 517. Van Gogh, Cypresses in the Moonlight,
Drawing (1890).

terribly aware of the spiritual conflicts in his own personal life and the life of his society. In his writing and painting he speaks of a world transformed, and as we can see, it is a world seen through the enraptured eyes of a mystic. On another occasion he writes that he is painting a landscape but fears that what he has done is after all *only* a landscape. His meaning is clear—that he tries to make his landscape convey some degree of the unfathomable mystery of life and creation.

As a colorist he introduces extremely bold ideas into art. His contemporaries found his bright contrasting colors garish and unpleasant, but today it is realized that they are deeply expressive of the intoxicating beauty he expounded. His color sense is equaled by his draftsmanship. In black and white drawings he simulates color values to an extraordinary degree. Swirling, twisting, gyrating linear patterns are used in the drawing done in 1890, *Cypresses in the Moonlight* (Fig. 517), much as in his paintings the heavily coiled rolls of pure pigment accentuate nervous movement. The slumbering village lies engulfed

by the mysterious orgiastic convulsion of light and the throbbing earth.

Though many artists felt Van Gogh's powerful influence, he was scarcely a master to attract the following Cézanne has had. His art was too purely personal and intimate; his method was created specifically to carry the weight of his unique visions. No one else could profitably employ his peculiar artistic language. At one time Van Gogh was associated with the painter Paul Gauguin (1848-1903), who in some respects is his French counterpart. Both were convinced of the corruption of their society and of modern culture generally. Van Gogh tried to reconcile himself to it by the fierce consuming mysticism of his art as earlier Daumier had through his moral and rational idealism. The gathering storm clouds culminating in World War I were manifest in many ways in the art of the late nineteenth century. Gauguin echoed something of the idealism of the Romantics in his dramatic flight from European civilization. Discovering the art forms of non-Mediterranean peoples and the

FIG. 518.   Gauguin, The Wave (1892).

simple patterns of primitive art, he formulated a style of flat decorative design. In the South Sea Islands he looked for a utopia among the Polynesians, only to find that the idyllic life described by Herman Melville had long since vanished. Under the French colonial policy the simple people had become demoralized and sickened by the white man's sharp exploitation and by his diseases. Nevertheless, Gauguin remained and made a life for himself among the native population. Through his art he created the substance of his dreams. What might have been a foolish gesture became a noble assertion of human dignity in the scores of paintings centering on the mysteries of folk customs and the exotic tropical landscape. *The Wave* (Fig. 518) of 1892 is representative of the way he combined broad flat areas of exotic color. The space pattern is consciously reduced in a tapestrylike surface that glows sensuously. The exotic people and foliage are rendered in decorative shapes. Gauguin and other Post-Impressionists anticipate the originality and the bold individuality that characterize the diverse activity in art in the twentieth century.

Detail of Picasso's Guernica, *Fig. 524.*

CHAPTER THIRTY-ONE

Painting in the Twentieth Century

Painting in the twentieth century is basically abstract and non-illusionistic. This assertion holds true despite the considerable amount of painting created in this period which continues to adhere to the aesthetic of Renaissance realism. The image of objects conceived in terms of solid forms enclosed in a defined space (Realism) no longer has power to move people as it once did, to stimulate their imagination or excite admiration. Naturally this holds true for the artists of our century somewhat more than for the general public which is slow in responding to changes, especially to aesthetic innovations.

Before exploring the recent aesthetic revolution, we are impelled to seek an explanation for so drastic a turn of events. Many people accustomed to the art of the old masters experience frustration when viewing works which often seem to deny any of the values of ordinary beauty or significance apparent in the older art. Because of its abstract character, the work of the modern artist has been called barbarous, infantile, and degenerate by a few responsible and many irresponsible critics. But when we look at the extensive collection of art in a representative museum we soon discover that what we term Realism is to be found in only few past art epochs.

The appearance of Cubism and the method of abstraction is no eccentricity of recent times, for such transformations are a recurrent phenomenon in art history. An equally radical reversal of style occurred at the end of the Middle Ages with the advent of the Renaissance. The changes in Italian and Flemish art after 1400 were no less remarkable than those that occurred shortly after 1900. Mediaeval painting (cf. Fig. 369) was in many respects like the new painting of our own age. Artists in both periods are concerned with ideas or concepts rather than realistic images. This method is employed in a child's drawing. When a child makes a picture of an apple he draws a circle or disk which is in fact a definition of a mental image. This image has no indication of mass or space which would create an illusion or imitation of an apple. Although the results of the methods of the mediaeval and modern masters are comparable in some ways to those of the spontaneous method used by children, they do not involve duplicating a preestablished mental image as is the case with children. The people of the Middle Ages rejected realism because, according to their philosophy and their religion, the external world of physical reality was of relatively little importance. The physical world was, at best, a kind of waiting room. Beyond it was the unquestioned reality of heaven or hell unseen by mortal eye.

When men of the Renaissance no longer considered the unseen world as ultimate reality, they created a doctrine that is generally called humanism. According to it, man is the measure, not God. Man becomes the explorer of a world which science clarifies and reason explains. Faith in man and his reasoning faculty replaced faith in God and His beneficences. The world view of our time quite naturally has many of the attributes of both mediaeval and Renaissance thought. But our age reserves judgment about life hereafter, and is skeptical about the ability of science to solve all human problems. Despite the violence and disruption, there is every reason to believe that our age will emerge from dangling doubt, from negative questioning. The work of artists, scientists, and statesmen demonstrates a sober and chastened faith in a new order for a horribly disrupted world. In all spheres, notably in physics, art, and politics, positive advances are being made against chaos. The work of Roosevelt, Einstein, Picasso, and Wright is that of heroic builders of strong foundations upon which a stable world structure can be erected.

The disappearance of the realistic image from painting was in itself a symptom of the upheavals in the general culture of our time. Its disintegration can be traced in the art of the nineteenth century. The Post-Impressionists, now universally acclaimed, were the incomprehensible artists of the late 80's and 90's just because they produced images so far removed from average understanding that only a very few at that time, even in France, found their work of any value. Yet they, especially Cézanne, were the seers of a new vision. By their resolute warping of space, by their placing of design above surface appearance, and by their systematic use of color for other purposes than simple description, they established precedents for the artists who came to maturity in the early twentieth century.

In 1905, before the Post-Impressionists attained any considerable public recognition, a new generation began to exhibit paintings whose like had never been seen. Objects were distorted; colors had a new intensity and were used without regard to their previously descriptive function. The time-honored Renaissance convention of space representation was often wholly abandoned for a flat two-dimensional treatment. These men—Matisse, Rouault, Marquet, Braque, and others—were popularly discredited and called

The Baltimore Museum of Art, Cone Collection.

FIG. 519. Matisse, Blue Nude (1907).

Fauves or wild beasts. Their artistic fathers were principally Gauguin and Van Gogh. Of this group Henri Matisse (1869-1954) attained commanding stature, deepening his perceptions of design and color through studies of Hindu sculpture, Persian miniatures, Greek vases, and any other source likely to contribute vitality and freshness. To some, Matisse is a skillful and imaginative decorator and little more. Yet if we compare an early work like *Blue Nude—Souvenir of Biskra* (Fig. 519) which he painted in 1907 with the *Lady in Blue* (Fig. 520) done in 1937, it becomes clear that his characteristic modulations of the human form resulted from a genuinely imaginative and structural response to visual experience. As the subtitle of the earlier painting indicates, it was suggested by exotic forms Matisse saw while traveling in the Near East. The massive blue contour lines, set off against a background of foliage variously green, rose,

ochre, and a pinkish violet, is in no way intended to simulate the proportions and profiles of nature. But the rhythmic movement it creates, and its vibrant color patterns constitute an experience that is at the same time vivid and alluring. The Lady in Blue is painted in more suave terms, but the precision and subtlety of the line that establishes both contours and textures express a concept no less positive than that in the Blue Nude for all it is more reticent. Here again color contributes a great deal—predominantly blue, with red and yellow in secondary roles, and minor touches of green, white, and black. At his most characteristic, as here, Matisse's designs are the pictorial epitome of elegance and charm.

Others of the Fauve group, similarly committed to strong color vigorously brushed in patterns either elemental in their simplicity or violently distorted (as some consider it), were Georges Rouault (1871-1958) and Georges Braque

Collection of Mrs. John Wintersteen, Villanova.

FIG. 520.   Matisse, Lady in Blue (1937).

(b. 1882). Rouault is notable as one of the few major painters of the early twentieth century to be concerned with religious and moral concepts; the somber powerful style in which he interprets them owes more than a little to his study of the jewellike color in mediaeval stained glass windows. Braque, on the other hand, soon moved to what was for him the more congenial structuralism of geometrical abstraction, or Cubism.

Although the Fauves indicated the general direction of twentieth-century artistic thought relatively early, it remained for the Spaniard, Pablo Picasso (b. 1881), to supply the basic grammar of modern art. At the age of twenty he went to Paris which, like a magnet, attracted the artistic talent of the world. A little younger than the Fauves, he was not drawn into their circle but worked then, as always, in a variety of styles. His early painting from 1901-1904, like *La Vie* (Fig. 521), is characterized by saturation of blue color with a corresponding melancholy pathos. Distortions reminiscent of El Greco and mediaeval sculpture (Fig. 297) are evident. Subsequently the melancholy note of the early works gives way to a new mood of romantic sentiment in his circus subjects, jugglers and acrobats. With these paintings done in 1905-1906 came new feeling for warmer colors, tans and pinks, and a new emphasis on classic form. In 1907 Picasso painted what has been called the first Cubist picture, *The Young Women of Avignon* (Fig. 522).

The significance of Picasso's picture lies in its definitions of a new world style. Plainly revealed is a sharp break even with his own early work, but notably with the five-hundred-year-old tradition of realistic art. Stemming from its implicit theory grew the great flower of his Cubist paintings and those of Braque, Fernand Leger, and Juan Gris. Their concentration on the disintegration and reintegration of natural form influenced the thinking of the Abstractionists in every country. Cubism began as a logical application of Cézanne's method (Fig. 512) which called for ordering, arranging, and imposing strict architectural procedure in pictorial design—in short, overleaping literal non-artistic vision. In searching for basic expressive forms Cézanne largely disregarded surface appearance and transformed familiar shapes; in building his images he ignored the traditional values of sentiment and beauty. He began to dispense with the Renaissance convention of defining space in Euclidean geometrical terms. One of the most characteristic features of the whole modern movement is its new conception of space.

Cubism had one of its clearest and most classic expressions as a basic style in the work of Picasso's friend and fellow Spaniard, Juan Gris (1887-1927). His *Still-Life with Poem* (Fig. 523), done in 1915, is a presentation of objects on a table without reference to the conventional notation of spatial relationship. As in a mediaeval painting, near and far are not considerations. In both modern and mediaeval painting objects exist in infinite space as opposed to the localized and particularized space which the Renaissance established. Here the objects—table top, playing card, and pipe—are not subjected to illusionistic treatment but are transposed into another key necessary for an effective presentation that stresses

formal inner relationship, cohesion, and inter-dependence of the objects. Even the pure illusion-ism of the poem that is seemingly tacked to the frame is subject to this order. In such interfunctional play of visual elements the modern style found its method and its logic.

This "flat, colored architecture," to use Gris' own term, is not making nothing of something. Cubism signalized a method for replacing out-worn materialism with a concept that implies a different philosophical view. It makes man the creator of his surrounding world rather than its exploiter or victim. The implicit method of this aesthetic revolution is to be found in all kinds of expression—in science and politics as well as art. It points to a conception of phenomena that stresses interrelationships of unifying elements rather than conflicts in diversity and isolation.

The Cleveland Museum of Art,
Gift of Hanna Fund, 1945.

FIG. 521.   Picasso, La Vie (1903).

FIG. 522.   Picasso, The Young Women of Avignon (1907).

In following his theory with extraordinary consistency, Gris was unwilling to deflect Cubism by making it a vehicle for sentiment or surface decoration or any element outside the most rigorous formal architectonic ones. Braque and Picasso, on the other hand, used it for the most diverse expression of psychological and personal feeling. From the first, Picasso's imagination was stimulated by the whole range of art history. Like other painters he absorbed into his work the heretofore neglected plastic ideas of Negro sculpture from the west coast of Africa, mediaeval wall paintings, and, of course, the Oriental and western masters. No brief account can more than mention the various turns and twists of his style. So vast was his all-consuming thirst for fresh stimulation in plastic ideas and so effective were his new ventures that he became the unrivaled leader of his age. In the 1930's he reached a kind of climax with such celebrated canvases as the Girl Before a Mirror, 1932, and *Guernica* (Fig. 524), painted in 1937. Both are masterworks of modern art, examples of the transformation effected by Cubism. In the former the figure of a girl exsists in infinite space, illuminated by the radiance of diamond-shaped patterns of color. The head is seen in a double image as though viewed simultaneously from various positions. Breasts and pelvic structure are presented in a kind of X-ray view. Freudian psychology, the light in mediaeval stained-glass windows, and the luminism of Vermeer's interiors intermingle here with renewed vitality.

Elements expressive of a specific feeling for violence and of tension (constant in our age) had for a long time been evident in Picasso's work—the orgiastic Dancers (1925), the heat of the Bull Fight (1934), the anguish of the Crucifixion (1930). These disturbing studies alternated with others of emotionally neutral structure. The Guernica resulted from the coincidence of political and artistic events. At the moment when Spain was plunged into a blood bath of civil war by General Franco aided by Hitler and Mussolini, Picasso was asked to contribute an artistic work for a world's fair in Paris. The great Guernica was his reply. Its theme is the bombing and destruction of the Spanish town of Guernica by the German air force. The painting, of mural proportions, is executed in black, white, and grays. Filled with symbolic images of specific character, it savagely probes an incalculably brutal act. In Picasso's words, "The bull is . . . brutality and darkness. . . . The horse represents the people . . . the Guernica mural is symbolic . . . allegoric." No single modern work has had the impact of this painting nor is there one that so surely illustrates the power of pictorial abstraction to create forcefully moving images in this idiom.

The abstraction in this painting is limited because it contains some recognizable objects like a horse, a bull, women, men, children, fire, etc. Some twentieth-century artists maintain that

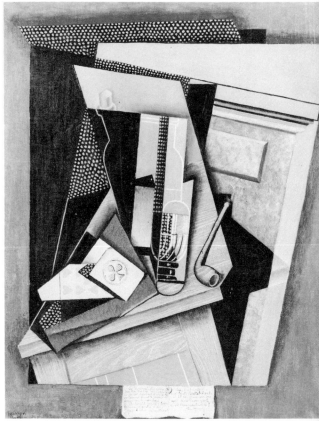

Collection of Mr. and Mrs. Henry Clifford, Radnor.

FIG. 523. Gris, Still-Life with Poem (1915).

painting, like music, may be freed of all representation and embody designs with no recognizable subject matter. One aspect of nonobjectivity as a concept is seen in the work of Piet Mondrian (1872-1944), a Dutch artist. His designs consist of balanced vertical and horizontal areas of color, subtly related in proportion and hue to each other and to the rectangle of the picture plane. These austere, purely geometrical compositions have influenced architecture and the industrial arts of the mid-twentieth century as well as the work of other painters.

Acceptance of the idea of nonobjectivity carries with it the possibility that formal relationships of shapes and colors may be inherently expressive, even if nothing immediately recognizable

Collection, the Artist. Courtesy, The Museum of Modern Art, New York.

FIG. 524. Picasso, Guernica (1937).

is involved. As early as 1891, Maurice Denis, a French painter and writer, suggested that a painting is primarily a two-dimensional plane on which colors are arranged in a certain order. It is such a concept that underlies the work of Wassily Kandinsky (1872-1944), illustrated by his painting called *Improvisation No. 30* (Fig. 525), done in 1913 and now in the Art Institute at Chicago. The title suggests the affinity with the nonrepresentational yet expressive art of music which Kandinsky sought to realize. In a book written a few years before, Kandinsky calls painting "the art of spiritual harmony." Both his writings and his painting make clear his feeling that "under the effect of the form and color combinations of the picture" the spectator shares the experience of the artist.

The term Expressionism has been applied to this concept of painting, in which the emphasis is less upon the definition of a systematic formal language, as in Cubism, than upon the energy of direct emotional statement. Without imitating Van Gogh the Expressionists gave their interpretation something of his vitality and passion. The painting of Franz Marc (1880-1916), Oscar Kokoschka (b. 1886), and more recently

George Grosz (1893-1959) and Max Beckman (1884-1950) shows variously elements of abstraction derived from the Cubists and from the study of primitive art. The Expressionistic painter is guided by impulse and passion to assert the excitement of life rather than its logic and form. Thus his art stresses spontaneous freedom in design and color and is thereby theoretically at the opposite pole from the more architectonic quality of Cubism.

Because the method of abstraction in both its Cubist and Expressionist aspects opened so many doors for expression there have been, in the past sixty years, a great many movements and schools, some of which are not localized in any city or country. The tendencies are often international and the methods interpenetrating. (Picasso, for instance, a Spaniard who works almost wholly in France, exemplifies half a dozen different styles. He may be at once a Cubist, a Surrealist, an Expressionist.) A number of painters called Surrealist or super-realist, who emerged after 1924, often have little in common save a name which has been thrust upon them. Surrealism, in general, exploits the mysteries of association, of strangeness, in appealing to subconscious feelings and impulses. Every image has about it a certain element of magic because it arouses in the observer responses on several levels of thought and feeling. The Surrealists create suggestive effects through distortions of space, double images, and grotesque juxtaposition of objects and ideas, just as Freud pointed out the distinction between recognition on the conscious plane and on the unguarded level of the subconscious. In sleep the unconscious element of thought is released in dreams. Surrealists seek to explore the borderland of dreamlike fantasy and the magic of the unreal world of imagination. The Spanish painter, Salvador Dali (b. 1904), created an international sensation with his well-advertised and sometimes trivial sexual fantasies that had an appeal for sensation-seekers. Since he depends upon an archaic realism in contriving his ingenious effects, his work is somewhere outside the realm of abstract painting.

Painting released from the rules of the realistic image and the Renaissance cage of space is an invitation to the free expression of psychic pressures and tensions, of fears and longings not ordinarily found in the more rationalistic confines of traditional art. Modern painting is sometimes a vehicle for a wholly novel type of pictorial humor, poetry, and fantasy. Marc Chagall (b. 1887) has enriched the world with his haunting pictures of childhood in a Russian peasant village. His remembrance of things past in *I and My Village* (Fig. 526), painted in 1911, is a fragment of memory, a kaleidoscope of feeling and images. In a painting so conceived, it stands to reason that the proportions and relationships of forms will have little connection with anything seen in nature. Instead, they are scaled in accordance with the painter's remembered emotional experience, and related in such a way that the nature of that experience is all the more vividly expressed. But if the illustration is inverted and what representational quality the various forms have is still further deemphasized, it will be seen that the whole is well organized in a simple pattern of diagonals with accentuating curves. In the painting itself the colors contribute in no small degree to the ingratiating effect of the whole.

Paul Klee (1879-1940) has a very special place among the twentieth-century artists who have explored the world of fantasy and imagination in their painting. A Swiss artist of German background, he once was a colleague of Wassily Kandinsky at the Bauhaus at Dessau (cf. pages 720-722) and contributed significantly to that school's reorientation of contemporary art. Klee is at the same time one of the most unpretentious and one of the most original spirits in the modern movement. His drawings, etchings, and paintings may look, at first, like doodles or a child's ideographs, but their inner meaning finally strikes with all the more force, like a delayed explosion. *Cat and Bird* (Fig. 527) painted in 1928 is such a work. The line that defines an almost banal image of a cat's head on observation becomes tense with savage lust, devouring the image of the bird. Klee often explores the "growth and progress of plants" and the anatomy of suffering and death. Frequently he expounds the psychic life of

The Art Institute of Chicago,
Arthur Jerome Eddy Memorial.

FIG. 525. Kandinsky, Improvisation No. 30 (1913).

Collection, Museum of Modern Art, New York, Mrs. Simon Guggenheim Fund.

FIG. 526.   Chagall, I and My Village (1911).

children—touchingly and fearsomely. Some of his studies are wholly abstract; yet even in them the artist is completely lucid, wholly concrete in projecting ideas. The mental image is his province; his magic is the sudden light of recognition. His voice is quiet, with its health, its humility, and its humor, but it sounds with indisputable authority. For all its striking individualism, Klee's art is sane and meaningful, unconcerned with the calculated enigma and created mystery that so often obscure the meaning of much of this century's painting.

The great transformation of Renaissance style to twentieth-century abstraction took place in Paris, the forcing hothouse of new aesthetic concepts. Until World War II, the City of Light attracted countless young painters from all over the world. Along with Spanish, Americans, Russians and Germans came the young artists of Mexico who were to play a momentous part in the cultural renaissance in that country. Mexico, a land with a dark and tragic history, emerged in the twentieth century from a mediaeval culture. Even today many of its millions are almost untouched by the industrial revolution. Though rich in its pre-Columbian history, in the vitality of its mixed races, and in natural resources, Mexico has peculiar, practical, and spiritual dilemmas unlike any other country. Its art reflects that unique status. When its artists came in contact with modern abstraction they modified the theoretical premises of Cubism in evolving their style. Diego Rivera (1886-1957) studied in his youth in Paris, where he painted abstract pictures. But the need for reform and social reconstruction in his country deflected his art toward social and dramatic expression on a popular level of realism. From 1922, when Mexican artists formed a syndicate to cooperate with the government in decorating public buildings, a great artistic resurgence took place. Reviving the medium used for the Renaissance mural painting, artists decorated acres of wall spaces using the technique of true fresco painting. Diego Rivera, José Orozco (1883-1949), and David Alfaro Siquerios (b. 1896) were leaders in the heroic effort to coordinate the work of artists with the national social program. The socialist revolution was carried on in the face of extremely strong religious and political opposition within and outside the country. The painters conceived of their art as a mighty instrument in the country's economic and political emancipation, a dramatic means of revealing the

history, philosophy, and aspirations of a people emerging from a heroic past into an equally heroic future.

Whereas Rivera's work has the virtues of lucidity and "readability," Orozco's painting is more daemonic, corrosive, and abstract. His figures are charged with terrible energy like those of Michelangelo, El Greco, and Goya, with whom he is often compared. As Rivera was called north to paint murals in San Francisco, Detroit, and New York, so Orozco also created important murals for Dartmouth College in Hanover, N. H., in New York City, and for Pomona College in California. The Dartmouth murals, painted in 1932-1934, deal with a legendary, historical, and spiritual account of the Americas. *Christ Cutting Down the Cross* (Fig. 528), a unit in that fresco, shows Christ as a stark emblem like the abstract images of Romanesque times. No one can escape the painter's meaning here as he presents an angry God destroying the sign which has become a mockery of divine love in a war-scarred Christian world. Not only in the Christ is there a link with mediaeval art but there is an equal link in the subordination of material reality to the all-embracing concept.

Orozco's grimly foreboding Christ and Picasso's Guernica (Fig. 524), both painted in the 1930's, were all too prophetic of the future. The note they sounded has echoed through western art since World War II. In a brief essay prefacing the catalogue of an exhibition presented by the Museum of Modern Art in 1959 called *The New Images of Man*, the philosopher Paul Tillich defines as follows the problem confronting the mid-twentieth century and its artists: "Humanity is not something man simply has. He must fight for it anew in every generation, and he may lose his fight." Viewed in this light, much that may seem ugly and repellent must be recognized as an all too discerning comment on the civilization of the period that produced it.

The years since World War II have been enormously productive. In the countries that overthrew totalitarian regimes, this can be understood as the inevitable consequence of being able once more to speak freely and honestly; in

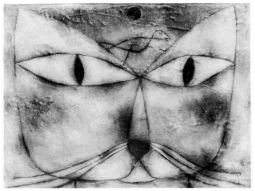

FIG. 527. Klee, Cat and Bird (1928).

others, this productivity is an aspect of the ferment and the challenge to tradition that invariably follow upheaval and change. Styles vary with each artist; and if there seems to be no sense of tradition, the very nontraditionalism of painting in the 1950's reflects the spirit of the time. A painting like *The Busy Life* (Fig. 529), done in 1953 by Jean Dubuffet (b. 1901), is the work of a man whom some consider one of the outstanding French artists since the war. Of considerable size and executed in strong, harshly dissonant color, the forms have the crude outlines of shapes scratched on a wall, and something of the dissociation characteristic of drawings by

children and insane people; Dubuffet has been interested in both forms of expression. His purpose is thus allied to that of Surrealism, although his method is different. The extent to which his imagination is expressed in the terms of his medium cannot really be sensed in a reproduction but is immediately evident in the work itself. In this, Dubuffet's work, whether or not it is actually influenced by the "action painting" (Fig. 545) of American abstract expressionism, clearly parallels it in significant respects.

As was stated earlier, any reasonably comprehensive impression of European painting since World War II would require comment on and

Baker Library, Dartmouth College.

FIG. 528.   Orozco, Christ Cutting Down the Cross (1934).

Artist's Collection.

FIG. 529.   Dubuffet, The Busy Life (1953).

illustration of the work of every artist of the period. Among them would have to be included Pierre Soulages (b. 1919) of France; Hans Hartung (b. 1904) of Germany; Francis Bacon (b. 1910) and William Scott (b. 1913) of the British Isles; and Afro (b. 1912), Giuseppe Capogrossi (b. 1900), and Alberto Burri (b. 1915) all of Italy—to mention but a few. All share with Dubuffet a concept of medium as a primary factor in the formation of style, and all have strongly individual manners of expression. In this, they too have contributed to the artistic climate of Europe in the 1950's which has found in the abstract expressionism of contemporary painting in the United States both creative interest and distinction.

Detail of Shahn's Handball, *Fig. 543.*

CHAPTER THIRTY-TWO

Painting in the United States

The discovery of the New World initiated a continuous over-flow of peoples from Europe, bringing ideas and institutions of the most diverse kinds. The English brought the austerity of Puritanism to their New England buildings, just as the Spanish brought, to Catholic lands, the splendors of baroque architecture. Such contrasts were inevitable in a hemisphere sparsely dotted with settlers representing crosscurrents of European thought that ranged all the way from mediaeval to Counter-Reformation. This intermingling of world thought was a basic factor in the development of America. The tide of immigrants, particularly from nations experiencing strong internal presssures, like the

German, Irish, and Italian, fertilized the new soil. Not least of the waves contributing to American thought was the advent in the 1930's of intellectuals uprooted by the catastrophe of Europe under Hitler. Today, past mid-century, the United States is producing valid symbols of itself not essentially on the plane of nationalism but on a plane commensurate with its position in world affairs.

When the American colonies seceded from England in the eighteenth century a new political unit was established, but a political organization obviously is not the same thing as a cultural tradition, being only one manifestation of a larger whole. The latter is involved and complex, requiring many generations to attain its peculiar qualities. A culture becomes integrated only after an organic way of life has been long established. Even now, after nearly one hundred and ninety years, our nation is still far from being a unified cultural entity. With a novel political organization, with widely disparate cultures occupying a territory almost the size of all continental Europe, the integration of our national life had, and still has, many obstacles to surmount. At first, only in New England was there a fairly stable society, based upon handicraft and agriculture. With the coming of the Industrial Revolution, that social unit was largely disrupted. Before the Civil War the South with its profitable plantation system, enjoyed an urbane and promising culture. But it was at this time, when the nation was in a position to realize its potentialities, that the Civil War inflicted a devastating blow to national morale; the decades that followed were the dreariest and most sordid we have endured. Yet paradoxically it was these very postwar years that witnessed the appearance of the painters who most deeply express the spirit of our national life. Painting appeared later than literature as an articulate and original expression for the simple reason that whereas books circulate freely and written language is almost universally comprehensible, works of plastic art were very scarce in our early days and their formal language was difficult to understand even in the best of circumstances. Thousands of miles away from European painting, the early Americans knew next to nothing of the technical practices of European art. The pressing need of making the wilderness habitable was a self-evident deterrent to the creation and patronage of the arts in our Colonial period.

An all too common misconception is that painting was frowned upon for religious reasons in Colonial America. An equally erroneous assumption that there was no painting to speak of in the English colonies before the middle of the eighteenth century has been disproved by the ever-increasing number of works brought to light by diligent research. It is now recognized that painting had a modest place in the colonies from fairly early times. It is understandable that almost without exception the existing examples are portraits, for there was scant demand for religious painting even in England in the seventeenth and eighteenth centuries; it stands to reason that there was even less demand in the young colonies. But there was a place for the portrait, not so much as a work of symbolic art as an appropriate part of the cultural furniture of families eager to retain ties with their inherited traditions and establish them for the future. Little is known of the anonymous craftsmen who filled this need for the seventeenth-century English colonists; many of them were doubtless sign painters who undertook portraits as well. Among them were men with untutored skill, unlimited patience, and an instinctive sense of design and pattern that could be genuinely expressive. Their paintings are sometimes called primitive—and so they are if the term means lacking in sophistication and academic competence. But the dogged fidelity to such literal facts as lace and ribbons and surface textures that most of them reveal also contributes to the homely charm that makes the most notable among them completely disarming of orthodox criticism.

The best of them are labors of love wholly unlike the later more or less facile commercial products. In 1674, an unknown artist in Boston painted the portrait, *Mrs. Freake and Baby Mary* (Fig. 530). A work of extraordinary charm, it is the type of picture made by someone wholly unlearned in technical resources of any school or tradition but with an instinctive sense for design

FIG. 530. Mrs. Freake and Baby Mary (1674).

in line and color and a solid craftsman's feeling for the medium of paint. Such untrained artists appear from time to time in our history and leave memorials of their spirit.

It was only natural that the portrait should first engross our early painters. Face paintings were in demand, and people were willing to reward the skillful artisan who could produce a valuable family record. Having a good likeness of its more distinguished members was almost a family duty in eighteenth-century America. In the seventeenth century when Holland emerged from political and military conflict, its first demand of its artists was portraits; in much the same matter-of-fact spirit, the colonists wanted to have their own images painted when they became conscious of their cultural and political attainments. More specifically, the popularity of the portrait in America was a direct heritage from the English, if one can speak of a "heritage" at a time when the colonies were simply an arm of the English nation. The English have always been patrons of portrait painting, as is evident in the activities of Hogarth, Reynolds, and Gainsborough (Fig. 484) in the eighteenth century.

The outstanding portraitist of our Colonial days was John Singleton Copley (1738-1815), a painter who gained fame not only in America but also in England. Trained under his stepfather and other teachers, he learned the methods that prevailed in the English school. Although his earliest pictures show a primitive awkwardness, he rapidly gained considerable mastery over his technique. He made no innovations in the methods of his contemporaries, but with a remarkably conscientious and searching eye he translated the spirit of his people into the paint of his canvas. His sobriety and reserve fit well the Colonial aristocrats who sat for him, but his reserve never becomes dryness or dullness. The likeness of his fellow Bostonian, the famous silversmith (cf. Fig. 635) and horseman *Paul Revere* (Fig. 531), was painted about 1765. It is typical of Copley that, striving for the individual and specific, he placed his sitter in a pose characteristic of his usual activity. Typical also was his

Museum of Fine Arts, Boston.

FIG. 531. Copley, Paul Revere (*ca.* 1765).

FIG. 532.   Stuart, Mrs. Perez Morton
(*ca.* 1802).

Late in the eighteenth century Europe offered strong inducements to the American artist. There could be found the schools and the patronage and the art that are so important to both student and mature master. Benjamin West (1738-1820), who had nearly all of his career in London, was the first American painter to gain European prestige. Though considered a member of the English school, as friend and teacher he assisted all his fellow countrymen who went to England to study. Among his American pupils was Gilbert Stuart (1755-1828), probably the ablest portraitist of the time. Everyone is familiar with his portrait of Washington, now in the Boston Museum of Fine Arts, if only from its use on our postage stamps. The stoic nobility shown in that portrait has been accepted as the most characteristic feature of our first President. But the Vaughn portrait of Washington is a far more subtly realized conception of the intimate character of the gallant Virginia country gentleman. Though no claim can be made for either as a great portrait with profound interpretive insight, both are admirable memorials to a great spirit. Most of our early portraits are of greater value as historical documents than for their artistic significance, though an occasional portrait reveals genuine pictorial inspiration. Such is Stuart's likeness of *Mrs. Perez Morton* (Fig. 532), painted about 1802, in the Worcester Museum of Art. Details of the background and parts of the costume were never finished, but the delicate modeling of the face in thin glazes of almost transparent pigment is fully realized. The difference between Stuart's freely brushed forms and Copley's linear patterns is obvious. That Stuart could make them expressive of character and personality as well as faithful to likeness and decorative is a major factor in the distinction accorded him among artists of the early Republic.

There is little if anything peculiarly American about the early portrait painters. When any origin can be determined for their style, it is usually English, as in Stuart's case. But as time went on, the influence of French methods became apparent. David's professional and highly disciplined manner (Fig. 488) contributed much to the development of such artists as Rembrandt

painstaking care to match every observed tint and hue in every detail on his palette before touching canvas with pigment. His eye was equally sharp for nuances of light and shade and the telling contour line. The finished work may appear primarily to be a drawing made in full color, but it is eminently convincing as a faithful account of appearance down to the most minute characteristic. In refusing to do anything from fancy, as he put it himself, his unquestioning faithfulness to what was before his eyes relates Copley and his craftsmen predecessors of the seventeenth century. But his greater technical training enabled him to establish a degree of visual truth in his portraits that was unsurpassed in his own time and seldom surpassed since. Being a Loyalist, he returned to England on the eve of the Revolution, thus ending his Colonial career in his late thirties. There he found patronage and honor, but his closer relation to the English tradition did not improve his style in his subsequent works.

FIG. 533.   Bingham, Fur Traders Descending the
Missouri (1845).

Peale and Samuel F. B. Morse (1791-1872) by
giving weight and substance where previously
the superficial and easy decorative effects of the
English style (cf. Fig. 484) had satisfied painters
and public alike. Morse could have had a splendid career as a painter had he not been discouraged
by lack of interest in his paintings and the immediate popular success of his invention of the
telegraph. His portrait of Lafayette in New
York's City Hall is a grand full-length picture of
surprising depth and power.

The Romantic movement which saw landscape painting elevated to first importance in
Europe through Constable, the Barbizon painters,
and others, was profoundly felt in America. The
New England landscape was celebrated in
Whittier's verse as early as 1831. Wordsworth's
nature poetry was appreciated as fully in America
as in England. As portraiture began to decline
before the Civil War, the landscape occupied the
talents of our painters more and more. Thomas
Cole (1801-1848), taught by an itinerant portraitist on the Ohio frontier, was deeply impressed by the wild and romantic aspect of the
untamed mountains and forests. Working in the
Catskills and along the Hudson River, he with
others formed the first group of landscape
painters in America.

Compared with a landscape by Bruegel (Fig.
452) or Poussin (Fig. 477) or Constable (Fig.
494), a Hudson River view may well seem a
little uninspired. In part this is because our early
landscapists could not apply the necessary techniques in using color and painting light which
were available to their European predecessors
and contemporaries. Even more, perhaps, it is a
consequence of the predominantly nationalistic
and literary sentiments they sought to express.
Over and over it is said that the American scene
should be painted because it is American, or because it has never been painted before. The results
are often no more than reasonably accurate indications of topography; at best they are little more
than merely picturesque. Exceptions to this are
some of George Caleb Bingham's paintings like
Fur Traders Descending the Missouri (Fig. 533)

done in 1845. A Midwesterner, Bingham studied painting at the Academy of the Fine Arts in Philadelphia where his teacher, John Neagle, taught him something of the method he himself had learned from Gilbert Stuart. Using the familiar theme of trappers bringing their wares to market, Bingham contrived a pattern of shapes completely faithful to fact; at the same time there is a sense of the romantic challenge in the still unexplored reaches of the great land that is created almost entirely by subtle nuances of light and color. The term genre—meaning the familiar or everyday—is as applicable to such a painting as to the seventeenth-century Dutch painters' interpretations of the things that were theirs and the world they lived in. And like them, this kind of painting communicates something of what made people think and feel and act and be what they were, instead of merely describing them.

The later development of American nature painting owes much to Winslow Homer (1836-1910), who brought to his subject a singularly sensitive and intelligent talent. When most American painters were absorbed by showy sentiment and patriotic bombast or almost wholly enthralled by the pretentiousness of Old World masterpieces, Homer was an outspoken realist. With pragmatic directness he studied the lakes and rivers, the fisherfolk and the northern trappers. There is an almost impersonal deliberation in his dispassionate record of outdoor life. Largely without reference to the knowledge and practice of centuries of painting, he contrived honest studies of immediate experience, finding for his pictures the colors that described veraciously the actual colors in nature. At the time Manet was shocking Paris with his original use of color, Homer, without any self-consciousness, was exercising the greatest freedom in its use. If he lacks the great assurance of his European contemporaries, he is at the same time not encumbered with their aesthetic theories.

In his early experience as an illustrator and pictorial journalist, Homer developed extraordinary sensitivity to expressive values and the means of integrating them with formal structure. In *The Life Line* (Fig. 534), which he completed in 1884, his concern was to convey the full drama of the unceasing conflict between man and nature. The colors are ominous in their somber scale. Winds whip the dark waves into a threatening melee of dashing spray and sliding volumes of water. Yet it does more than the most dramatic photograph of such a situation could, for the lines supporting the breeches buoy and the dark shapes of the man and woman are so related that not only the conflict but its ultimate outcome is brought directly to the observer. Without hesitation or groping, the artist says what he has to say. So deeply felt were his experiences of nature and so great was his artistic integrity that no note of half-realized sentimentality or any overtone of literary association detracts from the simple power of his direct statement. Perhaps his most significant contribution to American painting was his implicit acceptance of the life he knew as the proper theme of his art. To Americans of his time, accustomed as they were to finding models in the European past, this was no small cultural achievement.

In Albert Pinkham Ryder (1847-1917), nineteenth-century American painting has its profoundest spirit. He shares with Whitman and Melville the almost undisputed primacy in our artistic tradition. Furthermore, with them Ryder assumes a rank in art not confined to his own country but extending to the western world. Seen in this perspective, he belongs unquestionably with the Romantic school.

In nearly every respect Ryder's art differs from Winslow Homer's. Where the latter gives specific particulars about place and events, Ryder expresses his inner experiences. Of all his landscapes and marines, only three refer definitely to a specific place. He realized more fully than any other American painter of his time that the sphere of the artist is the mind, which transforms the raw stuff of the external world and gives it articulate meaning. Surface appearance means nothing to him except as it evokes a feeling beyond the realm of mere sensation. His groping efforts to express that thought comprehensibly are reflected in his painfully laborious methods of painting. Months and even years after a canvas was almost complete he still revised it;

Philadelphia Museum of Art.

FIG. 534.   Homer, The Life Line (1884).

he often called in paintings that had been sold to make additions and changes. In explaining his desultory methods he said, "Have you ever seen an inchworm crawling up a leaf or twig, and there clinging to the very end, feeling for something, to reach something? That is like me. I am trying to find something out there beyond the place on which I have a footing." These words are very like Van Gogh's. By concretion and concentration, Ryder packs into his art infinitely more than is seen or heard by the senses. Something of the resounding poetry and music of Chaucer, Shakespeare, and Wagner, whom he loved, emerges from the ghostly pale lights of his marine nocturnes. He gave his pictures poetic titles, like Toilers of the Sea and The Waste of Waters Is Their Home, and even wrote verses to accompany them. Though many of his canvases are inspired by literature, they are never mere illustrations any more than were those of Delacroix.

In all his paintings we feel the presence of the mysterious forces that lie in the unfathomed depths of nature, forces that Melville symbolized in the Great White Whale. For Ryder as for Melville, the sea had a peculiar fascination as a symbol of the incalculable destroyer and preserver. During his boyhood in New Bedford, the whaling port where since the seventeenth century men had wrested a living from the treacherous

FIG. 535. Ryder, Moonlit Cove.

interpreted. This independence, admirable because it showed that he could not be impressed by the studio small talk of ambitious simpletons, was at the same time a limitation. When French art was beginning to reform along the line taken by Manet, Renoir, Cézanne, and Van Gogh, Thomas Eakins was seemingly unaware of what they were achieving. Had he lived in Paris not from 1866 to 1869 but a few years later, his art might have taken a very different course.

When he returned to this country he set about soberly and sensibly to paint the scenes about him that he knew intimately: portraits of his friends, boat races, prize fights, the interiors of his fellow artists' studios, and the demonstration clinics of the hospitals. There is something of the old masters in Eakins, both in the learned technical methods he followed and in the self-assurance of his approach to his work. The searching realism of his painting and his friendship with the celebrated scientists of his native Philadelphia attest to his intense interest in scientific thought. "All the sciences," he said, "are done in a simple way; in mathematics, the complicated things are reduced to the simple things. So it is in painting. You reduce the whole thing to simple factors; you establish these and work out from them, pushing them toward one another. This will make strong work. The Old Masters worked this way." Walt Whitman, whose *Democratic Vistas* records the same acceptance of the American scene that characterizes Eakins' art, said, "I never knew of but one artist and that's Tom Eakins who could resist the temptation to see what they think they ought to see rather than what is." Certainly no painter was ever freer from pose and affectation than he. The popular American taste has always been more than tinged with the English concept of art as a decorative embellishment of life. For Eakins, art was no such thing, any more than it was for Ryder. To Eakins it was an instrument of almost scientific precision with which to formulate enduring monuments of human experience.

Everything Eakins painted has the authority of one who never questioned the validity of his conscious power to *see* and, by seeing, to understand. In this, he followed the path laid out a

sea, he must have been moved by the tragic beauty of the ocean. Its austere mystery is felt in his *Moonlit Cove* (Fig. 535). With the simple design of a boat and cliffs outlined against the moonlit sky swept by long low clouds, he gives utterance to the solitude of the soul of man. The illimitable plane of the sea, the inscrutable breadth of the sky, are conveyed by the coruscated light emerging from the enameled depths of the canvas.

Somewhere between Winslow Homer's romantic naturalism and Ryder's mysticism, the realism of Thomas Eakins (1844-1916) finds its place. Unlike the other two, Eakins based his technique on the tradition of European painting through his study in one of the celebrated academic studios in Paris. He had a surprising intelligence in regard to his training, for he realized that what he had to learn was simply the technique of painting, how to prepare a canvas and mix pigment, and the craft of picture-making. It must have been obvious to him, even in his youth, that his highly competent masters had little or nothing to teach him regarding what he should paint or how his subjects should be

century earlier by John Singleton Copley (cf. Fig. 531). Like Copley, Eakins realized that a portrait is much more than a delineation of features and hands and clothes. His portrait of *Riter Fitzgerald* (Fig. 536) was painted in the study where the books and other paraphernalia of the critic's profession provided a familiar and characteristic environment for his subject. The story is told of another man who wore a new suit when he came to sit for his portrait, only to have Eakins send him home to put on an old one. Only in the forms shaped by character and personality could the artist see what he sought—the planes and lines that bespeak the inner man to the eye trained to observe and the mind that is aware of what they mean. Eakins' portraits are sober and factual, restrained in color, solidly modeled, unrelieved by any technical tricks or decorative bravura. More often than not, they were too faithful and too probing for his subjects; they wanted something showier and more flattering. Not a few were rejected and returned to the artist.

Like Whitman, Eakins had the widest interest in all the life about him. His pictures of the prize ring are studied as intensely as his monumental paintings of the Gross Clinic and Dr. Agnew's Clinic. Perhaps his most dramatic work in both subject and treatment is The Salute. A prize fighter, nude except for shoes and loincloth, turns with lifted arm and face to receive the roar of adulation from the crowd. The painting records the exact moment when the lithe and muscular athlete, trained to an edge, holds the attention of the frantic mob. Calm and tense, he seems to be arrested for an instant by the torrent of applause that rushes upon him. Somewhat less intrinsically dramatic, *Between Rounds* (Fig. 537), painted a year later in 1899, is broader and more monumental in design. The background of the action is simplified by the accents of the horizontals and the subdued illumination of the scene. The white flesh of the boxer resting in his corner glows warmly in the murky atmosphere. The arrangement—the telegraphic reporter attentive at his key, the seconds busy with their fighter—is spontaneous and yet compact. Eakins never makes his figures more colorful

than they are, or his drama more intense than the actuality. There is a sober poetry about his staid realism that escaped the men of his own time; they found his art too severe, as the French found that of Courbet and Daumier lacking in elegance and charm. The great integrity of these men has been recognized in our own time for what it is—the highest gift of the artist.

Teaching for a time at the Pennsylvania Academy of the Fine Arts, Eakins influenced a great many younger painters. Early in the twentieth century, a group of them who had also been newspaper artists manifested a trend toward the same unsentimental realism that characterized Eakins' work. They were termed the "Ashcan School" by critics and by a public bemused by the pretentious elegance of the currently stylish painting by Europeans and by the Americans who emulated them. But to men like George Luks, Robert Henri, William Glackens, and others, the American scene, viewed as something that was the embodiment

Courtesy of the Art Institute of Chicago,
Friends of American Art Collection, Goodman Fund.

FIG. 536.   Eakins, Riter Fitzgerald
(1895).

Philadelphia Museum of Art.

FIG. 537. Eakins, Between Rounds (1899).

of our culture, provided the most appropriate theme for American painting. John Sloan (1871-1951) painted *McSorley's Bar* (Fig. 538) in much the same spirit as that in Bingham's Fur Traders (Fig. 533) and Eakins' Between Rounds (Fig. 537). The atmosphere of the Manhattan pub which catered only to men is well conveyed in colors that show Sloan's acquaintance with the more progressive traditions of European painting of his day, but they interpret something that is found only in America and they do it only as an American artist could have. At the same time it is significant that Sloan was one of the group of artists that was largely responsible for organizing the epoch-making exhibition of modern European painting in New York's Sixty-Ninth Regiment Armory in 1913 from which stemmed so many subsequent developments in American art.

In his own day, Eakins was eclipsed by a popular painter of talent who also studied in the Paris schools but a few years later than Eakins

and with quite different ultimate results. John Singer Sargent (1856-1925) was everything that Eakins was not. A cultured cosmopolite in background, he was taught in the *atelier* of a sophisticated portrait painter of eclectic derivation whose style Sargent mastered and exploited with facility and a certain dehumanized brilliance, impressing his clients with his unerring eye for the obvious and commonplace. He created a type of society-portrait that is somewhat more superficial than the transparent counterfeit of straight commercial work.

From the outwardly uncongenial atmosphere of American life following the Civil War, so admirably characterized by Lewis Mumford as the Brown Decades, an ever-increasing group of artists found haven in European capitals. Lack of patronage and prestige led many to seek recognition and guidance in countries with long-established traditions in the arts. Leaving her native Philadelphia, Mary Cassatt (1845-1926) developed under French Impressionism a

The Detroit Institute of Arts.

FIG. 538.   Sloan, McSorley's Bar (1912).

fluent and delicate style inspired largely by Degas. Her portraits of women and children are especially fine, but she must be considered a French painter because almost nothing in her manner of working or her expression suggests any but French influences.

By far the most publicized American painter of the time was James McNeill Whistler (1834–1903), also an expatriate with international standing. After receiving his early training in Paris, he exhibited with the progressive artists who were in revolt against the archaisms of the Academy. Maintaining that art was its own justification and should not concern itself with narration, description, or morality, he professed the theory of art for art's sake and projected his

aesthetic beliefs in witty and provocative paradoxes. Art, for him, had nothing to do with the mechanical finish so much prized by the Academicians or the elaborate literary and historical subject matter they employed. Here he was of the same mind as the creative French artists with whom he associated, though his own works fall short of their accomplishments. His paintings are basically decorative arrangements often similar to the flat patterns generally adopted by the French masters. Space and mass are subordinated to a fanlike surface spread of related color areas. The titles of his paintings—Nocturne, Symphony, Arrangement—suggest that his pictures were not studies of specific scenes but free organizations of color and tone. In his "arrangements" he only

National Gallery of Art, Washington, D.C., Rosenwald Collection.

FIG. 539.   Whistler, Il Traghetto, Etching (1880).

Collection of Whitney Museum of American Art, New York.

FIG. 540.   Prendergast, Central Park, Water Color (1901).

partly follows the general trend of modern art. There is nothing of the vigorous and sensuous color of Impressionism or the form-searching of Cézanne. Silver and gray heightened with warmer color notes in a screen effect is his usual formula, creating a half light where specific accents are softened and silhouettes converge.

In etching, however, Whistler made a real contribution, participating in the notable revival of the graphic arts in the nineteenth century. Here his talent for refinement in pattern and tone found an ideal medium. Etching is an intimate art in which subtleties of values and line play an all-important role, adapting it well to a temperament as sensitive to formal *nuance* as Whistler's. This is evident in *Il Traghetto* (Fig. 539), a Venetian scene etched in 1880. In the technique of preparing and printing the plates, in the refinements of the art, he was surpassed only by the great Rembrandt (Fig. 469). But in all his work there remains something attenuated and contrived. He skillfully adapted Oriental design, particularly that of the Japanese woodcuts. With sensitivity and taste he borrowed the rare tonalities of Velasquez' art for his own, but with a certain self-conscious aestheticism.

The development of Impressionism in France was inevitably felt by the painters on this side of the ocean. John Twachtman, Childe Hassam, William Glackens, and a score of other able painters were profoundly affected by French luminism. Their work, however, was not invested with the great imagination and penetrating realism of their predecessors Ryder and Eakins. The powerfully constructed art of Cézanne and Seurat was first appreciated in America by Maurice Prendergast (1861-1924). Perhaps the same intelligence that gave him a ready understanding of Post-Impressionism led him to evolve a style quite different from Cézanne's but animated by a similar desire to stabilize pictorial design. In his *Central Park* (Fig. 540) he is a highly imaginative and decorative figure painter, constructing his forms by broad touches of pure colors to create a glowing mosaic of great charm and depth of feeling.

The spectacular and, to many, bewildering work of the modern School of Paris was introduced to America in the famous New York Armory Show in 1913. Here for the first time the paintings of the Cubists and the *Fauves* or wild beasts, as they were called—Matisse,

Phillips Collection, Washington.

FIG. 541.   Marin, Maine Islands,
Water Color (1922).

Picasso, Braque—became known to the American public. Art dealers and enthusiasts widely publicized the theory of free expression that was behind the abstract treatment of the modern School of Paris. Although, in the judgment of most Americans (including many critics), the Armory Show was a cultural scandal, it gave some of our most able artists an opportunity to establish contact with significant world developments, a contact that has since been fruitfully maintained. Marsden Hartley (1877-1943), John Marin (1872-1953), Max Weber (b. 1881), Charles Demuth (1883-1935), and Georgia O'Keeffe (b. 1887) were in this group. Though not so radical as that of their European contemporaries, their work reveals genuine understanding of the expressive potential of abstraction.

John Marin's water color *Maine Islands* (Fig. 541), done in 1922, is an example. Heavily accented lines create an angular opening, softened occasionally by suggested curves within which the simplified shapes of islands and trees and planes of water make an abstract structural unity that still conveys a sense of the place, its space and atmosphere. Marin uses the exacting medium, water color, with the fullest awareness of its limitations and powers. The utmost assurance is required, for once a given hue is applied to the absorbent paper it cannot be

altered except by changing its character entirely; furthermore, there is not the freedom in such matters as texture that the painter in oils or more opaque mediums has. Hence a water color like *Maine Islands* is actually only a few planes of filmy, transparent, disembodied color. Yet they are so related that Marin's sense of what he called "the elemental big forms—Sky, Sea, Mountain, Plain" is fully communicated.

Several American painters accepted the concept of geometrical abstraction so completely that their work seems little more than uninspired imitation of the European innovators. Others, like Edward Hopper (b. 1882), fully understood the structural vigor of Cubist discipline but felt the need of remaining faithful to the expressive traditions they had inherited. Hopper might be characterized as having remained aware of the significance of factors apparent in American painting from Copley to Eakins and Sloane but as having regarded his world in a way that attains special meaning from the way he presented it. *Early Sunday Morning* (Fig. 542), painted in 1930, is at first a banal, even ugly city scene, in which the openings of doors and windows are repeated monotonously. Closer observation shows that these rectangles are spaced in a subtle rhythm accented by the simple color scheme. Even the black and white reproduction conveys some sense of the light that bathes this seemingly commonplace aspect of the American city and contributes a great deal to the feeling of the mystery inherent in mere existence. Hopper and Charles Burchfield (b. 1893) stand out among the many painters of the American scene in the 1930's for the quietly evocative power of their interpretations.

Ben Shahn (b. 1898) reveals even more clearly in *Handball* (Fig. 543), done in 1939, the effectiveness of structural logic in conveying the essence of things. The spare rectilinearism of his shapes could hardly have evolved without knowledge of Mondrian's ascetic manner (pages 613-614), but Shahn uses the armature of lines and planes in an almost lyric statement about a typical moment in American city life. Although his work in this vein seems at first glance to imitate photography, his use of tempera—at

FIG. 542. Hopper, Early Sunday Morning (1930).

least in this instance—makes possible distinctly pictorial effects of tint and surface textures.

Still another highly personal idiom that developed from geometrical abstraction is embodied in the work of I. Rice Pereira (b. 1907). Her *Spring, Twelve O'Clock* (Fig. 544), which she did in 1952, is based on a Mondrian-like system of rectangles that vary in size and color; she supplies additional variety and character by using different textures and patterns of stripes and dots. The resulting animation of surface, moreover, operates in space, an impression created by the angular pieces which look almost like a plastic or synthetic applied to the pigmented surface of the canvas, a technique with which the artist has experimented. The idea of combining pigments and nonpictorial materials is not new; it goes back to the assemblages of paper and other substances in the collages made by the later Cubists. Pereira's oil paintings show how industrial products of the mid-twentieth century, by enlarging the artist's technical repertory, may enhance both structural and expressive effect.

No period in American painting has offered greater variety than that since World War II. But in the comprehensive exhibitions presented periodically by such institutions as the Whitney Museum of American Art, the Pennsylvania Academy of the Fine Arts, and the University of Illinois, the dominant trend, far overshadowing any other mode or style, has been the increasing emphasis on some form of abstraction. Even within the limits of nonfigurative style, individual aspects of the idiom are numerous, the most distinctive being associated with the painters Jackson Pollock and Mark Rothko.

Of the two, Jackson Pollock (1912-1956) has been more publicized, chiefly because of his unorthodox technique. He executed his *Grayed Rainbow* (Fig. 545) in 1953 by pouring, spraying, whirling, and dribbling pigment from a scaffold raised above the canvas on the studio floor. The resulting pattern is a series of rhythmic, looping lines, smoothly flowing here, sharply jagged there, and coming to halt from time to time in massive clots. This pattern records or graphs the painter's movements back and forth along the platform above as he poured the paint, movements that some who watched him at work likened to a ballet dancer's. The term "action painting" that is often applied to Pollock's work is apt. For all its seeming novelty, Pollock's method is not without precedent; Kandinsky's *Improvisation No. 30* (Fig. 525) was likewise the result of creating free, nonassociative forms. Another parallel between the two artists is

Collection, The Museum of Modern Art, New York, Mrs. John D. Rockefeller, Jr. Purchase Fund.

FIG. 543.   Shahn, Handball (1939).

evident in their comments about their feelings while painting. Kandinsky said his work was done "rather subconsciously in a state of strong inner tension". Pollock often spoke of his designs as creating themselves; he himself could not know the outcome while he was "still in the painting," as he put it.

It stands to reason that whatever content a painting like Grayed Rainbow may have cannot be defined in traditional terms. Yet the individual seeing the canvas experiences the same compulsive rhythmic movement as Pollock did; it engenders a sense of depth as immediate as that of the two-dimensional plane on which this ordered color is arranged. Furthermore, it is an experience of pigment, of material facts of texture and fluent substance—in a word, of the medium in which the artist's interest was always

strong. Almost every one of Pollock's paintings reveals this characteristic, the prevailing dynamic rhythm being a direct expression of the particular medium used. Even if the significance

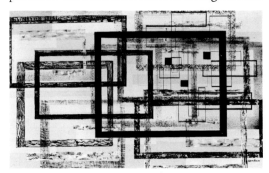

Collection of Mr. Henry F. Lenning, N.Y

FIG. 544.   Pereira, Spring, Twelve O'Clock (1952).

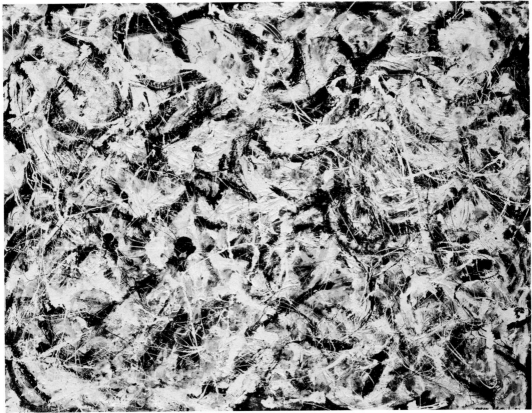

The Art Institute of Chicago, Gift of the Society for Contemporary American Art.

FIG. 545.   Pollock, Grayed Rainbow (1953).

or "reality" of such things is primarily pictorial, it is no less concrete.

Pollock's most characteristic paintings are very large (Grayed Rainbow is eight feet high). This quality is also a distinctive feature of the work of Mark Rothko (b. 1903). His *Orange and Yellow* (Fig. 546), which was painted in 1956, is over eight feet high and nearly six feet wide. But where the vast expanse of Pollock's canvas is filled with whiplash curves that swing the spectator with inexorable authority into their dynamic rhythm, he is confronted in the rectangles of Rothko's composition (orange for the larger one beneath and yellow for that above, separated and framed by pink bands) with a color sensation almost impersonal in its quietude. The observer is no less aware of the medium than in Pollock's work, and the monumental dimensions

make his feeling of being directly involved in experiencing its tangible, sensuous actuality equally as great. Vergil Barker phrases it as follows in his perceptive *From Realism to Reality:* "Rothko's kind of painting is what I interpret as the romantically classic climax to the theory of the self-sufficing reality of pigment." He goes on to say that as far as he can determine, "color produces the first individualized response of the whole human creature to visual experience." In the presence of such a painting as this, no one can be unaware of the powerful impact of sheer disembodied color, all the more challenging in its inscrutable impersonality for its sensuous, material tangibility. The works of Pollock and Rothko are thus pictorial statements about one of the overriding preoccupations of the mid-twentieth century—the quest of the absolute. In

FIG. 546.   Rothko, Orange and
Yellow (1956).

beginning this discussion of painting (page 413) we pointed out that line and color are the elemental facts of painting as an art. Pollock and Rothko have pushed their search for the fundamental reality of these facts—along with other painters who share this preoccupation—as close to the ultimate as any artists in the history of painting.

Obscure and baffling as the layman may find it, the abstract expressionism of the 1950's is a logical, even inevitable consequence of a trend which began in the late Renaissance with the idea fostered by the academies that art is at the same time esoteric yet understandable by those initiated into its mysteries. Strengthened early in the nineteenth century by the authority then assumed of subjective and emotional values as criteria (the phenomenon often called Romanticism), it was only natural that painters should insist more and more on holding their professional—i.e., pictorial—ideals paramount, regardless of public

disapprobation. This was true of other arts as well, as witness the protests against the music of Richard Wagner and Claude Debussy and the poetry of Walt Whitman. With the phenomenal expansion of scientific research and the industrial applications thereof in the twentieth century, the compartmentalization and specialization of knowledge and experience begun in the nineteenth century have reached such a point that an outstanding nuclear physicist of the postwar era once stated that he was illiterate in any but his own field. Yet there is no disposition to question the statement of the scientist or industrialist about truth as he sees it, from which it follows that what the painter has to say about painting should be accepted as equally authoritative. This is the position implicit in the concept of abstract expressionism.

Logical as this assumption may be, it does not convince those who feel that painting and the other arts are means of communication and must be understood. The fact that nuclear fission has affected the thought and action of a generation without being understood by more than a handful of people in that generation is not pertinent, in this way of thinking. The scientist may speak about the facts of the physical and astral worlds without being expected to say more, but the painter must concern himself with much besides the facts of line and color and pigment. There is an irrepressible feeling, almost an instinct, that an art like painting or sculpture should be in some way concerned with values that are human and not solely with those peculiar to the art and private to its practitioners.

Although this point of view has not been widely held by American painters since World War II, it has been upheld by some, notably Andrew Wyeth (b. 1917). Working quietly and on a scale that seems intimate in contrast to that in the giant canvases of Pollock and Rothko, Wyeth is a master of recording observed detail with meticulous craftsmanship. Yet unlike his contemporary expressionists, he has aimed—in his own words—". . . to escape from the medium with which I work. To leave no residue of technical mannerisms to stand between my expression and the observer. To seek freedom through

Collection of Mr. Robert Montgomery, N.Y.

FIG. 547. Wyeth, Chambered Nautilus (1956).

significant form and design rather than through the diversion of so-called free and accidental brush handling." Characteristically, much of Wyeth's painting is in tempera, one of the least sensuous pictorial media and one that is almost incapable of spectacular and dramatic effect. His color scheme is similarly restrained to browns, grays, blacks, and whites in generally subdued not to say somber effects. Yet for all this, in *Chambered Nautilus* (Fig. 547), done in 1956, the room with its wind-blown curtain is filled with light in space, or rather, as Vergil Barker has put it, with illumination that gives the forms a pictorial reality infinitely more moving and meaningful than ocular realism. Thus the minutely observed details are presented as if seen for the first time. Commonplace though they may be, the objects in a painting by Wyeth have the quality of being something more than they seem, because they have been observed by the eye of an artist; and the light his brush sheds on them is that of his imagination which allows us also to see something of the wonder he experienced.

THE MINOR ARTS

Detail of Fig. 557.

CHAPTER THIRTY-THREE

The Minor Arts: Pre-Classic and Classic

In all periods of world history, the visual arts have included other forms than those of architecture, sculpture, and painting —forms which are termed variously the minor arts, the useful arts, the decorative arts, or the functional arts. Whatever the name, it distinguishes them in purpose from the fine arts, for they are represented by objects that have utilitarian as well as aesthetic value. Indeed, it is usually the utilitarian function of the object that is the major factor in accounting for it, in contrast to the nonutilitarian purpose of the fine arts such as sculpture and painting. It is to architecture that the minor arts can be most directly compared in the sense of the utilitarian being equally important with the aesthetic or the expressive—in which usefulness is as vital a consideration as appearance. Even here, however, there is a significant difference—scale. For it is furniture and dishes, metal work and picture frames, rugs and carpets and vases that are the minor arts which contribute by the fitness of their design both to utilitarian purpose and to pleasure in the balance of form, flow of surface, rhythm of line, or contrast of texture that makes them as much works of art as they are effective tools.

The historical continuity of medium in the fine arts of architecture, sculpture, and painting is not found in the minor arts in anything like the same degree. This is largely a consequence of the different ways of living that prevail in different times and places and a more direct influence upon the functioning forms of the minor arts than upon the less utilitarian ones in the major categories. Thus, for all the important contrasts in form between a Greek temple and a modern office building, they nonetheless have more in common than do the crater in which the Greek mixed the wines for his banquets and the cocktail shaker that performs the same duty today. A mediaeval chalice is hardly comparable with either except in the most general terms. If, therefore, it seems difficult or impossible to discern a common quality or way of thinking in the many categories of the minor arts comparable to the sculptor's concern with plastic form or the architect's interest in space patterns or the painter's interpretation of three-dimensional experience in two-dimensional design, this is understandable in view of the variety of specific purposes the forms are intended to meet.

Although continuity and uniformity of purpose and form may be lacking in the minor arts in the same degree as in the major arts, in a given period they have much in common. This will be immediately evident in the more detailed discussion that follows; here we say only that the quality of an example of the minor arts is determined by the extent to which it reflects the characteristic formal and expressive values of its age. Thus, the organization of the mass and ornament of a Greek vase (Fig. 563) is as basically geometrical as it is in a contemporary statue or building (Fig. 250). The casket that enshrined the holy relics in a mediaeval church is built in an architectonic pattern that creates a microcosm of the church itself. An eighteenth-century chair (Fig. 629) has the same delicacy of scale and gracefulness of form as a painting by Watteau or Fragonard (Fig. 481); and the crystalline severity of plane and texture that characterizes a modern building or painting is directly paralleled in the contemporary forms of furniture and china. The term minor arts when applied to forms having such characteristics should therefore not be considered derogatory or condescending; its use is rather a generally accepted convention implying their utilitarian purpose as a primary factor.

There are two additional considerations of a general nature regarding the minor arts. The first—their importance in supplementing the major arts in certain periods—has been touched upon in other connections in this book. Thus the visual evidence of Greek painting before the fourth century B.C. is limited almost entirely to the ornament on vases and jars and the like, although we know from literary sources that there was monumental wall painting at least as early as the middle of the fifth century B.C. Small clay or terra-cotta models used for religious purposes tell us much about otherwise unrepresented phases of early Greek and Etruscan architecture. The sculptural tradition of one of the great branches of early mediaeval art, that of the Byzantine East, would be much less well known were it not for the carved ivory plaques that decorate the covers of manuscript books or are combined to form altarpieces and reliquary caskets. In such instances as these, it is the minor arts that make possible the comprehensive knowledge of a period and its way of thinking that is one of the fundamentals for interpreting and understanding human thought and experience.

It is in this same sense of the work of art as a human experience that the second general consideration concerning the minor arts is advanced. If the ancient Egyptian seems closer to us in the delightfully intimate figure of the little girl who is the handle of a perfume spoon (Fig. 550) than in the hieratic form of the Pharaoh (Fig. 240), it is because its everyday purpose is more readily paralleled in our own experience than is the mystical concept of deity on earth that underlies the monumental statue. The chest (Fig. 612) in which the Florentine bride treasured her wedding finery may arouse a homely emotion that is more immediate and moving than the wistful nostalgia of the classic gods and goddesses (Fig. 413) in the paintings that hung on her palace walls. Such reactions as these are admittedly sentimental rather than formal—anecdotal and literary rather than aesthetic—but to the extent that they lead to an understanding of a work of art as embodying human feeling and emotion, they contribute to the broadened experience that is the true end of knowledge.

PRE-CLASSIC MINOR ARTS

From earliest times man has sought to make the implements of his daily life and activity something more than tools—works of art as well as useful. Among the oldest such objects known is a *Reindeerhorn Dart-Thrower* (Fig. 548) that dates from the palaeolithic age of prehistory which ended about 10,000 B.C. This device enabled the hunter to hurl darts farther and with greater power than was possible with the arm alone; it served as a sort of extension of the arm. Since this mechanical function could have been performed quite as well by a straight stick with a notch at one end, obviously more than this was involved in both the choice of material and the way it was handled. The material was supplied by one of the animals which palaeolithic man depended on for his food, and it is carved in the form of another animal, the antelope. His motive in transforming inanimate material into a work of art—for his adaptation of the beast's head and forequarters to the cylindrical form of the piece of bone reveals a high degree of skill in selecting the memorable aspects of the animal for recording its appearance—can only be surmised, but two possibilities have been suggested. One is that the natural shape of the bone suggested the animal and the artist simply heightened this suggestion by carving a few lines as a sort of diversion or because of a subconscious and intuitive urge to render it into an attractive shape. The second is that manipulating the material in accordance with the artist's impulses would increase his power in the hunt by the magic influence exerted over his prey by its pictorial representation.

The first of these suggestions, motivation by aesthetic impulses, is apparently borne out by other examples of prehistoric art, such as many pottery vessels which have linear patterns purely decorative in character. On the other hand, the groups of painted animals found in one of the prehistoric caves at Altamira in Spain (Fig. 355), also of the palaeolithic period, comply in only the most elementary degree with generally accepted principles of composition and arrangement such as symmetry, accenting, and dramatic continuity. This leads to the conclusion that if the motivating impulse was only aesthetic, the primitive artist was able to see an order which is not clear today, whereas if the motive was magic, based on a superstitious belief that power was gained over the animals by the artist able to represent them, the lack of obvious design is not a major consideration. In the relatively late period of prehistory when the Dart Thrower was carved, both aesthetic and magic factors may have been involved, the aesthetic having more weight than in the wall paintings because of the less complex nature of the form and motive. However this may be, the Dart Thrower is an outstanding early example of the minor arts in its combination of pleasing appearance and utility of form.

In the more developed pre-classic cultures of Egypt and Mesopotamia and the Mediterranean and Aegean cities in Crete and Greece, the minor arts figure prominently. The discovery of metals and minerals and the evolution of processes for shaping them made available many of the materials that are still used for such purposes—gold and silver, glass and enamel, precious and semi-precious stones—and figure, along with more prosaic stone and wood and pottery, in the creation of utilitarian and decorative forms.

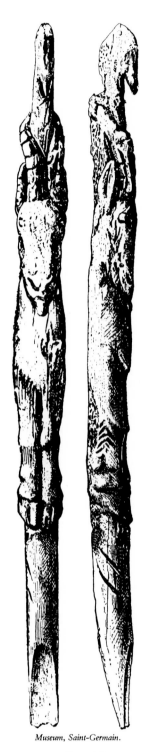

Museum, Saint-Germain.

FIG. 548.   Dart Thrower,
Reindeer Horn (Palaeolithic).

Many, in fact the majority of such objects have been preserved because all these cultures believed in the necessity of preserving by burial the body and possessions of the human being after death. Thus the Pharaoh of Egypt in his sarcophagus wears the jeweled necklace and breast ornament (Fig. 552) that symbolized with such opulence his semi-divine position in life, and his daughter's cosmetic container (Fig. 550) accompanies her in her tomb as it had on the dressing table in her palace. The golden cup (Fig. 560) of an ancient Greek warrior lies by his side in death as it had stood on his table in Vaphio, and the bull-headed harp (Fig. 556) of a Babylonian princess stood by her sarcophagus as it had by her throne. Thanks to this practice and the objects thus preserved, frequently as much is known about the way of living in long-since ended dynasties as about much of life today.

The *Falcon Head* (Fig. 549) in the museum at Cairo was excavated from the ruins of an ancient temple at Kôm-el-ahmar in Egypt. Of beaten gold, it dates from about 2700 B.C. and was originally part of a group symbolizing the protection of the king by the god Horus represented in Egyptian art with a falcon's head. This part of the figure was riveted to a bronze body after being beaten into shape, probably over a wooden form, and the eyes of red jasper were inlaid. To be noted is the craftsman's fine sense for his material—the flexible gold is rounded over to secure the maximum brilliance of surface—and also for the wild and savage spirit of the bird. In this latter respect the artisan shows himself one with his sculptor colleagues whose lively and spirited portrayals of animals are so often in striking contrast to the rigid and stylized monumental figures of human beings (cf. Fig. 233) which were executed under the immutable laws controlling such forms. This is not invariably true of the human form in Egyptian art, however, for in the *Perfume Spoon* (Fig. 550) the figure of the nude girl swimming behind a duck whose open back holds the perfume is natural in proportion and easy in movement. Of alabaster and slate, it dates from about 1450 B.C., in the general period of Egyptian history called the New Kingdom. It is not at all uncommon for the human

FIG. 549.   Falcon Head, Gold
(*ca.* 2700 B.C.).

form to decorate such utilitarian objects, another instance being the girl that forms the handle of a silvered bronze disk that was used as a *Mirror* (Fig. 551). It too is of the New Kingdom period. The figure is stylized to the extent necessary for it to serve as a handle but otherwise is surprisingly free and convincing in appearance. The object between the girl's head and the mirror disk is a papyrus capital; this parallels the practice of builders of the period who often employed human heads for capital decoration. Both objects are distinguished by the same sense of material that characterizes the gold falcon's head—the texture of the stone in the design of one and the

rhythmic flow of smooth metallic line that unifies the human with the geometrical form in the other.

Among the most spectacular examples of the minor arts in Egypt are the pectorals or breast ornaments that were part of the state costume of the ruler in his life and were placed on his mummy after death. A *Pectoral* (Fig. 552) of about 1850 B.C. in the Middle Kingdom period bears the name of Senusert II in the hieroglyphic cartouche flanked by two snakes in the upper portion. Below, kneeling, is a figure, presumably the monarch himself, with a falcon heraldically posed on either side. The material is gold with carnelian, lapis lazuli, and feldspar inlay. As a design, unity is attained through the symmetry of the arrangement, with the smoothly flowing curves of the various forms merging easily. Very effective too is the brilliant color pattern of the whole, a series of repeated accents in an abstract all-over pattern. Nor should the symbolism of the various details be overlooked—the *crux ansata* or cross of life that hangs from the snakes which are themselves a symbol of royal power, and the falcons representing the god Horus, protector of the Pharaoh. Such forms as these reveal the opulent and hieratic form of the minor arts in the official world of Egypt as the perfume container and mirror represent more intimate and personal aspects.

A *Throne of Tutankhamen* (Fig. 553) from his

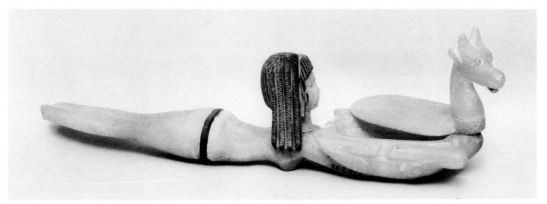

FIG. 550.   Perfume Spoon, Alabaster and Slate (*ca.* 1450 B.C.).

FIG. 551. Mirror, Bronze
(*ca.* 1450 B.C.).

FIG. 552. Pectoral of Senusert II,
Gold Inlaid (*ca.* 1850 B.C.).

back are comparable to the pectoral. The close-grained wood produces a different surface texture and scale, however, and the design as a whole provides for comfort in the gently curving lines of the seat.

The stoneworker and the potter are also represented in the minor arts of Egypt, along with the woodcarver and the goldsmith. *Alabaster jars* (Fig. 554) and other vessels, sometimes decorated with inscriptions but often without ornament, are a characteristic product of the

tomb is a further example of the minor arts of official Egypt. Of wood, it was among the many objects found in the subterranean burial place of this New Kingdom ruler. Although not one of the great figures in Egyptian history, his name is outstanding in the annals of archaeology because his tomb, which was virtually intact when discovered by Howard Carter in 1923, provided an unprecedentedly rich treasure of the burial paraphernalia of a Pharaoh. The body of the throne is cedar, and the carved ornament, consisting of symbolic figures of the king and the gods and hieroglyphic inscriptions, is covered in some places with gold leaf. The use of animals' claws for the feet is similar to the use of human figures as handles, as in the perfume spoon and the mirror (Figs. 550, 551), and the architectural details in the frame and the openwork of the

FIG. 553. Throne of Tutankhamen,
Cedar and Gold (*ca.* 1400 B.C.).

stoneworker; their simple curved outlines and the intrinsic texture of the material appeal more strongly to the modern eye, perhaps, than do the goldsmith's more striking works. The Middle Kingdom *Terra-Cotta Hippopotamus* (Fig. 555) is covered with a blue glaze over black papyrus buds and blossoms. This amusing example of Egyptian ceramic art is at the same time a well-composed form, as witness the appropriateness of the floral motives to the part of the animal's body on which they appear—opened blossoms

The Metropolitan Museum of Art,
Gift of Edward S. Harkness, 1917.

FIG. 555.   Terra-Cotta Hippotamus
(*ca.* 1900 B.C.).

The Metropolitan Museum of Art, Rogers Fund, 1921.

FIG. 554.   Alabaster Jar.

on the rotund body and the vertical accent of the buds on the shoulder and haunch. It is, moreover, another indication of the Egyptian artist's pleasure in identifying forms of nature that do not come within the rigid laws of hierarchic monumental art. Here again is evidence of a strong instinct for stylization such as is found in the monumental stone figures, but the terra-cotta animal appeals much more to a modern temperament, for it seems to reveal an aesthetic sense much more closely allied to our own than is the symbolic stylism of the statues. This figure and the similarly conceived forms discussed earlier impress us as having been made by human beings capable of human emotions, rather than by the strictly curbed and rigidly ruled artists

who in the larger figures are required to convey as directly as possible the sense of beings partaking alike of human and divine attributes.

The second pre-classic culture that developed in the Mediterranean world, that of the Near East or Mesopotamia, was also rich in the minor arts. Many small cult objects such as seals and rings might be used as examples; but the character of Mesopotamian art in this field is so well summed up by one object that it is used as the basis of discussion—the *Harp of Queen Shub' Ad* (Fig. 556), found in a tomb near Ur in Chaldaea by a joint expedition from the British Museum in London and the University of Pennsylvania Museum in Philadelphia. It is among the most ancient historical objects from the region, dating around 2500 B.C. The harp is of wood overlaid with carved shell and gold, with accenting details of blue lapis lazuli; the rich color effect stands for all that is exotic and Oriental in the popular mind. The bull's-head terminal has the same vigor of feeling present in the animal sculptures of the Mesopotamian style. A fine decorative effect results from the contrasting colors of the gold and the lapis lazuli details of the eyes, horn tips, and beard, from the contrasting textures of the stone and metal, and from the adjustment of the whole to its place on the front of the harp. The sumptuous exoticism of the whole accords well with the semi-barbaric Oriental character of Mesopotamian culture indicated in art and literature.

Pottery and metal work most completely represent the minor arts in the culture of the

University Museum, Philadelphia.

FIG. 556.   Harp of Queen Shub' Ad (*ca.* 2500 B.C.).

Aegean world that was the third pre-classic tradition to develop in the Mediterranean area. On the island of Crete, the sites of the great palaces built by the Minoan kings at Knossos and Phaistos and many less extensive sites have provided a considerable number of vases and jars whose ornament reveals a high degree of decorative skill. Abstract geometrical designs are frequent, but the motives derived from nature—flower and plant forms and the sea creatures that islanders would naturally be particularly interested in—are of the greatest interest, as in the *Lily Vase* (Fig. 557). The period in which the Cretan or Minoan potter achieved what now

appear to be his finest results is called Middle Minoan, from about 2100 to 1580 B.C.; the vase dates from the latter part of this epoch. Of great technical perfection as an example of ceramic method, the background is light and the bell and stem of the lilies are in dark tones. The pattern of blossoms is admirably adapted to the shape of the vessel, the long stalks rising from the base through the almost straight sides and flowering in a spreading design that fills the curved top, an effect that is satisfying both in representation and in adaptation to the form of the vase.

A little later than the Middle Minoan

example just discussed is the *Octopus Vase* (Fig. 558) found at Gournia in Crete; it dates from the Late Minoan period, probably about 1500 B.C. The color harmony is in browns, dark in the octopus and seaweed, light buff for the background. The theme of sea life is characteristic of this later period which preferred such motives to the geometrical and flower forms used earlier; in this respect it is interesting that the Aegean vase painter seldom represented the human figure, in contrast with the practice of contemporary mural decorators (cf. Fig. 359). As in the lily vase, the painter's primary concern is exactness of appearance stylized to achieve the maximum decorative effect. The octopus seems to float in the sea surrounded by seaweed, urchins, and anemones; the writhing tentacles float out to fill the bulbous contours of the jar in rhythmic linear patterns that are unified by the repeated dots and circles. If the effect is less restrained than the static simplicity of the lilies on the earlier vase, it nonetheless accords well with the sumptuous sophistication of life in the palace culture of the Late Minoan period.

The same freedom of design is found in two examples of Aegean metal work—a *Dagger from*

Museum, Candia.

FIG. 558.   Octopus Vase (*ca.* 1500 B.C.), from a reproduction.

Mycenae (Fig. 559) with a scene of cats hunting birds found in a grave at Mycenae, and the *Vaphio Cups* (Fig. 560), a pair of gold cups discovered at Vaphio, both cities on the mainland of Greece. The blade of the dagger is bronze and the inlaid figures of gold and silver are set off by a hard black paste-like substance. This method of working metal is called damascening and is particularly effective for contrasting colors, sheen, and textures. Here it shows dashing cats seizing fluttering birds in a scene of great animation, given continuity by the long flowing line of the river with fish swimming in it and bordered with papyrus plants. The design is well adjusted to the long tapering shape of the blade, and the repeated accents of the papyrus blossoms tie the whole together. An interesting point is the choice of motive, for the hunting cats, the river scene, and the papyrus plants are not native to the Greek mainland as the flowers and octopus of the Cretan vases were to the island, but are distinctly Egyptian. The possibility of the dagger having been made in Egypt cannot be overlooked, but it is more probable that relations between Egypt and Mycenae were such that the motive was transmitted from its place of origin to the other land.

Museum, Candia.

FIG. 557.   Lily Vase (*ca.* 1650 B.C.), from a reproduction.

National Museum, Athens.

FIG. 559. Dagger from Mycenae, Damascened Bronze (*ca.* 1400 B.C.),
from a reproduction.

The theme of the Vaphio cups, on the other hand, is intimately associated with Aegean culture. The bull figures prominently in scenes of religious rites and practices both in Crete (cf. Fig. 359) and on the mainland, probably as a symbol of fecundity in the semi-primitive worship of natural forms and principles that prevailed there. It is doubtless against some such background as this that the incidents on these cups must be interpreted. The left cup shows a wild bull dashing off in alarm on one side and hopelessly snared in a net on the other. The other cup shows a bull tied by one hind leg bellowing to a wild companion who is being decoyed by a cow on the other side. These cups are made by a technique called *repoussé*. The walls are hollow; the inner one is plain, the design being executed on the outer one by beating the malleable gold on a form of carved wood or terra cotta. There is less apparent concern in these cups with adapting the pictorial theme to the basic form than in the dagger or the vases; the head of the tethered bull is obscured by the handle, for instance, and the inconsistency between the stylized trees and the naturalistic animals must not be overlooked. But the vigorous plunge of the fleeing bull and its

National Museum, Athens.

FIG. 560. The Vaphio Cups, Gold (*ca.* 1400 B.C.), from reproductions.

desperate efforts to free itself from the net are well caught on the one cup, and its fatuous response to the lure of the decoy cow on the other is a masterpiece of animal characterization.

The pre-classic phase of western culture represented by the minor arts thus far considered is characterized by a primarily utilitarian and symbolic attitude toward the forms created. The idea of a vase or a piece of furniture as something that needs only aesthetic justification is characteristically modern; to the man of the ancient world, the desirability of an object lay in its usefulness or the excellence of its craftsmanship or its power as a symbol. A relief in an Egyptian tomb shows two stoneworkers carving vases; their conversation, indicated by hieroglyphics, has been translated: "This is a beautiful vase that I am making," "Indeed it is," which would seem to contradict the preceding statement. But the symbol translated as "beautiful" is used also to

mean "good" or "fine" in Egyptian writing, and the connotation usually permits the interpretation of "useful" or "well-made." At the most, the makers of these objects could have experienced only a pleasure in fine craftsmanship in the presence of these objects, a quite different emotion from an aesthetic response. As has been pointed out, this is also true of the concept of the major arts that prevailed at the time, a convincing demonstration of the honesty of purpose and sincerity of meaning that is one of the fundamental distinctions between ancient arts and those of today, wherein for the most part abstract aestheticism is considered the sole justification necessary for the existence of a work of art. It is this quality, too, that makes an ancient jewel or vase or chair as characteristic in its way of the culture that produced it as the temples or monumental stone figures with which it is contemporary.

THE MINOR ARTS OF GREECE AND ROME

The rich treasure of the minor arts in pre-classical Mediterranean cultures is a consequence of the burial cults in Egypt, Mesopotamia, and the Aegean phases of life in the Greek mainland and islands. For reasons pointed out elsewhere, such cults were not present in anything like the same degree in the classic world, a fact to which the relative absence of certain categories in the minor arts of Greece and Rome may be directly traced. The gold, silver, and jewels which once no doubt existed have long since been made into other objects; the wooden utensils and furniture that the dry air of a sealed Egyptian tomb preserved for centuries have disintegrated with time or been destroyed in the hearth fire of an insensitive owner; even bronze figurines and ornaments have crumpled with erosion or been melted to supply metal for other purposes. For the most part, it is only objects made of a material at once durable and inconvertible that today illustrate the classic genius in the minor arts, although indirect sources may shed some light on its products. Thus in the scene painted in the *Bowl of a Red-Figured Kylix* (Fig. 561), an early fifth-century drinking cup, the old man who is being served

with wine is sitting on a bench or stool whose legs terminate in a pair of scrolls like those of an Ionic capital (cf. Fig. 32). More developed is the form of Hegeso's chair on the stele carved in her

Museum, Corneto.

FIG. 561.   Bowl of a Red-Figured
Kylix (*ca.* 500 B.C.).

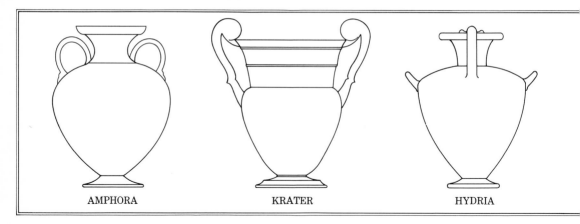

AMPHORA   KRATER   HYDRIA

FIG. 562. Greek Vase Shapes.

memory (Fig. 267); without superfluous ornament, consisting of legs fastened with pins to the horizontal slab of the seat and the upright of the back, it is rendered beautifully decorative by opposed yet complementary curves that are as subtle as the echinus of a Doric capital. Like the architectural forms with which it is contemporary, its design is simple yet effective by virtue of its refinement of functional form and its clear statement in visual terms of the nature of its matarial—wood in this case.

The largest single category of the Greek minor arts is the vases—jars, storage vessels, drinking cups, and the like. The baked clay of which they are made is one explanation of their preservation—lasting and durable, but of no great intrinsic value and inconvertible to other uses. Yet their importance as art objects is great, for, as already pointed out, the designs painted on them tell much that would otherwise hardly be known about the stages through which the Greek concept of significant form evolved.

Greek vases have many varied forms, determined by their use. The *Greek Vase Shapes* (Fig. 562) show a number of the more characteristic ones and the names that indicate their function. The amphora is a rather wide-mouthed jar used to store wine and oil; the somewhat similar hydria with a flattened lip and three handles was used for carrying and pouring water. The crater is a large open bowl in which water and wine were mixed at the banquet table; the kylix is a flat drinking cup; and a lekythos is a small flask-like container that could be corked to hold the oils for ceremonial rituals. The form in each case is well adapted to its use; the wine is poured from its container not directly into the cup but into the crater with its generous opening that even the most bibulous could dip into with his kylix, and the narrow neck of the lekythos permits the last drop of precious perfumed oil to be preserved.

The Greek vase was made or thrown on a rotating table or wheel from a mass of moist clay. The form was modeled by the potter who in all probability depended largely upon his instinct for determining the proper curvature of line and proportion of mass, being guided only by an inherent feeling for the most appropriate shape. When the fabric of the vase was completed, it was baked hard in an oven after which it usually had a characteristic red-brown color. Vessels intended for ordinary use might be left in this state, but it was more usual to paint the vessel on the outside and sometimes within as well. This was done with a liquid preparation called a slip. After its application, the vase was fired once more; this hardened the slip to a highly enameled and lustrous black glaze. This glaze sealed the porous clay on the inside; on the outside it sometimes simply covered the body of the vase with an even coat but more often it was applied to form a definite pattern. The following discussion is concerned with examples in the latter category for they involve problems of

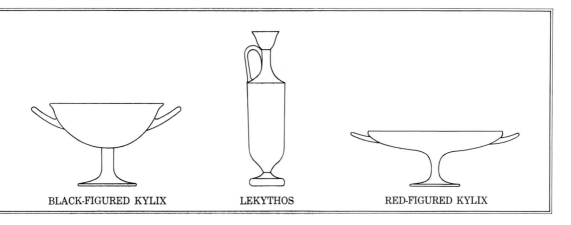

BLACK-FIGURED KYLIX   LEKYTHOS   RED-FIGURED KYLIX

composition and design and the creation of forms and figures that make these vases one of the most important classes of Greek art.

The history of Greek vase painting goes back to the earliest times of the classic tradition —the dim and darkened years of the ninth and eighth centuries B.C. when the fusion of Aegean culture with that of the invading barbarians from the north was still taking place. The great crater-like *Dipylon Vase* (Fig. 563) in the Metropolitan Museum dates from this period. It is over four feet high and was used as a funnel to pour libations on a grave, or as a container for ashes from a cremated body, funereal functions that also determine the decorative themes. Insofar as they involve figures, these represent the deceased on his bier on the top level, accompanied by his household and a procession of mourners; below are shown the funeral games celebrated in his honor, the chariot races and armed combats described in the twenty-third book of the *Iliad*. The figures are painted in a black glaze that technically is related to Minoan practice in the Aegean period, but the style of both figures and decoration is different. Strictly geometrical forms are used for the decoration, and the figures are reduced to similarly stylized geometrical elements—bodies and limbs consisting of triangles, with heads in profile. The armed warriors in the second level are thought of as standing behind their shields which are shaped like double-headed axes. Equally primitive is the filling of the

background of each figured panel with rosettes, dots, and zigzags. But the organization of the decorative scheme in horizontal bands, with the main subject in a large panel in the center of

The Metropolitan Museum of Art, Rogers Fund, 1914.

FIG. 563.   Dipylon Vase
(*ca.* 800 B.C.).

Museo Archeologico, Florence.

FIG. 564.   Klitias and Ergotimos, The François Vase,
Black-Figured Crater (*ca.* 560 B.C.).

the upper figured level, is more advanced than anything of its type in the Aegean period and reveals the sense of formal relationship between form and ornament that develops and prevails in all subsequent periods of Greek art.

This same decorative scheme—simplified, clarified, and yet more complexly organized—recurs in the *François Vase* (Fig. 564), a crater discovered in an Etruscan tomb in Italy but of Grecian origin. Inscriptions on it identify the subjects represented, dealing with the stories of Peleus and his son Achilles and also including episodes from the Trojan War. Other inscriptions also identify the vase as the work of the potter Ergotimos and the painter Klitias, a type of signature often found on later Greek vases and

revealing the equal esteem in which craftsman and painter were held. The François Vase, made in all probability about 560 B.C., is a fine example of the "black-figured" type of Greek vase painting that evolved from the process described above, although other colors are used as well—red and purple and some white. The subjects being primarily narrative, the composition of each frieze is more or less continuous and somewhat lacking in accent. Taken as a whole, however, the design builds up from the stylized ornament of the base through an animated frieze of grotesques into a figured frieze of some action. The main band, that where the vase is widest, is painted with a procession of figures moving in slow and stately accents. The upper two friezes are not as wide, and the decorative rhythm is speeded up. It is thus clear that the decorator was as much if not more concerned with the effect of his figures as elements in an abstract visual pattern controlled by the basic shape of the vase than with simply representing them or telling a story. The figures are much more realistic in general appearance and detail than those on the earlier funereal vase.

The black-figured technique of the François Vase is also used on *The Dionysos Kylix* (Fig. 565), painted by Exekias, one of the great masters of the style, probably about 540 B.C. The kylix being a drinking cup, its decoration deals appropriately with the Greek god of wine, Dionysos. Legend has it that when he was kidnaped by pirates who sought to carry him off in a ship to Egypt, he caused the mast to be transformed into a grapevine and the ship to stand still, whereupon the terrified pirates leaped into the sea and were changed into dolphins. Except for the sail, the forms are dark silhouettes against the lighter body of the cup; the details of the dolphins, the features of Dionysos' face, the outlines of the grapes and the like are incised in the black glaze so that after it was fired the light background shows through. It is with this exacting and inflexible technique that Exekias produced one of the masterpieces of decoration in the Greek minor arts. In a prevailingly symmetrical composition whose axis is established by the ship's mast, there is a fine balance between the pattern of grapes above and the dolphins below; the opposition and repetition of curving lines in the sail, the hull, the shapes of the dolphins in relationship to the circle of the cup bottom produce an effective sense of rhythmic movement.

Equally fine as a decorative composition is the scene of *Achilles and Ajax Playing Draughts* (Fig. 566) that Exekias painted on the side of an amphora which dates from about 540 B.C. The necessity for covering the entire exterior with decoration that the painter of the funereal vase (Fig. 563) felt is no longer sensed and even the less crowded compositional canon of the François Vase has been changed. Other than the main panel, on the broadest part of the vase, there is

Museum, Munich.

FIG. 565.   Exekias, The Dionysos Kylix, Black-Figured (*ca.* 540 B.C.).

only a band of stylized rays; the greater part of the outside is covered with a lustrous black glaze of great beauty in tone and texture. In the central panel, where the Greek heroes bend intently over their game, the curved lines of their backs repeat the profile of the vase, and their spears are at an angle that continues the line of movement created by the curved top of the handles where they join the body of the vase. The decoration thus reinforces the structural lines of the vase itself, but it is also of independent interest, for the figures are symmetrically placed yet varied in detail, resulting in a well-composed scene; they form a triangle whose apex is Achilles' helmet.

Considered only as a decorative medium, the black-figured style is eminently satisfactory; its material difficulties limit pictorial devices to silhouette and incision, both of which result in

Like the Dionysos painting by Exekias, this is on the bottom of a kylix or drinking cup, a vase that became increasingly popular during the fifth century B.C. when it was painted, probably around 500. Here the background is dark and the figures light; the lines that represent details and modeling are dark. Technically, this painting is the reverse of the earlier example; the reddish-brown clay of the vase is seen in the figures which are unpainted; the background is now painted. Now the lines in the figures are put on with a fine-pointed brush instead of being incised in the painted black slip as they were before. The greater freedom in drawing which this technique permits is immediately obvious in the multiplication of details, the variety of linear effects, and even some attempts to distinguish textures in the garments and to foreshorten the forms in depth.

The success of the more flexible red-figured technique in achieving greater pictorial complexity than was possible with the older method is seen in *Herakles and the Nemean Lion* (Fig. 567), a work by an artist called the Kleophrades Painter, who was active around 500 B.C. The subject is one of the labors of Herakles—his battle with the Nemean Lion—and the vase is a stamnos or wine jar. In the foreground, the heavily muscled giant is locked in a duel to the death with the lion; his club is at the left and his bow is hanging from a limb of the tree in the background. The ease with which these spatial relionships can be distinguished indicates the differing purpose of the Kleophrades Painter and Exekias. The master of the red-figured style is interested primarily in suggesting three-dimensional forms in depth, whereas Exekias is concerned almost solely with creating a pattern in a flat plane whose chief function is its relationship to the form of the object being decorated. As representation, the Kleophrades Painter's picture is very effective. The anatomy of the struggling giant is stylized but accurate, the chief trace of archaism being in the head. The legs and torso are shown in profile, and the artist has even dared to cover some parts of the body with others, for the plasticity of the observed portions allows the concealed ones to be inferred even if

Vatican Museum, Vatican City.

FIG. 566.   Exekias, Achilles and Ajax
Playing Draughts (*ca.* 540 B.C.).

forms that are two-dimensional and thus lie well on the surface to be decorated. When the human figure is portrayed, the result is similar to the schematic forms of archaic Greek sculpture with which these vases are contemporary (cf. Figs. 249-251). About the same time sculptors began to develop a figure style that more closely approximated nature, vase painters too began to explore the possibilities of forms that would be pictorially rather than decoratively functional. To achieve this, a more flexible medium had to be evolved and this—the red-figured style— made its appearance about 525 B.C. (Fig. 561).

not seen, an idea impossible with the black-figured reduction of the form to descriptive planes.

The vase painters of the middle and later fifth century continued to develop the representational resources of the red-figured style and were increasingly less sensitive to the structurally decorative function so ably achieved by the black-figured masters. The painting of Odysseus and the ghost of Elpenor (Fig. 361) on a vase now in the Museum of Fine Arts at Boston was executed about 440 B.C. The figures move freely and with ease, anatomically accurate and in well-observed foreshortened poses. The drawing is simple and linear, with little modeling by shadow. The forms are composed in a plane that lies parallel to the background, but in a way that

suggests the depth of the landscape setting. From this it is only a step to considering the dark picture field as space itself. The relationship of the figures in *Thamyris and the Muses* (Fig. 568) on an amphora of 420-400 B.C., which is attributed to the Meidias Painter, can be understood only if the background is thought of as a pictorial symbol of three-dimensional depth in which the plastically modeled forms can move freely. Such effects as these were probably suggested by the paintings of the wall decorators of the Golden Age in Greece, of whom Polygnotos was the most famous. Although these mural works are known only from descriptions, the history of contemporary vase painting indicates their increasing influence on the less monumental art as the century wore on. The result, as is

University Museum, Philadelphia.

FIG. 567.   The Kleophrades Painter, Herakles and the Nemean Lion,
Red-Figured Stamnos (*ca.* 500 B.C.).

The Metropolitan Museum of Art, Samuel D. Lee Fund, 1937.

FIG. 568. The Meidias Painter (attrib.),
Thamyris and the Muses,
Red-Figured Hydria
(420-400 B.C.).

tributed to the Achilles Painter, are on slender vases in which ceremonial oil could be brought to the tomb, a subject which often figures as decoration. Otherwise—and this too is illustrated in this example—the theme is allied in subject and interpretation to those of the sculptured funereal stele (cf. Fig. 267), such as a scene in the life of the deceased or the saying of farewells. Reticent alike in sentiment and in the beautifully simple draftsmanship, these are among the most appealing examples of Greek vase painting.

The Greeks placed great value on the works of the leading potters and vase painters. One evidence of this is the practice of signing vases, mentioned above in connection with the François Vase—a practice that enables the historian to associate with signed examples other examples in the same style that permit reconstruction of the artist's productive career. It also further affirms the value placed on the works themselves; for although many were made as containers for shipping wine and oil and other things, the presence of the François Vase—which was made in Athens and found in a tomb in distant Etruria—cannot be thus explained. A cup signed by the same Klitias who painted the François Vase was also found in Phrygia, far to the east of Greece; and other similar instances too numerous to mention indicate the esteem in which the works of the great ceramicists was held. It is a question, however, whether the value attached to them was for aesthetic or other reasons. In some cases they were certainly associative or sentimental; many drinking cups bear dedications to handsome youths much admired in their time who were doubtless boon companions in many a symposium. In other cases the name was probably valued as a trade-mark as Wedgwood and Lenox are today. Hence any inference that the vase was principally an object of visual admiration would probably have no better basis than in the case of the proud housewife of today.

The Greek's appreciation of decorative utilitarian forms in his painted vases is apparent also in a variety of metal objects that chance spared from the melting pot that was the fate of innumerable other examples. For instance, a

evident in the Meidias vase, was an almost complete abandonment of decorative for representational schemes. Intriguing though many of these later red-figured vases are for their often striking technical ingenuity, they cannot be ranked with the masterpieces of the late sixth century as examples of design integrated with form.

A third category of Greek vase painting in addition to the black- and red-figured types is the white-ground style. In this technique, which was practiced as early as the seventh century B.C. and continued in use from that time on, the clay of the vase was covered with a light-toned slip and the designs were drawn in dark outline. Various types of vase in this technique are known, including some fine drinking cups, but its most important and extensive use was in funereal lekythoi. *Mistress and Servant: Farewell* (Fig. 569), examples of the mid-fifth century at-

The Metropolitan Museum of Art, Rogers Fund, 1908.

FIG. 569.   The Achilles Painter (attrib.),
Mistress and Servant: Farewell, White-Ground
Lekythoi (*ca.* 450 B.C.).

Mirror (Fig. 570) consisted originally of a polished or silvered bronze disk supported by the figure of a girl with two sphinxes. The basic idea is not unlike that of the Egyptian mirror (Fig. 551), but the transition from the handle to the disk for which an architectural capital is used in the Egyptian example is handled less artificially here. Coins, too, give an excellent indication of the same attitude; symbols of place names, like the owl of Athena on the coins of Athens, are prominent in the decorative themes, sometimes combined with inscriptions. The *Decadrachm of Syracuse* (Fig. 571), in Sicily, struck about 480 B.C., is beautifully composed. Around the profile head representing the nymph Arethusa, who was especially honored in Syracuse, play four dolphins, a symbolic reference alike to the legend of the nymph and the nautical interests of the city; a literal inscription further identifies the origin of the piece. All these elements are wrought into a

The Metropolitan Museum of Art, Fletcher Fund, 1938.

FIG. 570. Mirror, Bronze
(6th cent. B.C.).

and neck, and the inscription is crowded between the head and the dotted rim of the coin. Obviously, where the designer of the Greek coin was considerably concerned with producing a combination of forms that would please the eye as well as indicate the character of the object, the Roman's only thought was to evolve a symbol of the emperor's promise to pay for value received. It is not inappropriate that a symbol of the ruler should replace that of the city or country, a practice that has continued from late classic to modern times.

The difference between the Greek and the Roman attitude of decorative functionalism in the minor arts is further illustrated by the silver *Bowl with Bust of Africa* (Fig. 573) on which a bust in high relief represents Africa in symbolic form; it was found in excavations at Boscoreale, a village not far from Pompeii, which also was buried in the eruption of Vesuvius in 79 A.D. As a demonstration of the handling of material to secure a striking effect, the dish is very fine; details like the serpent and the wild beasts—symbolizing, along with the plant forms and the horn of plenty, that continent's produce—are executed with great naturalism. In fact, naturalism is the keynote of the entire decorative scheme, for the bust and all its accessories look as if they had simply been applied to the bottom of the dish. This procedure effectively prohibits any practical use; imagine drinking from this cup in comparison with the Exekias kylix (Fig. 565). A utilitarian purpose was probably not intended—the plate is entirely ornamental in function—but the contrast with

circular pattern that lies well on the form of the coin. The irregular shape of Greek coins is due to the way they were made. A relatively thick piece of metal was placed between dies on which the face and reverse were incised, and a heavy blow was struck on the upper one; the edge of the metal disk was thus raised as it was squeezed out, forming a ridge that in some degree protects the relief pattern on the coin.

In turning from the minor arts of the Greeks to those of the Romans, a significant change in attitude is apparent. This change is indicated on a small scale, but no less clearly by comparing the Syracusan coin with one struck during the reign of Nero (A.D. 37-68) in Rome. Possibly the most obvious characteristic of the *Coin of Nero* (Fig. 572) is the naturalism of the head; it is a profile portrait which in a sense renders unnecessary the stolidly executed inscription surrounding it. Of composition and arrangement there is but little; there is an awkward space in front of the face

Museum of Fine Arts, Boston.

FIG. 571. Decadrachm of Syracuse,
Silver (480 B.C.).

University Museum, Philadelphia.

FIG. 572.   Coin of Nero, Gold
(*ca.* 50 A.D.).

Louvre, Paris.

FIG. 573.   Bowl with Bust of Africa,
Silver (1st cent. A.D.).

Greek practice is nonetheless illuminating. The Greek makes his utilitarian object decorative as well, whereas the Roman makes it striking at the cost of both decorative consistency and usefulness. This bowl was never intended as anything other than a "museum piece," treasured for the factual and naturalistic quality of its ornament and the intrinsic value of the material. Once the collectors' attitude is realized as being the primary

motivation in much of the Roman minor arts— the value of the object being determined by its cost, rarity, or curiosity—the contrast with the Greek forms in principle and result is easily understood.

This conception of ornament as something to be applied to the basic form of the object exemplified in the silver bowl from Boscoreale is also characteristic of the ceramic art of the Romans. The *Arretine Bowl* (Fig. 574), a vase with figures representing the four seasons, is an example of Arretine ware, so called because much of it was made in or near Arezzo; the characteristic red color is in the base clay and also in the glaze which hardens to a glossy coral color when fired. The body of the vase was formed on a wheel, but the decorative figures were made with moulds of baked terra cotta in which the ornament was incised in sunken relief. It was thus possible to make innumerable impressions of a given design, an instance of the mass-production methods the Romans followed in many of their artistic pursuits. In general shape the vessel is not unlike a Greek crater (Fig. 564), but the omission of handles is a characteristic indication of its purely decorative and nonutilitarian function.

Roman taste for the striking and extraordinary is shown by the popularity of cameos and related glass techniques in the minor arts.

The Metropolitan Museum of Art, Rogers Fund, 1910

FIG. 574.   Tigranes, Arretine Bowl,
Glazed Clay (10 B.C.-10 A.D.).

Cabinet des Médailles, Paris.

FIG. 575.   Augustus Deified,
Sardonyx Cameo (17 A.D.).

fication of the emperor that is its ultimate purpose, there are further parallels with contemporary sculpture. Cameo portrait medallions were also popular with the Romans, the variously colored layers permitting such effects as white for the flesh and brown for the beard, hair, and eyebrows.

The relative costliness of the semi-precious stone used for cameos and the limited size of available slabs restricted their general popularity. However, compensation was provided in the development, during the first century A.D., of new processes of handling glass. Although glass had previously been moulded like the clay or terra cotta of a vase, the discovery of the blowpipe method of forming glass vessels made possible such effects as those on *The Portland Vase* (Fig. 576) in the British Museum. By dipping the mass of molten blue glass that forms the background into opaque white, the vase when blown out was actually made in two layers; the outer one was cut away to form the desired design. The subject of the Portland Vase is

Cameos are cut from pieces of semi-precious stone like sardonyx which have alternate layers of different colors—brown and white in the *Augustus Deified* (Fig. 575)—through which the artisan cut to produce the contrasting effects characteristic of the medium. This cameo, in the Cabinet des Médailles in Paris, was executed in 17 A.D.; it is one of the largest examples known, measuring about ten by twelve inches. The subject is the protection by the deified Augustus of his successor Tiberius. Augustus is in the top level accompanied by deities of the Roman Pantheon; below are the members of his family with allegorical figures similar in import to those on the historical relief sculptures of the Ara Pacis and the Arch of Titus (Figs. 285, 286) with which they are roughly contemporary. The cameo shows a high degree of technical skill, the figures being cut in no less than five planes to produce the contrasting color effects that are so important in producing the illusion of real figures which constitutes its major stylistic quality. In this latter respect, as well as the glori-

British Museum, London.

FIG. 576.   The Portland Vase, Glass
(1st cent. A.D.).

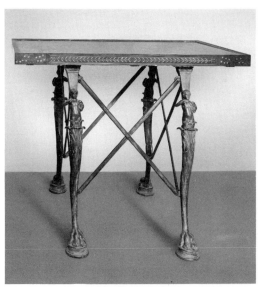

Museum, Naples.

FIG. 577.   Table from Pompeii,
Bronze, (1st cent. A.D.),
from a reproduction.

mythological—probably the wooing of Thetis by Peleus. The effect, enhanced by the semi-translucence of the material, is much like that of a painting, with its minutely differentiated planes and the resultant sense of depth in the third dimension; but as decoration for the curved walls of the vase it is open to the same criticism as the silver plate (Fig. 573).

Another use of glass developed by the Romans is seen in the mosaic ware or millefiori vases. These are made by fusing innumerable threads or strands of colored glass in a mould; when held to the light, the effect produced is aptly indicated by the Italian name—literally, thousands of flowers. The forms generally resemble vases carved in stone, a fact which suggests that they may have been intended to simulate vessels cut from the veined and colored marbles that abound in Italy but involving less effort in their creation.

The Roman fondness for elaborate decorative effects is illustrated by furniture as well as the objects already discussed. A *Table from Pompeii* (Fig. 577) is characterized in general by the lightness of proportion and delicacy of detail that are so apparent in the architecture and painting of that city. A comparison of its carefully calculated forms with those of the Greek chair in the Hegeso Stele (Fig. 267) is illuminating. The legs consist successively of the feet of animals, leaves composed to form cups, and the torsos and heads of cherubs, designed in a curve that is graceful and pleasing enough in itself but which lacks the sense of elastic support in the simpler lines of the Greek chair. Amid the display and opulent richness of the Roman house and its furnishings one longs for the straightforwardness and matter-of-fact appearance of their strictly utilitarian forms such as the aqueducts which supplied them with water (Fig. 61).

In the minor arts of Rome, the conception of an art form that has aesthetic rather than primarily utilitarian worth is apparent. This attitude —it cannot be characterized more completely than by calling it that of the collector—is entirely consistent with Roman practice in other fields. The intrinsic value or rarity of many Greek objects was the chief stimulus in accumulating the great collections of sculpture in Rome after the conquest of Greece, and these were the values the Roman asked for in objects made at his command. Deficient for the most part in the acute sensitiveness to formal quality that characterized the Greek temperament to a degree hardly conceivable today, the Roman desired ostentation and display more than anything else. Richness is likewise found in the minor arts of the Middle Ages, but it is motivated by quite different ideals.

Detail of Fig. 594.

CHAPTER THIRTY-FOUR

The Minor Arts of the Middle Ages and the Renaissance

During the Middle Ages and the Renaissance, the minor arts stand in much the same relationship to the major arts—architecture, sculpture, and painting—that has been observed in the earlier phases of western civilization. The figures of a Gothic ivory (Fig. 588) have the curving stance under pointed and cusped arches seen in their monumental counterparts that line the portals of a Gothic cathedral (Fig. 301). The forms supporting the Romanesque throne of a bishop (Fig. 599) are the brothers of those decorating the façade of a contemporary church

(Fig. 298). The composition of a Renaissance tapestry design (Fig. 604) has much in common with that of a great mural painting of the same period (Fig. 427). It is not surprising that this should be so, for during the time in question, the same artists were often commissioned in categories that today would be considered as involving separate ways of thinking—a distinction that mediaeval and Renaissance artists would not have been nearly so likely to make.

THE MEDIAEVAL PERIOD

The minor arts of the Middle Ages constitute one of the most varied and extensive categories of the art of that period, particularly in comparison with the preceding classic and pre-classic periods. Whether the need for utilitarian or symbolic objects was greater then than before cannot be said; but it is certain that their use by the Church was the reason for the creation of many of them and it is even more sure that had the Church not been instrumental in preserving them, an even smaller number would be in existence today than is the case. From literary sources we know that many objects of great intrinsic value and highly venerated for their religious associations were destroyed or melted down for the precious metals they contained. Since the number still in existence is very great, we can infer an almost incredible production during the mediaeval period as a whole. Without considering for the moment the needs of the laity for household implements and furniture, objects in the category of the minor arts had a large place in the Church. Altars were frequently covered or enclosed with decorated panels of gold and silver. The relics of saints were treasured in shrines of the same precious metals or of ivory or enamel. The books used for the service or in the libraries of cathedrals and monasteries were bound in elaborate covers decorated with ivory plaques, gold or silver filigree and precious stones. The vestments of priest and bishop were richly embroidered, and tapestries amazingly complex in form and color might cover the walls of the church itself. Every church that was the seat of a bishop or archbishop had an impressive throne of wood, stone, or metal in which he sat while taking part in the Mass. From these many and varied categories of the mediaeval minor arts a few examples are selected for discussion.

The Church's dependence both physically and intellectually upon the classic culture that eventually it almost entirely displaced was mentioned earlier; the same principle is apparent in much of the minor art of the Middle Ages. An objective illustration is supplied by *The Chalice of Suger* (Fig. 578), now in The National Gallery of Art in Washington, D.C. Commissioned by the famous Abbot Suger of the great abbey church of Saint-Denis in the outskirts of Paris, it consists of a sardonyx cup of antique origin; but the handles, rim, and base of gold filigree set with precious stones were executed during the primacy of Suger (1122-1151). Around the base is a series of medallions with figures of Christ and other Biblical characters in low relief, a symbolic device that identifies the Christian function of the object.

Ivory carving was widely practiced in the Middle Ages, and examples of this art provide a valuable continuity of medium in what is otherwise a field of such variety that clear-cut impressions of it are not easy to form. At the outset of the Christian era, the style of ivory carving was strongly influenced, as can easily be imagined, by the methods and ideas of the late antique. An example is the *Diptych of Anastasius* (Fig. 579), executed in 517 A.D. A diptych consists of two slabs of ivory hinged on the long sides, the outer faces decorated and the inner ones hollowed out to be filled with soft wax. The diptych under discussion was made to celebrate Anastasius' taking office as proconsul of one of the Roman provinces, an event signalized by the formal opening of the gladiatorial games and combats in his capital city. Such diptychs were given to the proconsul's guests as a souvenir score-card, the tallies marked in the wax with a sharp stylus. In this diptych, the outer faces of the ivory plaques show the consul giving the signal to

National Gallery of Art, Washington, D.C., Widener Collection.

FIG. 578.   The Chalice of Suger, Sardonyx
Mounted in Gold and Jewels (*ca.* 1140).

begin the games; at the top is an inscription with his name and office and immediately beneath are medallion portraits of the rulers he represents. The consul is seated under a canopy upon an elaborate throne with legs in the form of lions' forequarters. His scepter of office is held in one hand and the handkerchief whose fall is the starting signal is raised in the other; at the bottom are the games, with acrobats and wild beasts in the arena which opens out through doors at the sides. This decorative scheme with its combination of realistic and symbolic elements is in the characteristic Latin or western version of late classic style; the official figures above are in

rigid frontal poses and the more animated arena group below is seen as if from above. The artist's inability to suggest accurate relationships in the third dimension forces him to a purely descriptive procedure in which the distant forms are placed above those supposedly nearer. If the results lack decorative rhythm or grace, their flatness is at least somewhat in accord with the planar character of the ivory slab.

The antique sense of decorative form that the Latin artists of the Early Christian period had lost in their descriptive stylized figures was retained to some extent by their contemporaries in the eastern or Byzantine kingdom, whose capital was at Constantinople. The beautiful *Archangel* (Fig. 580), on a leaf from an ivory diptych of the sixth century in the British Museum, reveals its eastern origin in the Greek inscription as well as in the functional distribution of the drapery forms, in the solid if ill-articulated figure, and above all in the rhythm of line and surface which is so lacking in the Anastasius diptych. If the relationship of the figure to its arcade setting is somewhat ambiguous—the feet cover three steps at the bottom and appear to be at the back of the niche, and the left arm and the right hand are in front of the columns that enclose the figure—this is mentioned only to recognize the artist's sensitiveness to the decorative organization of what was doubtless a classic original and his relative lack of interest in its naturalistic qualities. The imposing *Throne of Maximianus* (Fig. 581)—he was bishop of Ravenna from 546 to 556—was probably executed about 500 A.D., some time earlier than

British Museum, London.

FIG. 580.   Archangel, Ivory
(6th cent.).

Bibliothèque Nationale, Paris.

FIG. 579.   Diptych of Anastasius, Ivory
(517).

the incumbency of the man whose name is associated with it. Of wood covered with elaborately carved ivory panels, it was made by Byzantine craftsmen who were working in Alexandria in Egypt, or by artists trained there. On the front are five panels showing John the Baptist and the four Evangelists framed by bands of elaborately carved foliage one of which encloses the monogram of Maximianus. The sides and back of the throne are decorated with foliate strips and with a considerable number of smaller slabs which tell the story of Joseph from the Old Testament and the Miracles of Christ from the New. The figures and foliage are very deeply carved, creating patterns in pronounced contrasts of light and shade which are at the same time rather naturalistic representations of form and elements in an abstract decorative pattern, for the varied scale of the figures and depth of the cutting are controlled by the location of the various panels on the throne. This work and the Archangel, which are roughly contemporary, give evidence of the

Byzantine artists' creative adaptation of the classic formal tradition to the needs of Christian expression, in contrast with the dull and spiritless forms used by the western or Latin craftsmen.

Although the Byzantine ivories are of historical importance in providing continuity of tradition, there is relatively little stone sculpture on a large scale from the eastern Christian world (cf. Figs. 289, 290). This was a consequence, in part at least, of the sentiment which led to the iconoclastic movement under Leo the Isaurian in 726 when the making of images was forbidden and many already in existence were destroyed. The iconoclastic edicts, however, did not apply with the same force to the small figures carved in ivory, and the creation of such masterpieces of decorative religious art as *The Harbaville Triptych* (Fig. 582)—a triptych because it has three panels instead of the two that a diptych has—was never entirely discontinued. The ivory worker was even permitted to use secular or pagan themes. One of the most attractive categories of the Byzantine minor arts is the *Casket* (Fig. 583); there were a series of fifty or more, dating from the late ninth or early tenth centuries, with representations of warriors, hunters, dancers, and the like. Ancient myths often supply the subject; the delicacy of carving, the unerring sense of scale that adapts the forms so well to the size of the object, and the rhythmic interplay of line and shadow and the color which often further accented the forms make them singularly well adapted to their purpose as jewel containers.

It was from the fusion and compromise of the Latin and Byzantine styles, to which was added the barbaric vigor of the Teutonic northern tribes (illustrated by an example of jeweled metal work shown in Fig. 590) that the attempt made by Charlemagne (724-814) to regenerate his kingdom intellectually and spiritually as well as politically is revealed in the minor arts. The *Crucifixion* (Fig. 584), in the cover of a manuscript book in the State Library in Munich, was carved about 870 and is thus later than Charlemagne's time, but the combination of stylistic elements resulted from this fusion. The classic element is strongest in the margin decoration,

Museo Arcivescovile, Ravenna.

FIG. 581. Throne of Maximianus,
Ivory (*ca.* 500).

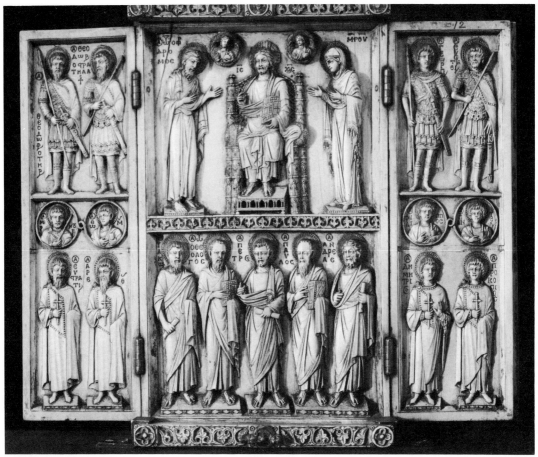

Louvre, Paris.

FIG. 582.   The Harbaville Triptych, Ivory (11th cent.).

the architectural details, and the use of figures to personify natural principles; the two in the lower corners, for example, represent Earth and Ocean and are taken directly from the kind of figure by which classic artists symbolized rivers and the like. Byzantine is the allover pattern of light and shade and, originally, of color; in this it resembles the Harbaville Triptych in principle though not in the sense of movement which is the Teutonic element in the relief. The artist who carved this panel probably had before him a manuscript book with illustrations like those in the Utrecht Psalter (Fig. 368); the animation produced by the waving lines of the ground, the energetic movement of the individual figures, and the pattern

of light and shade already mentioned are evidence of this. To these formal qualities should be added the Christian symbolism of the forms themselves. The subject is the Crucifixion; there are symbols of the sun and moon in the sky and personifications of the Church and Synagogue—the Old and New Dispensations—in the groups at the base of the cross. Below this are the Three Holy Women at the Tomb; and at the bottom, with the personifications of Earth and Ocean and the seated figure which is the city of Rome, is the Resurrection. As an embodiment of this subject, the book cover is more narrative or descriptive than formally interpretive in visual terms; the effect, especially when the rich border

FIG. 583. Casket, Ivory (ca. 900).

of gold work and jewels is taken into account, is nonetheless very striking and impressive.

Other elements than the above enter into the formation of mediaeval style. The ivory panel of an *Apostle* (Fig. 585) was carved in 1059 as part of the decoration of the casket in which the relics of Saints John and Pelagius were kept in the church of San Isidoro at León in Spain. The panel includes a contribution from the Moslem arts in the frame of the arch in which the figure stands. This—the so-called horseshoe arch—is more than a semicircle at the top and is very common in Moorish architecture; it was brought to Spain by the Moslems when they conquered that country in the eighth century. After the Christian reconquest in the eleventh century, many Moslems abjured their own faith and became Christians, but Moorish workmen were always employed in various capacities in the service of the Church. Their work, called Mozarabic, is often characterized by the mingling of western and Oriental qualities that appears here, for the style of the figure is derived from the Byzantine, and classic elements are also evident. The ivories carved in León—this is only one of a number—are more important than for these qualities, however; for it seems probable that the craftsmen who carved them also did the stone carving in the church of

San Isidoro itself, part of which was built in 1063; it is one of the earliest monuments embodying the full-fledged Romanesque style.

During the Romanesque period of the twelfth century, ivory carving continued to be one of the decorative arts, the carvings being used as a rule to ornament larger objects such as book covers, caskets, and shrines. An example is the large relief of *Christ Appearing to Two Apostles* (Fig. 586), now in the Metropolitan Museum of New York; in the lower part is His appearance to Mary Magdalene. It was probably carved about the middle of the twelfth century and comes from southwestern France or Spain. The fusion of earlier formal traditions that has been taking place in the Carolingian and eleventh-century ivories is now completed. The style is characteristically that of the monumental stone sculpture with which the portals of contemporary cathedrals and churches were being

FIG. 584. Crucifixion, Ivory (*ca.* 870),
Cover of ms. cim. 57.

S. Isidoro, León.

FIG. 585. Apostle, Ivory, (1059)
Casket of SS. John and Pelagius.

The Metropolitan Museum of Art, Gift of J. Pierpont Morgan, 1917.

FIG. 586. Christ Appearing to Two Apostles,
and Mary Magdalene, Ivory (ca. 1150).

decorated (cf. Fig. 297) as far as the proportions of the figures, the animated gestures, and the swirling folds and lines of draperies are concerned. Although subject matter and dogmatic values are still paramount, the admirable spacing of the groups in their framing mouldings is notable, as well as the way the heavier figures in the lower part create the visual effect of a base for the more slender ones above.

In the later Middle Ages or the Gothic period, ivory carving is illustrated by forms of varied character and purpose which are often self-sufficient rather than intended for use with a larger object. An example is an ivory diptych carved with scenes from *The Passion of Our Lord* (Fig. 587) which was once in the treasure of

Soissons Cathedral in France and is now in the South Kensington Museum in London; it dates from the late thirteenth century. Its intended purpose—for a private shrine rather than a great cathedral—is characteristic of the late Gothic period when it was carved. Beginning in the lower left part is the Betrayal, with the Trial and Flagellation on the right; the sequence then moves up to the Crucifixion on the right side and back to the left with the Entombment and Resurrection; it is concluded in the upper row with the Holy Women at the Tomb, the appearance to the Magdalene and the apostles at Emmaus, and Pentecost, again reading from left to right. The two panels of the diptych are thus complementary, unfolding to reveal for private meditation the story of Christ's last days on earth. Other than this, the setting and style of the figures are typical of the time. It is trite to mention the focusing of all mediaeval thought upon the Church and its ways of thinking; yet this is clearly the case here, for the figures in each of the three levels on both panels are placed under pointed arches framed with crocketed gables and pinnacles like those of the cathedral itself. The figures with their curving bodies, broad draperies, and bushy-haired heads are of the same style as the stone sculptures of the cathedral portals like the Vierge Dorée at Amiens (Fig. 304) and *Notre-Dame la Blanche* at Paris (Fig. 305).

The pathos that characterizes the telling of the gospel story in the diptych is even more apparent in the group of free-standing ivory figures in the *Deposition of Christ* (Fig. 588), or the taking of Christ's body from the cross, which is in the Louvre in Paris. It is also like the diptych in being an object for personal and private meditation, and the emphasis on sorrow and suffering is characteristic of the expressive aims of late Gothic art. Around the edges of the robes there are still traces of the colored decoration that once covered the ivory figures and made them even more jewellike than the semi-precious quality of the ivory suggests.

At the same time that late Gothic religious art was emphasizing the human emotive element in the Bible stories, an art of secular subjects was also developing. *Mediaeval Sports* (Fig. 589), two ivory reliefs in the Louvre, that originally came from a decorated writing tablet, are carved with scenes representing characteristic sports of the later fourteenth century, one being the familiar blindfold game known today as "hot-hand." Jewel caskets and mirror cases are other uses of ivory carving at this time; they are decorated with scenes of love, sport, jugglery, and other secular pursuits of the time. Of interest is the fact that, regardless of the character of the scenes, the setting almost invariably has the pointed and gabled arches that derive ultimately from contemporary church architecture; the basic decorative principle is that of the cathedral—multiplicity and variety of detail organized and related by the abstract order of the architectonic relationships of pointed arch and gable.

The importance of color in the art of the Middle Ages has been mentioned in other connections, particularly in the discussion of stained-glass windows in the churches. Color was also used to accent the sculptured figures in the portals and to give the interior further beauty, as many isolated fragments of painted ornament reveal even today. But it is hard to re-create the effect of this ornament on the weather-beaten exteriors of mediaeval buildings; except for one or two interiors, the overwhelming impression of the myriad hues of the windows can no longer be seen. What the mediaeval artist was striving for can be sensed nonetheless in the minor arts;

So. Kensington Museum, London.

FIG. 587.   The Passion of Our Lord,
Ivory (late 13th cent.).

the use of color in the ivories has already been indicated. But the effect is seen at its richest in the categories that directly involve the use of colored materials—work in gold, silver, and precious jewels, and the various enamel techniques.

The *Crucifixion* (Fig. 590), a jeweled golden book cover of a manuscript of the Four Gospels in the Morgan Library in New York, is one of the finest examples of Carolingian work in this category extant. In the center is the Crucifixion, executed in repoussé—that is, by being pounded out from the back—in a sheet of gold; above the inscription are symbolic figures of the sun and moon. In the four angles of the cross are clusters of gems in settings with figures above and below them; those above represent four angels, and those below are the Virgin and John the Beloved Disciple with two of the Marys who came to Christ's tomb. The cross is outlined with jewels and other jewels form a wide border around the entire cover. It was made in the workshop of the great abbey at Saint-Denis while that institution was under the patronage of Charles the Bald (823-877). Comparison with the contemporary ivory cover in Fig. 584 shows less interest in narrative in the gold cover and the greater stress on decorative effect. Symbolism is present as always, a particularly interesting detail being the representation of the moon and sun facing in opposite directions to portray the earth's darkening from the ninth to the twelfth hours while Christ hung on the cross. But the figures in the reentrant angles of the cross are placed decoratively rather than descriptively or symbolically and the symmetrical pattern that results is a major factor in the impressive effect created by this masterpiece of the goldsmith's art.

A later example of the use of precious metals in the minor arts in the Middle Ages is the golden *Virgin of Jeanne d'Evreux* (Fig. 591), which was executed in 1336 and is now in the Louvre. It is almost exactly contemporary with the stone *Notre-Dame la Blanche* (Fig. 305) and is closely related to it in style. The base is treated in characteristic Gothic fashion—the sides divided into panels by buttresslike forms with canopies and statues in the contemporary architectural

Louvre, Paris.

FIG. 588.   Deposition of Christ, Ivory (late 13th cent.).

manner. In this as in the innumerable shrines and reliquaries and other gold and silver objects made in the Middle Ages, the richness of the material is an important factor in the decorative effect and also in what might be termed one aspect of the usefulness of the objects themselves. For if such costly material can be used as the container for an object, the object must surely be of superlative value whether it is the written words of the Scripture, the relics of a holy saint, or the

Louvre, Paris.

FIG. 589. Mediaeval Sports, Ivory (14th cent.).

wafer used in the ceremony of the Eucharist. Thus it was not merely to delight the eye or to achieve display that the mediaeval artist used gold and silver and gems so lavishly, but to symbolize the even greater preciousness of the objects treasured within the containers he made.

On the side panels of the base of the golden Virgin there are a series of pictures; these are in enamel, the minor art of the Middle Ages which along with stained glass and manuscript illumination is most striking and brilliant in terms of color. Two methods of using enamel were extensively employed in the mediaeval period—cloisonné and champlevé. Cloisonné, the first to be developed, was most general in the Byzantine east, an example being a medallion representing *The Virgin* (Fig. 592). The illustration, which is the same size as the original, reveals the technique quite well. A design was formed on a plate of gold by soldering narrow strips or cloisons which were also of gold; the areas thus defined were then filled with a paste made of vitreous material colored with various kinds of metallic oxides which firing transforms into a hard, translucent substance. The surface was then polished, producing a brilliant pattern of gleaming colors defined and separated by the gold cloisons and made almost luminous by the

gold background shining through the glass-like enamel. The gold cloisonné enamels of Byzantium were usually on a rather small scale because of the costliness of the material. This, together with the somewhat restrictive nature of the technique, led to the employment of forms strongly stylized in pattern, although it is clear that this was in no way considered undesirable by the artists. The example in Fig. 592 dates from the eleventh century, but the technique had been practiced long before then. This medallion is one of a series used to decorate the frame of an icon or holy picture to which it was fastened by nails driven through the holes that are visible in the margin.

The Byzantine enamels were treasured both for their intrinsic value and for their religious associations and many found their way to western Europe. An Anglo-Saxon craftsman was possibly inspired by one when he created the scepter ornament called the *Jewel of Alfred the Great* (Fig. 593), now in the Ashmolean Museum at Oxford. The technique is the same as that in the Byzantine medallion, except that there is no backing and the effect of the light through the translucent enamel suggests that it is in fact the precious stone the name implies. Otherwise, the flat and linear pattern of the forms and their

FIG. 590.   Crucifixion, Gold and Jewels (9th cent.), Cover of ms. 1.

allows the period of its creation to be deduced—around 900.

The second technique, champlevé, is represented most extensively by western examples. It differs from cloisonné in that copper instead of gold is the background and the cells that are filled with paste are formed by gouging out the copper, leaving ridges between the enameled areas, instead of by fastening cloisons to it; the application of the enamel and its subsequent treatment are the same as in cloisonné. Because of its greater economy, this method was applied on an appreciably larger scale than the gold Byzantine enamels; after its first use in the eleventh century it is not uncommon to find shrines and altar frontals of considerable size decorated entirely in this way. The earliest examples known are Spanish or French in origin; its most extensive development occurred at Limoges in France—to such an extent, indeed, that the term "Limoges enamel" is almost a synonym for champlevé, which means literally "excavated field." A *Casket* (Fig. 594) in the Metropolitan Museum is a characteristic example of the late twelfth century. The side panel is the Crucifixion,

Louvre, Paris.

FIG. 591. Virgin of Jeanne d'Evreux, Gold and Enamel (1336).

schematic stylization make this a characteristically northern interpretation of the human figure, with its large head, long and pointed in shape (cf. Fig. 292). A Celtic inscription, "Alfred had me made," supplies the name of the object and

The Metropolitan Museum of Art,
Gift of J. Pierpont Morgan, 1917.

FIG. 592. The Virgin, Cloisonné Enamel (11th cent.).

FIG. 593.   Jewel of Alfred the Great,
Enamel (*ca.* 900).

legend that a Florentine enamel worker's practice of recording his designs by pressing paper on the inked ridges of his metal plates suggested the idea of making prints in that way. Although the specific details of this story are open to question, it is almost certain that the graphic art of metal engraving (cf. Figs. 408, 443) developed from practices used in fifteenth-century metal-working shops.

Any discussion of mediaeval minor arts must include textile designs. In spite of their inherent frailty, examples from relatively early times have been preserved, an indication in itself of the value placed upon them. An example is the fragment of silk whose woven pattern represents the *Annunciation* (Fig. 595); another part portrays the Nativity. It is in the treasury of the Vatican Sancta Sanctorum, dates from the sixth century, and came from Alexandria in Egypt. Most of the Early Christian textiles known are of eastern origin, particularly those of silk, for silk could be obtained only in the Orient at that time. Eastern too is the style, in its symmetry of two-dimensional forms and the stylized decorative

Christ sitting in judgment on the slanting top; figures in arcades fill out the ends of each section. The casket is bronze, with the heads of the figures modeled separately and attached to it. The backgrounds are decorated with vines done by a technique of light incisions called chasing; the robes of the figures and the half-rosettes in the margins are enameled. The colors are few, blue and green predominating with some accents of yellow and red, and there is no gradation or shading of their intensity; but the effect, combined with the gilt applied to the bronze of the background, is of great richness and splendor. Together with stained glass and manuscript illumination, enamel work is one of the most characteristically mediaeval of the minor arts; it continued to be practiced in some places in the Renaissance period. However, the aims of the later enamelers were influenced by those of painters rather than by the medium itself. It is worth noting that the art of enamel work probably was responsible to some extent for one of the most characteristic Renaissance artistic developments—the graphic arts. Vasari, the sixteenth-century Florentine art historian, relates a

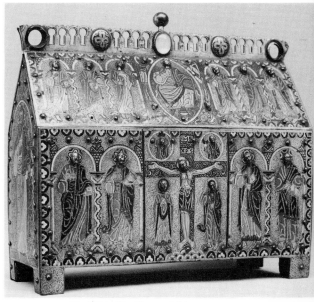

FIG. 594.   Casket, Champlevé Enamel
(late 12th cent.).

Cappella Sancta Sanctorum, Vatican City.

FIG. 595.   Annunciation, Silk (6th cent.).

foliage—characteristics that make the design particularly appropriate to the flat surface of the textile. Though there are no less than five tints, the effect as a whole is subdued; the colors are softly harmonious rather than striking. The preservation of such early examples of the textile arts was a consequence of the value placed upon them and the use to which they were put. Holy relics were wrapped in pieces of costly cloth to be placed in no less sumptuous caskets, a practice that has kept many of them in a surprisingly good state of preservation. They were also easily transported and many were exported from the Near East to western Europe.

Museum, Bayeux.

FIG. 596.   Norman Invasion of England, The Bayeux Embroidery
(late 11th cent.).

In western mediaeval Europe, the textile arts used wool and linen more extensively than silk, which was not produced outside of China before the sixth century and was always very costly. Such work as the Bayeux Embroidery showing the *Norman Invasion of England* (Fig. 596) by William the Conqueror would have been nearly impossible in the rarer material. Of linen, embroidered with blue, green, red, and yellow worsted, it is now 230 feet long and nineteen inches wide; there is some evidence that it has been shortened somewhat. According to tradition it was made by William's queen Matilda and her maids-in-waiting, but there is no direct evidence for this; the fact that it had been used since time immemorial to decorate the nave of Bayeux Cathedral in Normandy makes it not improbable that it was commissioned by Odo, William's bishop, who had his episcopal seat there. In any event, it probably dates from the late eleventh century; this date is also suggested by the style of the figures which is similar to that in Anglo-Norman manuscript illuminations of the period. The portions of the embroidery illustrated show Harold of England seated in his London palace after taking the crown left by Edward, an act considered disloyal by William to whom Harold had sworn fealty; the Normans are stocking their ships with armor and food in the next section;

the third shows them crossing the English Channel; the fourth is the Battle of Hastings with which this frieze-like embroidery comes to an end in the flight of the English after Harold's death. The lively and animated movement of the figures is one quality of the original that appears in the reproductions, but the equally vigorous effect of the varicolored worsteds on the creamy linen background can only be guessed. The grotesque animals and birds in the upper and lower margins of most of the embroidery are in the manuscript tradition of the time. Only at the end—as in the third and fourth parts here—does the main action spread into these margins; the sails of the ships extend to the top and the soldiers killed in battle are shown below the battle itself. Apart from its technical and decorative interest, the Bayeux Embroidery is of outstanding importance as one of the first extensive instances of secular subject matter in mediaeval art—and this in spite of its intended purpose as the decoration of a church.

Of all the textile arts in the Middle Ages, tapestry making is the most familiar and the most extensively represented. In tapestry, the design is woven into the fabric by a process in which the weft or woof, the name given the horizontal threads, is wound around the warp or vertical ones; the stitches are pressed tightly

against each other so that the warp is entirely covered by the woof. Tapestry weaving of this type apparently was practiced in Europe since the ninth century at least, but it was in the fourteenth century that the famous manufactory at Arras in Flanders was established to produce the tapestries that made the name of that city synonymous with the art. However, the whole area of the Low Countries and northern France is represented in the most ancient known examples of mediaeval tapestry, of which the outstanding single work is undoubtedly the one representing *The Apocalypse* (Fig. 597), now in the cathedral of Angers in France. In its entirety this tapestry was originally nearly 500 feet long and contained ninety scenes from the story of the end of the world related in the Book of Revelation in the New Testament. It was designed by a painter named Jean Bondol of Bruges on the basis of illuminations in a

thirteenth-century manuscript book that is still preserved in the Bibliothèque Nationale in Paris. It was woven in the workshop of Nicolas Bataille, a tapestry maker in Paris, between 1364 and 1380, for the Duke of Anjou, who ordered it for the decoration of his château at Angers and left it to that city's cathedral after his death. In spite of mutilation that has reduced its length to 328 feet and the total number of scenes to seventy-eight, it is still one of the most impressive examples of mediaeval tapestry extant when displayed over the nave arches of the cathedral. The part shown in Fig. 597 is based on Revelation xvi, 1—"And I heard a great voice out of the temple saying to the seven angels, Go your ways, and pour out the vials of the wrath of God upon the earth." At the left is John, who sees this as a vision; the angels are in the center; and the figures at the right symbolize the people of the earth upon whom the wrath of God is to

Cathedral, Angers.

FIG 597.   The Apocalypse; The Vials of the Wrath of God, Tapestry
(1364-1380).

FIG. 598.   Hunting the Unicorn: The Unicorn Defending Himself
(*ca.* 1500).

fall. The style is similar to that in contemporary manuscript illumination in the way the figures are represented and in the flower pattern of the background. Although the dyes used in the wool have faded somewhat, the effect is still one of great richness. The flatness of the design combines with the texture of the material which, although quite coarse at close view, is eminently fitted to make the tapestry most effective as a decorative adjunct to an architectural interior.

The growing secular interests of the late Gothic period are reflected in the tapestries of the fifteenth and early sixteenth centuries woven in the Low Countries, which continued to be the center of this activity. More than ever was their purpose utilitarian, for the wall hangings of many a great hall relieved the dark cold of the stone and made the damp rooms of palace or

San Niccola, Bari.

FIG. 599.   The Bari Throne (*ca.* 1100).

castle more comfortable. If the patronage was more secular, symbolism and allegory remained the choice of subject, as a series of six tapestries now in the Cloisters of the Metropolitan Museum clearly reveals. The subject of the series is *Hunting the Unicorn* (Fig. 598); in the episode illustrated, the fourth of the series, the unicorn defends itself from the hunters and their dogs. This was a popular allegory of the time, in which the unicorn is a symbol of purity and its capture is interpreted as the Incarnation of Christ since this could be effected only by a virgin. But the religious significance of the theme is not emphasized; it is rather the picturesque panoply of an aristocratic hunting party that is stressed in the realistically portrayed costumes and the flowers and trees and birds and castles that provide a background for the several episodes of the hunt. Though more naturalistic than the background in the Angers Apocalypse, these are woven into a fine decorative pattern that lies flat in the picture plane, making it an effective ornamental design. The color, too, is used with great skill; the foliage is green, with reds, yellows, blues, and oranges employed in the details of the figures; all this makes the white of the unicorn

Philadelphia Museum of Art.

FIG. 600.   Room from near Le Mans (15th cent.).

stand out as the decorative and dramatic center of each panel. The popularity of the subject is indicated by its use in one of the best-known late mediaeval tapestries, the famous Lady and the Unicorn in the Cluny Museum in Paris, which is contemporary with the Metropolitan tapestry; its general similarity in idea to the literary allegories like the famous *Roman de la Rose* so widely read at the time is obvious.

In making a general subdivision of the minor arts as a whole, it might be possible to distinguish between the decorative arts and the useful arts. The decorative would include the majority of the mediaeval examples thus far considered, for although there is a definite reason for their existence, the decorative function, as symbol or ornament, is still the primary one. The useful arts would include such things as furniture, in which usefulness is the major

consideration, the decorative effect secondary. One example of mediaeval furniture is *The Bari Throne* (Fig. 599) in the church of San Niccola in Bari in southern Italy, which was made for the bishop Elias about 1100. It represents the continuation of a classic tradition in using human figures called caryatids as supports (cf. Fig. 43). In this instance, these figures are among the earliest in the Romanesque style, being contemporary with those carved by Guglielmus on the façade of Modena Cathedral (Fig. 298) and having little in common expressively with the immobile maidens of the Erechtheum. Also to be noted is the decoration of the seat and arm supports which are carved in low relief with rosettes and grotesque animals; the backgrounds were originally filled in with a black paste that made the figures in the stone stand out prominently. Both technique and decorative detail

the stone buildings of the time—tracery and pinnacles and "linen-fold" motives—and is so placed as to accent the openings of doors and windows. The tapestry of the Coronation of the Virgin over the windows is in a style like that of the Unicorn Hunt. Much of the furniture of a Gothic room was built in, another instance of the fundamentally architectonic character of mediaeval art; in the Philadelphia Museum Room, this is true of the cabinet at the extreme left.

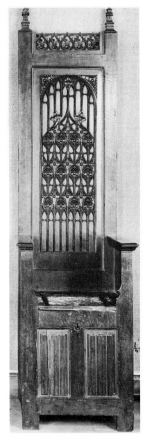

Philadelphia Museum of Art.

FIG. 601. Gothic Chair, Oak
(15th cent.).

are Byzantine, a fact which is not surprising in view of the close relationship always maintained between southern Italy and the Near East. As an example of Romanesque furniture, the Bari Throne is exceptional; although not all the chairs of the time were like it, it is characteristic of its period in the character of its ornament as well as in the solid massive proportions so appropriate to the stone from which it is made.

In the Gothic period wood was used quite extensively for furniture. The *Room from near Le Mans* (Fig. 600) in the Philadelphia Museum of Art is a characteristic late Gothic interior. The walls are wainscoted or paneled with wood; this paneling is carved with the motives employed in

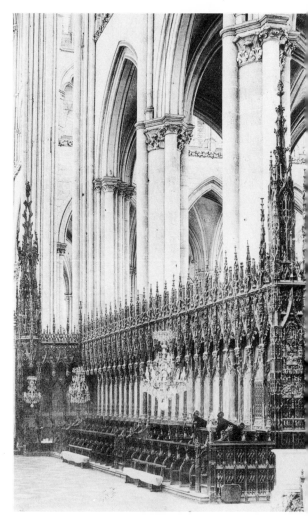

Cathedral, Amiens.

FIG. 602. Choir Stalls, Oak
(1508-1522).

Also to be noted are the heavy chest at the right with its similar decoration and some typical metal work in the wrought-iron hinges and handles, and the fifteenth-century walnut chair with its elaborately carved back standing between the windows. Decorative motives similar to those in the fifteenth-century room appear in a *Gothic Chair* (Fig. 601), of the same period, also in the Philadelphia Museum; its high back is typical. It has a dual purpose, being a chest as well as a seat. This was a common practice in mediaeval times that allowed the relatively complete furnishing of a room with minimum of separate pieces; it was not unusual, for instance, for a chest to serve also as table and bed.

Prominent in the furniture of the church were the *Choir Stalls* (Fig. 602) where the clergy participating in the Mass sat during the service. The seats are in an uninterrupted row; their high backs are elaborately carved with pointed arched canopies, pinnacles, cusps, and other architectural detail that makes them appropriate elements of the Gothic church interior. The backs are at the same time a screen to isolate the sanctuary from the ambulatory and a field for sculpture. Carving is also often present on the under side of the tipping seats; the motives on these misericords, as they are called, usually involve secular or genre subjects and are sometimes obscene, supplying the same contrast with the religious subjects elsewhere in the interior of the church as the grotesques and gargoyles on the

outside. Oak and walnut were most frequently used in Gothic furniture, and the design of the greater part of it bespeaks the nature of the materials. The proportions are heavy; the impression is one of massiveness enlivened by carving in the sharp lines and crisp planes possible with the close-fibered tough wood.

There is probably no period in the history of art in which distinguishing the so-called major and minor arts on the basis of expressive quality is more arbitrary than the Middle Ages. Certain categories of mediaeval art often considered as minor include some of the loftiest and most elevated embodiments of mediaeval faith that were created, notably manuscript illumination and stained glass. Even in the most humble chest or chair there is the sense of oneness with the great cathedrals—apparent in form as well as purpose—that reveals the consistency of thought during the period. In wood or gold, in enamel or wool, the mediaeval craftsman worked for the greater glory of the Church and of God just as his architectural and sculptural colleagues realized in their monumental stone symbols a reality transcending that of earthly experience. This perfect idealism, however, was short-lived. The infusion of more worldly values already noted in one or two instances became more and more persistent and the Renaissance period brought once more a different concept of the minor arts than that prevailing in the preceding epoch.

THE MINOR ARTS OF THE RENAISSANCE

The long-established historical convention of a sharp demarcation between the Middle Ages and the Renaissance is primarily for convenience. A broadly simplified study makes it possible only to see such obvious and significant contrasts as are present in characteristic expressions of the respective periods (cf. Figs. 100 and 130); it does not permit following the frequently almost imperceptible changes that lead from one form to another. So while it is illuminating to note the differences between the products of the mediaeval and Renaissance points of view in forms that are in the same medium and involve

similar technical procedures, it is even more important to note the special aptness of different mediums to different periods.

Enameling is a technical procedure that reached its highest point of expressive development in the Middle Ages and continued in the Renaissance. The Renaissance example illustrated, a triptych of the *Annunciation and Nativity* (Fig. 603), was made in Limoges in France as was the earlier Gothic enamel already discussed (Fig. 592); it dates from about 1500. Technically, it reveals a considerably greater dexterity in handling the medium, vitreous paste fired on a bronze

Philadelphia Museum of Art.

FIG. 603.   Annunciation and Nativity, Enamel
(*ca.* 1500).

plate, though the earlier dividing cloisons or ridges are no longer present; the enamel was spread with a brush or spatula. Nonetheless, the careful shading and hatching that model the forms, and the perspective devices used to suggest three-dimensional depth would have been impossible without extraordinary manual skill. But as a work of art in which the inherent quality of the material is a factor in creating expressive values, the Renaissance enamel is not as satisfactory as the mediaeval one, for the man who designed it was thinking not as an enameler but as a painter (cf. Fig. 377). If these panels were used to decorate a casket, the solid forms would seem to make bumps on its surface and their depth would be a denial of the flat plane whose function is to close in the side of the box. On the other hand, if they are thought of as a free decoration that hangs on the wall like a painting, the technical limitations still present in spite of the craftsman's considerable success in surmounting them make it at once apparent that a painter working in oils on panel or canvas could have secured even more impressive effects.

Tapestry is another medium that continued from mediaeval times into the Renaissance but at the cost of losing many of its inherent qualities to more pictorial conceptions. An outstanding example by reason of its designer's fame, and very influential because of it, is the series representing the Acts of the Apostles which Raphael designed for the Sistine Chapel in Vatican City.

There were eight pieces in all; the one illustrated, the *Miraculous Draft of Fishes* (Fig. 604), is related in Luke v, 1-11. By a happy circumstance, the cartoons or full-scale working models used by the weavers for this series have been preserved and are now in the South Kensington Museum in London; comparison with the finished tapestries reveals the faithfulness with which the Flemish craftsmen followed the patterns, for the weaving was done in Brussels, then the most important center of such activity, between 1515 and 1518. Their quality as works of art is indicated by the freedom with which cartoons and tapestries alike have been cited by critics and historians of art as examples of Raphael's developed style as a painter. The most casual observation reveals the absence of tapestry quality; the flatness of pattern, simplicity, and strength of drawing in two dimensions—and above all the texture of the material—that are fundamental to the medium are forsworn for magnificent pictorialism in the main subject and for an astonishingly accurate transcription of the effect of a carved stone relief in the lower border. The skill of the weavers in reproducing with unfailing accuracy every nuance of tone and color in the cartoon commands the greatest admiration, but the result is a "woven picture" instead of a tapestry in the expressive and decorative sense as well as technically, The side borders, with cherubs and foliage mingling in a type of decoration called *grotteschi* which Raphael had used in his decoration of the Vatican Loggie, have much more of the tapestry quality than the main subjects do.

Motives of this type are used extensively in one of the most ingratiating of Italian Renaissance decorative arts—the ceramic ware called majolica, an example of which is the *Adam and Eve* (Fig. 605). This ware has an earthen base covered with an enameled glaze containing a high percentage of tin. In earlier examples, of the fifteenth and early sixteenth centuries, these arabesque motives are used with naïve enjoyment of their supposedly classic elements but with very fine decorative effect; later on, the majolica artists also succumb to the pervasive practice of imitating pictorial models and the

Sistine Chapel, Vatican City.

FIG. 604. Raphael, Miraculous Draft of Fishes, Tapestry (1515-1518).

ware loses its originally attractive decorative character. The ceramic technique involving glazes containing tin was used for substantive or independent sculpture as well as for plates like

The Metropolitan Museum of Art, Rogers Fund, 1904.

FIG. 605. Orazio Fontana, Adam and Eve, Majolica (16th cent.).

POLIPHILO QVIVI NARRA,CHE GLI PARVE AN,
CORA DI DORMIRE,ET ALTRONDE IN SOMNO
RITROVARSE·IN VNA CONVALLE,LA QVALE NEL
FINE ERA SERATA DE VNA MIRABILE CLAVSVRA
CVM VNA PORTENTOSA PYRAMIDE,DE ADMI,
RATIONE DIGNA,ET VNO EXCELSO OBELISCO DE
SOPRA.LA QVALE CVM DILIGENTIA ET PIACERE
SVBTILMENTE LA CONSIDEROE.

LA SPAVENTEVOLE SILVA,ET CONSTI-
pato Nemore euafo,&gli primi altri lochi per el dolce
fomno che fe hauea per le feffe & profternate mébre dif,
fufo relicti,me ritrouai di nouo in uno piu delectabile
fito affai piu che el præcedente.El quale non era de mon
ti horridi,&crepidinofe rupe intorniato, ne falcato di
ftrumofi iugi. Ma compofitamente de grate montagniole di non tro-
po altecia. Siluofe di giouani quercioli, di roburi,fraxini & Carpi-
ni,& di frondofi Efculi,& Ilice,& di teneri Coryli,&di Alni,& di Ti,
lie,& di Opio,& de infructuofi Oleaftri, difpofiti fecondo lafpecto de
gli arboriferi Colli.Et giu al piano erano grate filuule di altri filuatici

The Library of Congress.

FIG. 606. Poliphilus Dreaming,
from the Hypernerotomachia Poliphili,
Woodcut and Metal Type (1499).

this; it is indissolubly associated with the della
Robbia family, whose products still ornament
with great charm the walls of many Florentine
Renaissance buildings.

There is no better illustration of the principle that every age must develop for itself the
forms expressive of its characteristic ideals than
the history of the book. As pointed out elsewhere, in the Middle Ages the written word had

transcendent value, being not merely the record
of mortal thought but the Word of God made
manifest in literal symbol. This idea is basic to
the whole concept of the illuminated manuscript, for the blaze of color and gold with which
the mediaeval artisan decorated his pages was
justified by the preciousness of the words inscribed thereon; and the essential fitness of the
handwritten word and the hand-illuminated
picture to the page of the book makes their
abstract identity clear to the beholder. But once
this ideal concept of the word was questioned,
as it was in the late Middle Ages, a new value was
developed to take its place, as is evident in any
example of late mediaeval illumination (Fig.
372). The reality of the word was lessened and
the reality of the picture increased; for the
spiritual experience that gave communal transcendental significance to the word is no longer
meaningful, and only in the objective evidence
of experience of the senses can a counterpart for
it be found. As an adjunct to the written word,
the picture as conceived by manuscript illuminators had lost its expressive validity just as the
designs of the enamelers and tapestry makers had
done.

The illuminated and handwritten book died
in the late Middle Ages; its place was taken by
the book printed from type and illustrated with
woodcuts such as *Poliphilus Dreaming* (Fig. 606).
The development of printing from movable
type was without doubt the most significant
single factor in the evolution of the Renaissance
and modern conceptions of life. The whole idea of
the handwritten book was based on the assumption of a limited privileged class—the clergy in
the early Middle Ages, the feudal aristocracy in
the later part—for each example was unique
and could be reproduced only by as long and
arduous a process as that by which the original
was created. The individualism of the Renaissance could not tolerate such a concept; once
the validity of individualism for all is established,
it follows that equal privileges must be enjoyed
by all, and the book, as a symbol of this, must
be available to all. Only by a mechanical means
of reproducing could this be realized; and the
development of the printing press supplied that

means. It has often been said that the printing press killed the Middle Ages; rather, the printing press is a symbol of the life that grew from the dust of an outworn and dying way of thinking, for only by such means could it find the expression it required.

The example of Renaissance illustrated printing in Fig. 606 is from a book published in Venice in 1499 by Aldus Manutius, one of the first to appreciate the potential humanistic value of the process. His avowed purpose of making the great literary classics available in the most perfect typographic form possible is indication of his more than mercenary motives; the result is a striking instance of a form developed in accordance with its inherent characteristics, for this is clearly a printed page and not a printed imitation of a manuscript like so many of the earliest incunabula—the Gutenberg Bible, for example—as the first printed books are sometimes called. The subject of the book was a long and involved semi-religious allegory called The Strife of Love in a Dream—*Hypnerotomachia Poliphili* in the original Latin title—which is hopelessly dull to modern readers. At the top of the page is a woodcut—the type of illustration first used in mechanical printing—and the beauty of the page lies in the completely satisfactory visual consistency in the linear effect of picture and type face, an identity of aesthetic character that in the mechanical process parallels that of the handwritten and hand-painted pages of the earlier manuscript books. Proportion and balance, variety and contrast are as carefully studied here as in any painting—as comprehensive an example as there is of the art of typography, the primary Renaissance contribution to the minor arts. A good case can be made for painting as the artistic medium most completely adapted to giving full expression to the Renaissance ideal. If this is true, the development of an illustrative style such as this can hardly be denied as being the most fruitful application of pictorial values to the decorative and complementary purposes that are an intrinsic quality of the minor arts.

Decorative wrought-iron forms are among the most attractive and individual contributions of the Renaissance to the minor arts. The utilitarian and ornamental function of this *Lantern* (Fig. 607) on the Strozzi Palace in Florence is a direct expression of the secular culture of the time in which a growing emphasis upon the owner's wealth and social position is apparent in the tendency toward more elaborate treatment of the palace exterior. The lantern holder is placed on the angle of the building, carried out from the wall on an ornamental bracket, the light source being inside the small enclosure formed by miniature pointed Gothic windows; the spreading spikes above enhance the scale of the holder and tie it into the architectural design of the building. The basic design is rather simple because the necessity of working quickly in the red-hot metal that the iron forger handles does not permit too detailed effects. These are achieved in the subsequent finishing and chasing

Strozzi Palace, Florence.

FIG. 607. Lantern,
Wrought Iron (1489).

Louvre, Paris.

FIG. 608.   Pisanello, Medal of John Palaeologos,
Bronze (1439).

of the form, but thanks to the effectiveness of the
large design they do not overshadow it. Gothic
and Renaissance forms are combined; the latter
predominate in the console brackets and the
base and cornice but, as noted, the little windows
of the lamphouse are Gothic. When this was
made, in 1489, the Renaissance style in architecture was well established in Italy (cf. Figs. 118,
119, 121). The occurrence of Gothic elements in
the design shows the general conservatism of
artisans and craftsmen who as a rule remain
faithful to outmoded styles after architects,
sculptors, and painters have adopted new ways.

Another characteristic type of Renaissance
metal work is the bronze medals and plaques of
the period. These were generally commemorative, and the artistic problem they presented
involved realizing an effective decorative relationship between the portrait bust of the
individual, the inscription identifying him or
stating the reason for making it, and the circular
field of the medallion. Because they are usually
on a rather small scale—rarely more than three
or four inches in diameter—the sculptural problem of the relief planes is also important. The
most famous Italian *médailleur* was Antonio Pisano,
usually called Pisanello (*ca.* 1395-1455), who is
also well known as one of the most important
painters of the early fifteenth century in northern
Italy. The *Medal of John Palaeologos* (Fig. 608)

*The Metropolitan Museum of Art,
Gift of J. Pierpont Morgan, 1917.*

FIG. 609.   Pendant, Gold, Enamel,
and Pearls (16th cent.).

was made by him to honor a dignitary of the court at Constantinople; it is a fine example of skill in relating the above elements as well as Pisanello's ability as a draftsman in reducing the profile head to a series of beautifully drawn lines that in few planes suggest the structure of the head and the character of the subject. This essentially Renaissance contribution to the minor arts began a practice that has continued down to modern times—the creation of commemorative medals and plaques.

Still another minor art in metal that was developed to an extraordinary degree in the Renaissance is gold and silver work. Again although only little of the vast amount in existence can be mentioned, Florence was a recognized center of the goldsmith's work in the fifteenth and sixteenth centuries and training in the ateliers of workers in precious metals was the lot of nearly every major sculptor and painter of the time, particularly in the earlier period. Their products were both ecclesiastic and secular, caskets and shrines for the former and jewelry for the latter being the most numerous classes. An example of the latter is a *Pendant* (Fig. 609) in the form of a mermaid in the Metropolitan Museum, which dates from the sixteenth century. It is somewhat larger than a comparable object today because its effect in the sumptuous costumes of the period had necessarily to be striking. Gems are usually of equal importance with the metal work and are cut much more simply than modern taste requires, being rounded over for the most part and cut in few facets. Pearls predominate in this Pendant; an irregularly shaped one—called "baroque"—is used for the body of the mermaid. Further examples of this branch of goldsmith work can be seen in many of the painted portraits of the time, especially those of the sixteenth century.

A name in the history of Renaissance goldsmith work that is known to many for reasons not specifically related to the visual arts is that of Benvenuto Cellini (1500-1571). His popular fame rests upon his *Autobiography*, in which the egotism that was his outstanding personal characteristic is the motivation for the telling of many picturesque incidents and the basis of much

Kunsthistorisches Museum, Vienna

FIG. 610.   Cellini, Salt Cellar of Francis I, Gold and Enamel (1543).

derogatory criticism of others. His achievement as a sculptor (Fig. 329) is considered elsewhere in this book, where it is characterized as reflecting his training and activity as a goldsmith. Of the many examples of goldsmith work attributed to him, including a jasper cup in a jeweled and enameled setting in the Metropolitan Museum, the only one that can certainly be considered his is *Salt Cellar of Francis I* (Fig. 610), in the Kunsthistorisches Museum in Vienna which he made in 1543. As an example of decoration, it is characterized by the same bravado that appears in the *Autobiography*. Technically it is the work of an accomplished manipulator of materials; there is incredibly fine detail in the bowls that hold the salt and pepper and their setting of waves, sea beings, and the like that accompany the nude figures of Neptune and a nereid on the top; similarly accomplished is the decorative gold work of figures and marine motives on the ebony base. But the forms are not original with Cellini, for he adapted them without change except in dimension from the powerful stone figures on Michelangelo's Medici Tombs (Figs. 147, 327); particularly flagrant is one whose

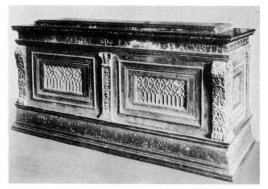

FIG. 611.   Table-Chest of Isotta
da Rimini, Oak (mid-15th cent.).

head is left unfinished in the gold work just as it
is on the tomb. This and the obvious disparity
between the monumentally conceived figures
and the relatively commonplace function of the
object illustrate the result of bringing into the
decorative arts a canon developed in a monumental medium, just as is the case with the
Renaissance enamel and tapestry discussed above
(Figs. 603, 604) and they indicate a debatable

conception of the essential character of the forms
that are copied and the one on which they are
used.

In no minor art is the character of the
Renaissance more clearly indicated than in its
furniture. The secularization that began in the
late Gothic period and was responsible for a perceptible increase in the utilitarian forms of
everyday living at that time was carried on and
amplified in the fifteenth and sixteenth centuries
and produced some of its most distinguished and
characterful results in Italy. An architectonic
form having been established in mediaeval furniture, it is not surprising to find it continued
but with a change in the character of the detail.
The *Table Chest of Isotta da Rimini* (Fig. 611), the
friend of Sigismondo Malatesta of Rimini who
was the humanist patron of Alberti in designing
the church of San Francesco (Fig. 119), combines
Gothic and Renaissance motives in a way
typical of the mid-fifteenth century. The treatment of the base as a pedestal rather than with
feet is characteristic, and its mouldings are essentially architectural, as is also true of the cornice-
like top; arabesqued pilasters and consoles divide
the side into panels filled with Gothic tracery.

FIG. 612.   Cassone, Oak (*ca.* 1475), from
the Strozzi Palace, Florence.

Davanzati Palace, Florence.

FIG. 613.   Bedroom.

The chest or *Cassone* (Fig. 612), dating *ca.* 1475, from the Strozzi Palace in Florence, now in the Metropolitan Museum in New York, is similarly organized in architectural terms with elaborate mouldings and heavy consoles, but the side panels are painted instead of being carved. This was a common practice in the fifteenth century when the most famous painters did not consider executing such decorations beneath them. Botticelli, to mention only one, is known to have painted a number of these *cassoni* with subjects from the myths of ancient Greece and Rome.

The somewhat sparse furniture of the Gothic room (Fig. 600) was increased in the Renaissance period, and although such an interior as the *Bedroom* (Fig. 613) in the Davanzati Palace in Florence might be considered somewhat bare by modern standards, it represents the

ideal of luxurious equipment of its time. The palace itself was built in the late fourteenth century, but the excellent restoration has brought into a harmonious relationship the products of later periods in the Renaissance. The heavy piece on the left wall in the illustration is called a *cassapanca*, from the Italian words *cassone* and *panca* which mean respectively chest and bench; it is a characteristic Florentine form and this example, with baroque figures in the cresting of the back, is of the seventeenth century. The bed, which dates from the sixteenth century, is typical in its massive proportions and the reduction of the ornament to a series of panels framed by mouldings; this is the more usual practice in the High Renaissance, replacing the painted or applied gesso (a kind of plaster or stucco) decoration that characterized the earlier furniture like the Strozzi *cassone*. These two pieces establish the

FIG. 614.   Chair, Wood and Leather
(late 16th cent.).

character of the room and although in different styles are quite in harmony as a result of two factors—the material of which they are made and their scale. The material, walnut, was used almost exclusively in Florence in the Renaissance; its close grain and texture permitted the most delicate carving and it has a very attractive color when waxed or oiled as these pieces are. The scale is rather large, but this again is in harmony with the size of the room and its relatively scanty furnishings: pieces of small size or delicate scale would not be particularly effective in such a setting. The chairs are of two types—a backed stool called a *sgabello* and the Renaissance form of the mediaeval folding type which is called a Dante chair; in both the seat is of wood with at best a thin pad of fabric or leather. Chairs upholstered in leather or textile (Fig. 614) are not found in any great number until the late sixteenth century, when the throne type previously limited to royalty or other persons of rank came into wider use.

Italian Renaissance furniture is distinguished

by local styles just as contemporary painting and architecture are. In northern Italy, for example, inlaying the object with other kinds and colors of wood was used extensively in Lombardy and Venice. A striking example of this method of woodworking, called *certosina* or *intarsia*, is seen in the decoration of an entire *Room from Gubbio* (Fig. 615) in the Metropolitan Museum in New York, which dates in all probability from the last half of the fifteenth century. The decorative scheme reflects the passionate interest of the period in perspective and foreshortening (cf. pages 364, 469); the craftsmen's skill in creating illusions of open cupboards or bookshelves, and of vast extension of the actual floor area by the converging lines of the patterns in the lower walls evidence a remarkable facility in the medium. These tricks do not themselves indicate good decorative sense, but continued study of the room soon makes them relatively subordinate because the fine feeling for the quality of the material itself is a much more lasting value. Contrasting textures and colors and the dull gleam of carefully treated surfaces are the outstanding elements in the effect of the room, which is one of the decorative masterpieces of the woodworker's art. The architectural membering by pilasters and panels and mouldings is in the current classicizing tradition.

One of the high points in glass blowing was reached in Venice in the sixteenth century where work in this medium, which the early Renaissance tended to use in an enamel technique, assumes a more independent character. Since its founding, the city had been a center for the glass industry in making colored cubes or *tesserae* for mosaics; it inherited from its Byzantine antecedents a taste for the deep and refulgent color that characterizes that process. In the later Renaissance, as the *Venetian Glasses* (Fig. 616) illustrate, this glassware tends toward forms of independent interest, depending upon brilliance, transparency, and color for effects in vessels that are essentially glasslike in shape and proportion. The crystalline bowls of these drinking glasses and the delicately curved stems could be the work only of a craftsman with an infallible sense of his material; each is intended for a specific

The Metropolitan Museum of Art, Rogers Fund, 1939.

FIG. 615.   Room from Gubbio, Intarsia (*ca.* 1470).

purpose that dictates its form. Later in the sixteenth and seventeenth centuries. Venetian glass is often more elaborate in form and decoration and reveals extraordinary dexterity in handling the glass, but it cannot vie with such examples as these in decorative quality.

Outside of Italy, the history of the minor arts during the Renaissance is a repetition of that in the major forms—the imposition of Italianate decorative detail on forms still structurally Gothic. A *Chair* (Fig. 617) of the sixteenth century in France is structurally much like the earlier Gothic example (Fig. 601). The ornament, however, is inspired by north Italian Renaissance models—cornice-like mouldings on the back and arms, and panels filled with arabesques of foliage,

The Metropolitan Museum of Art,
Bequest of Edward C. Moore, 1891.

FIG. 616.   Venetian Glasses
(16th cent.).

FIG. 617.   Chair, Oak
(16th cent.).

effectiveness of the *caquetoire* in both use and appearance in such circumstances.

In the fifteenth and sixteenth centuries, the distinction between decorative and useful categories in the minor arts largely determines the character of the results as a work of art. The decorative classification includes such things as the enamels, tapestries, and much of the gold work; the useful includes ironwork, glassware, and furniture. To sum up this discussion, in the decorative category there is a pronounced tendency to achieve effects imitating those of other arts, notably painting and sculpture, whereas in the useful arts the function of the object and its material control the design for the most part. The next chapter discusses the influence of new circumstances, differing uses, and, possibly more than ever, the availability of new materials that play their part in the ever-changing forms included under the general heading of the minor arts.

cherubs, and classic heads that are direct adaptations of the style current in the late fifteenth and early sixteenth centuries in Italy (cf. Figs. 122, 605). But it was in France that the practical conception of the chair as an object for easy and comfortable use began to develop, and the widest variety is found in the sixteenth and seventeenth centuries. Only one example can be shown, the light and easily portable form called *Caquetoire* (Fig. 618) or gossip chair—a name which illustrates alike the French genius for concise and illuminating terminology and the social conditions leading to its development; one has only to imagine an informally arranged group of the earlier stall chairs to perceive the greater

FIG. 618.   Caquetoire, Walnut
(16th cent.).

Detail of Fig. 643.

CHAPTER THIRTY-FIVE

The Minor Arts of the Post-Renaissance and Modern Periods

Drawing a hard and fast line between the Renaissance and Post-Renaissance periods in history is possibly even more arbitrary than establishing a distinction between the Middle Ages and the Renaissance, nor is it essential, except for expediency, to define the exact span of the modern age. But since some such distinction is necessary for clarity, the Post-Renaissance period is here considered as embracing the seventeenth and eighteenth centuries and the modern era as commencing in 1800. There is some justification for this division. The seventeenth century saw for the

FIG. 619.   Cabinet, Ebony, Ivory, and
Gilt Bronze (early 17th cent.).

Museum. This is true not only of the form which was extensively employed at that time in various types but also of the decoration. Legs and ornamental details that have been turned on a lathe now come into general use; the elaborate carved panels are similar in overall design to much contemporary work in Flanders which is directly comparable with the architecture of the period. The general effect of rich ornamentation combined with heavy and massive proportions is the touchstone of the style.

The Louis XIV period in the later seventeenth century contributes to the minor arts a style well in accord with the proud and opulent spirit of *Le Roi Soleil*. A *Cabinet* (Fig. 620) in the Louvre is the work of one of the leading designers of the period, A. C. Boulle, who is famous for the method of marquetry that his name is associated with. This consists of inlaying wooden panels, usually of ebony—considered to have an effect of magnificence lacking in the now outmoded oak or walnut—with a design formed by inset pieces of other woods or preferably of ivory, mother-of-pearl, bone,

first time a comprehensive political focus in the principle of absolutism that made France a world power whose essential character as a political entity was not modified until the closing years of the eighteenth. This modification was itself a manifestation of the changing philosophies of a world in which the Industrial Revolution was to stamp the nineteenth century with an unmistakable character that is only now being resolved into its basic and essential elements.

France's preeminence in seventeenth-century European culture is one of the fundamental facts in the history of the Post-Renaissance period, and this is recognized in selecting the majority of the examples of the period from French work. Furthermore, furniture supplies the the most consistently evolving forms, paralleling in character the architectural designs that provide a setting for them. Thus a characteristic example from the Louis XIII period in the early seventeenth century is a *Cabinet* (Fig. 619) of ebony, ivory, and gilt bronze in the Metropolitan

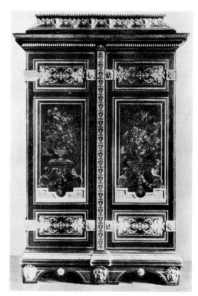

FIG. 620.   A. C. Boulle, Cabinet,
Inlaid Ebony (*ca.* 1650).

Montague House, London.

FIG. 621. A. C. Boulle, Desk,
Inlaid Ebony and Enamel
(late 17th cent.).

the effect was further enhanced by embroideries draped over it from caryatides that topped it by seven feet more. Less overwhelming in effect is a *Chair* (Fig. 622) in the Metropolitan Museum in New York; to be noted are the curving diagonal stretchers bracing the console legs, and the elaborate carving of the wooden portions. Tapestry, needlepoint, brocade, or velvet are the upholstery material; leather is seldom used.

One of the high points in the history of French decorative arts was reached in the eighteenth century in the reign of Louis XV and of Louis XVI. The pompous austerity that prevailed in the preceding century was considerably relaxed and the keynote of social usage was rather intimacy and refinement. The furniture and accessories of the period seen in the *Rice Room* (Fig. 623) in the Philadelphia Museum, present the varying aspects of both the earlier and later periods on a quite comprehensive scale. Dominating the room is the series of tapestries on the walls relating the story of Cupid and Psyche; these were designed by one of the most popular painters of the period, François Boucher (1703-1770), and executed between 1741 and 1770 in the famous Beauvais

brass, tortoise shell, and the like; brass or bronze appliqué work completes the very ostentatious effect. Elaborate though the decoration is, the structural form of the cabinet is relatively simple, with straight lines predominating and vigorous moulded profiles accenting top and base. Toward the end of the century this rectangular simplicity is modified as in the *Writing Desk* (Fig. 621) made by Boulle for Max Emanuel, Elector of Bavaria; the double curve in the legs —a form called cabriole—became very popular in the eighteenth century.

The chair is also important in the Louis XIV period; with strict protocol governing the seating at grand court functions, it is easy to see how essential it was that the occupant's social position be indicated by the shape and proportions of his chair. The throne of Louis XIV himself, for example, was of solid silver draped with crimson velvet; the back was eight feet high;

The Metropolitan Museum of Art,
Bequest of Benjamin Altman, 1913.

FIG. 622. Chair, Walnut and Tapestry
(late 17th cent.).

FIG. 623. The Rice Room.

tapestry factory in northern France. Like the Raphael tapestry (Fig. 604), the Boucher examples are primarily pictorial, but they are nonetheless extremely fine as decoration because the pictorial ideal is basically decorative. Particularly notable is the color scheme in rich but subdued tones well calculated to appear to advantage in the light from the crystal chandeliers.

Two styles and various materials are represented in the furniture of the room. The chairs with the delicately curved cabriole legs are in the Louis XV manner, upholstered in tapestry of flowers on a rose ground. The complex curves of the backs and arms in these examples is in the so-called rococo manner, a word derived from *rocaille* and *coquille* which mean respectively rock and shell; in this combination it refers to the irregularity of contour and surface that makes such furniture so effective a complement of the rococo interior (cf. Fig. 168). The Louis XVI style is seen in the tables and commodes with simpler lines in which rectangular and circular forms predominate and whose legs are straight though still richly carved. This tendency toward less complicated structural forms that characterizes the Louis XVI style in furniture in contrast to the Louis XV is one of the consequences of the increased interest in and knowledge of ancient classic art mentioned earlier; it will be noted in English forms, specifically in Robert Adams' designs in which it originated.

The tables and commodes in the Rice Room also illustrate a decorative technique developed by the cabinetmakers of the time; this is the applied ornament called ormolu, from the French *or-moulu*, meaning literally moulded gold. The piece was first cast in bronze and after being chiseled to the desired finish was covered with an amalgam of mercury and gold. It was then heated; this caused the mercury to vaporize and the gold to deposit on the bronze. The results thus produced were much more stable than when gold leaf was merely applied to the object; the fact that the mercury vapor freed in the process was usually fatal to the workmen was apparently not of much importance, in view of the widespread use of decorative motives thus created. In Fig. 623 the mounts on the tables and chests are ormolu—rosettes, medallions, and the like—and it was also employed for larger free forms like the candle sconces that flank the fireplace, and for clocks (cf. Fig. 621). On the furniture, its color and surface texture make it an admirable foil for the dark polished ebony which continued to be favored by the eighteenth-century cabinetmaker.

Other forms shown in the Rice Room illustration are the sculptured busts and the terracotta figurines on the chests in the room; Clodion was especially admired in the eighteenth century for his taste in such forms (cf. Fig. 337). Also to be noted are the various porcelain objects—chiefly vases and urns but also furniture mounts in the form of plaques. This is mostly Sèvres ware, made at the factory established at Vincennes in 1740 and granted royal patronage in 1745; here processes that created extraordinary charm of color and surface effects were developed during the eighteenth century. Their refinement and delicacy of form gives these porcelain objects a place in an ensemble which reveals throughout the elegance, gracefulness, and unerring taste that are characteristic of the "boudoir art" of the eighteenth century in France and that for sheer decorative effectiveness is equaled only with difficulty and certainly is unsurpassed in any other period or country.

England developed a furniture style in the eighteenth century that is no less distinguished than the French under Louis XV and XVI, although it is as individually English as the examples just discussed are French. Before that time, English furniture was more likely to be a variant or combination of continental styles, with Italian, Flemish, or French influences predominant according to the prevailing political tendencies. These are reflected in the names of the various modes—Tudor, Jacobean, William and Mary, Queen Anne, and the like—corresponding to the different monarchs or embodying the preferences resulting from their relationships to continental countries. One form deserves special notice because of its importance and popularity in the New World—the gate-leg table (cf. Fig. 180), which was evolved during the seventeenth century. The most characteristic examples date from Cromwell's time, ca. 1650; their massiveness is continued from sixteenth-century types but there is less decoration, the ornament being limited for the most part to the turned legs. Oak was most widely used in the Elizabethan and early Jacobean periods in the late sixteenth and early seventeenth centuries; walnut tended to replace it in the latter part of the seventeenth, in the William and Mary and Queen Anne styles.

In the Georgian period of the early eighteenth century there is continued assimilation of continental elements in English furniture—cabriole legs, ball-and-claw or hoof feet, masks, rock-and-shell motives derived from the baroque-rococo. A new material, mahogany, also appears; most of it imported from the New World, it was not much used by English cabinetmakers until the originally heavy import tax was lightened in 1733 and it became plentiful in England. Thereafter its strength, the ease of working it, and the attractive finish possible with it led to its supplanting native woods almost entirely by mid-eighteenth century. Mahogany is the wood most completely identified with the first of the famous eighteenth-century English furniture designers, Thomas Chippendale (1718-1779). In this connection, it should be stressed that other cabinetmakers than those most frequently mentioned in histories of furniture produced designs of great distinction. It was, in fact, by virtue of the general feeling for material combined with adaptation to purpose—the functionalism of design as against the chiefly decorative aims of the eighteenth-century French —that English furniture of the period as a whole achieved its undebatable preeminence. This quality combined with the now thoroughly assimilated stylistic elements of continental origin established the character of English furniture in this period.

Chippendale's primacy in the middle of the century is attributable to various factors. His designs show that he was a consummate master of his material; they are couched in terms that evolve naturally from pieces of wood that are joined to realize the utmost structural and decorative consistency. His influence became widespread through his publication in 1754 of *The Gentleman and Cabinet-Makers' Director* which included designs of inexhaustible variety— French, Gothic, Rococo, Chinese—but all conceived in essentially structural terms; it proved a fertile source of inspiration for the craftsmen and joiners of wood in England, Ireland, and the colonies. In this respect, the Chippendale style in the larger sense is comparable to the Georgian architectural style with which it is contemporary; it remains consistent and distinctive in spite of regional variations and even provincial awkwardness because it is expressed in terms of the material used.

An example of Chippendale's basic style, a mahogany *Full-Front Desk with Cabinet Top* (Fig. 624), reveals a fundamental simplicity of form

enlivened by the treatment of the surface and by well-chosen decorative details. These are never so prominent as to obscure the main structural lines, however; the impression of something solid and well made that can stand use is always foremost in a well-designed Chippendale piece. Although the fact that many of his designs were executed in collaboration with architects may have had something to do with this, his ability to create forms that look solid and graceful at the same time and are also easy and comfortable to use is his particular and personal distinction. He designed innumerable varieties of *Chairs* (Fig. 625)—ribbon-back, Gothic, Chinese—whatever the client's taste dictated but all having an unfailing quality that is his own. For example, whatever the pattern of the splat in the open back, it is always firmly fixed at the top and bottom; the legs, whether straight or subtly curved and with elaborate carving, rest solidly on the floor and give strong

FIG. 624. Chippendale, Full-Front Desk with Cabinet Top, Mahogany (*ca.* 1760).

Center: *The Metropolitan Museum of Art, Kennedy Fund, 1918.*
Right: *The Metropolitan Museum of Art, Bequest of John L. Cadwalader, 1914.*

FIG. 625. Chippendale, Chairs, Mahogany (*ca.* 1760).

support to the seat. In the more elaborately carved forms, the close texture of the mahogany makes possible a refinement of motive and a minuteness of scale that are essentially rococo in spirit, regardless of the specific character of the ornament.

One of the most novel features of eighteenth-century European style in the decorative arts is the use of Oriental themes and forms. This was a direct outcome of the opening of commercial relationships with the Far East (cf. pages 196-197) late in the seventeenth century and their exploitation in the following century that was systematized in the formation of the East India Company in 1708. This in itself might not have been sufficient to account for the *chinoiseries* and *singeries*—decorative patterns of pagodas, bamboo trees, people in Chinese costumes, and monkeys—that appear so frequently in French interiors of the time, nor could it entirely explain Sir William Chambers' constructing, about 1760, a Chinese pagoda in Kew Gardens in London, had there not existed a taste for the strange and exotic that was by way of being a reaction against the solemn and pompous dignity of the seventeenth-century manner. It is thus as another aspect of the refined frivolity of the rococo that Chippendale's Chinese designs must be considered; in his chairs the Oriental touch may be no more than a latticework. His *"Chinese"* Bed (Fig. 626) is more consciously derivative, however, with its curved canopy ending in flying dragons, the lattice back, and an elaborate decorative scheme in lacquer on the

So. Kensington Museum, London.

FIG. 626. Chippendale, "Chinese" Bed, Lacquer (*ca.* 1760).

FIG. 627.   Robert Adam, Chairs and Screen,
Painted Wood and Tapestry (1767).

posts and top. Even though this is more of a curiosity than anything else, it nonetheless quite completely embodies one aspect of the taste at the time.

Taste as a factor in the evolution of style accounts for the popularity later in the eighteenth century in England of the work of the Adam brothers (Robert, 1728-1792, and James, 1730-1794), who were among the most prominent figures in English architecture of their time (cf. pages 200-202). On his return to England in 1758 after four years of travel and study in Italy, Robert was so filled with enthusiasm for the arts of ancient Rome as newly revealed in the excavation of Herculaneum that the delicate classicizing style he developed in architecture (Fig. 173) and the decorative arts soon replaced in popularity both the Chippendale of the earlier eighteenth century and the baroque-rococo in architecture. A similar development for similar reasons has been mentioned in connection with the change from Louis XV to Louis XVI style in France. In England the difference is possibly even more pro-

nounced, however, because it involved a new canon of proportion and new materials as well as different formal qualities. The fact that the Adams were primarily architects and decorators rather than cabinetmakers underlies their conception of the interior as a consciously composed ensemble in which the design of furniture, lamps, hangings, carpets, and wall decorations is controlled by a single stylistic idiom—classic and Pompeiian in the majority of their designs. The unity of effect is clear, even though it differs from the eighteenth-century French interior already discussed (Fig. 623), in which what might be called the inherent and traditional stylistic sense of a number of craftsmen has produced a formal harmony, whereas the English ensemble is the result of a consciously contrived, not to say academic uniformity of detail.

Comparison of the Adam style in furniture, as exemplified in the *Chairs and Screen* (Fig. 627), with the earlier Chippendale reveals a different stylistic sense. The irregularity of detail and elaboration of form—rococo elements in the

FIG. 628. Wedgwood Ware (1780-1790).

earlier style—have given way to simplicity of basic shape and regularity of individual motives in the Adam. Tapestry backs, for example, replace the open splats, and the decorative motives are often classic mythological subjects. Mahogany is replaced by satinwood or harewood and painted decoration is often used, the colors being soft pastel shades that may be repeated in the walls of the room and in the accessory ceramic objects that are a characteristic detail of an Adam interior (Fig. 173). These were often based on Neo-classic designs by leading artists of the time and were made at the Wedgwood factory which was founded to supply objects of this type in England as the Sèvres plant did in France. Jars and vases and plaques to be set into the walls or on mantelpieces, such as the *Wedgwood Ware* in Fig. 628, are among the most characteristic products of this firm, the decoration being based for the most part on the refined and delicate classic style which the excavations of Pompeii and Herculaneum were then revealing and which were extraordinarily popular.

The Adam version of classic style is the basis of the two most generally accepted modes in late eighteenth-century furniture in England— Hepplewhite and Sheraton. The names are those of cabinetmakers who, like Chippendale, published books of furniture designs that had wide influence. George Hepplewhite collaborated with the Adam brothers on many of their designs and the work with which his own name is associated, such as the *Chair* in Fig. 629, represents an individual modification of their taste. Although he designed all types of furniture, chairs are most numerous in his published designs; the one shown in the figure is characteristic. The legs are rather sturdy, straight or very slightly curved and fluted or inlaid. The backs, however give an effect of fragility, with sweeping curves predominating in heart or shield shapes unsupported at the base. This specific point of contrast with Chippendale's style indicates a differing conception of design that is not without some significance. Chippendale is still the craftsman for whom function is primary and decorative effect subordinate; Hepplewhite's attitude, when carried to its logical conclusion, reduces the

FIG. 629.   Hepplewhite, Chair,
Satinwood (late 18th cent.).

chair to a decorative accessory, for the frailty of his designs is actual as well as seeming. Thomas Sheraton (1750-1806) also reflects the classic taste of the Adams in his designs, but by emphasizing straight lines and rectangular forms, he achieves somewhat more substantial effects than are found in Hepplewhite's work. His *Chairs* (Fig. 630), for example, have open splat backs with vases and lyres as motives, but a bottom rail makes them sturdier than Hepplewhite's. A *Commode* (Fig. 631), a type of cabinet evolved in England in the eighteenth century, is characteristic of his style in its simple lines, curving front, and the inlay of contrasting woods in harewood panels.

    In the English colonies in the New World, the familiar pattern of adapting and modifying the basic types of the mother country occurs in the minor arts as in architecture and painting. In discussing colonial architecture we pointed out that inasmuch as the first settlers in New England were from the lower middle classes in England, their architecture was not in the elaborate classicizing forms of Inigo Jones' Palladian palaces or Christopher Wren's baroque churches but were rather in the vernacular idiom of frame and fill construction, using wood and sparing of ornament. The furniture of the early Colonial period in the seventeenth century is of like character. The interior of the Capen House (Fig. 180), built at Topsfield, Mass., in 1683, has been

restored with furnishings of its period. Although in some respects it was more elaborate than most houses of the time, its furnishing is probably no more so than many others. Prominent is the gate-leg table with turned legs evolved in the mid-seventeenth century in England. In the background is a low heavy chest with turned feet and simple paneling on the front and ends; if less elaborately decorated than English chests of the late sixteenth century, the proportions are similar. The chairs are of the so-called ladder-back type in which horizontal slats replace the splats of the eighteenth-century English chairs; in these, the slats are flat instead of being turned or carved as in some earlier examples. The form as it appears here is still in part the product of turning, the posts and stretchers having been made in this way. Turning on a lathe as the principal technical method is also characteristic of the *Windsor Chair* (Fig. 632) which is distinguished by legs pegged into the wood or rush seat and a back of turned spindles in a carved or bent-wood frame. This type of chair was apparently used first in the vicinity of Windsor Castle in England (whence the name) about 1720; the earliest American examples date from after 1725. It is basically a woodworker's rather than a cabinetmaker's form and this is probably the reason for its considerable development in the

FIG. 630.   Sheraton, Chairs, Mahogany
(late 18th cent.).

colonies, its ease of manufacture, lightness, comfort, and variety of forms making it very popular. Being easily available, pine, maple, and birch were extensively employed in American furniture in the seventeenth century, as well as the traditional English oak. The wood, regardless of type, was often left unfinished after being smoothed, to acquire polish and color in normal use.

American furniture in the eighteenth century is the product of native craftsmen with highly developed manual skill who still worked in the same formal tradition as their English contemporaries, often with the same books and designs. Hence it is not surprising to find an identical sequence of styles; it is possible to speak of Chippendale and Sheraton styles in American furniture as in English, for the general characteristics are much the same. There is even a general parallel in the use of different materials at various times, for mahogany tends to replace oak and walnut in colonial furniture in the eighteenth century as it did in English products. There are differences, however, in the American tradition. The Chippendale style, for example, is popular for a longer period here and the eighteenth-century classicizing tendencies are not so pronounced. Certain types, moreover, continue to be used in the Colonies after they disappear in England, a case in point being the high chest which lost favor in England after the first quarter of the eighteenth century, the lower commode (Fig. 631) being preferred. The chest has various forms in colonial furniture, the most notable being the highboy which has cabriole legs of such height as to resemble a stand on which the chest apparently is placed, and the *Block-Front Chest-on-Chest* (Fig. 633) whose form is well described by the name. Though both these forms have English precedents, those developed in the Colonies are uniquely American. In the chest-on-chest that is illustrated there is a regional distinction in the block front, the term applied to the alternate recessed and protruding paneling on the lower part. The block front was a product of Rhode Island and was not made in other Colonies, which suggests, as is the case, that in furniture as in architecture in the eighteenth

The Metropolitan Museum of Art,
Gift of Alexander Smith Cochran, 1911.

FIG. 631.   Sheraton, Commode,
Inlaid Harewood (*ca.* 1800).

century there were local schools and styles within the larger framework of the period style as a whole.

Among the local styles in American furniture in this century, the style that developed in Philadelphia was one of the most distinguished. Various circumstances contributed to this; a large and prosperous merchant population with aspirations toward social position was one of the most important. Strong local pride was another factor responsible for the prevalence of the term "Philadelphia Chippendale" as a definite style in furniture; this also provides a clue to its formal quality. Upward of two dozen cabinetmakers are known who labeled their work as made in Philadelphia. A *Bedroom* (Fig. 634) in the fine Georgian house called Mount Pleasant, built on the Schuylkill River in what is now Fairmount Park in Philadelphia by Captain John MacPherson in 1761, contains a number of such pieces. The chest-on-chest in the background is believed to be the work of Jonathan Gostelowe (1744/5-1795); its cabriole feet, scroll pediment with latticework and flowered urn, and the elaborate brass mounts are typical details of Philadelphia Chippendale. It is mahogany, whereas the chest of drawers with the bowed front in the foreground is of walnut but in the same style; a label indicates that it also was made by Gostelowe. The two chairs in the room are likewise Philadelphia Chippendale; the one by the bed has a simplified "Gothic" back, the other has a very elaborate lyre splat. The four-poster bed with its needlework hangings and spread and the small three-legged table are consistent with the other pieces. Also in the Philadelphia style is the furnishing of the room from the Powel House in the Metropolitan Museum (Fig. 183), characterized by the elaborate carving on the cabriole legs of the chairs and tables. The sofa is less ornate, but its general lines and massive proportions are in the best colonial Chippendale tradition. Even the wall paper indicates the interest in Chippendale's style, for the Chinese motives reflect the same decorative taste that figures in some of his furniture designs, though not in any of the examples shown here.

Further details in the Powel room are of interest as representing the minor arts of eighteenth-century America. The elaborate carving of the mantelpiece and the frame on the chimney breast with its broken pediment reveal the same nicety of detail and vigor of line that characterize the decoration of the furniture. The crystal chandelier or luster and the little pottery figures on the mantel were probably imported from Europe but the taste they reveal parallels that of contemporary France and England. The silverware, on the other hand, is colonial and is a reminder of the flourishing trade in the manufacture and sale of such objects carried on in the New World in the eighteenth century. It is of historical as well as artistic interest that Paul Revere (cf. Fig. 531) was a silversmith of great renown; pieces by him, such as the *Urn-Shaped Silver* (Fig. 635), are in demand as much for their formal quality as for their associations. They are less ornate as a rule than contemporary European work but reveal to an extraordinary degree the

The Metropolitan Museum of Art, Gift of Mrs. Russell Sage, 1909.

FIG. 632. Windsor Chair, Pine (mid-18th cent.).

Henry Francis du Pont Winterthur Museum.

FIG. 633. Block-Front Chest-on-Chest, Mahogany (1765-1780).

Mount Pleasant, Philadelphia.

FIG. 634.   Bedroom (late 18th cent.).

unerring instinct of a master in his chosen field —the craftsman's sense of his material. Of similar character is another of the famed products of the century in American minor arts—the *Glassware* (Fig. 636) produced by Heinrich Wilhelm Stiegel at Mannheim in Pennsylvania. Their brilliant colors and occasional etched or painted designs are effective complements to their shapes which so clearly reveal the character of the substance of which they are made.

The craftsman's inherent sense of material was mentioned earlier in discussing the quality of Chippendale's furniture designs—the feeling for wood and its intrinsic properties that characterizes his most distinctive work. It is this characteristic that makes the Colonial adaptations

of his work as distinguished as the originals, for they were made by men of the same temperament who responded to the qualities described with intuitive perception. This, as well as the normal lag always apparent in comparisons of the cultural phenomena of mother country and colony, accounts for the belated appearance of the refined classicism of the Adams, of Hepplewhite and Sheraton, in the minor arts of the New World—in which a conscious aesthetic is coequal with the craftsman's feeling that was dominant in the earlier Chippendale period in both England and the colonies. A *Secretary-Bookcase* (Fig. 637) of mahogany and inlaid satinwood made in Philadelphia about 1790 has both Hepplewhite and Sheraton characteristics, a

chests and case pieces of this period were generally inlaid instead of being carved as was the earlier practice.

In the post-Revolutionary development in American furniture represented by this secretary-bookcase the outstanding characteristic is gracefulness of line and surface combined with delicacy of proportion and a pleasing sense of the decorative quality of materials. A high level of taste still prevailed in the cabinetmaker's craft, and its practitioners include some of America's outstanding designers—notably Samuel McIntire, "the woodcarver of Salem," Charles Bulfinch, and Robert Wellford. Works by men of their caliber have as great distinction as the best English furniture of the period. Duncan Phyfe (1768-1854) developed an adaptation of the classicizing Sheraton manner which is one of the most distinguished furniture styles of the period in either Europe or America. His shop was established in New York late in the eighteenth century

*The Metropolitan Museum of Art,
Bequest of A. T. Clearwater, 1933.*

FIG. 635.   Paul Revere, Urn-Shaped
Silver (*ca.* 1800).

Right: *The Metropolitan Museum of Art,
Gift of Mrs. Charles E. Atwood, 1924.*

FIG. 636.   Stiegel, Glassware
(late 18th cent.).

not uncommon mixture in furniture of the late eighteenth century in America because the handbooks of the various current English styles were used indiscriminately. In this piece, the general rectangularity of form and the pattern of the leaded glass in the bookcase doors are Hepplewhite, whereas the inlaid ornament of the lower part is more in the Sheraton manner although

Philadelphia Museum of Art.

FIG. 637.   Secretary-Bookcase,
Inlaid Mahogany (*ca.* 1790).

FIG. 638.   The Duncan Phyfe Room
(early 19th cent.).

and his most effective designs date from then and the first years of the nineteenth. *The Duncan Phyfe Room* (Fig. 638), *ca.* 1800, has been furnished with pieces from this period. The table is of the pedestal type which Phyfe frequently used, and the chairs and benches have the latticework and curved patterns inspired by Sheraton but given an individual quality all their own. In all these pieces, whether solid or veneered, the wood is important in the design; its beauty, accented by delicate carving or reeding appropriate in scale to the lightness of the forms. The subtle curves of the legs are well calculated to create the sense of elastic support

desired in this type of form. The upholstery textiles are soft in color as befits the impression of refinement and good taste throughout.

To the cabinetmakers of the later eighteenth century, the classic was a source of inspiration; to those of the early nineteenth century, it was a style to be copied. A mere glance at the *Cabinet* (Fig. 639) designed by Geoffroy Lemarchand in the Musée des Arts décoratifs in Paris shows how the entire concept of form has changed from one that combines a feeling for material with a taste for classic decorative motives to one that seeks to reproduce an effect first achieved in far different ways. For the massiveness

FIG. 639. Lemarchand, Cabinet,
Mahogany and Ormolu
(early 19th cent.).

work, the name being that of a character in a German comic weekly who was the personification of bourgeois tastelessness. Even though this general characterization does not do justice to an occasional piece whose sturdy simplicity gives some aesthetic pleasure, it is applicable to the greater part of the furniture of the period.

The examples of eighteenth-century furniture thus far considered were created by master designers working in cosmopolitan centers for aristocratic patrons. In the provinces—the outlying or rural district—such magnificent and ostentatious forms were seldom known; moreover, the cost of furniture by the famous cabinetmakers was too great for the average man. Yet from such circumstances as these have come many attractive pieces. French provincial furniture of the seventeenth and eighteenth centuries has a character all its own that results from the assimilation and modification of the more sophisticated ideas of Parisian cabinetmakers to local and regional tastes; the work of many an anonymous artisan is infused with the craftsman's sense of material and the intuitive feeling for distinguished design that are the key note of all effective forms in the minor arts. An example of such work in the American colonies is the *Painted Chest* (Fig. 640) made in eastern Pennsylvania in the eighteenth century. The wood is usually what is available—pine in this case—and it is worked by the simplest methods; the panels in the example illustrated are dovetailed at the angles. A simple carved decoration was sometimes used, but painting was more usual; the motives are varied—flowers, people, animals, and the like—treated with a naïve simplicity that seldom ventures beyond symmetry as the basic principle of design. The colors are simple too. These chests have a charm that is immediately sensed; it results in no small degree from the flat stylization that makes such patterns as these so fitting as decorative adjuncts of the object.

The minor arts of the eighteenth century are products of the last great period of hand craftsmanship, in which the artisan was guided as much by a feeling for his medium as by anything else. Without invalidating this general

of Lemarchand's Empire piece is the result of trying to reproduce in wood the heaviness of stone forms, in contrast with the massiveness intrinsic in Chippendale's methods of joining and construction. Other than this, the supposedly classic motives—lions' heads, busts, cherubs, nude goddesses, and various foliate forms, in gilded appliqué—show how completely the furniture designer's inspiration is controlled by the archaeologist's vision rather than by functional requirement or decorative fitness of form to material. Occasionally the earlier grace of line and form appears, as in the chaise longue in David's portrait of Madame Récamier, but uninspired heaviness and archaeological literalness are the usual order of the day. Even Duncan Phyfe's later work shows him sharing the general trend toward graceless heaviness; these pieces were popularly known as "Butcher's furniture." The name Biedermeier is often used broadly to mean early nineteenth-century furniture of this type; it is more specifically applied to the Empire style in Germany which was distinguished chiefly by its simplification of the decoration on French

Philadelphia Museum of Art.

FIG. 640.   Painted Chest (18th cent.).

statement, however it must be pointed out that toward the end of the period an ideal of judgment appeared that was not essentially artistic but rather was aesthetic in a dogmatic way; associative values and symbolic implications were stressed, rather than line and mass and texture and color. This shift in taste is one of the significant factors in the background of the minor arts in the nineteenth century. Another was the development of mechanical processes as aids to carving, weaving, painted decoration, and the like, the beginning of the mass production that was the contribution of the Industrial Age to modern culture. Another manifestation of this new era was the appearance of a type of patronage that was unknown or at most had very limited influence in preceding periods—the middle-class industrial worker who had sufficient income even at the low wages paid, to buy what he needed instead of making it himself. Thus the fundamental factors influencing nineteenth-century style in furniture, chinaware, decorative objects, and the like, are the general change in taste, the appearance of so large a demand for such things that it could not possibly be satisfied by traditional handicraft processes, and the development of mechanical methods of production to meet this need.

The mid-nineteenth century ideal in the minor arts had its most comprehensive statement in the displays in the Great Exhibition in London's Crystal Palace (Fig. 196) in 1851. This was one of the first of the expositions held at frequent intervals from the middle of the century to the present. They are another characteristic manifestation of the increasingly industrialized culture of the West, in seeking to emphasize the greatness of past achievement and pointing the way to further conquests. Albert, Prince Regent of England, who was primarily responsible for the idea of the Crystal Palace, stated that its purpose was to give "a living picture of the point of development at which mankind had arrived, and a new starting point from which all nations will be able to direct their future exertions." That this starting point was to be the machine was quickly apparent, for the crowds that thronged the Exhibition from its opening soon showed marked preference for the mechanical displays over all the others and the objects which attracted most attention were those produced by machine processes. One was a papier-mâché chair called *The Day Dreamer* (Fig. 641), described as follows in the official catalogue: "The chair is decorated at the top with two winged thoughts—the one with bird-like pinions and crowned with roses representing happy and joyous dreams, the other with leathern bat-like wings, unpleasant and troublesome ones. Behind is displayed Hope under the figure of the rising sun. . . ." The popular appeal of such an object was twofold. Its "symbolism" delighted an age that enjoyed sentimentality, and its material, being synthetic rather than natural, represented a triumph of mechanical ingenuity and also permitted unlimited reproduction. Such formal qualities as it has are exaggerations of the classicizing ornament of the eighteenth century; a leaf is not merely a decorative adjunct to the chair leg as it would be in Chippendale's design, it is actually the leg.

Textile designs were an important feature in the Exhibition because they represented one of the key industries of nineteenth-century industrial England. A *Tapestry Carpet* (Fig. 642), one of the many widely acclaimed achievements in this field, illustrates, like the chair, its designers' dependence for ideas on the craftsmen of the preceding century. In spite of all the mechanical aids available, the creators of this design tried only to reproduce the patterns of earlier similar objects, possibly one like that in the eighteenth-century French room shown in Fig. 623. But the difference in effect is unmistakable; the leaf patterns that lie flat in the plane of the carpet in the Rice Room and make it an admirable floor covering and ornament are treated by the nineteenth-century designer so naturalistically with modeling shadows and perspective foreshortening, as to create an illusion of actual stems and blossoms underfoot. The eighteenth-century patterns are also realistic; but in creating them on the loom the craftsman's sense of style and the minute individual variations in each recurrence of the motive produce something that is both decorative and vigorous, whereas the mechanically identical forms of the nineteenth-century carpet are stereotyped and dead. Neither the type of material nor the purpose of the object is a factor in the design—although both are absolutely fundamental considerations in any creative approach to the minor arts.

Prevalent as were the ideals implicit in the papier-mâché chair and the carpet during the nineteenth century, there were also certain more reassuring developments. The designs of John

H. Belter, an American cabinetmaker who worked in New York around 1850, have the overornate and naturalistic decoration that connotes Victorian taste, but his craftsmanship is excellent and his use of wood is sound. Sir Charles Eastlake attempted to establish a foundation for popular taste in his book, *Hints on Household Taste*, published in England in 1870 and reprinted widely in the United States; he hoped to adapt the then widely popular mediaeval forms to machine production by simplifying them. However praiseworthy his intentions, they were so distorted in the realization that his name is practically synonymous with the most completely unimaginative taste of the Victorian age. But it was such attitudes as his in attempting to substitute the machine for the craftsman simply to increase the production of traditional forms that were primarily responsible for a phenomenon in the minor arts of the nineteenth century which, although more or less isolated and with little immediate influence, is nonetheless of great importance—the Arts and Crafts Movement sponsored by William Morris (1834-1896).

The Arts and Crafts Movement was the outcome of an attitude that could have existed only in nineteenth-century England. There was first

FIG. 641. The "Day Dreamer," Papier-Mâché, Great Exhibition of 1851.

of all a feeling of aesthetic disgust for the cheap, shoddy, machine-produced objects that revealed lack of taste and of a genuine craft tradition. Second, there was a moral objection to those qualities as expressive of a brutal and debased philosophy that was a direct result of the industrialization of western culture by the machine, and the consequent emphasis on purely mercenary and materialistic values. Third, there was the now strongly ingrained habit of historical criticism that led men to turn for inspiration to other times when a more desirable way of thinking produced more beautiful forms. Because of these various considerations, William Morris found it impossible to expect his bride to live in the "immoral" atmosphere of a house built and furnished in the prevailing taste of the time; therefore he turned to the art of the Middle Ages as the sort of thing produced by men inspired by lofty and elevated ideals and for that reason, according to him, beautiful. With a group of associates and sympathizers who held similar ideals and were known as the Pre-Raphaelite Brotherhood, he attempted to bring about a return to the mediaeval tradition of fine handicraft motivated by considerations of taste that had no part in the industrial output of his time. An example of the products of his attitude is the *"Daisy" Wallpaper* (Fig. 643), one of many patterns that he designed. Morris had learned the lesson taught by mediaeval tapestries (Fig. 597) and made his pattern lie flat on the wall; it is stylized rather than naturalistic, clear and soft in color, light and delicate in drawing and tone. The motives are based on the foliate decoration of mediaeval illuminated manuscripts, and it was blocked and tinted by hand. The reforms Morris attempted are evident in other fields as well; the chair he designed and gave his name to is a frame made by simple joinery that supports loose cushions for seat and back; intended for comfort rather than display, it is noteworthy for its solid construction. Typography also attracted his attention; the hand-set pages of books printed at the Kelmscott Press have much the same brilliance of tone and effective relationship of type face and illustration as the fifteenth-century incunabula (Fig. 606) that were his models.

FIG. 642. Tapestry Carpet,
Velvet Pile, Great Exhibition of 1851.

Basic to Morris' conception of the arts was the principle that only hand craft could have aesthetic character. His opposition to the machine amounted to a phobia—a feeling that was no doubt amply justified by the machine products of his age but which he was concerned with only superficially since he condemned the tool rather than the inspiration that guided it. As the voice of one crying in the wilderness of tastelessness and mercenary values, his example was invaluable, because he kept alive the principle of formal values of line and mass and color as being essential and primary in the applied arts. But it

FIG. 643. William Morris, "Daisy" Wallpaper (late 19th cent.).

appropriate to its methods are the basis of modern applied arts. Realization of this fact is evident in various trends that developed toward the close of the nineteenth century in which a new conception of ornament is apparent. It was only natural that attempts to reform the aesthetic abuses of the mid-century undisciplined industrialism should be directed first toward this end, for it was in the stereotyped machine versions of traditional decorative forms that the limitations of mechanical processes were most obvious. Hence in the style called *Art Nouveau*, conceived by Henry van de Velde (1863-1939), there is no reference to traditional ornamental motives of acanthus leaves, ball and claw feet, pediments and scrolls, and the like. Instead, as shown in the *Art Nouveau Interior* (Fig. 644), the prevailing characteristic is the complex, subtly curved contour line that is the earmark of the style. This evolved from van de Velde's study and analysis of the functional nature of the form itself which he attempts to visualize in the type of curve in the design—slight and easy, for example, in members that support, and more vigorous and pronounced in those that provide a transition from one structural element to another. This is combined with a feeling for decorative color relationships in other elements in the room that derives from van de Velde's early training as a painter. The aesthetic unity of

was of value primarily historically, for his blind opposition to the creative possibilities of the machine and his attempt to revive the moribund handicraft tradition were in effect nothing more than a refusal to live in his own time and an effort to turn back the hands of the clock to an age forever gone.

Acceptance of the machine and of designs

FIG. 644. Van de Velde, Art Nouveau Interior (1906).

an interior by him is obvious, but it is also clear that it is often too important. To live constantly in a work of art is as artificial as living in surroundings without any formal character is degrading; overemphasis on aesthetic value is scant compensation for lack of comfort. In the hands of others, moreover, particularly when *Art Nouveau* forms went into industrial production, the subjective character of the style became apparent, for as long as a style is based on a decorative ideal there can be little structural foundation on which to work. The excesses to which *Art Nouveau* was carried in commercial exploitation cannot obscure the vital character of van de Velde's original work, but they also make clear the reason for its short life and ultimate discredit.

William Morris' Arts and Crafts Movement was one of van de Velde's inspirations in developing a new style; and if he was unable because of historical circumstance to make the machine an element in it, he sensed the weakness of Morris' theory and opened the way for further achievement by others. Publicizing that theory in Europe, for example, stimulated an interest in the applied arts and a revival of handicraft that were destined to make significant contributions in the early twentieth century. The *Deutsche Werkbund* was a craft organization founded in 1907; its avowed purpose was "to ennoble industrial labor through the cooperation of art, industry and handicraft." By virtue of the sincere idealism and intelligence of its members, it soon began to have some influence on German industrial design. From the beginning, the machine and its potentialities were accepted as basic factors, an attitude one of its members summed up as follows: "There is no fixed boundary line between tool and machine. Work of a high standard can be created with tools or with machines, as soon as man has mastered the machine and made it a tool. It is not the machines in themselves that make work inferior, but our inability to use them properly." This idea is expressed even more succinctly in the title of a paper by Frank Lloyd Wright in 1903—"The Art and Craft of the Machine"— then and for many years to come a lone figure

preaching the gospel of integrity in the artistic wilderness that was the United States early in the twentieth century.

The most casual survey of contemporary minor arts indicates the infinite variety in this category—greater, possibly, than at any other time in the history of western culture. The variety is qualitative as well as quantitative, ranging from superlatively fine design to the dullest and most stereotyped monotony. This is because of the circumstances controlling the creation of furniture and glassware and jewelry and hangings and all the myriad types that might be included—the extraordinary demands of an ever-increasing bourgeois class and their satisfaction by objects mass-produced for commercial profit for the most part but with growing realization of the possibility and necessity for producing objects of formal character and distinction even under such conditions. Although even a limited general examination of contemporary minor art is beyond this discussion, we must note what has without doubt been the most vital influence in shaping the significant trends therein since the First World War—the principles and practices of the Bauhaus.

FIG. 645. Martha Erps,
Knotted Wool Tapestry (1924).

FIG. 646.   Brandt, Coffee and Tea Pots, Metal (1926).

The Bauhaus idea stemmed originally from the attempt by the *Deutsche Werkbund* to synthesize "machine style" with the "arts and crafts" concept. It was formulated first at the Academy of Arts and Crafts in Weimar in Germany when Walter Gropius became director of that school in 1919 with the intention of making it a "consulting art center for industry and the trades." The name of the school was then changed to Bauhaus—its literal meaning is the "house of building"—and its aims and principles were defined. These were to provide designs for objects needed in modern living, instruction in

their creation to be given by teachers who ideally would be both artists and craftsmen, that is, have a sense of both formal character and the materials employed. It was with this in mind that many of the foremost artists of the time—architects, sculptors, and painters—as well as leading practitioners of the practical arts were on the Bauhaus staff in the early 1920's, making it a focal point of the progressive trends in the creative formal thought of the period. In 1925 the Bauhaus was moved from Weimar to Dessau; it was housed in buildings especially designed for it by Gropius. Among them was the famous workshop (Fig. 211), an outstanding example of the International Style of the period following World War I, in which designs created by students at the school underwent the ultimate test of determining their adaptability to mass production.

Stated briefly, the Bauhaus method involved concurrent instruction in crafts and in form so that when the material characteristics of a substance were being investigated, the form in which those physical properties could best be utilized was also being determined. Thus one preliminary to creating a *Knotted Wool Tapestry* (Fig. 645) involved handling and manipulating the yarn until the designer was thoroughly, almost instinctively, conversant with its tensile strength, texture, etc. Similarly the designer of the *Coffee and Tea Pots* (Fig. 646) worked with metal to acquire a feeling for it as material, and also the various processes of forming and shaping it. This was accompanied by more theoretical

Collection, The Museum of Modern Art, New York, Gift of Herbert Bayer.

FIG. 647.   Breuer, Tubular Metal Chair (1925).

studies concerning the use to which the objects were to be put, the form which was best suited for that use, and the abstract qualities of design which would give that form its maximum character as a work of art. The similarity of the tapestry to a painting of the type represented by Juan Gris' composition (Fig. 523) is considerable. The similarity illustrates the basic theory of the Bauhaus that formal character is an immutable quality regardless of the medium; a theory in accordance with the idea that designing such forms concerns the painter as much as the craftsman in textile. Likewise the Tea and Coffee Pots and the metal-framed building of the Bauhaus itself have more in common than the use of comparable materials, for the primary concern in each case is structural appropriateness.

The influence of Bauhaus ideas and products since the mid-1920's has been widespread. It is recognizable in many fields—household objects and accessories, textile design, ceramics, to mention some in which the original character of Bauhaus ideas has often been obscured in products that ape the superficial character of the originals without perceiving the motivation. But in other fields, notably typography whose modern phase may in a certain sense be said to date from the developments in the Bauhaus, and in furniture design, later work has unequivocally been directed along lines clearly defined by Bauhaus concepts. It was an instructor at the Bauhaus, Marcel Breuer, who designed the first *Tubular Metal Chair* (Fig. 647) in 1925, using the material not as a substitute for traditional

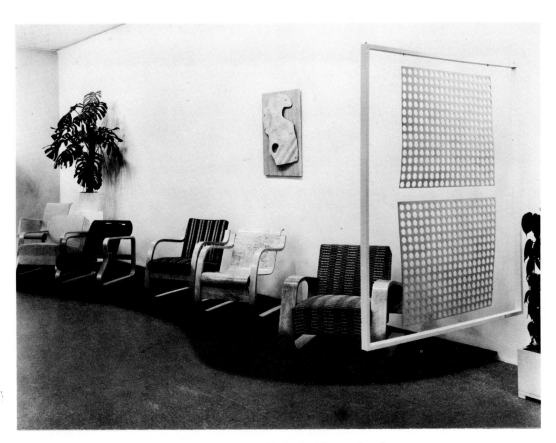

FIG. 648. Aalto, Chairs in Plywood and Upholstery (1934).

FIG. 649.   Eames, Furniture Units (1946).

substances, but studying the entire problem of the object, its use, and the materials and form which would most clearly and effectively incorporate all these, in accordance with the best Bauhaus theory. Today this chair may seem primitive, just as a 1925 automobile or airplane would. The vitality of the Bauhaus concept is shown by nothing more clearly than by the fact that during the short life of the school (it was closed in 1933 with the rise of the Nazi regime in Germany) the members of its staff were the first to improve their own ideas. Mies van der Rohe, who took over the direction of the school in 1930, was another pioneer in developing furniture forms in accordance with the inherent properties of metal and in being the first to utilize the spring quality of bent steel legs (cf. Fig. 213). Le Corbusier was also in the forefront of architects who realized the appropriateness of such forms as these to the International Style interior.

Possibly the Bauhaus' most significant contribution to effective design has been the demonstration of untold possibilities of the materials provided by modern industry when used intelligently and imaginatively. Along this line is the work of Alvar Aalto, a Finnish designer, who in 1932 made a chair of bent plywood and tubular metal and followed this a short time later with a series of *Chairs in Plywood and Upholstery* (Fig.

648). The nature of this material, made of thin veneers of wood glued together with the grain at right angles in alternate layers, is such that it can be manipulated and formed in an almost unlimited variety of curved shapes and planes, as is clear from the different designs in the illustration. Aalto's furniture is admirably suited to the contemporary interior by virtue of its fine proportion and its dependence upon inherent quality for decorative effect; moreover, it is characterized by pleasant texture and color that metal furniture cannot always equal.

The period since the end of World War II has been marked by resumption on an even larger scale of producing articles for the increasingly more complex life of the twentieth century, and by correspondingly greater opportunities for industrial and commercial designers. The United States is more and more appreciating well-designed as against unimaginative forms. Cases in point are the advances, some spectacular, in designing automobiles, in meeting the demands of television, and in developing more pleasing and less costly chinaware. In an effort to solve the problem of efficient yet formally distinguished interiors, many new ideas in designing furniture have been introduced. Outstanding in this respect is Charles Eames, whose *Furniture Units* (Fig. 649) are so designed that they may be purchased individually or combined in a number of different ways. The resultant patterns have a uniformly attractive consistency in much the same way and for the same reasons as the best of contemporary architectural design —through the recurrence of certain proportions that give rhythmic unity to the whole, but are not monotonous because the materials permit great variety of color and surface texture.

An important aspect of the arts of the machine today is the part played by new materials, and the result of different and more effective methods of processing old ones. The new plastics are in the first of these categories; the ease of handling and shaping these synthetic materials has made them specially popular. Aluminum is another comparatively recent development that is now extensively used. Originally classed as a rare metal because of high pro-

duction costs when it was first processed late in the nineteenth century, it is now one of the most widely used materials of its kind. The *Tea Kettle* (Fig. 650), designed by the Lurelle V. A. Guild and manufactured by the Aluminum Cooking Utensil Co. of the United States, is typical of the well-designed utilitarian objects which result from increased understanding of better ways of producing the metal and clearer insight into the value of more effective forms. Because of its lightness and relatively high resistance to staining and discoloration, aluminum is particularly favored for cooking utensils. The Tea Kettle has been designed with similar considerations of utility in mind. The base is broad, to provide the greatest possible surface for transmitting heat to the water inside, and the shape of the spout and its opening as well as the pitch have been

FIG. 650.   Tea Kettle, Aluminum
(1934).

controlled by the need for an efficient pouring device. This need is also responsible for the asymmetrical handle which aids in tilting the vessel; the plastic moulded band around it provides a firm grip that is insulated against the heat of the metal.

But it is not these matters of utility alone that concerned the designer of the Tea Kettle. The curve of the shoulder, the easy merging of the spout at its base with the main body of the kettle, and the slight recess around the knob on the top have nothing to do with mechanical efficiency. They have much to do, though, with its attractive appearance, and contribute directly to the visual satisfaction derived from looking at it.

Collection, The Museum of Modern Art, New York: Left, *Phyllis B. Lambert Fund;*
Center, *Gift of H. E. Lauffer Co.;* Right, *Gift of Marshall Field.*

FIG. 651.   Flatware, Stainless Steel (1957).

Stainless steel is another metal much used for utilitarian and well-designed objects today. An alloy of steel and chromium, it is, as the name implies, almost completely rustproof and non-corrosive. Thus it is particularly effective for *Flatware* (Fig. 651), especially for knives because blade and handle can be a single piece of metal. The three sets in the figure show the changing conception of form that has occurred since the earliest (on the extreme right) was produced in Germany in 1929. It is based on eighteenth-century designs in silver, notable for their elegance particularly in English work. The set in the center, designed in 1956 by the American Don Wallace, and that on the left designed by Bertel Gardberg of Finland in 1957, are quite

FIG. 652.   Electric Fan, Plastic and Rubber (1957).

different in shape. The American design was based on studies of changing habits of eating, and the suppression of the juncture between handle and blade is a departure from the traditional form that is made possible by the material. Nor is it entirely by chance that the easy flowing curves have something in common with many contemporary forms in other mediums (cf. Fig. 351). The sharp and angular lines of the Finnish design suggests the crystalline structure of the metal. As is true of the traditional silver flatware, considerable variety of color and texture can be achieved in stainless steel, and use gives it a soft sheen that adds to its attractiveness.

Another instance of a common form being given new character by taking advantage of technical innovations is the *Electric Fan* (Fig. 652) designed in 1957 by Peter Schlumbohm and produced by the Chemex Corporation. Mechanical movement of air has always been produced by agitated planes, whether palm leaves, textile, or metal. Schlumbohm's fan is no exception to this, but the planes are sheets of filter paper that whirl inside the rubber composite and gray plastic housing. When they become soiled, they can be removed and others installed. The simply curved planes and colors of the materials give the fan a decorative distinction quite different from the traditional electric fan with its metal blades and protective guard of wire rods.

Thus even extremely utilitarian household implements may be works of art that give pleasure in addition to serving an immediate mechanical function. It is by solving such problems as these that the commercial and industrial designer contributes to the art of the machine today.

Glossary

The references to figures are not exhaustive.

Abacus. A slab forming the crowning member of a capital. Figs. 31, 32.

Absidioles. Small apse-like projections from the ambulatory and transepts of a church. Figs. 75, 98.

Acanthus. A plant whose leaves are reproduced in stylized form on the Corinthian capital. Fig. 34.

Action painting. A certain type of abstract expressionism. Fig. 545.

Aerial perspective. The indication in pictorial art of the effect of light and atmosphere upon distant objects, giving thereby an impression of depth in the picture or relief. Fig. 399.

Akroterion. Ornament on the peak or corners of a classic temple pediment. Figs. 29, 251.

Ambulatory. Passageway around the apse of a church. Figs. 75, 98.

Amphora. Greek vase in the form of a jar, usually fairly large, with two handles connecting the wide mouth or the neck with the body. Used for provisions. Figs. 562, 566.

Applied order. Column and entablature attached to a wall or pier; decorative rather than structural in function. Figs. 49, 50, 52, 118, 126.

Apse. Semicircular or polygonal recess, covered with a half-dome or other vault; more particularly, the semicircular termination of the choir of a church. Figs. 63, 65, 71, 75, 98.

Aqueduct. A channel or conduit to conduct water, often supported on masonry arches. Fig. 61.

Arabesque. Florid design involving foliate scrolls and forms of animals and people, extensively used in Renaissance decoration. Figs. 122, 406, 604, 605.

Arcade. A series of arches resting on piers or columns. Figs. 65, 76.

Arch. A structural device, semicircular or pointed in shape, formed of separate truncated wedge-shaped blocks to span an opening. Fig. 2.

Architrave. The horizontal beam or lintel that is the lowest member of the entablature in the classic orders; more generally, a horizontal member spanning the distance between two vertical ones: a lintel. Figs. 31, 32.

Arris. The sharp ridge between two flutes of a Doric shaft. Fig. 31.

Art Nouveau. A short-lived style of architecture and its accessories, characterized by predominantly curvilinear patterns, that enjoyed some popularity in the 1890's and 1900's. Fig. 644.

Atrium. The open outer court of a Roman house, usually surrounded by a roofed gallery, Fig. 59; the open court before the narthex of a Christian basilica or church, Figs. 62, 87.

Baldacchino. A canopy over a tomb or altar. Fig. 132.

Balustrade. A handrail, usually supported by small pillars. Figs. 133, 135.

Baroque. Literally, irregular or fantastic; applied to art of the 17th and early 18th centuries; a style in which an artistic medium is handled freely to produce striking effects. Figs. 149, 150, 334, 335.

Barrel vault. A vault that is semicircular in section. Fig. 53, A.

Basilica. In Roman architecture, a rectangular building with nave and aisles used for business and judicial purposes, Figs. 51, 54, 55; in Christian architecture, a church of similar form, the longitudinal axis being the most important, Figs. 62-64.

Bay. An opening between two columns or piers, Fig. 31; more generally, a principal compartment or unit which is repeated to form an architectural design. See discussion of the Church at Vignory, Fig. 76.

Beam. A horizontal piece of wood, stone, or metal, used in the frame of a building: a lintel. Fig. 1.

Black-figured. The dominant style in Greek vase painting before the late 6th century B.C., in which the forms are black with incised details against a lighter background. Figs. 564-566.

Broken pediment. A pediment in which one or both of the cornices are not continuous; much used in baroque architecture. Figs. 149, 150.

Burin. A piece of sharply pointed metal, usually rectangular in section, set in a knob; it is used in engraving.

Buttress. A mass of masonry employed to counteract the lateral thrust of an arch or vault. Fig. 2.

Cabriole. Double-curved furniture leg, extensively used from the late 17th century on. Figs. 621, 623, 625.

Campanile. Italian word for bell tower; usually freestanding. Figs. 71, 78, 87, 113.

Cantilever. A horizontal member attached at one end to a vertical support, its stability depending upon the tensile strength of the material. A structural principle employed chiefly in steel construction. Fig. 3.

Capital. The part of a column or pilaster that rests on the shaft, acting as a transition from it to the architrave or arch, and usually decorated. Figs. 31, 32, 48, 294.

Caquetoire, also *caqueteuse.* A relatively light wooden chair with high back and curved arms that originated in France in the 16th century. Fig. 618.

Cartoon. A full-size preliminary sketch for a painting. Fig. 417.

Cartouche. An ornament of irregular or fantastic shape, on which armorial bearings or symbols are sometimes carved; frequently in baroque architecture. Figs. 149, 335.

Caryatid. A support in the form of a female figure that takes the place of a column. Fig. 43.

Cassapanca. A settee formed by adding arms and a back to a chest. Italian. Fig. 613.

Cassone. Italian, meaning a large chest. One of the most characteristic forms of Italian furniture. Figs. 611, 612.

Cella. The principal chamber of a classic temple in which the cult statue stood; sometimes used with reference to the entire walled portion of the building surrounded by the peristyle. Fig. 40.

Centering. The timber framework supporting an arch or vault during process of construction; it is removed after the insertion of the keystone which makes it self-supporting.

Champlevé enamel. A type of enamel in which the base, usually copper or bronze, is dug out leaving a design of ridges between shallow depressions which are filled with a vitreous paste that hardens after firing. Fig. 594.

Chevet. French, meaning literally pillow; term applied to the apsidal end of a French church, and including the semicircular or polygonal vault over the end of the choir, the ambulatory, and the absidioles. Fig. 98.

Chiaroscuro. Italian, meaning literally light-dark; applied to contrasts of light and shade by which various elements in a painting, statue, or architectural design are distinguished from one another. Fig. 416.

Choir. Specifically, the part of a church where the singers are accommodated; in general, the arm of the cross between the transepts and the apse. Sometimes referred to as the chancel. Figs. 75, 98.

Ciborium. See *Baldacchino.*

Cinquecento. Italian, literally "five hundred"; the 16th century.

Cire perdue. French, meaning literally lost wax. A method of casting statues in bronze or other metal in which the original figure is modeled in wax over a core; the wax flows out of the space between the core and the mould when melted by the hot metal which replaces it.

Clapboard. A flat piece of wood applied to the exterior of a building in such a way that its lower edge laps over a similar piece immediately below it making a weatherproof joint. Fig. 179.

Clearstory. The part of the elevation of a church that rises above the aisle and ambulatory roofs and is pierced with windows to illuminate the interior. Figs. 62, 64, 91, 101.

Cloisonné enamel. A process in which small strips or *cloisons,* often of gold, are soldered to a metal plate to form cells which are filled with a vitreous paste; the whole is fired and hardened and then polished. Fig. 592.

Codex. Latin term used for the first books made of pages fastened together on one side as distinguished from a *rotulus.* Figs. 367-370.

Collage. French, literally pasting. Used to describe the practice of some 20th-century artists in introducing paper or other nonpigmented material in a painting.

Colonnade. A series of columns connected by lintels, as contrasted with an arcade. Fig. 64.

Colonnette. A diminutive column.

Column. A vertical support, usually circular in section, with a base, shaft, and capital; distinguished from a pillar by the fact that there is a calculated ratio between its height and diameter. Figs. 31, 32.

Compound pier. A pier built up of various members, such as pilasters, shafts, colonnettes, etc., applied to a masonry core, the applied members corresponding to the arches and ribs of a vault. Figs. 86, 101.

Console. A bracket; a projecting member to support a weight, usually formed of scrolls or volutes in an S-shape; also known as a corbel. Fig. 48.

Corbel. A block of stone projecting from a wall, often carved, that supports cross beams, etc.

Corbel table. A projecting course of masonry resting on corbels which are often connected by small arches. Figs. 86, 87.

Cornice. A horizontal projecting member crowning an entablature or wall; also any crowning moulded projection. Figs. 31, 32, 116, 199.

Courses. The horizontal layers of stone or brick in masonry construction.

Crater, also *krater.* A vessel with wide mouth and broad body, used by the Greeks for mixing wine and water. Figs. 562, 563, 564.

Crocket. A carved projection from the edge of a gable, pinnacle, flying buttress, etc., in a Gothic building; usually in the form of a leaf. Fig. 100.

Crossing. The space formed by the intersection of nave and transepts in a church of cruciform plan. Figs. 75, 98.

Crown. The highest point in an arch or vault; the keystone. Fig. 2.

Crux ansata. The cross of life, an ideograph made up of forms embodying the male and female principles, used as a symbol of deity in Egyptian art. Figs. 239, 552.

Cuneiform. Term used in referring to the wedge-shaped marks that served the Mesopotamians as writing. Fig. 245.

Cupola. A dome or hemispherical covering; also applied colloquially to any small structure above the roof of a house. Figs. 58, 68, 131.

Damascene. The inlaying of metal with other metal or substance in a decorative design. Fig. 559.

Dentils. Small projecting blocks, suggesting somewhat a row of teeth, in Ionic and Corinthian cornices. Fig. 48,D,E,F.

Diaphragm walls. Walls whose primary purpose is to stiffen construction that is liable to be destroyed by intrinsic weakness or strain. See discussion of Sant' Ambrogio at Milan.

Dipylon vase. A type of crater used in Greece in archaic times to store the ashes of cremated bodies; so named because many examples were found in the cemetery near the Dipylon Gate of Athens. Fig. 563.

Dome. A hemispherical or polygonal vault. Figs. 58, 68. See also *Cupola.*

Drum. In a column, the circular sections that make up the shaft; Fig. 48,A,B. Also used with reference to the circular or polygonal wall on which a dome is placed, Fig. 131.

Eave. The lower edge of a roof that projects beyond the wall underneath.

Echinus. From a Greek word meaning sea urchin. The convex member of a capital that supports the abacus, usually parabolic or hyperbolic in profile. Fig. 31.

Egg-and-dart. A row of alternate ovoid and pointed members, usually carved, used as a decorative moulding. Figs. 32, 296.

Elevation. The vertical arrangement of the elements in an architectural design.

Engaged column. A member somewhat like a column but projecting from a wall, of which it is usually a part, instead of free-standing. Also known as an applied column. Figs. 49, 50, 52. See also *Applied order.*

Engraving. The process of cutting a design with a sharp instrument, called a burin, directly in a copper plate from which impressions are made on paper after being inked. Also applied to such an impression. Figs. 443, 446, 447.

Entablature. The part of a building of lintel construction above the columns, beneath the roof or the story above. Figs. 31, 32.

Entasis. A slight, almost imperceptible swelling in the profile of a column shaft. See discussion of the Doric order.

Etching. Engraving a metal plate by the corrosive action of an acid; or by direct application of a sharp instrument, when it is known as dry-point; also applied to the impression made on paper by a plate so prepared after being inked. Figs. 468, 469, 539.

Extrados. The outer curved surface of an arch or vault. Fig. 2.

Façade. One of the faces of a building, usually that containing the main entrance. Figs. 93, 99, 100, 114.

Faïence. See *Majolica.*

"False door." The simulated openings in the external and internal walls of a mastaba, for the use of the "ka" or spirit. Figs. 7, 9.

Fillet. A narrow flat surface separating two mouldings; the surface between two flutes of an Ionic shaft. Fig. 32.

Finial. The decorative foliate termination of a Gothic gable or buttress. Fig. 100.

Flutes. The vertical grooves in the shaft of a column, usually semicircular in section or in the form of a segment of a circle. Figs. 31, 32, 48.

Flying buttress. A bar of masonry, supported by an arch or arches, at right angles to the longitudinal axes of the interior spaces of a Gothic church whose vaults it supports by carrying their lateral thrusts over the side-aisle or ambulatory roofs to vertical piers rising from the outer walls. Figs. 96, 97.

Formal. Of or pertaining to form as an element of artistic style.

Fractional point of view. The concept evident in many early or primitive art forms in which an object is visually described as a combination of different parts rather than represented as an organic unity. Figs. 230, 233, 356.

Free-standing. A term applied to a column or carved figure which is not part of a wall or background.

Fresco. Italian, meaning literally fresh. A method of painting upon wet plaster with colors of pigment mixed with water which sink into the plaster and dry with it; also used with reference to a painting executed in this manner.

Frieze. An extended horizontal band, often decorated with carved figures and mouldings; the portion of an entablature between the architrave and the cornice. Figs. 31, 32.

Gable. The triangle formed by the end of a ridged roof and the similarly shaped wall enclosed by the horizontal and raking cornices; called a pediment in classic architecture. Figs. 28, 31, 179, 256.

Gesso. The mixture of plaster, water, and glue with which wooden panels are coated before being painted.

Girder. A horizontal beam that supports a vertical load and bears vertically upon its supports.

Gothic. Term first applied to mediaeval art during the Renaissance in a derogatory sense. Now used to designate the art of the later Middle Ages, after the Romanesque.

Grille. A grating or screen, usually of iron or a perforated stone slab, but sometimes of wood.

Groined vault. A vault formed by the intersection of two barrel vaults of equal span, either semicircular or pointed, the diagonal lines of the intersecting under surfaces being the groins. Figs. 53, 82, 84.

Guttae. From the Latin *gutta*, or drop. The small cylinders or truncated cones pendent from the mutules and regulae of the Doric entablature. Fig. 31.

Half-timber. A type of construction in which the spaces formed by the wooden beams of a building are filled with brick or clay, the beams being left exposed. Figs. 141, 142.

Haunch. The part of an arch or vault where the lateral thrusts are strongest, about midway between springing and crown. Fig. 2.

Hieroglyphs. The ideographs or picture-words the Egyptians used as writing. Figs. 234, 239, 356.

Hipped roof. A roof with inclined sides and ends, the diagonal lines formed by the intersecting planes being known as hips. Fig. 182.

Historiated capital. A capital with figures that generally illustrate a specific subject. Most frequently employed in Romanesque times. Fig. 294.

Hue. The name of a color—i.e., red, blue, yellow, green, etc.—for which the term color is more generally used alone.

Iconography. The traditional manner of representing a subject in art, governed by more or less fixed rules.

Illuminated manuscript. A book in which the text is written by hand and illustrated with drawings or small paintings. Frontispiece.

Impasto. Italian, literally paste. Refers to the physical body of the pigment of a painting, i.e., light or heavy.

Impost. The horizontal member from which an arch springs. Fig. 2.

Incunabula. Name applied to the earliest books printed from movable type. Fig. 606.

Intarsia. A type of wood inlay in wood much practiced in Renaissance Italy. Fig. 615.

Intensity of hue or color. Strength as compared with a standard gray; a coefficient of saturation.

Intrados. The inner curved surface of an arch or vault; also known as the soffit. Fig. 2.

Isocephalism. A convention by which all the heads in a row of figures are placed arbitrarily at the same height. Figs. 265, 295.

Joist. A horizontal timber in a floor or roof.

Keystone. The central voussoir of an arch which renders it stable when put in place. Fig. 2.

Kylix, also *cylix*. A shallow bowl, usually on a high footed stem and with two handles, used for drinking. Figs. 562, 565.

Law of frontality. A convention in archaic art in which a straight vertical line bisects the figure from the front, there being no movement to either side. Figs. 232, 236, 248, 250.

Leading. The strips of lead by which the pieces of a stained-glass window are held together. Fig. 371.

Lean-to. A supplementary structure added to a building, usually covered by a roof in a single slanting plane. Fig. 179.

Lekythos. A jug, usually rather slender, with a single handle, used for oil and perfume and as a funereal offering. Figs. 562, 569.

Linear perspective. A method of suggesting depth in space in pictorial art, based on the fact that receding parallel lines seem to converge on the horizon line. One of the first systems of linear perspective was evolved by Brunellesco.

Lintel. The horizontal beam in the post and lintel system, Fig. 1; also used with reference to an architrave.

Lithography. A reproducing graphic process invented by Alois Senefelder in 1796-1798, based on the chemical affinity of ink for grease. Stone blocks originally used, whence the name, but prepared metal plates now used. Fig. 503.

Majolica. A type of earthenware enameled with tin-base glazes, much used in Renaissance Italy. Fig. 605. Also known as faïence ware.

Mastaba. From the Arabian for bench. Used for the low masonry superstructure of the characteristic Old Kingdom tomb type in Egypt. Figs. 7, 11.

Meander. A motive used in classic mouldings, consisting of patterns formed by the intersection of straight lines. Also called fret and Greek key.

Medium. In general, the vehicle in which an artist expresses his ideas. Specifically in painting, the substance with which the painter mixes his pigments, i.e., water, oil, egg white, etc.

Memory picture. The portrayal of the most characteristic aspects of forms as seen in primitive and early art; an element in the *fractional concept*. Figs. 230, 238, 243, 354, 360.

Metope. The panel between two triglyphs in a Doric frieze, Fig. 31; originally an opening between two roof joists; sometimes carved, Figs. 252, 259, 264.

Miniature. A small drawing or painting in an illuminated manuscript. Figs. 366-370, 372.

Modillion. A console or bracket used to support a cornice. Fig. 48.

Monolith. Literally a single stone. Used to distinguish a column shaft cut from a single block of stone from one built up in drums.

Mosaic. A method of wall decoration in which designs are formed by setting cubes of colored glass or marble in wet plaster which holds them firmly in place on hardening. Figs. 362, 365.

Moulding. A projecting or depressed surface, either plain or decorated, used to ornament a wall surface, cornice, capital, etc. Figs. 42, 116.

Mullion. A vertical member dividing a window into separate lights, Fig. 118; also used to support the glass in a stained-glass window.

Mural. Of or pertaining to a wall; fresco paintings are sometimes called murals. Fig. 403.

Mutules. Projecting inclined blocks on the lower face of a Doric cornice from which guttae hang. Fig. 31.

Narthex. The entrance porch of a Christian basilica or church, usually colonnaded and originally opening directly into the atrium, Fig. 62; sometimes in two stories, Fig. 87.

Nave. The chief interior division of a church in Latin cross form, corresponding to the long arm but separated from the side aisles, Figs. 63-65, 98, 105; also applied to the corresponding portion of a Roman basilica, Figs. 51, 55.

Nave arcade. The arches and columns or piers separating the nave of a church of Latin cross form from the side aisles. Figs. 64, 97.

Necking. The band between the shaft and echinus of a classic column. Figs. 31, 32.

Niche. A recess in a wall, as a rule either circular or rectangular with a circular head, in which statuary may be placed. Figs. 58, 147.

Nimbus. Sometimes called a halo. The disk of light behind the head of Christ, the Virgin, saints, etc. Figs. 289, 295, 371, 382, 386, 389.

Obelisk. A tapering shaft of stone, generally rectangular in section and with a pyramidal peak; much used by the Egyptians as memorials. Fig. 130.

Order. A system governing the design of column and entablature in classic architecture. There are two main orders, the Doric and Ionic, and one subordinate order, the Corinthian, in Greek architecture. To these, the Roman added the Tuscan, somewhat resembling the Doric, and the Composite, a combination of Ionic and Corinthian. Figs. 31, 32, 48.

"Organic architecture." An architecture involving the use of vaults, supported by piers, buttresses, and ribs, whose form and arrangement are dictated by the part they play in maintaining the stability of the vaults.

Ormolu. Gilt bronze ornament much used in France in the 18th and early 19th centuries as a decorative accessory to furniture, etc. Figs. 621, 623.

Palmette. A certain type of stylized foliate form employed in classic mouldings; also known as anthemion. Fig. 42.

Pastel. A picture made with a crayon consisting of pigment mixed with some heavy binding medium such as gum; often classed with painting.

Pediment. A triangular space framed by horizontal and raking cornices; in classic architecture, above

the peristyle at the end of a temple, Fig. 29; in Renaissance architecture, a repetitive motive for window decoration, Fig. 125.

Peristyle. A row of columns, bearing architraves or arches, that surrounds the exterior of a building or the interior of a court. Figs. 29, 35, 117.

Perspective. The means by which three-dimensional effects can be suggested on a two-dimensional plane. See also *Aerial perspective, Linear perspective.*

Pier. A vertical support of masonry, built up in courses, distinguished from a column by greater massiveness and by a shape other than circular. Figs. 76, 86, 91, 101.

Pietà. Italian, meaning literally pity or compassion. A representation of the Virgin holding the dead Christ. Figs. 382, 437.

Pilaster. A flat rectangular member, projecting slightly from a wall or pier of which it forms a part, and furnished with a capital, base, etc., in the manner of an applied column, from which it differs chiefly in its rectangular section. Figs. 52, 115, 118.

Pillar. A vertical, isolated mass of masonry used as a support that is not strictly speaking a column or a pier; generally employed, usually incorrectly, to designate any vertical support; also applied to memorial shafts.

Pinnacle. A small decorative conical or pyramidal turret surmounting a buttress, tower, etc. Figs. 100, 110.

Plan. A diagram indicating by conventional means the general distribution of the various parts of a building on the ground or some specified level. Figs. 30, 63, 85, 98, 134.

Podium. A continuous base or pedestal for a monument or building. Figs. 44, 50.

Pointing. A mechanical process employed by sculptors to reproduce a clay or plaster model in stone, points on the model being indicated in the stone block by holes drilled to the proper depth.

Portico. An open vestibule or porch, its roof supported by a colonnade or an arcade on one side. Figs. 57, 114.

Post and Lintel. A structural system or unit of construction in which vertical supports bear the load of horizontal beams. Fig. 1.

Primary hue or color. The red, yellow, and blue components of the spectrum.

Pulvin. The inverted truncated pyramid between a Byzantine capital and the arch it supports. Also known as *stilt-block.* Figs. 70, 72, 365.

Putto. Italian, plural *putti,* meaning boy. Applied to the cherubs used in Italian Renaissance painting and sculpture. Figs. 315, 317, 404.

Pylon. The monumental gateway to an Egyptian temple; also the massive walls separating one court of an Egyptian temple from another; by extension, any gateway of classic design. Figs. 16, 18, 38.

Quattrocento. Italian, literally "four hundred"; the 15th century.

Quoins. Stones or blocks that project slightly at the angle of a building. Fig. 125. Sometimes spelled *coigns.*

Raking cornice. The sloping mouldings of a pediment. Fig. 31.

Red-figured. The dominant style in Greek vase painting after the late 6th century B.C., in which the forms are reserved in the base color of the vase fabric, and the details and background are painted on. Figs. 361, 561, 567, 568.

Regula. The block under each triglyph, beneath the taenia of the Doric entablature, from which guttae are pendent. Fig. 31.

Relief sculpture. Forms carved or cast in such a way that they are attached to a background. Figs. 252, 265, 286, 319.

Repoussé. French, meaning literally pushed back. Used to describe designs executed by hammering a sheet of metal over a form or mould. Figs. 560, 590.

Rib. An arch of masonry, usually moulded, forming part of the framework on which a vault rests and usually projecting slightly from its under surface. Figs. 83, 86, 94, 106.

Ribbed vault. A masonry vault with a relatively thin web supported by ribs. Figs. 86, 94, 95, 101.

Rinceau. French, meaning foliage. A band of carved foliate ornament used as a frieze or moulding. Figs. 50, 293, 296.

Romanesque. Term applied to the period from approximately 1000 to 1200 in European history and to the art then produced by virtue of its embodiment of some of the principles of Roman art without being actually like it.

Rotulus. Latin, meaning a scroll. Refers to the earliest form of book consisting of a long strip of papyrus, parchment, or paper, which was read by rolling the strip from one spindle to another. Fig. 366.

Rustication. A method of treating masonry walls in which the joints between the stones are recessed and the outer surfaces are left rough or project beyond the joints. Figs. 111, 116.

Salient buttress. A strip of masonry applied to the outer face of a wall at a point where the thrusts of a vault are concentrated. Fig. 87.

Secondary hue or color. The orange, green, and violet components of the spectrum.

Segmental pediment. A pediment whose upper profile is a section of a circle instead of triangular. Figs. 125, 133, 162.

Set-back. A step in the elevation of a skyscraper.

Severy. The triangular cell of a ribbed vault web between the diagonal and framing ribs. Fig. 95.

Sexpartite vault. A ribbed vault in which a transverse rib to the crown divides the under surface into six parts or cells. Fig. 91.

Sgabello. A backed, three-legged chair of Italian origin. Fig. 613.

Shaft. The vertical cylindrical or conoid section of a column between the base and the capital, usually rather slender. Figs. 31, 32.

Sizing. The preparation of a surface for the application of paint.

Soffit. The under side of an architectural member such as an arch, cornice, architrave, etc.

Spandrel. The triangular space formed by the curve of one-half of an arch and lines drawn vertically from its springing and horizontally from its crown, Fig. 2; also applied to the horizontal strips between the windows of a skyscraper, Fig. 210.

Spectrum. The pattern of hues or colors constituting white light as shown by analysis with a prism or spectroscope, ranging from red to violet.

Spherical pendentive. Mathematically, a triangular section of a hemisphere. In architecture, the inverted concave triangle of masonry placed upon a pier to sustain part of the weight of a dome. Figs. 66, 68.

Sphinx. Combination of a lion's body with the head of a human being or another animal. Figs. 11, 234.

Spire. An elongated rectangular or octagonal pyramid that terminates a tower. Figs. 99, 185. Sometimes called a steeple.

Splat. The thin, flat piece, solid or pierced and often decorated, in a chair back. Fig. 625.

Splaying. Cutting the sides of an opening in a wall diagonally in such a way that the inner opening is larger than the outer, or conversely. Fig. 80.

Springing. The point where an arch begins to curve over. Fig. 2.

Squinch. A beam or arch across the angle of a square or polygon, used to make the shape more nearly round to serve as the base of a dome. Fig. 86.

Stamnos. A Greek vase in the form of a jar with high shoulder and short neck and two horizontal handles; used for wine. Fig. 567.

Steeple. See *Spire.*

Stele. A slab of stone or a pillar erected as a memorial. Fig. 267.

Stilt-block. See *Pulvin.*

Stilted arch. An arch in which the springing is from a level above the impost. Fig. 82.

String course. Projecting horizontal course of masonry, often moulded, that marks off one story of an architectural elevation from another. Figs. 116, 125.

Stud. Angle beam connecting the vertical and horizontal members of a wooden house frame. Fig. 142.

Stylobate. Strictly, the outer part of the top step of a classic temple base; by extension, the topmost of the steps in its entirety. Figs. 31, 32.

Swag. A heavy garland of carved foliage used for architectural ornament. Figs. 126, 128, 162.

Taenia. The projecting band or fillet that crowns the Doric architrave. Fig. 31.

Tapestry. A textile in which a pattern or image has been woven. Figs. 597, 598, 604.

Tempera. A process of painting on a prepared panel with colored pigment mixed with egg.

Terra-cotta. Italian, meaning baked earth. A form of pottery, baked in moulds and used for architectural ornament, also as a protective sheath for the steel framework of modern buildings; also a sculptural medium.

Thrust. The force exerted horizontally outward by an arch or vault, created by the pressure of the wedge-shaped voussoirs against each other. Fig. 2.

Tie-rod. A rod, usually of iron, embedded in the masonry of an arch or vault at the springing and connecting its sides to counteract the lateral thrusts. Figs. 86, 115.

Tracery. Ornamental pattern of stone work in the windows of mediaeval buildings. Figs. 100, 101, 107.

Transept. The large division of a cruciform plan church at right angles to the axis of the nave; the cross arm. Figs. 63, 75, 98.

Transverse arches. The arches across the nave or side aisles of a mediaeval church, connecting corresponding piers or pilasters with each other. Figs. 81, 82, 86, 101.

Trecento. Italian, literally "three hundred"; the 14th century.

Triforium. The space between the sloping exterior roof over the side aisle of a church and the vault covering it on the inside; more generally, the story of an interior elevation immediately above the nave arcade. Figs. 76, 77, 80, 92, 97.

Triglyphs. The projecting blocks with vertical channels that alternate with the metopes in a Doric frieze. Fig. 31.

Trumeau. French, meaning pier. The member that divides a Gothic portal, often decorated with sculpture. Figs. 300, 304.

Truss. A framework of wood or metal beams, stiffened by cross braces; used for roofs, bridges, etc. Fig. 72.

Tympanum. The space bounded by the horizontal and raking cornices of a pediment or enclosed by the lintel and arch of a doorway. Figs. 31, 300.

Uraeus. The serpent symbol of Egyptian royalty, often used as a head ornament but sometimes separately. Figs. 239, 553.

Value. The proportion of light or dark in a hue or color; a high value has more light, a low one more dark.

Vault. A roof of masonry, constructed on the arch principle. Figs. 53, 84, 95. See also *Barrel vault, Groined vault.*

Vault web. The relatively thin fabric of stone or masonry that constitutes the expanse of a ribbed vault, supported by the ribs.

Volutes. The scrolls of an Ionic capital; also found in Corinthian and Composite capitals. Figs. 32, 34, 48, 117.

Voussoirs. The truncated wedge-shaped blocks of stone used in an arch or vault. Fig. 2.

Wainscot. The wooden sheathing of an interior wall, usually paneled. Figs. 180, 600.

Wedgwood. A type of ceramic ware developed in England in the 18th century, when it was characterized by use of various colors and by "classical" style and subject matter. Fig. 628.

White-ground. A type of Greek vase in which the background is a creamy white and the figures usually appear in outline. Fig. 569.

Windsor chair. A type of chair made of wood employing turned spindles for the back and sides instead of carved members; it originated in England in the early eighteenth century and was much used in the American colonies. Fig. 632.

Woodcut. A picture made by pressing on paper an inked block of wood that has been carved in such a way that a design stands out slightly from its surface in the manner of ordinary printing type. Fig. 384.

Ziggurat. Stepped pyramidal masonry mass with ramps for ascent and descent, developed in Mesopotamia. Figs. 20, 21.

Bibliography

Most of the books listed have been selected because they are generally available in English. A well-selected and more extensive bibliography is:

Lucas, E. Louise, *The Harvard List of Books on Art*, Cambridge, Harvard Univ. Press, 1952.

GENERAL REFERENCE WORKS

Art Index; a Cumulative Subject and Author Index to Fine Arts Periodicals and Museum Bulletins, N.Y., Wilson, 1930-
  Lists articles in magazines and other periodical publications, invaluable for recent and current material.
Chamberlain, Mary W., *Guide to Art Reference Books*, Chicago, American Library Assn., 1959.
Encyclopedia of World Art, N.Y., McGraw-Hill, 1959-
  A multi-volume project by international authors; titles are published each year.
Thieme, U., and Becker, F. (eds.), *Allgemeines Lexikon der bildenden Künstler von der Antike bis zur Gegenwart*, Leipzig, Engelmann, 42 vols., 1907-1961.
  The standard compilation of biographical and critical notices.

SERIES

Many volumes which first appeared in more expensive editions are available in relatively inexpensive paperback editions under the following imprints:

Avon	Harper Torchbook
Dell	Mentor
Doubleday Anchor	Meridian
Dover	Penguin

The following series are more specialized:

Pelican, published by Penguin Books, Harmondsworth, Middlesex, England, and Baltimore, Md.
  Monographs, in English, on specific periods in the history of art, with well-chosen and well-printed black-and-white illustrations and useful bibliographies.
Propyläen Kunstgeschichte, Berlin, Propyläen-Verlag, 16 vols., 1927-1934.

Each volume is a well-illustrated treatise, in German, on a broad phase of the history of art.
Skira, published by a Swiss firm, Skira International, in Geneva and New York City.
  These volumes deal with the history of painting and are illustrated in color.

GENERAL WORKS

Arnheim, Rudolph, *Art and Visual Perception*, Berkeley, Univ. of California Press, 1954.
Aronson, Joseph, *The Encyclopedia of Furniture*, N.Y., Crown, 1940.
Bell, Clive, *Art*, London, Chatto & Windus, 1949.
Birrell, Verla, *The Textile Arts*, N.Y., Harper, 1959.
Boger, Louise A., *The Complete Guide to Furniture Styles*, N.Y., Scribner, 1959.
Clark, Kenneth, *Landscape Painting*, N.Y., Scribner, 1950.
Clark, Kenneth, *The Nude*, Garden City, Doubleday Anchor, 1959.
Croce, Benedetto, *Aesthetic as a Science of Expression and General Linguistic*, N.Y., Noonday Press, 1953.
Doerner, Max, *The Materials of the Artist* (tr. Eugen Neuhas), N.Y., Harcourt, 1949.
Faison, S. L., Jr., *A Guide to the Art Museums of New England*, N.Y., Harcourt, 1958.
Fletcher, Banister, *A History of Architecture on the Comparative-Method*, London, Batsford, 1956.
Focillon, Henri, *The Life of Forms in Art*, N.Y., Wittenborn, 1957.
Friedländer, Max J., *Art and Connoisseurship*, London, Cassirer, 1942.
Fry, Roger, *Vision and Design*, London, Peter Smith, 1948.
Giedion, Siegfried, *Space, Time and Architecture*, Cambridge, Harvard Univ. Press, 1954.
Goldwater R., and Treves, M., *Artists on Art*, N.Y., Pantheon, 1945.
Gombrich, E. H., *Art and Illusion*, N.Y., Pantheon, 1960.
Greene, Theodore M., *The Arts and the Art of Criticism*, Princeton, Princeton Univ. Press, 1947.
Hamlin, Talbot, *Architecture Through the Ages*, N.Y., Putnam, 1953.

Holt, Elizabeth G., *A Documentary History of Art*, Garden City, Doubleday Anchor, 2 vols., 1957.

Ivins, William M., *How Prints Look*, N.Y., Metropolitan Museum, 1943.

Langer, Suzanne K. (ed.), *Reflections on Art; a Source Book of Writings by Artists, Critics and Philosophers*, Baltimore, Johns Hopkins Press, 1958.

Malraux, André, *The Voices of Silence*, N.Y., Doubleday, 1953.

Mayer, Ralph, *The Artist's Handbook of Materials and Techniques*, N.Y., Viking, 1957.

Morison, Stanley, *Four Centuries of Fine Printing*, N.Y., Barnes & Noble, 1960.

Mumford, Lewis, *The City in History*, N.Y., Harcourt, 1961.

Newton, Eric, *The Arts of Man*, Greenwich, New York Graphic Socy., 1960.

Newton, Eric, *Masterpieces of European Sculpture*, N.Y., Abrams, 1959.

Ogden, C. K., Richard, I. A., and Wood, J., *The Foundation of Aesthetics*, N.Y., International, 1931.

Panofsky, Erwin, *Meaning in the Visual Arts*, Garden City, Doubleday Anchor, 1955.

Panofsky, Erwin and Dora, *Pandora's Box*, N.Y., Pantheon, 1956.

Pearson, Ralph M., *Experiencing Pictures*, N.Y., Harcourt, 1932.

Peterdi, Gabor, *Printmaking: Methods Old and New*, N.Y., Macmillan, 1959.

Pevsner, Nikolaus, *An Outline of European Architecture*, Baltimore, Penguin, 6th (Jubilee) ed., 1960.

Pope, Arthur, *The Language of Drawing and Painting*, Cambridge, Harvard Univ. Press, 1949.

Read, Herbert, *Art and Society*, London, Faber & Faber, 1945.

Read, Herbert, *The Meaning of Art*, Baltimore, Penguin, 1959.

Rich, Jack C., *The Materials and Methods of the Sculptor*, N.Y., Oxford Univ. Press, 1947.

Robb, David M., *The Harper History of Painting: The Occidental Tradition*, N.Y., Harper, 1951.

Rosenau, Helen, *The Ideal City in Its Architectural Evolution*, London, Routledge & Kegan Paul, 1959.

Rothschild, Lincoln, *Style in Art*, N.Y., Yoseloff, 1960.

Sachs, Paul J., *The Pocket Book of Great Drawings*, N.Y., Dell, 1951.

Santayana, George, *The Sense of Beauty*, N.Y., Dover, 1955.

Shahn, Ben, *The Shape of Content*, Cambridge, Harvard Univ. Press, 1957.

Spaeth, Eloise *American Art Museums and Galleries; an Introduction to Looking*, N.Y., Harper, 1960.

Sterling, Charles, *Still Life Painting* (tr. James Emmons), Paris, Tisné, 1959.

Watrous, James, *The Craft of Old Master Drawings*, Madison, Univ. of Wisconsin Press, 1957.

Whyte, Lancelot, *Accent on Form*, N.Y., Harper, 1954.

Zigrosser, Carl, *The Book of Fine Prints*, N.Y., Crown, 1958.

PREHISTORIC ART

Bataille, Georges, *Prehistoric Painting: Lascaux*, N.Y., Skira, 1955.

Brown, Gerard B., *The Art of the Cave Dweller*, London, Murray, 1928.

Burkitt, Miles C., *The Old Stone Age*, London, Bowes & Bowes, 1955.

Frobenius, Leo, and Fox, D. C., *Prehistoric Rock Pictures in Europe and Africa*, N.Y., Museum of Modern Art, 1937.

Graziosi, Paolo, *Palaeolithic Art*, N.Y., McGraw-Hill, 1960.

Hawks, Christopher and Jacquetta, *Prehistoric Britain*, Harmondsworth, Penguin, 1949.

Laming, Annette, *Lascaux: Paintings and Engravings*, Baltimore, Penguin, 1959.

Newall, R. S., *Stonehenge*, London, Her Majesty's Stationery Office, 1955.

Raphael, Max, *Prehistoric Cave Paintings* (tr. Norbert Guterman), N.Y., Pantheon, 1945.

Spearing, Herbert G., *The Childhood of Art*, London, Benn, 1930.

Windels, F., *Lascaux Cave Paintings*, London, Faber & Faber, 1949.

EGYPTIAN ART

Aldred, Cyril, *The Development of Ancient Egyptian Art from 3200-1315 B.C.*, London, Tiranti, 1952.

Davies, Nina M., and Gardiner, Alan H., *Ancient Egyptian Paintings*, Chicago, Univ. of Chicago Press, 1936.

Edwards, I. E. S., *The Pyramids of Egypt*, Baltimore, Penguin, 1955.

Hayes, William C., *The Scepter of Egypt*, N.Y., Metropolitan Museum, 1953.

Lange, Kurt, and Hirmer, M., *Egypt*, London, Phaidon, 1956.

Ranke, Hermann, *The Art of Ancient Egypt*, London, Allen & Unwin, 1936.

Smith, Earl Baldwin, *Egyptian Architecture as Cultural Expression*, N.Y., Appleton-Century, 1938.

Smith, William Stevenson, *The Art and Architecture of Ancient Egypt*, Baltimore, Penguin, 1958.

Smith, William Stevenson, *A History of Egyptian Sculpture and Painting in the Old Kingdom*, N.Y., Oxford Univ. Press, 1946.

Vandier, Jacques, *Egypt: Paintings from Tombs and Temples*, N.Y., New York Graphic Socy. and UNESCO, 1954.

Wilson, John A., *The Culture of Ancient Egypt*, Chicago, Univ. of Chicago Press, 1956.

Woolley, Charles Leonard, *Digging Up the Past*, Baltimore, Penguin, 1954.

MESOPOTAMIAN ART

Frankfort, Henri, *The Art and Architecture of the Ancient Orient*, Baltimore, Penguin, 1955.

Parrot, André, *Sumer*, London, Thames & Hudson, 1959.

Schäfer, H., and Andrae, W., *Die Kunst des alten Orients*, Berlin, Propyläen-Verlag, 1925.

Woolley, Charles Leonard, *The Development of Sumerian Art*, London, Faber & Faber, 1935.

Woolley, Charles Leonard, *Ur of the Chaldees*, Baltimore, Penguin, 1954.

AEGEAN ART

Evans, Arthur J., *The Palace of Minos at Knossos*, London, Macmillan, 4 vols. in 6, 1921-1935.

Kantor, Helene J., *The Aegean and the Orient in the 2nd Millennium B.C.*, Bloomington, Principia Press, 1947.

Lorimer, Hilda L., *Homer and the Monuments*, N.Y., Macmillan, 1951.

Marinatos, S., and Hirmer, M., *Crete and Mycenae*, London, Thames & Hudson, 1959.

Pendlebury, J. D. S., *The Archaeology of Crete*, London, Methuen, 1939.

Pendlebury, J. D. S., *A Handbook of the Palace of Minos at Knossos*, N.Y., Macmillan, 1955.

Wace, Alan J. B., *Mycenae, an Archaeological History and Guide*, Princeton, Princeton Univ. Press, 1949.

GREEK AND HELLENISTIC ART

Beazley, J. D., and Ashmole, Bernard, *Greek Sculpture and Painting*, N.Y., Macmillan, 1932.

Bieber, Margaret, *The Sculpture of the Hellenistic Age*, N.Y., Columbia Univ. Press, 1955.

Buschor, Ernst, *Greek Vase-Painting* (tr. G. C. Richards , N.Y., Dutton, 1922.

Carpenter, Rhys, *The Esthetic Basis of Greek Art*, Bloomington, Indiana Univ. Press, 1959.

Carpenter, Rhys, *Greek Sculpture: A Critical Survey*, Chicago, Univ. of Chicago Press, 1960.

Casson, Stanley, *The Technique of Early Greek Sculpture*, N.Y. Oxford Univ. Press, 1933.

Collignon, Maxime, *Le Parthénon* (revised by G. Fougéres), Paris, Hachette, 1926.

Fyfe, D. T., *Hellenistic Architecture*, Cambridge, Cambridge Univ. Press, 1936.

Grinnell, Isabel H., *Greek Temples*, N.Y., Metropolitan Museum, 1943.

Hege, W., and Rodenwalt, G., *Olympia*, London, Sidgwick & Jackson, 1936.

Hoyningen-Huené, G., and Chisholm, H. J. (eds.), *Hellas*, N.Y. Augustin, 1944.

Lawrence, A. W., *Greek Architecture*, Baltimore, Penguin, 1957.

Lullies, R., and Hirmer, M., *Greek Sculpture*, London, Thames & Hudson, 1959.

Paton, J. M. (ed.), *The Erechtheum*, Cambridge, Harvard Univ. Press, 1927.

Pfuhl, Ernst, *Masterpieces of Greek Drawing and Painting*, N.Y., Macmillan, 1955.

Richter, Gisela M. A., *A Handbook of Greek Art*, N.Y., Phaidon, 1959.

Richter, Gisela M. A., *Kouroi; Archaic Greek Youths; a Study of the Development of the Kouros Type in Greek Sculpture*, N.Y., Phaidon, 1960.

Richter, Gisela M. A., *Sculpture and Sculpture of the Greeks*, New Haven, Yale Univ. Press, 1950

Robertson, D. S., *A Handbook of Greek and Roman Architecture*, Cambridge, Cambridge Univ. Press, 1954.

Robertson, Martin, *Greek Painting*, N.Y., Skira, 1959.

Rodenwalt, G., *Die Kunst der Antike*, Berlin, Propyläen-Verlag, 1927.

Swindler, Mary H., *Ancient Painting*, New Haven, Yale Univ. Press, 1929.

ROMAN AND ETRUSCAN ART

Goldscheider, L., *Etruscan Sculpture*, N.Y., Oxford Univ. Press, 1941.

Goldscheider, L., *Roman Portraits*, N.Y., Oxford Univ. Press, 1940.

Lehmann, Phyllis W., *Roman Wall Paintings from Boscoreale in the Metropolitan Museum of Art*, Cambridge, Archaeological Inst. of America, 1953.

Maiuri, A., *Roman Painting*, N.Y., Skira, 1953.

Nash, Ernest, *Roman Towns*, N.Y., Augustin, 1944.

Pallottino, M., and Hurliman, M., *Art of the Etruscans*, N.Y., Vanguard, 1955.

Robertson, D. S., *A Handbook of Greek and Roman Architecture*, Cambridge, Cambridge Univ. Press, 1954.

Scherer, Margaret R., *Marvels of Ancient Rome* (foreword by C. R. Morey), N.Y., Phaidon (for the Metropolitan Museum), 1956.

Smith, Earl Baldwin, *Architectural Symbolism of Imperial Rome and the Middle Ages*, Princeton, Princeton Univ. Press, 1956.

Strong, Eugénie S., *Art in Ancient Rome*, N.Y., Scribner, 2 vols., 1928.

MEDIAEVAL ART—GENERAL

Morey, Charles Rufus, *Christian Art*, N.Y. Longmans, 1935.

Morey, Charles Rufus, *Mediaeval Art*, N.Y., Norton, 1942.

BIBLIOGRAPHY

SYMBOLISM AND ICONOGRAPHY

Appleton, L. H., and Bridges, S., *Symbolism in Liturgical Art*, N.Y., Scribner, 1959.

Didron, Adolphe N., *Christian Iconography* (tr. E. J. Middleton), London, Bell, 2 vols., 1907.

Hirn, Yrjö, *The Sacred Shrine*, Boston, Beacon, 1957.

Jameson, Anna B. M., *Sacred and Legendary Art*, Boston, Houghton Mifflin, 2 vols., *ca.* 1911.

Künstle, Karl, *Ikonographie der christlichen Kunst*, Freiburg i. Br., Herder, 2 vols., 1926-1928.

Mâle, Émile, *L'art religieux du XIIe siècle en France*, Paris, Colin, 1947.

Mâle, Émile, *L'art religieux de la fin du moyen âge en France*, Paris, Colin, 1925.

Mâle, Émile, *The Gothic Image: Religious Art in France of the Thirteenth Century*, N.Y., Harper Torchbooks, 1958.

Mâle, Émile, *Religious Art from the Twelfth to the Eighteenth Century*, N.Y., Noonday Press, 1958.

EARLY CHRISTIAN AND BYZANTINE ART

Anthony, E. W., *A History of Mosaics*, Boston, Sargent, 1935.

Conant, Kenneth J., *A Brief Commentary on Early Medieval Church Architecture*, Baltimore, Johns Hopkins, Press, 1942.

Demus, Otto, *Byzantine Mosaic Decoration*, London, Kegan Paul, 1941.

Diez, E., & Demus, O., *Byzantine Mosaics in Greece: Hosios Lucas and Daphni*, Cambridge, Mass., Harvard Univ. Press, 1931.

Grabar, André, *Byzantine Painting*, N.Y., Skira, 1953.

Grabar, André, and Chatzidakis, M., *Greece-Byzantine Mosaics*, N.Y., New York Graphic Soc., and UNESCO, 1960.

Hinks, R. P., *Carolingian Art*, London, Sidgwick & Jackson, 1935.

Kirschbaum, E., *The Tombs of St. Peter and St. Paul* (tr. John Murray), N.Y., St. Martin's Press, 1959.

Kitzinger, Ernst, *Early Medieval Art*, London, British Museum, 1955.

Mâle, Émile, *The Early Churches of Rome* (tr. David Buxton), London, Benn, 1960.

Morey, Charles Rufus, *Early Christian Art*, Princeton, Princeton Univ. Press, 1953.

Morey, Charles Rufus, *The Mosaics of Antioch*, N.Y., Longmans, 1938.

Natanson, Joseph, *Early Christian Ivories*, London, Tiranti, 1935.

Nordenfalk, Carl, and Grabar, André, *Early Medieval Painting*, N.Y., Skira, 1957.

Rice, D. T., *The Art of Byzantium*, London, Thames & Hudson, 1959.

Smith, Earl Baldwin, *Architectural Symbolism of Imperial Rome and the Middle Ages*, Princeton, Princeton Univ. Press, 1956.

Smith, Earl Baldwin, *The Dome*, Princeton, Princeton Univ, Press, 1950.

Smith, Earl Baldwin, *Early Christian Iconography*, Princeton, Princeton Univ. Press, 1918.

Swift, E. H., *Hagia Sophia*, N.Y., Columbia Univ. Press, 1940.

Toynbee, J., and Perkins, J. Ward., *The Shrine of St. Peter*, N.Y., Longmans, 1956.

Volbach, W. F., *Early Christian Mosaics*, N.Y., Oxford Univ. Press, 1948.

Volbach, W. F., and Hirmer, M., *Early Christian Art*, London, Thames & Hudson, 1960.

Weitzmann, K., *Ancient Book Illumination*, Cambridge, Harvard Univ, Press, 1959.

Weitzmann, K., *Illustrations in Roll and Codex; a study of the Origin and Method of Text Illustration*, Princeton, Princeton Univ. Press, 1947.

EARLY MEDIAEVAL ART

Clapham, A. W., *English Romanesque Architecture Before the Conquest*, N.Y., Oxford Univ. Press, 1930.

Conant, Kenneth J., *Carolingian and Romanesque Architecture 800 to 1200*, Baltimore, Penguin, 1959.

De Wald, Ernest T., *The Illustrations of the Utrecht Psalter*, Princeton, Princeton Univ. Press, 1932.

Evans, Joan, *Art in Mediaeval France—987 to 1498*, N.Y., Oxford Univ. Press, 1948.

Fisher, E. A., *An Introduction to Anglo-Saxon Architecture and Sculpture*, N.Y., Praeger, 1959.

Goldschmidt, Adolf, *German Illumination*, Paris, Pegasus, 2 vols., 1928.

Henry, Françoise, *Irish Art in the Early Christian Period*, London, Methuen, 1940.

Leeds, E. T., *Early Anglo-Saxon Art and Archaeology*, N.Y., Oxford Univ. Press, 1936.

Porter, A. Kingsley, *The Crosses and Culture of Ireland*, New Haven, Yale Univ. Press, 1931.

Swarzenski, Hanns, *Monuments of Romanesque Art*, Chicago, Univ. of Chicago Press, 1954.

ROMANESQUE ART

Anthony, Edgar, *Romanesque Frescoes*, Princeton, Princeton Univ. Press, 1951.

Boase, T. S. R., *English Art, 1100-1216*, N.Y., Oxford Univ. Press, 1953.

Clapham, A. W., *English Romanesque Architecture After the Conquest*, N.Y., Oxford Univ. Press, 1934.

Clapham, A. W., *Romanesque Architecture in Western Europe*, Oxford, Clarendon, 1936.

Conant, Kenneth J., *Carolingian and Romanesque Architecture 800 to 1200*, Baltimore, Penguin, 1959.

Crichton, G. H., *Romanesque Sculpture in Italy*, London, Routledge & Kegan Paul, 1954.

Crosby, S., *The Abbey of St. Denis*, New Haven, Yale Univ. Press, 1942.

Decker, H., *Romanesque Art in Italy*, London, Thames & Hudson, 1960.

Gantner, J., Pobé, M., and Roubier, J., *Romanesque Art in France*, London, Thames & Hudson, 1959.

Gardner, Arthur, *An Introduction to French Church Architecture*, Cambridge, Cambridge Univ. Press, 1938.

Gardner, Arthur, *Medieval Sculpture in France*, Cambridge, Cambridge Univ. Press, 1931.

Millar, Eric G., *English Illuminated Manuscripts from the Xth to the XIIIth Century*, Paris, van Oest, 1926.

Nordenfalk, C., and Grabar, A., *Romanesque Painting*, N.Y., Skira, 1958.

Porcher, Jean, *Medieval French Miniatures*, N.Y., Abrams, 1960.

Porter, A. Kingsley, *Lombard Architecture*, New Haven, Yale Univ. Press, 1915-1917.

Porter, A. Kingsley, *Medieval Architecture*, New Haven, Yale Univ. Press, 2 vols., 1915.

Porter, A. Kingsley, *Romanesque Sculpture of the Pilgrimage Roads*, Boston, Marshall Jones, 10 vols., 1923.

Rickert, Margaret, *Painting in Britain—The Middle Ages*, Baltimore, Penguin, 1954.

Salmi, Mario, *Italian Miniatures*, N.Y., Abrams, 1956.

Stone, Lawrence, *Sculpture in Britain—The Middle Ages*, Baltimore, Penguin, 1955.

Stenton, Frank W., *The Bayeux Tapestry*, N.Y., Phaidon, 1957.

Webb, Geoffrey, *Architecture in Britain—The Middle Ages*, Baltimore, Penguin, 1956.

GOTHIC ART

Adams, Henry, *Mont-Saint-Michel and Chartres*, N.Y., Mentor, 1961.

Aubert, Marcel, *French Cathedral Windows*, N.Y., Oxford Univ. Press, 1939.

Boase, T. S. R., *English Art, 1100-1216*, N.Y., Oxford Univ. Press, 1953.

Bony, J., and Hurlimann, M., *French Cathedrals*, N.Y., Viking, 1961.

DuPont, J., and Gnudi, C., *Gothic Painting*, N.Y., Skira, 1954.

Fitchen, John, *The Construction of Gothic Cathedrals*, N.Y., Oxford Univ. Press, 1961.

Frankl, Paul, *The Gothic: Literary Sources and Interpretations Through Eight Centuries*, Princeton, Princeton Univ. Press, 1960.

Grodecki, Louis, *The Stained Glass of French Churches*, Paris, Éditions du Chêne, 1947.

Herbert, J., *Illuminated Manuscripts*, London, Methuen, 1912.

Houvet, Étienne, *La Cathédrale de Chartres*, Chelles, France, A. Faucheux, 7 vols., 1919.

Karlinger, Hans, *Die Kunst der Gotik*, Berlin, Propyläen-Verlag, 1927.

Katzenellenbogen, Adolf, *The Sculptural Programs of Chartres Cathedral—Christ, Mary, Ecclesia*, Baltimore, Johns Hopkins Press, 1959.

Lasteyrie, Robert de, *L'architecture religieuse en France a l'époque gothique*, Paris, Picard, 1926-1927.

Panofsky, Erwin, *Abbott Suger on the Abbey Church of Saint-Denis and Its Art Treasures*, Princeton, Princeton Univ. Press, 1946.

Panofsky, Erwin, *Gothic Architecture and Scholasticism*, N.Y., Meridian, 1958.

Pirenne, Henri, *Medieval Cities*, Princeton, Princeton Univ. Press, 1925.

Simson, Otto von, *The Gothic Cathedral*, N.Y., Pantheon, 1956.

Stoddard, Whitney S., *The West Portals of Saint-Denis and Chartres*, Cambridge, Harvard Univ. Press, 1952.

Ward, Clarence, *Mediaeval Church Vaulting*, Princeton, Princeton Univ. Press, 1915.

LATE MEDIAEVAL ART

Bühler, Curt F., *The Fifteenth Century Book* (The A. S. W. Rosenbach Lectures in Bibliography for 1958), Philadelphia, Univ. of Pennsylvania Press, 1960.

Friedlander, Max J., *Early Netherlandish Painting from Van Eyck to Bruegel*, London, Phaidon, 1956.

Huizinga, J., *The Waning of the Middle Ages*, Garden City, Doubleday Anchor, 1956.

Lassaigne, J., *Flemish Painting*, N.Y., Skira, 1957.

Meiss, Millard, *Painting in Florence and Siena After the Black Death*, Princeton, Princeton Univ. Press, 1951.

Panofsky, Erwin, *Early Netherlandish Painting*, Cambridge, Harvard Univ. Press, 2 vols., 1953.

Ring, Grete, *A Century of French Painting*, London, Phaidon, 1949.

Venturi, L., and Skira-Venturi, R., *Italian Painting*, N.Y. Skira, 1950.

Wescher, P., *Jean Fouquet and His Time*, N.Y., Reynal, 1947.

ITALIAN RENAISSANCE ART

Ackerman, James S., *The Architecture of Michelangelo*, London, Zwemmer, 1961.

Anderson, W. J., *The Architecture of the Renaissance in Italy*, N.Y., Scribner, 1927.

Berenson, B., *The Drawings of the Florentine Painters*, Chicago, Univ. of Chicago Press, 1938.

Berenson, B., *The Italian Painters of the Renaissance*, N.Y., Meridian, 1957.

Berenson, B., *Italian Pictures of the Renaissance*, N.Y., Oxford Univ. Press, 1932.

Blunt, Anthony, *Artistic Theory in Italy*, N.Y., Oxford Univ. Press, 1951.

Burckhardt, J. C., *The Civilization of the Renaissance in Italy* (tr. G. C. Middlemore), N.Y., Oxford Univ. Press, 1945.

Cellini, Benvenuto, *Autobiography* (tr. G. Bull), Baltimore, Penguin, 1956.

Cennini, Cennino, *Il Libro dell' Arte* (tr. and ed. D. V. Thompson, Jr.), New Haven, Yale Univ. Press, 1932-1933.

Clark, Kenneth, *Leonardo da Vinci*, Baltimore, Penguin, 1959.

Clark, Kenneth, *Piero della Francesca*, London, Phaidon, 1951.

DeWald, Ernest, *Italian Painting 1200-1600*, N.Y., Holt, 1961.

Freedberg, S. J., *Painting of the High Renaissance in Rome and Florence*, Cambridge, Harvard Univ. Press, 1961.

Friedlander, W., *Mannerism and Anti-Mannerism in Italian Painting*, N.Y., Columbia Univ. Press, 1957.

Goldscheider, L., *The Painting, Sculpture and Architecture of Michelangelo*, London, Phaidon, 1957.

Gould, C., *An Introduction to Italian Renaissance Painting*, London, Phaidon, 1957.

Hartt, Frederick, *Giulio Romano*, New Haven, Yale Univ. Press, 1958.

Heydenreich, L. H., *Leonardo da Vinci*, N.Y., Macmillan, 1954.

Janson, H. W., *The Sculpture of Donatello*, Princeton, Princeton Univ. Press, 1957.

Krautheimer, R. and T., *Lorenzo Ghiberti*, Princeton, Princeton Univ. Press, 1956.

MacLagen, Eric, *Italian Sculpture of the Renaissance*, Cambridge, Harvard Univ. Press, 1935.

Magnuson, Toril, *Studies in Roman Quattrocento Architecture*, Stockholm, Almqvist & Wiksell, 1958.

Marle, Raimond van, *The Development of the Italian Schools of Painting*, The Hague, M. Nijhoff, 19 vols., 1923-1938.

Mather, Frank Jewett, Jr., *A History of Italian Painting*, N.Y., Holt, 1923.

Panofsky, Erwin, *Renaissance and Renascences in Western Art*, Stockholm, Almqvist & Wiksell, 1960.

Panofsky, Erwin, *Studies in Iconology*, N.Y., Oxford Univ. Press, 1939.

Pope-Hennessey, J., *Sienese Quattrocento Painting*, London, Phaidon, 1947.

Sandberg-Vavalà, Evelyn, *Sienese Studies*, Florence, Olschki, 1953.

Sandberg-Vavalà, *Uffizi Studies*, Florence, Olschki, 1948.

Schmeckebier, L., *Handbook of Italian Renaissance Painting*, N.Y., Putnam, 1938.

Scott, Geoffrey, *The Architecture of Humanism*, Garden City, Doubleday Anchor, 1956.

Tolnay, Charles de, *Michelangelo*, Princeton, Princeton Univ. Press, 5 vols., 1943-1960.

Vasari, Giorgio, *The Lives of the Most Eminent Painters, Sculptors and Architects* (tr. A. B. Hinds), N.Y., Dutton, 4 vols., 1927.

Venturi, Adolfo, *A Short History of Italian Art* (tr. E. Hutton), N.Y., Macmillan, 1926.

Venturi, Lionello, *The 16th Century: From Leonardo da Vinci to El Greco*, N.Y., Skira, 1956.

Wittkower, R., *Architectural Principles in the Age of Humanism*, London, Warburg Inst., 1952.

Wölfflin, Heinrich, *Classic Art*, London, Phaidon, 1952.

RENAISSANCE ART OUTSIDE ITALY

Benesch, Otto, *The Art of the Renaissance in Northern Europe*, Cambridge, Harvard Univ. Press, 1945.

Blunt, Anthony, *Art and Architecture in France—1500 to 1700*, Baltimore, Penguin, 1953.

Gerson, H., and ter Kuile, E. H., *Art and Architecture in Belgium—1600 to 1800* (tr. Olive Renier), Baltimore, Penguin, 1960.

Kubler, G., and Soria, M., *Art and Architecture in Spain and Portugal and Their American Dominions—1500 to 1800*, Baltimore, Penguin, 1959.

Mather, Frank Jewett, Jr., *Western European Painting of the Renaissance*, N.Y., Holt, 1939.

Panofsky, Erwin, *Albrecht Dürer*, Princeton, Princeton Univ. Press, 2 vols., 1948.

Stange, Alfred, *German Painting: XIV-XVI Centuries*, N.Y., Macmillan, 1951.

Summerson, J. N., *Architecture in Britain—1530 to 1790*, Baltimore, Penguin, 1953.

Waterhouse, E. K., *Painting in Britain—1530 to 1790*, Baltimore, Penguin, 1953.

POST-RENAISSANCE ART

Blunt, Anthony, *Art and Architecture in France—1500 to 1700*, Baltimore, Penguin, 1953.

Florisoone, M., *Le dix-huitième siècle*, Paris, Tisné, 1948.

Fokker, T. H., *Roman Baroque Art: The History of a Style*, N.Y., Oxford Univ. Press, 1938.

Friedrich, C. J., *The Age of the Baroque, 1610-1660*, N.Y., Harper, 1952.

Fromentin, Eugène, *The Masters of Past Time: Dutch and Flemish Painting from Van Eyck to Rembrandt*, London, Phaidon, 1948.

Gerson, H., and ter Kuile, E. H., *Art and Architecture in Belgium—1600 to 1800* (tr. Olive Renier), Baltimore, Penguin, 1960.

Kimball, Fiske, *The Creation of the Rococo*, Philadelphia, Museum of Art, 1943.

Mahon, Denis, *Studies in Seicento Art and Theory*, London, Warburg Inst. 1947.

McComb, Arthur, *The Baroque Painters of Italy*, Cambridge, Harvard Univ. Press, 1934.

Powell, Nicolas, *From Baroque to Rococo: An Introduction to Austrian and German Architecture from 1580 to 1790*, N.Y., Praeger, 1959.

Slive, Seymour, *Rembrandt and His Critics*, The Hague, M. Nijhoff, 1953.

Summerson, J. N., *Architecture in Britain—1530 to 1830*, Baltimore, Penguin, 1953.

Sypher, Wylie, *Four Stages of Renaissance Style*, Garden City, Doubleday Anchor, 1955.

Waterhouse, E. K., *Painting in Britain—1530 to 1790*, Baltimore, Penguin, 1953.

Wittkower, R., *Art and Architecture in Italy—1600 to 1750*, Baltimore, Penguin, 1958.

Wölfflin, H., *Principles of Art History*, N.Y., Dover, 1950.

NINETEENTH-CENTURY ART

Baudelaire, Charles, *The Mirror of Art*, London, Phaidon, 1955.

Bell, Clive, *Landmarks in Nineteenth Century Painting*, N.Y., Harcourt, 1927.

Boas, George (ed.), *Courbet and the Naturalistic Movement*, Baltimore, Johns Hopkins Press, 1938.

Canaday, John, *Mainstreams of Modern Art*, N.Y., Holt, 1959.

Clarke, Kenneth, *The Gothic Revival*, London, Constable, 1950.

Condit, C. W., *The Rise of the Skyscraper*, Chicago, Univ. of Chicago Press, 1952.

Friedlander, Walter, *From David to Delacroix*, Cambridge, Harvard Univ. Press, 1952.

Fry, Roger, *Reflections on British Painting*, N.Y., Macmillan, 1934.

Gauss, C. K., *Aesthetic Theories of French Artists*, Baltimore, Johns Hopkins Press, 1949.

Giedion, Siegfried, *Space, Time and Architecture*, Cambridge, Harvard Univ. Press, 1954.

Hamilton, George Heard, *Manet and His Critics*, New Haven, Yale Univ. Press, 1954.

History of Modern Painting, 3 vols.: *From Baudelaire to Bonnard; Matisse, Munch and Rouault; From Picasso to Surrealism*, N.Y., Skira, 1949-1950.

Hitchcock, Henry-Russell, *Architecture—Nineteenth and Twentieth Centuries*, Baltimore, Penguin, 1958.

Hitchcock, Henry-Russell, *The Architecture of H. H. Richardson and His Times*, N.Y., Shoe String Press, 1961.

Hitchcock, Henry-Russell, and Johnson, Philip, *The International Style: Architecture Since 1922*, N.Y., Norton, 1932.

Hunter, Sam, *Modern French Painting, 1855-1950*, N.Y., Dell, 1956.

Klingender, Francis D., *Art and the Industrial Revolution*, London, Noel Carrington, 1947.

Novotny, Fritz, *Painting and Sculpture in Europe—1780 to 1880*, Baltimore, Penguin, 1960.

Pevsner, Nikolaus, *The Englishness of English Art*, London, Architectural Press, 1956.

Pevsner, Nikolaus, *Pioneers of Modern Design*, N.Y., Museum of Modern Art, 1949.

Rewald, John, *History of Impressionism*, N.Y., Museum of Modern Art, 1962.

Rewald, John, *Post-Impressionism from Van Gogh to Gauguin*, N.Y., Museum of Modern Art, 1956.

Richardson, E. P., *The Way of Western Art*, Cambridge, Harvard Univ. Press, 1939.

Selz, P., and Constantine, M. (eds.), *Art Nouveau*, N.Y., Museum of Modern Art, 1959.

Sloane, J. C., *French Painting Between the Past and the Present*, Princeton, Princeton Univ. Press, 1951.

TWENTIETH-CENTURY ART

Apollinaire, Guillaume, *The Cubist Painters*, N.Y., Wittenborn, 1949.

Barr, Alfred H., Jr., *Cubism and Abstract Art*, N.Y., Museum of Modern Art, 1936.

Barr, Alfred H., Jr., *Fantastic Art, Dada, Surrealism*, N.Y., Museum of Modern Art, 1948.

Barr, Alfred H., Jr., *Masters of Modern Art*, N.Y., Museum of Modern Art, 1954.

Barr, Alfred H., Jr., *Matisse—His Art and His Public*, N.Y., Museum of Modern Art, 1951.

Barr, Alfred, H., Jr., *Picasso—Fifty Years of His Art*, N.Y., Museum of Modern Art, 1946.

Behrendt, Walter C., *Modern Building*, N.Y., Harcourt, 1937.

Bell, Clive, *Art*, London, Chatto & Windus, 1949.

Blanshard, F. M. B., *Retreat from Likeness in the Theory of Painting*, N.Y., Columbia Univ. Press, 1949.

Canaday, John, *Mainstreams of Modern Art*, N.Y., Holt, 1959.

Duthuit, G., *The Fauvist Painters*, N.Y., Wittenborn, 1950.

Fry, Roger, *Vision and Design*, N.Y., Meridian, 1956.

Giedion-Welcker, C., *Contemporary Sculpture*, N.Y., Wittenborn, 1954.

Goldwater, R., *Primitivism in Modern Painting*, N.Y., Harper, 1938.

Gray, Christopher, *Cubist Aesthetic Theories*, Baltimore, Johns Hopkins Press, 1953.

Hayes, Bartlett H., and Rathbun, Mary C., *Layman's Guide to Modern Art*, Andover, Addison Gallery, 1954.

Hitchcock, Henry-Russell, *Architecture—Nineteenth and Twentieth Centuries*, Baltimore, Penguin, 1958.

Kahnweiler, D. H., *The Rise of Cubism* (tr. H. Aronson), N.Y., Wittenborn, 1949.

Kandinsky, Wassily, *Concerning the Spiritual in Art*, N.Y., Wittenborn, 1947.

Kaufmann, Emil, *Architecture in the Age of Reason*, Cambridge, Harvard Univ. Press, 1955.

Le Corbusier (Charles É. Jeanneret-Gris), *Toward a New Architecture* (tr. F. Etchells), N.Y., Payson, 1927.

Moholy-Nagy, Laszló, *The New Vision*, N.Y., Wittenborn, 1949.

Mondrian, Pieter C., *Plastic Art and Pure Plastic Art*, N.Y., Wittenborn, 1945.

Motherwell, Robert, *The Dada Painters and Poets*, N.Y., Wittenborn, 1951.

Read, Herbert, *A Concise History of Modern Painting*, N.Y., Praeger, 1959.

Read, Herbert, *The Philosophy of Modern Art*, N.Y., Horizon, 1952.

Ritchie, Andrew C., *Sculpture of the Twentieth Century*, N.Y., Museum of Modern Art, 1952.

Rosenblum, R., *Cubism and Twentieth Century Art*, N.Y., Abrams, 1960.

Rothschild, E. F., *The Meaning of Unintelligibility in Modern Art*, Chicago, Univ. of Chicago Press, 1934.

Schmeckebier, L. E., *Modern Mexican Art*, Minneapolis, Univ. of Minnesota Press, 1939.

Selz, Peter H., *German Expressionist Painting*, Berkeley, Univ. of California Press, 1957.

Selz, Peter H., *New Images of Man*, N.Y., Museum of Modern Art, 1959.

Seymour, Charles, Jr., *Tradition and Experiment in Modern Sculpture*, Washington, D.C., American Univ. Press, 1949.

Smith, G. E. K., *The New Architecture of Europe*, N.Y., Meridian, 1961.

Soby, James Thrall, *Modern Art and the New Past*, Norman, Univ. of Oklahoma Press, 1957.

Sweeney, J. J., *Plastic Redirections in Twentieth-Century Painting*, Chicago, Univ. of Chicago Press, 1934.

Taylor, Joshua C., *Futurism*, N.Y., Museum of Modern Art, 1961.

Valentiner, W. R., *Origins of Modern Sculpture*, N.Y., Wittenborn, 1948.

Whittick, A., *European Architecture in the Twentieth Century*, London, Crosby Lockwood, 2 vols., 1950-1953.

Zevi, Bruno, *Toward an Organic Architecture*, London, Faber & Faber, 1949.

AMERICAN ART—GENERAL

Andrews, Wayne, *Architecture, Ambition and Americans*, N.Y., Harper, 1955.

Andrews, Wayne, *Architecture in America: A Photographic History from the Colonial Period to the Present* (Introd. by Russell Lynes), N.Y., Atheneum, 1960.

Burchard, J. E., and Bush-Brown, A., *Architecture of America: A Social and Cultural History*, Boston, Little, Brown, 1961.

Hamlin, Talbot F., *The American Spirit in Architecture* (Pageant of America Series, Vol. 13), New Haven, Yale Univ. Press, 1926.

Larkin, Oliver, *Art and Life in America*, N.Y., Holt, 1960.

Mather, F. J., Jr., Morey, C. R., and Henderson, W. J., *The American Spirit in Art* (Pageant of America Series, Vol. 12), New Haven, Yale Univ. Press, 1927.

Mendelwitz, D. M., *A History of American Art*, N.Y., Holt, 1960.

Mumford, Lewis, *Sticks and Stones*, N.Y., Dover, 1955.

Pierson, W. H., and Davidson, M., *Arts in the United States; a Pictorial Survey*, N.Y., McGraw-Hill, 1960.

Tatum, George Bishop, *Penn's Great Town: 250 Years of Philadelphia Architecture Illustrated in Prints and Drawings* (Foreword by Theo B. White), Philadelphia, Univ. of Pennsylvania Press, 1961.

Tunnard, C., and Reed, H. H., Jr., *American Skyline*, N.Y., Mentor, 1956.

AMERICAN ART—COLONIAL

Briggs, Martin, *The Homes of the Pilgrim Fathers in England and America*, N.Y., Oxford Univ. Press, 1932.

Burroughs, Alan, *Limners and Likenesses*, Cambridge, Harvard, Univ. Press, 1936.

Christensen, E. O., *The Index of American Design*, N.Y., Macmillan, 1950.

Downs, Joseph, *American Furniture—Queen Anne and Chippendale Periods, in the Henry Francis du Pont Winterthur Museum*, N.Y., Macmillan, 1952.

Flexner, J. T., *First Flowers of Our Wilderness*, Boston, Houghton Mifflin, 1947.

Kimball, Fiske, *Domestic Architecture of the Colonies and of the Early Republic*, N.Y., Scribner, 1922.

Kubler, George, *The Religious Architecture of New Mexico*, Colorado Springs, Fine Arts Center, 1940.

Morrison, Hugh, *Early American Architecture*, N.Y., Oxford Univ. Press, 1952.

Phillips, John Marshall, *American Silver*, N.Y., Chanticleer, 1949.

Rogers, Meyric R., *American Interior Design*, N.Y., Norton, 1947.

Waterman, Thomas T., *The Dwellings of Colonial America*, Chapel Hill, Univ. of North Carolina Press, 1950.

AMERICAN ART—NINETEENTH CENTURY

Barker, Virgil, *American Painting, History and Interpretation*, N.Y., Macmillan, 1950.

Baur, John I. H., *American Painting in the Nineteenth Century*, N.Y., Praeger, 1953.

Born, W., *American Landscape Painting,* New Haven, Yale Univ. Press, 1948.

Born, W., *Still-Life Painting in America*, N.Y., Oxford Univ. Press, 1947.

Coolidge, John P., *Mill and Mansion*, N.Y., Columbia Univ. Press, 1942.

Hamlin, Talbot F., *Greek Revival Architecture*, N.Y., Oxford Univ. Press, 1944.

Lipman, Jean, *American Primitive Painting*, N.Y., Oxford Univ. Press, 1942.

Lynes, Russell, *The Taste Makers*, N.Y., Harper, 1954.

Mumford, Lewis, *The Brown Decades*, N.Y., Dover, 1955.

Richardson, E. P., *American Romantic Painting*, N.Y., Weyhe, 1944.

Scully, V., *The Shingle Style*, New Haven, Yale Univ. Press, 1955.

Sullivan, Louis, *Kindergarten Chats and Other Works*, N.Y., Wittenborn, 1947.

Sweet, Frederick A., *The Hudson River School and the Early American Landscape Tradition*, N.Y., Whitney Museum, 1945.

White, Theo B. (ed.), *Philadelphia Architecture in the Nineteenth Century*, Philadelphia, Univ. of Pennsylvania Press, 1953.

AMERICAN ART—TWENTIETH CENTURY

Barker, Virgil, *From Realism to Reality in Recent American Painting*, Lincoln, Univ. of Nebraska Press, 1959.

Baur, John I. H., *New Art in America: Fifty Painters of the Twentieth Century*, N.Y., Praeger, 1957.

Baur, John I. H., *Revolution and Tradition in Modern American Art*, Cambridge, Harvard Univ. Press, 1951.

Brown, Milton, *American Painting from the Armory Show to the Depression*, Princeton, Princeton Univ. Press, 1955.

Drexler, A., and Daniel G., *Introduction to Twentieth Century Design*, N.Y., Museum of Modern Art, 1959.

Hitchcock, Henry-Russell, *In the Nature of Materials: The Buildings of Frank Lloyd Wright*, N.Y., Duell, Sloan & Pearce, 1942.

Hunter, Sam, *Modern American Painting and Sculpture*, N.Y., Dell, 1959.

Ritchie, Andrew C., *Abstract Painting and Sculpture in America*, N.Y., Museum of Modern Art, 1951.

Ritchie, Andrew C., *Sculpture of the Twentieth Century*, N.Y., Museum of Modern Art, 1952.

Wright, Frank Lloyd, *Modern Architecture*, Princeton, Princeton Univ. Press, 1931.

Chronological Table

The majority of the monuments discussed are listed in this table;
the italic numbers after the titles are figure numbers.

Date	Architecture	Sculpture	Painting	Minor Arts
Aurignacian Magdalenian		Menton. *229*	Bison Cow. *354*	
ca. 3200		Narmer Palette. *230*		
ca. 2750	Step Pyramid. *10*			
2700–2600	Pyramids, Gizeh. *11*			
ca. 2700		Sumerian Noble. *242*		Falcon Head. *549*
ca. 2600	Mastaba, Ptahotep. *9*	Menkaura. *231*		
ca. 2550		Sheikh el-Beled. *232*		
ca. 2500				Gold Harp. *556*
ca. 2300		Hunting Hippo. *233* Naram-Sin Stele. *243*		
ca. 2100	Ziggurat, Ur. *20*			
ca. 1950– ca. 1400	Knossos. *24*			
ca. 1900	Beni-Hasan. *356*			Hippo. *555*
ca. 1850				Senusert Pectoral. *552*
ca. 1800	Beni-Hasan. *13*	Sphinx of Sesostris III. *234*		
ca. 1500	Stonehenge. *6* Deir el-bahari. *15*	Snake Goddess. *248*	Toreador. *359*	Octopus Vase. *558*
ca. 1450		Thutmose III. *236*	Nobleman Hunting. *357*	Bronze Mirror. *551*
ca. 1400	Luxor. *17*			Tutankhamen Throne. *553* Dagger, Mycenae. *559* Vaphio Cups. *560*
ca. 1350	Mycenae. *26*			
ca. 1325	Mycenae. *27*	Negro Captives. *238*		
ca. 1300		Seti I Offering. *239*		
1257	Abu Simbel. *19*			
ca. 1250		Rameses II. *240*		
ca. 1225	Tiryns. *28*			
ca. 1180			Girl Acrobat. *358*	
ca. 1100	Khons Temple. *16*			
ca. 900		Assurnasirpal II. *245*		
ca. 875		Winged Man-Lion. *247*		
ca. 800				Dipylon Crater. *563*
706	Khorsabad. *21*			

Date	Architecture	Sculpture	Painting	Minor Arts
ca. 650		Wounded Lioness. *246*		
ca. 600		Saïtic Head. *241*		
		Apollo. *250*		
6th cent.				Mirror. *570*
ca. 570	Ishtar Gate. *23*			
ca. 560		Victory of Delos. *251*		François Vase. *564*
ca. 550	Paestum. *35*	Hera of Samos. *249*		
		Perseus and Medusa. *252*		
ca. 540				Exekias, Dionysos. *565*
ca. 500				Kleophrades Vase. *567*
490–480		Euthydikos Statue. *253*		
ca. 480		Aegina Sculpture. *254*		Coin, Syracuse. *571*
ca. 475		Delphi Charioteer. *255*		
ca. 460		Olympia Sculpture. *256–259*		
ca. 450		Doryphorus. *260*		White Lekythoi. *569*
		Athena Lemnia. *263*		
447–432	Parthenon. *39, 40*			
ca. 445		Parthenon Metope. *264*		
442–438		Parthenon Frieze. *265*		
ca. 440		Pericles. *266*	Odysseus-Elpenor. *361*	
438–433		Parthenon Pediment. *261, 262*		
437–432	Propylaea. *38*			
ca. 421		Paionios Victory. *268*		
421–406	Erechtheum. *41–43*			
420–400				Meidias Vase. *568*
ca. 410		Nike Balustrade. *269*		
ca. 400		Hegeso Stele. *267*		
Late 4th cent.	Priene. *46*			
ca. 350	Theatre, Epidauros. *45*	Head from Tegea. *272*		
334	Lysikrates Monument. *44*			
ca. 325		Praxiteles, Hermes. *270*		
ca. 320		Apoxyomenos. *274*		
ca. 310			Alexander Mosaic. *362*	
2nd cent.			Herakles, Telephos. *363*	
ca. 240		Dying Gaul. *277*		
237–212	Edfu. *18*			
180–160		Pergamon Altar. *278*		
ca. 150		Aphrodite of Melos. *276*		
ca. 50		Laocoön. *280*		
		Terme Boxer. *281*		
16	Maison Carrée. *50*			
ca. 15		Augustus, Prima Porta. *284*		
13		Ara Pacis. *285*		
1st cent. A.D.	House of Vetii. *60*			Silver Bowl. *573*
	Pont du Gard. *61*			Portland Vase. *576*
				Table, Pompeii. *577*
A.D. 17				Augustus Deified. *575*

Date	Architecture	Sculpture	Painting	Minor Arts
ca. 50		Peasant and Cow. *279*		
50–79			Paris on Mt. Ida. *364*	
75–82	Colosseum. *52*			
ca. 82	Arch of Titus. *49*	Titus Reliefs. *286*		
112	Trajan Forum. *51*			
120	Pantheon. *57, 58*			
211–217	Caracalla Baths. *56*			
ca. 215		Caracalla. *283*		
Late 4th cent.		Two Brothers Sarcophagus. *288*		
310–*ca.* 320	Basilica of Maxentius. *54, 55*			
315		Arch of Constantine. *287*		
ca. 330–354	Old St. Peter's. *62–64*			
Early 5th cent.		Theodorus Sarcophagus. *290*		
ca. 400		Berlin Sarcophagus. *289*		
425	Sta. Sabina. *65*			
6th cent.				Ivory Angel. *580* Annunciation Textile. *595* Maximianus Throne. *581* Anastasius Diptych. *579*
ca. 500				
517				
526–547	San Vitale. *70*		Abraham Mosaic. *365*	
532–537	Hagia Sophia. *67–69*			
534–539	S. Apollinare in Classe. *71, 72*			
Early 8th cent.			Joshua Rotulus. *366*	
762–776		Sigwald Relief. *292*		
772–795	S. Maria in Cosmedin. *73*			
792–805	Chapel, Aachen. *74*			
9th cent.				Crucifixion, gold. *590*
ca. 800			Book of Kells. *367*	
ca. 830			Utrecht Psalter. *368*	
ca. 870				Crucifixion, ivory. *584*
ca. 900				Byzantine Casket. *583* Alfred Jewel. *593* Triptych, ivory. *582* Madonna, cloisonné. *592*
11th cent.		Madonna Orans. *291*		
ca. 1000			Otto III Gospels. *369*	
1007–1015		Hildesheim Doors. *293*		
ca. 1050	Church, Vignory. *76*			
1059				Apostle, León. *585*
1063–1272	Cathedral, Pisa. *77, 78*			
ca. 1068	Caen, S. Étienne, façade. *93*			
Late 11th cent.				Bayeux Embroidery. *596*

Date	Architecture	Sculpture	Painting	Minor Arts
ca. 1080	Morienval. *82* S. Ambrogio. *85–87*			
ca. 1080– 12th cent.	S. Sernin. *81*			
1093–1133	Cathedral, Durham. *89, 90*			
Early 12th cent.		Bari, S. Niccola. *296*		
ca. 1100	N.-D. du Port. *75, 79, 80*	Modena Sculpture. *298*		Bari Throne. *598*
ca. 1110		Vézelay Capitals. *294*		
ca. 1115	Caen, S. Étienne, vaults. *91*			
ca. 1135		Isaiah, Souillac. *297*		
ca. 1135–1140	N.-D. la Grande. *88*			
ca. 1140				Suger Chalice. *578*
ca. 1145	Chartres, façade. *99*			
ca. 1150		Chartres, west portal. *299*		Christ, ivory. *586*
Late 12th cent.		S. Trophime, façade. *295*		Champlevé Casket. *594*
ca. 1160	S.-Germain-des-Près. *96*			
ca. 1185			Flying Fish. *frontispiece*	
1220	Cathedral, Salisbury. *103–105*			
1220–1230		Amiens, portal. *300–302*		
1220–ca. 1300	Cathedral, Amiens. *97, 98*			
Late 13th cent.				Passion, ivory. *587* Deposition. *588*
1260		Pisa Pulpit. *309*		
ca. 1265		Vierge Dorée. *304*	Coppo, Madonna. *385*	
ca. 1285			de Lisle Psalter. *370* Cimabue, Madonna. *386*	
ca. 1296			Giotto, St. Francis. *387*	
1296–1461	Florence, Cathedral. *113*			
1298	Palazzo Vecchio. *111*			
Late 13th– 14th cent.	Carcassonne. *108*			
14th cent.				Sports, ivory. *589*
ca. 1305		G. Pisano Madonna. *310*	Giotto, Madonna. *388*	
ca. 1306			Giotto, Arena Chapel. *389, 390*	
1308	Pont Valentré. *109*			
1311			Duccio, Maestà. *391*	
ca. 1318			Duccio, Betrayal. *392*	
ca. 1330		N.-D. la Blanche. *305*		
1336				Evreux Virgin. *591*
1337–1340			A. Lorenzetti, City. *394*	
1342			P. Lorenzetti, Birth of Virgin. *393*	
ca. 1350	Cathedral, Exeter. *106*			
1364–1380				Angers, Apocalypse. *597*
1395–1403		Sluter, Moses. *306*		
ca. 1410	Canterbury, Nave. *107*			
1413–1416			Limbourg, Heures. *372*	
ca. 1416		Donatello, Zuccone. *314*		

Date	Architecture	Sculpture	Painting	Minor Arts
ca. 1420–1429	Pazzi Chapel. *114, 115*			
1423			Buxheim, St. Christopher. *384* Fabriano, Magi. *395*	
1425–1438		Quercia, Fall. *313*		
1425–1447		Ghiberti, Doors. *311, 312*		
ca. 1427			Masaccio, Carmine, Frescoes, *398, 399*	
1428–1433		Donatello, Annunciation. *315*		
ca. 1430		Donatello, David. *316*		
1432			Van Eyck, Ghent Altarpiece. *373, 374*	
1434			Van Eyck, Arnolfini. *375*	
ca. 1435			Rogier, Descent. *376*	
ca. 1437–1445			Fra Angelico, Descent. *396*	
1439				Pisanello, Medal. *608*
1443	Jacques Cœur's House. *110*			
1444		Donatello, Gattamelata. *317*		
1444–1459	Medici-Riccardi Palace. *116, 117*			
ca. 1445			Fouquet, Charles VII. *381* Veneziano, Madonna. *401*	
1446–1455	Rucellai Palace. *118*			
1448–1457			Mantegna, St. James. *406*	
ca. 1450			Lochner, Magi. *383* Castagno, Crucifixion. *403* Lippi, Madonna. *404*	
1450–1468	S. Francesco, Rimini. *119*			
1454		Tonnerre Holy Sepulcher. *307*		
ca. 1457			Uccello, Battle. *400*	
1459			Gozzoli, Magi. *405*	
ca. 1465		Verrocchio, David. *321*	Avignon Pietà. *382* Piero della Francesca, Resurrection. *402*	
1468		Rossellino, Palmieri. *318*		
ca. 1470		Pollaiuolo, Hercules. *320*		Room from Gubbio. *615*
1474			Mantegna, Ceiling. *407*	
ca. 1475			Van der Goes, Nativity. *377* Pollaiuolo, Nudes. *408*	Cassone. *612*
ca. 1480			Schongauer, Virgin. *443*	
1480			Ghirlandaio, Last Supper. *409*	

Date	Architecture	Sculpture	Painting	Minor Arts
1481	Vendramini Palace. *120*		Leonardo, Adoration. *416*	
1482–1487	S. Satiro. *121, 122*			
ca. 1488			Botticelli, Venus. *413*	
1488		Verrocchio, Colleoni. *322*		
1489				Strozzi Lantern. *607*
ca. 1490			Memling, Madonna. *378*	
1493	Rouen, Palais de Justice. *112*			
1495			Perugino, Pietà. *411*	
ca. 1495–1498			Leonardo, Last Supper. *418*	
1497–1498			Dürer, Four Horsemen. *444*	
ca. 1498			Leonardo, St. Anne. *417*	
1499				Poliphilus Dreaming. *606*
Early 16th cent.	Rouen Cathedral, façade. *102*	Princeton, Saint. *308*		
16th cent.				Pendant. *609*
				Walnut Chair. *617*
ca. 1500				Unicorn Tapestry. *598*
				Enamel Triptych. *603*
1500			Gentile Bellini, True Cross. *410*	
1500–1504			Signorelli, Damned. *412*	
1501–1505		Michelangelo, Bruges Madonna. *324*		
1502	S. Pietro in Montorio. *123*			
1503			Leonardo, Mona Lisa. *420*	
ca. 1504			Giorgione, Christ. *432*	
1504		Michelangelo, David. *323*	Dürer, Fall of Man. *445*	
ca. 1505			Bosch, Christ Before Pilate. *379*	
1506–1667	St. Peter's. *129*			
ca. 1508			Giorgione, Sleeping Venus. *431*	
1508–1522				Amiens Stalls. *602*
1509–1510			Raphael, Alba Madonna. *429*	
1509–1511			Raphael, School of Athens. *427*	
1509–1512			Michelangelo, Sistine Ceiling. *421–425*	
ca. 1510			Giorgione, Three Philosophers. *433*	
1511			Massys, Deposition. *380*	
1513–1516		Michelangelo, Slave. *325*		
1514			Dürer, Melencolia I. *446*	

Date	Architecture	Sculpture	Painting	Minor Arts
ca. 1515			Raphael, Sistine Madonna. *428* Raphael, Baldassare Castiglione. *430*	
1515			Grünewald, Isenheim Altarpiece. *448, 449*	
1516–1518			Titian, Assumption of the Virgin. *435*	
1517–1546	Farnese Palace. *124–126*			
1518–1524	Azay-le-Rideau. *138*			
1519–1534	Medici Chapel. *147*			
ca. 1520	Compton Winyates. *141*			
1520			Correggio, Ascension. *438*	
1523			Correggio, Madonna. *439* Holbein, Erasmus. *451*	
1525–1533		Michelangelo, Medici Tombs. *327, 328*		
1535	Massimi Palace. *127, 128*			
ca. 1539			Holbein, Henry VIII. *450*	
1541–1548	Louvre, Court. *139*			
1543				Cellini, Salt Cellar. *610*
1546	Campidoglio. *133, 134*			
1548		Cellini, Perseus. *329*		
1549	Vicenza, Basilica. *135*	Goujon, Innocents. *331*		
Late 16th cent.				Wood chair. *614*
1552–1564	Ecouen. *140*			
1552–1591	Vicenza, Villa Rotonda. *137*			
1556–1566	Vicenza, Valmarana Palace. *136*			
1558–1590	St. Peter's, Dome. *131* St. Peter's, Nave. *132*			
1559			Titian, Europa. *436*	
1565			Breugel, Summer. *452*	
1566			Breugel, Wedding Dance. *453*	
1568–1579	Longleat. *143*			
1568–1584	The Gesù. *148*			
1571	Warwick, Lord Leicester's Hospital. *142*			
1573–1576			Titian, Pietà. *437*	
1578–1585			Veronese, Triumph. *442*	
1580–1588	Wollaton Hall. *144, 145*			
1583		Giov. da Bologna, Rape of Sabine Women. *330*		
1584		Pilon, René Birague. *332*		
1587			Tintoretto, Paradise. *441*	
1594			Tintoretto, Last Supper. *440*	

Date	Architecture	Sculpture	Painting	Minor Arts
ca. 1600			El Greco, Cardinal Guevara. *472*	
Early 17th cent.				Ebony Cabinet. *619*
1600–1614			El Greco, Toledo. *473*	
1602–1604			Caravaggio, Entombment. *454*	
1605–1613	St. Peter's, Façade. *130*			
1606–1608			El Greco, Nativity. *471*	
1607–1611	Hatfield House, *146*			
1614			Rubens, Lamentation. *455*	
1615–1624	Luxembourg Palace. *155*			
ca. 1618			Rubens, Leucippus. *457*	
1619–1622	Banqueting House. *162*			
1624			Hals, Cavalier. *461*	
1624–1708	Versailles. *158*			
ca. 1631			Brouwer, Smokers. *459*	
1632			Rubens, Garden of Love. *456*	
			Rembrandt, Anatomy Lesson. *463*	
ca. 1635		Bernini, Costanza Buonarelli. *334*	Van Dyck, Charles I. *458*	
1635–1638	Blois, Orléans Wing. *156*			
ca. 1636			Rembrandt, Saskia. *465*	
1638			Rembrandt, Fall. *468*	
ca. 1642	Acoma, San Estevan. *181*			
1646		Bernini, Theresa. *333*		
1647–1651		Four Rivers Fountain. *335*		
1648			Rembrandt, Samaritan. *467*	
			Lorrain, Embarkation. *478*	
ca. 1650				Boulle Cabinet. *620*
1650			Velasquez, Innocent. *474*	
ca. 1651			Poussin, Matthew. *477*	
1651			Poussin, Holy Family. *476*	
1654			Rembrandt, Bathsheba. *466*	
1656	S. Maria della Pace. *149*		Velasquez, Maids of Honor. *495*	
1658			Rembrandt, Woman. *469*	
1661–1662			Rembrandt, Syndics. *464*	
1662–1667	San Carlo. *150*			
1662–1684	Versailles, Gardens. *161*			
1664			Hals, Lady Regents. *462*	
ca. 1665			Vermeer, Girl with Jug. *470*	
1667–1670	Louvre, Colonnade. *157*			

Date	Architecture	Sculpture	Painting	Minor Arts
Before 1669	Whipple House. *179*			
ca. 1670		Girardon, Nymphs. *336*		
1671–1680	St. Mary-le-Bow. *164*			
1674			Mrs. Freake. *530*	
1675–1710	St. Paul's. *163*			
1678	Versailles, Galerie des Glaces. *160*			
1683	Capen House. *180*			
ca. 1700–1725	Spanish Steps. *153*			
1705–1724	Blenheim. *165*			
1711	Swan House. *166*			
ca. 1718			Watteau, Cythera. *479*	
ca. 1720			Watteau, Drawing. *480*	
1727–1744	Christ Church. *185*			
1728	Hôtel de Biron. *167*			
ca. 1740	Hôtel de Soubise. *168*			
1740			Chardin, Saying Grace. *483*	
1743	Vierzehnheiligen. *169*			
1745			Hogarth, Countess' Dressing Room. *485*	
1748	Strawberry Hill. *174*			
Mid-18th cent.				Windsor Chair. *632*
1753–1763	Place de la Concorde. *170*			
1758–1788	Mount Vernon. *184*			
ca. 1759	Longfellow House. *182*			
ca. 1760				Chippendale Desk. *624* Chippendale Bed. *626*
1760	15 St. James' Sq. *172*			
1761			Greuze, Village Bride. *486*	
1762–1768	Petit Trianon. *171*			
1767				Adam Furniture. *627*
ca. 1768	Powel Room. *183*			
Late 18th cent.				Hepplewhite Chair. *629* Mt. Pleasant. *634*
ca. 1773			Fragonard, Lover Crowned. *481*	
1775			Gainsborough, Mrs. Graham. *484*	
1784			David, Horatii. *487*	
1785–1790	Va. State Capitol. *187*			
1788		Houdon, Voltaire. *338*		
1792–1865	U.S. Capitol. *190*			
Early 19th cent.				Duncan Phyfe Room. *638* Cabinet. *639*
ca. 1800				Sheraton Commode. *631* Revere Silver. *635*

Date	Architecture	Sculpture	Painting	Minor Arts
1800			David, Mme. Hamelin. *488*	
			Goya, Charles IV. *492*	
ca. 1802			Stuart, Mrs. Morton. *532*	
1805		Canova, Pauline Borghese. *339*		
ca. 1814			Ingres, Odalisque. *490*	
1817			Géricault, Races. *496*	
1818–1824	2nd Bank of U.S. *188*			
ca. 1820	Spencer House. *189*			
1824			Delacroix, Scio. *497*	
1826			Constable, Salisbury. *494*	
1832			Ingres, Bertin. *489*	
1834			Daumier, Legislature. *503*	
1835		Rude, Marseillaise. *341*	Turner, Parliament. *495*	
1840–1865	Parliament. *175*			
1843		Powers, Greek Slave. *340*		
1843–1850	Bibl. Ste.-Geneviève. *176, 177*			
ca. 1845			Daumier, Side Show. *504*	
1845			Bingham, Fur Traders. *533*	
Late 19th cent.				Morris, Wallpaper. *643*
ca. 1850	Wedding-Cake House. *191*			
1850–1851	Crystal Palace. *196*			
1851			Corot, La Rochelle. *499*	Day Dreamer. *641*
			Millet, Gleaners. *501*	Carpet. *642*
1854			Delacroix, Galilee. *498*	
1859–1879	St. Patrick's. *192*			
1861–1874	Paris Opéra. *178*			
1863			Manet, Déjeuner. *506*	
1863–1868		Carpeaux, Flora. *342*		
ca. 1865			Courbet, Preparation. *502*	
1866			Corot, Agostina. *500*	
1871–1883	Brooklyn Bridge. *197*			
1872–1887	Boston, Trinity. *193*			
1873–1877			Cézanne, Still Life. *511*	
1874			Monet, Seine. *507*	
1880			Whistler, Traghetto. *539*	
1882	Stoughton House. *194*			
1884			Homer, Life Line. *534*	
1884–1886			Seurat, Grande Jatte. *514*	
ca. 1885			Renoir, Mother and Child. *509*	
1885–1887	Marshall Field Bldg. *195*			
1887		St. Gaudens, Adams Memorial. *344*		
1888			Van Gogh, Café. *516*	

Date	Architecture	Sculpture	Painting	Minor Arts
ca. 1890			Cézanne, Card Players. *513*	
1890			Van Gogh, Cypresses. *517*	
1890–1891	Wainwright Bldg. *199*			
1892			Gauguin, Wave. *518*	
1895			Renoir, Bather. *510*	
1896–1904	Wertheim Store. *207*			
1898		Rodin, Kiss. *343*		
1898–1906			Cézanne, Bathers. *512*	
1899			Eakins, Between Rounds. *537*	
1899–1904	Schlesinger-Mayer Bldg. *200*			
1901			Prendergast, Central Park. *540*	
1902		Maillol, Mediterranean. *345*		
1903			Picasso, La Vie. *521*	
1905–1906	Unity Temple. *205*			
1906				Van de Velde, Room. *644*
1907			Matisse, Blue Nude. *519* Picasso, Avignon. *522*	
1908–1909	Gamble House. *206*			
1909	Robie House. *203, 204*	Barlach, Sorrowing Woman. *347*		
	A. E. G. Factory. *208*			
1910–1913	Woolworth Bldg. *202*			
1911			Chagall, Village. *526*	
1912			Sloan, McSorley. *538*	
1913		Brancusi, Pogany. *349*	Kandinsky, Improvisation. *525*	
1913–1927	Stuttgart Station. *209*			
1915			Gris, Still-Life. *523*	
1922			Marin, Maine Islands. *541*	
1922–1926	Nebr. State Capitol. *201*			
1923	Millard House. *219*			
1924				Knotted Tapestry *645*
1925		Meštrović, Lady. *346*		Breuer, Chair. *647*
1926	Bauhaus. *211*			Bauhaus Coffee and Tea Pots. *646*
	Oud Houses. *214*			
1926–1930		Lipchitz, Figure. *350*		
1928			Klee, Cat. *527*	
1929–1930	Savoye Villa. *212*			
1930	Brno House. *213*		Hopper, Sunday. *542*	
1930–1932	Phila. P.S.F.S. Bldg. *210*			
1931–1939	Rockefeller Center. *225*			
1933–1934	Mackley Houses. *224*			
1933–1935	Penguin Pool. *215*			

Date	Architecture	Sculpture	Painting	Minor Arts
1934			Orozco, Christ. *528*	Aalto, Chairs. *648* Aluminum Kettle. *650*
1936		Milles, Orpheus. *348*		
1936–1937	Falling Water, *221*			
1936–1939	Johnson Bldg. *220*			
1937			Matisse, Lady in Blue. *520* Picasso, Guernica. *524*	
1937–1943	Rio Ministry. *217*			
1939	Welwyn House. *216* Dunsmuir Flats. *218*		Shahn, Handball. *543*	
1940	Goetsch-Winckler House. *222*			
1946		Moore, Figure. *351*		Eames, Furniture Units. *649*
1947–1951	Termini Station. *226*			
1952		Lassaw, Kwannon. *352*	Pereira, Spring. *544*	
1953			Dubuffet, Busy Life. *529* Pollock, Grayed Rainbow. *545*	
1956		Gabo, Form. *353*	Rothko, Orange and Yellow. *546* Wyeth, Nautilus. *547*	
1957				Stainless Steel Ware. Chemex Fan. *652*
1958	Seagram Bldg. *227*			
1958–1960	Univ. of Pa. Lab. *228*			
1959	Guggenheim Mus. *223*			

Illustration Index

Works of art illustrated are listed by title and artist, and architectural examples will also be found listed by place.

ILLUSTRATION INDEX

General Index

Numbers in *italics* indicate pages with illustrations.

Format by Susan Bishop
Set in Monotype Bembo
Composed by Santype Ltd.
Printed by The Murray Printing Company
Bound by Haddon Bindery, Inc.
HARPER & ROW, PUBLISHERS, INCORPORATED